The **Rough Guide** to

Romania

written and researched by

Tim Burford and Norm Longley

D0071760

ROUGH
GUIDES

www.roughguides.com

Contents

Romanian architecture
colour section
following p.152

The great outdoors
colour section
following p.312

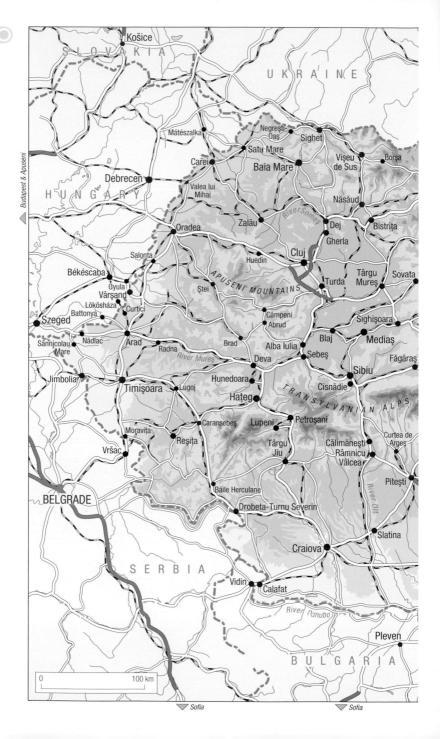

Budapest & Apuseni

Košice

S L O V A K I A

U K R A I N E

Mátészalka

Negreşti-Oaş   Sighet

Satu Mare

Carei   Baia Mare   Vişeu de Sus   Borşa

Debrecen

Valea lui Mihai

Năsăud

H U N G A R Y

Zalău   *River Someş*   Dej   Bistriţa

Oradea   Gherla

Salonta   Huedin   Cluj

Békéscaba   Târgu Mureş   Sovata

Gyula   A P U S E N I   M O U N T A I N S   Turda

Vărşand   Ştei

Lököşháza   Curtici   Câmpeni

Battonya   Abrud   Sighişoara

Szeged

Sânnicolau Mare   Nădlac   Arad   Radna   Brad   Blaj   Mediaş

Alba Iulia

River Mureş   Deva   Sebeş   Făgăraş

Jimbolia   Hunedoara   Sibiu

Timişoara   Lugoj   Cisnădie

Hațeg   T R A N S Y L V A N I A N   A L P S

Caransebeş   Lupeni   Petroşani

Moraviţa   Curtea de Argeş

Reşiţa   Târgu Jiu   Călimăneşti

Vršac   Râmnicu Vâlcea

Piteşti

Băile Herculane

BELGRADE   Drobeta-Turnu Severin   *River Olt*

Slatina

S E R B I A   Craiova

Vidin   Calafat

River Danube

Pleven

B U L G A R I A

0   100 km

▽ *Sofia*   ▽ *Sofia*

4

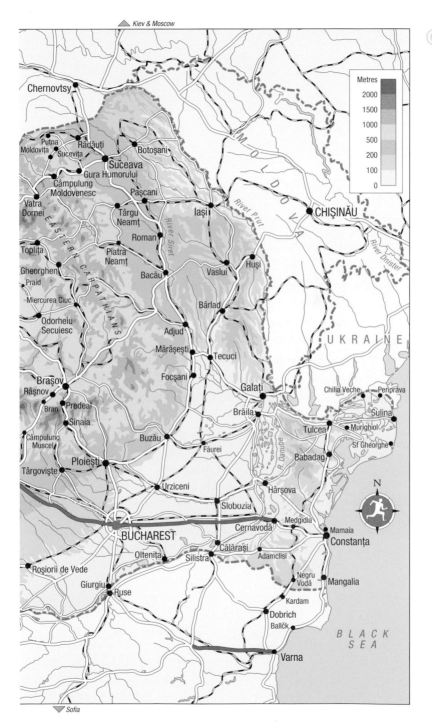

Kiev & Moscow

Metres	
2000	
1500	
1000	
500	
200	
100	
0	

Chernovtsy

Putna
Moldoviţa Rădăuţi
Sucevita Botoşani
Suceava
Gura Humorului
Câmpulung
Moldovenesc Paşcani
Vatra
Dornei Târgu Iaşi CHIŞINĂU
Neamţ
Roman
Topliţa Piatra
Neamţ
Gheorghen Bacău Vaslui Huşi
Praid
Miercurea Ciuc
Odorheiu Bârlad
Secuiesc
Adjud
Mărăşeşti Tecuci
Focşani
Braşov Galaţi Chilia Veche Periprava
Râşnov
Bran Predeal Brăila Sulina
Sinaia Tulcea Murighiol
Câmpulung Sf Gheorghe
Muscel Buzău
Ploieşti Făurei Babadag
Târgovişte
Urziceni Hârşova
Slobozia
BUCHAREST Cernavodă Medgidia Mamaia
Olteniţa Călăraşi Adamclisi Constanţa
Roşiorii de Vede Silistra Negru
Giurgiu Vodă Mangalia
Ruse Kardam
Dobrich
Ballčk
Varna

MOLDOVA

River Prut
River Siret
River Dnister

UKRAINE

EASTERN CARPATHIANS

R. Danube

BLACK
SEA

N

Sofia

5

Introduction to

Romania

Travel in Romania is as rewarding as it is challenging. The country's fantastic mountain scenery and great diversity of wildlife, its cultures and people, and a way of life that at times seems little changed since the Middle Ages, leave few who visit unaffected. Rather than expecting an easy ride, try to accept whatever happens as an adventure – encounters with Gypsies, wild bears and tricky officials are likely to be far more interesting than anything purveyed by the tourist board.

Romanians trace their **ancestry** back to the Romans, and have a noticeable Latin character – warm, spontaneous, anarchic and appreciative of style and life's pleasures. In addition to ethnic Romanians, one and a half million Magyars pursue a traditional lifestyle long since vanished in Hungary, while dwindling numbers of Transylvanian Germans (Saxons) reside around the fortified towns and churches their ancestors built in the Middle Ages to guard the mountain passes. Along the coast, in the Delta and in the Banat, there's a rich mixture of Russians, Ukrainians, Serbs, Slovaks, Bulgars, Gypsies, Turks and Tatars.

Two decades of rule under the dictator Nicolae Ceaușescu took Romania to the brink of ruin, with economic collapse, a widely condemned village systematization programme and continual repression by the feared Securitate all contributing to a dramatic deterioration in living standards. Although it's now more than twenty years since Ceaușescu's overthrow in what was

Europe's bloodiest revolution of 1989, the country is, in many ways, only just emerging from his shadow – though Romania's admission into NATO in 2004 and then, somewhat more controversially, the **European Union** in 2007, has at least cemented its place in the wider international community. However, the latter has made little tangible difference to the lives of ordinary Romanians, who remain among Europe's poorest cousins.

As fascinating as the major towns and cities are – such as the capital, Bucharest, Braşov, Sighişoara, Timişoara and, most enchantingly, Sibiu – Romania's charm essentially lies in the remoter, less visited regions. Almost any exploration of the **villages** of rural Romania will be rewarding, with sights as diverse as the log houses in Oltenia, Delta villages built of reeds, and the magnificent wooden churches, with their sky-scraping Gothic steeples, of Maramureş, not to mention the country's abundance of more traditional churches, which reflect a history of competing communities and faiths. Moreover, Romania offers some of the most varied and unspoilt wilderness anywhere on the continent, from the majestic peaks of the Carpathian mountains and the verdant, rolling hills of Bucovina to the extraordinary wetlands of the Danube Delta.

Fact file

• Occupying an **area** of some 237,000 square kilometres, and with a **population** of around 23 million, Romania is one of central-eastern Europe's largest nations. Its capital, Bucharest, lies in the far south of the country on the plains of Wallachia, located between the Danube and the mountainous region of Transylvania to the north. The highest peak is Moldoveanu (2544m), in the Carpathian mountains.

• The constitution sets in place a **parliamentary system of government**, elected every four years, with the prime minister at its head – the president is head of state.

• **Tourism** is one of the fastest-growing sectors of the Romanian economy, with mountain, coastal and health spa resorts absorbing the bulk of the country's tourist traffic. Romania's most important **exports** are textiles and footwear, metal products, and machinery and equipment, and its main trading partners are Italy and Germany.

• Romania's most famous **historical figure** is Vlad Ţepeş (c.1431–76), also known as Vlad the Impaler and, more familiarly, as Dracula.

Where to go

The first point of arrival for many visitors to Romania is the capital, **Bucharest**. While not an easy city to love – its wide nineteenth-century Parisian-style boulevards are choked with traffic, once-grand *fin-de-siècle* buildings are crumbling and the suburbs are dominated by grim apartment blocks – its myriad cultural institutions, surprisingly abundant greenery and lively Old Town nightlife certainly reward patience.

From the capital, most visitors make a beeline for the province of **Transylvania** to the north, setting for the country's most thrilling scenery and home to its finest cities: the gateway to Transylvania is **Braşov**, whose medieval Old Town is a good introduction to the Saxon architecture of the region, which reaches its peak in the fortified town of **Sibiu** and the jagged skyline of **Sighişoara**, Romania's most atmospherically sited town and the birthplace of Vlad the Impaler (Dracula). The Saxon influence is further evident in the surrounding villages in the form of numerous citadels and churches, with particularly fine examples at Biertan, Prejmer and Viscri.

North and west of here, the great Magyar cities of **Târgu Mureş**, **Cluj** and **Oradea** have retained a wealth of medieval churches and streets, as well as impressive Baroque and Secession edifices. To the southwest of the country, near the border with Serbia, is **Timişoara**, source of the 1989 Revolution and a hugely enjoyable place to spend a day or two.

The best of Romania, though, is its countryside, and in particular the wonderful mountain scenery. The wild **Carpathians**, forming the frontier between Transylvania and, to the east and south, Moldavia and Wallachia, shelter bears, stags, chamois and eagles; while the Bucegi, Făgăraş and Retezat ranges and the Padiş plateau offer some of the most undisturbed and spectacular hiking opportunities in Europe. The **Black Sea coast** has a multiplicity of brash resorts, notably Mamaia, though it's not without its charms, not least the old port of Constanţa.

Spas

Romania boasts one-third of all Europe's mineral springs, and around 160 **spa resorts** (*băile*), many of which were made fashionable by the Habsburgs during the nineteenth century.

Spa holidays are tremendously popular, the theory being that you stay in a resort for about eighteen days, following a prescribed course of treatment, and ideally return regularly over the next few years. However, if you can get cheap accommodation, a spa can also make a good base for a one-off holiday. In any case, it's worth bearing in mind that even the smallest spas have campsites and restaurants.

The basic treatment naturally involves drinking the **waters**, which come in an amazing variety: alkaline, chlorinated, carbogaseous, and sodium-, iodine-, magnesium-, sulphate- or iron-bearing. In addition, you can bathe in hot springs or sapropelic muds, breathe in foul fumes at mofettes, or indulge in a new generation of complementary **therapies** such as ultrasound and aerosol treatment, ultraviolet light baths, acupuncture and electrotherapy.

The spas all have their own areas of specialization: Sovata is the best place for **gynaecological problems**; Covasna, Vatra Dornei and Buziaş deal with **cardiovascular complaints**; Călimăneşti-Căciulata, Slănic Moldova, Sângeorz-Băi and Băile Olăneşti with **digestion**; and others (notably Băile Herculane and Băile Felix) with a range of **locomotive and rheumatic ailments**. Mountain resorts such as Sinaia, Băile Tuşnad and Moneasa treat **nervous complaints** with fresh air, which has an ideal balance of ozone and ions.

Just north of here, the waterlogged **Danube Delta** is a place set apart from the rest of the country, where life has hardly changed for centuries and where boats are the only way to reach many of the settlements. During spring and autumn, especially, hundreds of species of birds from all over the Old World migrate through this area or come to breed. While not quite as remote, the northern region of **Maramureş**, bordering Ukraine, retains an almost medieval-like feel, its villages renowned for their fabulous wooden churches. Close by, sprinkled amid the soft, rolling hills of **Bucovina**, are the wonderful painted monasteries, whose specimens of religious art are among some of the most outstanding in Europe.

When to go

The **climate** is pretty crucial in deciding where and when to go to Romania. **Winters** can be fairly brutal – snow blankets much of the country, temperatures of minus fifteen to twenty degrees are not uncommon, and a strong, icy wind (the *crivaţ*) sweeps down from Russia. Conditions improve with **spring**, bringing rain and wildflowers to the mountains and the softest of blue skies over Bucharest, and prompting the great migration of birds through the Delta. By May, the lowlands are warming up and you might well find strong sunshine on the coast before the season starts in July. Although by far the hottest time of the year, **summer or early autumn** is the perfect time to investigate Transylvania's festivals

▼ City Hall, Braşov

▲ Skiers in Poiana Braşov

and hiking trails (though brief but violent thunderstorms are common in the Carpathians during this period), and to see the painted monasteries of Bucovina, while flocks of birds again pass through the Delta towards the **end of autumn**.

Average daily temperatures

	Jan	Feb	Mar	Apr	May	Jun	Jul	Aug	Sep	Oct	Nov	Dec
Braşov (The mountains)												
(˚C)	1	1	6	11	16	19	21	21	18	13	7	2
(˚F)	34	34	42	52	61	66	69	69	65	55	45	36
Bucharest												
(˚C)	-3	-1	4	11	17	21	23	22	18	12	5	1
(˚F)	26	31	40	52	62	69	71	70	65	53	41	34
Constanţa (The coast)												
(˚C)	-1	1	3	13	19	24	26	26	22	17	11	6
(˚F)	31	34	39	55	66	75	79	79	70	62	52	43
Timişoara (The Banat)												
(˚C)	-2	1	5	11	16	20	20	18	18	12	6	1
(˚F)	28	34	41	52	61	67	67	65	65	53	43	34

29

things not to miss

It's not possible to see everything Romania has to offer in one trip – and we don't suggest you try. What follows is a selective and subjective taste of the country's highlights: outstanding architecture, natural wonders, spectacular hikes and unforgettable festivals. They're arranged in five colour-coded categories, so you can browse through to find the very best things to see, do, buy and experience. All highlights have a page reference to take you straight into the guide, where you can find out more.

01 **Peleş Castle, Sinaia** Page **129** • Once a refuge for Ceauşescu and visiting dignitaries, Peleş remains the country's most opulent palace.

02 Bucharest Page **49** • Romania's noisy, chaotic capital boasts a number of terrific museums, some surprisingly appealing architecture and some flourishing nightlife.

03 Danube Delta Page **338** • Bordering Ukraine, this remote and beautiful landscape has an abundant array of wildlife, and offers some of the finest birdwatching in Europe.

04 **Black Sea** Page **352** • Strewn with lively resorts and long sandy beaches, the Black Sea coast offers opportunities aplenty for activities, while Constanţa offers some cultural respite.

05 **Karst formations** Page **214** • Romania's impressive karst landscape offers fantastic subterranean wonders, including Cetăţile Ponorului in the Apuseni mountains.

07 **Maramureş** Page 277 • Romania's remote, northernmost region is also its most beguiling, with villages seemingly lost in time and ancient customs still very much alive.

06 **Fortified churches** Pages **150** & **156** • Scattered among the lush green hills of southern Transylvania are dozens of marvellous fortified Saxon churches, such as those at Mălâncrav and Viscri.

08 **Sheep's cheese** Page **37** • Fresh from the highland pastures, a sample of tasty sheep's cheese is a must.

09 **Bear and wolf tracking** Page **145** • Get on the trail of Romania's largest carnivores, and if you're lucky you may even get to see one of these magnificent creatures up close.

10 **Vişeu de Sus train ride** Pages **302–303** • Jump aboard the early-morning logging train for a slow, meandering ride up the picturesque Vaser valley.

11 **Constantin Brâncuşi** Page **110** • Romania's greatest sculptor has bequeathed an impressive legacy of striking works of art, such as the *Endless Column* in Târgu Jiu.

13 **Pageant of the Juni** Page **139** • Dancing, costumes and brass regiments constitute Braşov's liveliest event.

12 **Sibiu** Page **158** • Beautiful squares and architecture, terrific museums and some fabulous festivals make the once great Saxon town of Sibiu one of Romania's most alluring destinations.

14 **Braşov** Page **134** • Shadowed by mountains and containing a fine Baroque centre, this erstwhile Saxon settlement is one of Transylvania's most appealing cities.

16 **Village homestays** Page **34** • Wonderful rural retreats offering cheap, friendly and relaxing accommodation and great home-cooked food.

15 **Wooden churches of Maramureş** Page **286** & *Romanian architecture* colour section • The landscape of this isolated region is dominated by marvellous wooden churches, characterized by their magnificent spires.

17 **Bicaz gorges** Page **240** • Take a drive through the majestic Bicaz gorges, bisected by sheer, 300m-high limestone cliffs.

18 **Skiing** Page **141** & *The great outdoors* colour section • Hit the slopes in Poiana Braşov, Romania's premier ski resort, or many of the country's other fast-developing centres.

19 Merry Cemetery, Săpânţa Page **295** • True to its name, the Merry Cemetery is a riot of beautifully carved and brightly coloured wooden headstones.

20 Timişoara Page **323** • The crucible of the 1989 revolution, this most cosmopolitan of Romanian cities incorporates handsome architecture, fine parks and a vibrant arts scene.

21 **Measurement of the Milk Festival** Page **217** • Enjoyable and unusual spectacle in which shepherds vie to see who has the most productive animals.

22 **Bucovina hills** Page **259** • Cloaked in beech, fir and pine, the gorgeous rolling Bucovina hills are a walker's paradise.

23 **Țuică** Page **37** • A typically powerful Balkan brandy, Romania's national drink should be tried at least once.

25 **Dracula** Page **403** • The tomb at Snagov, old castle ruins at Poienari, the Princely Court at Târgoviște and the birthplace in Sighișoara – the Dracula legend is alive and kicking.

24 **Sighișoara** Page **151** • A brooding skyline of ramparts, towers and spires marks Sighișoara out as Transylvania's most atmospheric medieval town.

26 **Hiking in the Făgăraş mountains** Page **146** • The spectacular peaks of the Făgăraş are the highest in Romania, providing access to some of the Carpathians' most rewarding hikes.

27 **Painted monasteries** Pages **259**, **263** & *Romanian architecture* colour section • Nestled behind huge walls, the monasteries of southern Bucovina and Moldavia are renowned for their magnificent exterior frescoes.

28 **Folk and Gypsy music** Page **392** • Don't miss the chance to experience the wild, irrepressible sounds of Romanian folk and Gypsy music.

29 **The Carpathian range** Pages **126**, **145** & **146** • One of Europe's least spoilt mountain ranges, the Carpathians are full of wildlife as well as first-class hiking trails.

Basics

Basics

Getting there

Flying is the easiest way to reach Romania, with several airlines now operating direct from the UK. Flying from North America, Australasia or South Africa will entail one or more changes. Travelling to Romania from the UK by train is a long haul, though with a rail pass you can take in the country as part of a wider trip. Driving there will involve a journey of some 2000km; an absorbing trip but one best covered slowly.

Airfares are highest from June to August, and drop during the "shoulder" seasons – March to May and September to October. The best prices appear during the low season, from November to February, excluding Christmas and New Year when fares are hiked up and seats are at a premium.

You can often cut costs by going through a specialist flight agent, who in addition to dealing with discounted flights may also offer student and youth fares and travel insurance, rail passes, car rental, tours and the like. Some agents specialize in charter flights, which may be cheaper than scheduled flights, but departure dates are fixed and cancellation penalties high.

Flights from the UK and Ireland

Flying from the UK to Romania takes approximately three and a half hours. British Airways and TAROM, the Romanian national carrier, both have **daily direct scheduled flights** from London Heathrow to Bucharest Henri Coandă airport. **Fares** can be obtained for around £110–130 return, including tax. Of the **budget carriers**, WizzAir flies from London Luton to Bucharest Baneasa and Cluj (in Transylvania); while Blue Air also flies from London Luton to Baneasa. Fares can be obtained for as little as £60–70 return, including tax.

Another possibility is to fly to one of the **neighbouring countries** and continue your journey overland. Budget airlines easyJet, Ryanair and WizzAir all fly from the UK to Budapest, in Hungary, from where there are cheap onward connections by bus or train to Romania. EasyJet also fly from London to Sofia, in Bulgaria.

Aer Lingus has direct flights from Dublin to Bucharest Henri Coandă, while Blue Air flies from Dublin to Bucharest Baneasa.

Flights from the US and Canada

There are **no direct flights from the US or Canada to Romania**, so you'll have to fly into a major European hub and continue the journey from there. From the east coast of the US, expect to pay around US$750 low season and US$1100 high season; and from the west coast around US$1100 low season and US$1500 high season. From Canada, expect to pay around Can$1300 low season and Can$1600 high season.

Flights from Australia, New Zealand and South Africa

There are **no direct flights from Australia or New Zealand to Romania**, so you'll have to change airlines, either in Asia or Europe, although the best option is to fly to a Western European gateway for a connecting flight. A standard return fare from eastern **Australia** to Bucharest, via London, with Qantas, is around Aus$2200 low season and Aus$2700 high season. The same routes apply for flights from **New Zealand**, with a standard return fare from around NZ$2400 low season and NZ$3000 high season.

Similarly, there are no direct **flights** from South Africa, so you'll have to change airlines at one of the main European gateways. A standard return fare from Johannesburg to Bucharest, via Frankfurt or Vienna (with South African Airways or a

Five steps to a better kind of travel

At Rough Guides we are passionately committed to travel. We feel strongly that only through travelling do we truly come to understand the world we live in and the people we share it with – plus tourism has brought a great deal of **benefit** to developing economies around the world over the last few decades. But the extraordinary growth in tourism has also damaged some places irreparably, and of course **climate change** is exacerbated by most forms of transport, especially flying. This means that now more than ever it's important to **travel thoughtfully** and **responsibly**, with respect for the cultures you're visiting – not only to derive the most benefit from your trip but also to preserve the best bits of the planet for everyone to enjoy. At Rough Guides we feel there are five main areas in which you can make a difference:

• Consider what you're contributing to the **local economy**, and how much the services you use do the same, whether it's through employing local workers and guides or sourcing locally grown produce and local services.

• Travel with a purpose, not just to tick off experiences. Consider **spending longer** in a place, and getting to know it and its people.

• Give thought to how often you **fly**. Try to avoid short hops by air and more harmful night flights.

• Consider **alternatives to flying**, travelling instead by bus, train, boat and even by bike or on foot where possible.

• Make your trips "**climate neutral**" via a reputable carbon offset scheme. All Rough Guide flights are offset, and every year we donate money to a variety of charities devoted to combating the effects of climate change.

leading European airline), is around ZAR9500 low season and ZAR11,500 high season.

By train

Travelling **by train** is likely to be considerably more expensive than flying, though it can be a leisurely way of getting to the country if you plan to stop off in other parts of Europe along the way.

The shortest journey takes about 36 hours, with a standard second-class **return ticket**, incorporating Eurostar, costing around £350. From London St Pancras International, take the Eurostar to Paris Gare du Nord, and then walk next door to the Gare de l'Est for a train to either Munich or Vienna, where you change for Budapest. In Budapest, change again for the last leg to Romania. Tickets are usually valid for two to three months and allow unlimited stopovers.

Deutsche Bahn is the best option for making seat reservations on continental trains and its website (⊛www.bahn.de) is an excellent resource for checking railway timetables, while The Man in Seat Sixty-One

(⊛www.seat61.com) is another excellent source of information on most aspects of rail travel in Europe. Thomas Cook's red-covered European Rail Timetable, which details schedules of the main Romanian train service, is the most useful printed source for timetables.

Rail passes

If you're taking in Romania as part of a wider trip, there are a number of **rail passes** available. The **InterRail Pass** (⊛www .interrailnet.com) is available to European residents only (or those who have been resident in a European country for at least six months), and you will be asked to provide proof of residency before being allowed to buy one. They come in over-26 and (cheaper) under-26 versions, and cover up to thirty countries.

There are two types of pass. The **Global Pass** covers all thirty countries (one month of continuous use costs €599 for over-26s/€399 for under-26s; 22 days continuous €469/309; 10 days in 22 €359/239; 5 days in 10 €249/159). InterRail

Passes do not include travel between Britain and the continent, although holders are eligible for discounts on rail travel in Britain and Northern Ireland and cross-Channel ferries, as well as reduced rates on the London–Paris Eurostar service.

The other InterRail scheme is the **one-country pass**, which allows you to travel a certain number of days during a one-month period. For Romania, eight days in one month costs €139 over-26s/€90 under-26s; six days in one month €119/77; four days in one month €89/58; three days in one month €71/46.

Non-European residents qualify for the **Eurail pass** (@www.eurail.com), which must be bought before arrival in Europe (or from RailEurope in the UK). The pass allows unlimited travel in Romania and twenty other European countries, and is available in increments of fifteen days (€511 over-26s/€332 under-26s), 21 days (€662/429), one month (€822/535), two months (€1161/755) and three months (€1432/933).

The One-Country Pass for Romania allows unlimited travel on a select number of days over a two-month period, with five days costing €139 for over-26s/€111 for under-26s, and ten days (€242/195). Furthermore, there's the Select Pass, which allows travel in three (from €211), four (from €235) or five (from €260) bordering countries over a selected period of time (five, six, eight, ten or fifteen days within a two-month period); and the Regional Hungary-Romania Pass (from €133), which allows unlimited travel between five and ten days over a two-month period.

By car from the UK

Driving to Romania, a distance of some 2000km from London, can be a pleasant proposition. However, it's really only worth considering if you are planning to travel around Romania extensively or want to make various stopovers en route.

Once across the channel, the best **route** (around 30hr at a leisurely pace with plenty of stops) is through Belgium, Germany, Austria and Hungary, passing Brussels, Frankfurt, Nuremberg, Regensburg, Linz, Vienna and Budapest, and then taking the E60 down to the Borş border crossing near Oradea or the E75/E68 to Nădlac near Arad. Detailed printouts of the route can be obtained from the websites of Michelin (@www.viamichelin .com), the AA (@www.theaa.com) or the RAC (@www.rac.co.uk). See p.32 for details of driving within Romania.

Airlines, agents and operators

Airlines

Aer Lingus @www.aerlingus.com.
Air Canada @www.aircanada.com.
Air France @www.airfrance.com.
Air New Zealand @www.airnewzealand.com.
Blue Air @www.blueairweb.com.
British Airways @www.ba.com.
easyJet @www.easyjet.com.
KLM (Royal Dutch Airlines) @www.klm.com.
Lufthansa @www.lufthansa.com.
Qantas Airways @www.qantas.com.
Ryanair @www.ryanair.com.
South African Airways @www.flysaa.com.
TAROM @www.tarom.ro.
WizzAir @www.wizzair.com.

Agents and operators

North South Travel UK ☏01245/608 291, @www.northsouthtravel.co.uk. Friendly travel agency, offering discounted fares worldwide. Profits are used to support projects in the developing world, especially the promotion of sustainable tourism.
STA Travel UK ☏0871/2300 040, US ☏1-800/781-4040, Australia ☏134 782, New Zealand ☏0800/474 400, South Africa ☏0861/781 781; @www.statravel.co.uk. Worldwide specialists in independent travel; also student IDs, travel insurance, car rental, rail passes, and more. Good discounts for students and under-26s.
Trailfinders UK ☏0845/058 5858, Ireland ☏01/677 7888, Australia ☏1300/780 212; @www.trailfinders.com. One of the best-informed and most efficient agents for independent travellers.
Travel CUTS Canada ☏1-866/246-9762, US ☏1-800/592-2887; @www.travelcuts.com. Canadian youth and student travel firm.
USIT Ireland ☏01/602 1906, Northern Ireland ☏028/9032 7111; @www.usit.ie. Ireland's main student and youth travel specialists.

Specialist operators

Adventure Center US ☏1-800/228-8747 or 510/654-1879, @www.adventurecenter.com. Eight-day culture and wildlife tours in the Carpathians, staying in guesthouses.

Avian Adventures ☎01384/372 013, ⓦwww
.avianadventures.co.uk. Ten-day birding tour of the
Danube Delta and Transylvania.

Balkan Holidays ☎0845/520 1260, ⓦwww
.balkanholidays.co.uk. Southeastern Europe
specialists offering package deals to the coast, as well
as ski packages in Poiana Braşov and flights.

Birdfinders ☎01258/839 066, ⓦwww
.birdfinders.co.uk. Ten-day birdwatching tour of the
Danube Delta in April.

Dream Tours International US ☎1-800/260-
1068 or ☎818/956-8397, ⓦwww.dreamtoursint
.com. Eight- and twelve-day tours of Romania,
including Transylvania and the Bucovina monasteries,
as well as Dracula tours.

Eastern Eurotours Australia ☎1800/242-353 or
07/5526-2855, ⓦwww.easterneurotours.com.au. A
range of seven- to ten-day tours throughout Romania,
including Transylvania, the painted monasteries and
Dracula.

Equine Adventures ☎0845/130 6981, ⓦwww
.equineadventures.co.uk. Horseriding specialists
offering eight- and ten-day tours through
Transylvania.

Exodus ☎0845/805 5344, ⓦwww.exodus
.co.uk. Eight-day culture and conservation tours
in the Carpathians, with accommodation in local
guesthouses. In Ireland, contact Worldwide Adventures
☎01/679-5700.

Explore Worldwide ☎0845/013 1537, ⓦwww
.explore.co.uk. Eleven-day tours (with some hiking)
of the Maramureş villages, the painted monasteries of
Bucovina, and the Danube Delta.

Hooked on Cycling ☎0151/740 985, ⓦwww
.hookedoncycling.co.uk. Eight-day self-guided
cycling tour (easy to moderate) through the
Carpathians, staying in local guesthouses.

Inghams ☎020/8780 6680, ⓦwww.inghams
.co.uk. Ski packages in Poiana Braşov.

Limosa Holidays ☎01692/580 623, ⓦwww
.limosaholidays.co.uk. Spring and autumn birding
tours in the Danube Delta and along the Black Sea
Coast, and a two-country (with Hungary) Birds and
Bears trip.

Martin Randall Travel ☎020/8742 3355,
ⓦwww.martinrandall.com. Seven-day tours of
Bucovina's painted monasteries, with accommodation
in comfortable three- and four-star hotels.

Naturetrek ☎01962/733 051, ⓦwww.naturetrek
.co.uk. Wide range of tours, including the wildlife
of Transylvania, birds of the Danube Delta, and wild
flowers in the Carpathians.

Quest Tours and Adventures US ☎1-800/621-
8687, ⓦwww.romtour.com. Wide range of tours and
fully customized packages, including monastery and
Dracula tours, as well as Bucharest city packages.

Ride World Wide ☎01837/82544, ⓦwww
.rideworldwide.com. Seven-day riding holidays in the
Carpathians between April and Oct; four to six hours'
riding daily and accommodation in local guesthouses.

Romania Travel Centre ☎0800/132 973,
ⓦwww.romaniatravelcentre.com. Romania
specialists offering a comprehensive programme
including Bucharest city breaks, coastal, ski and spa
holidays, eco-tours and biking trips. Flights and tailor-
made accommodation deals too.

Transylvania Uncovered ☎01539/531 258,
ⓦwww.beyondtheforest.com. Comprehensive
Romania specialists offering package and special
interest tours (wilderness, wine and culture, riding,
spas, Dracula), flights, accommodation, car hire and
rail tickets.

Travelling Naturalist ☎01305/267 994,
ⓦwww.naturalist.co.uk. Spring, autumn and winter
birdwatching tours to the Danube Delta, and a
summer Flowers of the Carpathians trip.

Vamos Travel ☎01926/330 223, ⓦwww
.vamostravel.com. Various offerings including
Bucharest city breaks (plus stag weekends), the
painted monasteries and Dracula tours.

Wilderness US ☎1-800/368-2794, ⓦwww
.wildernesstravel.com. Twelve-day hiking and
sightseeing expedition throughout the Carpathians,
incorporating two nights in mountain chalets.

Rail contacts

European Rail UK ☎020/7619 1083, ⓦwww
.europeanrail.com.

Europrail International Canada ☎1-888/667-
9734, ⓦwww.europrail.net.

Eurostar UK ☎0843/218 6186, ⓦwww.eurostar
.com.

Rail Europe UK ☎0844/848 4064, US
☎1-800/622-8600, Canada ☎1-800/361-7245;
ⓦwww.raileurope.co.uk.

Ferry contacts

P&O Ferries UK ☎08716/642 121, ⓦwww
.poferries.com.

Sea France UK ☎0871/423 7119, ⓦwww
.seafrance.com.

Stena Line UK ☎0844/770 7070, ⓦwww
.stenaline.co.uk.

Getting around

Most Romanian towns are easily reached by train, and although it is not the fastest or cleanest system in the world, it is remarkably cheap and reliable. In the absence of a coordinated bus network, maxitaxis (minibuses) are everywhere, linking many of the larger centres and often providing a more direct and frequent mode of transport than trains. Driving is another attractive proposition, enabling you to visit anywhere you please, and in your own time.

By rail

The **SNCFR** (*Societatea Naţională a Căilor Ferate Române*, generally known as the **CFR**, or ChéFéRé) network covers most of the country. Tickets are incredibly cheap – a 100km trip (second class) is around €3–8 – though this is offset by the aged carriages and bizarre timetable. However, many routes are wonderfully scenic, particularly in Transylvania.

There are several types of train: **Intercity** ("IC") and **Rapid** ("R") services, halting only at major towns, are the most comfortable and expensive, while **Accelerats** ("A") have more frequent stops, and are the standard means of inter-urban travel. The painfully slow **Personal** ("P") trains should be avoided where possible, unless you're heading for some tiny destination. **EuroCity** ("EC") and **EuroNight** ("EN") trains are international services.

Train **timetables** (*orar trenurilor*) are displayed in stations and CFR offices; arrivals are on a white board, departures on a yellow one. Watch out for services that run only during certain seasons (*circulă numai*, eg *Intre 9.V şi 8.IX* – between May 9 and Sept 8), or only on particular days (1 represents Mon, 2 represents Tues and so on; *nu circula Sâmbata şi Duminica* means the service doesn't run on Sat or Sun). If you're planning to travel a lot by train, try to get hold of the notoriously elusive national **CFR timetable**, the *Mersul Trenurilor*, issued each December. Otherwise, check out the web version, ⓦ www.cfr.ro. In any case, you should always check at the station. Details of main **routes** are given in the text, and summarized at the end of each chapter.

Left luggage offices (*bagaje de mână*) exist in most train stations, where you'll usually have to pay around €1.

Tickets

Fares (calculated by distance travelled) are extremely low; for example, a journey of 100km on an Intercity service will cost around €9 second class, and around €12 first class (around €8/10 on a Rapid, €5/7 on an Accelerat, and €3/5 on a Personal), which makes travelling first class a bargain. Supplements (with a seat reservation) are required on Intercity, Rapid and Accelerat services, costing around €5, €4 and €2 respectively for a 100km journey. In most stations, **tickets** are now computerized, with all information on one piece of paper. In smaller places, however, your ticket (*bilet*) will usually be accompanied by a second piece of card, indicating the service (*nr. trenului*), your carriage (*vagon*) and reserved seat (*loc*). These **tickets** are sold only an hour before departure time, and usually at specific windows for each train, which can lead to a bit of a scrum; at these non-computerized stations it's easier to book a day ahead (or seven days for services to the coast during summer) at the **Agenţia CFR in town**.

Return tickets (*bilet dus întors*) are rarely issued except for international services. Many long-distance overnight trains have **sleeping cars** (*vagon de dormit*) and couchettes (*cuşete*), for which a surcharge of around €10–15 and €6–10 respectively (depending upon how many berths there are) is levied.

By bus or maxitaxi

Romania's **bus network** consists of a hugely confusing and poorly coordinated array of private companies, and is really only useful if you're planning to visit some village not served by train. In the countryside, knowing when and where to wait for the bus is a local art form, and on Sundays many regions have no local buses at all.

A popular mode of road transport is **minibuses**, or **maxitaxis**. The advantage they have over trains is the frequency and speed of services. That said, passengers are usually crammed aboard with scant regard for comfort, and there's generally very little luggage space available. Moreover, the speed and recklessness of some of the driving leave a lot to be desired. Expect to pay around €4.50 from Bucharest to Piteşti (100km), or €8 from Bucharest to Braşov (250km). Maxitaxis often begin and end their journeys from the local bus or train station. Main bus and maxitaxi routes are listed in the "Travel Details" section at the end of each chapter in this Guide.

All towns have **local bus services**, and in the main cities you'll also find **trams** (*tramvai*) and **trolley buses** (*troleibuz*). Tickets are normally sold in pairs (around €0.30) from street kiosks. Validate them yourself aboard the vehicle; stiff fines apply if you don't.

By car

Driving in Romania is, on the whole, an attractive proposition. Outside the major towns and cities, you'll find the roads relatively traffic-free, and many routes, particularly through Transylvania, are wonderfully scenic. That said, the overall state of the roads varies enormously (roadworks grind on interminably), while Romanian driving habits often leave much to be desired.

There are presently just two motorways (*autostrada*) in Romania, the A1 between Bucharest and Piteşti, and the A2 between Bucharest and Cernavodă, just short of Constanţa. The **main roads** (*Drum Naţional* or DN) are, generally speaking, in good condition. The quality of the **county roads** (*Drum Judeţean*), however, is variable, while many of the local roads are disintegrating – potholes are a particularly nasty hazard. Being such a big country, long distances are best covered at a steady pace, especially if driving in the more mountainous regions where greater powers of concentration are required.

Aside from the very Balkan habit of overtaking at absurdly risky moments, other potential hazards include horses and carts, which are commonplace in rural areas, and stray dogs – squashed canines lying on the side of the road are an all too common sight. For these reasons, it's best to **avoid driving after dark** wherever possible.

If bringing your own car into the country you must purchase an electronic vignette (*rovigneta*); upon purchase (€7 for a month or €13 for three months and available from border entry points, petrol stations and post offices), you receive an invoice, and your car details are recorded onto a database.

Driving rules and regulations

Traffic drives on the right and speed limits for vehicles are 50km/h in built-up areas, 90km/h on the open road (100km/h on European roads, denoted by E), and 130km/h on the motorway. Otherwise, the most important rules are the wearing of **seat belts** and the use of dipped headlights outside towns and cities. It is forbidden to use a hand-held **phone** while driving, and **drinking** and driving is severely punished. **Police** (*poliţia*) are empowered to levy on-the-spot **fines** for road traffic offences, but they cannot collect them; instead you'll be issued with a ticket (typically €40–80); if you settle up within 48 hours – at a town hall or one of the CEC savings banks – then you'll only have to pay half the fine. If you have an **accident**, you're legally obliged to await the arrival of the police. You can get **technical assistance** and information from **ACR** (Romanian Automobile Club), whose main Bucharest offices are at Str. Tache Ionescu 27 (☏021/315 5510) and Şos. Colentina 1 (☏021/635 4140). In the event of a **breakdown**, call ACR's 24-hour **breakdown service** on ☏021/222 2222, whereupon an English-speaking operator will direct you to the nearest point of assistance.

Petrol stations (*benzinarie*) can be found almost everywhere, even in the most rural backwaters – the best and most common are those run by ROMPETROL, OMV-PETROM, LUKOIL (Russian) and MOL (Hungarian), many of which have good refreshment and toilet facilities; avoid the small, private stations, where fuel may be dirty or diluted. Lead-free fuel (*fără plomb*), which costs around €1.10 per litre, is the most common. Credit cards are accepted at most stations. While most service stations operate from around 7am to 8 or 9pm, quite a few are open around the clock, usually located on the outskirts of larger towns and cities.

Car rental

Renting a car is simple enough, provided you are 21 or older, and hold a valid national driving licence. You can order a car through rental agencies in your home country, which sometimes works out cheaper, particularly if you book online. Most of the major companies have branches in Bucharest (and Henri Coandă airport) and the other major cities. **Costs** are not especially cheap; expect to pay around €45–50 for a day's hire (unlimited mileage), and around €35–40 per day for seven day's hire or more. You may find that **local companies**, such as Pan Travel (see p.207), offer better deals.

Car rental agencies

Auto Europe ⓦ www.autoeurope.com.
Avis ⓦ www.avis.com.
Budget ⓦ www.budget.com.
Carhire3000 ⓦ www.carhire3000.com.
Dollar ⓦ www.dollar.com.
Europcar ⓦ www.europcar.com.
Hertz ⓦ www.hertz.com.
Holiday Autos ⓦ www.holidayautos.co.uk.
National Car Rental ⓦ www.nationalcar.com.
Rental Car Group ⓦ www.rentalcargroup.com.
Skycars ⓦ www.skycars.com.
SIXT ⓦ www.sixt.com.
Thrifty ⓦ www.thrifty.com.

Cycling

Given the mountainous terrain and the poor state of many of the country roads, you'll need to be fit and self-reliant to **cycle** around Romania. Cycle shops are few and far between, although most village mechanics can manage basic repairs. Carry a spare tyre and a few spokes, and check carrier nuts regularly, as the potholes and corrugations will rapidly shake them loose. A touring bike is better than a mountain bike unless you want to go off-road; with the immense network of forestry roads (*Drum Forestiere*) and free access to the hills, genuine mountain-biking is wonderful here. If you do bring your own bike, avoid cycling in **Bucharest**, where the roads are too hazardous. Carrying your bike by train is easiest on Personal services, where you can simply put it in the carriage; on Accelerats, it can be stored in the baggage van (this should be indicated on the timetable) and a good tip is necessary to ensure that it's properly guarded.

Hitchhiking

Hitchhiking (*autostop* or *occasie*) is an integral part of the Romanian transport system to supplement patchy or nonexistent services on back roads – it's even common (although illegal) on the *autostrada*. It's accepted practice to pay (a very small amount) for lifts; although this is often waived for foreigners, make sure you've got some small change to hand if you think it would be good to give the driver some money. As anywhere, however, it's not a foolproof pursuit, so caution should be exercised.

By plane

Romania has a well-integrated **plane network**, serving most of the larger cities. **TAROM**'s domestic **services** depart most days from Bucharest's Henri Coandă airport to Bacau, Baia Mare, Cluj, Constanţa, Iaşi, Oradea, Satu Mare, Sibiu, Suceava, Timişoara and Târgu Mureş. In addition, **Carpatair** (ⓦ www.carpatair.com), with its hub in Timişoara, operates flights out of Arad, Bacau, Bucharest, Cluj, Constanţa, Craiova, Iaşi and Sibiu. Singles are around €40–50.

Accommodation

You should have little trouble finding a bed in Romania, whatever the season. Hotels run the full gamut from plush, top-end establishments, to flea-pit dives with an intermittent water supply. There are a good number of youth hostels, in addition to a spread of private rooms and village homestays, the last of which typically offer wonderfully peaceful retreats.

In summer, it's safer, though only really essential on the coast, to make advance hotel **reservations**. If you're keen to save money on accommodation and you're travelling around a lot, you can use the **trains** to your advantage. On the long overnight journeys by Rapid or Accelerat train, it only costs a little more to book a comfortable sleeping car or couchette.

Hotels and pensions

Hotels use the traditional five-star **grading system** for classification, although in many cases this often gives only the vaguest idea of **prices**, which can fluctuate wildly according to the locality and season. For example, in Bucharest you can get some excellent deals at many high-end hotels in summer when the traditional business market is slack, while along the coast prices can drop by as much as a third outside July and August.

Outside Bucharest and the coast, the average three-star hotel can cost anything between €30 and €60 for a double room. Moreover, the ratings are not always indicative of the quality of a place, particularly at the lower end of the scale, where standards can vary tremendously. The plushest four- and five-star hotels offer all the luxuries one would expect, while three-star hotels can be unpredictable in terms of both quality and cost; you should, however, expect a reasonable standard of comfort, as well as private bathroom, TV and minibar, in most. Anything with three stars and above is almost certain to have internet access, either wi-fi or cable.

In some of the most basic places you may find that **hot water** is only available for a few hours a day (*cu program*), while it's not unusual to find some hotels in smaller towns doubling up as the local nightclub.

There are now a high number of **pensions** throughout the country; these are often smaller and more personable than hotels, as well as offering much better value for money. You may also come across **sport hotels** (an old East European institution), which were traditionally intended for visiting teams and school groups, but which now admit tourists too. Although often very basic, they invariably offer a clean and cheap place to bed down for the night.

Village homestays and private rooms

Village homestays (*agroturism*) – rural farmhouse-style accommodation – offer visitors the opportunity to spend some time with a Romanian family (most of whom won't speak English) in often lovely surrounds. The downside is that many places are in fairly remote locations, and are therefore difficult to reach without your own transport. Homestays are **graded** according to a **daisy classification system**; four or five daisies (of which there are few) denotes a house with large, well-furnished rooms with private bathroom or shower/toilet, while one or two daisies represents a more basic place offering shared shower and toilet facilities. Expect to pay €10–15 per person per night depending upon the category; many places also offer breakfast (around €3) and dinner (€5–7) upon request. The excellent website ⓦwww.ruralturism.ro lists a number of homestays throughout the country. The official nationwide body for homestays is **ANTREC** (the National Association of Rural, Ecological and Cultural Tourism; ⓦwww .antrec.ro).

You'll also come across many places advertising private rooms (*cazare* or *camere*

Accommodation price codes

Hotels listed in this guide have been coded according to the scale below. Prices given are for the cheapest **double room** available during peak season. Though you will generally pay for your room in lei, the codes are expressed in euros as many hotels are priced this way.

❶ €20 and under   ❹ €41–50   ❼ €76–90
❷ €21–30   ❺ €51–60   ❽ €91–105
❸ €31–40   ❻ €61–75   ❾ €106 and over

de inchiriat), particularly in the more touristed areas of Transylvania and along the coast. Indeed, in places like Braşov, Sighişoara and in some of the coastal resorts, you're likely to be greeted by people at the train station offering a room. Expect to pay no more than €10 for a bed, though breakfast is unlikely to be provided.

In the countryside, where there is a strong custom of hospitality, people may take you in and refuse payment, but you should offer something anyway, or come armed with a few packets of coffee, which make welcome presents.

Hostels

Romania has a rapidly expanding network of **youth hostels** (Ⓦ www.hihostels-romania .ro), with around half a dozen in Bucharest, as well as excellent options in Braşov, Cluj, Sibiu, Sighişoara and Suceava, and even in smaller towns and resorts such as Deva, Miercurea Ciuc and Vama Veche. Expect to pay around €10–12 for a dorm bed, €15–20 for a bed in a double room, and €25 for a single-bed room – breakfast is usually extra.

While **student accommodation** is largely in short supply, you may find the odd student residence willing to let out a bed, though these are largely available only in July and August – however, these are unlikely to be advertised, so ask for details at the local tourist office or town agency.

Cabanas

In the countryside, particularly in the mountainous areas favoured by hikers, there are well over a hundred **cabanas** or hikers' huts, ranging from chic alpine villas with dozens of bedrooms to fairly primitive chalets with bunk beds and cold running water. The hikers' cabanas are generally friendly and serve as useful places to pick up information about trails and the weather. Some (mainly in the Bucegi range) can be easily reached by cable car, while others are situated on roads just a few kilometres from towns; however, the majority are fairly isolated and accessible only by mountain tracks or footpaths. The location of the cabanas is shown rather vaguely on an ONT map, Cabane Turistice, but more precisely on hiking maps. Cabanas are supposed not to turn hikers away, but in the Făgăraş mountains, in particular, it might be wise to **book in advance**, by phone or through a local agency. Beds in remoter areas cost about €3–4, a little more for a private room or in one of the more comfortable cabanas.

Camping

Romania has a reasonable spread of **campsites** throughout the country, which vary in quality from very rudimentary places with minimal facilities, to first-class sites with **cabins** or bungalows (căsuțe) for rent, hot showers and even a restaurant. You'll generally pay about €3 per person per night, plus €5 for a car, though an ISIC student card may secure a thirty- to fifty-percent reduction.

In the mountains, though certain areas may be designated as a camping area (loc de campare), these are few and far between. However, providing you don't light fires in forests, leave litter or damage nature reserves, officialdom turns a blind eye to tourists **camping wild**, or, at the worst, may simply tell you to move along.

If you're planning to do a lot of camping, an **international camping carnet** is a good investment. The carnet gives discounts at member sites and serves as useful identification. Many campsites will take this instead of making you surrender your passport during your stay, and it covers you for third-party insurance when camping.

In the **UK and Ireland**, the carnet is available to members of the AA or the RAC, or the **Camping and Caravanning Club** (☎024/7669 4995, ⓦwww.campingandcar avanningclub.co.uk), the **CTC** (☎0870/873 0061, ⓦwww.ctc.org.uk), or the **Carefree**

Travel Service (☎024/7642 2024), which provides the carnet free if you take out insurance with them.

In the **US and Canada**, the carnet is available from home motoring organizations, or from **Family Campers and FCRVers** (FCRV; ☎1-800/245 9755 or 716/668 6242, ⓦwww.fcrv.org).

Food and drink

Romanian cuisine tends to be filling and wholesome rather than particularly tasty or imaginative, with menus dominated by meat, in common with the rest of the Balkans. Similarly, the range and quality of restaurants remains fairly average, the one exception being Bucharest, where it's possible to enjoy some superb cooking from a number of different countries. For a glossary of food and drink terms, see p.421.

Breakfast and snacks

Unless you're staying in a four- or five-star hotel, where a full buffet is usually available, **breakfast** (*micul dejun*) typically consists of a light meal of bread rolls with butter and jam, and the ubiquitous omelette, and you might also be offered some salty cheese or a long, unappealing-looking skinless sausage.

For **snacks**, known as *gustări* (also the Romanian word for hors d'oeuvres), head to a bakery (*brutărie*), which you can find everywhere. Just about all of these dispense *covrigi*, plain or seeded bread rings straight from the oven, sold as a bunch and tied to a piece of string. Bakeries are also good for *pateuri*, flaky pastries stuffed with cheese, meat or fruit fillings, and brioche, a Moldavian speciality. Street vendors and beer gardens dispense a variety of grilled meats, the most popular of which are *mititei* (more commonly known as *mici*), succulent grilled beef rissoles served with a dollop of mustard.

Restaurants

Given the affordability of eating out in Romania, it's best to go **upmarket** if you

can, since the choice of dishes in cheaper **restaurants** is invariably very predictable.

It's always worth enquiring *Care feluri le serviţi astazi, vă rog?* ("What do you have today?") or *Ce Óhmi recomandaţi?* ("What do you recommend?") before studying the menu too seriously. An increasing number of restaurants, including some of the better establishments, now offer daily set menus, typically a three- or four-course meal for around €5, which is usually offered Monday to Friday between noon and 5 or 6pm. While not exactly haute cuisine, these meals are cracking value.

Self-service **Autoservire canteens** are fairly commonplace, particularly in the coastal resorts. A far cry from the grisly canteens that Ceauşescu intended to make the mainstay of Romanian catering, these uncomplicated venues offer simple, cheap meals.

Inevitably, standards of **service** vary depending upon the type of establishment, but generally speaking don't expect anything but the most perfunctory of service, while in some places you'll be greeted (and served) with total indifference. Outside Bucharest and some of the larger cities, you'll find few staff speak English.

The concept of no-smoking in Romanian restaurants is almost nonexistent, and although a number of establishments have a **no-smoking** section, this remains the exception rather than the rule.

Generally speaking, in better restaurants you should be able to get a decent two-course meal, with a glass of wine or beer, for €10–12.

Romanian cuisine

Perhaps the most authentic Romanian dish is *sarmale* – cabbage leaves stuffed with rice, meat and herbs, usually served (or sometimes baked) with sour cream or horseradish; they are sometimes also made with vine leaves (*sărmăluţe in foi de viţă*) or, in Maramureş, with corn (*sarmale cu pasat*). *Mămăligă*, maize mush or polenta, often served with sour cream, is authentic country fare. Stews (*tocane*) and other dishes often feature a combination of meat and dairy products. *Muşchi ciobanesc* (shepherd's sirloin) is pork stuffed with ham, covered in cheese and served with mayonnaise, cucumber and herbs, while *muşchi poiana* (meadow sirloin) is beef stuffed with mushrooms, bacon, pepper and paprika, served in a vegetable purée and tomato sauce.

Keep an eye out for **regional specialities** (*specialităţile regiunii*). Moldavian cooking is reputedly the best in Romania, featuring rissoles (*pârjoale*), and more elaborate dishes such as *rasol moldovenesc cu hrean* (boiled pork, chicken or beef, with a sour cream and horseradish sauce), *tochitură moldovenească* (a pork stew, with cheese, *mămăligă*, and a fried egg on top), *rulade de pui* (chicken roulade) and *pui Câmpulungean* (chicken stuffed with smoked bacon, sausage, garlic and vegetables). Because of Romania's Turkish past, you may come across moussaka and varieties of pilaf, while the German and Hungarian minorities have contributed such dishes as smoked pork with sauerkraut and Transylvanian hotpot.

Cakes and desserts are sticky and very sweet. Romanians enjoy pancakes and pies with various fillings, as well as Turkish-influenced baclava and *savarină* (crisp pastry soaked in syrup and filled with whipped cream).

Romanian cheese (*brânză*) is mainly handmade from sheep's milk (although EU hygiene rules are threatening this practice) by shepherds who spend the summers in the hills with their flocks. The standard hard cheese is known as *caşcaval*, while *caş* is a less salty version of feta, and *telemea* is a soft and creamy white cheese matured in brine.

Vegetarian food

The situation for vegetarians remains predictably dull. You can try requesting something *fără carne, vă rog* ("without meat, please"), or check *este cu carne?* ("does it contain meat?"), but you're unlikely to get very far. It's worth asking for *ghiveci* (mixed stewed veg); *ardei umpluţi* (stuffed peppers); *ouă umpluţe picante* or *ouă umpluţe cu ciuperci* (eggs with a spicy filling or mushroom stuffing); *ouă româneşti* (poached eggs); or vegetables and salads. However, in practice you're likely to end up with omelette, *mămăligă* or *caşcaval pané* (cheese fried in breadcrumbs).

Drinks

Most cafés (*cafenea* or *cofetărie*) serve the full range of beverages, from coffee (and occasionally tea) to soft drinks and beer, while many also offer cakes, pastries and ice cream. Romanians usually take their coffee black and sweet in the Turkish fashion; ask for *cafea cu lapte* if you prefer it with milk, or *fără zahăr* without sugar. Other types of coffee, such as cappuccino, are invariably hit-or-miss affairs, ranging from good quality to insipid cups with a dollop of cream on top. **Bars and pubs** run the full gamut, from dark rough-and-ready dives to flash, modern concerns. A *crama* is a wine cellar, while a *gradina de vară* is a terrace or garden, usually offering *mititei* as well as beer.

The **national drink** is *ţuică*, a tasty, powerful brandy usually made of plums, taken neat. In rural areas, home-made spirits can be fearsome stuff, often twice distilled (to over 50 percent strength, even when diluted) to yield *palincă*, much rougher than grape brandy (*rachiu* or *coniac*). Most **beer** (*bere*) is European-style lager (*bere blondă*).

Silva (from Reghin), Valea Prahova (from Azuga), Ciucaş (from Braşov), Ursus (from Cluj), Ciuc (from Miercurea Ciuc), Timişoreana (from Timişoara) and Haţeg are probably the best regional brews, while Bergenbier and Eggenburger are acceptable mass-produced brands; you will also occasionally find brown ale (*bere neagră* or *brună*). Beer is usually sold by the bottle, so a request for *o sticlă* will normally get you one of whatever's available; draught beer is known as *halbă*.

Romania's best **wines** – and they are pretty good – are the white Grasa from Cotnari, near Iaşi; Tamaioasa, a luscious, late-harvested Moldavian dessert wine; Fetească Neagră, the blackberryish reds from Dealu Mare, east of Ploieşti; and the sweet dessert wines from Murfatlar (notably Merlot and Cabernet Sauvignon, and white Muscat Ottonel). They can be obtained in most restaurants, while some places may just offer you a choice of red or white. Sparkling (*spumos*) wines from Alba Iulia and Panciu (north of Focşani) are very acceptable. Wine is rarely sold by the glass, but it does no harm to ask – *Serviţi vin la pahar?*

Festivals

While Romania is not particularly known for its range of festivals, there are a number of increasingly diverse events taking place throughout the country, especially in music and film. Inevitably, the cities – in particular Bucharest, Cluj and Sibiu – boast the most impressive roster of events, though there remains an excellent spread of local festivals based around strongly rooted seasonal traditions.

Aside from the main festivals listed below, there are dozens of other, more local, events taking place across the country, some of which are also described in this guide. However, obtaining information on dates and locations for most festivals is notoriously difficult, so contact a tourist office or local agency wherever possible.

May

Measurement of the Milk Festival Ciucea, first or second Sunday of May. Hugely entertaining gathering in which shepherds compete to see who has the most productive flock.

Pageant of the Juni Braşov, first Sunday after Easter. Colourful parade in which the town's youth don elaborate costumes and ride through town on horseback, accompanied by brass bands.

Europafest Bucharest, second week of May. A dynamic week of pop, rock, jazz and blues constitutes the capital's foremost contemporary music festival.

International Theatre Festival Sibiu, two weeks end of May ⓦ www.sibfest.ro. Wonderful open-air jamboree serving up classical, rock and world music, alongside contemporary dance, film, theatre and art.

June

Transylvanian International Film Festival Cluj, beginning of June ⓦ www.tiff.ro/en. Romania's premier film festival puts on ten days of top-quality domestic and international movies shown around the city's many picture houses.

July

Girl Fair of Muntele Găina Avram Iancu, the closest Sunday to July 20. The match-making origins of this boisterous event, taking place atop Mount Găina, have largely given way to a feast of music and dance, though it remains a hugely enjoyable spectacle.

Medieval Arts Festival Sighişoara, last weekend of July. Medieval Transylvania comes to life in the town's atmospheric citadel, with street performers, open-air concerts and handicraft displays.

International Romani Art Festival Timişoara, end of July 🌐 www.iraf.ro. A colourful celebration of Gypsy art and culture, with music, theatre, photography and fire shows, as well as lots of activities for children.

August

Songs of the Olt Călimăneşti, first week of August. Superb gathering of musicians and folklore ensembles from Oltenia performing in the streets of this small spa town.

Anonimul Film Festival Sfântu Gheorghe, mid-August 🌐 www.festival-anonimul.ro. International independent film fest with an eclectic mix of long and short films, competitions and open-air screenings, all in a delightful Delta setting.

Felsziget Târgu Mureş, end of August 🌐 www .felsziget.ro. Romania's biggest rock festival features a roster of big-name international bands performing over four days.

Stufstock Vama Veche, last week of August 🌐 www.stufstock.com. With a nod to Woodstock, Romania's hippest, most alternative festival sees a plethora of rock gigs taking place on stages strung along the beachfront; the festival also incorporates Filmstock, with nightly screenings, as well as many other cultural happenings.

Transylvanian International Guitar Festival Cluj 🌐 transilvaniaguitar.ro. Brings together some of the world's foremost guitarists, and stages competitions, lectures and workshops.

September

Plai Festival Timişoara, second week of September 🌐 www.plai.ro/en. The "Field Festival" is three days of top-class world and jazz music, plus theatre, art, photography and literature.

George Enescu Festival Bucharest, every odd-numbered year 🌐 www.festivalenescu.ro. Three weeks of world-class classical music staged in the stunning surrounds of the Romanian Atheneum.

Sachsentreffen Biertan, second or third Saturday of September. Annual gathering of Saxons, both from the region and those returning from Germany.

October

Astra Sibiu, mid-October 🌐 www.astrafilm .ro. Well-established international festival of film documentary, with presentations and screenings from around the world.

Plum Brandy Festival Vălenii de Munte, end of October. Plum brandy producers from all over Romania gather and compete to see who has the country's finest brew.

December

Winter Customs Festival Sighet, end of December. Ancient pagan and Christian beliefs are celebrated in this vibrant coming together of costume, street theatre and music.

Sports and outdoor activities

Romania's sporting pedigree is strong, thanks largely to the exploits of the tennis player Ilie Nastase and the legendary gymnast Nadia Comaneci, both of whom achieved significant success and fame during the 1970s. Sporting triumph in the 1980s and 1990s came on the football field, with notable achievements by both the country's leading club side, Steaua Bucharest, and the national team, led by the mercurial Gheorghe Hagi.

Football

In 1986 **Steaua Bucharest** became the first team from behind the Iron Curtain to lift the **European Cup** (the Champions' League), defeating Barcelona on penalties. Although Inter Milan allegedly offered to build a Fiat car plant in Romania in order to get their hands on Gheorghe Hagi, players were only able to move freely to West European clubs after 1990: by 1992, nine of the national team were playing abroad.

Romania progressed to the quarter finals of the **1994 World Cup**, a tournament at which **Gheorghe Hagi** was arguably the best player. Dubbed the "Maradona of the Carpathians" – as much for his temperament as for his magical left foot – Hagi is a legend in Romania; born in Constanţa, he played for the local side before transferring to Steaua Bucharest on the orders of Ceauşescu's son Valentin, who effectively ran the team. After the revolution, he moved to Real Madrid for £1.8m, and after the 1994 World Cup to Barcelona, before flitting around a succession of lesser European clubs. Since Romania's last World Cup appearance in 1998, the only bright spots have been qualifications for the 2000 and 2008 European Championships.

For decades the **domestic game** was dominated by the three big Bucharest clubs: **Steaua** (traditionally the army team), **Dinamo** (the police and Securitate), and **Rapid** (rail workers), who regularly carved up the championship between them. In recent years, however, several other, much smaller, clubs – notably CFR Cluj and Unirea Urziceni – have claimed the national title, thanks largely to huge financial investment; both of these clubs have also appeared in the Champions' League. Every town has its stadium (*stadion*), and you should have no problem catching a game. **Matches** are usually played on Saturdays from August to May, with a break from November to February, and **tickets** for league games cost roughly €4–10.

Outdoor activities

The Romanian countryside lends itself perfectly to a multitude of **outdoor activities**, from hiking, skiing and cycling in the Carpathians to birdwatching in the Danube Delta – activities which can be done either individually or as part of a group tour.

Although two-thirds of Romania is either plains or hills and plateaux, the country's geography is dominated by **mountains**, which almost enclose the "Carpathian redoubt" of Transylvania, and merge with lesser ranges bordering Moldavia and Maramureş. Throughout these areas, there are opportunities to pursue several outdoor activities – hiking, skiing, caving and even shooting rapids. The **Danube Delta** is a totally different environment, unique for its topography – of which only one-tenth is dry land – and as a wildlife habitat attracting some three hundred species of bird during the spring and autumn migrations. A wide number of tours and trips are offered by a host of agencies in the UK (see pp.29–30), and, to a lesser degree, in North America (see pp.29–30) and Australasia (see pp.29–30).

For more on these activities, see "The Great Outdoors" colour section.

Travel essentials

Addresses

Addresses are written as Str. Eroilor 24, III/36 in the case of apartment buildings, ie Street (Strada) of Heroes, number 24, third floor, apartment 36. Some blocks have several entrances, in which case this is also given, eg scara B. Each district of Bucharest has a *sector* number, while in some towns each district (*cartier*) is named. In small villages, houses simply have a number and no street name. Streets, boulevards (*bulevardul*), avenues (*calea* or *Şoseaua*) and squares (*piaţa*) are commonly named after national heroes like Stephen the Great – Ştefan cel Mare – or Michael the Brave – Mihai Viteazul – or the date of an important event, such as December 1, 1918, when Transylvania was united with the Old Kingdom.

Children

Most of the better-quality hotels cater for **children**, while most restaurants (at least those of a decent standard) should be able to provide highchairs for younger children and babies. Most car rental firms provide child or baby seats for a small extra charge. Most supermarkets, and many smaller shops, are well stocked with the requisite nappies (diapers), baby food and so on.

In big coastal resorts and at Poiana Braşov there are **kindergartens** for the benefit of holidaymakers. A few train stations have a specially heated room for mothers with babies (*camera mama şi copilul*). The most obvious child-friendly destinations are the beaches along the coast, which, on the whole, are clean and safe, while there are enough water parks and fairgrounds in most resorts for further stimulation. You'll also find that most large towns have a good puppet theatre (*Teatrul de Păpuşi*).

Rail transport is free for under-5s, and half-price for under-10s. On TAROM flights, children under 2 pay only ten percent, and those up to the age of 12 receive a 33-percent discount.

Costs

Generally, costs are reasonably **low** in Romania, particularly when it comes to dining and public transport. If you're on a tight budget, you could get by on around £20/€25/$35 a day, staying in a hostel or private accommodation, eating in cheap diners and using public transport. Those on a moderate to mid-range budget (cheap to mid-range hotels, better restaurants and car rental) can expect to spend around £60/€70/$95 a day. If you want to splash out on the best hotels, restaurants and car rental, count on spending upwards of £100/€120/$150. In Bucharest, and, to a lesser degree, the coast, costs are appreciably higher than elsewhere.

Museum **admission** charges are extremely low, the typical fee being €1–2, though some of the major attractions (such

as the Palace of Parliament and Peleş Castle) will charge around three times that amount – moreover, these attractions may levy a fee (often twice the amount it costs to actually get in) for the use of cameras/camcorders. The more expensive hotels, flights, car rental and excursions are sometimes priced in **euros**, but must usually be paid for in **lei**.

Crime and personal safety

Romania remains generally **safe**, and it's unlikely that you'll have any problems; violent crime against tourists is almost nonexistent and petty crime rare. The major thing to watch out for is **pickpockets**, in particular on public transport in Bucharest, where thieves are adept at relieving tourists of their belongings; wearing a (hidden) moneybelt is advisable. Another, albeit far less common, occurrence in Bucharest, is the self-styled tourist police; typically, two or three men (the fact that they are plain clothed is a bit of a giveaway) will approach you demanding to see your passport – in such circumstances simply ignore their demands and walk off. If they persist, insist that they accompany you to the nearest police station, which should be enough to put them off.

Take care on overnight trains, shutting the door of your sleeper compartment as securely as you can (there are no locks) and keeping valuable possessions close at hand.

If your **passport** goes missing while in Bucharest, telephone your consulate immediately; anywhere else, contact the police. Thefts and other losses can be reported to the police who will issue the paperwork required for insurance claims back home, though only slowly and with painstaking bureaucratic thoroughness.

One of the legacies of Ceauşescu's systematization policy of the 1980s, when people were forced to move into concrete apartment blocks, was that thousands of dogs were abandoned and left to roam the streets. The problem is not as bad as it once was, but stray dogs remain a common nuisance, particularly in the cities, and you'll see plenty of them wandering the roadsides; should you feel threatened, just walk on slowly. For all emergency services dial ☎112.

Culture and etiquette

Although **tipping** is not obligatory, it is polite to round the bill up to a convenient figure in restaurants and when taking a taxi. In common with much of the Balkans, **smoking** is commonplace, and although officially banned in restaurants, this is ignored by many establishments. Moreover very few have non-smoking sections. On trains, smoking is allowed only in corridors or vestibules; buses are smoke-free.

Most public **toilets** are no longer the pits they used to be; some charge a small fee, particularly in the larger train stations. In any case, you should carry a supply of paper. "*Barbaţi*" means men and "*Femei*" means women.

It's rare for Romanian men to subject **female tourists** to **sexual harassment**. Romanians (both male and female) are highly tactile, so you may find yourself being prodded more than you care for. Most trouble is alcohol-fuelled, so it's best to avoid going alone to any but the classiest bars. Within earshot of other people, you should be able to scare away any local pest by shouting *lasaţi-ma in pace!* ("Leave me alone!") or calling for the *poliţia*.

Electricity

220 volts; a standard continental adaptor enables the use of 13-amp, square-pin plugs.

Entry requirements

Citizens of the EU, US, Canada, Australia and New Zealand can enter Romania with just a passport and may stay in the country for up to ninety days. Similarly, most other European citizens can enter the country without a visa, though can only stay for thirty days. However, **visa requirements** do change, so it's always advisable to check the current situation before leaving home.

Gay and lesbian travellers

The communist regime was relentlessly **homophobic**, and sexual relations between consenting adults of the same sex were illegal. The law against homosexuality was repealed in 2000, but the majority of the population remains largely **unsympathetic** towards the gay and lesbian community, and there are very few manifestations of gay life, even in Bucharest. That said, the first **Gay Pride** was held in Bucharest in 2005 and is now an annual event, usually taking place in May or June. Elsewhere, **Gay Film Nights** is now a major gay and lesbian film festival held in Cluj each October. **Accept** (PO Box 34–56, Bucharest ☎021/252 5620, ⓦwww.accept-romania.ro) is a Bucharest-based organization involved in the promotion of gay and lesbian activities in Romania, and they also offer counselling and HIV testing services.

Health

No **vaccinations** are required for Romania, although having hepatitis A, polio and typhoid boosters would be wise if you're planning to stay in remote areas where hygiene can sometimes be an issue. There's a **reciprocal health agreement** between Romania and Western countries (including the UK, US, Canada, Australia and New Zealand), so emergency treatment (excluding drugs) is free.

Summers can be blisteringly hot, particularly along the coast, so make sure you take a high-factor **sun cream**, and strong **insect repellent** if visiting the Danube Delta. Conversely, inclement weather in the **mountainous regions**, particularly at higher altitudes, can present potential dangers – take appropriate clothing, sufficient provisions and equipment, and keep an eye on the weather. **Tap water** is safe to drink practically everywhere, though bottled water (*apă minerala*) is widely available. Avoid any contact with **stray dogs**, as there's a very slight risk of **rabies**.

All towns and most villages have a **pharmacy** (*farmacie*), where the staff – in the big towns at least – may understand English, French or German. Pharmacies are typically open Monday to Saturday from 9am to 6pm, though all cities and most towns should have at least one that's open 24 hours – failing that, dial the emergency number displayed in the pharmacy window.

In Bucharest, the British and American embassies can supply the address of an English-speaking **doctor or dentist**, and there's a special clinic for treating foreigners. In **emergencies**, dial ☏112 or ask someone to contact the local casualty (*staţia de salvare*) or first-aid (*prim ajutor*) station, which should have ambulances. Each county capital has a fairly well-equipped county **hospital** (*spital judeţean*), but hospitals and health centres (*policlinics*) in smaller towns can be poor.

Insurance

Even though EU health-care privileges apply in Romania, you'd do well to take out an **insurance policy** before travelling to cover against theft, loss, and illness or injury. A typical travel insurance policy usually provides cover for the loss of baggage, tickets and – up to a certain limit – cash or cheques, as well as cancellation or curtailment of your journey. Most of them exclude dangerous sports unless an extra premium is paid.

Internet

Wi-fi is now widespread throughout the country. Most **hotels** – at least three-star and upwards – offer free wi-fi for their guests (either in the lobby or the rooms themselves) or, failing that, they'll have a cable connection, and **cafés**, even in the smaller towns, now have wi-fi, though you'll be obliged to buy a drink.

Internet cafés are now the exception rather than the rule, and even then most of these places are full of kids playing games, while connections can be dreadfully slow; expect to pay around €1 per hour.

Laundry

There are several **laundrettes** in Bucharest, but elsewhere they can be almost impossible to find; it's usually a choice between washing clothes yourself or paying a hotel to do it.

Living in Romania

Opportunities for working in Romania are relatively few. The most traditional form of work abroad, **teaching English**, is one option. The British Council (Ⓦwww .britishcouncil.org/work/job) recruits TEFL teachers and provides information about study opportunities and teacher development programmes in Romania. **International House** (Ⓦwww.ihworld.com) also offers TEFL training and recruits for teaching positions. They have branches in Bucharest, at Str. Lanariei 93–95 (☏021/335 4490, Ⓦwww.ih.ro), and in Timişoara, at B-dul C.D. Loga 11 (☏0256/490 593, Ⓦwww.ihtm.ro). The **TEFL** website (Ⓦwww.tefl.com) is also worth a look.

You could also get involved in one of the country's **summer work camps** or **field research** projects. **Earthwatch Institute** (Ⓦwww.earthwatch.org) is a long-established international charity with environmental projects and **archeological digs** in Romania. **Volunteers for Peace** (Ⓦwww.vfp.org) is another non-profit organization offering summer work camps, including work in Romanian **orphanages**.

Rough Guides travel insurance

Rough Guides has teamed up with WorldNomads.com to offer great travel insurance deals. Policies are available to residents of over 150 countries, with cover for a wide range of adventure sports, 24hr emergency assistance, high levels of medical and evacuation cover and a stream of travel safety information. Roughguides.com users can take advantage of their policies online 24/7, from anywhere in the world – even if you're already travelling. And since plans often change when you're on the road, you can extend your policy and even claim online. Roughguides .com users who buy travel insurance with WorldNomads.com can also leave a positive footprint and donate to a community development project. For more information go to Ⓦwww.roughguides.com/shop.

Mail

Post offices (*poştă*) are usually open Monday to Friday from 7am to 8pm, and on Saturdays from 8am to noon. **Stamps** (*timbru*) and prepaid envelopes (*pliicuri*) can be bought here. Sending mail home from Romania costs around €0.70 to overseas destinations – and takes about five days to Britain, and two weeks to North America and Australasia.

Maps

Nearly all the best **maps** of Romania are published outside the country, but they are available through most good map outlets, including a few shops in Romania itself. The country map published by the ADAC (the German motorists' association) is very detailed (at 1:500,000), as is the Szarvas/Kárpátia/Top-O-Gráf atlas (including city plans), which can be bought at Shell fuel stations in Romania (and through Stanfords bookstore in the UK). Other quality maps are produced by Falk (1:1,000,000), Cartographia (1:750,000) and Szarvas/Kárpátia/Dimap (1:700,000), along with a Kümmerley & Frey map of Romania and Bulgaria (1:1,000,000), and The GeoCenter Euromap (1:800,000), which includes Moldova. Cartographia and Falk also publish good maps of **Bucharest**, while Top-O-Gráf/Freytag & Berndt produce maps of Transylvanian cities such as Cluj. DIMAP also publishes maps of most tourist areas.

The maps produced by the **national tourist offices** are fairly poor, though just about adequate for **motoring**, but the campsite and cabana maps are useful for hikers. There are also good **hiking maps** of the major mountain massifs, by Editura Pentru Turism and Abeona in Bucharest and Editura Focul Viu in Cluj (available from bookstores as well as tourist offices). Hikers should also look out for the booklet *Invitaţie Ón Carpaţi*; the text is Romanian, but it contains detailed maps of the region's 24 main hiking areas, showing trail markings, huts, peaks, and so on (reproduced in *The Mountains of Romania* – see p.407).

Media

Western newspapers are almost impossible to track down in Romania, though the more upmarket hotels may have same-day editions. The very few **English-language publications** that exist are to be found in Bucharest; *Nine O'Clock* (Ⓦwww.nineoclock.ro), a reasonably informed, though not particularly well-written, daily newspaper available free in hotels, and *Bucharest Business Week* (Ⓦwww.bbw.ro), a standard business weekly with the occasionally enlightening article, are useful. Of the **listings magazines**, *Bucharest In Your Pocket* (Ⓦwww.inyourpocket.com/Romania/bucharest) is by far the most informative and up to date.

Romanian television offers the standard diet of news, soaps and gameshows. Once restricted to two hours a day, with half of that devoted to Ceauşescu's feats – ironically, it was TV that played a crucial role in his overthrow – these days there is no shortage of programming. Any decent hotel will have satellite TV, with CNN and BBC World most likely to feature. More annoyingly many restaurants deem it necessary to feature huge plasma screens in their establishment. Like many of the foreign-language programmes on Romanian TV, films at the **cinema** are shown in their original language with Romanian subtitles.

Money

Romania's unit of **currency** is the leu (abbreviation RON) – meaning "lion" (plural **lei**). Coins (*bani*) come in denominations of 1, 5, 10 and 50; and there are notes of 1, 5, 10, 50, 100, 200 and 500 lei. The **exchange rate** is currently around L5 to £1, L4.20 to €1 and L3 to US$1 – for current rates, check the websites Ⓦwww.xe.com or Ⓦwww.oanda.com.

If you need to change money, you're best doing so at a bank (*banca*); these are generally open Monday to Friday between 9am and 4 or 5pm. Alternatively, private exchange offices (*casa de schimb valuta*) can be found in most towns, some of which may be open 24 hours. As a rule, neither exchange offices nor banks charge commission. If taking **cash**, a modest denomination of euros or US dollar bills is advisable, though pound sterling is also accepted in most places. Make sure that you get rid of any unwanted lei before you leave the country, as it's unlikely you'll be able to change them once outside Romania.

Cash machines (*Bancomats*) are ubiquitous, even in the smallest towns, including many railway stations. **Credit cards** are accepted in most of the better hotels, restaurants and shops.

By far the most recognized **travellers' cheques** are American Express, either sterling or dollars. Although it may not be required in all instances, make sure you have your passport when changing travellers' cheques (or cash). Also note that, in some banks, you may have to show the receipt from the issuing bank, or another cheque to prove continuity of serial numbers.

Opening hours and public holidays

Opening hours in Romania are fairly unreliable and weekends can be like the grave, with a surprising number of restaurants and cinemas closing mid-afternoon or not opening at all. **Shops** are generally open from 9 or 10am to 6 or 8pm on weekdays, with department stores and some food stores opening from 8am to 8pm Monday to Saturday and from 8.30am to 1pm on Sunday. If you're trying to sort out flights, visas or car rental, be aware that many **offices** are closed by 4pm.

Museums (*muzeu*) are generally open Tuesday to Sunday from 9 or 10am to 5 or 6pm, though some do also close on Tuesdays. For the opening hours of **post offices, banks, pharmacies and restaurants**, see the relevant sections.

Public holidays in Romania are on **January 1 and 2** (New Year); Easter Monday; **May 1** (Labour Day); **December 1** (National Day) and **December 25 and 26** (Christmas).

Phones

Most **public phones** are orange **cardphones**, used both for internal and international calls. **Phone cards** (*cartelă telefonică*) cost €2 and €5; insert them with the gold lozenge foremost and facing upwards, and after a few seconds you should get a sign indicating that you can dial; at the end, wait until the message *scoateți cartela* indicates you can remove the card. Most towns have a **Romtelecom office** (usually open weekdays 6.30am–10pm, sometimes seven days a week), where the staff will connect your call. You'll normally pay the three-minute minimum in advance, and the balance afterwards.

Calls to Britain **cost** about €1 a minute, and to North America and Australasia €2; from card phones they cost a bit more, so the cards don't last long.

The main **mobile phone providers** in Romania are Cosmote, Orange and Vodafone. If staying for any length of time you might as well buy a local SIM card from any of these providers (typically costing €5), which you can then top up by voucher. All mobile numbers are designated by a phone code beginning with ☏07. Calling a mobile from within Romania, you must dial all the numbers; calling from abroad, you need to drop the "0".

Time

Romania is two hours ahead of **GMT**, seven hours ahead of **Eastern Standard Time** and ten hours ahead of **Western Standard Time**: clocks go forward one hour for the summer at the same time as other European countries.

Tourist information

Ensure that you pick up as much **information** as possible before you leave your own country, as getting hold of it in Romania is nigh on impossible. The **Romanian tourist board** has a site at ⊛www.romaniatourism .com, with a UK branch at 22 New Cavendish St, London W1G 8TT (☏020/7224 3692), and another at 355 Lexington Ave, 19th Floor, New York, NY 10017 (☏212/545 8484). Tourist offices in Romania remain few and far between, though most, but by no means all, cities will have one; you may also chance upon the odd one in smaller towns; elsewhere, most places should have an agency (usually more concerned with selling package trips) where you might be able to extract some basic advice, and possibly a map.

Travellers with disabilities

Very little attention has been paid to the needs of people with disabilities in Romania, and there's no sign of any change in attitude. Getting around is a major problem, as public transport is often inaccessible and cars with hand controls are not available from rental companies. The only place where facilities for disabled people are likely to be anything like comprehensive are in some of the classier hotels. Perhaps the best solution is to book a stay in a spa, where there should be a degree of level access and some awareness of the needs of wheelchair users.

Make sure you carry a **prescription** for any drugs you need, including the generic name in case of emergency, and spares of any special clothing or equipment, as it's unlikely you'll find them in Romania.

Guide

Guide

Bucharest

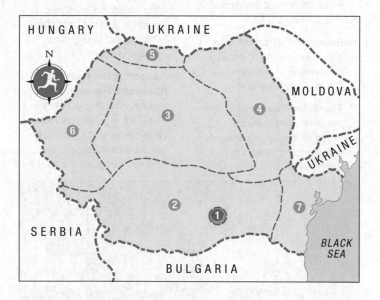

CHAPTER 1 # Highlights

✳ **National Art Museum** The country's biggest and best collection, the highlight of which is the spectacular Gallery of Romanian Medieval Art. See p.61

✳ **Museum of the Romanian Peasant** A superb display of traditional textiles, ceramics, carvings and replica buildings in the city's most enjoyable museum. See p.68

✳ **Palace of Parliament** Take a tour around the colossal centrepiece of Ceauşescu's Centru Civic. See p.70

✳ **The historic quarter** Escape the downtown concrete jungle with a ramble around the crumbling streets of Bucharest's old quarter, replete with cafés and bars. See p.72

✳ **Herăstrău Park** Combine a leisurely stroll through Bucharest's largest and greenest park with a cruise on the adjoining lake. See p.76

✳ **Village Museum** A varied assemblage of dwellings, churches, windmills and other structures from all over Romania, and the best place in the capital to buy craft souvenirs. See p.76

✳ **Concert at the Romanian Atheneum** The city's most beautiful building is also the venue for regular top-class classical concerts, including the biannual George Enescu Festival. See p.65 & p.81

▲ Fountain, Piaţa Unirii

Bucharest

or many people, initial impressions of **BUCHAREST** (Bucureşti), a sprawling, dusty city of some two million people, are less than favourable. As Romania's centre of government and commerce and site of its main airport, most visitors to the country will find themselves passing through the city at some point, but its chaotic jumble of traffic-choked streets, ugly concrete apartment blocks and monumental but mostly unfinished communist developments is often enough to send most travellers scurrying off to the more obvious attractions further north. Yet it's a city that rewards patience, with a raft of terrific museums, first-rate restaurants and bars, and, behind the congested main arteries, some superb architecture and abundant greenery.

The architecture of the old city, with its cosmopolitan air, was notoriously scarred by Ceauşescu's redevelopment project in the 1980s, which demolished an immense swathe of the historic centre – including many religious buildings and thousands of homes – and replaced it with a concrete jungle, named the **Centru Civic**. The centrepiece of this development was an enormous new palace for the communist leader, now known as the **Palace of Parliament**, which is Bucharest's premier tourist attraction. Other sites that justify a visit to the city include the superb **National Art Museum**, housing a fine collection of Romanian medieval art, the **Village Museum**, an assemblage of vernacular buildings garnered from Romania's multifarious regions, and, best of all, the **Museum of the Romanian Peasant**, with its marvellous exhibits on peasant life and several superbly reconstructed buildings. There's plenty of greenery to explore, too – most obviously the **Cişmigiu Gardens** in the heart of the city, or the more expansive **Herăstrău Park**, with its large lake, to the north. Bucharest is also the only Romanian city that can boast a clutch of international-class restaurants, as well as a bar and club scene that now rates among the best in the Balkans.

From Bucharest, there are excellent rail and road connections to the rest of the country, but local bus and train services to the towns and villages in the immediate vicinity are often limited or tortuous. There are, however, some enjoyable visits to be had outside the capital, most notably the lake and monastery at **Snagov**, the palace at **Mogoşoaia** and the village of **Clejani**, known for its outstanding Gypsy music.

Some history

According to legend, Bucharest was founded by a shepherd called **Bucur**, who built a settlement in the Vlăsia forest. It was recorded as a nameless "citadel on the Dâmboviţa" in 1368, and named as Bucharest in an edict from the time of Vlad the Impaler (ruled 1456–76). Over the centuries, both Târgovişte and Bucharest have served as the **Wallachian capital**, but the latter finally secured its claim in 1659, its position at the convergence of the trading routes to Istanbul outweighing the defensive advantages of Târgovişte's location in the Carpathian foothills.

As the boyars (nobles) moved into the city they built **palaces** and **churches** on the main streets radiating from the centre; these streets were surfaced with timber baulks and known as "bridges" (*poduri*). Despite earthquakes and periodic attacks by Turks, Tatars, Austrians and Russians over the course of its history, the city continued to grow and to modernize. New **boulevards** were driven through the existing street pattern in the 1890s, after the style of Haussmann's Paris, and they still form a ring road and the main north–south and east–west axes of the city today. Most of the major buildings, such as the **Romanian Atheneum** and the **Cercul Militar**, were designed by French or French-trained architects and built in the years immediately before World War I.

It was around this time that the city was dubbed the "Paris of the East", as much for its hectic and cosmopolitan social scene as for its architecture. The Romanian aristocracy was among the richest and most extravagant in Europe, but this lifestyle depended on the exploitation of the poor, and in Bucharest the two coexisted in what Ferdinand Lasalle described as "a savage hotchpotch", with beggars waiting outside the best restaurants, and appalling slums within a few steps of the elegant boulevards.

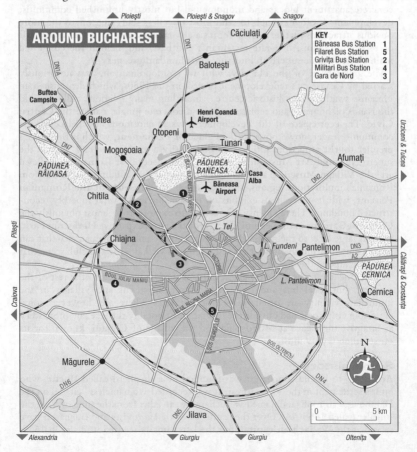

By 1918, the city's population had grown to 380,000 and roads such as Podul Mogoşoaiei, Podul de Pământ and Podul Calacilor were widened, paved and renamed as the Calea Victoriei, Calea Plevnei and Calea Rahovei respectively, in honour of the battles of the 1877–78 War of Independence from Turkey. After World War II, the city was ringed with ugly apartment buildings, first in areas such as "Red Griviţa", which the Allies had bombed flat (aiming for the rail yards), then expanding into the surrounding countryside.

A massive **earthquake** in 1977 reduced large parts of the city to rubble and left over 1500 people dead. While this prompted the construction of several major city projects, including a new metro system and an airport, it also provided Ceauşescu with the perfect excuse to implement his megalomaniac vision for the city. In 1984, and in order to create a new **Centru Civic**, Ceauşescu had most of the area south of the centre levelled, which entailed the demolition of thousands of homes, as well as churches, a monastery and a hospital.

In December 1989, the city found itself at the centre of the most violent of the popular **revolutions** sweeping across Eastern Europe that year; nearly three hundred people were killed in the uprising. Ceauşescu's execution did not, however, mark a complete end to the violence, and the following summer similar scenes erupted when miners from the Jiu Valley were brought in to stamp out student protests against the government, which resulted in a further seven deaths.

Although the post-communist era has brought back conspicuous consumption to the city, evidenced by the proliferation of luxury hotels, a raft of new shopping centres, and a stream of new restaurants, bars and clubs, these are largely for the benefit of tourists.

Arrival

While city transport is pretty good during the day, it's almost nonexistent at night, and street lighting throughout Bucharest leaves much to be desired. It is therefore best to avoid arriving late at night, unless you're willing to take a taxi to your hotel (see p.56).

By air

Bucharest has two international airports, both located on the DN1 road north of the city: the main one, **Henri Coandă** (often still referred to as Otopeni), is 16km north of the centre. The cheapest way to the city is by **express bus** #783 (5.30am–11.50pm Mon–Fri every 15min, Sat & Sun every 30min; journey time 45min; €2, return ticket only), which departs for Piaţa Unirii, stopping at Băneasa Airport, Piaţa Presei Libere, Arcul de Triumf, Piaţa Victoriei, Piaţa Romană and Piaţa Universităţii along the way. Buses leave from outside the domestic arrivals hall, one floor below international arrivals; buy your ticket from the booth by the stop. Express bus #780 (5.30am–11pm Mon–Fri every 20min, Sat & Sun every 30min; journey time 40min; €2, return ticket only) heads directly to the Gara de Nord – useful if you're staying in the area or need to make a train connection. There is also a **train** operating between the airport and the Gara de Nord (hourly 7.19am–9.19pm; from Gara de Nord hourly 7.10am–8.10pm; journey time 30min; €1.50 single ticket), although this does involve a fifteen-minute minibus transfer between arrivals and the airport train station.

If you opt for a **taxi**, avoid all offers from anyone within the terminal (you will almost certainly be ripped off), as well as the official (and very expensive) airport taxi company. Instead head through to departures and grab a taxi as it drops somebody off. Alternatively, call one of the reputable city companies (see p.56), though bear in mind that they are only allowed to pick up from the car park entrance; expect to pay around €12 to the city centre.

The much smaller and primitive **Băneasa Aurel Vlaicu Airport**, 8km closer to the centre, is used primarily by budget airlines; from here you can also catch express buses #783 and #780, as well as buses #131 and #335 to Piaţa Romană, or bus #205 to the Gara de Nord – all of these depart from the main road opposite the exit. Similarly, avoid all offers from any of the taxi drivers and call one instead.

By train

Virtually all international and domestic services terminate at the **Gara de Nord**, to the northwest of the centre. Although a much cleaner and less intimidating place than it used to be, you may still be accosted by any number of oddball characters, variously offering transport, accommodation or some other service – just ignore them and walk away. **Luggage** can be stored at the *bagaje de mână* (€1.50; open 24hr) on the concourse opposite platforms 4 and 5.

It's a thirty-minute walk from the Gara de Nord to the city centre; head right along Calea Griviţei to reach Calea Victoriei, the city's main north–south axis. Alternatively, you could take the metro (line M1) to Piaţa Victoriei, where you can change onto line M2 to reach Piaţa Universităţii, the nearest stop to the heart of the city, and Piaţa Unirii, in the Centru Civic. There are hordes of taxi drivers waiting to pounce as you leave the station, but be careful only to use a reputable company (see p.56), which shouldn't cost more than a couple of euros. Buses and trams from the Gara de Nord run around the centre rather than straight through it.

By road

Driving in Bucharest is not recommended for those of a nervous disposition. Approaching from Transylvania on the DN1 you'll pass both airports before reaching Şoseaua Kiseleff, which leads directly to the centre. The approach from Giurgiu (the point of entry from Bulgaria) on the DN5 leads through high-rise suburbs until B-dul Dimitrie Cantemir finally reaches the Piaţa Unirii. Likewise, the A1 motorway from Piteşti and the west brings you in through serried ranks of apartment blocks before reaching the Cotroceni Palace. The DN3 from the coast leads through the modern suburb of Pantelimon before reaching the older districts along B-dul Carol I.

Bucharest doesn't have a central **bus station**, which makes locating buses for specific destinations almost impossibly difficult. Instead, it has a smattering of stations on the edge of town which primarily serve the local villages: Filaret, on Piaţa Filaret (in Bucharest's first railway station, built in 1869), which sends buses south and southeast towards Giurgiu and Olteniţa; Băneasa, on B-dul Ionescu de la Brad, serving Snagov, and Ploieşti to the north; Militari, B-dul Păcii (Metro Păcii or bus #785), for points west; and Griviţa, Şos. Chitilei 221 (at the Mezeş terminal of tram #45), serving Târgovişte. Maxitaxis (for Braşov, Piteşti, Sibiu and other destinations) depart from a small bay opposite Gara de Nord, while there's another departure point at Str. Ritmului 35, to the northeast of town near Gara Obor.

Information and tours

Bucharest has two **tourist offices**; the main one is in the Piaţa Universităţii underpass (Mon–Fri 9am–6pm, Sat 9am–1pm; ☎021/305 5500), with another small booth on the concourse in the Gara de Nord (daily 9am–8pm); materials are fairly scant at both, though they can supply you with a free **city map** and are very helpful with general enquiries. For all-round information, including up-to-date events listings, your best bet is the highly informative and on-the-ball *Bucharest In Your Pocket*, available free from hotels and bookshops, and published bimonthly. *Nine O'Clock*, the (poorly written) main English-language newspaper, is available free from major hotels and airline offices.

The best of the city's **sightseeing tours** is run by Jolly Tours (℡021/321 5240, Ⓦwww.jollytours.ro), who run three- or four-hour themed trips (€30–50) including a guide, transport and museum entrance fees – bookings should be made at least a few hours in advance. Longer tours, including excursions to other parts of the country, can be arranged upon request. They can also be contacted through reception at the *Athénée Palace Hotel*.

City transport

Public transport is a little chaotic, but has improved over recent years, and remains extremely cheap. Apart from some express buses on the main axes, most **bus** and **tram** routes avoid the central zone, though this is covered by the **metro system**. Beyond the downtown thoroughfares, many roads are still so poor that buses and trams seem set to rattle themselves to pieces, and trolley buses frequently slip from the wires and stall. **Pickpockets** are rife on all forms of public transport so be extremely vigilant with your belongings.

Buses and trams

There is a flat fare of about €0.40 on **trolley buses** (*troleibuz*), **trams** (*tramvai*) and most **buses** (*autobuz*), all of which run from around 5am until 11.30pm. You need to buy tickets in advance from street kiosks (roughly Mon–Fri 6am–8pm, Sat 7am–7pm, Sun 7am–2.30pm) and punch them in one of the machines once aboard. It costs around €2 for day passes and €5 for weekly passes, both representing excellent value. It costs about double the standard fare to travel on the city's express buses, using tickets with a magnetic strip, also bought in advance from the kiosks (day and weekly passes not valid). Ticket inspectors are ubiquitous, and travelling without a valid ticket will result in a fine of around €12.

Key bus and trolley-bus routes	
North–south	along B-duls Magheru and Bălcescu: #783 (express)
	along Calea Dorobanţilor: #131 and #301
East–west	(north of the centre)
	from Gara de Nord along B-dul Dacia (via Piaţa Romană): #79 and #86
	along B-dul Dacia: #133
	along B-duls Regina Elisabeta and Carol I (via the university): #66 (Metro Obor), #69 (Gara Obor).
	from Gara de Nord to Str. Baicului (Gara Obor): #85
East–west	(south of the centre)
	along Splaiul Independenţei and B-dul Unirii: #104 (Opera–National Stadium), #123 (Gara de Nord–Vitan)
East	from Piaţa Rosetti: #63 (to Metro Obor).

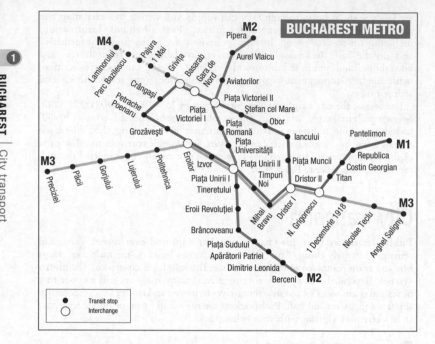

The metro

Opened in 1979 in order to serve the working-class suburbs, the Bucharest **metro** is not the most user-friendly system in the world – signposting is confusing, lighting is poor and announcements are barely audible, but it is clean, safe and absurdly cheap. Trains run from 5.30am until 11.30pm, with magnetic tickets costing around €0.75 for two rides and €2.50 for ten. The M1 line (shown in yellow on maps) runs from Pantelimon in the east of the city to Dristor, before looping around the city centre; the M2 (blue), runs north–south straight through the centre; the third, M3 (red), runs east–west sharing the M1 tunnel for some of the way; the M4 (green) links Gara de Nord with 1 Mai in the northwest, although you'll have little reason to use this line.

Taxis

Bucharest's **taxi** drivers have a deserved reputation for harassing and ripping off foreigners, and though the situation is not nearly as bad as it once was, you should still be wary. As a rule, trustworthy companies have their name and phone number plastered across the top or side of the taxi, while the fare (*Pornire* – starting price, and *Pret km* – price/km) should be displayed on the driver and passenger doors. Your safest bet is to call one of the following recommended taxi companies: Autogeneral (☎021/9401), Cobalescu (☎021/9451), Cristaxi (☎021/9461) and Meridian (☎021/9444), each of which should have an operator who speaks English. The same can't be said for the majority of drivers in the city, so make sure you have the address written down just in case. Prices are very cheap, and you should expect to pay around €0.30–0.50 per kilometre.

Accommodation

The range and quality of accommodation in Bucharest has improved markedly in recent years. The city is now awash with high-end **hotels**, aimed primarily at the business market, though there are an increasing number of more affordable places available. There are around half a dozen **hostels** in the city, most of which are centrally located, as well as a growing selection of **private rooms** and **apartments**. Bucharest's one **campsite** is located way out to the north of the city between the two airports.

Hotels

Hotel star ratings give a fair indication of standards, but in many cases the prices are absurdly high. That said, it is possible to get some big discounts in many of the upmarket hotels during the summer when the traditional business market is slack, so it's always worth enquiring. The city's hotels are evenly spread, though the most characterful places are sited in the areas around **Piaţa Revoluţiei** and the historic quarter. Many of the city's best privately run hotels are located north of the centre, with a smattering further south towards **Piaţa Unirii**. The cheapest location is around the **Gara de Nord**, which remains a rather seedy (though perfectly safe) area. Most of the higher-end hotels offer airport pick-ups and transfers.

Around the Gara de Nord

Andy Str. Witing 2 ☎021/300 3050, ⓦwww .andyhotels.ro. Just across from the station, this place is not exactly brimming with character, but its large, comfortable and neatly decorated rooms make it a decent option. ❻

Cameliei Str. Cameliei 37 ☎021/318 3726, ⓔrezervari@hotel-cameliei.ro. Tucked away behind the market, this quiet little budget hotel offers very cheap rooms, though they are somewhat careworn. Breakfast not available. ❹

Das President B-dul D. Golescu 29 ☎021/311 0535, ⓦwww.daspresident.ro. Directly opposite the *Andy*, this is one of the better options in this area, both for price and cleanliness, offering a range of adequately furnished rooms with private and shared bathrooms. ❸–❹

Elizeu Str. Elizeu 11–13 ☎021/319 1735, ⓦwww .hotelelizeu.ro. A bright and pleasant hotel, featuring spotless, mint green rooms with comfy leather sofas and a/c. Located just off B-dul Golescu, midway between Gara de Nord and Gara Basarab. ❺

Hello Calea Griviţei 143 ☎0372/121 800, ⓦwww .hellohotels.ro. The most comfortable hotel in the vicinity, this large, hospitable place offers good-sized rooms with lots of pine furnishings, wall-mounted TVs and splashes of colour. Lots of triples too. ❻

Ibis Calea Griviţei 143 ☎021/300 9100, ⓦwww .ibishotel.com. Immediately next door to *Hello*, this is much like any other *Ibis* in the world, though its neat, clean and functional rooms are a cut above most places hereabouts. ❻

Around Piaţa Romană and Piaţa Revoluţiei

Athénée Palace Hilton Str. Episcopiei 1–3 ☎021/303 7777, ⓦwww.hilton.com. Despite some stiff competition, this remains the city's most opulent and best-serviced hotel, with sumptuous rooms (doubles €250) and first-rate facilities, including sauna, gym and a gorgeous basement pool. It's the most famous hotel in Romania, with a long history of intrigue and espionage. ❾

Capital Plaza B-dul Iancu Hunedoara 54 ☎0372/080 080, ⓦwww.capitalplaza.ro. A 10min walk from both Piaţa Romană and Piaţa Victoriei, this mid-sized hotel offers real comfort in handsome, generously sized rooms decorated in subtle greens and browns. Doubles from €175. ❾

Carpaţi Str. Matei Millo 16 ☎021/315 0140, ⓦwww.hotelcarpatibucuresti.ro. The only real budget hotel in the downtown area, with a great central location to boot; numerous different rooms, including singles and doubles with and without bathrooms and TVs. ❸–❹

Christina Str. Ion Slatineanu 13 ☎021/210 7303, ⓦwww.hotelchristina.ro. A superbly conceived, eco-driven hotel just a short walk from Piaţa Romana. Each room is painted in one of four warm tones (grape-green, pink, lilac and yellow) and furnished with ergonomically designed beds, strip lighting and hanging artwork. Originality and comfort at its best. ❼

Grand Hotel Continental Calea Victoriei 56 ☎0372/010 300, ⓦwww.continentalhotels.ro. This wonderfully renovated late nineteenth-century

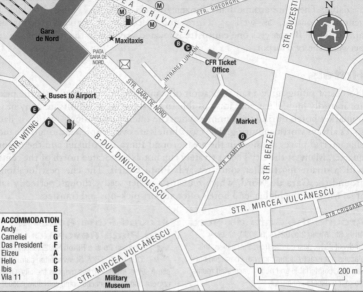

AROUND THE GARA DE NORD

Gara Basarab & A

B-DUL GH. DUCA

CALEA GRIVITEI

STR. GHEORGHE POLIZU

STR. BUZEŞTI

N

Gara de Nord

Maxitaxis

PIAŢA GARA DE NORD

INTRAREA LUNCANI

CFR Ticket Office

STR. GARA DE NORD

City centre

Buses to Airport

STR. WITING

STR. CAMELIEI

STR. BERZEI

B-DUL DINICU GOLESCU

Market

STR. MIRCEA VULCĂNESCU

STR. CRIŞANA

STR. MIRCEA VULCĂNESCU

Military Museum

ACCOMMODATION	
Andy	E
Cameliei	G
Das President	F
Elizeu	A
Hello	C
Ibis	B
Vila 11	D

0   200 m

building just south of Piaţa Revoluţiei lays fair claim to the city's most stylish hotel; big, high-ceilinged rooms (doubles €320) furnished in classic French style, with luxurious beds, glass-partitioned bathrooms and a stack of other neat little touches. ⑨

Moxa Str. Mihail Moxa 37B ☎021/650 5555, ⓦwww.hotelmoxa.ro. Very classy boutique hotel just off Calea Victoriei with gorgeous rooms complete with leather furnishings and wood-panelled flooring. Gym, sauna and fitness suite and a delicious Swedish buffet breakfast too. ⑧

Novotel Calea Victoriei 37B ☎021/308 8500, ⓦwww.novotel.com. Another glass behemoth, this one distinguished by a faux Neoclassical facade – a replica of the Old National Theatre which stood here before being bombed during World War II. The rooms (doubles €250), meanwhile, are as plush as anything else In the city, while there's a golf simulator and swimming pool for active types. ⑨

Opera Str. Ion Brezoianu 37 ☎021/312 4855, ⓦwww.thhotels.ro. Lovely hotel in a super location next to the Cişmigiu Gardens; the attractive, a/c and originally furnished rooms (doubles €140) incorporate some thoughtful touches, such as

tea- and coffee-making facilities, neat desk lamps, and pictures of old Bucharest on the walls. ⑨

Between Piaţa Universităţii and Piaţa Unirii

Flowers B&B Str. Plantelor 2 ☎021/311 9848, ⓦwww.flowersbb.ro. Handy location close to Piaţa Universităţii, this sweet little bed and breakfast is a welcome alternative to the city's hotels; warm, cosy rooms painted in a rich peachy colour, and a summery terrace on which to take breakfast. Take bus #69 or #85 to B-dul Carol I from where it's a 5min walk south. ⑤

Hostel Mioriţa Str. Lipscani 12 ☎021/312 0361, ⓦwww.hostel-miorita.ro. Terrifically located in the historic quarter's most famous street, this is a pleasant and unassuming pension-style establishment containing six homely en-suite rooms with a/c. Breakfast is in the restaurant next door. ④

Intercontinental B-dul N. Bălcescu 4 ☎021/310 2020, ⓦwww.ichotelsgroup.com. This towering city landmark remains the businessmen's and journalists' hotel of choice – it was from here that many watched the revolution unfold – and has all the class you'd expect of a five-star establishment. Immaculate rooms (doubles €260), marble-tiled bathrooms and top-notch facilities, including sauna, gym and (very small) rooftop pool; the citywide views are unbeatable. ⑨

K&K Hotel Elisabeta Str. Slănic 26 ☎021/311 8631, ⓦwww.kkhotels.com. Part of the hip Austrian-run chain of luxury boutique hotels, this is as cool as it gets; superbly designed rooms (doubles €160) – warm brown/ beige tones, lots of smooth wood and soft armchairs – state-of-the-art amenities and service of the highest order. ⑨

Marriott Grand Calea 13 Septembrie 90 ☎021/403 1000, ⓦwww.jwmarriott.ro. Originally conceived by Ceauşescu as a hotel for Communist Party hacks, this is now one of the most sumptuous establishments in town. Over 400 rooms (doubles €240) of unbridled luxury, each with separate bath and shower; it also boasts a couple of high-class restaurants and a sports bar (see p.80). Bus #385. ⑨

Rembrandt Str. Smărdan 11 ☎021/313 9315, ⓦwww.rembrandt.ro. This tall, narrow building conceals sixteen beautifully conceived rooms (doubles €120). Alluring wood furnishings – including the floor and panelling behind the bed – set the tone, along with sumptuous beds, etched glass windows and Tiffany-style lamps. ⑨

Suter Inn Str. Aleea Suter 3 ☎021/337 3939, ⓦwww.suterinn.ro. Anonymous-looking but warm, welcoming and cheap guesthouse near Carol Park, with rooms furnished throughout in bold red and black colours (even down to the toilet seat). Tram #32 or bus #232 to Piaţa Libertăţii, then walk uphill. ⑥

Tania Str. Şelari 5 ☎021/319 2758, ⓦwww .taniahotel.ro. Pleasant small hotel located in a quiet part of the Old Town, with reasonably sized,

sunny and thoroughly modern rooms. Breakfast is extra but this is a good-value place. ⑥

North of the centre

Avis B-dul Aerogarii 10 ☎021/232 4478, ⓦwww .avishotel.ro. A short hop from Băneasa airport, this decent hotel is perfect if flying in late, departing early, or just stopping over for the night; very reasonably priced for an airport hotel. ⑥

Casa Victor Str. Emanoil Porumbaru 44 ☎021/222 5723, ⓦwww.casavictor.ro. A pleasant private hotel with twenty tastefully decorated rooms in a quiet residential street just five minutes' walk from the Aviatorilor metro. ⑥

Floreta de Aur Str. Aviator Popa Marin 2 ☎021/230 6496. Great-value place frequented in the main by athletic types using the adjoining sports facilities; big square rooms (singles, doubles and triples), each with fridge and TV. ⑤

Piccolo Mondo Str. Clucerului 9 ☎021/260 0682, ⓦwww.piccolomondo.ro. Located in a pleasant, leafy street running parallel to Şos. Kiseleff (near the Arc de Triumf), *Piccolo* is better known for its excellent restaurant (see p.80), but the rooms here are tidy, spacious and some have balconies. ⑦

Residence Str. Clucerului 19 ☎021/223 1978, ⓦwww.residencehotels.com.ro. A few paces along from *Piccolo Mondo*, this is one of Bucharest's best small hotels; elegantly furnished with plush red carpets, wrought-iron beds, desks and chairs, carved wooden cupboards, wall pictures and pot plants. Small basement spa too. Doubles from €140. ⑨

Triumf Şos. Kiseleff 12 ☎021/222 3172. A huge red-brick building in the indigenous neo-Brâncovenesc style, set in parkland (with tennis courts) just off this main boulevard. There's still a whiff of the state-owned about this place, manifest in the phenomenally dull rooms and antiquated bathrooms, but the location is lovely and it's by far the cheapest option in this part of town. ⑥

Hostels

Bucharest has a handful of small **hostels**, all of which are fairly centrally located and open year-round. Booking ahead is advisable in the summer months. Pretty much all of these places offer a discount for stays of longer than a week. Note that none has representatives at the train station.

Alex Villa Str. Avram Iancu 5 ☎021/313 3198. A quiet, simple hostel east of Universităţii, with a/c dorms sleeping between four and nine (€10); free internet access, laundry and breakfast not included. Take bus #85 from the station to the junction of B-dul Carol I and Piaţa Protopopescu, from where it's a 2min walk.

Butterfly Villa Str. Stirbei Vodă 96 ☎021/314 7595, ⓦwww.villabutterfly.com. Small, cheerful and colourful hostel with cosy four-, six- and eight-bed dorms (€12), doubles (€13/person) and singles (€28). Breakfast and internet included, laundry extra. Bus #178 from Gara de Nord to Cişmigiu Gardens, walk back 100m to Str. C. Stahi and it's on your right by the black gate.

Funky Chicken Str. General Berthelot 63 ☎021/312 1425, ⓦwww.funkychickenhostel.com. Just around the corner from *Butterfly Villa*, this friendly, informal place has four-, six- and eight-bed dorms. Breakfast not included, but self-catering facilities available. Cheapest of the bunch at €8 per dorm bed.

Midland Hostel Str. Biserica Amzei 22 ☎021/314 5323, ⓦwww.themidlandhostel.com. Centrally located hostel, just off Piaţa Romană, with a range of modern dorms sleeping between six and

fourteen (€12–14), plus a comfortable lounge and fully equipped kitchen. Internet and breakfast included, laundry extra.

Vila 11 Str. Institutul Medico Militar 11 ☎072/249 5900, ©vila11bb@hotmail.com. Welcoming, family-run B&B-style place in a peaceful back street just five minutes' walk from the station. Three- and six-bed dorms (€10) as well as doubles with private or shared bathroom (€25/30) and one single (€20). Exit Gara de Nord by platform one, head north along B-dul Golescu for 200m, turn left up Str. Vespasian, and first left again. Price includes a pancake breakfast.

Camping and private accommodation

Bucharest's one **campsite**, the *Casa Alba* (☎021/361 7730, ⓦwww.casaalba.ro; open year-round), is situated out towards Henri Coandă Airport in the Pădurea Băneasa woods at Aleea Privghetorilor 1–3. It's a large, well-guarded site with excellent facilities, including a wide range of cabins (❸–❹), some with showers and cooking amenities; there's also a restaurant on site. To get there, take bus #301 from Piaţa Romană (or #783 if coming from Henri Coandă) and get off at the Băneasa restaurant stop, the fifth one after Băneasa Airport.

In recent years, numerous agencies have emerged offering **private rooms** and **apartments**, and these generally represent good value. Two of the better ones are Relax Comfort Suites, at B-dul Nicolae Balcescu 22 (☎021/311 0210, ⓦwww .relaxcomfort-suites.ro), and Professional Realty (☎021/232 0406, ⓦwww .accommodation.com.ro), both of which have centrally located rooms and apartments from around €40 per day.

The City

The heart of the city is the **Piaţa Revoluţiei**, site of the old Royal Palace and the scene of Ceauşescu's downfall. It lies halfway along Bucharest's historic north–south axis, the **Calea Victoriei**, which is still the main artery of city life. Buses heading north and south, however, use the scruffy boulevards east of Calea Victoriei; the main junction along them is the **Piaţa Universităţii**, scene of major events immediately after the 1989 revolution.

Just to the south of here lies the scruffy but atmospheric **historic centre**, a pleasant antidote to the noisy, modern surrounds, which is in a permanent state of regeneration. Beyond this, across the River Dâmboviţa, is the contrasting cityscape of Ceauşescu's compellingly monstrous **Centru Civic**, whose centrepiece, the extraordinary **Palace of Parliament**, is the city's main tourist attraction. Just west of the centre are the **Cişmigiu Gardens**, a tranquil space and a popular place for assignations, and beyond here the grand **Cotroceni Palace**.

North from Piaţa Victoriei, along the broad sweep of Şoseaua Kiseleff, lie Bucharest's two best museums – the **Museum of the Romanian Peasant** and the **Village Museum**, the latter sited in leafy **Herăstrău Park**, on the shores of the lake of the same name.

Piaţa Revoluţiei and around

Piaţa Revoluţiei (Square of Revolution), a large, irregularly shaped square sliced down the middle by Calea Victoriei, was created in the 1930s to ensure a protective

The fall of the Ceauşescus

Romania's revolution was the most dramatic of the popular revolts that convulsed Eastern Europe in 1989. On the morning of December 21, 1989, a staged demonstration – organized to show support for the **Ceauşescu** regime following days of rioting against it in Timişoara – backfired. Eight minutes into Ceauşescu's speech from the balcony of the Central Committee building, part of the eighty-thousand-strong crowd began chanting "Ti-mi-şoa-ra"; the leader's shock and fear were televised across Romania before transmissions ceased. From that moment, it was clear that the end of the Ceauşescu regime was inevitable. Though the square was cleared by nightfall, larger crowds poured back the next day, emboldened by news that the army was siding with the people in Timişoara and Bucharest. Strangely, the Ceauşescus remained inside the Central Committee building until midday, when they scrambled aboard a helicopter on the roof, beginning a flight that would end with their **execution** in a barracks in Târgovişte, on Christmas Day.

The revolution was tainted by having been stage-managed by the **National Salvation Front (FSN)** that took power in the name of the people. The FSN consisted of veteran communists, one of whom later let slip to a journalist that plans to oust the Ceauşescus had been laid months before. Among the oddities of the "official" version of events were Iliescu's speech on the Piaţa Revoluţiei at a time when "terrorist" snipers were causing mayhem in the square, and the battle for the Interior Ministry, during which both sides supposedly ceased firing after a mysterious phone call. Given the hundreds of genuine "martyrs of the revolution", the idea that it had been simply a ploy by Party bureaucrats to oust the Ceauşescus was shocking and potentially damaging to the new regime – so the secret police were ordered to mount an investigation, which duly concluded that while manipulation had occurred, the Russians, Americans and Hungarians were to blame.

field of fire around the Royal Palace in the event of revolution. While Romania's monarchy was overthrown by other means, the square fulfilled its destiny in 1989, when the Ceauşescus were forced to flee by crowds besieging Communist Party headquarters; two days of fighting left the buildings around the square burnt out or pockmarked with bullet holes – with the conspicuous exception of the Central Committee building, which was at the centre of the storm.

The Royal Palace and National Art Museum

The most imposing of the buildings surrounding the Piaţa Revoluţiei is the former **Royal Palace**, which occupies most of the western side of the square. When the original single-storey dwelling burnt down in 1927, the king, Carol II, decided to replace it with something far more impressive. The surrounding dwellings were razed in order to build a new palace, with discreet side entrances to facilitate visits by Carol's mistress, Magda Lupescu, and the shady financiers who formed the couple's clique. However, the resultant sprawling brownstone edifice has no real claim to elegance and the palace was spurned as a residence by Romania's postwar rulers, Ceauşescu preferring a villa in the northern suburbs pending the completion of his own palace in the Centru Civic.

Since 1950, the palace has housed the **National Art Museum** (Muzeul Naţional de Artă; Wed–Sun: May–Sept 11am–7pm; Oct–April 10am–6pm; €4; ⓦ www.mnar.arts.ro) in the Kretzulescu (south) wing. During the fighting in December 1989, this building was among the most seriously damaged of the city's cultural institutions, and over a thousand pieces of work were destroyed or damaged by gunfire and vandals. After a massive reconstruction project, during which time many of the items were repaired, the museum reopened and now

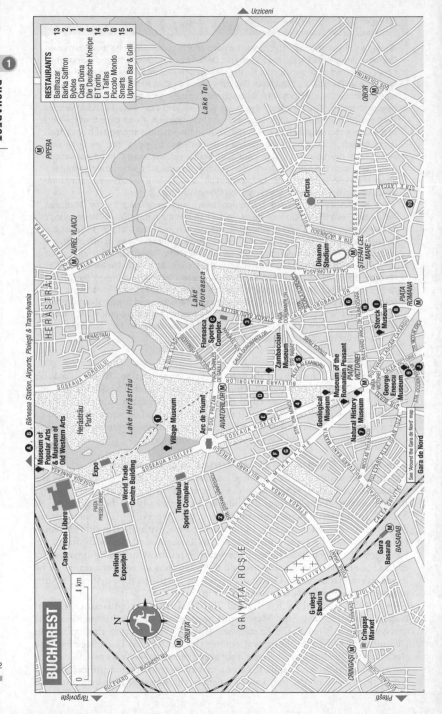

BUCHAREST

RESTAURANTS	
Balthazar	13
Barka Saffron	2
Byblos	1
Casa Doina	4
Die Deutsche Kneipe	6
El Torito	14
La Taifas	9
Piccolo Mondo	15
Smarts	G
Uptown Bar & Grill	5

0   1 km

N

Urziceni

Lake Tei

PIPERA

AUREL VLAICU

OBOR

ŞOS COLENTINA

ŞOS ŞTEFAN CEL MARE

CALEA FLOREASCA

HERĂSTRĂU

S. HERĂSTRĂU

CALEA LA PIPERA

Lake Floreasca

Circus

ŞTEFAN CEL MARE

STR V. LASCĂR

Dinamo Stadium

BULEVARD GH. VĂCĂRESCU

A, B Băneasa Station, Airports, Ploieşti & Transylvania

Museum of Popular Arts & Museum of Old Western Arts

ŞOSEAUA BĂNEASA

ŞOSEAUA NORDULUI

Lake Herăstrău

Herăstrău Park

B-DUL EVAD

PIAŢA CHARLES DE GAULLE

Floreasca Sports Complex

STRADA RADU BELLER

CALEA DOROBANTILOR

Zambaccian Museum

PIAŢA DOROBANTILOR

ALEEA ALEXANDRU

PIAŢA ROMANA

Storck Museum

Village Museum

Arc de Triumf

B-DUL PREZAN

AVIATORILOR

ŞOSEAUA KISELEFF

BULEVARD AVIATORILOR

STR RABAT

STR PARIS

Museum of the Romanian Peasant

PIAŢA VICTORIEI

BULEVARD IANCU DE HUNEDOARA

George Enescu Museum

CALEA VICTORIEI

Expo

Casa Presei Libere

PIAŢA PRESEI LIBERE

World Trade Centre Building

Pavilion Expoziţei

Tineretului Sports Complex

SOSEAUA KISELEFF

STR. MINCU

Geological Museum

Natural History Museum

BULEVARD NICOLAE BĂLCESCU

BULEVARD LASCĂR CATARGIU

BULEVARD DACIA

STR. OCCIDENT

STR. BUZEŞTI

GRIVIŢA-ROŞIE

BULEVARD ION MIHALACHE

STRADA URDA

STR ŞTEFAN SĂNDESCU

BULEVARD BANU MANTA

NICOLAE TITULESCU

CALEA GRIVIŢEI

GRIVIŢA

BUCUREŞTI NOI

Giuleşti Stadium

CALEA GIULEŞTI

CRINGAŞI

Cringaşi Market

CALEA CRINGAŞI

ŞOSEAUA GIULEŞTI

Gara Basarab

BASARAB

CALEA PLEVNEI

BULEVARD DINICU GOLESCU

Gara de Nord

See Around the Gara de Nord map

BULEVARD ALEXANDRU I. CUZA

CALEA GRIVIŢEI

Piteşti

Târgovişte

Pipera

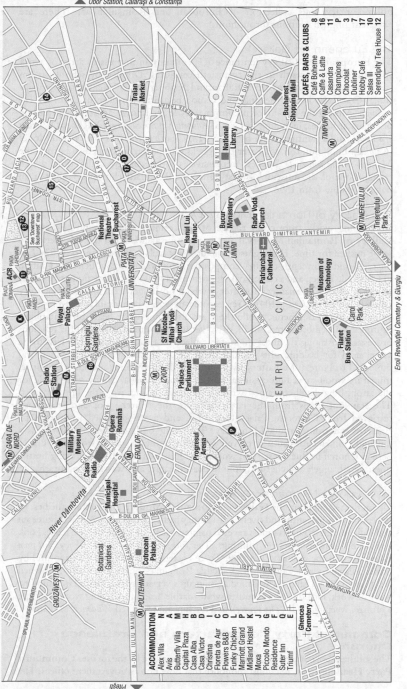

holds a marvellous collection of European and Romanian art. There are excellent English captions throughout.

The European Art Gallery

The **European Art Gallery** (entrance A1) contains an impressive array of work spanning the fourteenth to the twentieth centuries. Divided by schools, it has particularly fine paintings from Italian and Spanish artists, including an exceptional *Crucifixion* by Da Messina, and Cano's beautifully mournful *Christ At The Column*. Among the line-up of predominantly lesser-known artists is a sprinkling of superstar names, including El Greco (*Adoration of the Shepherds*), Rubens (*Portrait of a Lady*), and a painting apiece by Sisley (*The Church in Moret in Winter*) and Monet (*Camille*). Look out, too, for Peter Brueghel's spectacularly detailed and gruesome *Massacre of the Innocents*. No less impressive is the decorative art section, which contains one of the museum's oldest items, the Reichsadlerhumpen Goblet from Bavaria, dating from 1596.

The Gallery of Romanian Medieval Art

Comprising works from every region of the country, the museum's exhaustive **Gallery of Romanian Medieval Art** is quite spectacular, and the one section to see if pushed for time. Highlights of the first few halls include a fresco of *The Last Supper*, a mid-fourteenth-century composition retrieved from St Nicholas's Church in Curtea de Argeş, and a carved oak door from 1453 with shallow figurative reliefs from the chapel of Snagov Monastery (which no longer exists). The Monastery Church in Curtea (see p.104) is represented by some remarkably well-preserved icons and fresco fragments, while there are also some quite beautiful Epitaphios, liturgical veils embroidered on silk or velvet which were usually used for religious processions. Among the most memorable pieces is a sumptuous gilded Kivotos (a vessel used for holding gifts) in the shape of an Orthodox church, which was presented to Horezu Monastery by Constantin Brâncoveanu, and some exquisite, miniature wood-carved processional crosses from Moldavia, chiefly remarkable for the astonishing detail contained within – typically, scenes from the life of Christ. The standout items from the latter halls are the church door and iconostasis retrieved from Cotroceni Palace (see p.74), and a wood-carved iconostasis by Brâncoveanu from Arnota Monastery. Trumping both of these, however, is a 6m-high, nineteenth-century carved walnut iconostasis taken from the Prince Şerban Church in Bucharest. The workmanship is extraordinary, featuring, in the finest detail, angels and cherubs, double-headed eagles and warriors on horseback.

The Gallery of Romanian Modern Art

Up on the second floor, the **Gallery of Romanian Modern Art** features the best of the country's nineteenth- and twentieth-century painters, including Aman, Andreescu and Pallady, and Romania's most revered painter, Nicolae Grigorescu (see p.96). Look out for his brilliant character paintings, *The Turk*, *Jew with a Goose*, *Gypsy Girl from Gherghani* and the dramatic *The Spy*. There's a terrific assemblage of sculpture, by Storck, Paciurea and Constantin Brâncuşi, Romania's one truly world-renowned artist (see p.111). Using various media, Brâncuşi's versatility is displayed in a sublime body of work, including the beautiful white marble head of a sleeping woman (*Sleep*), a bronze, weeping nude (*The Prayer*), and the limestone-carved *Wisdom of the Earth*.

Communist Party Headquarters and Creţulescu Church

The southeastern corner of Piaţa Revoluţiei is dominated by the **former Communist Party Headquarters**, a Stalinist monolith that now houses government offices. The famous balcony where Ceaușescu delivered his last speech is surprisingly near ground level, and quite unmarked by bullet holes. Ironically, it was from the same spot, two decades earlier, that Ceaușescu had drawn cheers of approval for his denunciation of the Soviet invasion of Czechoslovakia, and made his vow that Romania would defend its own independence – casting himself as a "maverick Communist" whom Western leaders could embrace. It was a delusion that persisted almost until the end; as Romanians point out, the honorary knighthood bestowed on Ceaușescu by Buckingham Palace in 1978 was only revoked after the revolution began. There are now two very contrasting memorials dedicated to those who died in the revolution: directly in front of the headquarters is a marble **memorial** with the inscription *Glorie Martirilor Nostri* ("Glory to our Martyrs"). Just across the way, and more controversially – as much for its brute ugliness as for anything else – a nameless triangular **column** shoots upwards with what looks like a bird's nest sprouting from its upper reaches (it's known locally as the "Olive on a Stick"). Below, the semi-circular wall is inscribed with the names of those who perished.

Across from the memorial stands the **Crețulescu Church** (Biserica Crețulescu), which was also seriously damaged during the fighting. Bucharest's most celebrated church – high and narrow with mock arches, bricks laid in saw-toothed patterns around the towers and elaborate carvings over the entrance – is built in the style created by Constantin Brâncoveanu, a seventeenth-century ruler of Wallachia who set out to forge a distinctive national genre of architecture (see p.112). It was paid for in 1720 by the boyar Iordache Crețulescu and his wife Safta, Brâncoveanu's daughter. Sadly, little remains of its frescoes by Tattarescu, or of the one on the porch, which features scenes from the Apocalypse.

Piața Enescu and around

Piața Enescu sits just to the north of Piața Revoluției, and is notable for a couple of historically and culturally important buildings. Its northern side is filled by the **Athénée Palace Hilton Hotel**, which, since it was built in 1912, has been one of the most prestigious hotels in Bucharest. For decades the hotel was also a notorious hotbed of espionage, beginning in the 1930s when the liveried staff and almost all the characters who populated the lobby spied for the king's police chief, for the Gestapo or for British Intelligence. Symbolic of that fevered, corrupt era, Bucharest's elite would sometimes party here through the night while police were shooting strikers in the "Red" Grivița district only a kilometre or so away. During the early 1950s the hotel was extensively refurbished as an "intelligence factory", with bugged rooms and tapped phones, to reinforce the reports of its informers and prostitutes.

To the east stands the **Romanian Atheneum** (Ateneul Român), a magnificent Neoclassical structure built in 1888 almost entirely from funds generated from Bucharest's citizens, after the original patrons ran out of money. Take a look inside at the rampantly *fin-de-siècle* dome decorated with lyres, or, better still, try and catch a concert by the resident George Enescu Philharmonic Orchestra (see p.81). To the south is the **University Library**, totally gutted in December 1989 but now rebuilt and housing offices. Glance upwards at the surrounding residential buildings, however, and you'll see that many of these are still quite heavily pockmarked with bullet holes. Just behind the library, at Str. Rosetti 8, is **Theodor Aman's House** (Tues–Sun 9am–5pm; €1.50), one of many "memorial houses" of notable artists dotted around the city. Aman (1831–91) trained in Paris before returning to be the first director of the Bucharest Art College. A somewhat academic painter, he was a leading member of the group of Francophile intellectuals (with fellow Romanians the painter Gheorghe Tattarescu and the sculptor

Karl Storck) that dominated Bucharest's cultural life in the late nineteenth century. Built in 1868 to Aman's own designs and decorated by himself and Storck, the house now contains a number of family portraits as well as some finely sculpted pieces, wooden chests and tables.

Calea Victoriei

Originally built in the late seventeenth century as a wood-paved avenue named Podul Mogoşoaiei, **Calea Victoriei** ("Avenue of Victory") has been Bucharest's most fashionable street since wealthy boyars first built their residences along it. The arrival of the boyars encouraged Bucharest's most prestigious shops to open along the avenue and, after it was repaved and took its present name in 1918, strolling along the avenue became *de rigueur*, causing the writer Hector Bolitho to remark that "to drive down the Calea Victoriei between twelve and one o'clock will prove you a provincial or a stranger". Along the street were "huddles of low, open-fronted shops where Lyons silk and Shiraz carpets were piled in the half-darkness beside Siberian furs, English guns and Meissen porcelain", while lurking in the side streets were starving groups of unemployed, lupus-disfigured beggars and dispossessed peasants seeking justice in the capital's courts. An avenue of marked contrasts, the quieter northern end still seems verdant and sleepy with touches of Old-World elegance, while to the south it becomes an eclectic jumble of old apartment buildings, glass and steel facades and glossy shops.

The one real point of interest along the northern stretch is the Cantacuzino Palace at no. 141. Fronted by a superb, early twentieth-century, clamshell-shaped *porte-cochère* topped with fluttering cherubs, this was the brief one-time residence of Romania's national composer, George Enescu (1881–1955). It now houses the **George Enescu Museum** (Tues–Sun 10am–5pm; €1.50; Ⓦwww .georgeenescu.ro), several rooms packed with memorabilia and personal effects – his childhood violin, coat and tails, batons, manuscripts, concert programmes and some excellent photographs. There's also a lengthy audiovisual presentation, which is as informative about Romanian folk music as it is about Enescu's work. Enescu actually eschewed the palace, preferring instead to live – in 1945–46 – in the pavilion to the rear which has been left *in situ*. It's surprisingly modest, with just two bedrooms and a music room with piano. For more on Enescu, see the box on p.392.

From the Enei Church to the River Dâmboviţa

South of Piaţa Revoluţiei, and beyond the *Grand Hotel Continental*, the **Pasajul Victoriei** ("Victory Passage") sneaks one block further east to Str. Academiei and the smoke-blackened **Enei Church**, built in 1702; the church is also known as the Dintr-o zi or "(Made) In One Day" church, as that's precisely how long it took to erect. Back on Calea Victoriei, the street continues down to the noisy junction with B-dul Regina Elisabeta, Bucharest's main east–west axis. Dominating the area is the Neoclassical **Cercul Militar** ("Army House"), which replaced the previous monastery church of Sărindar in 1912. It was originally built to cater to the social, cultural and educational needs of the Romanian army, and remains an important centre for military activity. Across B-dul Regina Elisabeta, an alleyway just beyond *Pizza Hut* slips off to the courtyard of the picturesque **Doamnei Church** (Biserica Doamnei), built in 1683 under the orders of Princess Maria, wife of Prince Şerban Cantacuzino. Despite ongoing renovation work it's still possible to view the gloomy interior frescoes, while, architecturally, the most impressive aspect is the porch, featuring a thick-set stone portal and octagonal stone pillars, the first of their kind in Bucharest.

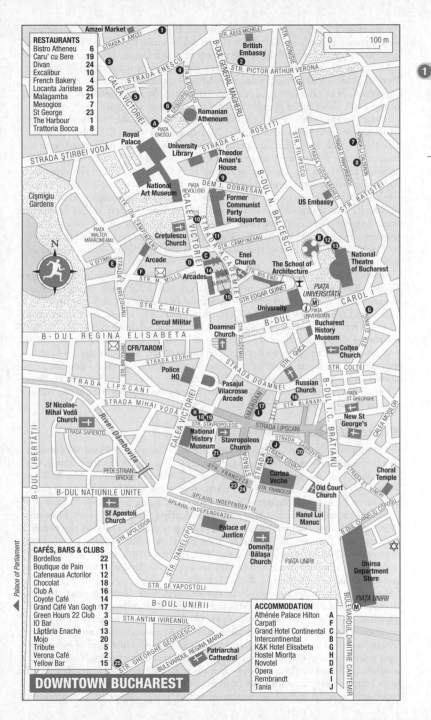

RESTAURANTS

Bistro Atheneu	6
Caru' cu Bere	19
Divan	24
Excalibur	10
French Bakery	4
Locanta Jaristea	25
Malagamba	21
Mesogios	7
St George	23
The Harbour	1
Trattoria Bocca	8

CAFÉS, BARS & CLUBS

Bordellos	22
Boutique de Pain	11
Cafeneaua Actorilor	12
Chocolat	18
Club A	16
Coyote Café	14
Grand Café Van Gogh	17
Green Hours 22 Club	3
IO Bar	9
Lăptăria Enache	13
Mojo	20
Tribute	5
Verona Café	2
Yellow Bar	15

ACCOMMODATION

Athénée Palace Hilton	A
Carpaţi	F
Grand Hotel Continental	C
Intercontinental	B
K&K Hotel Elisabeta	G
Hostel Miorita	H
Novotel	D
Opera	E
Rembrandt	I
Tania	J

DOWNTOWN BUCHAREST

0   100 m

Palace of Parliament

A short walk further down Calea Victoriei is Bucharest's **police headquarters**, now screened by a tall fence after it was stormed by a mob in 1990, an attack Iliescu used as his pretext for calling in the miners to smash the student opponents (see p.382). Directly opposite the headquarters, an inconspicuous portal leads into the **Pasajul Macca-Vilacrosse** ("Vilacrosse Passage"), whose glass roof and gracefully curved arcade of cafés give an idea of why Bucharest once claimed to be the "Paris of the East", although its grandeur has faded badly over the years.

Housed in the former Post Office building at no. 12 is the **National History Museum** (Muzeul Naţional de Istorie; Wed–Sun 10am–6pm; €2), a disappointing affair largely due to the fact that a much vaunted overhaul seems destined never to happen, hence the majority of exhibits are not on display. Until it does, and in addition to the regular schedule of temporary exhibitions held in the capacious foyer, you can view the modern lapidarium in the courtyard, housing plaster casts from Trajan's Column covered with depictions of his Dacian campaigns, as well as Greek, Roman and medieval tombstones and carvings. Better still, a basement vault exhibits Romania's **national treasures**: a dazzling display of gold and jewellery, from prehistoric finds (see particularly the elaborate Coţofeneşti helmet) to Queen Marie's crown and the casket said to hold her heart, to the sceptres of Ferdinand I and Carol II.

Another building worth more than a passing glance is the **National Savings Bank**, directly opposite the museum. Designed by French architect Paul Gottereanu in the 1890s, its grimy Neoclassical facade features an impressive high arch linked together by two solid Corinthian pillars. From here, it's a short walk to the **River Dâmboviţa**. An old saying has it that whoever drinks the "sweet waters" of the Dâmboviţa will never wish to be parted from Bucharest, to which one nineteenth-century traveller retorted that anyone who ever did "would be incapable of leaving the city for ever afterwards". Always prone to flooding, the Dâmboviţa was canalized in the 1880s and now passes underground at Piaţa Unirii. The river marks the abrupt transition from the fabric of the old city to the arbitrarily imposed pattern of the Centru Civic.

Piaţa Victoriei and around

Continuing north along Calea Victoriei, you eventually reach **Piaţa Victoriei**, a vast circular space around which crazed drivers maniacally jockey for position. On the east side of the square stands the main government building, the hulking Palaţul Victoria, completed in 1944 but even then already showing a chilly Stalinist influence in its design. On the north side, along Şos. Kiseleff, there is a cluster of museums. At no. 1 is the **Grigore Antipa Natural History Museum** (Muzeul de Istorie Naturală; Tues–Sun 10am–6pm; €2), named after the conservationist and founder of Romanian icthyology. A small aquarium aside, the museum's collection consists of some 300,000 items, including a 4.5m-high skeleton of a dinosaur unearthed in Moldavia, over 80,000 butterflies and moths, and the obligatory selection of stuffed animals.

Housed in an imposing, neo-Brâncovenesc red-brick building next door is Bucharest's finest museum, the **Museum of the Romanian Peasant** (Muzeul Ţăranului Român; Tues–Sun 10am–6pm; €2). On show is a wonderful display of traditional peasant artefacts from all regions of Romania, including colourfully woven linen and textiles, carvings, ceramics and a superb collection of wood and glass-painted icons. Of the several impressively reconstructed buildings dotted around the museum, the most eye-catching is an eighteenth-century **windmill** from Haţeg county, an enormous contraption that took three years to piece back together. Similarly, a thick-set peasant dwelling from Gorj county, comprising three rooms and a loft for storage, and originally displayed at the Village Museum up the road, took around a year to reconstruct. There is an incomplete timber church from Hunedoara, around which lie some of its furnishings – altar doors, a holy table, church bells and so on. A wooden church, typical of those found in Maramureş, stands on a neat patch of grass at the rear of the museum. Located here, too, is the museum shop, which sells a beautiful assortment of rugs, costumes and other folksy objects, and to the rear, a pleasant café. The entire premises were actually occupied by the Museum of Communist Party History until 1990, and there are still remnants from this time in the small basement, which contains a curious collection of paintings and busts of former communist leaders. On one wall, as if displayed reluctantly, is a rare picture of Ceauşescu – most images of the dictator were destroyed following his execution.

Southeast of here, in between B-dul Lascăr Catargiu and B-dul Iancu de Hunedoara at Str. V. Alecsandri 16, the fabulous **Storck Museum** (Wed–Sun 9am–5pm; €2) is one of Bucharest's lesser-known delights. Inside is a superb collection of sculpted works by Frederic Storck (1872–1942), whose father, Karl, was the first Romanian teacher of sculpture, as well as numerous paintings and murals by his wife Cecilia. They actually lived in the house next door; the museum building was originally built as a workshop.

The Centru Civic

In 1971, Ceauşescu visited North Korea and returned full of admiration for the grandiose avenues of Kim II Sung's capital, Pyongyang. Thirteen years later, inspired by what he had seen, Ceauşescu set out to remodel Bucharest as "the first socialist capital for the new socialist man", and to create a new administrative centre which was to be "a symbolic representation of the two decades of enlightenment we have just lived through". In truth, of course, this **Centru Civic** was meant to embody the state's authority and that of Ceauşescu himself. Implementing this megalomaniac vision entailed the demolition of a quarter of Bucharest's historic centre (about five square kilometres), said to be slums damaged by the 1977 earthquake, but in fact containing nine thousand largely undamaged nineteenth-century houses, whose forty thousand inhabitants were relocated in new developments on the outskirts of the city. There was worldwide condemnation of this vandalism, particularly since many old churches were to be swept away. Though some of the churches were in the end reprieved, they are now surrounded by huge modern apartment blocks and are separated from the urban context that gave them meaning. The core of the complex was largely completed by 1989, just in time for the dictator's overthrow.

Uniting the two halves of the Centru Civic is **Bulevardul Unirii**, at 4km long and 120m wide, slightly larger – intentionally so – than the Champs-Élysées after which it was modelled. Midway along is **Piaţa Unirii** ("Square of Union"), an oversized expanse of concrete dominated by traffic, and notable only as a key metro interchange, as the site of the city's main department store – the slicked-up Unirea – and as the best place to view the extraordinary Palace of Parliament.

From Piaţa Unirii it's a short walk up B-dul Corneliu Coposu to the junction of Str. Sf Vineri; a few paces along to the left, at no. 9, is the **Jewish Choral Temple**, a red-brick structure built in 1857, which still serves the city's dwindling Jewish community (services daily 8am & 7pm). A five-minute walk to the right along Str. Sf Vineri brings you to the **Great Synagogue**, at Str. Mămulari 3, which now houses a **Museum of Jewish History** (Muzeul de Istorie al Evreilor din Romania; Mon–Thurs 9am–2pm, Fri till noon, Sun till 1pm; free). There's a fairly comprehensive collection of books and paintings, as well as a handful of

Jewish ritual objects, though the most impressive exhibit is an elegant sculpture commemorating the lives of some 350,000 Jews deported in 1944.

The Palace of Parliament

Dominating the entire project from the western end of B-dul Unirii is the colossal **Palace of Parliament** (Palatul Parlamentului), claimed to be the second-largest administrative building in the world – after the Pentagon – measuring 270m by 240m, and 86m high. It epitomizes the megalomania that overtook Ceauşescu in the 1980s; here he intended to house ministries, Communist Party offices and the apartments of high functionaries. Built on the site of the former Spirei Hill, which was razed for this project, the sheer size of the building can only be grasped by comparison with the toy-like cars scuttling past below. It has twelve storeys, four underground levels (including a nuclear bunker), a 100m-long lobby and 1100 rooms, around half of which are used as offices while the remainder are redundant. The interiors are lavishly decorated with marble and gold leaf, and there are 4500 chandeliers (11,000 were planned), the largest of which weighs 1.5 tonnes, but the decoration was never finished due to the Ceauşescus' ever-changing whims. They were demanding patrons, allowing little more than a technical role to the architects, of which there were around seven hundred – one staircase was rebuilt three times before they were satisfied. Meanwhile, the floor pattern – which mirrors the layout of the building itself – was apparently designed that way so Ceauşescu wouldn't get lost.

This huge white elephant was officially known as the Casa Republicii, then as the Casa Poporului, but more popularly as the Casa Nebunului ("Madman's House"), before taking on its present name. The new government spent a long time agonizing about an acceptable use for it, and in 1994 it was finally decided to house the Senate and Parliament here; it is now also used for international conferences.

There are several different **tours** available (daily 10am–4pm); the standard one (€6, plus €8 for use of cameras) is a 45-minute trek through ten of the most dazzling, most representative or simply the largest of the halls, such as the extraordinary, glass-ceilinged **Sala Unirii** ("Unification Hall"), where legendary Romanian gymnast Nadia Comaneci was married in 1996. One of the last rooms you're led to is the Alexandru Ioan Cuza room, whose balcony offers defining views of the city. Other tours (€8–10) take in the basement, terrace or both. Although it's possible to turn up and take in a tour, you'll most likely have to wait some time before there are enough of you to make up a group – in which case you're best off calling beforehand (☏021/311 3611); you will also need to bring your passport. The entrance is from A3 (right-hand side as you face it; metro Izvor).

National Museum of Contemporary Art

Located in the building's west wing (to the rear of the Palace) is the **National Museum of Contemporary Art** (Muzeul Naţional de Arta Contemporana; Wed–Sun 10am–6pm; €2). Accessed via a specially constructed glass annex and external elevators (which, as they take you up, give you some idea of the breath-taking scale of this building), it's a superbly designed space. The works on display are exclusively by Romanian artists, and mostly take the form of sculptures, collages and montages – there's also a rare print from 1978 entitled *Removing Mihai Vodă Church*, in reference to the repositioning of the church when Ceauşescu set about demolishing the area. Up on the third floor, an enormous darkened room holds a series of curious multimedia installations, including several large screen projections, one of which has a woman serenely desecrating her kitchen, and another of a naked man balancing on a circle of chairs. It's a bit of a slog to get here, as you have to walk round the palace – walk up Calea 13 Septembrie and it's the second entrance on the right.

The churches of the Centru Civic

Hidden away among the rows of new buildings that make up the Centru Civic are numerous tiny Orthodox churches thankfully reprieved from demolition. In Bucharest, you'll frequently find churches in inappropriate places – such as the courtyards of apartment buildings – where the city planners have built around them, but here the churches seem even more disregarded and incongruous than elsewhere. The most striking example of this is the **Mihai Vodă Church** (Biserica Mihai Vodă), built by Michael the Brave in 1591; to make way for the Centru Civic development, in 1985 the church was moved 279m east on rails to Str. Sapienţei 4, which entailed the demolition of the church's medieval cloisters and ancillary buildings. What's more, as it's now standing on a concrete platform, the church will probably collapse when the next major earthquake hits Bucharest. A similar fate probably awaits the wretched-looking **Sf Apostoli Church** (Biserica Sfinţii Apostoli), five minutes south of here at Str. Sf Apostoli 33A; this grey, largely seventeenth-century structure was embellished in 1715 with a fine little steeple by Stefan Cantacuzino, a portrait of whom is just about visible inside the almost pitch-black interior. Located in slightly more civilized surrounds, just behind the Palace of Justice at Str. Sf Apostoli 60, is the late nineteenth-century **Domniţa Bălaşa Church** (Biserica Domniţa Bălaşa), one of the most popular churches in the city. Named after Constantin Brâncoveanu's sixth daughter, Doamna – a statue of whom stands in the garden in front of the church – this orange-brick edifice is actually the third church on this site, the previous two having burnt down in the eighteenth century. The interior, one of the most complete in the city, features a beautiful wooden cross-shaped chandelier.

On the southern side of B-dul Unirii, at Str. Antim 29, is the **Antim Monastery** (Mănăstirea Antim), a large walled complex built in 1715 upon the orders of polymath Antim Ivireanul. The centrepiece of this tranquil space is a beautifully proportioned red-brick church, featuring a superb stone portal and sculpted wooden doors. At the top of Aleea Dealul Mitropoliei stands the **Patriarchal Cathedral** (Patriarhia), built from 1655 to 1668 and seat of the Romanian Orthodox Church. The interior contains the most dazzling of the city's iconostases, as well as a couple of exquisitely carved side altars. Completing the set of buildings here is the Brâncoveanu-commissioned campanile, the **Patriarchal Palace** (built in 1875) and the former **Palace of the Chamber of Deputies** (1907).

South of the Centru Civic

From Piaţa Unirii, B-dul Dimitrie Cantemir runs south about 1km to the much older Calea Şerban Vodă. The two roads cover the site of Podul Şerban Vodă, destroyed by a fire in 1825. This was the route taken by merchants and Turkish officials heading for the Sublime Porte of Constantinople, the Sultan's Court. The two roads meet at the north end of **Tineretului Park** ("Youth Park"), which contains a fairground and a lake, as well as the Uman crematorium, a strange, rather Masonic chapel filled with caskets of ashes. To the west is the more popular and formal **Carol I Park**; its tatty southern end, site of a brutal monument which once held the remains of Gheorghiu-Dej and other communist leaders, gives way to a lovely green space bisected by a long promenade and a smaller lake – during the summer you can hire rowing boats (daily 10am–8pm; €3 for 1hr). A short walk north of the lake is the **Museum of Technology** (Muzeul Tehnic; Wed–Sun 9.30am–4pm; €1), an oddball place intended to assert Romania's technological fecundity, particularly several "firsts", such as the metal-bodied aeroplane (1912) and the streamlined motor car (1923). Ironically, it's the names of British, French and German firms that dominate the collection.

Ten minutes' walk south along Calea Șerban Vodă, at the junction of the highways to Oltenița and Giurgiu and opposite the Eroii Revoluției metro, is the **Heroes of the Revolution Cemetery** (Cimitirul Eroii Revoluției); buried here, in neat rows of identical white marble graves, are more than 280 "Heroes of the Revolution", gunned down by "terrorists" in 1989. Despite the traffic roaring by, it's an affecting place, and even more poignant given that some of the victims were as young as 13. To the left of the cemetery stands the Church of the Martyr Heroes. Neighbouring **Bellu Cemetery** is the resting place of some of Romania's greatest writers, including Mihai Eminescu (see p.248).

Nicolae Ceaușescu and his wife Elena are buried in **Ghencea Cemetery**, southwest of the city along Drumul Sării; you can get here by bus from Eroii Revoluției metro station (#173; Mon–Fri only) and from Piața Unirii (#385; nearest stop at the junction of Drumul Sării and Calea 13 Septembrie). Originally buried under pseudonyms, their graves were subsequently marked with their own names. However, doubts existed for years as to whether the Ceaușescus were actually buried here, and in 2010 both were exhumed (Nicolae in the black coat he was wearing when executed), primarily to satisfy the remaining family members. His grave is surrounded by a small black fence on the left side of the central alley before the chapel, while Elena's grubby little plot is on the opposite side of the alley. Ask one of the guards to show you if you can't find them. Note that photos are not permitted. Next door is a military cemetery, a surreal forest of propeller blades marking the graves of airmen.

The historic quarter

Bound by Piața Unirii to the south, Calea Victoriei to the west, and B-dul I. C. Brătianu to the east, the historic quarter – an area more commonly known as Lipscani – was mercifully spared Ceaușescu's bulldozers, and it now offers a welcome respite from the concrete monotony of the Centru Civic. A picturesque and agreeably ramshackle maze of streets and decrepit houses, Bucharest's oldest neighbourhood has been undergoing painfully slow regeneration for years, and while many parts of it remain desperately run-down, there's been a massive recent influx of cafés and bars into the area, making it *the* place to party in town.

It was here that Prince Vlad Țepeș ("Vlad the Impaler", otherwise known as Dracula – see p.403) built a **citadel** in the fifteenth century. The building was severely damaged during Țepeș's attempt to regain the throne in 1476 (in which he succeeded, only to be murdered a few months later), and was further damaged by various earthquakes and fires over the following centuries; it was subsequently auctioned off as wasteland. Thus, little remains of the ancient citadel – just some of the walls, arches and shattered columns of the **Curtea Veche** ("Old Court"), at Str. Franceză 60 (Tues–Sun 9am–5pm; free), most of which was uncovered during excavations in the late 1960s. The adjoining **Old Court Church**, established by Mircea Ciobanul ("Mircea the Shepherd") from 1546–58, is the oldest church in Bucharest. It is a typical example of sixteenth-century Wallachian church architecture, with horizontal bands of brick facing and rows of small niches beneath the cornice. Inside, a dazzling iconostasis brightens up an otherwise gloomy interior. Across from the church, at Str. Franceză 62, an austere, badly graffitied building conceals Bucharest's most famous hostelry, **Hanul lui Manuc** ("Manuc's Inn"). Built as a *caravanserai* (inn) in 1808 by a wealthy Armenian, Manuc-bey Mirzaian, it was the site of talks for the Treaty of Bucharest, which put an end to the Russo-Turkish War of 1806–12. For years a dodgy state-run hotel and restaurant, it now sits forlornly awaiting its fate. From Str. Franceză work your way up Str. Selari, where the **Glassblowers' Courtyard** at no. 9 holds an artisan's workshop, and on to Str. Lipscani, a lively thoroughfare named after the merchants from Leipzig who traded here in the eighteenth century. This whole area is a labyrinth of little shops, interspersed with arcades, such as the Hanul cu tei at no. 63.

The Old Town's most arresting site is the diminutive **Stavropoleos Church** (Biserica Stavropoleos) on Str. Stavropoleos. Built between 1724 and 1730 for the first Phanariot ruler, Nicolae Mavrocordat, the church has a gorgeous, almost arabesque, facade, with a columned portico carved with delicate tracery – stalks, leaves and stylized flowers. The interior, now fully restored, has a splendid iconostasis, featuring, in the upper part, medallions of the prophets and, in the middle and lower portions, scenes from the life of Christ. Have a look up at the beautiful dark blue star-flecked cupola. On this same street, at no. 5, you'll also find the *Caru' cu Bere* ("The Beer Cart"), an ornately decorated tavern dating from 1875 that's now one of the most popular eateries in the city (see p.79). A couple of streets further north, on Str. Doamnei, stands the brazenly colourful, corkscrew-domed **Russian Church** (1905–09). The church, faced with yellow brick, Art Nouveau green tiling and pixie-faced nymphs, has a small interior, featuring frescoes blackened with age and smoke.

Piaţa Universităţii and around

Piaţa Universităţii is the focus of city life and traffic, and was one of the key sites of the 1989 revolution, as evinced by the numerous memorials (note the ten stone crosses in the road island) to those killed at Christmas 1989 and in June 1990. The latter marks the date on which miners, under Iliescu's orders, drove out students who had been on hunger strike since April 30, causing the square to be nicknamed Piaţa Tiananmen. The most poignant of the memorials is the black cross and wall plaque at B-dul Bălcescu 18, some 200m north of the *Intercontinental* hotel – this marks the spot where the first victim, Mihai Gătlan, aged 19, fell, at 5.30pm on December 21.

West of the square, occupying the first block on B-dul Regina Elisabeta, is **Bucharest University**, whose frontage is lined with statues of illustrious pedagogues and statesmen, as well as a regular crop of bookstalls. Established in 1859 after the union of Wallachia and Moldavia, the university equipped the sons of bourgeois families to become lawyers and men of letters until the communists took over in 1949. Technical skills and education for women were subsequently given top priority, but since the revolution, business studies and foreign languages have overtaken them in popularity. Just behind here, on Str. Edgar Quinet, is the **School of Architecture**, built between 1912 and 1927 in the neo-Brâncovenesc style – ornate pillars, prominent, richly carved eaves and a multitude of arches.

Just north of the square, adjacent to the *Intercontinental*, the **National Theatre of Bucharest** resembles an Islamicized reworking of the Colosseum; it was a pet project of Elena Ceauşescu, who had the facade rebuilt twice, and the roof once, before she was satisfied. On the southwest corner of Piaţa Universităţii, the **Bucharest History Museum** (Muzeul Municipal Bucureşti; Tues–Sun 9am–5pm; €1.50) traces the city's evolution, with a limited but reasonably enlightening collection of old documents, coins, photographs and prints – there are also some rusting street signs from old Bucharest. The neo-Gothic building was built as the Suţu Palace in 1834; its superb *porte-cochere* was added later in the century.

Across the road from the museum lie two ancient and much-loved churches: in front of the hospital of the same name and period is the **Colţea Church** (Biserica Colţea), dating from the beginning of the eighteenth century and with a richly ornamented interior. Some 200m further south, the late sixteenth-century

New St George's Church (Biserica Sf Gheorghe Nou) was the largest church to be built in the city during the reign of Constantin Brâncoveanu, who, it is alleged, was reburied under the church in 1720 after his wife brought him back from Istanbul. The grey-brick interior is enlivened by paintings, murals and sculptures by Mutu, Popp and Caragea. A suitably grand bronze statue of Brâncoveanu, completed by Karl Storck, stands in front of the church.

West of Piaţa Universităţii

Heading west of Piaţa Universităţii, midway along B-dul Regina Elisabeta, the lovely **Cişmigiu Gardens** (Gradina Cişmigiu) were laid out as a park on land bequeathed to the city in 1845. Originally belonging to a Turkish water inspector, the gardens now fittingly contain a serpentine lake upon which small rowing boats and pedalos glide, rented by couples seeking solitude among the swans and weeping willows (rental May–Sept daily 10am–9pm; €4/hr, from a kiosk by the waterside). Otherwise, the gardens provide a tranquil space, with workers snoozing beneath the trees at lunch times and pensioners meeting for games of chess. At the park's northern end, a Roman garden contains busts of some of Romania's literary greats while, for kids, there's an attractive little playground next to the lake.

A few hundred metres beyond Cişmigiu, on B-dul Kogălniceanu, stands the mint-green **Opera Română**, a drab 1950s building containing a collection of operatic costumes, scores, photographs and posters. Although these are not particularly interesting, do try and catch one of the highly regarded performances here if you get the chance (see p.81). Looming over the Opera building is the monstrous **Casa Radio** ("Radio House"), another of Ceauşescu's unfinished projects. Initially intended to house the National History, Army and Communist Party museums, as well as Ceauşescu's tomb, it has long been rumoured that it will become, as the name implies, a radio centre.

Cotroceni Palace and the Botanical Gardens

From the Opera Română, buses and trolley buses trundle south across the river along B-dul Eroilor Sanitari to the Cotroceni Palace, passing an area of lovely bourgeois villas, each one individually designed. The **Cotroceni Palace** (Palatul Cotroceni) was built as a monastery by Şerban Cantacuzino between 1679 and 1682 and served as a base for the Austrian army in 1737, the Russian army in 1806, and Tudor Vladimirescu's rebels in 1821. Damaged by numerous fires and earthquakes over the course of its history, the original building was demolished in 1863 and the palace rebuilt from 1893 to 1895 to provide a home for the newly wed Prince Ferdinand and Princess Marie. Under communism, it served as the Palace of the Pioneers – the "Pioneers" being the Soviet-bloc equivalent of the Boy Scouts. A new south wing was added during restoration following the 1977 earthquake, and this is now the presidential residence. In 1986, Ceauşescu had the church demolished, apparently because it spoilt the view. It's only possible to visit the palace on a guided tour, which must be booked in advance (Thurs–Sun 9.30am–5.30pm; passport required; €6; ☏021/317 3107). Tours pass first through the remains of the monastery, where the Cantacuzino family gravestones are kept, then through the new rooms from the 1893–95 rebuild, decorated in an eclectic variety of Western styles. Enter the palace at B-dul Geniului 1.

On the other side of Şoseaua Cotroceni lie the university's well-tended **Botanical Gardens** (Grădina Botanică; daily 8am–8pm; €1.50), which contain pine trees and lily ponds, as well as glasshouses and a botany museum (Tues, Thurs & Sun 9am–1pm).

The National Military Museum

A short way north of the Opera Română, in a former army barracks at Str. Mircea Vulcănescu 125, is the **National Military Museum** (Muzeul Militar Național; Tues–Sun 9am–5pm; €2). The first part of the museum is an intermittently interesting trawl through Romania's military history, featuring an impressive array of weapons, banners and uniforms. The one section of the museum that really merits a visit, however, is the exhibition on the 1989 revolution. It's a deeply moving presentation, comprised mainly of personal belongings donated by families of soldiers and civilians killed during the fighting – from glasses, watches and medals to more sobering items such as torn and blood-splattered clothing and bullet casings. The main exhibit is the pistol, walkie-talkie and blood-soaked uniform of **General Vasile Milea**, Minister of Defence at the time of the revolution, who was executed for refusing to carry out orders to shoot upon the civilians. There are also some rare English-language newspaper editions from that time, including many graphic images of the dead and those mourning the dead. Despite the voluminous display of memorabilia on view in the remainder of the museum, Romania has rarely gone in for martial adventures; from 1958, it was the only Warsaw Pact country without Soviet troops on its soil. Ceaușescu called vociferously for disarmament, announcing peace proposals and cuts in the defence budget. Post-communist Romania has become more involved in international concerns, contributing peace-keepers to the former Yugoslavia, as well as deploying troops in both Iraq and Afghanistan.

The northern suburbs

The **Șoseaua Kiseleff**, a long, elegant avenue lined with lime trees, extends north from Piața Victoriei towards the Herăstrău Park and the Village Museum, one of Romania's best open-air museums, before heading out towards the airports and the main road to Transylvania. Modelled on the Parisian *chaussées* – though named after a Russian general – Șoseaua Kiseleff is a product of the Francophilia that swept Romania's educated classes during the nineteenth century; it even has its own Arc de Triumf.

East of Șoseaua Kiseleff, beyond B-dul Aviatorilor at Str. Muzeul Zambaccian 21, the **Zambaccian Museum** (Muzeul Zambaccian; Wed–Sun 11am–7pm; €2) is another little gem to rank alongside the Storck Museum. This little-known museum houses a small but terrific collection of art accumulated by wealthy businessman Krikor H. Zambaccian (1889–1962), and is notable for its paintings by established Romanian artists such as Grigorescu, Andreescu and Lucian, and French artists Renoir and Matisse; it is also home to the only painting in the country by Cézanne, as well as a few pieces of sculpture from Brâncuși and Storck.

About 1km north along Șoseaua Kiseleff you'll come to the **Arc de Triumf**, built in 1878 for an independence parade, and patched together in 1922 for

---

The Skopți

The Skopți coachmen, who worked along the Șoseaua Kiseleff until the 1940s, made up one of the curiosities of Bucharest. Members of a dissident religious sect founded in Russia during the seventeenth century – and related to the Lipovani of the Danube Delta – the Skopți ritually castrated themselves in the belief that the "generative organs are the seat of all iniquities", interpreting literally Christ's words on eunuchs in the Gospel of St Matthew. This was done after two years of normal married life – a period necessary to ensure the conception of future Skopți. Driving *droshkys* pulled by black Orloff horses, the coachmen wore caftans sprouting two cords, which passengers tugged to indicate that the driver should turn left or right.

another procession to celebrate Romania's participation on the winning side in World War I and the gains achieved at the Versailles peace conference. Originally made of wood, it was more fittingly rebuilt in stone from 1935 to 1936, in the style of the Arc de Triomphe in Paris.

Herăstrău Park

Immediately beyond the Arc is **Herăstrău Park**, which is best reached by metro – the Aviatorilor stop is at its southeastern corner. Paths run past formal flower-beds to the shore of **Lake Herăstrău**, one of the largest of a dozen lakes strung along the River Colentina. These lakes, created by Carol II to drain the unhealthy marshes that surrounded Bucharest, form a continuous line across the northern suburbs. Arched bridges lead via the small and fragrant Island of Roses to numerous lakeside snack bars and restaurants, from where you can rent rowing boats (€2/hr) or take a thirty-minute lake cruise (€1.50); tickets for both (May–Sept) must be bought from the windows opposite the departure point. Located near the park's other entrance, which is at the northern end of Şoseaua Kiseleff, near Piaţa Libere, is the **Expo** – a large pavilion selling mostly clothes – and a creaky old fairground.

The residential area east of the park is one of Bucharest's most exclusive neigh-bourhoods. It is where the communist elite once lived, cordoned off from the masses they governed; the Ceauşescus lived in the Vila Primavera, at the east end of B-dul Primăverii. The area is still inhabited by technocrats, favoured artists and members of the elite.

The Village Museum

Another of Bucharest's worthwhile sights is the **Village Museum** (Muzeul Satului: Mon 9am–5pm, Tues–Sun 9am–7pm; €2) on the shores of Lake Herăstrău – the entrance is on Şoseaua Kiseleff, just up from the Arc de Triumf. Established in 1936, this wonderful ensemble of over three hundred dwellings, workshops, churches, windmills, presses and other structures from every region in the country illustrates the extreme diversity of Romania's folk architecture.

Most interesting are the oak houses from Maramureş with their rope-motif carvings and shingled roofing, and their beamed gateways carved with animals and hunting scenes, Adam and Eve and the Tree of Life, and suns and moons. Other highlights are the heavily thatched dwellings from Sălciua de Jos in Alba county; dug-out homes, or "pit" houses (with vegetables growing on the roof) from Drăghiceni and Castranova in Oltenia; colourfully furnished homesteads from Moldavia; and windmills from Tulcea county in the Delta. Keep an eye out, too,

---

The Băneasa bridge

The bridge immediately north of Băneasa Station, where the DN1 crosses the River Colentina, was the scene of a **crucial battle** in August 1944. The success of the August 23 coup against Marshal Antonescu (see p.379) meant that Hitler's oil supplies were more than halved, which is reckoned to have shortened the war in Europe by at least six months. However, at the time just 2800 Romanian troops faced between twenty thousand and thirty thousand Germans, mostly at Băneasa and Otopeni. King Mihai offered the Germans safe passage out of Romania, but they responded by bombing Bucharest. The bridge was held by a Romanian lieutenant and a handful of men until August 25, when Romanian reinforcements began to arrive from Craiova. Allied help finally came the following day when four hundred American planes bombed the German positions, and by August 27 Bucharest had been cleared of German forces (only to be occupied by the Red Army four days later).

for the beautiful wooden church from the village of Dragomireşti in Maramureş. Mud-brick dwellings from the fertile plains ironically appear poorer than the homes of peasants in the less fertile highlands where timber and stone abound, while the importance of livestock to the Székely people of Harghita county can be seen by their barns, which are taller than their houses. The terrific souvenir shop here is the best place in the city to buy folk art objects, including textiles and costumes, ceramics and woodenware.

Piaţa Presei Libere

Şoseaua Kiseleff ends at **Piaţa Presei Libere** ("Free Press Square"), in front of **Casa Presei Libere** ("Free Press House"), a vast white Stalinist building, which was once the centre of the state propaganda industry. Little seems to have changed, as the free publishing industry is still largely corralled into this one building. Until 1989, the pedestal in front of the building accommodated a huge statue of Lenin, before he was carted off to Mogoşoaia Palace (see p.86) and unceremoniously dumped there.

Some 500m further north of here, by the Băneasa train station just off the Bucureşti–Ploieşti Highway, are Bucharest's two least-known museums. Both of these eccentric buildings on Str. Dr Minovici were constructed in the early twentieth century, specifically to hold the private collections of the oil-rich Minovici family. Built in 1905 in the style of a fortified manor house, the **Museum of Popular Arts** (Tues–Sun 9am–5pm; €1) at no. 2 exhibits woven blankets, Transylvanian blue pottery, painted Easter eggs, spinning wheels, musical instruments, furniture and beautiful peasant garments – there's also a tiny Orthodox chapel with eighteenth-century icons. Next door at no. 3, constructed in 1910 in a bizarre fusion of English Tudor and Italian Renaissance styles, the **Museum of Old Western Arts** (Thurs–Sun 9am–5pm; €1) is filled with hunting trophies and weapons, Flemish tapestries, Florentine furniture, German and Swiss stained-glass windows, and a fine rug from Mosul in Iraq.

Eating and drinking

Between the World Wars, Bucharest was famed for its bacchanals, its gourmet cuisine and its Gypsy music – but all this ended with the puritanical postwar regime of communism. However, Bucharest's **restaurant** scene has improved immensely in recent years, and while French and Italian kitchens dominate, there's been a welcome diversification in the types of cuisines available, with fusion, Asian and South/Central American foods slowly making their mark. Alfresco dining is extremely popular, which is handy in a city that can be stifling in the summer.

Bucharest now has some genuinely enjoyable **cafés**, many of which offer food and alcoholic beverages, while the city's many fine **patisseries** dispense freshly baked sweet and savoury pastries, cakes and confectionery. Look out, too, for the kiosks doling out *gogoş*, large, elongated doughnuts that come with a choice of fillings.

Cafés and patisseries

Ana Pan Str. Radu Beller 8. Clean and modern sit-down/takeaway patisserie with more than a dozen outlets around the city, serving croissants, sweet and savoury pastries, tarts and yoghurts.
Boutique de Pain Str. Academiei 28. Somewhat anonymously located just down from the former

Communist Party headquarters, this tidy, diner-style establishment rustles up food with a French twist (breads, croissants and tarts) alongside great coffee and cooling summer drinks (frappes and smoothies).
Café Boheme Str. Caderea Bastilliei. A short walk from Piaţa Romana, this is a lovely spot to come

and relax. Aside from the prolific range of coffees (including flavoured, iced, Turkish), this is one of the best places in town for a hot toasted sandwich or omelette breakfast.

Caffe and Latte B-dul Schitu Măgureanu 35. In a lovely leafy location across from the Cişmigiu Gardens, this is one of the city's most enjoyable cafés, run by happy smiling staff. Excellent coffees, fruit and chocolate shakes, and pastries.

Casandra B-dul Magheru 32. A friendly sit-down place serving savoury bites, fancy biscuits and cakes (including strudel and baklava), and small cups of coffee.

Chocolat Calea Victoriei 12a (located on Str. Stavropoleos) and Str. Radu Beller 13. Hugely popular chain of chocolatiers where you can select from a prodigious list of chocolate-flavoured drinks, pastries, cakes and confectionery, in addition to some fabulous French breads.

Grand Café Van Gogh Str. Smărdan 9. This most enjoyable of Old Town cafés features a coolly lit, orange-tinted interior furnished with high, window-facing tables, and also has one of the best terraces going. Excellent coffee, draught beer and food, including breakfasts, toasted sandwiches and platters.

Hobby Café Str. Negustori 34. Wonderfully conceived backstreet café where visitors can kick back with a coffee or beer at the same time as participating in a range of activities, such as painting, drawing and photography.

IO Bar Str. Demetri Dobrescu 5. This former Securitate hideout, gutted during the revolution – as evidenced by the superb wall-length black-and-white prints depicting these events – has been stunningly revamped into offices and a café. It's a friendly and relaxing venue, perfect after an afternoon at the National Art Gallery across the road.

Panipat B-dul Bălcescu 24 (24hr), Gara de Nord (24hr), Str. M Rosetti 15, B-dul Brătianu 44, Şos. Ştefan cel Mare 48 and B-dul Kogălniceanu 55. Established franchise patisserie with good takeaway buns, pizzas and cakes, including strudel.

Serendipity Tea House Str. Dumbrava Roşie 12. Enchanting little tea house serving up a wide range of hot and chilled teas, though the house variety – a fruity blend of roses and strawberries – is particularly delicious. Terrific place to come with a book and some time to spare.

Verona Café Str. Pictor Arthur Verona 13. An extension of the café in the Cărtureşti bookshop (see p.82), this summer-only affair to the rear of

the shop is a cool garden terrace that's conducive to more contemplative drinking.

Snacks, sandwich bars and fast food

Frufru Str. Batiştei 1–3. Behind the *Intercontinental* hotel, this funky little place doles out tubs of fresh pasta, soups and salads, to eat in or take away.

Gregory's Str. Lipscani 27 and other outlets around the city. Decent sandwich shop with baguettes, wraps, pies, salads and a good range of deli products.

Omnivore's Dilemma Calea Victoriei 214. Unassuming little place offering a selection of hot and cold light bites, including some good daily specials, as well as teas and coffees. Closed Sun.

Snack Attack Piaţa Dorobanţi and other outlets around the city. Bright and fashionable outlets serving the freshest and tastiest sandwiches, baguettes, soups and salads, as well as juices and desserts (yoghurt, panacotta, cheesecake).

Spring Time Str. Academiei 35 and other outlets around the city. It's not sophisticated, but this Lebanese-run fast-food chain has a wide range of foods to take away or eat in.

Restaurants

Around Piaţa Revoluţiei

Bistro Atheneu Str. Episcopiei 3 ☎021/313 4900. Across from the Atheneum concert hall, this homely little restaurant – its walls cluttered with bells, instruments and old Bucharest street signs – has been keeping pre- and post-concert punters happy for years with its tasty Romanian and continental food. Reservations advised at weekends.

Excalibur Str. Academiei 39–41. Settle down at large round wooden tables and get stuck into big platters of juicy smoked meats at this medieval-themed restaurant located in a cellar opposite the former Communist Party headquarters. Terrific value daily set menus for €4 (between noon and 4pm).

French Bakery Str. Nicolae Golescu 17. Beautifully decorated bistro specializing in top-end French cuisine. Lighter offerings include *bouillabaisse*, quiche and soufflés, alongside mouthwatering mains like duck steak, *coq au vin* and *steak au poivre*. The desserts – notably the tarte tatin – are sublime, while the wine list rounds things off superbly.

La Taifas Str. Gheorghe Manu 16. Well-established, popular and personable bistro with a large terrace and two salon-style rooms, each brightly painted and warmly decorated. The menu – notable for its delicious grilled and fried meats (such as the lamb mix) – is chalked up on a board and brought to your table. Excellent three-course lunch menu for €5 (12.30–2.30pm).

The Harbour Piața Amzei 10–22. Unsurprisingly the theme here is nautical, with fishing regalia suspended from the walls and ceiling, and waiters in daft sailor get-up. The food, such as home-made sausages with mashed potato, and lamb stew, is simply done but very tasty.

East of Bulevardul G. Magheru and Bulevardul N. Bălcescu

Balthazar Str. Dumbrava Roșie 2 ☎021/212 1460. Superb contemporary fusion restaurant offering an intriguing Franco-Asian menu – includes Peking duck blinis, coconut shrimp, and tuna steak with almond flakes and black rice. The great-looking surrounds (burgundy walls, white drapes and glitterballs) and impeccable service make it worth the expense.

El Torito Str. Iancu Capitanu 30. Bright, funky and friendly Mexican venue, whose specialities – tacos, burritos, enchiladas, quesadillas and the like – are made from the freshest, most authentic ingredients. Factor in a terrific drinks menu and great music, and you've got a cracking evening. Tram #21 along Calea Moșilor.

Mesogios Str. Calderon 49 ☎021/317 1355. Long-standing and beautifully turned out, this restaurant is the place to come for seafood. All manner of treats to feast on, including cuttlefish, monkfish, octopus, red snapper and squid, to name but a few – though it is at the higher end of the price scale.

Smarts Str. Alexandru Donici 14. Cosy, tightly packed restaurant – all chunky tables and thick wooden beams – of an international bent but veering towards Belgian food; their steaks are among the best in the city, while the freshwater fish pancakes make for an unusual entrée. Neat little inn-style bar downstairs, too, where you can sample Belgian beers.

Trattoria Bocca Str. Calderon 41. Housed in a delightful-looking villa a few paces down from *Mesogios*, this quiet and friendly *trattoria* offers a highly creditable, affordably priced Italian menu, with the emphasis on steaming plates of fresh pasta. The burgundy walls give the interior a pleasantly polished feel alongside the sunny little side terrace.

The historic quarter

Caru' cu Bere Str. Stavropoleos 5. Often the first stop for tourists, thanks to the fabulous surrounds,

featuring splendid decor and high Gothic vaulted ceilings. Decent Romanian food too, such as *mititei* (grilled spicy sausages), Moldavian *tochitură* (pork stew) and *mămăligă* (polenta). The daily set menus are good value (noon–6pm; €6).

Divan Str. Franceză 46–48. Turkish/Middle Eastern restaurant rustling up a host of impressively authentic and beautifully presented *meze* and main dishes (aubergine salads, *dolma*, *kofte*, lamb kebabs, spiced minced meat-covered *lahmacun*). The terrace is impressive too, a huddle of low tables surrounded by colourfully cushioned benches – a relaxing place to try an absinthe or water pipe.

Locanta Jaristea Str. George Georgescu 50–52. South of B-dul Unirii, *Locanta* dishes up some of the best and most unusual Romanian food in the city, such as grilled pigeon, boiled goat and roast boar or bear. The room is styled on early twentieth-century Bucharest, while the lush red carpets, tall-backed chairs and smartly attired waiters add to the overall sense of effortlessness.

Malagamba Str. Sf Dumitru 2. The predominantly Italian fare at this bright and modern restaurant, named after a local 1940s jazz musician, is a cut above most food in town; fresh pasta and risottos form the mainstay of the menu, though there are plenty of attractive alternatives such as baked dorada and grilled monkfish. It has an above-average selection of domestic and foreign wines too.

St George Str. Franceză 44. A complimentary shot of țuică to start things off, followed by a delicious and wholesome plate of typically calorific Hungarian fare – thick dumpling soup, Hortobagy pancakes (beef-filled crepes), goose liver – and, finally, a pancake dessert accompanied by a glass of sweet Tokaj Aszú. The authentic Magyar decor and resident Gypsy band (neither too loud nor invasive) round things off superbly.

North of the centre

Barka Saffron Str. Av. Sănătescu 1. This eternally popular, informal and enchanting little Indian–fusion restaurant has an appealing choice of chicken- and lamb-based curries, alongside some spicy Sri Lankan and Caribbean dishes. Bus #82 from Gara de Nord.

Byblos Parc Herăstrău. Relocated to the shores of Lake Herăstrău, *Byblos* is another well-established fixture on the city's dining scene; a fabulous combination of top-notch Italian food, film screenings and live music on the green, well-shaded terrace make this place well worth a visit. Metro Piața Aviatorilor.

Casa Doina Şos. Kiseleff 4. Occupying a prime location on the edge of a wooded park, this late nineteenth-century building accommodates an elegant and formal restaurant (no shorts allowed), serving an upscale expensive take on Romanian dishes, though the real joy is the sprawling leafy terrace.

Die Deutsche Kneipe Str. Stockholm 9. Terrific, family-run restaurant in a quiet residential street, offering gut-busting portions of succulent German sausages served with lashings of sauerkraut and washed down with German Pils or keg beer. Tricky to find; take a left off Calea Dorobanţilor down Str. Madrid, then left again. Closed Sun.

Piccolo Mondo Str. Clucerului 16. Bucharest's top Lebanese restaurant is a handsome affair, listing a long menu of salads, kebabs (including a good choice for vegetarians), yoghurt-based dishes, and cured meats. Post-meal, enjoy a smoke on a hookah pipe.

Uptown Bar and Grill Str. Rabat 2. Another pleasantly secluded place just off B-dul Aviatorilor (or a ten-minute walk from Piaţa Dorobanţilor). Delicious crepes, salads, pastas, grilled meats and seafood at slightly higher than average prices – try and grab a table in the elegant horseshoe-shaped conservatory.

Nightlife and entertainment

Bucharest does not immediately strike visitors as a place bursting with **nightlife**, but this is partly because, like the best of the city's restaurants, many places are discreetly tucked away or concentrated in unlikely areas of the city. That said, the historic Old Town quarter has undergone a remarkable resurgence, and on any given night you'll find the tightly packed ranks of cafés and **bars** full to the gills. The **club** scene, too, is developing, and in addition to the growing number of bars that double up as clubs there are now some choice venues scattered around town, increasingly catering to a more discerning range of musical tastes. Bucharestians, however, have long been starved of decent **live music**, a situation reflected in the dearth of venues, though this is slowly improving.

Bars and clubs

Bordellos Str. Selari 9–11. Vibrant bar on one of the Old Town's less hectic streets, with a better than average choice of draught beers and a tasty selection of tapas; the raised terrace is the business for people-watching and it's also the best venue in town to watch televised football.

Cafeneaua Actorilor B-dul Bălcescu 2. A warren of dark stepped corridors and secret corners marks this long-established pub out as the preferred post-show haunt of actors performing at the nearby National Theatre. Located to the north of the theatre just a few steps away from the *Intercontinental*.

Champions Calea 13 Septembrie 90, on the first floor of the *Marriott Grand* hotel. Thoughtfully designed, American-style sports bar with large plasma screens for all your sporting kicks and an impressive array of superstar memorabilia, including George Foreman's gloves and Dan Marino's helmet, as well as items belonging to local heroes Ilie Năstase, Gheorghe Hagi and Nadia Comaneci.

Club A Str. Blănari 14. Forty years old and still going strong, the "Young Architects' Club", as it is

popularly known, is something of a Bucharest institution; an energetic, proactive venue with good (often live) music, cheap drinks and a happy, youthful crowd. Occasionally features theatre, foreign films and jazz. Closed Sun & Mon.

Coyote Café Calea Victoriei 48–50 (Pasajul Victoriei). One of the better live music venues in town, the warren-like *Coyote* lays on a varied programme of rock concerts (usually Thursday to Sunday), but is otherwise a cool place to down a few beers. Closed Mon.

Dubliner B-dul N. Titulescu 18. The original expat hangout, ten minutes' walk west of Piaţa Victoriei, this is as close to a good old-fashioned boozer as you'll find, offering a decent range of beers, pies and steak sandwiches, and lots of televised sport.

Green Hours 22 Club Calea Victoriei 120. *Green Hours* remains Bucharest's jazz club of choice; an intimate cellar bar with live turns most evenings and, in summer, gigs taking place in the leafy courtyard, itself a great place to kick back.

Lăptăria Enache 4th floor of the National Theatre, B-dul Bălcescu 2. Massive outdoor terrace bar, invariably rammed, with occasional live jazz and film screenings.

Mojo Str. Gabroveni 14. A good-time atmosphere is guaranteed in this rollicking Old Town hangout split over three levels. The basement Brit Room plays host to weekend gigs (both by the entertaining house band and visiting groups), the ground floor operates as a conventional bar, while karaoke is belted out in the top-floor acoustic lounge.

Salsa III Str. Mihai Eminescu 89. Fabulous party place where the locals (and exponents of all abilities) indulge in a more sophisticated mode of dancing – Latino and salsa.

Tribute Calea Victoriei 118. Along with *Mojo*, this is Bucharest's most happening live music venue; aside from the resident house band, the club – with its first-rate acoustics – provides a consistently exciting programme of rock gigs most nights. Closed Mon and Tues.

Yellow Bar Str. Edgar Quinet 10. Funky café/bar with plush leather sofas, tunes just on the right side of loud and a good-looking crowd.

Entertainment

Bucharest's cultural forte is undoubtedly **classical music**, and it's possible to catch some top-drawer concerts in several locations around town. **Opera**, **ballet** and **theatre** performances, too, are invariably excellent, with ostentatious sets and huge casts. Prices for performances are incredibly cheap, typically costing between €2 and €10. Note that most **theatres** and **concert halls** close during the summer, but over the rest of the year check *Bucharest In Your Pocket* for the most up-to-date listings.

Classical music, opera and ballet

Several internationally acclaimed musicians have cut their teeth with the **George Enescu Philharmonic Orchestra**, which plays in the architecturally and acoustically superb **Romanian Atheneum** at Str. Franklin 1, near Piaţa Enescu (box office Tues–Fri noon–7pm, Sat & Sun 4–7pm; ☎021/315 2567, ⓦwww.fge .org.ro). The **Romanian National Opera** (Opera Română), at B-dul Kogălniceanu 70 (box office daily 10am–1pm & 2–7pm; ☎021/313 1857, ⓦwww.operanb.ro), is the principal venue for operatic and ballet performances, with other productions taking place at the **Teatrul Opereţa** (☎021/313 6348) next to the National Theatre, at B-dul Bălcescu 2. There are also high-quality concerts at the **Sala Radio**, Str. Berthelot 62 (box office daily 10am–6pm; ☎021/314 6800), which is home to the National Radio Orchestra and the enormous **Sala Palatalui**, behind the Royal Palace at Str. Ion Câmpineanu 28 (box office Mon–Fri 10am–6pm; ☎021/315 7372), which hosts all manner of musical concerts.

Theatre

The huge **National Theatre**, at B-dul Bălcescu 2 (box office Mon 10am–4pm, Tues–Sun until 7pm; ☎021/314 7171, ⓦwww.tnb.ro), with its three auditoriums, is the premier venue for domestic and foreign theatre productions (unfortunately, none in English). Other venues with productions that might just surmount linguistic barriers are the excellent Tăndărică Puppet Theatre, at Str. E. Grigorescu 24 (☎021/315 2377, ⓦwww.teatrultandarica.ro); the Comedy Theatre at Str. Sf. Dimitru 2 (☎021/315 9137, ⓦwww.comedie.ro) and the State Jewish Theatre, at Str. I. Barasch 15 (☎021/323 3970).

The permanent big-top **circus** (Circul Globus) is at Aleea Circului 1 (box office Wed–Sun 10am–6pm; ☎021/210 4998; Metro Ştefan cel Mare), with performances at 3pm on Saturdays and 3pm and 6pm on Sundays, though it's closed through the summer months. The circus is also the venue for Micul Paris ("Little Paris"), a lively **cabaret** show set in 1930s Bucharest featuring superb singing and music, much fancy footwork and extravagant costumes. The show is staged every Saturday at 10pm with tickets costing upwards of €20. Note that the show finishes just after midnight when most public transport has shut down – if you need a taxi, contact one of the recommended companies (see p.56).

Cinemas

Cinemas are plentiful, and while the majority are, predictably, suburban multiplexes, there are still a few places in the centre where it's possible to catch a film. The major multiplexes are IMAX/Cinema City in the Palace Cotroceni complex (see below), the Hollywood Multiplex in the Bucureşti Mall (see below) and Movieplex at the Plaza Romania Mall, B-dul Timişoara 26. The best of the city-centre cinemas (where films are much cheaper) are Cinema Pro, a one-screen cinema at Str. Ion Ghica 3, and Patria and Scala, on B-dul Magheru 12 and 2 respectively. The Elvire Popesco Hall, in the French Institute at B-dul Dacia 77, is usually a good place to catch world films, while the Cinematecă, at Str. Eforie 2, shows a good selection of screen classics. Prices are cheap at around €3–6.

Sports and activities

Bucharest's only major spectator sport is **football**, with the country's three biggest clubs resident in the city: by far the most famous is the army team and former European Cup winners, **Steaua Bucureşti** (B-dul Ghencea 35; tram #8 or #47, trolley bus #69), followed by the one-time Securitate team, **Dinamo Bucureşti** (Şos. Ştefan cel Mare 9; Metro Ştefan cel Mare), then the rail-workers team, **Rapid Bucureşti** (Şos. Giuleşti 18; Metro Cringaşi). Tickets (€4–10) can be bought at the stadia before each game.

The best of the city's relatively few **sporting facilities** is the Diplomatic Club, Str. Al Minovici 1 (Tues–Sun 9am–10pm; ☎021/224 2941), which has two **swimming** pools (one for kids), **tennis** courts and Bucharest's only golf course (albeit just seven holes). There's also an excellent **swimming pool**, as well as tennis courts, at the Daimon Sports Club (at Str. Piscului 10; daily 8.30am–11pm; ☎021/330 5071) in Tineretului Park. Blue Ciel is a large open-air swimming venue north of the city at Str. Giuseppe Verdi 2 (daily 9am–9pm; ☎021/230 0895). The Herăstrău complex, at Şos. Nordului 5–7, also has a handful of tennis courts. Other options include the indoor and outdoor pools at the *Radisson* hotel, at Calea Victoriei 63, while it's also possible to swim safely in the city lakes – Floreasca (Metro Aurel Vlaicu), Strauleşti (western terminus of trolley bus #97) and Băneasa (bus #131 or #205).

Shopping

Bucharest is now awash with **shopping malls**, most of which are located on the outskirts of the city and are open daily between 10am and 10pm. The largest **complex**, and the easiest one to get to, is the AFI Palace Cotroceni, just beyond the Cotroceni Palace on B-dul Vasile Milea (Metro Politehnica), followed by Băneasa Shopping City out near Băneasa airport, and the Bucureşti Mall, south of the centre at Calea Vitan 55–59 (buses #123 and #124). The most central is the Unirea department store on Piaţa Unirii.

The best of several very good bookshops in Bucharest is the terrific Cărtureşti, at Str. Pictor Arthur Verona 13 (daily 10am–10pm), where you can find an extensive selection of English-language **books** including Romanian history and politics, fiction and non-fiction, and some excellent children's books – there's a gallery and tearoom here too. The large Sala Dalles, at B-dul Bălcescu 18 (Mon–Fri 10am–10pm, Sun 10am–8pm), carries a decent range of English-language books and translated Romanian literature, and is also the best place to pick up **guidebooks and maps**. Next door to each other at Calea Victoriei 45 (by the Creţulescu church) are Humanitas (Mon–Sat 10am–7pm, Sun 10am–5pm), which has a varied selection of

Bucharest's Festival Calendar

Bucharest is not traditionally known for its **festivals**, and while there's generally a dearth of exciting events, this is slowly changing, partly due to the increased willingness of Western acts to perform in the country. The highlight of the city's cultural offerings is the biennial (odd numbered years) **George Enescu Festival** (Ⓦwww .festivalenescu.ro) in September, which features three weeks of classical concerts by some of the world's finest musicians. The event features a full programme of concerts at the Atheneum and Sala Palatalui, as well as recitals, movie screenings, events on Piaţa Revoluţiei and exhibitions on Enescu. Taking place in the second week of May, **Europafest** (Ⓦwww.europafest.ro) is the year's most eclectic event, a gathering of Europe-wide artists performing pop, jazz, blues and classical music concerts, plus workshops, competitions and jam sessions at venues around the city. The big screen is represented courtesy of the **Bucharest International Film Festival** (B-EST IFF; Ⓦwww.b-est.ro) in April, which features an impressive roster of both new domestic and foreign (mainly European) movies.

titles on Romania, and Anthony Frost (Mon–Sat 10am–7pm, Sun 10am–2pm), devoted exclusively to English-language titles, mostly fiction. Foreign newspapers and magazines are tricky to come by, but the kiosks in the higher-end hotels might have same-day foreign editions. Cărtureşti is also the best place to find Romanian **music**. Otherwise try Muzica at Calea Victoriei 43 (Mon–Fri 9.30am–7pm, Sat 9.30am–2.30pm), or Diverta, with shops at B-dul Magheru 9 and Str. Rosetti 14 (both Mon–Sat 10am–10pm, Sun 10am–2.30pm).

For **antiques**, head for the streets around the historic quarter; two of the best places are the Hanul cu Tei bazaar, at Str. Lipscani 63–65 (Mon–Fri 10am–6pm, Sat 10am–2pm), and the lovely Thomas Antiques, at Str. Covaci 19 (same hours). For craftwork and traditional **souvenirs**, try Romartizana, at Calea Victoriei 16–20 (Mon–Fri 10am–8pm, Sat 9am–1pm), or, better still, make your way out to the Museum of the Romanian Peasant (see p.68) or the Village Museum (see p.76). Every Saturday and Sunday there's a terrific **peasant market** (Targul Ţaranului), down on Calea Rahovei (tram #32 from Piaţa Unirii), where you can pick up all manner of fresh foodstuffs, while there's also a vast Sunday-morning **flea market** (Târgul Vitan) on Calea Vitan, fifteen minutes' walk south of the Dristor I metro station, alongside the Dâmboviţa embankment. Beware of pickpockets at these last two places.

Listings

Airlines TAROM has offices at Spl. Independenţei 17 (Mon–Fri 9am–7.30pm, Sat 9am–2pm; ☏021/316 0220, Ⓦwww.tarom.ro), and Str. Buzeşti 59, just off Piaţa Victoriei (Mon–Fri 8am–8pm, Sat 9am–2pm; ☏021/204 6464); Carpatair (☏0372/744 357, Ⓦwww.carpatair .com) is based at Henri Coandă Airport; Blue Air (☏021/208 8686, Ⓦwww.blueairweb.com) and WizzAir (Ⓦwww.wizzair.com) are based at Băneasa Airport. Air France, Calea Buzeşti 85 (☏021/206 9200); Austrian Airlines, Aleea Alexandru 9A (☏021/204 4560); British Airways, Calea Victoriei 15 (☏021/303 2222); Lufthansa, Aleea Alexandru 9A (☏021/204 8410).

Airport information Henri Coandă ☏021/204 1000 (Ⓦwww.otp-airport.ro); Băneasa ☏021/232 0020 (Ⓦwww.baneasa-airport.ro).

Bicycle hire There are a number of bike hire places around the city, the best of which are La Pedale, with outlets in Herăstrău Park and Kiseleff Park (at junction of Str. Ion Mincu and Şos Kiseleff) – they offer free hire for two hours; and Raitabike, Str. Ion Brezoianu 35 (€1.50/hr).

Buses Atlassib, B-dul Gh. Duca 4 (☎021/222 4735), for buses all over Europe; Double T, Calea Victoriei 2 (☎021/313 3642), for buses to Central Europe; Eurolines Touring, Str. Reinvierii 3–5 (☎021/316 0890), for buses to Germany; Murat, Str. Axinte Uricariul 8 (☎021/316 5520), for buses to Istanbul.

Car rental Avis, Str. Mihail Moxa 9 (☎021/210 4344, ⓦwww.avis.ro); Budget, *Howard Johnson* hotel at Calea Dorobanţilor 5–7 (☎021/210 5089, ⓦwww.budget.com.ro); Europcar, Str. Grigore Mora 17 (☎021/310 1797, ⓦwww.europcar.com.ro); Hertz, B-dul Natiunile Unite 3 (☎021/335 7533, ⓦwww.hertz.com.ro). All these companies have outlets at Henri Coandă Airport. A good local company is Rodna Cars at Băneasa (021/230 4159, ⓦwww.rodna-trans.ro).

Car repairs ACR has its head office at Str. Tache Ionescu 27 (☎021/315 5510) and technical assistance centres at Calea Dorobanţilor 85 (☎021/211 1835) and Spl. Independenţiei 204 (☎021/212 6433). These should be open 24hr.

Embassies and consulates Bulgaria, Str. Rabat 5 ☎021/230 2150, ⓦwww.bgembassy-romania.org; Canada, Str. Tuberozelor 1–3 ☎021/307 5000, ⓦwww.canadainternational.gc.ca/romania; Hungary, Str. Prof. Dr. Dimitrie Gerota 63–65 ☎031/620 4300, ⓦwww.mfa.gov.hu; Ireland, Str. Buzesti 50–52 ☎021/310 2161, ⓦwww.embassyofireland.ro; Moldova, Aleea Alexandru 40 ☎021/230 0474, ⓦwww.romania.mfa.md; Serbia, Calea Dorobanţilor 34 ☎021/211 9871; UK, Str. Jules. Michelet 24 ☎021/201 7200, ⓦwww.ukinromania.fco.gov.uk; Ukraine, B-dul Aviatorilor 24 ☎021/230 3660; US, Str. Tudor Arghezi 7–9 ☎021/200 3300, ⓦwww.romania.usembassy.gov.

Health For emergency treatment, you should go to the Emergency Clinic Hospital (Spitalul Clinic de Urgenţa), at Calea Floreasca 8 (Metro Ştefan cel Mare; ☎021/599 2300), or the private Bio-Medica International Centre, Calea Floreasca 111–113 (☎021/311 7793, for emergencies ☎0722/338 383). Your embassy can recommend doctors speaking your language. There's excellent dental treatment available at the German-run B.B. Clinic, Str. Ionescu Gion 4 (☎021/320 0151).

Internet Wi-fi is now available in many bars and cafés, some of which you'll have to pay for (or buy a drink), though is free in all KFC, McDonald's and Pizza Hut outlets. There are relatively few places in Bucharest where you can find cafés with PCs, but the best is the Orange Studio at B-dul Lascăr Catargiu 51 (Mon–Fri 9am–9pm, Sat 9am–4pm), which also has printing facilities. There's also Acces Internet, B-dul Lascăr Catargiu 6 (daily 24hr); British Council, Calea Dorobanţilor 14 (Mon 3–7pm, Tues–Fri 11am–7pm, Sat 10am–1pm); Cyber Espace, inside the French Institute at B-dul Dacia 77 (Mon–Sat 10am–8pm). Expect to pay around €1 for an hour online.

Laundry Immaculate Cleaners, Str. Polonă 76 (Mon–Fri 8.30am–8.30pm, Sat 9am–5pm; ☎021/211 4413); Nufărul, Calea Moşilor 276 (Mon–Fri 7am–8pm, Sat 9am–1pm; ☎021/210 1441); also at Str. Stirbei Vodă 4 and Str. Mendeleev 6.

Pharmacies Sensiblu Pharmacy has dozens of outlets throughout the city (Mon–Fri 8am–10pm, Sat & Sun 9am–9pm), including a 24hr pharmacy at Str. Radu Beller 6. Help Net pharmacy has 24hr outlets at B-dul Ion Mihalache 92 and B-dul Unirii 27.

Police Each sector has its own police station, but the most central is at B-dul Lascăr Catargiu 22 (☎021/212 5684). Traffic accidents (with damage) should be dealt with at Str. Logofăt Udrişte (☎021/323 3030).

Post office The main post office is at Str. Matei Millo 10 (Mon–Fri 7.30am–8pm). There are bigger offices at B-dul Regina Elisabeta 45 (Mon–Fri 7.30am–8pm, Sat 8am–2pm) and near the train station on Str. Gara de Nord (same times).

Supermarkets Mega Image, basement of the Unirea department store, & B-dul N. Titulescu (both Mon–Thurs 8.30am–9.30pm, Sun 8.30am–6pm); Nic, Piaţa Amzei (24hr). Best of the daily markets are Piaţa Dorobanţi, Calea Dorobanţilor, Piaţa Amzei, near Piaţa Romană, and Piaţa Matache, behind the CFR office near the Gara de Nord.

Trains CFR's advance booking offices are at Str. Domniţa Anastasia 10–14 (Mon–Fri 8am–8pm, Sat 9am–1.30pm; ☎021/313 2642), and next to the *Ibis* hotel at Calea Griviţei 139 (same times; ☎021/212 8947). You can also buy national and international tickets from Wasteels in the Gara de Nord (Mon–Fri 8am–7pm, Sat 8am–2pm; ☎021/317 0370, ⓦwww.wasteels.ro); foreign currencies are accepted here.

Around Bucharest

If you travel to Snagov by road, you'll pass through the area most notoriously affected by Ceauşescu's **systematization** programme (see box opposite). **Baloteşti**, just north of Henri Coandă Airport, consists of stark modern apartment buildings, housing people displaced from villages such as Dimieni, which lay just east of the airport. Vlădiceasca and Cioflinceni, just off the DN1 on the road to Snagov, were bulldozed in 1988, and the inhabitants resettled in Ghermăneşti, on the western outskirts of Snagov.

Four kilometres east of Baloteşti is **Căciulaţi**, built as a planned estate village by the Ghica family, whose villa – now the property of the Romanian Academy – was occupied by the Securitate; over three hundred bodies, unrecorded victims of the communist police state, were found buried in its run-down park in the mid-1990s. Seven **trains** a day from Bucharest (to Urziceni) stop here, and, of these, five continue on to **Greci**, another 10km east. A couple of kilometres south of Greci is the **Căldăruşani Monastery**, which is beyond the reach of public transport from Bucharest. This inconvenience didn't stop the world press from

Systematization

Systematization was Ceauşescu's policy to do away with up to half of the country's villages and move the rural population into larger centres. The concept was first developed by Nikita Khrushchev in the Soviet Union in 1951, to combat the movement of younger people to the towns by **amalgamating villages** to raise the standard of rural life. In 1967 Ceauşescu reorganized Romania's local government system and announced a scheme to get rid of up to 6300 villages and replace them with 120 new towns and 558 agro-industrial centres.

His declared aim (based on an original idea in Marx and Engels' *Communist Manifesto*) was "to wipe out radically the major differences between towns and villages; to bring the working and living conditions of the working people in the countryside closer to those in the towns". Ceauşescu thought that by herding people together into apartment buildings so that "the community fully dominates and controls the individual", systematization would produce Romania's "new socialist man". However, the project was forgotten while Ceauşescu was preoccupied by other projects such as the Danube–Black Sea Canal and Bucharest's Centru Civic, but he relaunched it in March 1988, when he was becoming obsessed with increasing exports and paying off the national debt.

Ceauşescu was determined to **revolutionize agriculture** by increasing the growing area, while also further increasing centralization and reducing the scope and incentive for individual initiative. While the peasants had previously been able to support themselves with their own livestock, there was to be no accommodation for animals in the new blocks. To add insult to injury, the peasants were to receive derisory compensation for their demolished homes and then be charged rent. The model development was to be the **Ilfov Agricultural Sector**, immediately north of Bucharest, where the first evictions and demolitions took place in August 1988. Only two or three days' notice was given before shops were closed down and bus services stopped, forcing the people into the designated villages. Entire communities were removed to blocks in Otopeni and Ghermăneşti, where up to ten families had to share one kitchen and the sewage system had not been completed. In other villages across the nation, ugly **concrete Civic Centre buildings** began to appear in the centres of the planned New Towns.

There was widespread condemnation of this scheme that was set to uproot half of the rural populace; in August 1988, the Cluj academic **Doina Cornea**, one of the country's few open dissidents, wrote an open letter (published in the West) in protest, pointing out that the villages, with their unbroken folk culture, are the spiritual centre of Romanian life, and that to demolish them would be to "strike at the very soul of the people". She was soon placed under house arrest, but the campaign abroad gathered pace. Approximately eighteen villages had suffered major demolitions by the end of 1989, when the scheme was at once cancelled by the FSN, the new ruling party following the revolution.

mobbing it when tennis stars Mariana Simionescu and Bjorn Borg were married here in 1980. The church where the wedding took place was built in 1638 (in exactly 100 days) by Matei Basarab and is noted for its school of icon painting, established in 1787. Among the many icons on display here are eight by the juvenile Grigorescu (see box, p.96), who studied at the school from 1854 to 1855. The monastery is now home to some thirty monks and over 150 boys attending the priest school. You may also be given a short guided tour of the church and the ossuary, where a large number of monks' skulls are held.

Snagov

SNAGOV, a sprawling village 40km north of Bucharest, is the most popular weekend destination for Bucharestians: its beautiful 19km-long lake has water-sports facilities and a reserve for water plants, such as Indian waterlily, arrowhead and oriental beech. In the centre of the lake is an island occupied by a **monastery** built in 1519. King Mihai and later Ceauşescu and other high functionaries had their weekend villas around the shore, and the lake was also the scene of the summit which saw Yugoslavia's expulsion from the Warsaw Pact in 1948. Bălcescu and other revolutionaries of 1848 were held in the monastery's prison, as was the Hungarian leader Imre Nagy following the Soviet invasion of 1956.

Visitors now come here principally to seek the **tomb of Dracula**, sited in front of the church altar. Though lacking identifying inscriptions, it's likely that this is indeed the burial place of Vlad the Impaler: the richly dressed corpse exhumed in 1935 had been decapitated, as had Vlad, whose head was supposedly dispatched, wrapped and perfumed, as a gift to the Sultan. Vlad's murder is believed to have occurred in the forests nearby, and the monks would have been predisposed to take the body, since both Vlad and his father had given money to the monastery. Indeed, Vlad is thought to have had quite a hand in its development, insisting that several features be added, including, appropriately enough, a prison and torture chamber. To get across to the island, you can hire a rowing boat (€5 from the jetty on the southern shore of the lake, just past the Complex Astoria; see below); follow the reeds round to the left until the monastery comes into view. Give yourself a good couple of hours to make the trip over and back. Note that you must be appropriately dressed to gain admittance to the monastery.

Around half a dozen **buses** a day make the rather long-winded trip from the Băneasa bus station – located 500m west of Băneasa Airport on B-dul Ionescu de la Brad 1 – to Snagov. Get the driver to drop you off at the fork in the road 1km beyond the village, and walk the remaining half a kilometre or so to the **Complex Astoria**, a large leisure park on the lake's southern shore. Although it's unlikely you'll need, or want, to stay here, the complex contains the down-at-heel *Snagov Minihotel* (☎021/313 6782; ❹), which also has villas (❼) and bungalows (❸). There's better accommodation in the village of **Ghermăneşti**, 2km south of Snagov, namely the roadside *Pension Galanton* at Ghermăneşti 18 (☎021/351 0639; ❹), which has smartly furnished rooms, restaurant and pool. The bus to Snagov stops in the village.

Mogoşoaia

The lovely **palace** at **Mogoşoaia** (Tues–Sun 10am–6pm; €2), 10km northwest of Bucharest along the DN1, is perhaps Wallachia's most important non-religious monument. Designed by Constantin Brâncoveanu between 1698 and 1702 as a summer residence for his family, it's a two-storey building of red brick with a fine Venetian-style loggia overlooking a lake. After Brâncoveanu's execution, the palace became an inn, then, after a fire destroyed the interior, a warehouse. Towards the end of the nineteenth century, the palace was passed to the Bibescu family (descendants of Brâncoveanu), before finally being handed over to the state in 1956.

At the end of the long drive, which extends from the main road up to the palace, you pass the small St George's Chapel (built in 1688) before entering the complex proper through the entry tower; to the left is the L-shaped great house, to the right, the old kitchen, and straight in front, the main palace building. Its interior is now given over to a series of rather dull, furniture-less rooms (thanks to Ceauşescu, who requisitioned it all), occasionally brightened up with tapestries, vestments and icons, while the fine vaulted cellar to the left of the entrance contains a stack of stoneworks. The lush gardens, and the lake behind the main building, do, however, make a visit worthwhile, and there's some good rambling to be had in the nearby woods. Hidden away on waste ground behind the old kitchen wall is a huge statue of Lenin, removed from Piaţa Presei Libere and dumped here after the 1989 revolution; next to the prostrate Russian leader is the statue of the former communist prime minister Petru Groza. The easiest way to get to Mogoşoaia is to make your way up to the Laromet tram terminus (trolley bus #97), and then take a maxitaxi from there.

Clejani

Some 40km southwest of Bucharest is the small village of **CLEJANI**, renowned throughout the region as a centre for **Gypsy music**; the world-famous band Taraf de Haidouks (see p.394 & p.401) hails from here, as well as a number of other very talented musicians. If you're a fan of such music, or if you're just interested in experiencing Gypsy culture close up, then take half a day to visit the village – and, if you're lucky, you may get to hear some of the spellbinding music first-hand.

The village itself is unremarkable, but the Gypsy settlement – little more than a dusty, mud-dried street lined with crumbling, one-roomed homes – is easily found; upon arriving at the village from Vadu Lat (see below), take the first left, continue walking for 400m and you'll find the settlement on your right. While you're here, there's a good chance that you'll find a group happy to put on an impromptu **performance**. It's expected that you'll offer some money in return for the band's efforts (€10–15 would be appropriate), and a few bottles of beer wouldn't go amiss either. While at the settlement, have a wander around; it's likely you'll get invited into someone's house, which will give you the opportunity to witness first-hand the paucity of Gypsy life.

To get to Clejani from Bucharest, take one of the six daily **trains** from the Gara Basarab to Vadu Lat (the last train back to Bucharest is at 9.19pm). From the station, it's a 3km walk: turn right and continue along the tracks for 100m until you come to some steps set into an embankment; from here, walk along the path across the field until you come to the main road, then turn left and carry on walking for 2km – there's also a good chance you'll be able to hitch a ride.

Travel details

Trains

Bucharest to: Baia Mare (2 daily; 13hr); Braşov (every 45–60min; 2hr 30min–4hr 45min); Cluj (6 daily; 8hr–11hr 15min); Constanţa (8–15 daily; 2hr 30min–5hr 30min); Craiova (hourly; 3hr–4hr 30min); Galaţi (5 daily; 3hr 30min–4hr 30min); Giurgiu Nord (2 daily; 1hr 45min); Iaşi (6 daily; 6hr 30min–7hr 15min); Mangalia (4–7 daily; 3hr 45min–5hr 15min); Oradea (3 daily; 11hr 45min);

Pitești (9 daily; 1hr 40min–2hr 30min); Ploiești (every 40–60min; 45min–1hr 45min); Satu Mare (2 daily; 14–15hr); Sibiu (3 daily; 6hr 30min–7hr 30min); Sighișoara (8 daily; 5hr 15min–5hr 45min); Suceava (6 daily; 6hr 20min–7hr); Târgoviște (7 daily; 1hr 25min–2hr 15min); Timișoara (6 daily; 8hr 15min–9hr 30min).

Buses and maxitaxis

Bucharest to: Brașov (every 30–45min; 2hr 45min); Constanța (every 45min; 3hr 30min); Pitești (every 30–45min; 1hr 45min); Ploiești (hourly; 1hr 20min); Sibiu (hourly; 4hr 30min); Sighișoara (8 daily; 5hr 30min); Sinaia (every 30–45min; 2hr); Târgoviște (10 daily; 1hr 30min); Târgu Mureș (8 daily; 6hr 30min).

Flights

Bucharest to: Arad (12 weekly; 1hr); Baia Mare (5 weekly; 1hr 15min); Cluj (2–3 daily; 1hr);

Constanța (4 weekly; 1hr); Iași (3 daily; 1hr 10min); Oradea (6 weekly; 1hr 20min); Satu Mare (6 weekly; 1hr 15min); Sibiu (10 weekly; 45min); Suceava (2–3 daily; 1hr 45min); Timișoara (3–4 daily; 55min).

International trains

Bucharest to: Belgrade, Serbia (1 daily; 12hr 50min); Budapest, Hungary (3 daily; 14hr); Chișinău, Moldova (1 daily; 12hr 30min); Istanbul, Turkey (1 daily; 19hr); Prague, Czech Republic (2 daily; 23hr); Sofia, Bulgaria (2 daily; 10hr); Thessaloniki, Greece (1 daily; 18hr); Vienna, Austria (2 daily; 17hr).

International buses

Bucharest to: Chișinău, Moldova (4 daily; 8hr); Istanbul, Turkey (3 daily; 11hr).

Wallachia

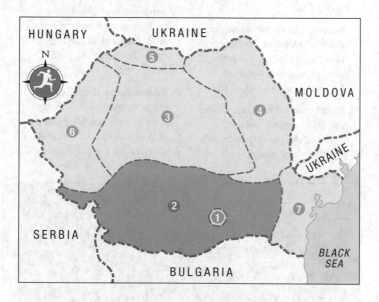

CHAPTER 2   # Highlights

* **Curtea de Argeş** Attractive small town with two of the region's most striking ecclesiastical monuments – the Princely Church and Episcopal Church. See p.104

* **Dracula's Castle** Take Vlad's trail up to the dramatically sited Poienari Castle – the real Dracula's castle. See p.106

* **Bujoreni open-air museum, Râmnicu Vâlcea** Fascinating assemblage of local buildings and other structures from the Olt valley region. See p.107

* **Brâncuşi's sculptures, Târgu Jiu** Outdoor collection of some of the great Romanian's most famous sculptures,

including the *Endless Column*. See p.110

* **Horezu Monastery** Brâncoveanu's marvellous seventeenth-century complex, featuring the Great Church replete with Byzantine frescoes. See p.112

* **Tismana garden festival** Listen to shepherds' panpipes and check out traditional clothes and rugs at this annual music and crafts festival in August. See p.114

* **Kazan gorge** Bisected by the Danube, the sheer cliffs of the Kazan gorge offer some of Wallachia's most dramatic scenery. See p.116

▲ Horezu Monastery

2

Wallachia

C enturies before the name "Romania" appeared on maps of Europe, foreign merchants and rulers had heard of **Wallachia**, the land of the Vlachs or Wallachs, known in Romanian as Țara Romaneasca ("Land of the Romanians"). A distant outpost of Christendom, it succumbed to the Turks in 1417 and was then largely forgotten until the nineteenth century. Occasional travellers reported on the region's backwardness and the corruption of its ruling boyars, but few predicted its sudden union with Moldavia in 1859 – the first step in the creation of modern Romania. Today, in the highlands and on the Bărăgan Steppe – where pagan rites such as the festivals of Ariet and Căluș are still practised – peasant life largely follows the ancient pastoral cycle, but industrialization and collective farming have wrought huge changes to the region's wide-open plains. The region is mainly comprised of flat and featureless agricultural land, and is in many ways the least interesting of Romania's three principal provinces, but as it is home to the nation's capital, **Bucharest**, people will invariably find themselves passing through en route to Transylvania, the coast, or Bulgaria.

The most rewarding part of Wallachia is its western half, known (after its chief river) as Oltenia, which stretches from Bucharest to the Iron Gates on the Danube. Here, the foothills of the Carpathians are largely scenic and unspoilt, and possessed of the region's most attractive and historically interesting towns, such as **Curtea de Argeș**. Both **Poienari Castle**, north of Curtea de Argeș, and the town of **Târgoviște** have strong connections with Vlad Țepeș – better known as **Dracula** – who once ruled Wallachia, even though modern myth links him with Transylvania. In addition, a string of fine monasteries, such as **Horezu** and **Arnota**, runs along the foothills; most were razed at the behest of "progressive" despots (who otherwise spent their time fighting the Turks and repressing their own peasantry), but were rebuilt in the late seventeenth century in the distinctively Romanian style developed by Constantin Brâncoveanu. The remainder of the region is dominated by large industrialized centres, such as **Ploiești**, **Pitești**, **Craiova** and **Târgu Jiu**, the last of which does at least have the work of Romania's world-renowned sculptor Constantin Brâncuși as an incentive to visit. Otherwise, there's a fine excursion to be had up along the **Kazan gorge**, where the Danube marks the border with Serbia.

Getting around the region is easy enough: trains fan out from Bucharest in all directions, serving most places listed here, while regular maxitaxis shuttle between towns and link the capital to destinations as far afield as Craiova and Târgu Jiu. Note that tourist information is pretty much nonexistent throughout the region.

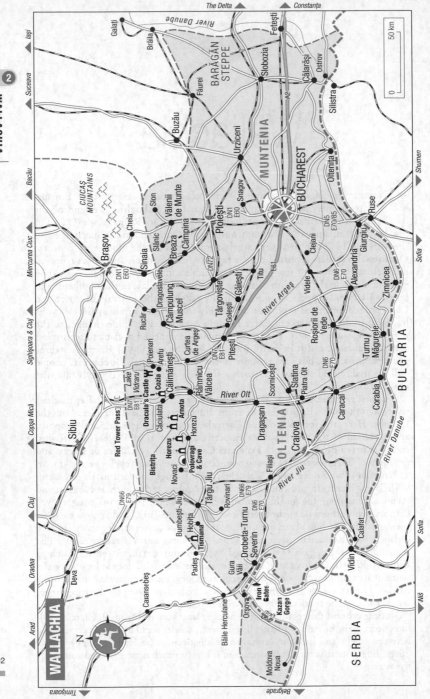

WALLACHIA

N

The Delta · Constanța

River Danube

BARĂGĂN STEPPE

MUNTENIA

BUCHAREST

Galați
Brăila
Fetești
Slobozia
Călărași
Ostrov
Silistra
Făurei
Buzău
Urziceni
Oltenița
Ruse
Slon
Vălenii de Munte
Snagov
Ploiești
Clejani
Cheia
Slănic
Câmpina
Breaza
Târgoviște
Titu
Videle
Alexandria
Giurgiu
Brașov
Sinaia
Dragoslavele
Golești
Găiești
Rosiorii de Vede
Zimnicea
CIUCAȘ MOUNTAINS
Rucăr
Câmpulung Muscel
Pitești
Turnu Măgurele
Poienari
Curtea de Argeș
Arefu
Scornicești
Slatina
Piatra Olt
Corabia
Lake Vidraru
Cozia
Călimănești
Râmnicu Vâlcea
River Olt
Caracal
BULGARIA
Dracula's Castle
Căciulata
Arnota
River Argeș
Dragășani
Red Tower Pass
Bistrița
Horezu
Horezu
OLTENIA
Craiova
Vidin
Polovragi & Cave
Novaci
Filiași
Calafat
Târgu Jiu
Rovinari
River Jiu
Bumbești-Jiu
Hobița
Pades
Tismana
Drobeta-Turnu Severin
River Danube
Gura Văii
Băile Herculane
Iron Gates
Orșova
Kazan Gorge
Caransebeș
Deva
Moldova Nouă
SERBIA

50 km
0

Iași ▲
Suceava ▲
Bacău ▲
Miercurea Ciuc ▲
Sighișoara & Cluj ▲
Copșa Mică ▲
Cluj ▲
Oradea ▲
Arad ▲
Timișoara ▼

Shumen ▲
Sofia ▲
Sofia ▼
Niș ▼
Belgrade ▼

Sibiu

DN1 E60
DN72
DN1 E60
DN5 E70/85
DN6 E70
E81
DN7 E81
DN66 E79
DN6 E70
DN66 E79
A2
E60
E81
E60

Ploieşti, Târgovişte and Piteşti

The large industrial towns of **Ploieşti** and **Piteşti** are typical of much of Wallachia as a whole, and while neither is very attractive nor possesses much in the way of sights, they do serve as useful springboards for more enticing destinations in the region. Ploieşti lies on the principal road and rail line between Bucharest and Transylvania, with a couple of sites of interest to the north, while Piteşti is situated astride the main routes from Bucharest to Câmpulung and the Argeş and Olt valleys. The most worthwhile of the three major towns north and northwest of Bucharest is **Târgovişte**, the old capital of Wallachia, boasting several ancient churches and the ruins of Vlad Ţepeş's court.

Ploieşti

An oily smell and the eerie night-time flare of vented gases proclaim **PLOIEŞTI** as Romania's biggest oil town. In 1857, the world's first oil wells were sunk here and in Petrolia, Ontario; the first ever refinery was built in Ploieşti, and in 1858 Bucharest became the first city in the world to be lit by oil lamps. By the outbreak of World War I, there were ten refineries in the town, all owned by foreign oil companies; these were wrecked in 1916 by British agents to deny them to the Germans, and patched together again only to be destroyed once more, this time by the retreating German forces in 1918. However, it was the townsfolk who really paid the price, when Allied aircraft carpet-bombed Ploieşti in 1944 – hence the town centre's concrete uniformity today.

Arrival and information

Generally speaking, **trains** to and from Transylvania use Ploieşti Vest station, southwest of town at the end of Str. Mărăşeşti, while those to and from Moldavia use Ploieşti Sud, 1km south of town on Piaţa 1 Decembrie 1918; trains from Bucharest may arrive at either. The two stations are linked by bus #2, which stops near the post office in the centre of town. The **bus station** is 200m west of the Sud train station.

Accommodation

Central B-dul Republicii 1 ☎0244/526 641, ⓦwww.thr.ro. Modern hotel on the main boulevard with two categories of room, with the larger four-star ones more comprehensively furnished. ❼–❽
Phoenix Str. Făt Frumos 15 ☎0244/510 094, ⓔhotel.phoenix@yahoo.com. On a residential street a couple of blocks north of the Gara Sud, this quiet place offers clean, comfortable and generously sized rooms. Good value. ❹
Prahova Plaza Str. Dobrogeanu-Gherea 11 ☎0244/526 850, ⓦwww.hotelprahova.ro. Unprepossessing high-rise block concealing modestly

sized but fancy, well-furnished rooms, featuring lots of burgundy and dark wood. ❾
Sud Str. Depoului 4 ☎0244/597 411. It's not pretty, but it's cheap, convenient for the train and bus stations, and each room has TV, bathroom and a/c. ❸
Vigo Hotel B-Dul Independenţei 28 ☎0244/514 501, ⓦwww.vigohotel.ro. In a lovely white *belle époque* building midway between the stations and town, this is by far the town's classiest establishment. Colourful, individually fashioned rooms each have ergonomically designed beds, hydro-massage baths and many other neat little touches. ❾

The Town

While there's little to detain you in Ploieşti, the town does have several moderately interesting museums (all open Tues–Sun 9am–5pm; €2). The most enjoyable is the **Art Museum** (Muzeul de Artă) at B-dul Independeţei 1, a fine Neoclassical building holding a healthy collection of paintings by many of Romania's foremost artists, including Aman, Luchian, Pallady, Petrascu and

Grigorescu. Close by are two of the country's more unusual museums; at Str. Bagdazar 10 the intermittently interesting **Oil Museum** (Muzeul Naţional al Petrolului) offers a comprehensive account of the oil industry's origins in Romania, while the **Clock Museum** (Muzeul Ceasului), at Str. Simache 1, has an engagingly varied collection of clocks and timepieces.

The huge Neoclassical Palace of Culture at Str. Cătălin 1, the **Museum of Human Biology** (Muzeul de Biologie Umană), has eye-catching displays on evolution, anatomy and ecology which make it one of the most striking museums of its kind in Romania. In the same building, the **Ethnography Museum** (Muzeul de Etnografie) houses more conventional displays of peasant costumes and artefacts, mostly from the Carpathian foothills; while the **History and Archeology Museum**, at Str. Toma Caragiu 10 (Muzeul de Istorie şi Arheologie Prahova), displays relics from the Neolithic to Roman periods, as well as sixteenth-century armour, nineteenth-century furniture and portraits (including one each by Mişu Popp and Sava Henţia, and a few Grigorescu sketches), plus a room on postal history including fascinating 1920s postcards.

Eating and drinking

While there's nowhere worthwhile to **eat** in the very centre of town, there are some choice places in the area of pre-World War I villas just southwest of the Clock Museum. Opposite the museum the fairly upmarket *Bulevard* covers the whole gamut of soups, salads, pastas and grilled meat dishes, as does the *Vienna Café*, across the road in a beautiful villa at Str. Ana Ipătescu 3 – its cool, sprawling terrace, set below huge wooden beams and white drapes, is also the most agreeable

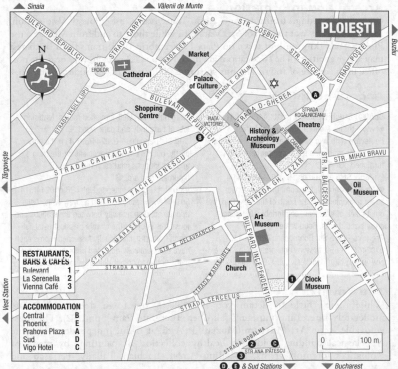

PLOIEŞTI

RESTAURANTS, BARS & CAFÉS
Bulevard 1
La Serenella 2
Vienna Café 3

ACCOMMODATION
Central B
Phoenix E
Prahova Plaza A
Sud D
Vigo Hotel C

0 100 m

The Ploieşti ploy

In 1940 it was feared that Germany would occupy Romania – as in World War I – to guarantee oil supplies from what was then Europe's second-largest producer (after the Soviet Union). The neutral Romanian government gave tacit support to Anglo–French plans to **sabotage the oil wells**, thus making a German invasion pointless, but technical problems and bad luck meant that these never went ahead. The back-up plan, to stop the oil barges reaching Germany along the Danube by sinking barges in the Iron Gates gorge and blocking the navigable channel, was a greater fiasco: the Germans soon found out about the British barges making their way upstream from Galaţi, and forced the Romanian authorities to expel the crews (naval ratings ill-disguised as art students).

A third plan involved the RAF bombing the oil wells from its bases around Larissa in Greece. However, the 660km route would have taken the early Wellington bombers over Musala, the highest peak in southeastern Europe, at close to their maximum altitude. Following severe maintenance problems, the plan was abandoned. It wasn't long before the Allies were driven out of Greece, allowing the Axis powers access to Romania's oil wells, from which they subsequently obtained a third of their aviation fuel. On August 1, 1943, 178 new American Liberator B-24Ds took off from bases in North Africa to strike **Ploieşti** in the **longest-range bombing raid** yet attempted; although 440 aircrew were killed and 220 captured, a heavy blow was dealt to the Nazi war machine. By 1944, continuing raids from Italy had succeeded in halving oil production, despite terrible Allied losses.

place in town to grab a beer. Close by, at Str. Bobâlna 9, *La Serenella* is a decent Italian restaurant. The indoor **market** behind the Palace of Culture has a good stock of bread, fruit and dairy products.

Câmpina

From Ploieşti, the main DN1 road heads north towards the Prahova valley and Transylvania. Thirty-two kilometres along the road lies **CÂMPINA**, another of Romania's key oil towns which, like Ploieşti, was heavily bombed during the war.

Despite the town's lack of visual appeal, it has two tourist sights that just about make a stopoff worthwhile. Around 1km north of the centre, across the rail tracks and up by the bend in the road, the **Nicolae Grigorescu memorial house** (Tues–Sun 9am–5pm; €2) at B-dul Carol I no. 166, was where the artist spent the last years of his life (see box, p.96). The house was largely destroyed during World War I, before Grigorescu's son had it restored and then moved in himself. Most of Nicolae's possessions survived intact, some of which are on display here (notably a fine collection of leather-bound French books in his library), in addition to a healthy number of paintings including a self-portrait.

Further along the road at no. 145 is **Hasdeu Castle** (Tues–Sun 9am–5pm; €2), an odd cruciform structure with battlements and buttresses, built between 1894 and 1896 by historian and linguist Bogdan Petriceico Hasdeu (1838–1907), one of the progenitors of the nationalist and anti-Semitic philosophy that infected Romanian politics throughout the twentieth century. He built the castle as a memorial to his daughter Julia, to plans he claimed were transmitted by her in séances. After finishing high school, Julia went to study in Paris, and would have been the first Romanian woman to receive a doctorate from the Sorbonne had she not died of tuberculosis in 1888, aged just nineteen. Among the many items retained within the castle is the desk she used in France. She also left three volumes of plays and poetry, all published after her death.

Nicolae Grigorescu

Romania's most famous painter, **Nicolae Grigorescu**, was born in 1838 and came to Bucharest at the age of ten to train as a church painter; his earliest signed works, dating from 1853, are in the church of Sf Constantine and Helena in Baicoi (near Ploieşti). Grigorescu subsequently worked in Căldăruşani (1854–55), in Zamfira (1856–58), and in Agapia (1858–60), where his work represents the high point of **Romanian classicism**. Here he met Kogălniceanu, who arranged a grant for him to study in Paris, where he became a friend of Millet, joining the Barbizon group and beginning to paint *en plein air*. In 1869 he returned to Romania, where he painted society portraits, but also toured the Prahova, Dâmboviţa and Muscel counties painting local characters in a mobile studio in an adapted coach. From 1877–78, he accompanied the army in the War of Independence, producing, among others, major works of the battle of Griviţa. His first solo exhibition in 1881 was a great success, and from 1881 to 1884 he lived in Paris, developing a more Impressionist style. He kept a studio there until 1894, although from 1890 he spent increasing amounts of time with his companion Maria Danciu in **Câmpina**, where he died in 1907.

The **train** station is 3km west but is connected to the centre by frequent maxitaxis, while the **bus** station is south of town on Str. Bălcescu. If you do need to **sleep** here the unappealing choices are the *Hotel Muntenia*, in the centre at B-dul Carol I no. 61 (℡0244/333 090; ➍), or the hostel-like *Casa Tineretului*, in front of the bus station at Str. Bălcescu 50 (℡0244/334 540; ➊).

Breaza

The small town of **BREAZA**, just a few kilometres north of Câmpina on a loop road off the DN1, is ideal for a quiet stopover en route towards the Prahova valley. There are some excellent examples of the local architectural style – many houses have carved wooden verandas – but Breaza's one real sight is the small Orthodox **Church of Sf Nicolae**, just south of the centre. Finished in 1777, the church's interior is totally covered in paintings; of special note is that of the *Last Judgement* in the porch.

Arriving by **train** entails a 2km walk (500m of which is a steep climb) on Str. Căpriou into town; **maxitaxis** to Bucharest (every 2hr) leave from the park in the centre of town, and there are others to Sinaia and Câmpina (every 10min and 15min respectively). The best of the several **pensions** in town is *Casa Ionuş* at Str. Morii 7 (℡0730/247 430; ➌), which has a handful of colourfully designed en-suite rooms. To find it, walk north of the park for 400m, turn right on Str. Morii, then left down the driveway after 200m. There are also double rooms (➏), suites (➐–➑) and apartments (➒) at the *Lac de Verde* **golf club** (℡0244/343 525, ⓦwww.lacdeverde.ro), 1.5km west of town at Str. Caraiman 57 (it's signposted). The short but scenic nine-hole course (€25 for nine holes, €35 for eighteen holes) is one of the few in Romania. From Breaza, trains and maxitaxis continue north to Sinaia and Buşteni and on into Transylvania.

The Teleajen valley

From Ploieşti, the much quieter DN1A runs along the lovely **Teleajen valley** into the foothills of the Carpathian mountains; public transport along this route is poor, but it is well worth considering if you have your own car or bike.

The main place of interest is **VĂLENII DE MUNTE**, served by trains from Ploieşti 30km to the south. Located at the northern end of the main thoroughfare,

B-dul N. Iorga, is a fine **memorial house** (Tues–Sun 9am–5pm; €2), dedicated to the great historian and former prime minister Nicolae Iorga, who lived here from 1910 until his murder by the Iron Guard in 1940. Ironically, Iorga founded the National Democratic Party, a predecessor of the Guard. As well as some beautiful furniture, many of Iorga's personal effects – books, handwritten letters, family photos and portraits – have been neatly preserved. Look out, too, for a painting by Grigorescu. There's also a good ethnographic collection in the neighbouring wing, featuring some superb icons painted on glass and wood. If you need to break a journey here, there's the very good-value **hotel** *Capitol*, 400m south of the house at B-dul N. Iorga 50 (☎0244/281 965; ❸). The train and bus stations are just south of here.

From Vălenii, a minor road heads west for 11km to **SLĂNIC** (sometimes known as Slănic Prahova, to distinguish it from Slănic Moldova, to the north). Here, the Muntele de Sare, or Salt Mountains – a product of the salt mining that has taken place in the area since at least 1532 – stand between two lakes in which you can swim in summer. The town's salt-working heritage is displayed in the tiny **Museum of Salt** (Muzeul Sării; daily 9am–7pm; €1), housed in the Casa Cămărăşiei (the former Salt Chancellery built in 1800) at Str. 23 August 9. More worthwhile is the **Unirea Mine Complex** (Minier Unirea; Tues–Fri 9am–3pm, Sat & Sun 8am–5pm; €3), a ten-minute walk east of here across the bridge, which displays scenes from Romanian history carved in salt. A lift drops 210m below the surface to the former salt mine, converted in 1970 into a sanatorium for lung disorders and a tourist attraction, with sculptures of Roman and Dacian gods and of historical figures such as Mihai Viteazu and Mihai Eminescu carved from the salt walls. Slănic lies at the end of a rail line from Ploieşti Sud via Ploieşti Vest; three of the four daily trains do the distance in 80–90 minutes, but the early afternoon train (in each direction) stops for 35 minutes in Plopeni. Of the handful of **places to stay** in Slănic, the best is the *Baie Roşie* resort (☎0244/240 131; ❻) at the entrance to the village, which also has two outdoor pools, one of which contains salt water. Non-guests can use the pool complex for €7.

The DN1A continues north along the Teleajen valley past the Suzana nunnery (built in the eighteenth century and rebuilt in 1835–38 with icons by Tattarescu) to the pleasantly relaxed resort of **CHEIA**, 35km north of Vălenii, at the foot of the Ciucaş mountains; minibuses to the resort meet trains at Măneciu, 17km north of Vălenii. Cheia has a good stock of *agroturism* guesthouses that make useful bases for exploring the surrounding area; you can either take pot luck by wandering around looking for signs, or book ahead through the Prahova branch of Antrec (☎0244/592 915, ✉prahova@antrec.ro). There are also hotels here, including the *Cheia* (☎0244/294 331; ❸), a giant A-frame construction with a restaurant and sauna. From Cheia, the DN1A continues due north into the **Ciucaş mountains**, a compact range of weirdly eroded conglomerate outcrops and pillars, with fine open walking country all around.

The Bratocea Pass is away to the northwest, between the Roşu and Ciucaş mountains. At the foot of the mountains, 7km from Cheia, is the *Muntele Roşu* cabana (☎0244/294 370; ❶), from where it's a two-hour walk, marked with yellow stripes, up to the *Ciucaş* cabana (❶). From the pass the road leads downhill all the way past the *Babarunca* cabana (☎0268/274 885; ❶) into Săcele and Braşov.

Târgovişte

TÂRGOVIŞTE, 50km west of Ploieşti on the DN72, was the capital of Wallachia for more than two centuries, vestiges of which can be seen in the old Princely Court complex, the town's principal attraction and the one major reason for

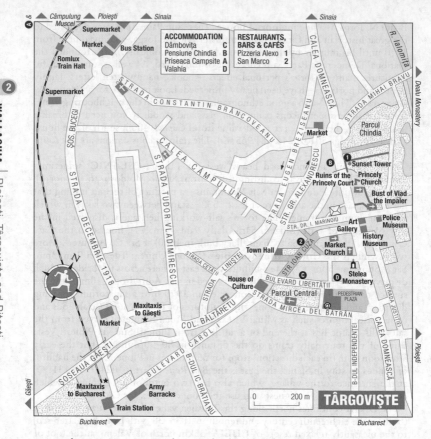

coming here. In recent times, the town has been best known as an industrial centre, producing equipment for the oil industry, but it gained notoriety when Nicolae and Elena Ceauşescu were executed in its army barracks on Christmas Day, 1989.

Arrival, information and accommodation

Târgovişte's **train station** is southwest of town on Piaţa Gării, from where it's a pleasant fifteen-minute walk to the centre along B-dul Carol I, lined with trees and attractive villas; alternatively, bus #5 will take you into town. Now largely screened by trees, the barracks to the right of the station as you exit is where the Ceauşescus were executed, but be warned, it's forbidden to take any pictures. Maxitaxis for Bucharest arrive and depart every half-hour or so from a point 200m to the left of the station as you exit. The large and disorganized **bus station** is 1km west of town by the Romlux train halt and linked to the centre by buses and maxitaxis along Calea Câmpulung. There's **internet access** at Arena Computers, on Mircea del Bătrân.

The town's dour **accommodation** possibilities boil down to the communist-era *Dâmboviţa*, at B-dul Libertăţii 1 (☎0245/213 370, ⓦwww.hoteldambovita.ro; ❹); the marginally gloomier *Valahia*, 200m further along at no. 7 (☎0245/634 491; ❹); and the *Pensiune Chindia* (☎0245/620 013; ❷), with four rooms above a café-bar opposite the Princely Court at Calea Domnească 200. The Priseaca **campsite** is 7km out along the Câmpulung road, reached by bus #18.

The town and around

The **Princely Court** (Curtea Domnească; Tues–Sun 9am–5pm, approx. May–Sept until 7pm; €1.50) lies north of the centre on Calea Domnească (on some maps this is still shown as Str. Bălcescu). Now a mass of crumbling ramparts, with a few well-preserved sections, it was once the royal seat of Wallachia (from 1415–1659), from where 33 *voivodes* (princes) exercised their rule – all of whom are denoted on the inside wall of the southern gate, the entrance to the complex. The Princely Court figured large in the life of **Vlad the Impaler** (see p.403), who spent his early years here, until he and his brother Radu were sent by their father to Anatolia as hostages. Following the murder of his father and his eldest brother, Mircea, who was buried alive by Wallachia's boyars, Vlad returned to be enthroned here in 1456, and waited three years before taking his revenge. Invited with their families to feast at court on Easter Sunday, the boyars were half-drunk when guards suddenly grabbed them and impaled them forthwith upon stakes around town, sparing only the fittest who were marched off to labour on Vlad's castle at Poienari (see p.106). Dominating the complex is the 27m-high **Sunset Tower** (Turnul Chindiei), built during the fifteenth century and originally used as a watchtower for Vlad's soldiers; from the top there are some terrific views of the complex and the rest of the town. Nearby stands the handsome **Princely Church**, built in 1583 and painted in 1698, where Vlad's successors used to attend services sitting upstairs in a special section screened from the congregation. Presently being renovated, the interior contains a vast iconostasis, as well as dozens of frescoes of Wallachian princes, such as Basarab, Cantacuzino and Brâncoveanu.

South of the Princely Court is a trio of museums (all Tues–Sun 9am–5pm; €1), the most worthwhile of which is the **Art Museum** (Muzeul de Artă), in the former prefecture. Renovated after a lengthy period of neglect, the building houses works by Grigorescu, Petrascu and Pallady, though the highlight is a collection of seventeenth-century wall-length frescoes – mostly of venerated saints – retrieved from the Princely Church. Next door, the **History Museum** (Muzeul de Istorie) was set up in the former Law Courts by Ceaușescu in 1986, and the first floor, now used for temporary art shows, was devoted to his achievements. Set back slightly from these two is the unlikely sounding **Museum of the Romanian Police** (Muzeul Poliției Române), not surprisingly the only one of its kind in the country. As well as charting the history and evolution of the Romanian police, it also exhibits costumes garnered from numerous forces from around the world, including an old-fashioned British bobby's uniform.

A couple of minutes' walk west of here, along Str. Stelea, you'll come to the **Stelea Monastery**, a striking building in the same Moldavian Gothic style of the famous Church of the Three Hierarchs in Iași (see p.245), its exterior carved with chevrons and rosettes studded with green discs. Built in 1645 by Moldavia's Basil the Wolf as part of a peace agreement with the Wallachian ruler, Matei Basarab, it inspired the design of many Wallachian churches. The monastery was closed from 1863 to 1992 (although it served as a parish church), but is once more in use. It houses a rare seventeenth-century iconostasis and Byzantine-influenced frescoes, of which the more interesting were painted from 1705–06 under Constantin Brâncoveanu.

Three kilometres northeast of town (bus #7), the graceful bulk of **Dealu Monastery** rises upon a hill. Built in 1501, it set the pattern for much of Wallachian church architecture – with its towers above the *pronaos* and cornice arcades separated by cable moulding – until the advent of the Brâncovenesc style at the end of the seventeenth century. Inside, beneath a marble slab topped by a bronze crown, lies the **head of Michael the Brave** – severed within a year of his conquest of Transylvania and Moldavia, which put paid to the unification of Romania for another 250 years. The inscription reads: "To he who first united our homeland, eternal glory".

Eating and drinking

Places to eat in town are few and far between, though *San Marco*, at Str. Alexandru Ioan Cuza 22, is a most agreeable **restaurant** serving above-average pasta dishes. More generally, this sociable pedestrianized street is replete with terrace cafés, such as *Queen's Corner* and the very loud *Mushu*. Beyond this central core there's *Pizzeria Alexo*, set in attractive garden pavilions on the north side of the Sunset Tower – this is also a relaxing place for a beer.

Piteşti and around

Situated 100km northwest of Bucharest, **PITEŞTI** is another of Wallachia's industrial towns, and in truth it's one of the grimmest, though it does make a useful base for forays up into the Argeş valley. Much of the town's architectural charm has been lost to earthquakes and subsequent rebuilding, and these days it's dominated by the woodworking and petrochemical industries, and by the Renault (formerly Dacia) factory – origin of most of Romania's cars – 11km north in Mioveni.

The heart of the town is Str. Victoriei, a broad, pedestrianized thoroughfare lined with shops, cafés and hotels, with a couple of minor sights located at either end. Standing on a solitary patch of grass at its eastern end is the seventeenth-century **Princely Church** of Constantin Şerban, and at the other end, at B-dul Republicii 33, is the town's **art gallery** (Galeria de Artă; Tues–Sun 9am–5pm; €1), which houses a good sample of works by some of Romania's finest painters – Grigorescu, Pallady and Iser – as well as some intriguing wooden pieces by Gheorge Călineşti, one of the country's foremost sculptors.

South of B-dul Republicii on the parallel Str. Călinescu, the **County Museum** (Muzeul Judeţean; Tues–Sun 9am–5pm; €1), housed in the turn-of-the-twentieth-century prefecture building, offers a standard review of the region's history, as well as a dull natural history section. In front is the odd conjunction of anti-tank guns

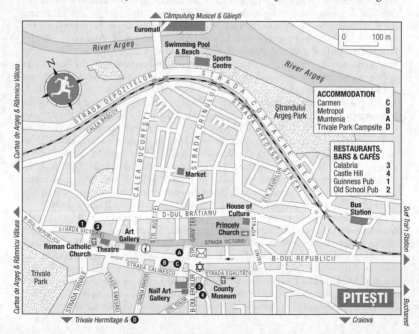

Piteşti prison

For older Romanians, Piteşti is synonymous with its **prison**, the scene under the early Stalinist regime of some of the most brutal psychiatric abuse anywhere in the Soviet bloc. In May 1948, there were mass arrests of dissident students, and from December 1949 about a thousand of them were brought here, to the "Student Re-education Centre", for a **programme** aimed at "re-adjusting the students to communist life" and eliminating the possibility of any new opposition developing. In fact, it simply set out to destroy the personality of the individual: by starvation, isolation, and above all by forcing prisoners to torture each other, breaking down all distinctions between prisoner and torturer, and thus between individual and state. "United by the evil they have both perpetrated and endured, the victim and the torturer thus become a single person. In fact, there is no longer a victim, ultimately no longer a witness", as Paul Goma put it in his book *The Dogs of Death*. Sixteen students died during this atrocious "experiment".

The programme was extended to Gherla and other prisons and the Danube–Black Sea Canal labour camps, but security was looser here and the torture stopped when word got out. The experiment was abandoned in 1952, when the Stalinist leader Ana Pauker was purged; it was claimed that the authorities had not been involved, and in 1954, those running the Piteşti prison were tried secretly for murder and torture. The leader of the "Organization of Prisoners with Communist Convictions", Eugen Turcanu, was executed along with several of his henchmen, while others were sentenced to forced labour for life. Nevertheless, because of the guilt of all involved – both prisoners and guards – there followed a conspiracy of silence, which only began to break in 1989.

and a small botanical garden, and to its east a new wing housing the **Naïf Art Gallery** (Galeria de Artă Naivă; Tues–Sun 9am–5pm; €1), featuring a typically exuberant collection of works by unschooled local painters. A synagogue survives nearby at B-dul Noiembrie 1. The seventeenth-century **Trivale Hermitage**, southwest of the centre in Trivale Park, is nothing special, but it's a lovely twenty-minute, traffic-free walk to it up Str. Trivale through fine oak woods. Alternatively, maxitaxis and bus #8 run from the station up Str. Smeurei just to the east, leaving you in the midst of modern apartment blocks immediately above the hermitage. The **Ştrandului Argeş Park**, facing the gigantic new Euromall shopping centre across the Argeş, contains a sports centre, outdoor pool and small beach area, all of which get very crowded in the warmer months.

Practicalities

The town's **train station** is 1km to the southeast, linked to the centre by buses #2, #8 and #19 and frequent maxitaxis; trains serving Curtea de Argeş also call at Piteşti Nord, in the northern suburbs. The disorganized **bus station** is to the northwest of the train station on Str. Târgul din Vale. Limited **tourist information** is available from the county's Centru de Informare Turistică, a few paces from the art gallery at Pasajul Victoriei 89 (Mon–Fri 8am–4pm; ☏0727/341 728).

There's plenty of **accommodation** available in the centre, all of it very average; the *Muntenia*, on Piaţa Muntenia (☏0248/210 880, ✉hotel@turism-muntenia.ro; ❹–❺), is an ugly concrete mass, though the variously priced rooms are perfectly adequate. Close by, at B-dul Republicii 84, *Carmen* (☏0248/222 699, ⓦwww .hotel-carmen.ro; ❸–❹) has a mix of older and newer rooms, some of which overlook the park; and just off B-dul Republicii at Str. Panselelor 1, the *Metropol* (☏0248/222 407; ❸) offers modest, garishly coloured rooms. There are also chalets (❷) in the Trivale Park **campsite** (☏0248/634 190).

There's precious little in the way of decent **places to eat**, though *Calabria*, across from the County Museum at Str. Eroilor 5, is an atmospheric Italian place dishing up pasta and spaghetti, as well as good pizza, and just around the corner at Str. Primăverii 11, *Castle Hill* offers similar fare. The liveliest **drinking** spots are the *Old School Pub* and the *Guinness Pub*, a few paces away from each other at Str. Victoriei 30.

Goleşti

The village of **GOLEŞTI**, 8km east of Piteşti just off route 7 (the road running parallel to the Bucharest–Piteşti highway), is the junction from the Bucharest–Piteşti railway to the branch to Câmpulung Muscel. It was once the fiefdom of the Golescus, one of the leading liberal families of nineteenth-century Wallachia – not only were they active members of both the 1821 and 1848 revolutions, but they also worked in favour of Romanian union in 1859 and Romanian independence in 1877. Their home – now at the heart of a very enjoyable open-air **Museum of Fruit and Vine Growing** (Muzeul Viticulturii şi Pomiculturii; April–Sept Tues–Sun 9am–6pm; Oct–March 8am–4pm; €1.50) – is in fact a *conac* or summer residence (winters would be spent in Bucharest or Paris), and is beautifully cool, with authentic furnishings and historical displays. The museum itself is behind the house, settled among plum and pear orchards, and comprising over one hundred structures from Romania's fruit- and vine-growing communities, mainly dwellings (including dug-out homes, or "pit houses"), but also churches, wine presses and wells. The oldest structure is the wooden church of Drăguteşti, built in 1814. Over the gateway is the immaculately restored *foişor* or watchtower of Tudor Vladimirescu, leader of the 1821 peasant revolt, who was captured here and taken to Târgovişte to be executed. Beside this stands an early nineteenth-century schoolhouse, which still retains some original fixtures and fittings, including German, Greek and Latin textbooks, and a sandbox that was used for practising writing. There's also an interesting little **Ethnographic Museum** in the grounds, exhibiting various viticultural implements, peasant costumes and craftworks.

The village church, across the road from the museum's main gate, dates from 1646 and contains the tombs of the Golescu family; take a look, too, at the fine iconostasis carved from yew tree wood and the stone portal separating the *naos* and *pronaos*. If the church is closed, ask in the village for the caretaker who will let you in. You can get to Goleşti by one of the regular maxitaxis which depart from the Bălcescu hospital in Piteşti (on B-dul I.C. Brătianu), or by train from Piteşti; Goleşti station is a ten-minute walk from the village centre.

Câmpulung Muscel

Câmpulung, or **CÂMPULUNG MUSCEL** (as it is properly known), 53km north of Pitesţi, dates back to pre-Roman times and has played an important role in Wallachia's history, including a stint as the region's first capital after the *voivodate* was forged around 1300. Today, there are a couple of minor attractions to while away an hour or two, and it's a convenient place to break a journey to Transyl-vania. About 500m north of the train station on Str. Negru Vodă, Câmpulung's main drag, is the town's major sight, the **Negru Vodă Monastery**, attributed to its namesake, Romania's legendary thirteenth-century Black Prince. The present building, incorporating stonework from the original, was completed in 1837; the infirmary chapel to its rear dates from 1718. The monastery's most striking feature is the massive seventeenth-century gate tower, with its heavy beech gates, and a twelfth-century stone carving of a doe to the left as you enter; this was brought from a nearby Dominican monastery and is remarkably Western European in style.

Continuing north, Str. Negru Vodă brings you to Str. Republicii (forking off to the left), which forms the southbound stretch of the centre's one-way system (Str. Negru Vodă forms the northbound). Housed in a fine seventeenth-century building at Str. Republicii 5 is a fabulous little **Ethnographic Museum** (Muzeul de Etnografie; Tues–Sun 9am–5pm; €1), containing some exquisitely crafted furniture, colourful regional costumes, and a stock collection of farming and cooking implements. Beyond here, where Strs. Negru Vodă and Republicii meet (continuing as the north- and southbound sides of one divided main road), is the Bărătei complex, where the chunky fourteenth-century **Roman Catholic Church of St James** houses the tombstone of Count Laurentius of Campo Longo, the inscription on which, dating from 1300, is the oldest Romanian document. It's also worth seeing the mid-seventeenth-century parish house and the bell tower, built in 1730 and raised at the end of the nineteenth century. Walking up from here, take a look up at the wonderful neo-Brâncovenesc buildings with their pillars and wrought-iron balconies.

The **town museum** (Muzeul Câmpulung Muscel; Tues–Sun 9am–5pm; €1) is just north at Str. Republicii 119, opposite the *Hotel Muscelul*. It offers a fairly standard overview of the region's history, in Romanian only, in addition to a dusty collection of artwork by the likes of Luchian, plus a couple of sketches by Pallady. There's also coverage of the **Roman fort**, or *castrum*, of Jidava, part of the Limes Transalutanus defensive line, which was destroyed by the Goths in 244 AD. The fort's remains, by the Pescăreasa rail halt 6km south of town en route to Piteşti, have been preserved and can be visited (Tues–Sun 9am–5pm); there's also a small museum here housing a few excavated fragments and a mock-up of how the camp would have looked.

Practicalities

Trains from Goleşti (just east of Piteşti) terminate at Câmpulung Station, 2km south of town, and are met by maxitaxis. Otherwise, there are regular maxitaxis to and from Piteşti at the following locations: the main bus station, located to the east of town across the river at Str. I.C. Frimu; just north of the Negru Vodă Church; and a small terminal by the bridge just south of the town centre.

A couple of agreeable **places to stay** are *Pensiunea Nico Pardon*, Str. Negru Vodă 122 (℡0248/510 858, @pensiunea.nico.pardon@yahoo.com; ❸), though it's actually located in a residential street behind the Bărătei complex; and, further north at Str. Negru Vodă 180, *Pensiunea Hangiţa* (℡0248/511 805, @www.hangita.ro; ❸); breakfast costs extra at both. There are also several agrotourism programmes in **Lereşti**, 8km north of town (and reached by regular maxitaxis). **Homestays** here (and in equally attractive villages such as Rucăr, Dâmbovicioara and Dragoslavele) can be booked through the local Antrec office in Rucăr (℡0248/542 230, @arges@antrec.ro), or you can just try your luck where you see a sign for *Agroturism* or *Cazare*.

The best **place to eat** here is the small *Brâncovenesc* restaurant, opposite the *Nico Pardon* pension at Str. C. Brâncoveanu 50, which offers a lengthy Romanian menu; and there's the good little *Iepuraşul* patisserie opposite the *Hotel Muscelul*.

North to Transylvania

The scenery becomes increasingly dramatic on the road north from Câmpulung into Transylvania. Eight kilometres beyond Câmpulung (at the junction of a lovely road to Târgovişte, to the right), a road branches left to the village of **Nămăesti** (served by maxitaxis), site of a gorgeous little rock church complete with an ancient icon (said to miraculously cure ailments) and cells hewn from sandstone by sixteenth-century monks. Today, the small monastery complex is inhabited by a handful of nuns.

Some 3km further along the road to Braşov, the austere, lighthouse-shaped **Mateias Mausoleum** marks the spot where Romanian troops managed to repel a major German offensive over 45 days in 1916. More than two thousand Romanians lost their lives, their remains now kept in a large glass chest in the ossuary. The walls and ceiling of the mausoleum, meanwhile, are beautifully decorated with mosaics, depicting scenes of war as well as some of Romania's most prominent historical figures, including Mircea the Old, Constantin Brâncoveanu and Vlad Ţepeş. There's also a small **museum** (daily 9am–5pm) up the steps, containing artefacts, photographs and a working diorama retelling the events of the battle.

Beyond the monument, the road continues to the villages of **Dragoslavele** and **Rucăr**, with their traditional wooden houses and verandas. Dragoslavele also has an eighteenth-century wooden church; homestays are available at both villages (see p.103 for the Rucăr Antrec office). From Rucăr, the road continues up in a series of hairpin bends towards the Bran (or Giuvala) Pass, encountering the **Bridge of the Dâmboviţa**, a spectacular passage between the Dâmboviciorei and Plaiu gorges to the north and the yet narrower Dâmboviţei gorges to the south (see p.144 for the continuation of the route beyond the Bran Pass).

Curtea de Argeş, Arefu and Poienari Castle

After the Old Courts of Bucharest and Târgovişte, Wallachia's Dracula trail continues west via the attractive little town of **Curtea de Argeş**, another former princely capital that still boasts some interesting churches and palace ruins, to the remains of **Dracula's Castle** at **Poienari**. Although the tourist industry focuses on Bran castle in Transylvania (see p.142), which has almost no connection to the Dracula myth, the castle at Poienari was once Vlad the Impaler's residence, and its location in the foothills of the Făgăraş mountains makes for a wonderfully dramatic setting.

Curtea de Argeş

CURTEA DE ARGEŞ, Wallachia's second capital (after Câmpulung and before Târgovişte), lies some 36km northwest of Piteşti, and is easily accessible by road or rail. At the beginning of the main through street, B-dul Basarabilor, stands the **Court of Argeş**, the oldest church in Wallachia. Enclosed by a wall of river boulders, the thirteenth-century complex (Tues–Sun 10am–6pm; €1) was rebuilt in the fourteenth century by Radu Negru, otherwise known as Basarab I, the founder of Wallachia. Its **Princely Church** (in which the early Basarab rulers are buried) was constructed in 1352 and its interior decorated with frescoes in 1384; later restoration work has now been largely removed to reveal the original frescoes, which are fully in the Byzantine tradition but wonderfully alive and individual, reminiscent of Giotto rather than the frozen poses of the Greek masters. To its east are the remains of a palace and tower, and to the north those of the later palace of Neagoe Basarab. Across the square, in the pink and white painted villa at Str. Negru Vodă 2, the **town museum** (Muzeul Municipal; Tues–Sun 9am–4pm; €1) displays a rather mundane collection of local artefacts; however, do look out for a six-hundred-year-old stone slab bearing the coat of arms of Vlad Ţepeş's father, Vlad Dracul. Across the main road to the east are the ruins of the fourteenth-century Church of San Nicoara, and up the hill beyond, the equally ruinous seventeenth-century Olarie (Potters') church.

More visually impressive is the monastery, or **Episcopal Church** (daily 8am–7pm), about 1.5km north of the court at the end of B-dul Basarabilor, (reached by maxitaxis from the town centre). Resembling the creation of an inspired confectioner, it's a boxy structure enlivened by whorls, rosettes and fancy trimmings, rising into two twisted, octagonal belfries, each festooned with little spheres and the three-armed cross of Orthodoxy. Next to a restaurant in the park across the road, **Manole's Well** is a spring said to have been created by the death of **Manole**, the Master Builder of Curtea de Argeş. Legend has it that Manole was marooned on the rooftop of his creation, the Episcopal Church, when Prince Neagoe Basarab, who had commissioned him to build it, ordered the scaffolding to be removed, to ensure that the builder could not repeat his masterwork for anyone else. Manole tried to escape with the aid of wings made from roofing shingles – only to crash to his death, whereupon a spring gushed forth immediately. The story is perhaps that of a crude form of justice, for legend also has it that Manole had immured his wife within the walls of the monastery – at the time it was believed that *stafia* or ghosts were needed to keep buildings from collapse.

The current Episcopal Church is not Manole's original creation of 1512–17 but a re-creation of 1875–85 by the Frenchman Lecomte de Noüy, who grafted on all the Venetian mosaics and Parisian woodwork; he wanted to do the same to the Princely Church, but the historian Nicolae Iorga managed to get legal backing to stop him. Inside the garish red, green and gold interior lie the tombs of the church founder and kings Carol I (1866–1914) and Ferdinand (1914–27).

Practicalities

It's a five-minute walk to the Old Town centre from the ornate Mughal-style **train station** and the adjacent **bus station** – turn left out of the stations on Str. 1 Mai and then right up Str. Traian and left on Str. Negru Vodă. This continues as B-dul Basarabilor; it's one-way northbound, so maxitaxis loop south on Str. 1 Mai. Moving on by train, your only option is one of the five daily services to Piteşti; there's more choice at the bus station, with services to Arefu, Bucharest, Câmpulung, Braşov, Râmnicu Vâlcea and Sibiu. **Maxitaxis** run from outside the Princely Church (every 15min) as far as Bascov – get another maxitaxi there on to Piteşti, 10km to the south.

The town's two perfectly decent **accommodation** options are on B-dul Basarabilor, namely the tidy *Pensiunea Montana*, halfway along at no. 72 (☎0248/722 364; ❸), and the *Posada* hotel, some 300m further up at no. 27 (☎0248/721 451, Ⓦwww.posada.ro; ❸-❹), which has two categories of room, though there's marginal price difference. For **food**, try the *Crama Basarabilor* a few paces north of the Princely Church, serving soups and salads, and meats prepared on a spit in the terraced garden. The *Restaurant Laura*, by Manole's Well, has a nice terrace around a pool and serves adequate Romanian food as well as pizza. Taking the first road east south of the monastery and turning right at the end on to Str. Episcop Nichiţa, you'll come to the *Restaurant Sârbesc*, serving Serbian food.

Arefu and Poienari Castle

Twenty-five kilometres north of Curtea de Argeş is **AREFU** (or Aref), a long, ramshackle village 3km west of the valley road – if you're travelling by car, be warned that the surface from the main road to the village is very rough. It was to here, in 1457, that the survivors of Vlad the Impaler's massacre in Târgovişte (see p.99) were marched to begin work on his castle. This is the real Dracula's Castle, which Vlad began work on in 1457 – his only connection with the better-known one at Bran is that he may have attacked it once. Situated on a crag north of the village, the moody **POIENARI CASTLE** (Cetatea Poienari: daily 9am–5pm; €1), 4km north on the road from Arefu, can only be reached by climbing 1480 steps (about a 30min walk) from the hydroelectric power station (and a kiosk selling refreshments), which proves a powerful disincentive to most visitors. There are plenty of maxitaxis from Curtea de Argeş, but only as far as Arefu, so you'll need to walk (or hitch a lift) beyond there. Struggle to the top and you'll find that the citadel is surprisingly small, one-third having collapsed down the mountainside in 1888. Entering by a narrow wooden bridge, you'll come across the crumbling remains of two towers within; the prism-shaped one was the old keep, Vlad's residential quarters, from where, according to legend, the Impaler's wife flung herself out of the window, declaring that she "would rather have her body rot and be eaten by the fish of the Argeş" than be captured by the Turks, who were then besieging the castle. Legend also has it that Vlad himself escaped over the mountains on horseback, fooling his pursuers by shoeing his mount backwards – or, according to some versions, by affixing horseshoes that left the impression of cow prints. **Private rooms** (❶) are available both in Arefu and in the two villages preceeding Arefu, Corbeni and Căpăţânenii Pământeni, where you can try places (advertising *camere* or *cazare*) at random.

You can continue up the twisting road to **Lake Vidraru**, held back by a spectacular dam (165m), 4km from Poienari. Four hundred metres beyond the dam is the *Casa Argeşeana* cabana (☎0248/721 451; ❶), essentially a **restaurant** but with a few **beds** available too. A further 8km on, above the main road beside the lake, is the *Cabana de Pesti* (☎0248/506 047; ❹), an attractive hotel popular at weekends with local fishermen; comfortable rooms are complemented by an outstanding fish restaurant. Beyond the lake, the **Transfăgăraşan Highway** continues across the **Făgăraş mountains** and into Transylvania (see p.147).

The Olt valley

The **River Olt** runs south from its source in Transylvania through the Red Tower Pass below Sibiu, carving a stupendous 50km gorge through the Carpathians down into Wallachia, where it passes through **Râmnicu Vâlcea**, 34km west of Curtea de Argeş, and continues south to the Danube. In Wallachia, the valley can best be approached by road from Piteşti and Curtea de Argeş or from Târgu Jiu further to the west. **Trains** from Piatra Olt, midway between Piteşti and Craiova, head north up the valley to Podu Olt and Sibiu, with slower services stopping at the villages in between; there's also an increasing supply of buses following the valley between Râmnicu Vâlcea and Sibiu.

Râmnicu Vâlcea

Sprawling across successive terraces above the River Olt, **RÂMNICU VÂLCEA** is a typically systematized town, with many communist era apartment blocks and more modern malls, but there are half a dozen attractive old churches as well as an excellent open-air museum here.

Just about everything of interest is on, or just off, the town's main street, Calea lui Traian, which runs along the western side of the main square, Piaţa Mircea cel Bătrân; on the north side of the square is the sixteenth-century **Church of the Annunciation** (Buna Vestire). This was established between 1545 and 1549 by Mircea the Shepherd and rebuilt in 1747 by the citizens of Sibiu. Going a block west to reach Calea lui Traian at the fantastic Palace of Justice (Palatul de Justiţei) and heading north, you'll pass two more old churches: **St Paraschiva**, built between 1557 and 1587, and **All Saints**, built between 1762 and 1764 in a post-Brâncovenesc style with distinctive oblique cable mouldings that make the towers seem twisted. A few paces along at Calea lui Traian 143, the **County Museum** (Muzeul Judeţean; Tues–Sun 10am–6pm; €1) holds a better-than-average hoard of local archeological finds. Behind the museum at Str. Carol I no. 25 is a modern villa housing the **art gallery** (Muzeul de Artă; Wed–Sun 10am–6pm), with works by the customary Romanian artists, Grigorescu and Pallady. Another five minutes north, at Str. Carol I no. 53, is the **Bishopric** (Episcopiei), a wonderfully tranquil complex, with three small churches set in well-kept lawns. It dates from the sixteenth century, although the main church, with its Tattarescu paintings, was only built in 1856, after a fire destroyed the original. Further north, at Calea lui Traian 351, the **Citadel Church** (1529) still stands amid the remains of its fortifications.

At the northern town limits is the superb **Bujoreni open-air museum** (Muzeul Satului Vâlcea; Tues–Sun 10am–6pm; €1), a fine ensemble of some eighty structures laid out as per a typical village from the Vâlcea region. It's possible to enter a good cross section of these units, including a splendidly preserved inn (1899), one of the village's largest buildings and its social focus, a perfectly furnished village school (1904), complete with period books and maps, and a *cula* or watchtower, dating from 1802. The oldest building is the church (1785), complete with a candelabrum featuring wooden eggs hanging below wooden birds, and some original icons. To get here, take a **maxitaxi** from town, or walk south for fifteen minutes from the Bujoreni train station.

Practicalities

The **train station** is east of the centre on Str. V. Popescu, from where it's a ten-minute walk along Str. Regina Maria (50m to the left of the station as you exit) to Piaţa Mircea cel Bătrân and Calea lui Traian. From the **bus station**, south of the river on Str. G. Coşbuc, it's a short walk to the left along Str. Dacia and right on Calea lui Traian to cross the bridge into the centre.

The best of the town's **hotels** is the warm, welcoming and colourfully decorated *Castel*, a five-minute walk north of Piaţa Mircea cel Bătrân at Str. Praporgescu 5 (℡0250/730 003, ⓦwww.hotel-castel.ro; ❹). Situated on the slopes of the hills immediately west of town, at Str. Badescu 20, the *Gemina* (℡0250/735 101; ❸–❹) has tidy rooms with lofty views of the town and surrounding hills; it's a ten-minute walk past the art gallery and up the hill. Located on the southern outskirts (served by the Halta Ostroveni rail halt) is the *Popas Ostroveni*, a basic **campsite** with chalets (℡0250/736 601; ❶).

For something to **eat**, head for the rustically themed *Hanul Haiducilor* at Calea lui Traian 171 and tuck into big bowls of Romanian stew (*tocane*) and plates of sausages (*mititei*). Otherwise the Romanian-Mediterranean restaurant in the *Castel* hotel is well worth a visit (and they've got a lively sports bar across the road), and there are two branches of the cracking *Boromir* patisserie – one at Str. Târgului 2, a modern circular building on the east side of Piaţa Mircea cel Bătrân, and the other by the shopping mall on Calea lui Traian. The central **market** is behind the *Galeriile Romarta* on the south side of Piaţa Mircea cel Bătrân.

Călimăneşti–Căciulata

The twin settlements of **CĂLIMĂNEŞTI–CĂCIULATA** mark the entrance to the Olt valley, a deep twisting gorge of great beauty and the site of several monasteries, the most notable of which are **Cozia** and **Turnul**. While the main road runs along the Olt's west bank, a lesser road (as far as Cozia) and the rail line follow the other side of the defile.

A fading spa town 15km north of Râmnicu Vâlcea, **Călimăneşti** is home to the **Songs of the Olt folklore festival**, with musical groups from all over Oltenia, usually combined with a **pottery fair** during the first week in August. It's also the location for **Ostrov island**, a municipal park and the site of a tiny **hermitage**, built from 1520–22 for Despina, wife of Neagoe Basarab, with painted frescoes dating from 1752–60. The hideous green-faced women in the porch are no indication of the beautiful paintings inside; to get there, walk across a bridge opposite the *Hotel Central*.

The nearest **train station** is actually in the village of Jiblea just to the south, although the station itself takes Călimăneşti's name; buses run every twenty minutes from here into Călimăneşti, then to its twin town of Căciulata and onwards as far as Cozia Monastery. In fact the station is only 1km from Călimăneşti, and it takes just ten minutes, walking beside the train tracks, then turning left along Str. Vlahuţă, to reach the dam that carries the main road across the Olt into town.

The only **hotel** in Călimăneşti itself is the *Central* at Calea lui Traian 398 (☎0250/750 990; ❷), an enormous gone-to-seed spa hotel built in 1886 and remodelled 24 years later by the same architect. There's stacks more accommodation 2km to the north (take the paved path on the river embankment rather than the road) in **Căciulata**, a one-street spa town lined with villas, many of which advertise *cazare* or *camere* (rooms). The most prominent hotel here is the *Traian* (☎0250/750 780; ❷), with clean and good-value rooms that belie the grim exterior; just behind it there's the *Vila Flora* (same no; ❹), a small villa complete with spa facilities. Rather grander is the modern *Orizont* at Calea lui Traian 495 (☎0350/805 993, ⓦwww.hotel-orizont.ro; ❺). There is also a **campsite**, the *Ştrand*, across the road from the *Traian* hotel.

Cozia and Turnul

Beautifully pitched amid elegant pine trees and fragrant rose bushes, **Cozia Monastery**, 1km north of Căciulata, is the earliest example of Byzantine architecture in Wallachia. Built by Serb architects in 1388 – thanks to the patronage of Vlad Ţepeş's grandfather, Mircea the Old (who is buried within the monastery) – the church's principal architectural features include alternating bands of brick and stone, filigree latticework and fluted, false pillars. The church portico was added by Constantin Brâncoveanu in the early eighteenth century, although it's not a particularly striking example of the Brâncovenesc style. The monastery also houses a small **museum of religious art**, exhibiting a dazzling collection of church treasures – mostly seventeenth- to nineteenth-century icons. Across the road is the impossibly slender Bolniţa, or **Infirmary Church**, built between 1542 and 1543, with murals dating from the same period. About 300m south of the church stands the *Cozia* motel (☎0350/801 975; ❷), where maxitaxis from the south terminate, and opposite, the tidy *Vila Liliacul* (☎0250/750 440; ❸). Just to the north, a dam takes you across the Olt to the reconstructed Arutela *castrum*, a fort built in 137 AD as part of the Limes Alutanus, the Romans' defensive line along the Olt.

About 3km north of Cozia Monastery, on the east bank of the River Olt near the Mânăstirea Turnu train halt, is **Turnul Monastery**, based around rock cells hewn by hermits from Cozia at the end of the sixteenth century. From here, it's a five- to six-hour walk up a steep trail marked by red stripes to the *Cozia* cabana (❶), situated near the summit of the **Cozia massif**. Sheltered from northeasterly winds by the Făgăraş mountains, this has the mildest climate of all Romania's ranges, enabling oak, walnut and wild roses to grow at altitudes of up to 1300m. Both sides of the Olt north of Căciulata are now protected as part of the Cozia National Park.

Târgu Jiu and around

Forewarned about **TÂRGU JIU** and the surrounding **Jiu valley**, visitors often decide to ignore them completely – but the town does merit a visit on the strength of its association with Romania's foremost sculptor, Constantin Brâncuşi. Ranged along the valley, from Petroşani to Rovinari, are the **coal and lignite mines** that traditionally supported all the country's other industries. For the most part, this is a bleak landscape made grimmer by slag heaps, pylons and the mining towns themselves, while the sandbanks in the river are almost solid coal dust. Under communism, the **miners** were lauded as the aristocrats of the proletariat, but had to be placed under **martial law** in 1985, when Ceauşescu demanded ever higher output and halved their pay when quotas weren't achieved. After the revolution of 1989, the miners were used as Iliescu's **shock troops**, rushed on special trains to Bucharest to terrorize the opposition as required, and even to precipitate the resignation of prime minister Petre Roman himself.

Arrival, information and accommodation

The **train** and **bus stations** are just a stone's throw apart on Str. Titulescu, a twenty-minute walk east of town. Târgu Jiu is on the Simeria–Petroşani–Craiova train line, with a few trains continuing to Arad, Cluj, Craiova, Deva and Bucharest. Buses and maxitaxis run to Bucharest, Cluj, Horezu, Râmnicu Vâlcea, Drobeta-Turnu Severin, Sibiu, Timişoara and most surrounding villages.

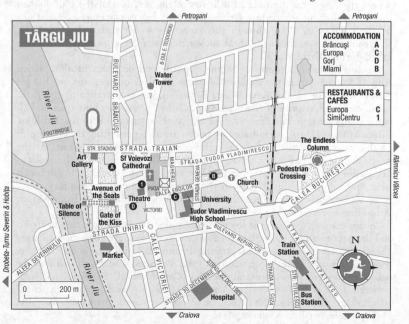

The town's **hotels** are nothing special, but they're inexpensive: by far the best is the *Europa* at Calea Eroilor 22 (℡0253/211 810, Ⓦwww.hotelrestauranteuropa.ro; ❺), with polished rooms and colourful, good-sized bathrooms. A short walk east at no. 27 there's the reasonable *Miami* (℡0253/218 407; ❸), while the *Brâncuşi*, at B-dul C. Brâncuşi 10 (℡0253/215 981, Ⓦwww.hotelbrancusi.ro; ❹), has tidy, albeit gaudy, rooms. Cheapest of all is the *Gorj* at Calea Eroilor 6 (℡0253/211 567; ❷–❸), whose mix of old and new rooms is not nearly as grim as the exterior might suggest. **Homestay accommodation** in the area (❶) can be arranged through the Guardo Tours agency, just behind the cathedral at Str. Tudor Vladimirescu 17 (℡0253/223 081, Ⓔgorj@antrec.ro).

There's a distinct paucity of **places to eat** in town, the only worthwhile **restaurant** being the one in the *Hotel Europa*, serving Romanian-Italian food. For **drinking**, try the *SimiCentru*, a decent little bar with a busy outdoor garden on the west side of Piaţa Victoriei.

The Town

Although Târgu Jiu has no links with coal mining, it still suffered the gross "modernization" imposed by Ceauşescu on Romania's coal-mining centres, with homes knocked down to make way for unattractive and impractical concrete blocks. Nevertheless, this busy, dusty town does hold one singularly important attraction (or attractions) – namely the monumental sculptures that **Constantin Brâncuşi** (see box opposite) created in the late 1930s as a war memorial for the town of his boyhood. He offered a series of twelve sculptures, but completed only four before he died – indeed, these were the only large-scale projects by Brâncuşi to bear fruition anywhere. The most iconic of his works, in a park at the eastern end of Calea Eroilor, is the **Endless Column** (*Coloană Infinita*), a vast 30m-high totem pole of smooth rhomboidal blocks, whose rippling form is emulated in many of the verandas of the old wooden houses throughout the region. Brâncuşi actually began working on variations of the column in 1918, though this structure wasn't installed until 1937, following a request from the local authorities to create a memorial for those killed during World War I.

Brâncuşi's other sculptures lie at the opposite end of Calea Eroilor, which runs 1.7km west from the *Endless Column* to the park on the banks of the Jiu River: the **Gate of the Kiss** (*Poarta Sărutului*), at the entrance to the park, opens onto the **Avenue of Seats** (*Aleea Scaunilor*), flanked by lime trees and 30 stone chairs (not intended for sitting on), which in turn leads to the **Table of Silence** (*Masa Tăcerii*), surrounded by twelve stools representing the continuity of the months and the traditional number of seats at a funeral feast. At the north end of the park, in a villa purpose-built for Ceauşescu, is the modern **art gallery** (Tues–Sun 9am–6pm; €1), though there's nothing by Brâncuşi here, instead just a clutch of rather ordinary contemporary paintings with some eighteenth- and nineteenth-century icons, including one from Mount Athos in Greece.

Cutting through the centre of town, Calea Eroilor is a surprisingly narrow street, and the vista east from the park to the *Endless Column* is blocked by a modern, ugly church. However, there are some striking architectural pieces amid the concrete, most notably around the pedestrianized Piaţa Victoriei, where you will find the neo-Brâncovenesc prefecture and the tiny **Cathedral of SS Voievozi**, built between 1749 and 1764. On Str. Unirii, the Tudor Vladimirescu high school stands diagonally opposite the Rectorat of the Constantin Brâncuşi University, both splendid neo-Brâncovenesc piles.

Constantin Brâncuşi

One of the greatest sculptors of the twentieth century, **Constantin Brâncuşi** was born in 1876 in a peasant cottage at Hobiţa, some 28km west of Târgu Jiu. He came to town at the age of nine to work as an errand boy, and later learned the techniques of the local woodcarvers, who chiselled sinuous designs on rafters, verandas and wells in the region. Through the sponsorship of local boyars, he was able to attend an art college in Craiova and went on to the **National School of Fine Arts** in Bucharest, before arriving at the Ecole des Beaux Arts in Paris in 1904, with a government scholarship of 600 Lei. He stayed in France for over fifty years, helping create a revolution in sculpture with his strikingly strong and simple works. With a circle of friends that included Picasso, Gide and Pound, he was at the centre of the intellectual ferment of Paris at its height.

He worked briefly in Rodin's studio, then, in company with Amadeo Modigliani, discovered the primitive forms of African masks and sculptures, concentrating thereafter on stripping forms down to their fundamentals. In 1907, he claimed that "what is real is not the exterior form but the essence of things", a credo which he pursued for the rest of his career. In 1920, his *Prinţesa X* was removed by police from the Salon des Indépendents because it was considered obscenely phallic; it was bought by Fernand Léger and Blaise Cendrars, but Brâncuşi never exhibited in Paris again. A different sort of scandal followed in 1926 when Brâncuşi took his *Măiastra* (*Magic Bird*) with him to New York. US Customs classified it as "a piece of metal" and levied import duty of $10; Brâncuşi appealed against the decision, thereby starting a furore which made him a household name in America. During that same trip, the photographer Edward Steichen gave credibility to Brâncuşi's work by publicly announcing that he had bought one of the sculptor's bronze *Birds in Flight* for $600 – by 1967, it was worth $175,000. Brâncuşi died in 1957, with his series of sculptures for Târgu Jiu unfinished, and is buried in Montparnasse cemetery in Paris. You'll find examples of his work in Craiova and Bucharest as well as Târgu Jiu, and also in London, New York and Philadelphia; his last studio is preserved in Paris.

East of Târgu Jiu

Away from the industry of the Jiu valley, there are plenty of tranquil villages where traditional customs are still a part of everyday life. Moreover, the area east of town has particularly impressive **cave formations** and important **monasteries**, though most of these sights are poorly served by buses from Târgu Jiu and Râmnicu Vâlcea. **POLOVRAGI**, 48km east of Târgu Jiu and dominated by the Căpăţânii mountains, is home to one of the great Wallachian fairs: the *Nedeia*. An occasion for highlanders to dress up, dance and do deals face to face in the old fashion, the *Nedeia* usually occurs on the Sunday between July 14 and 20. If your visit doesn't coincide with the fair, the main sites of interest are north of the village, where a forestry road runs into the 1.6km-long **Olteţu gorges**, beyond which, 3km from the main road, you'll find the **Polovragi Monastery and cave**. The small monastery was originally built in 1470, then rebuilt by Brâncoveanu in 1647; the later **Bolniţa Church** (1736), on the same site, is definitely worth the trip for its fine frescoes. Further on, lurking behind the eastern rockface at the mouth of the gorge, is the Polovragi cave, once believed to be the abode of Zalmoxis, the Dacians' chief deity. Now fully illuminated and open for guided tours (daily 9am–5pm; €2), it was first explored in 1860 by the French naturalist Lancelot, and is renowned for the stalactites in its "Candlesticks Gallery".

From Baia de Fier, 7km west of Polovragi and 5km north of the main road from Târgu Jiu to Râmnicu Vâlcea, a road leads 3km north to a beautiful grotto in the smaller **Galbenul gorges**. Although only two passages out of the ten kilometres of convolutions that make up the so-called **Women's Cave** (Peştera Muierilor; daily 9am–5pm; €2) have been illuminated, it's an impressive sight nonetheless; halfway in, multicoloured stone columns resemble petrified wood, while in the lower passage the skeletons of 183 cave bears have been discovered. The cave gets its name from the human skeletons – mainly those of women and children, and dating from prehistoric times – found on its upper levels. From the cave and nearby *cabana*, a footpath leads up to the **Rânca tourist complex** (℡0244/461 542; ❷–❸) 15km away in the Parâng mountains in Transylvania; the basic accommodation is useful mainly for hikers in the summer.

Horezu and the monasteries

Set amid apple and plum orchards, sweet chestnut trees and wild lilac, 16km east of Polovragi on the main road to Râmnicu Vâlcea, is the small town of **HOREZU** – so-called after the numerous owls (*huhurezi*) that reside here (the town is also shown as Hurez on some maps). Although wooden furniture and wrought-iron objects are also produced here, Horezu is best known for its **pottery**, especially its plates, which by tradition are given as keepsakes during funeral wakes. The Cocoşul de Horezu **pottery fair**, held on the first Sunday of June, is one of the year's biggest events in the area – though if you miss it, you can still see many wares displayed in dozens of roadside huts just east of the centre. There's also an exhibition of local pottery in a large hut by the car park leading up to Horezu monastery, where you can view and buy items.

The real attraction, however, lies near the village of Romanii de Jos, around 3km northeast of town, turning off the main road 2km east of town. Built between 1691 and 1697, and now a UNESCO World Heritage Site, **Horezu Monastery** (Mănăstirea Hurezi) is the largest and finest of Wallachia's Brâncoveanu complexes, and is the site of the school which established the Brâncovenesc style. The complex is centred around the **Great Church**, built in 1693 and entered via a

---

Constantin Brâncoveanu

Constantin Brâncoveanu (1654–1714) became ruler of Wallachia in 1689 after the usual Byzantine family intrigues, and was instrumental in bringing about a cultural renaissance by establishing a printing press in Bucharest and a school of architecture and sculpture at the monastery of Horezu. He created an **architectural style** that was a fusion of Western (especially Venetian) Renaissance and Ottoman elements, characterized by a harmonious layout and fine ornamental stone carving, especially on balconies, external staircases and arcades. In the early twentieth century a neo-Brâncovenesc style was very popular, especially in Wallachia and Moldavia, as an expression of the new nation's cultural identity.

Politically, he sought to distance Wallachia from its Ottoman overlords (partly because he wanted to keep some of the massive taxes they demanded to use for his building projects). At the outbreak of a Russo-Turkish War in 1710 he sought alliances with the Russians, as well as the Habsburgs, while also being prepared to fight on the Turkish side if they seemed likelier winners. However, he was arrested, tortured and (with his four sons and grand treasurer Enache Văcărescu) executed in 1714 in Constantinople. He was succeeded by his cousin Ştefan Cantacuzino, who was soon deposed and executed by the Ottomans and replaced by Nicolai Mavrocordat, the first Phanariot ruler of Wallachia (having already been the first Phanariot ruler of Moldavia).

In 1992 Brâncoveanu, and those executed with him, were declared saints and martyrs by the Romanian Orthodox Church, honoured as protectors of the Orthodox faith against Islam. Nevertheless, to the outside world it is his artistic and cultural achievements that are his lasting legacy.

marvellous ten-pillared porchway and doors of carved pearwood. Inside, the **frescoes**, once tarnished by the smoke from fires lit by Turkish slaves who camped here, have been restored, and you can now make out portraits of Constantin Brâncoveanu and his family, Cantacuzino and Basarab, as well as scenes from Mount Athos and the Orthodox calendar. To the right of the church as you enter is a vacant tomb, which was Brâncoveanu's intended resting place – as it is, he is buried in St George's Church in Bucharest (see p.74).

Opposite the church is the nuns' domed refectory, which contains some more but poorly preserved frescoes and, to the left, another Brâncoveanu porch, featuring a splendid stone balustrade carved with animal motifs. In one of the upper cloisters, there's a collection of sacral art, mainly seventeenth-century icons. Set apart to the north and west are the small hermitages of the Holy Apostles and of St Stephen, built in 1700 and 1703 respectively. The chapel of St Michael outside the gates was built by Brâncoveanu for the local villagers.

If you're looking to stay the night, there's basic but very cheap **accommodation** in the centre of Horezu at the *Hotel Horezu* (☎0250/861 040; ❷), behind the bus station, and, 300m further along at Str. Căpitan Maldăr 5, the *Pensiunea Criveanu* (☎0250/860 038; ❷), a family guesthouse. The *Trei Stejari* campsite, 2km back out on the road to Târgu Jiu, has tiny, bunker-like huts sleeping two (☎0250/860 570; ❶).

Six kilometres on towards Râmnicu Vâlcea on the DN67, a left turn at Coşteşti leads another 6km north to **Bistriţa Monastery**, funded by the boyars of Craiova in the fifteenth century. You will, however, need your own transport, as bus services no longer run here. As well as three churches, dating from the sixteenth and seventeenth centuries, there is a cave containing two more chapels; the relics of St Gregory the Decapolite were hidden in one of these during the Turkish wars. A nun can lead you to the cave along the precipitous cliffside path. The seventeenth-century **Arnota Monastery** stands on a hill, 4km north of Bistriţa beyond a large quarry; by financing the construction of this monastery, *voivode* Matei Basarab guaranteed himself a tasteful burial place within its church surrounded by his chattels and murals of his wife, of which only fragments remain. As so often in this area, the porch is the work of Brâncoveanu.

West of Târgu Jiu

The small scenic towns and villages to the west of Târgu Jiu are a complete contrast to the flat, grimy mining areas to the east and south. Buses run from Târgu Jiu along the DN67d, stopping close to most of the sites of interest. From Peştişani, 21km west of Târgu Jiu, it's 3km south to the small village of **HOBIŢA**, birthplace of Constantin Brâncuşi (see p.111). The sculptor's childhood home has been turned into a small **museum** (Wed–Sun 9am–5pm; €1); if it's closed, you can ask in the shop at the crossroads for the museum's custodian to let you in. It's an attractive, traditional cottage, surrounded by plum and cherry trees. You'll learn relatively little about Brâncuşi here, but it's worth seeing the ceramics and textiles displayed inside, and the intricate spiral motifs on the veranda posts. One hundred metres away on the same road is the *Popas* pension, where you can sleep in *căsuţe* (wooden cabins; summer only; ❶) by a ford which leads into a wood dotted with Brâncuşi-esque sculptures left by a 1981 summer-school group. Further south, at the edge of the same wood, but reached by the main road through the village, is the village cemetery, with a tiny wooden chapel; even if it's closed, it's possible to enter the chapel's roof space by a ladder from the open porch to admire the skill of the local carpenters. There's also accommodation at the east end of Peştişani at the *Pensiunea Casa Brâncuşi* (☎0253/277 279; ❷).

TISMANA, just north of the DN67d another 7km west, harks back to the region's traditional pastoral ways. **Tismana Monastery**, 3km to the north of the village, is the oldest in Romania, founded in 1375 by St Nicodim, a member of the Basarab royal family, whose hermit-like cave is just to the right of the monastery gate, and whose tomb is to the right as you enter the church porch. Surrounded by a high wall during the reign of Matei Basarab, the monastery served as a meeting place for rebels in the 1821 rising led by Tudor Vladimirescu. Tismana is the setting for the annual **Tismana Garden Festival** of music and crafts on August 15, where the most popular instrument is the *nai* or shepherds' panpipes. You'll find wooden utensils, sculptures, embroidered clothing and Oltenian rugs on sale during the festival, while there are also stalls all year in the car park, selling good ceramics as well as trashy souvenirs. The monastery has a modern guesthouse (❶), and the *Gura Plaiului* youth hostel (☎0253/374 238; ❶) is right at the entry to the car park. Tismana also has some good **homestay** possibilities – contact the Guardo Tours Agency in Târgu Jiu (see p.110) or scout around the village, where *Pensiunea Magnolia* (☎0727/292 096; ❷), about 1km north of the main road at no. 15, has rooms with and without bathrooms.

Drobeta-Turnu Severin and the Danube

Drobeta-Turnu Severin lies in the far west of the region, on the north side of the **River Danube**, the country's natural border with Serbia and Bulgaria. The river narrows below Moldova Veche before surging through the **Kazan gorge** towards Orşova, only to be tamed and harnessed by the dam at the mighty **Iron Gates**, before reaching the town. Motorists driving down from Moldova Veche can see something of this magnificent panorama (the rail journey is less scenic); but if you're coming from Târgu Jiu, the real landscape feast doesn't start until you reach Drobeta-Turnu Severin. The shortest route from Târgu Jiu is via the badly surfaced DN67. By train, you'll have to travel down to **Filiaşi** to join the Craiova–Drobeta-Turnu Severin line.

Drobeta-Turnu Severin

Dubbed the "town of roses" for its beautiful parks, notably the archeological park around the Museum of the Iron Gates, with its lovely roses and walnut trees, the modern appearance of **DROBETA-TURNU SEVERIN** (usually known simply as Severin) belies its origins as the Dacian settlement of Drobeta, more than two thousand years ago. Its Roman conquerors left more enduring landmarks, however, notably the ruins of **Trajan's bridge**, which Apollodorus of Damascus built to span the Danube at the order of the emperor in 103–105 AD. As the travel writer Patrick Leigh Fermor put it, "two great stumps of his conglomerate masonry still cumbered the Romanian side", and these can be seen from the train or from the grounds of the **Museum of the Iron Gates** (Muzeul Porţile de Fier; Tues–Sun 9am–5pm; €1.50) down by the Danube on the east side of town. Divided up into several sections, it's a bit hit and miss: the most enjoyable is the ethnographic section, featuring a lovely assortment of rugs, costumes, ceramics and painted chests, while the aquarium, with tanks full of unusual species from the Danube, will keep kids happy. Otherwise, the natural science, archeological and historical departments are missable, if only because all captions are in Romanian. Nearby, within the museum precincts, or *Parc Arheologic*, are the remains of a Roman bath and the foundations of both the fort that guarded Trajan's bridge and the fourteenth-century **Metropolitan's Basilica**. The small **art museum** (Muzeul de Artă; Tues–Sun 10am–6pm; €1) at Str. Rahovei 3

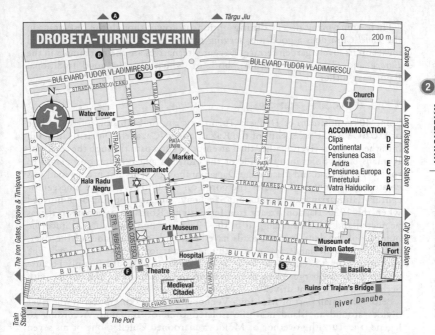

holds a few works by important Romanian painters, including several still-life paintings and nudes by Pallady.

A few minutes' walk south of the art museum, across B-dul Carol I and down past the hospital, stand the tower and walls of a **medieval citadel** dating from the thirteenth century. Heading back north, the lively daily market is on Piaţa Unirii, while just to the west are a **synagogue** (finally being refurbished) and the site for a new Orthodox cathedral, and the *Hala Radu Negru* market hall, which now houses a huge furniture and textile store.

Practicalities

From the **train station** it's a fifteen-minute walk east along B-dul Carol I to the centre, while the main **bus station** is to the east of the centre on Str. Topolniţei (buses #1 and #45), with services west to Băile Herculane and Timişoara in the Banat and east to Târgu Jiu and Râmnicu Vâlcea.

In a town flush with **hotels**, the best is the *Clipa* at Str. Brâncoveanu 165 (☎0352/401 723, ⓦwww.hotelclipa.ro; ❹), with rooms furnished in smooth pine. Similarly appealing is the *Pensiunea Europa* a few paces along the road at B-dul Tudor Vladimirescu 66 (☎0252/333 737, ⒺOffice@pensiunea-europa.ro; ❹). Agreeable, and slightly cheaper, alternatives include the *Continental*, at B-dul Carol I no. 2 (☎0252/306 730, ⓦwww.continentalhotels.ro; ❹), which has average-looking but fairly priced rooms offering river views, and *Pensiunea Casa Andra*, occupying a nice old building further along the riverfront at Str. Coşbuc 2 (☎0352/401 444, ⒺReceptie@casa-andra.ro; ❸). The real budget choice is the *Tineretului* youth hostel, just north of the *Europa* at Str. Crişan 25 (☎0252/317 999; ❶). The *Vatra Haiducilor* (Outlaws' Hearth) **campsite** is 3km north along Str. Crişan in the Crihala forest. Antrec, at Str. I.L. Caragiale 39 (☎0252/333 023, ⒺMehedinti@antrec.ro), can arrange **homestay accommodation** (❶) in the county.

There aren't many decent **dining** options in town, though the restaurant in the *Hotel Clipa* does a good job, serving up hot sandwiches, pasta and grilled meats on its lovely garden terrace. Decent alternatives are the restaurants in the *Europa* and *Casa Andra* pensions, both of which also do good traditional Romanian dishes.

The Kazan gorge

Some 40km upstream of Drobeta-Turnu Severin, on both sides of the village of **DUBOVA**, the sheer cliffs of the **Kazan gorge** (Cazanele Dunării) fall 600m into the tortuous river. Rather than attempt to cut a path through the rock, the Romans bored holes into the side of the cliff and added beams and planks to roof over the road and discourage Dacian ambushes. The first proper road was created on the northern side of the gorge on the initiative of the nineteenth-century Hungarian statesman Count Szechenyi, but had not long been finished when the 1920 Trianon Treaty transferred it to Romania, whereupon it was neglected and finally submerged in the 1970s by the rising waters. Since the building of the dam, modern roads have been built on both sides of the river, and the dramatic landscape makes this an excursion not to be missed. The authorities aren't keen on tourists canoeing down the Danube (mainly because of the industrial barges using the river and the proximity of the border with Serbia), but it's a great drive.

Before the small port of **Moldova Veche**, a further 37km upstream, the river divides around an island near the isolated **rock of Babakai**. According to legend, the Turkish governor of Moldova marooned Zuleika, one of his seven wives, here because she had attempted to elope with a Hungarian noble. Admonished to "Repent of thy sin!" (*Ba-ba-kai*) and left to die, Zuleika was rescued by her lover, who later had the joy of taunting the mortally wounded governor with the news that Zuleika was alive and had become a Christian. Another legend refers to the caves near the ruined fortress of **Golubac**, just downstream on the Serbian bank of the river, where St George is said to have slain the dragon. Thereafter, its carcass has reputedly fed the swarms of bugs that infest the town of the same name.

The Iron Gates

The **Iron Gates** is a cliff-lined stretch of the River Danube which once had a formidable reputation, owing to the navigational hazards (eddies, whirlpools and rocks) that formerly restricted safe passage during the two hundred days of the year when the river was in spate. The blasting of a channel in 1896 obviated these terrors, and the building of a **hydroelectric dam** at Gura Văii, 10km upstream of Drobeta-Turnu Severin, finally tamed the river.

Conceived in 1956, the Porţile de Fier I hydroelectric project was undertaken as a joint venture; Romania and Yugoslavia (as it was then) each built a 1GW turbine plant and locks for shipping on their respective banks, linked by a slipway dam and an international road crossing. That task took from 1960 until 1972 and raised the river level by 33m. Romantics have deplored the results; the damming has submerged two places worthy of footnotes in history – the island of **Ada Kaleh** and old **Orşova** – and reduced the Danube's peak flow, so that the pollution of Central Europe is no longer flushed out to sea but gathers here, killing fish and flora. On the E70 (DN6) 10km west of Drobeta-Turnu Severin, the dam can be reached by bus #3 (*Baraj*) from the local *autogara* at the junction of Str. Traian and Str. Calărasi, just east of the Roman fort in Severin.

Southern Wallachia

In many respects, **southern Wallachia** is tedious, uninviting terrain, for while the Subcarpathians provide varied scenery and picturesque villages, below them stretch kilometres of featureless plains, dusty or muddy according to the season, with farms lost amid vast fields of corn or sunflowers. Although the large industrial town of **Craiova** has a few rewarding museums, the only obvious reason for venturing into this region is to cross the **border to Bulgaria**: there are crossing points at Calafat, 87km southwest of Craiova, and Giurgiu, some 60km south of Bucharest.

Craiova

Almost every locomotive on the tracks of Romania originally emerged from the Electroputere workshops of **CRAIOVA**, which also exports to Hungary, Bulgaria, China and even Britain. The city is also a centre for the Romanian automobile industry, the Oltcit works having produced many of the country's cars, first in collaboration with Citroën, then, as Rodae, with Korea's Daewoo conglomerate. After Daewoo's worldwide collapse in 2002, the government bought back the factory and in 2007 sold it to Ford. These industries are here because of the ready availability of oil, whose presence is attested to by the derricks surrounding what is

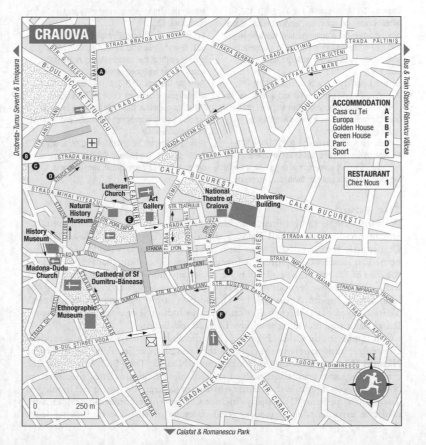

▼ Calafat & Romanescu Park

now the chief city of Oltenia and capital of Dolj county. Craiova does have a longer history than it might appear from its industrialized heritage, having begun its life as the Roman town of Pelendava, and **Michael the Brave** (see p.374) began his career here as deputy governor. Today it's a sprawling and hectic place, but you may find yourself breaking a journey to or from Bulgaria here, in which case there is a cluster of impressive museums to while away the time.

Arrival and information

Craiova's **train** and **bus stations** are located side by side northeast of the centre on Str. Dacia, from where it's a twenty-minute walk along B-dul Carol I (or minibuses #1, #5, #12 and #29) to the main through road, Calea Bucureşti. There are two train lines between Craiova and Bucharest: the main route crosses the southern plains by way of Caracal, Roşiori de Vede and Videle (with express trains continuing to Timişoara), while the second is a non-electrified line via Piteşti. The best place for **information** is the Mapamond agency at Str. Olteţ 2, though it's actually located up a flight of stairs just off Calea Unirii (Mon–Fri 9am–6pm, Sat 9am–2pm; ☎0251/415 071, ✉travel@mapamond.ro), which also acts as an Antrec agent booking **homestay accommodation** (❶) in the surrounding villages.

Accommodation

Casa cu Tei Str. Amaradia 4 ☎0372/981 433, ⓦwww.casacutei.com. The "Linden House" is the city's most restful accommodation: fourteen large and well-equipped rooms housed in a large villa-style building just a short walk uphill from the centre. ❼

Europa Calea Unirii 10A ☎0251/412 321, ✉cmitrita@yahoo.com. A solid and quiet three-star place in a handy central location and well set back from the main road; rooms are neat if a little ordinary. ❺

Golden House Str. Brestei 18 ☎0251/406 270, ⓦwww.goldenhouse.ro. Set in the middle of extensive, fragrant gardens, this large villa is by far the most luxurious place in town, with gorgeous,

artfully decorated rooms, swimming pool and a fine restaurant. ❾

Green House Str. Fraţii Buzeşti 25 ☎0251/411 352, ⓦwww.green-house.ro. A modern building slightly south of the centre offering comfortable, sunny rooms and good service. ❹

Parc Str. Bibescu 12 ☎0251/417 257, ✉office @hotel-parc-craiova.ro. Once the Communist Party's guesthouse, this rather austere looking building now conceals well-renovated rooms, some with balconies. ❺

Sport Str. Brestei 25 ☎0251/412 022, ⓦwww .hotel-sport.ro. The friendly *Sport* is the cheapest option in town, offering small, simple rooms. ❸

The Town

Built from 1900–08 by a French architect for one of Romania's richest men, the elegant neo-Baroque **Mihail Palace**, at Calea Unirii 15, was home to Nicolae Ceauşescu in the early 1950s when he was local party secretary, and since 1954 has housed an excellent **art gallery** (Muzeul de Artă; Tues–Sun 10am–5pm; €1). At the core of the museum's collection are two rooms housing half a dozen pieces by Brâncuşi (including versions of *Mlle Pogany* and *The Kiss*), a room of paintings by local artist Theodor Aman (1831–91), and two dozen paintings by Grigorescu. There's also plenty of French decorative art, including Sèvres porcelain, and some Italian paintings, including works by Bassano and Bellotto.

Continuing south, Calea Unirii becomes the pedestrianized axis of the modern city centre; immediately to the right on the main plaza, at Str. Popa Şapcă 4, is the **Natural History Museum** (Muzeul Ştiinţele Naturii; Tues–Sun 9am–5pm; €1), offering the usual grim assortment of stuffed animals. Southwest of the museum, on Str. Madona-Dudu, is the **History Museum** (Muzeul de Istorie şi Arheologie; Tues–Sun 9am–5pm; €1). Displays include Oltenia's oldest archeological remains, medieval ornaments and frescoes, good coverage of the War of Independence

Crossing into Bulgaria: Calafat and Giurgiu

The neat, orderly town of **Calafat**, 84km southwest of Craiova, is one of the two major border crossings into Bulgaria. After extensive delays the bridge across the Danube is due to be completed by 2011, but until then the crossing to Bulgaria is by ferry to Vidin. It's less than ten minutes' walk straight ahead from the train station (just east of the port) to the centre of Calafat, marked by a war memorial; to the right is the market, and to the left is the House of Culture (Casa de Cultură), next to a couple of cafés and snack bars. If you need to **stay**, there's the *Hotel Panoramic*, located just one block inland from the port at Str. 22 Decembrie 1 (℡0251/232 960; ❸).

The second major crossing point into Bulgaria, and more convenient if travelling from Bucharest, is at **Giurgiu**, 64km due south of the capital. So-called fast trains take one hour and forty-five minutes to crawl from Bucharest's Gara de Nord to Giurgiu Nord Station just outside the town; alternatively, you can travel from the Gara de Nord to Videle and wait for a connection to Giurgiu Station, in the town next to the bus terminal. The 3km-long **Danube Bridge** is open 24 hours a day. If you need to stay, there's the small and basic *Hotel Victoria* (℡0246/212 569; ❸), five minutes from Giurgiu station at Str. Gării 1, hidden behind a block of flats to the right, or the slightly more comfortable *Vlaşca* at Str. Portului 12 (℡0246/215 321; ❹). You'll also find a **campsite** nearby on the Danube meadow (Lunca Dunării); plenty of buses run out this way from the town centre. Further east, a ferry across the Danube from Călăraşi to Silistra is in operation.

(1877–78) and World War I, and some Brâncovenesc art. Opposite this is the **Madona-Dudu Church**, rebuilt in 1936 to house an icon of the Virgin.

Immediately to the south on Str. Matei Basarab is the **cathedral of Sf. Dumitru-Băneasa**, built in 1652 but thoroughly transformed in 1889 by Lecomte de Noüy – it's less gloomy than most Orthodox churches, with a gorgeous golden glow to its frescoes. Occupying the former governor's residence, or *Casa Băniei* (dating from 1699), just across from the cathedral is the very worthwhile **Ethnographic Museum** (Muzeul de Etnografie; Tues–Sun 9am–5pm; €1), with a fabulous assortment of local costumes, ceramics from Horezu, porch pillars and some exquisitely carved staffs; the stunning cellar holds a superb assemblage of agricultural and viticultural implements, all with English captions. On the southern edge of the city (down Calea Unirii) is the superb **Romanescu Park**, laid out by French architects in 1901–03, with a zoo and lake and the first cable suspension bridge in Europe.

Eating, drinking and entertainment

You'll find the best **food** in the restaurants of the *Golden House* and *Casa cu Tei* hotels. For traditional Romanian fare, there's the inconspicuous-looking but really rather good *Chez Nous* at Str. Traian Demetrescu 8, which also has a small garden terrace out back. During warmer weather a succession of outdoor cafés dot Calea Unirii, which becomes a lively *passegiata* at sundown. The *Teatrul Naţional Marin Sorescu*, just west of the university at Str. A.I. Cuza 11 (℡0251/413 677), is home to one of Romania's leading theatre companies.

Travel details

Trains

Câmpulung to: Goleşti (5 daily; 1hr 5min–1hr 50min).

Craiova to: Bucharest (12 daily; 3hr–4hr 15min); Calafat (4 daily; 3hr 15min); Drobeta-Turnu Severin (10 daily; 2hr 35min–3hr 10min); Filiaşi (10 daily; 25min–1hr); Piatra Olt (10 daily; 45min–1hr

30min); Piteşti (5 daily; 2hr 15min–4hr); Sibiu (2 daily; 4hr); Târgu Jiu (10 daily; 1hr 30min–2hr 45min); Timişoara (8 daily; 5hr–6hr 30min).

Curtea de Argeş to: Piteşti (5 daily; 40min–1hr).

Drobeta-Turnu Severin to: Băile Herculane (9 daily; 45min–1hr 10min); Caransebeş (9 daily; 2hr 5min–3hr 15min); Craiova (12 daily; 1hr 40min–3hr 10min); Orşova (8 daily; 25–45min); Timişoara (9 daily; 3hr 15min–5hr 15min).

Piatra Olt to: Călimăneşti (7 daily; 1hr 30min–3hr 15min); Râmnicu Vâlcea (10 daily; 1hr 10min–2hr 40min); Sibiu (5 daily; 3hr 10min–6hr); Turnu Monastery (3 daily; 3hr 15min–3hr 30min).

Piteşti to: Bucharest (10 daily; 1hr 30min–2hr 40min); Câmpulung Muscel (4 daily; 1hr 55min–2hr 10min); Curtea de Argeş (5 daily; 45min–1hr); Goleşti (10 daily; 15min); Titu (10 daily; 55min–1hr 30min).

Ploieşti to: Braşov (every 30min–1hr; 2hr 10min–3hr 20min); Bucharest (every 20min–1hr; 40min–1hr 35min); Iaşi (5 daily; 6hr); Slănic Prahova (4 daily; 1hr 20min–2hr); Suceava (8 daily; 5hr 30min–6hr); Târgovişte (4 daily; 1hr 40min); Vălenii de Munte (4 daily; 1hr 10min).

Râmnicu Vâlcea to: Călimăneşti (10 daily; 20–40min); Craiova (3 daily; 2hr); Piatra Olt (10 daily; 1hr 10min–2hr 40min); Podu Olt (5 daily; 2hr 20min–3hr); Sibiu (6 daily; 2hr–3hr 40min).

Târgovişte to: Bucharest (5 daily; 1hr 20min–2hr); Ploieşti (4 daily; 1hr 30min–1hr 50min); Titu (8 daily; 30–45min).

Târgu Jiu to: Filiaşi (10 daily; 1–2hr); Petroşani (8 daily; 1hr 10min–1hr 45min); Simeria (4 daily; 2hr 50min–3hr 45min); Subcetate (3 daily; 2hr 20min–3hr 10min).

Titu to: Târgovişte (9 daily; 30–45min).

Buses and maxitaxis

Călimăneşti to: Cluj (5 daily); Sibiu (10 daily); Voineasa (6 daily).

Câmpina to: Bucharest (every 2 hours); Sinaia (every 15min); Ploieşti (every 15min).

Câmpulung to: Braşov (5 daily); Bucharest (8 daily); Curtea de Argeş (1 daily); Lereşti (hourly); Piteşti (hourly); Ploieşti (2 daily); Râmnicu Vâlcea (2 daily); Rucar (8 daily, weekends 5 daily); Târgovişte (2 daily).

Craiova to: Băile Herculane (4 daily); Bucharest (hourly), Calafat (12 daily); Drobeta-Turnu Severin (6 daily); Piteşti (every 45min); Râmnicu Vâlcea (8 daily); Târgu Jiu (10 daily); Timişoara (8 daily).

Curtea de Argeş to: Arefu (up to 12 daily); Bucharest (hourly); Câmpulung (1 daily); Râmnicu Vâlcea (2 daily).

Drobeta-Turnu Severin to: Baile Herculane (5 daily); Craiova (6 daily); Orşova (10 daily); Râmnicu Vâlcea (3 daily); Târgu Jiu (3 daily); Timişoara (5 daily).

Giurgiu to: Bucharest (every 30min).

Horezu to: Bistriţa monastery (3 daily); Bucharest (3 daily); Hateg (4 daily); Horez monastery (5 daily); Râmnicu Vâlcea (hourly); Sibiu (5 daily); Târgu Jiu (5 daily).

Piteşti to: Braşov (2 daily); Bucharest (every 30min); Câmpulung (hourly); Craiova (3 daily); Gaieşti (every 45min); Râmnicu Vâlcea (every 45min); Târgovişte (1 daily); Târgu Jiu (2 daily).

Ploieşti to: Breaza (every 30–45min); Bucharest (every 30min); Câmpulung (2 daily); Sinaia (every 30–45min); Slanic Prahova (up to 4 daily); Târgovişte (every 45–60min).

Râmnicu Vâlcea to: Bistriţa monastery (6 daily Mon–Fri, 3 daily Sat–Sun); Bucharest (hourly); Câmpulung (3 daily); Cluj (8 daily); Cozia (hourly); Craiova (7 daily); Curtea de Argeş (7 daily); Drobeta-Turnu Severin (3 daily); Horezu (hourly); Piteşti (every 45min); Sibiu (hourly); Târgovişte (1 daily); Târgu Jiu (5 daily); Timişoara (4 daily); Voineasa (3 daily).

Târgovişte to: Braşov (4 daily); Bucharest (hourly); Câmpulung (4 daily); Piteşti (1 daily); Ploieşti (every 45–60min); Sinaia (3 daily).

Târgu Jiu to: Baia de Aramă (3 daily); Baia de Fier (3 daily); Bucharest (6 daily); Cluj (7 daily); Craiova (hourly); Drobeta-Turnu Severin (3 daily); Horezu (12 daily); Petroşani (7 daily); Piteşti (5 daily); Polovragi (6 daily); Râmnicu Vâlcea (4 daily); Sibiu (4 daily); Timişoara (6 daily); Tismana (5 daily).

International trains

Craiova to: Belgrade (1 daily; 9hr 45min); Budapest (1 daily; 13hr).

Drobeta-Turnu Severin to: Belgrade (1 daily; 8hr).

Giurgiu Nord to: Istanbul (1 daily; 16hr); Kiev (1 daily; 29hr); Moscow (1 daily; 42hr); Ruse (4 daily; 30min); Sofia (2 daily; 7hr 30min–8hr 15min); Thessaloniki (1 daily; 15hr 30min).

International ferries

Călăraşi to: Silistra, Bulgaria (6 daily).

Calafat to: Vidin, Bulgaria (hourly 5.30am–midnight daily; 24hr in summer, with crossings at least every 3 hours overnight).

Transylvania

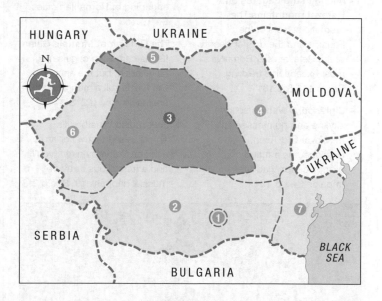

CHAPTER 3 # Highlights

✳ **Braşov** Wander the beautiful Baroque streets and medieval ramparts of Braşov's Old Town. See p.134

✳ **Wildlife-watching in the Carpathians** Take to the woods on the trail of the brown bear, lynx, chamois and wolf. See p.145

✳ **Hiking in the Făgăraş and Retezat mountains** The dramatic schists of the Făgăraş and the quieter beauty of the Retezat offer Romania's most exceptional trekking. See p.146 & p.181

✳ **Sighişoara** With its spiky skyline and quintessentially medieval Old Town, Sighişoara is a fitting birthplace for Vlad the Impaler. See p.151

✳ **Saxon fortified churches** Biertan's Saxon church is the most prominent of the massive and austerely fortified churches that dominate many of the region's villages. See p.156

✳ **Sibiu** With its gorgeous cobbled squares, outstanding museums and colourful festivals, this is the most engaging of Romanian cities. See p.158

✳ **The Girl Fair at Muntele Găina** Its matchmaking origins may have faded, but the annual Girl Fair is still a magnificent spectacle. See p.213

✳ **Folk music** Whether it's an organized festival or an average Saturday night, you'll find a marvellous array of musical happenings. See p.218

▲ Piaţa Sfatului, Braşov

Transylvania

Thanks to Bram Stoker and Hollywood, **Transylvania** (from the Latin for "beyond the forest") is famed as the homeland of Dracula, a mountainous place where storms lash medieval hamlets, while wolves – or werewolves – howl from the surrounding woods. The fictitious image is accurate up to a point: the scenery is breathtakingly dramatic, especially in the Prahova valley, the Turda and Bicaz gorges and around the high passes; there are spooky Gothic citadels, around Braşov and at Sibiu, Sighişoara and Bran; and there was a Vlad, born in Sighişoara, who earned the grim nickname "The Impaler" and later became known as **Dracula** (see p.403).

But the Dracula image is just one element of Transylvania, whose near 100,000 square kilometres take in alpine meadows and peaks, caves and dense forests sheltering bears and wild boar, and lowland valleys where buffalo cool off in the rivers. The **population** is an ethnic jigsaw of Romanians, Magyars, Germans and Gypsies, among others, formed over centuries of migration and colonization. Most Hungarians view Erdély ("the forest land", their name for Transylvania) as a land first settled by them but "stolen" in 1920 (with the signing of the Trianon Treaty) by the Romanians, who continue to oppress some two million Magyars. Romanians, who call it Ardeal, assert that they appeared first in Transylvania and that for centuries it was the Magyar minority who oppressed them. Since 1920, the Romanian majority has been boosted by peasants brought in from Moldavia and Wallachia to form a new industrial proletariat. The revolution of 1989 enabled Transylvania's German population to return to their ancestral homeland, leaving the Hungarians as the region's main minority group. Meanwhile, Transylvania's Gypsies (Ţigani) still go their own way, largely unconcerned by prejudice against them. The result is an intoxicating brew of characters, customs and places that is best taken in slowly.

For the visitor, most striking of all are the *Stuhls*, the former seats of Saxon power, with their medieval streets, defensive towers and fortified churches. **Sighişoara**, the most picturesque, is their greatest legacy and an ideal introduction to Transylvania, followed by the citadels and churches of **Braşov** and **Sibiu**, and smaller settlements like **Cisnădioara**, **Hărman**, **Prejmer**, **Viscri** and **Biertan**. The other highlight of this southeastern corner is the castle at **Bran**, which looks just how a vampire count's castle should: a grim facade, perched high on a rock bluff, its turrets and ramparts rising in tiers against a dramatic mountain background. Travelling west, routes towards the Banat and Hungary pass through southwestern Transylvania, a region of peaks and moorland peppered with the citadels of the Dacians, rulers of much of Romania before the Roman conquest. To the north and east, Transylvania has a more Hungarian flavour: cities such as **Cluj** and **Târgu Mureş** have a strong Magyar influence, while **Miercurea Ciuc**

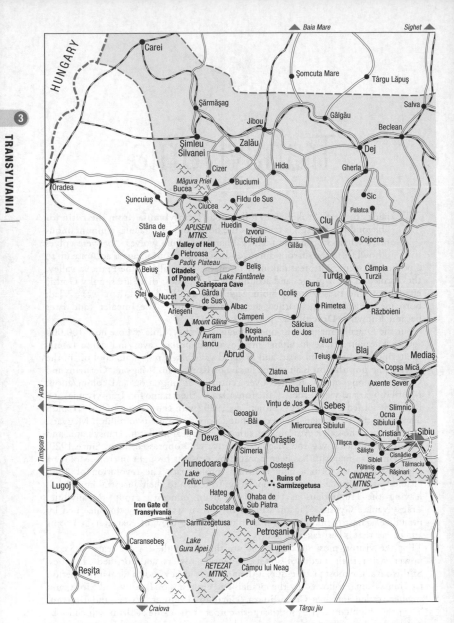

and **Sfântu Gheorghe** are the cultural centres of the Székely, a closely related ethnic group. The **Carpathian mountains** are never far away in Transylvania, and for anyone fond of walking this is one of the most beautiful, least exploited regions in Europe. **Hikes** to stunning places in the Făgăraş, Apuseni and Retezat

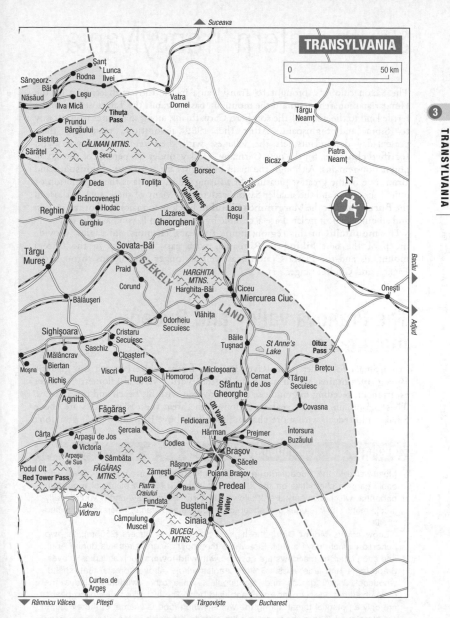

▲ Suceava

TRANSYLVANIA

0   50 km

Sanţ
Lunca
Rodna   Ilvei
Sângeorz-
Băi
Leşu
Năsăud
Ilva Mică
Vatra
Dornei
Târgu
Neamţ
Prundu
Bârgăului
Tihuţa
Pass
Bistriţa   CĂLIMAN MTNS.
Sărăţel
Secu
Borsec
Bicaz
Piatra
Neamţ
Deda
Topliţa
Upper Mureş Valley
Brâncoveneşti
Reghin   Hodac
Gurghiu
Lăzarea
Gheorgheni
Lacu
Roşu
Târgu
Mureş
Sovata-Băi
Praid
SZÉKELY
HARGHITA
MTNS.
Corund
Harghita-Băi
Bălăuşeri
Ciceu
Miercurea Ciuc
Oneşti
Vlăhiţa
LAND
Odorheiu
Secuiesc
Sighişoara
Cristaru
Secuiesc
Băile
Tuşnad
St Anne's
Lake
Oituz
Pass
Mălâncrav
Saschiz
Cloaşterf
Bretcu
Moşna
Biertan
Viscri
Rupea
Homorod
Micloşoara
Cernat
de Jos
Târgu
Secuiesc
Richiş
Sfântu
Gheorghe
Agnita
Covasna
Făgăraş
Feldioara
Olt Valley
Cârţa
Arpaşu de Jos
Şercaia
Hărman
Prejmer
Întorsura
Buzăului
Victoria
Codlea
Arpaşu
de Sus
Sâmbăta
Podul Olt
FĂGĂRAŞ
MTNS.
Râşnov
Braşov
Săcele
Red Tower Pass
Zărneşti
Poiana Braşov
Piatra
Craiului
Bran
Predeal
Lake
Vidraru
Fundata
Buşteni
Câmpulung
Muscel
Sinaia
Prahova Valley
BUCEGI
MTNS.
Curtea de
Argeş

▼ Râmnicu Vâlcea   ▼ Piteşti   ▼ Târgovişte   ▼ Bucharest

N

Bacău ▶

Adjud ▶

ranges can last several days, but it's perfectly feasible to make briefer yet equally dramatic forays into the Piatra Craiului or Bucegi mountains, or to one of Transylvania's many spectacular gorges.

Southeastern Transylvania

The Saxon colonists, brought to Transylvania in the thirteenth century by the Hungarian monarchy to guard the mountain passes against the Tatars, settled in the fertile land to the north of the southern Carpathians, along the routes from Braşov to Sibiu and Sighişoara. After the 1989 revolution, many of their present-day descendants left the villages, with their regimented layouts and **fortified churches**, for the new Germany – today, under ten percent of the Saxon population remains. Although the main highlights are at **Braşov**, **Sighişoara** and **Bran**, one of the greatest pleasures of visiting Transylvania is the exploration of quiet backwaters and the smaller Saxon settlements. Many of these, such as those in the **Burzenland** or the **Mărginimea Sibiului**, lie close to major road or rail routes, and all but the most isolated are accessible by bus or train if you have the time.

The **mountains** in this region, home to bears, chamois and eagles, provide much of the best **hiking** in Romania, with easy day-walks in the Bucegi mountains and the Piatra Craiului, as well as longer expeditions through the Făgăraş and Cindrel ranges.

The Prahova valley and Bucegi mountains

From Sinaia to Predeal, the River Prahova froths white beneath the gigantic **Bucegi mountains**, which overhang Buşteni with a vertical kilometre of sheer escarpment, receding in grandiose slopes covered with fir, beech and rowan trees. These mountains are the real attraction of the area: the easiest walks are above Sinaia and Predeal, with more challenging hikes above Buşteni. Even if you don't

---

Hiking in the Bucegi mountains

Most walks in the **Bucegi mountains** (Munţii Bucegi) are easy day-hikes, with cable cars an alternative on the steeper sections. There are plenty of **mountain cabanas**, which in theory aren't allowed to turn hikers away, and if you're really stuck, maps show refuges and sheepfolds (*refugiu* and *stână*), where you may find shelter.

Snow covers **Mount Omu**, the highest point of the Bucegi (2505m), for two hundred or more days a year. Elsewhere the snow generally retreats during April, and soon after the meadows are covered with **wildflowers** such as ladies' gloves, grape-ferns and edelweiss. Golden eagles circle above forests that shelter woodcock, hazel grouse and nightingales, while other **wildlife** includes the Carpathian red deer (around Bran) and wild boar. The last, like wolves and bears, are only a potential threat during the winter (when food is scarce) or if their litters are threatened. Above the forest, on the cliffs to the north of the massif, you may well see chamois.

A good hiking **map** is *Five Mountains from the Carpathians Bend* (also covering the Piatra Craiului – see p.144), which has English-language notes. Otherwise, the Romanian-language **maps** of the mountains shouldn't be hard to understand if you refer to the vocabulary on p.425.

stop off to hike in the range (or ride up by cable car), the valley's upper reaches are unforgettable: sit on the west side of the train for the best views.

The stunning **Prahova valley**, dotted with fantastic caves and other karstic phenomena, is shadowed by the DN1 (E60) highway and the Bucharest–Braşov **railway**: express services take three hours to Braşov, stopping en route at Ploieşti (see p.93) and the resorts of **Sinaia**, in northern Wallachia, and **Predeal**, in Transylvania proper. Slower trains stop at the smaller towns and villages – change at either Sinaia or Predeal for **Buşteni**, served by Personals and some Accelerats. The DN1 has been largely modernized, the railway is being largely rebuilt, and construction of a motorway to link Bucharest, Braşov, Cluj and Oradea is under way, if delayed by funding issues. Frequent local buses and maxitaxis link Ploieşti, Sinaia, Buşteni and Azuga.

Sinaia

SINAIA, 122km from Bucharest, was the preserve of hermits and shepherds until King Carol I built his summer home, Peleş Castle. Once an exclusive aristocratic resort, it is nowadays full of holidaymakers here to walk or ski in the dramatic **Bucegi mountains**. Though actually in the province of Wallachia, it has much in common with the neighbouring Transylvanian towns and is included in this chapter for convenience.

Arrival and information

Steps lead up from Sinaia **train station** to the main street, B-dul Carol I; turning left here takes you through the town centre to the **tourist information centre** (with free internet access), in front of the town hall at B-dul Carol I 47 (Mon–Fri 8.30am–4.30pm; ☏0244/315 656, ✉contact@infosinaia.ro). Plentiful **buses** and **maxitaxis** between Bucharest, Sinaia, Braşov and nearby towns run along Strada Gării, stopping at the station; local **minibuses** run from B-dul Carol I up to the hillside areas of Platoul Izvor and Furnica. There's an hourly service (8.40am–6.40pm, Tues from 11.40am) to the *telegondola* and the *Taverna Sârbului* restaurant (see p.130) and occasionally all the way to Cota 1400, the roadhead at the mid-station of the Bucegi cable car.

Ski gear can be bought or rented at Snow, by the cable-car terminal at Str. Cuza Vodă 2 (daily 9am–6pm; ⊛www.snow-sinaia.ro). The Sinaia Forever **festival** takes place on the last weekend of September.

Accommodation

The town is well served with **hotels**, many catering to package tourists. The *El Dorado* **youth hostel**, at Str. Avram Iancu 14 (☏0244/312 667; ❶), has utilitarian rooms (some with bathroom and TV). There are also a few **villas** inside Peleş Park (☏0244/310 353; ❹–❺), while touts at the station and on the way into town offer **private rooms** (❶) – before agreeing to anything, though, insist on knowing the exact location, as some are far from the centre. The *Izvorul Rece* **campsite** is south of Sinaia at km118 (☏0244/314 881, ⊛www.motelizvorulrece.ro). The **cabanas** at the *Piscu Câinelui* (☏0244/315 492; ❶) and *Schiorilor* (☏0244/313 655, ⊛www .cabana-schiori.ro; ❶) at Drumul Cotei 7 are small but right on the edge of town (the latter's restaurant is also recommended, especially for the *ciorbă de burta*).

Anda B-dul Carol I 30 ☏0244/306 020, ⊛www.hotelanda.ro. Smaller than the town's other ski hotels, this is a polished, modern and comfortable place. Pleasant wine-cellar restaurant, too. ❻

Caraiman B-dul Carol I 4, in Dimitrie Ghica Park ☏0244/311 542, ✉palace@rdslink.ro. Sinaia's first hotel, opened in 1881, is a decent enough place, even if the rooms are a little cramped and the furnishings somewhat dated. ❹

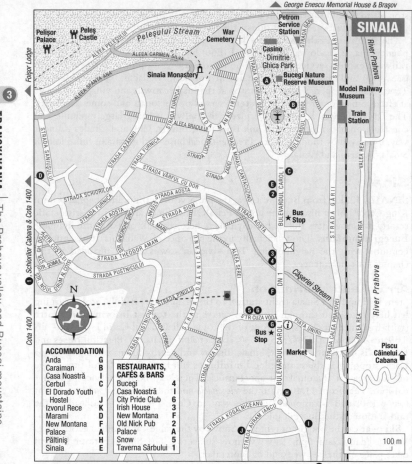

▲ George Enescu Memorial House & Braşov

SINAIA

ACCOMMODATION
Anda	G
Caraiman	B
Casa Noastră	I
Cerbul	C
El Dorado Youth Hostel	J
Izvorul Rece	K
Marami	D
New Montana	F
Palace	A
Păltiniş	H
Sinaia	E

RESTAURANTS, CAFÉS & BARS
Bucegi	4
Casa Noastră	I
City Pride Club	6
Irish House	3
New Montana	F
Old Nick Pub	2
Palace	A
Snow	5
Taverna Sârbului	1

▼ **K**, Ploieşti & Bucharest

Casa Noastră B-dul Republicii 9 ☎0244/314 556, ⓦwww.casanoastrasinaia.ro. Odd-looking, narrow wooden high-rise, with simple wood-furnished rooms, including triples and quads. Breakfast is extra. ❸

Cerbul B-dul Carol I 19 ☎0244/312 391, ⓦwww.cerbul.ro. Good-value hotel with modern (if not particularly stylish) rooms, some with shared showers. Breakfast is extra. ❹

Marami Str. Furnica 52 ☎0244/315 560, ⓦwww.marami.ro. One of Sinaia's more welcoming hotels, this has large, well-equipped rooms, each furnished in a different colour. Sauna, jacuzzi, gym and a very good bar-pizzeria. ❹

New Montana B-dul Carol I 24 ☎0244/312 751, ⓦwww.newmontana.ro. This large hotel on the main street is as slick as you'd expect from a hotel

catering in the main to big ski groups, with pool, sauna and gym. ❻

Palace Str. Octavian Goga 4 ☎0244/312 051, ⓔpalace@rdslink.ro. In the park by the casino, this *belle époque* gem has been well modernized while retaining its charm. ❻–❼

Păltiniş B-dul Carol I 67 ☎0244/314 651, ⓦwww.hotelpaltinis.ro. Hulking grey neo-Brâncovenesc pile atop two floors of treatment rooms; rooms with shared and private bathroom. Breakfast is extra. ❷–❸

Sinaia B-dul Carol I 8 ☎0244/302 900, ⓦwww.hotelsinaia.ro. Along with the *New Montana*, this is the town's main ski hotel; it has a swimming pool, gym and sauna, and some rooms have balconies. ❼

The Town

Sinaia's **train station** is a historical site in itself; here, the Iron Guard murdered the Liberal leader Ion Duca in 1933, just three weeks after he had taken office as prime minister. In the original station building, immediately to the north, is a British-run model railway exhibition (daily 10am–6pm; €1.50), popular with families. From here, steps lead to **Dimitrie Ghica Park**, home to red squirrels and several fine neo-Brâncovenesc buildings, as well as a portakabin housing the Bucegi Nature Reserve Museum (daily 9am–5pm; €1), offering a limited overview of the mountains' flora and fauna. Beyond the park, a World War I military cemetery also houses a poetic **memorial** to the US airmen killed over Romania in World War II; a footpath leads off Str. Mănăstirii up to **Sinaia Monastery** (€1 at busy times), founded by Prince Mihai Catacuzino in 1690, following a pilgrimage to Mount Sinai. His **Old Church** (Biserica Veche), decorated with a fine *Last Judgement* soon after it was built, is not the one before you as you enter, but is hidden through a passageway to the left. The **Great Church** (Biserica Mare), added in 1846, is distinguished by a fine Brâncovenesc-style porch and an unusual green enamel belt with a twisted rope motif encircling the building. Four of the five fresco portraits on the inside west wall, painted by the Dane Aage Exner in 1903, are of King Carol I, Queen Elisabeta, their youngest daughter Maria, and Cantacuzino himself. There are currently around a dozen monks here.

Just behind the monastery, a long cobbled path lined with souvenir stalls leads to one of Romania's most popular and rewarding sights, **Peleş Castle** (Muzeul National Peleş; Wed 11am–5pm, Thurs–Sun 9am–5pm; €4, €10 for use of camera). Set in a large park landscaped in the English fashion, and named after the Peleş stream which flows nearby, the castle outwardly resembles a Bavarian Schloss. Built between 1875 and 1883 for Carol I, and largely decorated by his eccentric wife Elisabeta (better known as the popular novelist Carmen Sylva), it contains 160 rooms, richly done out in ebony, mother of pearl, walnut and leather – all totally alien to the traditional styles of Romanian art – and stuffed solid with antiques and copies of paintings housed in Bucharest's National Art Museum. How a man of such reputedly austere tastes as Carol managed to live here is something of a mystery, and indeed it hasn't been lived in since his death in 1914. Following the monarchy's demise, Peleş was opened to the public in 1953, with a temporary interruption when the Ceauşescus appropriated it as a "state palace". In 2008 the castle was finally handed back to the king, reuniting Mihai with his birthplace and childhood home; it will remain open to visitors, as will Pelişor, which is still state property.

To **visit the castle**, follow signs to a ticket window and then to the separate entry for foreigners. You then wait in the entry hall for a guide to take you on a 45-minute tour of eighteen rooms on the ground floor, and the newly opened Imperial Suite, decorated for Kaiser Franz Josef's visit in 1896. Note that the only toilets are by the path up to the castle.

The first room (the Reception Hall) is startling, awash with fantastic walnut carvings, alabaster reliefs and French tapestries, to say nothing of the 16m-high glass ceiling that opens up in summer. You continue through several more extravagantly decorated rooms, including the Florentine Hall, with kitschy Murano chandeliers; a Moorish hall based on the Alhambra and containing a Carrera marble fountain; and the Louis XIV room (with paintings by a young Gustav Klimt) housing Romania's first cinema. A short walk up the hill stands **Pelişor Palace** (same hours and price), built between 1899 and 1903 for Ferdinand and Marie, Carol I's heirs. Although its exterior is also in the German Renaissance style, the interior is far more restrained and mostly Art Nouveau. The one exception is the dazzling Gold Room, covered in 24-carat stucco gold leaf and home to a Tiffany lamp from Chicago. Although Ceaușescu used Pelișor Palace to host foreign dignitaries such as Colonel Gadaffi, he much preferred the seclusion of the **Foişor Lodge**, a little above Pelișor. Finished in 1878, it was home to Queen Elisabeta from 1914, and then to Prince Carol (later King Carol II) and Princess Helen from 1921; here, Carol met the Jewish Magda Lupescu, who for thirty years remained his mistress and the power behind the throne, outraging Romanian society, which tended towards anti-Semitism. The lodge is now used for government protocol, but the park is open to the public (Wed–Sun 9am–4pm).

Across the DN1 from the lower gate of the Peleș park, signs lead to the **George Enescu Memorial House** (Tues–Sun 10am–5pm; €2; ⓦ www.casa-enescu.ro), in Cumpătu, 2km north of the town centre. Known as the **Vila Luminiş** (Sunshine House), it was built for the great composer-violinist in 1921–6 in the style of a *conac* (Turkish administrator's house); he spent his summers here until 1946, when he left the country for good. The ground floor contains Oriental, Biedermeyer and traditional Romanian furnishings, and Enescu's Ibert piano; upstairs are his simple bedroom (as well as student Yehudi Menuhin's more conventional room) and his workroom, looking west to the peaks of the Bucegi, and home to photos, posters and scores of his works. Tours of Enescu's house are accompanied by his lushly romantic music, CDs of which are for sale.

Eating and drinking

The best and most interesting **food** in Sinaia, as long as you're not vegetarian, is at the *Taverna Sârbului*, ten minutes north by car (or hourly minibus – see p.127) en route to Cota 1400 at Calea Codrului 39. This hugely popular and convivial Serbian restaurant dishes up gargantuan portions of meat-heavy cuisine, typically *čorba pasulj* (bean soup with smoked meat), *čevapi* (grilled rissoles of meat) and *pljeskavica* (oversized burger). Otherwise, in the centre of town, the *Bucegi* at B-dul Carol I 22 has great pizza, game (roast bear, boar and venison) and excellent vegetarian choices. Next door, the *Irish House* (daily 8am–midnight) has a predict-able slant to its dishes, namely Dublin chicken's liver, Irish breakfast and "Irish salad", as well as Romanian dishes, pizza and pasta. Other decent options are *Snow* (next to the shop of the same name – see p.127), an après-ski-type place doling out big bowls of steaming soup and mixed grills, and to the south of the centre, the *Casa Noastră* hotel has excellent *crama* and *terasa*, although the folk music in the huge main restaurant is pretty cheesy. Other hotels offering good **dining** include the *Palace* and *New Montana*.

For a **drink**, most people congregate at *Snow*, the *Irish House* or the *Old Nick Pub*, at B-dul Carol I 22a. The *City Pride Club*, below *Snow* at B-dul Carol I 24 (ⓦ www .cityprideclub.ro), has DJs from 10pm.

Around Sinaia

From a terminal on Str. Cuza Vodă, a **cable car** (*telecabina*; summer Tues–Sun 8.30am–5pm; €4 single, €7 return) whisks you to an altitude of 1400m (**Cota 1400**) at the roadhead halfway up the hill, site of a hotel and numerous cabanas. From here, another cable car (same hours; €7 single from Sinaia, €13 return) runs to **Cota 2000**, and a chairlift (Wed–Mon 9am–5pm) to **Cota 1950**, both just a five-minute walk from the *Miorița* cabana (☎0244/312 299; ❶) on Mount Furnica. To the south, below Cota 1950, is the *Valea Dorului* cabana (☎0244/313 531; ❶), from where there's a three-hour circular walk to the beautiful **Lacuri tarns**, following a path marked with yellow crosses (outwards) and red stripes (returning). Alternatively, you can reach Cota 1400 with the new **telegondola** from Cota 998, 150m above the *Taverna Sârbeasca* (summer 9am–7pm; spring/autumn 9am–6pm;

winter 8.30am–5pm; Tues from noon all year; €2.30/4 single/return); it carries mountain bikes, and is reached by an hourly minibus (see p.127).

Heading north from Mount Furnica, it's an attractive and easy 45-minute walk to the **Piatra Arsă cabana**. Here, blue triangles lead down to Buşteni (2hr) via **La Scari**, a spectacular "stairway" hewn into rock, while another path (marked with blue stripes) drops westwards into the central depression of the Bucegi, reaching the *Peştera* hotel (℡0372/378 372, ⓦwww.pestera.ro ❹) and monastery in about an hour (for routes north from *Peştera*, see p.133). Just west of the *hotel*, past the **Peştera Ialomiţa** – a 400m-long cave with a walkway but no lighting (bring a flashlight) – an unmarked path leads up through the Batrâna valley past several waterfalls, the "Gorge of the Bear" and two natural bridges. Half an hour to the south lies the *Padina* cabana (℡0726/576 868, ⓦwww.cabana-padina.ro; ❶), from where a rough road continues past more caves and gorges to a camping spot near **Lake Bolboci**, eventually emerging from the Izvorasu valley just south of Sinaia.

Buşteni

BUŞTENI, 10km up the valley from Sinaia, is a small, bustling resort overshadowed by the sheer peaks of Caraiman (2384m) and Coştila (2490m), separated from each other by the dark Alba ravine and Europe's highest conglomerate cliffs. Caraiman is marked by a huge cross (a 1920s war memorial), and Coştila by a TV tower that looks like a space rocket. Buşteni is a good base for walking in the mountains to east and west, but there's nothing much in the town itself, other than a church founded by Carol I and Queen Elisabeta in 1889, the house of writer **Cezar Petrescu** (1892–1961), in a handsome villa north of town on Str. Petrescu, and the **Cantacuzino Castle**, less than 1km east of the station on Str.Zamora. This was built in 1911 by Prince Gheorghe Cantacuzino, known as "The Nabob" because of his fabulous wealth, and was recently restituted to his heirs, who sold it to a consortium which plans to develop a Swiss-style resort, with five-star hotel, aquapark and spa (ⓦwww.cantacuzinocastle.ro); at the moment all that's open is the *Nababu Café* (10am–4pm daily).

Practicalities

The **train station** is in the centre of town on the DN1, from where it's just a few hundred metres south to a clutch of **hotels**, including the *Caraiman* at B-dul Libertăţii 89 (℡0244/320 156; ❸), which has small but decent rooms, including triples and quads. Another couple of hundred metres south and to the right at the country's oldest paper mill is the *Silva* at Str. Telecabiniei 36 (℡0244/321 412, ⓦwww.hotelsilva.ro; ❸–❺), a large package tourist place with two- and three-star rooms. Back down on the same road, at no. 22 (it's set back from the road and has no sign), the *Villa Laura* guesthouse (℡0241/606 136, ⓔrezervari @paradistours.ro; ❸) has clean and comfortable en-suite double rooms, some with little kitchen areas; there are also rooms at no. 26. North of the station, at B-dul Libertăţii 153, the conspicuous *Hotel Alexandros* (℡0244/320 138, ⓦwww.hotel-alexandros.ro; ❹–❺) is another comfortable place. The friendly and informal *Motel Maximilian* is across the tracks to the southeast (in the Zamora quarter), at Str. Pescariei 8 (℡0244/323 297; ❶); it's most easily reached by car (take the first turning on the left south of Str. Telecabinei). It's also worth enquiring at the **tourist agency** (daily 10am–6pm; ℡0244/320 027) at B-dul Libertăţii 202, about **villas** and **private rooms** (❶); you'll also see *Oferim cazare* signs on houses that offer accommodation.

The best of a rather poor bunch of **restaurants** is *Bistro Le Petit Gourmand*, a friendly little place opposite the *Caraiman* serving grills, pasta and salads – the

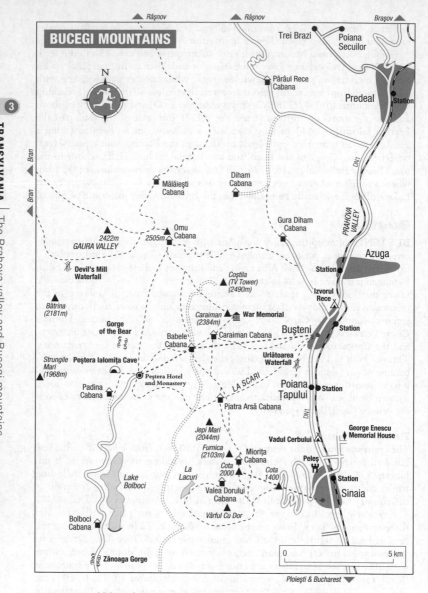

BUCEGI MOUNTAINS

Răşnov · Răşnov · Braşov
Trei Brazi · Poiana Seculor
Pârâul Rece Cabana
Predeal · Station
N
Mălăieşti Cabana
Diham Cabana
Gura Diham Cabana
PRAHOVA VALLEY
2422m GAURA VALLEY · Omu Cabana · 2505m
Azuga · Station
Devil's Mill Waterfall
Coştila (TV Tower) (2490m)
Izvorul Rece
Bătrina (2181m)
Caraiman (2384m) · War Memorial · Buşteni · Station
Gorge of the Bear
Babele Cabana · Caraiman Cabana
Strungile Mari (1968m) · Peştera Ialomiţa Cave
Urlătoarea Waterfall
Peştera Hotel and Monastery
Padina Cabana
Poiana Ţapului · Station
LA SCĂRI
Piatra Arsă Cabana
Jepi Mari (2044m)
Furnica (2103m) · Miorita Cabana
Vadul Cerbului
George Enescu Memorial House
La Lacuri · Cota 2000 · Cota 1400
Peleş
Lake Bolboci
Valea Dorului Cabana
Station · Sinaia
Vârful Cu Dor
Bolboci Cabana
Zănoaga Gorge
0   5 km
Ploieşti & Bucharest

Caraiman itself has the cosy *Rustic* restaurant, with a similar menu plus pizza.
There are lots of snack places by the cable-car terminal, and beer and wi-fi at *Pub 39*, at Str. Libertăţii 39.

Around Buşteni

From the *Hotel Silva*, an easy path marked with red dots leads to the **Urlătoarea waterfall** and back to the road at **Poiana Ţapului** (2hr). A harder footpath, marked with blue crosses, and a **cable car** (Wed–Mon 8.30am–3.45pm in summer; €7 each way) take you 1235m up the Jepi valley to the **cabanas** at *Caraiman* (☎0734/659 590; ❶) and *Babele* (☎0723/191 265; ❶). The latter offers a panoramic view, and is only five minutes' walk from an impressive skull-like rock formation, the **Babele Sphinx**. From here, you can walk (1hr) or ride the cable car (daily 8am–4pm) down to the *Peştera* hotel and monastery (see p.131). North of *Babele*, a path marked by yellow stripes leads to **Mount Omu** (4hr), also reached by a blue-striped path up the Ialomiţa valley from *Peştera* (1–2hr). There's a small hut here (☎0244/320 677; closed winter), without running water.

Though completely cloudless days are rare in the vicinity of **Mount Omu**, it is possible to see the **Burzenland** to the north, the ridge of the Piatra Craiului to the west and the **Făgăraş range** beyond. From Omu, a path marked with red stripes descends a glacial valley past eroded rock "chimneys" to the **Mălăieşti** chalet (2–3hr); two other paths lead down to **Bran** in about six hours – the route indicated by yellow triangles is easier going, while the path marked with red crosses drops down the superb Gaura valley past the **Cascada Moara Dracului** ("Devil's Mill Waterfall"), a fitting approach to "Dracula's Castle" in the village below.

There's more accommodation in **AZUGA**, a couple of kilometres north of Buşteni, which is known mainly for its brewery and bottle factory but also has a couple of ski runs. It's also the location of the **Rhein Azuga Cellar**, at Str. Independenţei 24, owned by the British company Halewood, who make wine in the Dealu Mare region just south of the Prahova Valley. They offer wine-tasting sessions along with a tour of the cellars (9am–5pm; €5); there's a shop here plus the super *Pensiunea Rhein*, with restful, rustically styled rooms (☎0244/326 560, Ⓦwww.halewood.com.ro; ❹). Otherwise, there's the *Hotel Azuga*, on the main DN1 at Str. Victoriei 87 (☎0744/966 188; ❹); the *Pensiunea Căprioara*, at Str. Valea Azugii 38 (☎0244/326 310; ❷), and *Pensiunea Flora*, at Str. Florilor 50 (☎0722/354 718; ❷).

Predeal

PREDEAL is further from the more spectacular peaks that dominate Sinaia and Buşteni to the south, but is a popular centre for winter sports and easy strolls. There's a wide range of **accommodation**, which can be booked through the **tourist office** (Mon–Fri 8am–4pm, Sat & Sun 9am–2pm; ☎0268/455 330, Ⓦwww.predeal.ro) in a striking modern building outside the train station, itself a decent piece of communist modernism. There's a good chance that you'll be offered a room while near the station. The best option in the centre is the *Carmen*, just south of the station at B-dul Săulescu 121 (☎0268/456 517, Ⓦwww .carmen-ana.ro; ❷–❸); although a little unkempt externally, the rooms are tidy and brightly furnished. There are several other options further north, on Str. Trei Brazi, the road leading up to the mountainside *Trei Brazi* cabana (see p.134); the first of these is the *Orizont* (☎0268/455 150, Ⓦwww.hotelorizont.ro; ❹), a good modern hotel with a pool, sauna and tennis courts. Better still are the *Relax Comfort Suites* (☎0268/455 795, Ⓦwww.predealcomfort-suites.ro; ❼) 500m up the hill, whose rooms come with wrought-iron furnishings and huge corner baths. Moving further up, the *Vila Select* (☎0268/456 579, Ⓦwww.vila-select.ro; ❸) makes for a quiet, pleasant stopover. The welcoming *Fulg de Nea* cabana at Str. Teleferic 1 (☎0268/456 089, Ⓦfulgdenea.com; ❷), at the foot of the Clăbucet chairlift, has rudimentary, but perfectly acceptable, accommodation.

A couple of half-decent **restaurants** are *Casa Ana*, B-dul Săulescu 2 bis, and *Hanul Domnitorilor*, Str. Libertăţii 90, both serving Italian food. The 24-hour Casa Ana store at B-dul Săulescu 127 has good supplies for hiking. The best **bar** in town is at the *Fulg de Nea*; in a similar vein there's the *Guinness Pub* at B-dul Săulescu 32. **Ski equipment** can be rented at the *Fulg de Nea* (which also has mountain bikes – €15/day), or the adjacent Clăbucet-Sosire chairlift terminal.

Around Predeal

There's good **walking** in these hills, not as dramatic as in the Bucegi but with fine views to the high peaks and cliffs, and plenty of **cabanas** to aim for. *Gârbova* (☎0244/360 723, ⓦwww.cabanagirbova.ro; ❶) and *Susai* (☎0268/457 204; ❶) are within a few kilometres of the Clăbucet-Plecare chairlift. In the foothills of the Bucegi massif, northwest of Predeal, are the hotel-like *Trei Brazi*, 5km west of Predeal at the top of Str. Trei Brazi (☎0244/455 150; ❹); the *Poiana Secuilor* (☎0745/339 694; ❶), a short walk east; and the *Pârâu Rece* complex, 2km west of *Trei Brazi* just off the Predeal–Râșnov road, which also has camping (☎0268/456 491; ❶). The *Diham* cabana (☎0726/203 262, ⓦwww.diham.ro; ❶) is higher up and further south, with a slalom run nearby.

Brașov

The medieval Saxons, with an eye for trade and invasion routes, sited their largest settlements within a day's journey of the Carpathian passes. One of the best placed, **BRAȘOV** (Kronstadt to the Saxons and Brassó to the Hungarians), grew prosperous and fortified as a result, and for many centuries its Saxons constituted an elite whose economic power long outlasted its feudal privileges. During the 1960s, the communist regime drafted thousands of Moldavian villagers to Brașov's new factories, making it Transylvania's second-largest city. The economic collapse in the 1980s led to the **riots** in November 1987 and December 1989; since then more factories have closed, but tourism has become almost as important.

The town's proximity to a host of attractions, such as the **Piatra Craiului mountain range**, the alpine resort of **Poiana Brașov**, the fortified **Saxon churches** of **Hărman** and **Prejmer**, and "**Dracula's Castle**" at **Bran**, makes it an excellent base.

Arrival and information

Brașov is a major rail junction, served by long-distance **trains** from every corner of the country. The **train station** is over 2km northeast of the Old Town, right in the heart of Brașov's drab new concrete suburbs. Bus #4 will take you down to **Parc Central** (also known as Titulescu), and Livada Poștei. Buy a **day pass** (€1.50) if you expect to make several bus trips.

The town has no less than four **bus stations**: most long-distance buses and maxitaxis use **Autogară 1**, by the train station (☎0268/427 267). Buses from Pitești and Râmnicu Vâlcea use both this terminal and **Autogară 2** at Str. Avram Iancu 114 (☎0268/426 332), which also serves Bran and Curtea de Argeș, while services from the villages just east of Brașov use **Autogară 3**, 1km northeast of the main train station at Str. Harmanului 47 (☎0268/332 002). Finally, the **Autogară Bartolomei**, northwest of town on Calea Făgărașului, handles international services. Autogară 2 is reached by buses #12 and #22 from the centre, and bus #23 from the train station to Stadion Tineret (Youth Stadium), from where you can cut through to Autogară 2. Trolley bus #1 serves Autogară 3. Bus 2 runs to Bartolomei from in front of the train station, and local trains from Zărnești and Sibiu call at the nearby Bartolomei station. You can **rent a bicycle** from Active Travel at: Str. Toamnei 2 (Mon–Fri, 8am–6pm, Sat 10am–1pm; ☎0268/321 252, ⓦwww.activetravel.ro); bikes can be

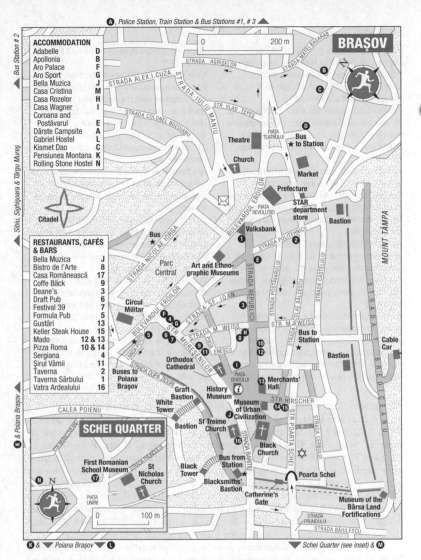

BRAȘOV

0   200 m

ACCOMMODATION
Adabelle	D
Apollonia	B
Aro Palace	F
Aro Sport	G
Bella Muzica	J
Casa Cristina	M
Casa Rozelor	H
Casa Wagner	I
Coroana and Postăvarul	E
Dârste Campsite	A
Gabriel Hostel	L
Kismet Dao	C
Pensiunea Montana	K
Rolling Stone Hostel	N

Citadel

RESTAURANTS, CAFÉS & BARS
Bella Muzica	J
Bistro de l'Arte	8
Casa Românească	17
Coffe Bäck	9
Deane's	3
Draft Pub	6
Festival 39	7
Formula Pub	5
Gustări	13
Keller Steak House	15
Mado	12 & 13
Pizza Roma	10 & 14
Sergiana	4
Șirul Vămii	11
Taverna	2
Taverna Sârbului	1
Vatra Ardealului	16

SCHEI QUARTER

First Romanian School Museum

St Nicholas Church

0   100 m

TRANSYLVANIA | Brașov

repaired at Str. Avram Iancu 84. The city **tourist office** is in the Council House on
Piața Sfatului (daily 9am–5pm; ☎0268/419 078, ⓦwww.brasov.ro), though it's of
rather limited help. A more useful source of information is Roving Romania
(ⓦwww.roving-romania.co.uk).

Accommodation

There is stacks of accommodation in Brașov, from some very characterful **hotels**
and **pensions** to some smart little **hostels** and lots of private offerings. There are
also a number of decent places to stay outside the city, in particular on the road out
towards Poiana Brașov.

Hotels

Adabelle Str. Pieții 5 ☎0268/411 080, ⓦwww
.adabelle.ro. Despite its hostel-like appearance, this
tidy youth hotel has modern, well-equipped
en-suite rooms, with plasma TV and wi-fi. Rates
include breakfast and dinner. ❺

Apollonia Str. Neagoe Basarab 7 ☎0268/476 163,
ⓦwww.hotelapollonia.ro. Smart, unassuming little
hotel in a peaceful location close to the centre.
Sauna, massage, gym and swimming pool cost
extra. ❼

Aro Palace B-dul Eroilor 27 ☎0268/478 800,
ⓦwww.aro-palace.ro. Above what must be
Romania's largest hotel lobby, the Aro Palace has
Brașov's most luxurious and expensive rooms; ask
for a view of Mount Tâmpa. The spa has two pools
and a gym. ❾

Aro Sport Str. Sfântu Ioan 3 ☎0268/478 800,
ⒺFoffice@aro-palace.ro. On a narrow side street
behind the Aro Palace, this is a very basic, hostel-
like place, with shared toilet and shower facilities.
However, it's cheap, reasonably cheerful and very
central. ❶

Bella Muzica Piața Sfatului 19 ☎0268/477 956,
ⓦwww.bellamuzica.ro. In a lovely 400-year-old
Neoclassical building, this gem of a hotel has
modestly sized but sumptuously furnished rooms,
each with thoughtful little touches such as wood-
framed mirrors, pictures and plants. Its superb

restaurant is a few steps down the road (see
p.139). ❻

Casa Cristina Str. Curcanilor 62A ☎0722/322
021, ⓦwww.casacristina.ro. High up above Schei
on an unpaved road, the comfortable rooms have
great views over the city; there's a kitchen and
drinks machine but no breakast. ❷

Casa Rozelor Str. Michael Weiss 20 ☎0268/475
212, ⓦwww.casarozelor.ro. In a former salt
warehouse, the "House of Roses" has magnificent
apartment-style rooms; the bare brick walls
remain, combined with an outstanding fusion of
contemporary and period furnishings and original
artwork. ❼

Casa Wagner Piața Sfatului 5 ☎0268/411 253,
ⓦwww.casa-wagner.eu. This understatedly elegant
pension has twelve rooms, beautifully furnished
with lots of wood and brass, some overlooking the
square. Very good value. ❻

Coroana Str. Republicii 62 ☎0268/477 448,
ⓦwww.aro-palace.ro. A muddy grey building
concealing two rather careworn and rudimentary
hotels – the one-star Postăvarul and the two-star
Coroana. ❷–❻

Pensiunea Montana Stejerișului 2A ☎0268/472
731, ⓦwww.casa-montana.ro. Excellent bed and
breakfast, on the road up to Poiana Brașov, with
marvellous views over the city. ❹

Hostels, private rooms, camping and cabanas

Brașov has three **hostels**, all in the Schei quarter – from the train station take bus
#50, #51 or #52 to the quarter's main square, Piața Unirii, and it's a couple of
minutes' walk. The clean and welcoming *Rolling Stone*, at Str. Piatra Mare 2a
(☎0268/513 965, ⓦwww.rollingstone.ro), has modern dorms (❶) as well as three
very comfortable double rooms (❸), one of which is en suite; there's also a pleasant
terrace with pool and basement bar. The *Kismet Dao* at Str. Democrației 2b
(☎0268/514 296, ⓦwww.kismetdao.com; ❷–❸) also has dorms (❶) and private
rooms (❸). Both have laundry facilities and all prices include breakfast and internet
access. The new *Gabriel Hostel*, at Str. Vasile Saftu 41A (☎0744/844 223), has
dorms (❶) with kitchen and segregated male and female bathrooms.

Closer to the centre or the station, your best option may be a **private room** (❶),
likely to be in a modern apartment block; there are many people offering these on
arrival at the train station, the most likely suspects being Maria and Grig Bolea
(☎0744/816 970); the helpful Eugene (☎0722/542 581, Ⓔejrr68@yahoo.com);
Gigi and Diana Borcea (☎0268/416 243), and Gabriel Ivan (☎0744/844 223).
Beds are available in apartments right on Piața Sfatului, including through Ileana
Dascalu (☎0268/410 076) and Iulian Niță (☎0723/159 991). Most of these will
happily arrange local excursions.

The **Dârste campsite** (☎0268/339 967, ⓦwww.campingdirste.ro) is about
7km from Brașov's centre, on the Bucharest road. Take bus #17 from the centre or
#35 from the station out along the main highway until it turns off for Săcele; the
campsite is fifteen minutes' walk further south along the DN1 at km160. The site

has reasonable facilities including a restaurant plus bungalows sleeping two to four people (❷—❹) with 24-hour hot water.

The Town

Most visitors make a beeline for the largely Baroque **Old Town**, coiled beneath Mount Tâmpa and Mount Postăvaru. The hub of the city's social and commercial life is **Strada Republicii**, which leads to **Piața Sfatului**, a strikingly handsome, quintessentially Germanic town square dominated by the **Black Church**. Close by are the medieval ramparts and, beyond here, the Schei quarter.

Piața Teatrului and around

Buses from the train station will set you down near **Piața Teatrului**, from where it's a short walk to the major sights. Near the square are some stark reminders of the events of December 1989; in a small park by the post office stand thirty headstones, memorials to those gunned down, including a girl of six caught in crossfire. Across the road, at the head of Str. Republicii, stands the heavily pockmarked **Volksbank building**, the only edifice still exhibiting any damage. From here, it's a pleasant stroll down pedestrianized **Str. Republicii** (Purzengasse), a wide boulevard that's at its best during the warmer months when cafés and bars spill out across it.

Two minutes southwest of the Volksbank building, at B-dul Eroilor 21, the **Ethnographic Museum** (Muzeul de Etnografie; Tues–Sun: summer 10am–6pm; winter 9am–5pm; €1) has a modest but enlightening display on the regional textile industry and local costume – the pick of the exhibits is a still-functioning Jacquard weaving loom from Germany (ask for a demonstration). There's also a neat selection of craftworks for sale, together with books and CDs. Next door, the **Art Museum** (Muzeul de Artă; same times and admission) has a large selection of canvases by Grigorescu, Aman and Tattarescu, as well as works by Brașov-born **János Máttis-Teutsch** (1884–1960), one of the most influential of modern Romanian artists. He was a painter, sculptor, writer and teacher who exhibited with avant-garde groups in Berlin, Budapest and Bucharest before returning to figurative art. The decorative arts collection in the basement is also worth a peek.

Piața Sfatului

Local legend tells that when the Pied Piper enticed the children from Hamelin in Germany, they vanished underground and emerged in Transylvania near what is now Brașov's main square, **Piața Sfatului** (Council Square). It is lined with sturdy merchants' houses, their red-tiled roofs tilted rakishly, presenting their shop fronts to the Casa Sfatului (Council House) in the centre of the square, which was built by 1420, rebuilt in the eighteenth century, and now houses the tourist office and **History Museum** (Tues–Sun 10am–6pm; €2). The dusty exhibits here tell the story of the Saxon guilds – locksmiths, goldsmiths, milliners and so on – who dominated Brașov and met in the Hirscher Haus or **Merchants' Hall** (Casa Negustorilor) on the eastern side of the square. Built in the "Transylvanian Renaissance" style in 1544–5, this now contains shops, a wine cellar and the *Casa Hirscher* restaurant. Facing it at Piața Sfatului 15 is the new **Museum of Urban Civilisation** (Tues–Sun summer 10am–6pm; winter 9am–5pm; €2), which will display re-creations of shops and homes. Through an archway at Piața Sfatului 3, you'll find the **Orthodox cathedral**, built in Byzantine style in 1896; its dark, richly painted interior features an 8m-high iconostasis and marble paved flooring from 1963, while the brightly coloured wall paintings in the courtyard are more recent, dating from 2003. Across the square, and similarly hidden away down an

3

alley at Str. Bariţiu 12, the eighteenth-century **Sf Treime (Holy Trinity) Church** also features an elaborately decorated altar screen.

To the southwest, the square is dominated by the pinnacles of the town's most famous landmark, the **Black Church** (Biserica Neagră; Mon–Sat 10am–3.30pm; €1.50), stabbing upwards like a series of daggers. Allegedly the largest Gothic church between Vienna and Istanbul, it took almost a century to complete (1383–1477) and is so-called for its once soot-blackened walls, the result of a great fire started by the Austrian army that occupied Braşov in 1689. It's a classic example of a three-nave hall church, though its interior is largely devoid of colour or ornamentation and the main altar is memorable only for its size. The exceptions to this are the mostly seventeenth-century **Turkish prayer mats** hung in isolated splashes of colour along the balconies and walls of the nave – a superb collection built up from the gifts of local merchants returning from the east; there's also a fine tympanum of the *Virgin and Child with Two Saints* in the south porch. The four-thousand-pipe organ is one of the largest in southeastern Europe, and it's worth trying to catch one of the regular recitals. On the last pillar to your left as you enter, look out for four bullet holes, left by shots fired through the nearby wooden door as people cowered inside during the fighting in 1989. To the south and west of the church are the buildings of the **Honterus Gymnasium**, the still-prestigious Saxon school named after the apostle of Luther's Reformation in Transylvania.

A short walk east of Piaţa Sfatului, at Str. Poarta Schei 27, is Braşov's Moorish-style **synagogue** (Mon–Fri 9am–1pm), built in 1901 and now beautifully restored. Just to its east is Str.Sforii (Rope Street), the narrowest alley in Romania, although at 1.3m it's more than twice as wide as some in the City of London.

The fortifications and Mount Tâmpa

With the threat of Turkish expansion in the fifteenth century, Braşov began to fortify itself, assigning the defence of each bastion or rampart to a particular guild. The length of **fortress wall** along Str.Brediceanu, at the foot of Mount Tâmpa, has recently been refurbished, along with the Bastion Funarilor (Ropemakers' Bastion). Good **views** of the Old Town can be had from here, but the best are from the forested heights of **Mount Tâmpa** (967m), accessible by cable car (Tues–Fri 9am–5.30pm, Sat & Sun 9am–6pm; €2 up, €3 return) from the terminal behind the Bastion Funarilor, or by various winding trails; a pretty dodgy path leads about 200m from the terminal to the viewpoint by the Hollywood-style "Braşov" sign that's visible all over town.

Of the original seven **bastions**, the best preserved is that of the Weavers (Bastionul Ţesătorilor), at Str. Coşbuc 9, with three tiers of wooden galleries and meal-rooms in which the townsfolk stocked bread, meat and other provisions in case of siege. The top two floors are now unsafe, but the ground floor houses the **Museum of the Bârsa Land Fortifications** (Tues–Sun 10am–6pm; winter 9am–5pm; €1), recalling the bad old days when the surrounding region was repeatedly raided by Tatars, Turks and, on a couple of occasions, by Vlad Ţepeş. The fortifications survived these onslaughts, but those caught outside didn't fare so well. When Ţepeş attacked Braşov in 1460, he burnt the suburbs and impaled hundreds of captives along the heights of St Jacob's Hill to the north of the city. On the west side of the Old Town, the **Bastionul Graft** (1494), squeezed between stream and walls on the traffic-free Str. După Ziduri, houses a dull collection of weapons (Tues–Sun 9am–5pm; €2). From here steps lead up to the **Blacksmiths' Bastion** (Bastionul Fierarilor) and the **Black and White Towers** on Calea Poienii, all of which are also open, with another display of medieval weapons in the fourteenth-century Black Tower (Turnul Negru; Tues–Sun 10am–6pm; €1).

The Schei quarter

During the heyday of Saxon rule, the Romanian-speaking population was compelled to live beyond the citadel walls, in the southwestern district of **Schei**. They could only enter the centre at certain times, and had to pay a toll at the gate for the privilege of selling their produce to their neighbours. The Poarta Schei, the gate on the street of the same name, was built in 1825–8 by Emperor Franz I, next to the splendid **Catherine's Gate** (Poarta Ecaterinei) of 1559, which bears the city's coat of arms. Today, Schei is a peaceful residential dead-end whose main sight is the **Church of St Nicholas**, on Piaţa Unirii, ten minutes' walk from Poarta Schei. A fetching amalgam of Byzantine, Baroque and Gothic, it was the first Orthodox church to be built in Transylvania by the *voivodes* of Wallachia, between 1493 and 1564; it was extended and the clocktower added in 1751, with interior frescoes realized in the nineteenth century by the Braşov-born painter Mişu Popp. On the left as you enter the churchyard is the first **Romanian-language school**, established in the fourteenth century; it is now a museum (daily 9am–5pm; €1), exhibiting the first Romanian-language textbooks, a printing press, and costumes worn in the Pageant of the Juni.

Eating and drinking

Outside Bucharest, Braşov has the best selection of **restaurants** in Romania. **Drinking** options, too, are plentiful, particularly during the warmer months when the cafés and bars spill out onto Piaţa Sfatului and along Str. Republicii.

Restaurants

Bella Muzica Str. Gheorghe Bariţiu 2 ℡0268/477 956. Deep inside a gorgeous, low-ceilinged cellar, this is one of Braşov's classiest restaurants. The food is a curious mix of Mexican and Hungarian cuisines, while the surrounds – dim table lamps and soft background music – are delightful. Perfect for a romantic evening out.

Bistro de l'Arte Piaţa Enescu 11 ℡0268/473 994. Tucked away in a little courtyard, this cosy low-key place offers a limited menu of excellent French-influenced food, but is worth a visit just for its delicious fondue. Cracking breakfasts, too (except Sun).

Casa Românească Piaţa Unirii 15. The only really decent place to eat in Schei (and handily located for the hostels) – there's nothing fancy about it, but the tasty Romanian food is inexpensive and there's regular live music.

Gustări Piaţa Sfatului 14. Though far from the flashiest restaurant on the main square, this is, as any local will tell you, the place to choose for wholesome Romanian food, served with a smile.

The Pageant of the Juni

The **Pageant of the Juni** (Sărbătoarea Junilor) is held on the Sunday after Easter, traditionally the one day of the year when Romanians could freely enter the Saxon city. The name derives from the Latin for "young men", and on this day the town's youths dress up in costumes and, accompanied by brass bands, ride through town in seven groups such as the Juni, the Old (ie married) Juni, and the Dorobanţi and Roşiori, named after famous regiments.

The parade assembles in the morning on **Piaţa Unirii**, the historic heart of Schei. It then marches to Piaţa Sfatului, circles it three times, returns to the Schei backstreets, then climbs a narrow valley northwest to the **Gorges of Pietrele lui Solomon**. Here, spectators settle down to watch the Round Dances (Horăs). The Horă, which still has the power to draw onlookers into its rhythmically stepping, swaying and stamping circles, served as a sanction in village society – miscreants seeking to enter the circle (and so re-enter society) were shamed when the dancing immediately ceased, resuming only when they withdrew.

Keller Steak House Str. Apollonia Hirscher 2. One of the country's few genuine steak houses, this well-turned-out establishment also has pasta, salads, a terrific Romanian menu and a very good wine list.
Pizza Roma Str. Apollonia Hirscher 2/Str. Republicii. Friendly, partly non-smoking Italian places serving up decent pizza and big bowls of fresh salad.
Sergiana Str. Mureşenilor 27. In an attractive maze of cellars with lots of hidden alcoves, the *Sergiana* has a long menu of traditional and modern Romanian dishes – a fun place to eat.
Şirul Vămii Str. Mureşenilor 18 ☏0268/477 725. Second only to *Bella Muzica*, this handsome-looking

restaurant offers pricey but high-class (Belgian, French and Italian) food, fine wines and impeccable service.
Taverna Str. Politehnicii 6 ☏0268/474 618. Intimate, warm and classy restaurant serving plates of spicy mixed meats and fish, with lots of veggie options, such as mushroom stew with sour cream, or spinach purée with egg.
Taverna Sârbului Str. Republicii 55. This splendid brick cellar (reached through a small courtyard), with thick wooden tables and bench seating, is the place for fantastically tasty portions of meat-heavy Serbian food.

Cafés and bars

The **cafés** along Str. Republicii and around Piaţa Sfatului are much of a muchness, but more than suffice for a relaxed evening's drinking; the pick of the pavement cafés is *Mado*, Str. Republicii 10 and Piaţa Sfatului 11, a pair of colourful coffee-houses with a good selection of cakes and ices. The queen of Braşov's cake shops, however, is the old-style *Vatra Ardealului*, Str. Bariţiu 14, with its tremendous selection of sticky things, and good coffee too; for German baking, head for *Coffé Bäck*, at Str. Mureşenilor 16.

The most popular **bars** are *Deane's*, Str. Republicii 19, a decent Irish boozer that puts on some varied entertainment including karaoke on Thursdays and live jazz on Fridays; and *Draft Pub*, Str. Mureşenilor 27, a bare-brick bar that offers a range of draught lagers as well as Guinness. Other possibilities include *Festival 39*, Str. Republicii 62, which boasts a long cocktail list and wacky decor, and the *Formula Pub* at B-dul Eroilor 29, which can pass the time while you're waiting for a bus at Livada Poştei, or if you're a fan of Formula 1 – most of these places stay open until around 2am.

Entertainment

Classical concerts by the Braşov Philharmonic take place in various venues: enquire at the box office at Str. Hirscher 10 (Mon–Fri 10am–5pm; ☏0268/477 813) – tickets are inexpensive but usually sell out well in advance. The municipal **theatre** is on Piaţa Teatrului, at the east end of B-dul Eroilor (box office Tues–Fri 11am–7pm, Sat & Sun 3–7pm; ☏0268/418 850); the less appealing **Opera** – mainly staging operettas and musicals – at Str. Bisericii Române 51 (☏0268/415 990, ⓦwww .opera-brasov.ro); and the **puppet theatre** beside the Centrul Cultura Reduta next to the Philharmonic. Note that little happens at any of these between mid-June and mid-September. There are no **cinemas** near the city centre; the main ones are the *Patria* (B-dul 15 Noiembrie), *Cosmos* (Str. Uranus 1) and *Bulevard* (B-dul Griviţei 47).

Other than the **Pageant of the Juni** (see p.139) and the cheesy **Golden Stag** pop music extravaganza, which takes over Piaţa Sfatului (and national TV) in late August or early September, Braşov doesn't have any major festivals. That said, smaller-scale events include the **Springtime Jazz and Blues Festival** in early May; the **International Chamber Music Festival** in the first week of July; and the rather anonymous **Oktoberfest Beer Festival** in early October.

Shopping

Braşov is a good place to buy books and outdoor gear, and the food markets are reasonable. The STAR **department store** is at Str. Bălcescu 62 (Mon–Sat

9am–8pm, Sun 10am–3pm), and there are some fascinating **antique** and **junk** shops on Str. Coresi. Shops selling English-language books include Coşbuc, Str. Republicii 29 (Mon–Fri 8am–8pm, Sat 10am–4pm); Carturești, Piaţa Sfatului 20 (Mon–Sat 10am–9pm, Sun 10am–7pm); Okian, Str. Mureşenilor 1 (Mon–Fri 10am–6pm, Sat 9am–1pm); and Şt. O. Iosif, Str. Mureşenilor 14 (Mon–Fri 8am–8pm, Sat 10am–4pm), which also sells useful **maps**. Expert Store, Str. Bariţiu 10 (Mon–Fri 10am–7pm, Sat 10am–3pm), is an excellent **mountain-gear** shop. The central food **market** is next to the STAR department store, and there's another behind the apartment blocks opposite the train station. Also near the station, in the Unirea mall just to the west, is the *Penny Market* **supermarket**. On the last weekend of each month a **Slow Food market** is held on Piaţa Sfatului, bringing producers from as far afield as Maramureş.

Listings

Football FC Braşov play at Stadion Tineret on Str. Stadionului.

Hospitals County Hospital, Calea Bucureşti 25–27 (☎0268/135 080); Emergency Military Hospital, Pieţei 9 (☎0268/416 393); Clinica Romano Americana, Str. Traian 10 (☎0268/332 023).

International bus tickets Tickets for Budapest can be bought from Autogară 1; for buses to Germany (and beyond), go to the Autogară Bartolomei (see p.134); AtlasSib, Piaţa Teatrului 2 (☎0268/412 313); Double-T, Piaţa Sfatului 25 (☎0268/410 466); or Touring-Eurolines, Piaţa Sfatului 18 (☎0268/474 008).

Internet access CyberCafé, Str. Republicii 58 (Mon–Fri 11am–9pm, Sat & Sun 12.30–9pm); Internet Café, Str. Michael Weiss 11; Internet Caffé, Str. Republicii 41 (24hr); ReD NeT, Str. Bariţiu 8; and on the mezzanine floor of the train station.

Pharmacy Farma Plus, Str. Republicii 27 (daily 8am–midnight; ☎0268/143 560).

Police Str. Titulescu 28 (☎0268/407 500).

Taxis Braşov has hordes of taxis, but you're best sticking to the following: Martax (☎0268/313 040), Rey Taxi (☎0268/411 111), BraTaxi (☎0268/315 555) or Tod (☎0744/321 111).

Train tickets For international tickets, go to Wasteels at the station (Mon–Fri 8am–7pm; ☎0268/424 313, ❦www.wasteels.ro).

Around Braşov

Braşov sits right at the foot of the mountains, and there are opportunities for hiking and skiing just a few kilometres from the city at **Poiana Braşov**. The most popular excursion is to the castle of **Bran**, and in spite of the crowds it's well worth a visit. Better still, though, is the ruined fort at **Râşnov**, approximately halfway between Braşov and Bran. The Bucegi mountains, to the south, and the Făgăraş range to the west, including Romania's highest peaks, can both be reached by train. Between these two ranges lies the very distinctive ridge of the **Piatra Craiului**, a single block of limestone that offers a marvellous, if tiring, day's walking.

Poiana Braşov

POIANA BRAŞOV sits at an altitude of 1000m on a shoulder of the spectacular Mount Postăvaru, 12km south of Braşov (20min by bus #20, every 30min from Livada Poştei, by the Parc Central). It's Romania's premier **ski resort**, and while it's a great place to learn to ski, with lots of English-speaking instructors, experienced skiers may soon be bored. **Ski gear** can be rented at several places, as can **mountain bikes**; **horseriding** is also available.

The **hotels** are usually filled by package groups, but they may have space out of season. The *Alpin* (☎0268/262 343, ❦www.hotelalpin.ro; ❾) has the best facilities and serves a hearty buffet breakfast, but the most attractive hotels include the

Sport (☎0268/262 313, ⓦwww.anahotels.ro; ⑥); the *Poiana Ursului* (☎0268/262 216, ⓦwww.poianaursului.ro; ⑥) and the *Tirol* (☎0268/262 460, ⓦwww .hoteltirol.ro; ⑥), which has an excellent restaurant. One of the best of the many **villas** dotted around the resort is the welcoming *Vila Zorile*, Str. Poiana Ruia 6 (☎0268/262 286, ⓦwww.vila-zorile.ro; ⑦), locally famed as where Jude Law and Nicole Kidman stayed while filming *Cold Mountain*. There's also a fair chance that you'll be approached by locals offering **apartments** (❷–❺), which can be good value.

The resort's **restaurants** go in for folk architecture and music, as you'd expect with names like *Şura Dacilor* (Dacians' Barn) and *Coliba Haiducilor* (Outlaws' Hut), both offering pretty authentic, pork-heavy cuisine.

Râşnov

Thirty minutes from Braşov by bus or train, and 12km west of Poiana Braşov by a back road (where much of 2003's blockbuster *Cold Mountain* was filmed), is **RÂŞNOV** (Rosenau), where a **ruined fort** (daily 8am–8pm; €1.50), founded around 1225 by the Teutonic Knights, crowns the fir-covered hill that overlooks the town. The fort was only ever captured once, in 1612, when the Hungarian prince Gabriel Báthory cut off its water supply. It last saw action during the 1848 revolution, after which it was abandoned, only being restored recently. A small **museum** inside the fort holds mostly weapons and torture implements, along with a seventeenth-century female skeleton, found during excavations inside the citadel; there is also a small snack bar. The best reason for visiting the fort, however, is to take in the glorious mountain **views** across to the Piatra Craiului.

To get there on foot, head through the archway and up the steps opposite the BCR bank on Piaţa Unirii, just south of the Lutheran church. You can also get there by road from the **hotel** *Cetate* (☎0268/230 266; ❸), on Str. Cetăţii (the Poiana Braşov road, starting from the southern end of Piaţa Unirii). A much better place to stay is the terrific-value *Pension Stefi*, near the steps leading up to the fort, at Piaţa Unirii 5 (☎0368/592 019, ⓦwww.hotelstefi-ro.com; ❷); you'll find plenty of signs for other guesthouses.

Bran and around

The small town of **BRAN** (Törzburg), 28km southwest of Braşov, commands the entrance to the pass of the same name, once the main route into Wallachia. The Saxons of Kronstadt (Braşov) built a castle to safeguard this vital trade artery between 1377 and 1382 (replacing a wooden castle raised in 1212 by the Teutonic Knights), and although what's now billed on every tourist brochure as **Dracula's Castle** (Muzeului Castel Bran; May–Oct Mon noon–6pm, Tues–Sun 9am–6pm; Nov–April Tues–Sun 9am–4pm; €5; ⓦwww.bran-castle.com) has only tenuous associations with Vlad the Impaler – it's likely he laid siege to it in 1460 when he attacked the Burzenland – Bran does look like a vampire count's residence, perched on a rocky bluff and rising in tiers of towers and ramparts from the woods against a glorious mountain backdrop.

The castle now looks much as it would have done in the time of its most famous resident, **Queen Marie of Romania**. A granddaughter of Queen Victoria who married Prince Ferdinand in 1893, Marie soon rebelled against the confines of court life in Bucharest – riding unattended through the streets, pelting citizens with roses during the carnival and appointing herself a colonel of the Red Hussars. Her popularity soared after she organized cholera camps in the Balkan war and appeared at the Paris peace conference in 1919, announcing "Romania needs a face, and I have come to show mine". Confiscated by the communists, the castle was returned in 2009 to Marie's grandson Dominic von Hapsburg, but will continue to be open to the public.

Marie called Bran a "pugnacious little fortress", but whether because of her spirit pervading the rooms or the profusion of flowers in the yard, it seems a welcoming place, at odds with its forbidding exterior. Inside it's a warren of spiral stairs, ghostly nooks and surprisingly cosy rooms. Not surprisingly, it can get horribly crowded: the trick is to arrive as the castle opens – the bus parties will be arriving as you leave. In the grounds, the open-air **Village Museum** (Muzeul Satului; same hours; €2) comprises some fine examples of local architecture, including a sawmill, fulling mill (used in the manufacture of cloth) and, most impressively, a large house dating from 1843, including a cellar, and stables.

By the road south, the **Ancient Customs House Museum** (Vama Medievală; same hours; €2) predictably stresses the trade links from the earliest times between the Vlachs on either side of the Carpathians, and displays examples of foreign goods. There's a hectic market at the castle gate, but inevitably there's lots of Dracula tack (and a Haunted Castle); for authentic **folk art** go to the entrance to the Village Museum. Bran holds its village **festival** on August 9 (the Feast of St Pantelimon).

Aside from its castle, Bran is a good base for **hikes** into the Bucegi mountains to the east (see p.126) and onto the narrow ridge of the **Piatra Craiului**, the eastern extremity of the Făgăraş mountains, to the west (see p.144).

Practicalities

Buses run from Braşov's *Autogară* 2 via Râşnov and Bran to Moeciu de Jos, 3km south of Bran (Mon–Fri every 30min, Sat & Sun hourly); the two or three buses from Braşov south to Piteşti and Câmpulung Muscel also call at Bran. Note that **parking** near the castle costs about twice as much as in a city centre. There's no tourist office in Bran, but you can get (scant) **information** from Antrec at Str. Moşoiu 10 (℡0268/236 355), which can also set you up in **private accommodation** (❷–❹) – big business in Bran, and usually full at weekends.

The best **hotel** is the *Hanul Bran*, a five-minute walk north of the castle at Str. Principală 384 (℡0268/236 556, Ⓦwww.hanulbran.ro; ❷–❹), with a new wing supplementing the older, fairly antiquated rooms. Another reasonable place, with an outdoor pool, is the *Popasul Reginei*, across the small park near the castle at Str. Dr. Aurel Stoian 398 (℡0268/236 834, Ⓦwww.popasulreginei.ro; ❸). Under 1km from the centre on the Braşov road, and 100m up Str. Aluniş, the pleasant *Club Vila Bran*, Sohodol 271A (℡0268/236 554, Ⓦwww.vilabran.ro; ❷), is actually a complex of villas, with indoor pool and a *stâna traditional* (sheepfold-restaurant); midweek off-season rates are remarkably good value. Another 2km towards Braşov, the *Hotel Wolf* complex (℡0268/419 576, Ⓦwww.complexulwolf.ro; ❹) has fresh, modern rooms, a swimming pool and a bowling alley. There are also quite a few independent **guesthouses**, the best of which is the British-run *The Guesthouse* (℡0744/306 0625, Ⓦwww.guesthouse.ro; ❷), opposite the *Hanul Bran* at Str. Moşoiu 365A. Other good ones are *Pensiunea Iulia*, nearby at Str. Bologa 20 (℡0268/236 966; ❷); and the *Pensiunea Piatra Craiului*, 1km south at Str. Principală 425 (℡0745/851 120, Ⓦwww.pensiuni-munte.ro; ❷), which has a trout pond for guests' use. The *Taverna Lupilor*, in the *Wolf* complex, is easily the best **restaurant** hereabouts, serving hunter-style dishes (deer stew and roast boar) in a heavily rustic setting – there's a **supermarket** here, too (Mon–Sat 8am–9pm, Sun 9am–7pm). Otherwise, the restaurant in the *Popasul Reginei* is good, as is the *Restaurant Bran Parc*, by the Parc Central on Str. Sextil Puşcariu, or there's the *Cheile Castelului* for pizza, below the castle near the *Vama*.

Moeciu and Fundata

In **MOECIU**, just southwest of Bran, there are plenty of **guesthouses**, all very clean with lots of stripped pine and big breakfasts. **Buses** terminate just beyond the junction at km105; there's a group of three good guesthouses 2.5km up the Moeciu de Sus road (Str. Cheia) in Moeciu de Jos. Call in advance at *Mariana Olteanu*, no. 427A (☎0268/419 477; ❸), *Liliana Urzica*, no. 433 (☎0268/237 233, ✉ovyonut @yahoo.com; ❶), or *Camelia*, no. 436 (☎0268/236 233, ✉pensiuneacamelia @yahoo.com; ❷), and they'll pick you up. In Moeciu de Sus (Upper Moeciu) itself, 8km south of the junction, the best **place to stay** is the *Casa Orleanu*, also known as the *Centru de Ecologie Montană*, at no. 125 (☎0745/978 023, ⓦwww.cem.ro; ❷); you can get information on local wildlife here.

In the foothills of the Piatra Craiului, west of the Bran–Fundata road, hide tiny settlements where more genuine *agroturism* pensions are springing up. The best are in Măgura – the *Cabana Montana*, at no. 44 (☎0744/801 094; ❶); *Vila Hermani*, at no. 130 (☎0745/512 096, ⓦwww.cntours.ro; ❷); and the *Villa Park Hostel* (☎0749/213 119; ❶).

Atop the spectacular **Bran** or **Giuvala Pass** (1290m), 14km south of Bran, **FUNDATA** is one of the highest villages in Romania, and is served only by occasional Braşov–Câmpulung buses. Little more than a scattering of small farmhouses, it hosts the popular **Mountain Festival** (Nedeia Muntelui) on the last Sunday of August. The underlying purpose is to transact business: exchanges of handicrafts, livestock and (formerly) of pledges of marriage. As Fundata straddles the border between Transylvania and Wallachia, the festival was important as a means of maintaining contacts between ethnic Romanians in the two provinces.

Zărneşti and the Piatra Craiului

Mountains dominate the skyline around Bran. To the southeast is the almost sheer wall of the **Bucegi range** – it takes about eight hours to hike from Bran to Mount Omu, where there's a cabana. To the west, gentler slopes run up to the **Piatra Craiului**, a 20km-long narrow limestone ridge, known as the Royal Rock. Now a national park, it's punctured with karst caves along its eastern face, and is home to Carpathian bears (see box opposite), lynx and chamois, as well as the endemic Piatra Craiului pink.

The gateway to the park, and a good starting point for hikes, is the town of **ZĂRNEŞTI**, some 25km west of Braşov and reachable by bus and train via Râşnov. About 1.5km east of the town centre, along a gravel road heading up the Bârsa Mare Valley (see below), is the new **Piatra Craiului National Park visitor centre** (Str. Topliţa 150; ☎0268/223 008, ⓦwww.pcrai.ro), an overly conspic- uous structure where you can pick up a few leaflets. They can also point you towards the various agencies in the area offering **wildlife-watching** trips, such as bear-watching and wolf-tracking, as well as a host of other leisure pursuits and guided tours (see box opposite).

Several **guesthouses** here offer superb home cooking, including the homely *Pensiunea Mosorel*, Str. Dr Ioan Şenchea 162 (☎0745/024 472; ❷), which also allows camping in the large back garden, and the *Wolf House*, Str. Metianu 108 (❸), owned by the people who run Transylvanian Wolf (see box opposite). They use local produce and fresh herbs, and offer cooking courses in winter (€25/person). The large rooms all have private bathrooms and traditional furniture. *Elena*, Str. Piatra Craiului 43 (☎0268/223 070, ⓦwww.pensiuneaelena.ro; ❷), is another good option.

From Zărneşti, it's 12km (under three hours' walk) on an awful road up the Bârsa Mare valley to the *Plaiul Foii* cabana (☎0722/357 739, ⓦwww.cabanaplaiulfoii .ro; ❶), the main centre for **hiking** in this area. It's really a hotel restaurant, with

Wildlife-watching and other activities

The **Piatra Craiului National Park** is ideal for all kinds of outdoor pursuits. Organized by a number of different agencies – mostly members of the **Association of Ecotourism in Romania** (Ⓦwww.eco-romania.ro), dedicated to nature conservation and sustainable tourism development – there's a multitude of things to see and do, from observing animals in the wild to sporting activities and guided walks.

The most popular of these is **bear-watching**, which gives visitors a rare chance to observe these animals in their natural habitat – gathering at dusk, you are taken up to a forest hide, where the chances of seeing a brown bear are rated at around seventy percent (€35, plus €25 for the use of cameras; Carpathian Tours; ☏0745/512 096, Ⓦwww.cntours.ro). While you're less likely to see wolves, **wolf-tracking** is also popular, with the excellent Transylvanian Wolf (☏0744/319 708, Ⓦwww.transylvanianwolf.ro; €70/group). Other companies with similar programmes include Active Travel at Str. Toamnei 2 (Mon–Fri 8am–6pm, Sat 10am–1pm; ☏0268/321 252, Ⓦwww.activetravel.ro), Absolute Carpathian (☏0788/578 796, Ⓦwww.absolute-nature.ro) and Discover Romania (☏0268/472 718, Ⓦwww.discoveromania.ro). Equus Silvania (☏0268/228 601, Ⓦwww.equus-silvania.com), 50km west of Braşov in the village of Şinca Nouă, offer **horseriding** lessons and guided one- and two-day trips.

single, double and triple-bedded rooms, some with showers, and a campsite; note, though, that the water isn't safe to drink. The best day hike from here leads to the *Curmătura* cabana at 1470m (☏0745/454 184; ➊), where camping is also available – there's good food here, too. It begins with a stiff climb (3–4hr, following red cross markings, and using fixed cables in places) to the main ridge 1400m above, and continues north along its knife-edge (following red dots), finally descending (following yellow stripes) to the right to the cabana or to the left to Zărneşti. It's a demanding route and you should be properly equipped with boots, waterproofs and plenty of water.

Făgăraş and around

FĂGĂRAŞ (Fogarasch), 54km west of Braşov, is scarred by communist town planning and chemical works. Nevertheless, it's a good jumping-off point for hikes in the mountains to the south, and for exploring the Saxon villages just north, and it does have some small-town charm and some affordable hotels. Founded by Hungarians and Saxons, from 1366 it and the surrounding duchy of Amlaş were under Wallachian rule for a century; when Vlad the Impaler was deposed in 1460, he set out on a murderous rampage towards the Burzenland, razing the **citadel** of Făgăraş en route. The present walls and moat were built after this, with a Renaissance mansion raised inside; but after 1688 it was largely abandoned until it housed political prisoners in 1948–60.

From the **train station** 1km south of the centre, turn left along Strada Negoiu and you'll pass between the market and an abandoned synagogue to reach the modern town centre and the fortress, now housing a moderately good **museum** of local history (Tues–Sun 9am–4pm). One block west is Piaţa Republicii, still the town's social hub.

Local **buses** run from outside the train station to Agnita, Ucea and Sâmbăta de Jos; buses to Sibiu, Braşov and international destinations leave from the south-eastern side of the central roundabout. **Tourist information** is available in the

Hiking in the Făgăraş mountains

The **Făgăraş range**, composed mainly of crystalline schists with occasional limestone outcrops, is a series of pyramidal crests, linked by narrow ridges, that harbours more than seventy **lakes** at heights of 1800 to 2250m. Up to about 2000m the mountainsides are covered with spruce forests sheltering deer, bears, chamois and other **wildlife**; above this level snow may linger as late as June.

Most **hiking routes** are well marked and easy to follow with Dimap's *Munţii Făgăraşului* **map**, which can be bought in Braşov, Bran, Făgăraş or Sibiu, or in the cabanas in the mountains. It's useful, but rarely essential, to **reserve accommodation**. Always carry ample food and water, waterproofs and good boots – the weather is very changeable on the ridge.

Almost invariably, the starting point is one of the settlements along the Olt valley, where marked routes lead from the train stations to the mountains. All trains stop at **Ucea**, from where buses head south to **Victoria**, a town dominated by its chemical works; the decent *Hotel Central* is at Str. Libertăţii 20 (☏0268/241 309, ⓦwww.hotelcentral-victoria.ro; ❸). From the bus station, follow the main road uphill to the works gates and then the route marked with red triangles round to the right (west). A forestry track becomes a steep trail climbing past the *Turnuri* cabana (☏0740/247 362, ⓦwww.turnuri.ro; ❶) to the basic *Podragu* cabana (closed mid-Oct to May; ☏0745/319 766, ⓦwww.podragu.ro; ❶) at 2136m, reached in eight to ten hours. From *Podragu*, follow the **ridge path** marked with red stripes, either eastwards past Romania's highest peak, **Moldoveanu** (2544m), descending by the Sâmbăta valley to the friendly *Valea Sâmbatei* cabana (☏0731/340 914, ⓦwww.simbata.ro; ❶) and the *Complex Turistic Sâmbăta* (with a monastery and accommodation – see opposite), from where occasional buses head to Făgăraş and Victoria, 11km west; or west to **Bâlea Lake** (2034m). The *Bâlea Lac* cabana (☏0788/609 930, ⓦwww.balealac.ro; ❸) also has a decent restaurant-bar and an attractive *terasa* by the lake. In winter you can stay in their *Ice Hotel* (☏0740 692 757, ⓦwww.icehotel.ro; ❺), or just stop in for a cocktail in the *Ice Bar*. From here you can descend either by the Trans-Făgăraş Highway (usually June–Sept) or by a cable car (daily 9am–6pm; €4 each way) to the *Bâlea Cascada* cabana (☏0269/211 703, ⓔbaleacascada@yahoo.com; ❶), and from there to Cârtişoara, the DN1 and the Cârţa rail halt. There's decent accommodation at the *Vama Cucului* cabana (☏0744/393 264, ⓦwww.vamacucului.ro; ❷) and the *Pensiunea Pâraul Rece* (☏0744/545 550, ⓦwww.paraulrecebalea.ro; ❷), both about 5km south of Cârtişoara.

Casa Municipal de Cultură at Str. Mihil Viteazul 1, across the road east of the castle (☏0268/210 000, ⓔfagaras@brasovtourism.com). Opposite the station at no. 125, the *Meridian 25* (☏0268/212 409; ❷) is a simple, clean and friendly **hotel**. On the way into town, the warm and friendly *Roata* is a block east of the market at Str. V. Alecsandri 10 (☏0268/212 415; ❶); immediately south at no. 12 is the fancier *Flora* (☏0268/215 103, ⓦwww.pensiunea-flora.ro; ❷). The *Pensiunea Vanessa*, in the centre at Piaţa Republicii 15 (☏0268/215 989, ⓦwww.pensiuneavanessa.ro; ❷), has been nicely modernized. The best place in town is the *Bulevard*, at B-dul Unirii 1A (☏0268/212 411, ⓦwww.hotel-bulevard.ro; ❸), although its balconies over the DN1 are unappealing. It also has the best **restaurant** in town, and there's the *Derby Pub & Pizza* on Str. Republicii between Piaţa Republicii and the citadel.

Around Făgăraş

Wallachian rule gave rise to characteristic local art forms still evident in the villages surrounding Făgăraş, such as the icons on glass in the gallery at **Sâmbăta**

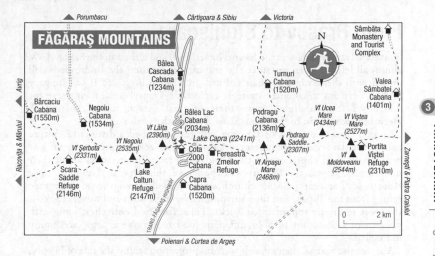

Monastery, founded in 1696 by Constantin Brâncoveanu, 27km southwest of the town, while the fifteenth-century church at Vad, reached by buses east to Şinca, also has a collection. There's plenty of accommodation in **SÂMBATA DE SUS**, including *Casa Maria* (☎0268/243 290; ❷) and *Villa Emma* (☎0724/317 162; ❷), and a decent restaurant at the *Complex Sâmbata* (☎0744/332 805, ⓦwww .complexsambata.ro). On the DN1 exactly 99km west of Braşov, the ruined Cistercian monastery of **Cârţa** (Kerz) is the oldest Gothic building in Transylvania, founded in 1202 and rebuilt after the Tatar attack of 1241; it was dissolved in 1474, but the choir remains intact and in use as the village church (the key is at Str. Principală 110; ☎0269/521 125). The Dutch-owned *De Oude Wilg* campsite is at Str. Prundului 311 (☎0269/521 347, ⓦwww.campingdeoudewilg.nl). The **Transfăgărăşan Highway** (labelled "the best road in the world" by TV's *Top Gear* programme) starts 1km west of Cârţa. The Saxon village of **ŞOARŞ** (Scharosch), 10km north of Făgăraş, offers good **homestays**; contact Mihai Patrichi, Str. Principală 155 (☎0268/267 415, ⓔpatrichimihai@yahoo.com; ❷), or *Casa Andradei*, Str. Principală 164 (☎0268/285 428, ⓦwww.andrada-house.ro; ❶); bikes and excursions are also available. There's **horseriding** at the Dutch-owned *Merlelor Inn* at Str. Principală 143, Halmeag (☎0312/263 520, ⓦwww.merlelor .com), 17km east of Făgăras.

The rare buses heading north from Făgăraş to Agnita and Rupea (via Lovnic) pass through Saxon villages with fine **fortified churches**. Villagers still dress up in embroidered costumes for **New Year celebrations** – particularly at Şercaia, Arpaşu, Porumbacu de Jos and Porumbacu de Sus – and gather en masse for the **Flowers of the Olt Festival** (Florile Oltului) at the small town of **AVRIG**, 50km west of Făgăraş, on the second Sunday in April. In Avrig the outlines of Europe's most easterly **Baroque garden** can be seen at the Brukenthal summer residence, just west of the central crossroads at Str. Lazăr 39 (usually open; free). Laid out in 1760, it's being restored by the Brukenthal Foundation (ⓦwww.brukenthal.org), which offers tours at weekends (2pm & 4pm). Beyond Avrig, the road forks (with two motels at the junction), the DN1 heading north to Sibiu, the DN7 veering south to Tălmaciu and the Red Tower (Turnu Roşu) Pass, and on into Wallachia. Travelling by train, you may need to change at Podul Olt to reach Piatra Olt in Wallachia; these services pass several of the monasteries in the Olt valley (see p.106–109).

From Braşov to Sighişoara

Southern Transylvania was the **Saxon heartland**, and although the Saxons have almost all left for Germany since the end of communism, the landscape is still dotted with the vestiges of their culture. In 1143, King Géza II of Hungary invited Germans to colonize strategic regions of Transylvania, their name for which was Siebenbürgen, from their original "seven towns", of which Hermannstadt (**Sibiu** to the Romanians) became the most powerful.

Around them, hundreds of farming villages developed a distinctive culture and vernacular style of architecture. Although the Székely, just north, put low walls about their churches and the Moldavians raised higher ones about their monasteries, it was the Saxons who perfected this type of building; their Romanesque and early Gothic churches were initially strengthened to provide refuge from the Tatars, and then surrounded by high walls and towers to resist the more militarily sophisticated Turks. These **fortified churches**, some with warrens of storerooms to hold sufficient food to survive a siege, are highly individual.

Alas, for the Saxons, their citadels were no protection against the tide of history, which steadily eroded their influence from the eighteenth century on and put them in a difficult position during World War II. Although many bitterly resented Hitler's giving northern Transylvania to Hungary in 1940, there were others who embraced Nazism and joined the German army. As collective punishment after the war, all fit Saxon men between the ages of 17 and 45, and women between 18 and 30 (30,000 in all), were deported to the Soviet Union for between three and seven years of slave labour; many did not return, and those who did found that much of their property had been confiscated.

Though **road** and **rail** routes diverge in places, it's fairly easy to reach settlements along the Olt valley in particular; however, there are many more well worth discovering in the side valleys that can only be reached by occasional buses, by car, bike or on foot. In summer, many Saxons return from Germany to their home villages, but at other times you're likely to be the only visitor.

Hărman

Erected in the fifteenth century, the immense **fortification system** surrounding the church of **HĂRMAN** (Honigberg), 12km northeast of Braşov, once consisted of three concentric walls (the outermost wall has since gone), with the inner wall, some 12m high, reinforced with seven towers. Entered via a long narrow passageway, the **church** (summer Tues–Sun 9am–noon & 1–5pm; winter Tues–Sun 10am–6pm; €1) itself is a Romanesque basilica, dating from 1293 and displaying clear Cistercian influence. Of particular importance are fifteenth-century frescoes of the *Last Judgement* and the *Crucifixion*, uncovered only in the 1920s – they are in the east tower of the ring wall, currently closed for refurbishment.

Hărman is served by regular **buses** (Mon–Fri hourly, Sat & Sun every 2hr) from Braşov's *Autogară 3*; in addition, buses from *Autogară 1* towards Târgu Secuiesc and Sfântu Gheorghe, and maxitaxis to Prejmer, will drop you by Hărman **train** station, 1.5km from the centre along Str. Gării and served by the same five trains a day that go on to Prejmer. While it's unlikely you'll need to stay here, there is **accommodation** at the *Dynasty Club* (☎0744/560 287; ➍), just down from the church, and the arty (but unmarked) *Country Hotel* at Mihai Viteazul 441 (☎0740/090 987; ⓦwww.thecountryhotel.info; ➏), which offers good dinners too.

Prejmer

PREJMER (Tartlau), 7km to the east, and off the main road (but on the railway), is the most comprehensively fortified and perhaps the most spectacular of all the region's **churches** (May–Oct Tues–Fri 9am–5pm, Sat 9am–3pm; Nov–April Tues–Sat 9am–3pm) – now on UNESCO's World Heritage list. Access to the inner precinct and church is through a 30m-long vaulted gallery, in the centre of which is a sliding portcullis. The cross-shaped church was built by 1225, but was taken over by the Cistercians in 1240 and enlarged in their Burgundian early Gothic style. The crossing and choir have splendidly worn stonework, while the nave has late Gothic vaulting, and there's a fine Gothic altarpiece of the *Passion* (1450–60).

After the Turkish campaign of 1421, the church was surrounded by a five-towered wall, 12m high, lined two centuries later with four tiers of rooms, used variously for storage and refuge – many of these have been cleaned up and can now be viewed, including one housing a mocked-up classroom. Two of the four towers on the exterior of the outer wall have since been demolished, and, as at Hărman, the moat has been filled in. There is even a small **museum** (same hours – ask the caretaker if closed), boasting fine examples of Saxon costume.

Prejmer is served by frequent **maxitaxis** (to Lunca Calnicu) from Brașov's Str. Harmanului, at the east end of B-dul Gării, and by **buses** from *Autogară* 3 to Vama Buzaului (2–5 daily). There are also six **trains** a day in each direction; note that the Ilieni train stop is closer to the town centre than Prejmer station proper. *Pensiunea Silvia*, at Str. Carpaților 1203 (℡0745/056 027; ❷), has seven decent rooms; the attractive *Gasthof Wolf*, across the road from the church, calls itself a "Chillout Caffe", while there's 24-hour drinking at the *Rustic Pub*, at the main road junction.

The Olt valley

Further north, following the River Olt towards Sighișoara, there are many more Saxon villages with fortified churches; Personal trains between Brașov and Sighișoara (5 daily) stop at most, including **FELDIOARA** (Marienburg), where the Teutonic Knights built a citadel, refashioned into a basilica after 1241; **ROTBAV** (Rothbach); **MAIERUȘ** (Nussbach); and **APAȚA**, just across the Olt from **AITA MARE** (Nagyajta). The DN13 (E60) bypasses Maieruș, swinging left across the wooded Perșani mountains, but an attractive minor road follows the east side of the Olt.

A few kilometres north of Aita Mare in the remote village of **MICLOȘOARA** (Miklósvar), the sixteenth-century manor house of the Kálnoky family is a rare example in Romania of the Italian Renaissance style. Count Kálnoky's four **guesthouses** (℡0742/202 586, ⓦwww.transylvaniancastle.com; ❹) are beautifully furnished in Székely and Saxon style; meals are also available, and a full programme of activities – including cultural and wildlife tours, riding and hiking trips – is included. The count also manages Prince Charles's lovely houses in Viscri (see p.150) and the tiny village of **Zalánpatak**, in the middle of nowhere between Sfântu Gheorghe and Baraolt, where the forests are full of bears and other wildlife. Micloșoara is reached by daily **buses** from Sfântu Gheorghe and Brașov to Baraolt, or guests can be collected from Brașov or the airports of Bucharest, Cluj or Târgu Mureș.

Around 17km north of Micloșoara is the Almaș cave in the gorge of the Vârghis (Vargyas) river, a system that continues for a total of 7.5km on four levels and where the **Pied Piper** legendarily surfaced with the children of Hamelin (who became the Saxon colonists of Transylvania).

Viscri

The village of **VISCRI** (Deutsch-Weisskirch) is 80km northwest of Braşov, off the main E60 and south along a badly resurfaced road. Set, gleaming white, upon a small hill and screened by trees, its Saxon **fortified church** is one of Romania's most impressive, and is on UNESCO's World Heritage list. It's largely thirteenth-century Gothic, with fortified walls added in 1525, and an assortment of towers from the fifteenth, seventeenth and eighteenth centuries. The interior is surprisingly small, with wooden lofts, painted with red, seventeenth-century motifs, set on rickety pillars.

There's an interesting little **museum** on the Saxon community in one of the towers, featuring a collection of costumes and other personal effects donated by Saxons leaving the village. It's also worth seeing the **Lard Tower** (Speckturm), where each family would lock away a side of bacon, stamped with their house number, in readiness for the next siege. The village, overwhelmingly populated by Roma, and with less than thirty Saxons left, nevertheless has a forceful Saxon local councillor, Caroline Fernolend, who has worked with the Mihai Eminescu Trust (see box below) to restore the church and at least the facades of over fifty buildings. The village is also prospering thanks to a somewhat less likely source, namely **sock-making**. What started a few years back as a small-scale operation involving

Rural tourism

Ceauşescu's **systematization** policy, aimed at demolishing many of Romania's villages and moving the inhabitants to concrete apartment blocks, had hardly got started before his downfall; but it had attracted protests from Prince Charles, among others, and the Belgian organization Opération Villages Roumains. The programme was immediately scrapped by the new FSN government, but far more irresistible forces were about to strike Romania's rural way of life.

Many people who had lived by subsistence farming, more or less without money, learned about consumer goods and a more modern lifestyle from the suddenly omnipresent television, leading many to go abroad in search of paid work. This money, plus ludicrously generous and unchecked EU agriculture grants, led to many older houses being demolished and replaced by ugly new piles, ruining the traditional vernacular appearance of many villages. Meanwhile the villages themselves were dying as young people left, while EU-inspired regulations aimed, for instance, to end traditional cheese-making and remove horsecarts from the roads.

It was clear to many that **rural tourism** was one of the best options for bringing cash into the villages and keeping people on the land; but with a government that was only interested in beaches, skiing and Dracula tourism, it was left largely to foreign NGOs to put together networks of **guesthouses** and help the owners bring them up to acceptable standards. The OVR took an early lead, together with the **Mihai Eminescu Trust**, formed to support dissident intellectuals, which had then joined the fight against systematization. Prince Charles entered the fray again, both as the MET's patron and buying and restoring his own houses. The Lutheran church, with German support, has worked hard to save the Saxon fortified churches and opened guesthouses in parish houses, while the Transylvania Trust and various Hungarian bodies did a fantastic job at Rimetea, turning back the tide of modernization and creating some delightful guesthouses, now serving as a model for other projects. ADEPT, working to preserve Transylvania's landscape and biodiversity, is involved with local tourism projects, while the Association of Ecotourism in Romania also has a few guesthouses among its members, together with various hiking and horseriding agencies.

In 2010 the Ministry of Tourism relaunched Romania's tourism brand, focusing on the "Carpathian garden" and ignoring the Black Sea beaches altogether.

a handful of people has grown into a fairly substantial cottage industry, and over a hundred villagers are now involved in the manufacture of socks and other woollen goods, largely for export to Germany.

There are now ten family guesthouses – contact Caroline Fernolend at no. 13 (☎0740/145 397, ✉dwk@zappmobile.ro; ➊), her sister Gerhild Gross at no. 61 (the second house on the left after the school; ☎0742/077 506) or their mother, Frau Dootz, at no. 141; they also hold the church key. The MET also has a guesthouse, at Str. Principală 63, sleeping two people in each of two separate buildings; contact Andrea Rost (☎0745/924 558 or 0723/150 819, ✉guesthouses @mihaieminescutrust.org; ➎); meals and transfers can be provided. Another conservation NGO, Pro Patrimonio, owns a guesthouse on the main street, sleeping three people in each of its two wings – contact Annette or Roman Schorb (☎0788/086 918, ✉viscri@gmx.net; ➎), or ask at the ADEPT tourist office in Saschiz. There's a rough bar, a simple yet homely **café** in a restored barn, but no grocery shop, though food can be bought from villagers.

Cloaşterf and Saschiz

On the E60 north of the Viscri turning, it's a further 20km to a left turn and the village of **CLOAŞTERF** (Klosdorf) where many houses have been restored with funding from the Mihai Eminescu Trust. Standing within a simple square wall in the centre of the village is the **church**, a modest Saxon construction finished in 1524 and with three of its four original towers remaining – the freestanding bell tower, meanwhile, dates from 1819. The key can be obtained from no. 99, about 200m back down the road near the entrance to the village. The former bell-ringer's house just inside the church entrance has been converted into a simply furnished **guest room** (➌), complete with minimal outdoor washing facilities and composting toilet. There's a small fridge and two-ring stove, or meals can be provided – contact the Mihai Eminescu Trust for details (see box opposite).

The E60 bisects the village of **SASCHIZ** (Keisd), 7km north of Cloaşterf, where around fifty Saxons still reside. The roadside church is unusual in that it's not surrounded by walls, while its magnificent bell tower is almost identical to the Clock Tower in Sighişoara. In times of trouble the villagers fled instead to a **citadel**, built in the fourteenth century and now in ruins; it makes a lovely half-hour walk from the church, across the small covered bridge and following the signs.

Facing the church at Str. Principală 166, the **tourist office** (May–Oct daily 9am–6pm; ☎0265/711 635, ⊛www.fundatia-adept.ro) is run by the British-led non-profit ADEPT (promoting sustainable rural development in the region). They publish excellent hiking maps and wildlife guides, and the staff can advise on any aspect of visiting the surrounding villages. They have the church key and also arrange excursions, for instance to a *stâna* (sheepfold), or a beekeeper, producing delicious wildflower meadow honey.

Sighişoara

A forbidding silhouette of battlements and needle spires looms over **SIGHIŞOARA** (Schässburg to Germans and Segesvár to Hungarians) as the sun descends behind the hills of the Târnava Mare valley; it seems a fitting birthplace for Vlad Ţepeş, "The Impaler" – the man known to so many as **Dracula**. Visually archaic even by Romanian standards, Sighişoara is on UNESCO's World Heritage list and makes the perfect introduction to Transylvania, especially as the Budapest–Bucharest express trains stop here.

During the last weekend of July, sometimes later, a lively **Medieval Arts Festival** takes over the streets of the citadel, starring costumed musicians and street performers. There's also an Inter-ethnic Cultural Festival in August.

Arrival and information

The **train and bus stations** are fifteen minutes' walk north of the centre, across the Târnava Mare River; outside the train station you'll see an antique locomotive that once ran on the Sibiu–Agnita–Sighișoara line. The official **tourist information centre** is at Piața Goga 8 (℡0265/770 415, ⓦwww.infosighisoara .ro), but you may find the Cultural Heritage Info Center more useful, in a cellar opposite the Clock Tower at Piața Muzeului 6 (℡0788/115 511, ⓔsighisoara @mioritics.ro). Here you can arrange city tours (donation welcome) or cycle tours of the area. There's **internet access** in the Catacombe (Mon–Fri 11am–7pm, Sat noon–4pm), the basement of the House on the Rock, on Piața Cetății, and in the *Burg Hostel* (see opposite).

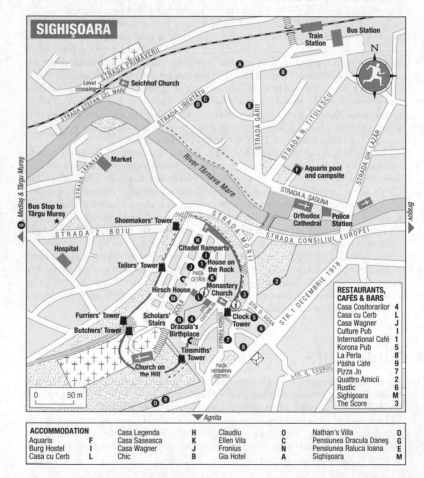

RESTAURANTS, CAFÉS & BARS

Casa Cositorarilor	4
Casa cu Cerb	L
Casa Wagner	J
Culture Pub	1
International Café	1
Korona Pub	5
La Perla	8
Pasha Cate	9
Pizza Jo	7
Quattro Amicii	2
Rustic	6
Sighișoara	M
The Score	3

ACCOMMODATION							
Aquaris	F	Casa Legenda	H	Claudiu	O	Nathan's Villa	D
Burg Hostel	I	Casa Saseasca		Ellen Vila	C	Pensiunea Dracula Daneș	G
Casa cu Cerb	L	Casa Wagner	J	Fronius	N	Pensiunea Raluca Ioana	E
		Chic	B	Gia Hotel	A	Sighișoara	M

Romanian architecture

Romania manifests a wonderful array of architectural styles, from Romanesque, Baroque and Gothic to indigenous forms such as Brâncovenesc, though modern developments have largely centred on the often brutal communist-style structures. In particular, Romania's entangled history of competing faiths accounts for an extraordinary diversity of church design, collectively representing a form of architectural heritage unique in Europe today.

Biertan citadel ▲

Sucevița monastery ▼

Medieval architecture

During the thirteenth and fourteenth centuries, many Saxon towns were fortified in order to withstand the constant threat of Ottoman and Tatar raids. Invariably sited on a hillock in the centre of the village, the key component of any **fortification** was the church, either a Romanesque basilica or a single-nave Gothic structure. The most important and powerful Saxon settlements were the cities of **Brașov**, **Sibiu** and the wonderful medieval town of **Sighișoara** (see p.151), but it's the fortifications in the smaller villages that exert the greatest pull, such as **Prejmer** (see p.149), one of the largest citadels in Transylvania, **Biertan** (see p.156), a commanding structure set in two and a half rings of walls, and the delightful church at **Mălâncrav** (see p.156), one of the few villages in the region to retain a sizeable Saxon population.

Throughout the fifteenth and sixteenth centuries, the so-called Moldavian style – integrating Gothic and Byzantine – came to the fore, and was manifest most spectacularly in the painted monasteries of **Bucovina** (see p.259). These magnificent monuments typically feature a large fortified enclosure with thick-set walls and an imposing entrance gate, offering refuge from Turkish invaders. Above all, though, it's the exterior wall paintings that stand out – startlingly detailed compositions depicting mythological beliefs and biblical events, the most striking being the *Siege of Constantinople* at **Moldovița** (see p.265), the *Ladder of Virtue* at **Sucevița** (see p.266), and, most splendid of all, the *Last Judgement* at **Voroneț** (see p.262).

Seventeenth- and eighteenth-century architecture

Seventeenth-century architecture was largely influenced by the Brâncovenesc school, so called after the former Wallachian ruler Constantin Brâncoveanu. An elegant fusion of Baroque, Renaissance and Ottoman styles, this form of architecture was particularly prominent in Wallachia; Horezu monastery (see p.112), and Mogoşoaia Palace (see p.86), near Bucharest, are first-rate examples.

While Baroque was the dominant architectural style in the eighteenth century, it's the wonderful wooden churches of **Maramureş** that stand out from this period. Of the forty or so wooden churches that remain, many are in a parlous state, though many more have been renovated in recent years, and eight are on UNESCO's World Heritage list. These were constructed by locally trained carpenters, who adopted and refined the Gothic style hitherto prominent in the churches of Transylvania. Their distinguishing features are a steeply sloping shingled roof (in many cases a double roof), a porch (*privdor*) at the western end, and a slender bell tower adorned with miniature turrets – the churches at **Şurdeşti** and **Bârsana** (see p.287 and p.299) are perhaps the finest examples in the region. The marvellous, if mostly decaying, frescoes are naïf in style, and were usually executed at the hands of unknown local artists. In most cases they conform to the universal Orthodox pattern, depicting scenes from the Old and New Testaments, the most common iconographical themes being the *Last Judgement* and the *Passion*.

▲ Quiet reflection at Horezu monastery

▼ Fresco at Horezu

▼ Wooden gate, Maramureş

Secession-era house, Oradea ▲

Redesigned Securitate building, Bucharest ▼

Nineteenth- and twentieth-century architecture

Nineteenth-century Romanian architecture drew on a combination of Romantic and Neoclassical elements, and nowhere was this more pronounced than in **Bucharest**, where many French-designed buildings were fashioned, such as the magnificent Romanian Atheneum and the Cantacuzino Palace – the city thus earned the title of the "Paris of the East". The Romanian architect and Parliamentarian Ion Mincu was particularly influential in this trend, the Palace of Justice in Bucharest being his most significant project. The Secessionist (or Art Nouveau) movement, meanwhile, was fairly restrained, though there are some fine examples throughout the Banat, and in particular in **Oradea** and **Timişoara**.

A sustained period of industrialization after World War II led to a dramatic growth in the urban population. Not long after, Ceauşescu implemented his notorious **systematization** policy, whereby whole villages were razed and its inhabitants forced into multistorey apartment blocks in reconstructed towns and cities. Monumental public buildings were erected and many urban centres – particularly those in Wallachia and Moldavia – were bequeathed Civic Centres (Centru Civic), monochrome concrete jungles meant to symbolize the heart of the community. While contemporary architectural styles have increasingly been integrated into the fabric – such as the brilliantly redesigned former Securitate building in Bucharest – it's the Centru Civic that remains the defining symbol of much of modern architecture in Romania.

Accommodation

Over the last few years, numerous **hotels and pensions** have opened in restored buildings in the citadel, while several **hostels** have appeared near the station, which is where you'll also find people offering **private rooms** (around €10/person) – some are in the citadel, such as Cristina Faur's lovely family house at Str. Cojocarilor 1 (☎0744/119 211, ✉cristinafaur2003@yahoo.de), with a dorm room sleeping six, plus en-suite doubles, kitchen and laundry facilities. There's **camping** (and cabins) at the *Aquaris* swimming pool at Str. Titulescu 2 (☎0265/772 110, ⊛www.aquariscamp.net).

Hostels

Burg Hostel Str. Bastionului 4–6 ☎0265/778 489, ⊛www.ibz.ro. Less welcoming than the other hostels, but it's right in the citadel, with a range of rooms, from dorms with shared facilities to single, double and triple en suites. Laundry and breakfast available for an extra charge. ❶–❷

Ellen Villa Str. Libertăţii 10 ☎0265/776 402, ✉office@elenvillahostel.com. Very pleasant hostel with a pretty, shaded garden just five minutes' walk from the stations; four- and eight-bed dorms, free internet and laundry, breakfast is extra. ❶

Gia Youth Hotel Str. Libertăţii 41 ☎0265/772 486, ⊛www.hotelgia.ro. Very accommodating place with clean and colourful six-bed dorms plus rooms for two, three or four. No breakfast, but there's a kitchen available. ❷

Nathan's Villa Str. Libertăţii 8 ☎0265/772 546, ⊛www.nathansvilla.com. A similar standard to the *Ellen Villa*, but much livelier; large dorms and some doubles. Breakfast included. ❶–❷

Hotels

Casa cu Cerb Str. Şcolii 1 ☎0265/774 625, ⊛www.casacucerb.ro. Named after the painting of the stag on its corner, this classy, warm and welcoming hotel has ten beautifully furnished rooms, with wrought-iron beds, sofas and corner tubs. Breakfast is extra. First-class restaurant, too. ❹

Casa Legenda Str. Bastionului 8bis ☎0744/632 775, ⊛www.legenda.ro. Along an alley just north of Piaţa Cetăţii, this low-key pension offers five very attractive, highly individual themed rooms. ❸–❺

Casa Saseasca Piaţa Cetăţii 12 ☎0265/772 400, ⊛www.casasaseasca.com. Another fine new pension in the citadel, this lovely place has good-looking rooms, its furnishings hand-painted with pretty floral motifs. ❸

Casa Wagner Piaţa Cetăţii 7 ☎0265/506 014, ⊛www.casa-wagner.com. A nicely restored hotel with antique decor – the rooms are large, comfortable and tastefully decorated, but staff can be dour. ❺

Chic Str. Libertăţii 44 ☎0265/771 046, ⊛www.sighisoara-tourism.com. Simple place opposite the station, with clean and modernish rooms with and without bathrooms. The downstairs restaurant/bar can get a little noisy. ❶–❷

Claudiu Str. Ilarie Chendi 28 ☎0265/779 882, ⊛www.hotel-claudiu.com. Lovely, restful little hotel just south of the citadel with colourfully furnished rooms and friendly staff. Secure parking. ❸

Fronius Residence Str. Scolii 13 ☎0265/779 173, ⊛www.fronius-residence.ro. A gem in a quiet location near the foot of the Scholars' Stairs, with large, beautifully furnished rooms, a cosy bar and a great breakfast. ❹

Pensiunea Dracula Daneş ☎0265/772 211, ⊛www.dracul.ro. Near the village of Daneş, 6km west of town, this is better than the name might lead you to imagine, with a fabulous swimming pool and horseriding on offer. ❸

Pensiunea Raluca Ioana Str. Gării 11 ☎0265/771 156, ⊛www.pensiuearalucaioana.ro. Near the station, this clean and friendly guesthouse has tasteful en-suite rooms, kitchen and breakfast facilities. ❷

Sighişoara Str. Şcolii 4 ☎0265/771 000, ✉rezervare@sighisoarahotels.ro. In the former Bishop's Palace, the *Sighişoara* has four floors (but no lift) of big, bright rooms (some with a/c), a very good restaurant and pleasant *terasa* at the rear. ❻

The Town

Of overwhelming interest to most is the Old Town or **citadel**, which dominates the newer quarters from a rocky massif whose slopes support a jumble of ancient, leaning houses, their windows overlooking the steps leading up from Piaţa Hermann Oberth to the main gateway. The **lower town** holds little of note, though is useful for things of a practical nature.

Clock Tower

Above the gateway rises the mighty **Clock Tower** (Turnul cu Ceas), where each night at midnight one of seven wooden figures emerges from the belfry to gaze over the lower town; two figures, representing day and night, face the upper town. The tower was raised in the fourteenth century when Sighişoara became a free town controlled by craft guilds, each of which had to finance the construction of an eponymous bastion and defend it during wartime. The Clock Tower, however, was different in that it belonged to the town council. The clock was added in 1604; the tower was rebuilt after a fire in 1676, and in 1894 the roof was covered in colourful glazed tiles.

Originally a Saxon town known as Castrum Sex (Fort Six), Sighişoara grew rich on the proceeds of trade with Moldavia and Wallachia, as the **History Museum** in the tower attests (Tues–Fri 9am–6.30pm, Sat & Sun 10am–5.30pm). In a curious and somewhat random collection – Gothic furniture, pharmaceutical objects and the like – the best display is on **Hermann Oberth**, one of the fathers of space travel, born in Sighişoara in 1894. In 1923, he published the ground-breaking book *The Rocket into Interplanetary Space*, then worked in Berlin – launching his first rocket there in 1931 and teaching Werner von Braun – at Peenemünde, on the V2 rocket, and in the 1950s and 1960s on the American space programme. The main reason for climbing the tower, though, is for the marvellous **views** of the crooked lanes and orange-roofed houses below, and the thickly forested hills of the Târnava Mare valley in the distance.

Below the Clock Tower is an old **torture chamber** (same hours as History Museum), containing a handful of devilish implements – note the innocuous-looking ladder, upon which victims were stretched out while being roasted alive. A few paces across from the tower, on the corner with Str. Cositorarilor, there's a small **museum** of medieval weapons (same times as History Museum).

Vlad's birthplace

In around 1431, in or near a three-storey house at Piaţa Muzeului 6, within the shadow of the Clock Tower, a woman whose name is lost to posterity gave birth to a son called Vlad, who in later life earned the title of "The Impaler". Abroad, he's better known as **Dracula**, derived from Dracul or The Devil – referring to his father, **Vlad Dracul**, whom the Holy Roman Emperor Sigismund of Hungary made a knight of the Order of the Dragon in 1431. At this point, Vlad Dracul was merely the guard commander of the mountain passes into Wallachia, but in 1436 he secured the princely throne of Wallachia and moved his family to the court at Târgovişte. Vlad's privileged childhood there ended several years later, when he and his brother were sent by their father as hostages to the Turkish Sultan; living there in daily fear of rape and of the executioner's silken cord, Vlad observed the Turks' use of terror, which he would later turn against them. Nowadays, his birthplace contains a tacky, and not particularly good, restaurant.

The rest of the citadel

To the north of the Clock Tower stands the **Monastery Church** (Tues–Sat 10am–5pm, Sun 11.15am–3pm), now Lutheran, which has a stark, whitewashed interior hung with colourful carpets similar to those in the Black Church at Braşov. Established by 1298, the church was progressively rebuilt between 1484 and 1680. In summer, there's also an organ recital on Fridays at 6pm.

From Piaţa Muzeului it's just a few steps to **Piaţa Cetăţii** (Citadel Square), the heart of the upper town and particularly lively in the summer when a clutch of cafés spills out into the square. The square is surrounded by some fine, recently restored sixteenth-century buildings, such as the **Casa cu Cerb** (*Haus mit dem*

Hirschgeweih or *Stag House*) – now a fine pension and restaurant – and the House on the Rock opposite it, itself housing a super little café.

Heading south from Piaţa Cetăţii, up Str. Şcolii, you reach the impressive **Scholars' Stairs**, a steep, covered wooden staircase of 175 steps and 29 landings that dates from 1642. At the top, the fine murals and wooden balconies of the Bergschule, or School on the Hill, built in 1619, are being restored. Dominating the hill is the main Saxon church, aptly named the **Church on the Hill** (daily 10am–5pm) – built between 1345 and 1525, it has been beautifully restored, with faded murals and memorial stones surviving in an otherwise bare interior, as well as three Gothic altars. Massively buttressed and with few windows, it is a cool and restful place. Opposite the church door is the **Saxon cemetery** (daily 9am–4pm), a weed-choked mass of graves spilling beside the ruined citadel walls.

Of the citadel's original fourteen **towers**, named after the guilds responsible for their upkeep, nine survive, the most impressive being the hexagonal Shoemakers' Tower (Turnul Cizmarilor), the Tailors' Tower (Turnul Croitorilor) and the Tinsmiths' Tower (Turnul Cositorarilor); the last of these, best viewed from the gateway of the *Pfarrhaus*, below the Church on the Hill, has a fine wooden gallery and still shows traces of its last siege in 1704. The Furriers' Tower (Turnul Cojocarilor), on the west side of the citadel, is being restored by the Mihail Eminescu Trust for exhibitions on traditional crafts and Transylvania's built heritage.

The lower town

The **lower town** has little of the character of the citadel, but there's a nice ambience around **Piaţa Hermann Oberth**, where townsfolk gather to consume coffee, beer or pizza, conversing in Romanian, Magyar and, occasionally, antiquated German. **Strada 1 Decembrie** has a fine array of Baroque facades, and there's a striking synagogue at Strada Tache Ionescu 13. The **Mill quarter**, between the citadel and the river, was partially cleared before 1989 for redevelopment as a Civic Centre, and the area is still in limbo. Taking the footbridge over the river, you come to the Romanian **Orthodox Cathedral**, built in the Byzantine style in 1937. Its gleaming white, multifaceted exterior is in striking contrast to the dark interior.

The **market**, off Str. Târnavei, sells food daily but is particularly recommended on Wednesdays and Saturdays, when craft items such as carved wooden spoons are sold for far less than in the citadel's stalls.

Eating and drinking

The best **restaurants** are in the hotels and pensions. During the summer Piaţa Cetăţii is taken over by **cafés**, most of them linked to the various hotels and pensions surrounding the square. The best is the *International Café*, in the House on the Rock at Piaţa Cetăţii 8 (closed Sun) – there's a delicious range of home-made cookies, cakes and quiches, and their organic apple juice and spiced cider are great refreshers in hot weather. Hidden away at the southern end of the citadel at Str. Cositorarilor 9, the lovely *Casa Cositorarilor* is a peaceful spot for breakfast, coffee and cake, or a glass of wine.

Drinking options are more limited, with most people ending up in one of the convivial pizzeria-pubs on Piaţa Oberth such as *La Perla*, at no. 15, or *Pizza Jo*, at no. 7. *The Score*, Str. Goga 3, is a sports pub with good burgers and wi-fi, and the *Pasha Café*, Str. Chendi 20, is a dark, arty spot. The *Culture Pub*, in the basement of the *Burg Hostel*, has **live music** and stays open until 3am, and for dancing there's the *Korona Pub* (closed Sun), beneath the Clock Tower.

Restaurants

Casa cu Cerb Str. Şcolii 1. The *Stag House*, in the hotel of the same name, offers high-class international and Romanian food, beautifully presented with gorgeous surrounds and impeccable service.

Casa Wagner Piaţa Cetăţii 7. Another polished restaurant along the lines of *Casa cu Cerb*, this bright, handsome place offers an upscale take on Romanian dishes.

Quattro Amicii Str. Octavian Goga 12. Next to the scruffy field in the lower town, this is the best pizzeria going; the large terrace is a good venue for crisp, oven-baked pizzas and fresh salads.

Rustic Str. 1 Decembrie 1918 58. Low-key restaurant whose traditional Romanian food – such as *mititei*, *sarmalute* and Transylvanian goulash – is very good. Non-smokers have one table secreted away behind a glass partition. Good breakfasts.

Sighişoara Str. Şcolii 4. As classy as the hotel it's located in, the Romanian food on offer here is top-notch. You can eat in the large green terrace or the lovely cellar restaurant – the service is spot-on.

From Sighişoara to Sibiu

The main **approach to Sibiu** follows the Târnava Mare River west from Sighişoara. From the train or the DN14, you'll see water buffalo pulling wagons or wallowing in the river, and glimpse fortified Saxon churches in villages off the main road. The area south and west of Sighişoara is particularly good for leisurely exploration, its villages all accessible from Sighişoara by bus, or on tours run by Eyetours (☎0788/314 009 or 0752/328 149, ⓦwww.eye-tours.com).

Mălâncrav

Around 7km west of Sighişoara, a side road heads south to Laslea and **MĂLÂNCRAV** (Malmkrog), a picturesque little village nestling at the head of a narrow wooded valley 13km from the DN14. More Saxons remain here, proportionally, than in any other village, and there are still church services every Sunday, as well as early July's *Kronenfest*, bringing together Saxons from the whole region. The diminutive stone-built **church**, idyllically set on a small hillock, was built in the late fourteenth century and surrounded by low walls in the fifteenth century; it is noted for its altarpiece (c.1520) and lovely fourteenth- and fifteenth-century frescoes, especially those of *Genesis* and the *Life of Christ*, on the north wall. For access, ask at the *Pfarrhaus* (parish house; ☎0744/645 473, ⓔmalmkrog@evang.ro) or no. 140, on the main street just below the church (☎0745/924 558). Facing the church is a seventeenth-century Hungarian **manor house**, an unusual presence in Saxon villages at that time. This has been renovated by the Mihai Eminescu Trust, and is now a **guesthouse**, with five en-suite bedrooms, a library and a stately drawing room. The Trust also has a guesthouse at no. 139, for up to five adults (to book either of these contact ☎0754/212 372, ⓔguesthouses@mihaieminescutrust.org), as well as an organic orchard with ancient varieties of apple, pear, plum and walnut, producing wonderful apple juice. It's a delightful hike south over the watershed to **STEJĂRIŞU** (Probstdorf), 2km off the Sibiu–Sighişoara road, where there's a small museum in the Saxon church (ask at no. 70 for access: ☎0720/899 936), and three families offer simple accommodation (€5/person).

Biertan and around

Continuing west along the DN14, a turning at **Şaroş pe Târnave**, 26km from Sighişoara, leads 9km south to **BIERTAN** (Birthälm); travelling by train, you'll need to get off at Mediaş and catch a bus (Mon–Fri); otherwise, a taxi from Sighişoara should cost no more than €10. The best approach to the village, however, is the four-hour hike through fields and woods from Brateiu (Pretai), the first rail halt east of Mediaş, via the tiny villages of Aţel (Hetzeldorf) and Dupuş (Tobsdorf), all three with fortified churches. Aţel has a functional Gästehaus (☎0269/204 865, ext 114; ❶) should you want to stop over, and five buses a day from Mediaş (Mon–Fri); the church key is at the *Azil de Bătrâni*, no. 171 (☎0269/515 710).

Biertan is home to the best known of all the Saxon **fortified churches** (Mon–Sat 10am–1pm & 2–7pm, Sun 9–11am & 2–7pm), high on a hill within two-and-a-half rings of walls linked by a splendid covered staircase, not dissimilar to that in Sighişoara. Completed as late as 1522 on the site of a Catholic basilica, and now on UNESCO's World Heritage list, this was the seat of the Lutheran bishops from 1572 to 1867, and their fine upright gravestones can be seen inside the Bishops' Tower – one of seven. The interior is a classic late Gothic hall church, with intricate stone-ribbed vaulting. Other notable features are the altarpiece (1483–1515), comprising no less than 28 panels; the extraordinary sacristy door, with no fewer than nineteen locks, and a room where couples wanting to divorce were supposedly shut up together for two weeks (there's now a small museum here).

For **information**, ask at the Sachsenbischof bookstall at the church entrance (daily May–Sept 10am–1pm & 2–7pm; April & Oct 10am–1pm & 2–5pm; closed Nov–March). The most restful **place to stay** is the *Casa Dornröschen* (☎0269/868 293, Ⓔcucausbuc@gmail.com; ❷), actually within the church grounds – it's down the path from the archway at the church entrance. Other guesthouses (❶) are *Pension Otto* at Str. Bălcescu 29 (☎0757/094 793); *Pensiunea Todoran Maria*, Str. A. Vlaicu 42 (☎0269/868 189); and *Pensiunea Tiriba Ana*, Str. A. Vlaicu 31 (☎0269/868 277). Just below the church, the medieval-themed *Unglerus* **restaurant** is good for a hearty meal, though rather group-oriented; it also has rooms (☎0269/806 699 or 0751/147 936; ❷), with bikes available (€10/day). Various festivals are held here, though not every year, including Transylvania Fest (the last weekend of July 2011) and the **Sachsentreffen** or Saxon Meeting, when many Saxons return from Germany to meet up, drink and dance (next one mid-September 2012).

Five buses a day (Mon–Fri; one on Sat) run from Mediaş to Biertan, continuing 6km south to **RICHIŞ**, where the fine Dutch-run *La Curtea Richvini* guesthouse (☎0269/258 475, ⓌWWW.richis.eu; ❷) is in the former Parish House at Str. Principală 5; camping is also available. There's a fourteenth-century fortified church too; the key is at no. 87 (☎0269/258 429).

In **COPŞA MARE**, 2km east of Biertan, the massive three-naved Gothic basilica was built by the early fourteenth century, with its choir added in 1519; the keyholder lives at the church. The delightful ⚑ *Copşamare Guesthouses* (no. 216; ☎0746/046 200; ⓌWWW.copsamare.ro; ❹) consist of three beautifully restored homes, with traditional style meeting Italian flair, and great service. A textile museum is also being set up in the village.

Mediaş

The main town between Sighişoara and Sibiu is **MEDIAŞ** (Mediasch), which, despite being ringed by tanneries and chemical works (now closed) fed by the Târnava Mare valley's methane reserves, gets more attractive the further in you venture. Originally an Iron Age and then a Roman settlement, Mediaş was a predominantly Saxon town for many centuries, walled and with gate towers, two of which remain on Str. Cloşca, east of the bus station. After 1918, and the construction here of Transylvania's first gas pipeline, it developed into an industrial – and largely Romanian – town.

From the **train station** on Str. Unirii, turn right to reach the **bus station**, a few minutes' walk away opposite the synagogue; from here, head left up Str. Pompierilor and then take a right down Str. Roth to the town centre, **Piaţa Regele Ferdinand I**, an attractive triangular space ringed by brightly painted two-storey townhouses and pavement cafés. The **Schuller House** (Schullerhaus), at no. 25, was built in 1588 and once hosted the Transylvanian Diet, but now houses temporary art shows.

Just up from the square, along Str. Johannes Honterus, is the fifteenth-century **Evangelical Church**, its 68.5m bell tower slightly askew; the church (Mon–Fri

10am–3pm) is a true citadel, surrounded by store rooms, high ramparts and towers (in one of which, the Tailors' Tower, Vlad the Impaler was imprisoned in 1467). The church interior is highly ornamented, with Anatolian carpets, superbly preserved frescoes, a colourful Baroque organ (used for recitals at 7pm on Mondays June–Sept), and three superb Gothic altars, including a Crucifixion with a view of Vienna painted in 1474–79. If the church is closed, ask at the parish office at the top of the courtyard. For a limited insight into the history of the town, and a better wildlife display, visit the **town museum** (Tues–Sun 9am–5pm) in a former monastery east of the centre at Str. Mihai Viteazul 46.

Tourist information and maps are available at the Kastell bookshop, Piaţa Enescu 8 (May–Oct Mon–Sat 10am–6pm, Sun 11.30–6pm; Nov–April Mon–Fri 10am–6pm). There's some good **accommodation** in town, the best being the *Hotel Traube*, Piaţa Regele Ferdinand I 16 (℡0269/844 898, ℮traube@dafora.ro; ❻), whose fantastically comfortable rooms feature an appealing mix of wrought-iron and handcrafted wooden furnishings; there's also the small but pleasant *Select*, at Str. Petőfi 3 (℡0269/834 874; ❸), and the *Central*, Str. Eminescu 4 (℡0269/841 787, ℮hotcentral@yahoo.com; ❷), a communist relic but very affordable.

Buses run from the bus station to Agnita, Sibiu and Târgu Mureş, and the surrounding villages. Some especially picturesque villages with fortified churches lie along the road to Agnita, notably **Moşna** (Meschen), 10km south and reached by eight buses (Mon–Fri). Its church, built in 1491, has a 50m tower, and the key is at Str. Cetăţii 531 (℡0269/862 154).

Copşa Mică to Ocna Sibiului

You may find you have to change trains for Sibiu in **COPŞA MICĂ** (Kleinkopisch), 13km west of Mediaş, but there isn't anything to stop for. There are good fortified churches in **Valea Viilor** (Wurmloch, 4km south of Copşa Mică), **Axente Sever** (Frauendorf) and **Agârbiciu** (Arbegen). Valea Viilor's church is on UNESCO's World Heritage list, with its key at no. 211 (℡0269/515 266); Axente Sever's church houses an excellent new museum (April–Oct Mon–Sat 10am–6pm, Sun noon–6pm), and there's also a guesthouse within its walls (℡0269/847 328, ℮rodi .stef@yahoo.com; ❸). Four buses a day (Mon–Fri) run from Mediaş to Valea Viilor, while the other two are visible just east of their rail halts. It's possible to follow easy hiking trails from Agârbiciu to Valea Viilor and Moşna to Biertan.

The main road south to Sibiu (DN14) passes through rolling hills and orchards, and more Saxon villages with doughty fortress-churches, notably **Slimnic** (Stolzenburg), which is interesting because the church, begun in 1450, was never finished, but the ruins of a substantial fortress around it survive. Along the railway, slightly to the west, there's little worth stopping for other than **OCNA SIBIULUI** (Salzburg), a bathing resort with fizzy, salty water, which bubbles up in four lakes formed in abandoned salt-workings. The grand *fin-de-siècle* spa building has been restored, and fine new hotels are opening (℡0269/577 348, ℗www.ocnasibiului .ro). The nearest train stop to the spa is Băile Ocna Sibiului, 2km north of Ocna Sibiului station proper, with a decent **campsite** adjacent.

Sibiu

"I rubbed my eyes in amazement," wrote Walter Starkie of **SIBIU** (Hermannstadt in German and Nagyszeben in Hungarian) in 1929. "The town where I found myself did not seem to be in Transylvania, for it had no Romanian or Hungarian character-istics: the narrow streets and old gabled houses made me think of Nuremberg."

Nowadays, the illusion is harder to sustain, in a city surrounded by high-rise suburbs and virtually abandoned by the Saxons themselves, but the Old Town is still a startling sight, with many of its houses painted sky blue, red, apricot or pea green. Split into a **historic centre** and a lower **new town**, Sibiu has many fine old **churches** and some of Romania's best museums, as well as the remains of the **bastions** and fortifications. Founded by 1191, Sibiu was the chief city of the Transylvanian Saxons, dominating trade with Wallachia through the Olt gorge. In 1241 their citadel was destroyed by the Tatars, leaving only a hundred survivors; the townsfolk surrounded themselves with four rings of walls (including a new lower town) by 1452, defences which repelled the Turks three times but were largely demolished in the nineteenth century. Now, the wheel has turned, and Sibiu has stronger trading links with Germany than any other Transylvanian town, and has even elected a Saxon mayor, who has been so successful that he ran for prime minister in 2009.

Arrival and information

Sibiu's **bus and train stations** are next to each other on the northeast side of town. The rail service is poor, but bus services are increasing, reaching as far afield

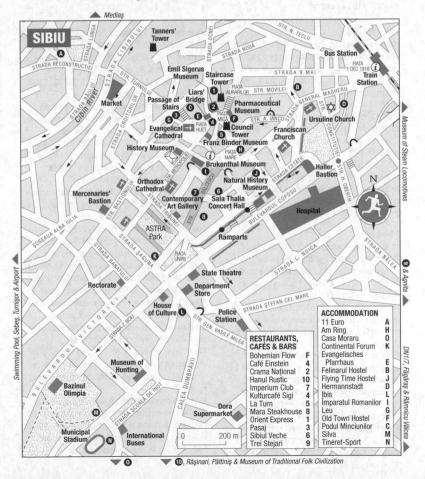

as Bucharest, Cluj, Constanţa and Timişoara. To reach the centre, cross Piaţa 1 Decembrie 1918 (still generally known as Piaţa Gării) and follow Str. General Magheru up the hill. Most international buses call next to the *Tineret-Sport* hotel – tickets available from the travel agency across the road (☎0269/232 826). The **airport** (☎0269/229 161) is on the western edge of town, served by bus #11.

The **tourist information office** is at Str. Brukenthal 2 on the north side of Piaţa Mare (Mon–Fri 9am–5pm, Sat & Sun 9am–1pm; ☎0269/208 913, Ⓦwww .sibiu.ro); there are also kiosks at the airport and the station (Mon–Fri 9am–5pm), where you can leave luggage (€2). The **Lutheran Pfarrhaus**, Piaţa Huet 1 (☎0269/211 203), sells a leaflet (currently in German only, with English summaries) describing the town's Kulturweg circuit of information signs, as well as a book listing accommodation and walks in the Saxon villages to the north. Kultours, Piaţa Mică 16 (daily 9am–7pm; ☎0269/216 854, Ⓦwww.kultours.ro) has **bikes for hire** (€12/day).

Accommodation

Sibiu has a decent, if largely uninspiring, range of **hotels**, **hostels** and **guesthouses**, mostly fairly central.

Hostels

Felinarul Hostel Str. Felinarul 8 ☎0269/235 260, Ⓦwww.felinarulhostelsibiu.ro. Run by a Romanian-Irish couple, this aims to be a "boutique hostel" and largely succeeds, with its peaceful atmosphere and traditional furniture; it's between the station and the centre. ❷

Flying Time Pub-Hostel Str. Gheorghe Lazăr 6 ☎0369/730 179, Ⓦwww.sibiuhostel.ro. The funkiest hostel in town, with four dorms, one double room, and a café and pub-pizzeria with DJs. ❷

Old Town Hostel Piaţa Mică 26 ☎0269/216 445, Ⓦwww.hostelsibiu.ro. Fabulously located, this has three large, bright dorms, laundry facilities and wi-fi (but no lockers) – breakfast is not included but there is a kitchen. ❷

Hotels

11 Euro Tudor Vladimirescu 2 ☎0269/222 041, Ⓔcontact@11euro.ro. Unmissable yellow and orange brick building in a quiet spot across from the Cibin River; it's a decent place, with some refurbished rooms. ❷

Am Ring Piaţa Mare 14 ☎0269/206 499, Ⓦwww .amringhotel.ro. The location is wonderful, the rooms are delightful, with excellent bathrooms, but it's two floors up with no lift; there's also a decent restaurant (in the courtyard and cellar) and terrace café. ❼

Casa Moraru Str. A. Vlahuţă 11A ☎0269/216 291, Ⓦwww.casamoraru.ro. A family hotel with good facilities, including in-room hair dryers, a good restaurant and bar, plus sauna and pool. ❸

Continental Forum Str. Unirii 10 ☎0372/692 692, Ⓦwww.continentalhotels.ro. Newly refurbished, this slick business hotel is the grandest place in town, but there are good offers to be had online. ❾

Evangelisches Pfarrhaus Piaţa Huet 1 ☎0269/211 203, Ⓔgast@evang.ro. The Lutheran parish house provides clean, simple, hostel-style accommodation. No breakfast. ❷

Hermannstadt Str. Blănarilor 13 ☎0269/212 368, Ⓦwww.pensiuneahermannstadt-sibiu.ro. The handiest place for the station (but also very close to the centre), this breezy little guesthouse has modern, a/c rooms. Breakfast is extra. ❸

Ibis Calea Dumbravii 2 ☎0269/218 100, Ⓦwww .ibishotels.ro. Beautifully refurbished communist tower, now as reliable as every other *Ibis*. ❻

Împaratul Romanilor Str. Bălcescu 4 ☎0269/216 500, Ⓦsibiu.imparatulromanilor.ro. Traditionally the city's most opulent hotel, and in a great location. ❺

Leu Str. Moş Ion Roată 6 ☎0269/218 392. Secreted away at the bottom of the "Passage of Stairs", this simple, hostel-style pension has a dorm plus double and triple en-suite rooms. ❶–❷

Podul Minciunilor Str. Azilului 1 ☎0269/217 259, Ⓦwww.ela-hotels.ro. The "Liars' Bridge" guest-house, just down from the bridge and first on the left, is a friendly, old-fashioned place with six simple en-suite rooms. Breakfast not available, but there's a coffee machine and fridge. ❷

Silva Aleea Eminescu 1 ☎0269/243 985, Ⓦwww .hotelsilvasibiu.com. Pleasant, welcoming hotel by an attractive park, nicely refurbished with spacious rooms. ❹

Tineret-Sport Str. Octavian Goga 2 ☎0269/233 673, Ⓦwww.hotelsportsibiu.ro. Not exactly the best location – next to the football stadium – but the rooms are cheap and relatively modern, with bathroom and TV. Breakfast is extra. ❷

The Old Town

The Old Town centres on three conjoined squares – **Piaţa Mare** (Grosser Ring), **Piaţa Mică** (Kleiner Ring) and **Piaţa Huet** (Huetplatz). Heading west from the train station along Str. Magheru (Sporergasse), you'll pass a **synagogue** (still used in summer by Sibiu's remaining handful of Jews) and the **Ursuline church** (1474–78), now shared by Greco-Catholic and Roman Catholic congregations. Forking right onto Str. Avram Iancu brings you to the Casa Böhel at no. 16, one of the oldest houses in town, built in the first half of the fourteenth century and newly restored.

Piaţa Mare

Traditionally the hub of public life, the resplendent **Piaţa Mare** (Large Square) is surrounded by the renovated premises of sixteenth- and seventeenth-century merchants. Its north side is dominated by a Roman Catholic church (1726–33); to its left, at Piaţa Mare 5, the eighteenth-century **Brukenthal Palace** was the home of Samuel von Brukenthal (see box, p.162), governor of Transylvania from 1777 to 1787. Built in 1778–85 by a Viennese architect in a refined late Baroque style, the palace now houses Transylvania's finest art collection, partly assembled by von Brukenthal himself and opened to the public in 1817, three years before the Louvre in Paris. Before entering, note the splendid portal, incorporating a gilded coat of arms (in the centre) and two large urns atop the side pillars.

As well as an extensive array of Romanian and Western art, the **Brukenthal Museum** (Muzeul Brukenthal; Tues–Sun 10am–6pm; closed Tues Nov–April & 1st Tues of month; €3, €7.50 combined ticket for Sibiu's six main museums) includes fifteenth- and sixteenth-century Transylvanian wooden religious sculptures and eighteenth-century Romanian icons. While the first floor is somewhat disappointing, the real treasures lie on the second floor: beautifully presented in spotlit glass cases, the chief paintings are Antonello de Messini's *Crucifixion*, Pieter Brueghel's *Massacre of the Innnocents*, and, most famously, Jan van Eyck's exquisite *Man in Blue Turban*.

Heading from here towards Piaţa Huet, you'll pass near the **History Museum** (same hours; €3), in the Old City Hall (Primăria Veche; 1470–91) at Str. Mitropoliei 2 (Fleischergasse); the arcaded courtyard is worth a look (daily 10am–6pm; €0.25) even if you choose not to go inside to view the interesting exhibits on local history or the collection of silverware (€1 extra).

Piaţa Huet and Piaţa Mică

On **Piaţa Huet**, the massive **Evangelical Cathedral** (daily: summer Mon–Sat 9am–8pm, Sun 11am–8pm; winter 9am–3pm; €0.25), built in three phases between 1320 and 1520, dominates its neighbours, the Saxons' Brukenthal Gymnasium (Grammar School; 1782) and *Pfarrhaus* (Parish House; 1502). There's a fresco of the *Crucifixion* (1445) by Johannes von Rosenau on the north wall of the choir, showing Italian and Flemish influences, and the **tomb of Mihnea the Bad**, Dracula's son, is in the crypt; Mihnea was *voivode* of Wallachia for just three years before being stabbed to death in 1510 on leaving the cathedral. There's also a fine array of funerary monuments here, including a well-tended memorial to the dead of World War I. The cathedral **tower** (visits Mon–Sat noon & 4pm) is worth the climb for its expansive views over the city. By the cathedral, the thirteenth-century **Passage of Stairs** (Pasajul Scărilor) descends into the lower town, overshadowed by arches and the medieval citadel wall. The cathedral houses Romania's largest church organ, and in summer there's a regular programme of concerts.

From Piaţa Huet it's a short hop into **Piaţa Mică** (Kleiner Ring or Small Square), where a miniature urban canyon drops below the elegant wrought-iron Iron

The roots of homeopathy

Baron **Samuel von Brukenthal**'s achievements as governor of Transylvania were many, but his role in the development of **homeopathy** was the widest-ranging and ultimately most important.

It was Brukenthal who paid for **Samuel Hahnemann** (1755–1843) to complete his medical degree in Germany and then brought him to Sibiu as his private doctor. In recompense, Hahnemann spent the best part of two years (1777–79) cataloguing Brukenthal's immense library of 280,000 books, including a large collection of rare manuscripts and books by medieval alchemists and physicians such as Paracelsus and Rumelius; it was his study of these authors that laid the basis of his lifetime's work. In 1779, Hahnemann returned to Germany, married and had children – although desperately poor, he pursued his studies, driven by his dissatisfaction with the conventional medicine that he was obliged to practise, while gradually formulating his own theories. Although homeopathy was eventually marginalized by conventional (allopathic) medicine, by the 1870s this had itself absorbed key homeopathic principles, such as the abandonment of complex mixtures of drugs and the adoption of theories of disease based upon infectious agents.

In recent times, Romania was one of the first countries to legitimize homeopathy, due to the shortage of medicines and medical equipment under Ceauşescu. From 1995 only qualified doctors were allowed to practise homeopathy (although those already registered as homeopaths were permitted to continue).

Bridge (Podul de Fier). Built in 1859, it's nicknamed the **Liars' Bridge** (Podul Minciunilor), the story being that if someone tells a lie while standing on it the bridge will collapse. Ceauşescu managed to give a speech from it and survive, although he disliked the town and never returned.

By the bridge, at Piaţa Mică 21, the handsome, arcaded Hall of the Butchers' Guild (Fleischerhalle) houses the **Emil Sigerus Museum of Saxon Ethnography** (Tues–Sun 10am–6pm; €2), a limited collection of household goods plus a craft shop. On the eastern side of the square, at no. 26, the **Pharmaceutical Museum** (Muzeul de Farmacie; Tues–Sun 10am–6pm; €1.50) preserves the interior of an ancient pharmacy – beautiful carved walnut shop-fittings and a laboratory stuffed with flutes, scales and copper pans – and also commemorates Samuel Hahnemann, founder of homeopathy, who lived in Sibiu in the 1770s (see box above). The Casa Hermes (Hermeshaus) at no. 11 houses the **Franz Binder Museum of Ethnology** (Muzeul de Etnografie Universale Franz Binder; Tues–Sun 10am–6pm; €2), based on the collection of Franz Binder (1820–75), who spent thirty years in Africa as a merchant and plant collector. As well as items from Africa, Binder garnered all manner of objects from far-flung places, such as Chinese vases and Japanese statuettes. To return from Piaţa Mică to Piaţa Mare, cut through the gate below the **Council Tower** (Turnul Sfatului; daily 10am–6pm; €0.50), built in the thirteenth century as part of the city's second ring of fortifications, and rebuilt in 1588; climb the 111 steps for fine **views** of the city.

Alternatively, a passageway leads down through the **Staircase Tower** (Finger-lingsstiege) at Piaţa Mică 24 via Piaţa Aurarilor to Str. Movilei, a street pockmarked with medieval windows, doorways and turrets. Down in the rambling lower town northwest of the squares are the octagonal brick **Tanners' Tower** (Turnul Pielarilor), on Str. Pulberăriei, reached via Str. Valea Mare, and a busy food **market** beside the river on Piaţa Cibin – the site of the first settlement in Sibiu.

Over to the east, near the train station, the enjoyable **Museum of Steam Locomotives** (daily 8am–8pm; €1) is an open-air collection of over thirty engines, as well as snow ploughs and steam cranes – rail enthusiasts will love it. To get there, cross the bridge to the left of the station, descend the steps and go south along Str. Dorobanților; after 300m or so (at house no. 26), turn sharp right to the rail tracks and go left through the arch.

The New Town

In Saxon times, Sibiu's promenade was the Heltauergasse, now **Strada Bălcescu**, leading south from Piaţa Mare to Piaţa Unirii, and this is still the heart of the modern city. At the northern end of the street is Sibiu's oldest hotel, the **Împăratul Romanilor**, still recognizable as the grand establishment once patronized by the likes of Johann Strauss and Eminescu. The design of the hotel, which dates from 1895, was a reaction against the militaristic architecture that had previously dominated the town; this can be seen to the southeast in the three rows of **ramparts and bastions** on either side of B-dul Coposu, where three mighty **towers** were built in the late fourteenth century and manned by members of the Carpenters', Potters' and Arquebusiers' (later the Drapers') guilds. To the east, a theatre was built on the base of the **Powder Tower** (Pulverturm) in 1788, burnt down in 1948, and has now been restored as the Sala Thalia concert hall. Just beyond it, at Str. Cetăţii 1, the **Natural History Museum** (same hours as Brukenthal Museum; €2) has the standard collection of stuffed wildlife. The **Haller Bastion** (1552) at the northern end of Str. Cetăţii, and the Soldisch or **Mercenaries' Bastion** (the last to be built, in 1627) further west on Str. Bastionului, also survive.

Sibiu developed as a centre of intellectual and cultural life during the nineteenth century, and the first congress of **ASTRA** – the Association for the Propagation of Romanian Culture in Transylvania – was held in 1861 on **Strada Mitropoliei**, a street east of the Mercenaries' Bastion that is full of significance for Romanian nationalists. No. 19 was the home of Zaharia Boiu (1834–1903), poet and founder of the first Romanian-language school in Sibiu, while Avram Iancu and Mihai Eminescu both stayed in houses here. Furthermore, opposite the **post office** is the **Orthodox Cathedral** (1902–06), based on the Aya Sofya in Istanbul, which is embellished with all manner of neo-Byzantine flourishes and frescoes, plus mosaics from Munich. Between the cathedral and Piaţa Unirii is the **ASTRA Park**, lined with busts of Romanian worthies; in 1905, ASTRA opened a library and museum overlooking the park in a fine building at Str. Lupaş 5. A block east from the park, at Tribunei 6, you'll find the Brukenthal Museum's **Contemporary Art Gallery** (same hours; €1.25).

Southwest of Piaţa Unirii, at Str. Şcoala de Înot 4, the **Museum of Hunting** (same hours; €1.50), once the home of a Habsburg general, is worth a brief visit to see his collection of weapons, medals and stuffed animals.

Outside the centre

Southwest of the centre along Calea Dumbrăvii (bus #13, leaving the train station at 47 minutes past the hour), on the edge of the Dumbrava Forest, the superb **Museum of Traditional Folk Civilization** (daily: May–Oct 10am–8pm; Nov–April 9am–5pm; €5; ⓌÆwww.muzeulastra.ro) is the best open-air museum in Romania (generally known as the Muzeul ASTRA). Set against a mountain backdrop, it offers a fantastic insight into Romanian rural life, with almost 150 structures divided up into themed areas. Highlights include the many neatly thatched or wooden-roofed homesteads with their adjoining workshops (such as blacksmiths', wheelwrights', weavers' and potters'), several windmills, and two wooden churches, both still in use. You'll also notice numerous *troiţas*, stone crosses used as places of worship in villages where no church existed. It's worth buying the excellent guiding leaflet.

The museum grounds are the venue for a couple of annual **festivals**, namely the Craftsmen's Fair in mid-August (usually around the 15th) and, in September, the Festival of National Traditions, featuring folk costumes from across Romania, music, dance and much merriment. There's also an excellent little **information office** (daily 9am–3pm) in a converted hut near the entrance, and a good **restaurant** (see below).

Bus #10, from the bridge south of the train station on B-dul Coposu, takes you to Turnişor, dropping you outside the *Pfarrhaus* at Str. Bielz 62 (Kirchgasse). To Romanians, Turnişor is simply a suburb of Sibiu, but to its German populace it's a distinct village, Neppendorf. Originally Saxon, its population was boosted in the eighteenth century by an infusion of Austrian Protestants, expelled by their Catholic neighbours. Although the two groups never mixed in other villages throughout the region, here the Saxons and Landler intermarried – yet they are still seated separately in the church, with Landler women on one side of the nave and Saxon women on the other. The **church** was never fortified – the villagers fled to Sibiu when the Turks came to burn their settlement in 1493 – but internally it's typical of Saxon village churches, with lovely paintings on the gallery; ask at the *Pfarrhaus* for the key. There's also an excellent **museum** in the north transept, mapping the history of the village, with lots of old photos and plenty of text (all in German). Today, there are only about 200 Germans in Turnişor, compared to some 4000 before World War II. Visible from trains to the north of Turnişor station is an amazing Gypsy palace, resembling a Japanese castle with multiple Gothic spikes.

Eating and drinking

While Sibiu has plenty of **restaurants**, they're not particularly varied and there's often little to distinguish one from another. For daytime snacks, there's *Dori's*, at Piaţa Mică 3 (Mon–Fri 8am–7pm, Sat 8am–2pm).

There's a healthy spread of nice **cafés and bars** on the two main squares, Piaţa Mare and Piaţa Mică, and along Str. Bălcescu, most with convivial streetside *terasas*. The best of these is the cute, classy *Imperium Club*, Str. Bălcescu 24, with regular sessions of quality jazz, piano and stand-up. Below the Liars' Bridge at Str. Ocnei 8, *Orient Express* is an attractive arty café (daily to midnight), often with live piano or poetry. At the splendid *Trei Stejari*, at the corner of Stradas Oberth and Fabricii, big jugs of beer on the enormous rambling *terasa* are the order of the day, thanks to the brewery next door.

There are various **venues** open to 2am or later around Piaţa Mică, including *Café Einstein* at no. 13 (ⓦwww.cafeeinstein.ro); *Kulturcafé Sigi* at no. 16 (ⓦwww .kulturcafe.ro); the long-established and bohemian *Crama Naţional*, below no. 18 (daily 6pm–2am); and *Bohemian Flow* below the *Old Town Hostel* at no. 26 (daily 4pm–2am).

Restaurants

Hanul Rustic Museum of Traditional Folk Civiliza-tion. With traditional Romanian food and decor, this place does a roaring trade with locals and tourists alike; the entrance is on the Răşinari road, about 1km or so beyond the museum's main entrance (see p.163).

La Turn Piaţa Mare 2. Nothing extraordinary, but the setting, in a quiet cobbled corner next to the Council Tower, and the juicy mixed grills, make a visit worthwhile.

Mara Steakhouse Str. Bălcescu 21. Just about the best restaurant on this busy street, this pleasingly simple and convivial joint serves Romanian staples, including game (deer, wild boar and bear). Decent breakfasts, too.

Pasaj Str. Turnului 3A. Sprightly pizzeria with a cool brick interior, also offering a varied selection of salads and pasta, as well as chicken, beef and vegetarian options (and wi fi)

Sibiul Veche Str. Papiu Ilarian 3. Just off Str. Bălcescu, this claustrophobic *crama*, with walls strewn with regional objects, offers some of the most authentic Romanian food (*sarmale, mămăligă*) in town. As befits its rather touristic bent, there's regular live folk music.

Entertainment

Classical concerts are held in the Sala Thalia, Str. Cetății 3 (tickets daily 10am–4pm; €1.50–5). The **state theatre** is at B-dul Corneliu Coposu 2 (☎0269/217 577); tickets can be bought at the Agenție Teatrala, Str. Bălcescu 17 (Mon–Sat 11am–6pm), or at the theatre one hour prior to performances.

Sibiu has one of Romania's liveliest and most varied **festival** rosters. The best is the superb **International Theatre Festival**, over ten days usually beginning at the end of May – there are nightly happenings (classical, rock and world music concerts, contemporary dance) on an open-air stage on Piața Mare, plus a multitude of different events (installations, films, plays and photographic/art exhibitions) taking place elsewhere around town. There's also a **Jazz Festival** at the beginning of May, a **Pottery Fair** on the first weekend of September and, in October, the **ASTRA Film Fest** and **International Festival of Documentary Film and Anthropology**.

Listings

Car rental Autonom, Str. Bălcescu 1 (☎0269/235 538, ⓦ www.autonom.com); Toro, Str. Filarmonicii 5 (☎0269/232 237, ⓦ www.tororent.ro).
Hospital B-dul Spitalelor, opposite the Haller Bastion.
Internet Silence Internet Café, Str. Mitropoliei 27 (daily 9am–10pm).
Libraries The British Council library is at the university's central library (Biblioteca Centrală), B-dul Victoriei 10 (☎0269/446 077).
Pharmacy Farmasib, Str. Bălcescu 53 (daily 9am–10pm), has an urgent night-time service.

Sport Facilities are clustered around the open-air swimming pool, the Ştrand, on Şos. Alba Iulia (bus #17), and there's an indoor, Olympic-sized swimming pool on B-dul Victoriei. At Str. Şaguna 2, the Baia Neptun (Tues–Sat 8am–8pm) has a 20m pool, plus sauna and massage treatments. Sibiu's football team, FC InterSibiu, plays in the Municipal Stadium in the Parc sub Arini.
Train tickets The CFR office is at Str. B ălcescu 6; international bookings Mon–Fri 10am–5.30pm.

Around Sibiu

Buses serve many of the **old Saxon settlements** around Sibiu. Many of these villages have sizeable Romanian and Gypsy populations, now far outnumbering the Germans, but most have fortified churches and rows of houses presenting a solid wall to the street – hallmarks of their Saxon origins. After 1989, most Saxons left for Germany and their culture has largely vanished from this region, but church restoration and cultural projects are now gathering pace.

South of Sibiu are the **Cindrel** (or **Cibin**) mountains, where enjoyable day walks and longer hikes can be taken from the small ski resort of Păltiniş.

Cisnădie and Cisnădioara

Two or three buses an hour (or roughly one every two hours at weekends) leave Sibiu's bus station for **CISNĂDIE** (Heltau), 12km south, known to the Turks as the Red Town, both for the colour of its walls and the blood that was shed attempting to breach them. A long square leads to the largely Romanesque **church** (daily 9am–2pm & 3–6pm), a formidable bulk protected by a double wall and a moat. You can also ascend the massive thirteenth-century **tower**, climbing through a succession of lofty vaults linked by creaking ladders and narrow stairways to the belfry. From here, the view of Cisnădie's angular courtyards and red rooftops is superb, while just visible in the distance below the Cindrel mountains is the conical rock overlooking the village of Cisnădioara. The church grounds are the unlikely setting for a small **Museum of Communism** (daily 9am–2pm & 3–6pm; €1), containing newspaper clippings, a calendar used for bread rationing, and objects belonging to former party members. The only **accommodation** is 2.5km south along Str. Cetății towards Sadu, at the comfortable and friendly *Cerbul Carpatin* (☎0269/562 937; ④).

From central Cisnădie, it's a 3km walk west along Str. Măgurii and the valley road towards the striking 70m-high rock that looms over **CISNĂDIOARA** (Michelsburg), also reached by around eight buses a day (Mon–Fri only) from Sibiu. Crowning the summit of the hill is the tiny **Romanesque church**, built in 1223, which frequently withstood Tatar attacks; the villagers defended it by hurling down rocks which had previously been carried into the citadel by aspiring husbands, the custom being that no young man could marry until he had carried a heavy rock from the riverbed up the steep track. The interior is bare save for a tiny stone altar, but the **views** over the church's 2m-high ring wall to the snow-streaked peaks of the Făgăraş mountains are superb. The stiff fifteen-minute climb to the church begins near the bus stop in the centre of the village – there's usually someone present to collect the €2 fee, but if not (and the gate is shut), go to house no. 246 or call ☎0269/564 332.

Follow the main road down through the village and you will pass a few shops and rows of neat, unmistakably German houses, now holiday homes. The best accommodation in the village is the *Pension Subcetate* (☎0740/220 049, ⊛www .sub-cetate.ro; ❸), just down from the path leading up to the church – a lovely, homely place with bright rooms and traditionally painted furniture, it also has a very good restaurant. A British couple offers accommodation (with or without meals) in two nicely refurbished Saxon houses in the lower part of the village, with a swimming pool and bar (☎0742 247 664, ⊛www.secrettransylvania.co.uk; ❸).

Răşinari and Păltiniş

From Sibiu, hourly buses trundle for 12km to **RĂŞINARI**, a tight-packed village with a painted Orthodox church built in 1752, and an **ethnographic museum** (Tues–Sun 10am–5pm), showing the usual range of local costumes and pottery. However, it's more noteworthy for the **Pastoral Album Folklore Festival**, held on the third Sunday of April. There are several appealing **guesthouses** in the village, all on Str. Goga, including the *Phoenix* at no. 777 (☎0745/308 034; ❷), and the *Badiu* at no. 786 (☎0269/557 359; ❷). Răşinari is connected to Păltiniş by road and by a mountain trail (marked with red stripes; 6 or 7hr).

PĂLTINIŞ (Hohe Rinne; 1442m), 22km from Răşinari, is primarily a minor **ski resort**, but also attracts summer hikers. Three **buses** a day (#22) come here from the train station in Sibiu. You should phone directly to book a bed at the central *Casa Turistilor* (☎0269/574 035; ❷), or the *Hotel Cindrel* (☎0269/574 056, ⊛www.hotelcindrel.ro; ④); you'll also find various guesthouses plus the HI-affiliated *Hostel Păltiniş* (☎0269/210 934, ⊜sibiu@e-tineret.ro; ❶), a fairly old-school centre for youth groups.

The Cindrel and Lotrului mountains

Păltiniş makes a good starting point for walks into the **Cindrel and Lotrului mountains**, one of the lesser-known sections of the Transylvanian Alps; the mountains offer high open hikes on quiet trails, and easier terrain than the **Parâng range** to the west. It's only two or three hours' walk north from Păltiniş, predominantly downhill, through the **Cibin gorges** (Cheile Cibinului), past Lake Cibin, to the *Fântânele* cabana (☎0741/251 554; ❶), following the red dots beyond the *Casa Turistilor*. From here, you can push on in a couple of hours either to **Sibiel** village (see below) following blue dots, or direct to Sibiel rail halt following blue crosses.

However, the route barely takes you above the tree line, so it's worth trying some **overnight hikes**. A two-day route, marked with red triangles, leads south via the former *Gâtu Berbecului* cabana and a forestry road along the Sadu valley and the Negovanu Mare (2135m) in the Lotrului mountains to Voineasa in the Lotru valley. If you take this route you'll need to camp, but the more popular route is to the west, into the **Parâng mountains**, east of Petroşani (see p.182), with well-spaced cabana accommodation. This route, indicated by red stripes, follows a ridge to the *Cânaia* refuge (5–6hr; ☎0746/788 218; ❶) and then continues over open moorland (poorly marked with red stripes and red crosses – be careful not to lose your way) to *Obârşia Lotrului* (another 9–10hr), at the junction of the north–south DN67C and the east–west DN7A, both largely unsurfaced. There's a cabana here (☎0744/700 180; ❶), as well as camping and the odd guesthouse. This is the gateway to the Parâng mountains, an alpine area with beautiful lakes; the red crosses continue up to the main ridge, from where red stripes lead you west to Petroşani.

The Mărginimea Sibiului

West of Sibiu, the DN1/7 (E68/E81) and the railway pass through the **Mărginimea Sibiului** (Borders of Sibiu), an area that's fairly densely populated, mostly by Romanians rather than Saxons, with a lively folklore recorded in small ethnographic museums in most villages. There are many sheep-raising communities here, and you'll see flocks on the move, with donkeys carrying the shepherds' belongings. Personal trains between Sibiu and Vinţu de Jos (the junction just beyond Sebeş) halt a short distance from several settlements en route.

Cristian

The first of the accessible villages, 10km from Sibiu by Personal trains and bus #20 (hourly), is **CRISTIAN**, where a double wall protects the fifteenth-century Saxon church of Grossau, with a Romanesque portal and massive towers. An earthquake in 1850 partially destroyed the church, after which the tower was extended with the addition of four turrets – there are superb views from the top. Since the mid-eighteenth century, when some 150 Austrian migrants arrived, the village has been largely dominated by a Protestant population, who fled here to avoid Catholic oppression. Indeed, there were still some three thousand Germans living here in the mid-1970s, but that number has dwindled to just forty. The entrance (€1) is on the main road at Str. X 40 (at the bus stop), or call ☎0269/579 690. From April on the village is home to dozens of **storks**, who construct their impressive, and improbably bulky, nests atop telegraph poles and chimneys, where two dozen nesting platforms have been fitted – affording fabulous photo opportunities. The village has a few guesthouses and one **hotel**, the *Spack* (☎0269/579 262; ❸), just north of the **train** station (walking towards the church) at Str. II 9; it's a clean, homely little place owned by a Saxon family, but without a restaurant. The main road passes to the north of all of the villages after Cristian, and some of the train stations – notably those for Sălişte and Tilişca – lie several kilometres north of the villages they serve, making public transport slightly problematic; however, there are good guesthouses in every village.

Sibiel

It's 8km west through Orlat to the Sibiel train station, from where a smaller road continues for 3km to **SIBIEL**, a sheep-raising community with a strong tradition of **witchcraft**. Perhaps understandably, the villagers fear witches and ghosts more for their attacks on livestock than on people, blowing horns on St George's Day to prevent witches (*strigoi*) from stealing their ewes' milk. In the grounds of the Orthodox church (built in 1765), the rather good **Museum of Icons Painted on Glass** (daily 8am–1.30pm & 2–8pm; €1) has more than 700 icons, mostly painted by naïve (or peasant) artists from Transylvania and Moldavia; from here, a footpath leads uphill past a ruined citadel to the *Fântânele* cabana (❶) and through the Cibin gorges to Păltiniș in eight hours (see p.166). Opposite the church gate at no. 325, the welcoming pension *Adriana* (☎0269/552 573; ❷) has several cheap and cosy rooms, with dinner available upon request – the family also produce their own painted icons, which you can buy. There are plenty of other guesthouses, including the *Pensiunea Morariu* at no. 309 (☎0265/552 619; ❷) and *Casa Stanca* at no. 306 (☎0265/552 583; ❷).

Săliște and Tilișca

Continuing north from Sibiel, the road meets the route east back to the main DN1/7 at **SĂLIȘTE**, famous for its peasant **choir**, which performs occasionally in the community centre, and for its cooperative, which produces carpets and embroidered costumes, the latter worn during Săliște's **Meeting of the Village's Sons festival** (December 28). From a distance, the village church could almost be Saxon, but it is in fact firmly Orthodox. Just beyond it, at Piața Eroilor 8, is the **Ethnographic Museum**, displaying local costumes and artefacts; ask at the *Primaria* for entry or call a day ahead (☎0269/553 086). Near a watermill ten minutes' walk along the Tilișca road at Str. București 21, lives Radu Ilieș, probably the last craftsman making the distinctive black felt hats worn by men in this area, who lets visitors watch him as he works.

Costumes are more likely to appear during the course of everyday life at **TILIȘCA**, wedged between two wooded hills about 3km west; this is a less spoilt settlement than Săliște and one that can trace its origins back to Dacian times. Standing in the heart of the village is the **church**, built in 1782, painted a lovely sky blue and decorated, just below the eaves, with a belt of exterior frescoes depicting various saints. Continuing down Str. Școlii you'll come to the Ethnographic Museum in a restored wooden house opposite the *Primaria*, where you should ask for admission. Halfway along Str. Școlii, at no. 535, is the smart *Pensiunea Irina* (☎0269/554 009 or 0744/313 102, ⓦwww.pensiuneairinasibiu.ro; ❷). There's also accommodation in Săliște, at *La Salisteana*, Str. Băii 13 (☎0269/553 121, ⓦwww.salisteanca.com; ❷), and *Casa Rudi & Ella*, Str. Luncii 14 (☎0269/553 753, ⓦwww.casa-rudi-ella.ro; ❷), where there's also camping space.

Miercurea Sibiului, Băile Miercurea and Câlnic

Road and rail are reunited at **MIERCUREA SIBIULUI** (Reussmarkt), a village whose name derives from the Romanian word for Wednesday, the traditional market day here. In the centre of the village is a small, well-preserved thirteenth-century basilica, fortified during the fifteenth century, with food stores on the inside of its oval ring wall. Trains and buses also stop 5km further on at **BĂILE MIERCUREA**, a modest spa resort with a run-down campsite, tourist cabana (❶) and a hotel-restaurant on the main road. A few kilometres west, a handful of cabins (❶) stand at the junction to **CÂLNIC** (Kelling/Kelnek), 3km south of the DN1/7, where a massive keep, built around 1300, and a very simple Roman-esque chapel of the same period, are enclosed within one-and-a-half rings of walls that resisted several Turkish sieges. The castle has recently been restored and opened to visitors, with temporary exhibits in the chapel; local trains halt at Cut, just northwest of the road junction, or you can get a bus at 11.30am from Sebeș. In Gârbova, on a back road between Miercurea Sibiului and Câlnic, the Dutch-owned Urwegen guesthouse and Poarta Oilor campsite is at Str. M. Eminescu 573 (☎0258/748 001, ⓦwww.guest-house-urwegen.com; ❹).

Sebeş

The town of **SEBEŞ** grew up on the proceeds of the leather-working industry, trading mainly with Wallachia; as Mühlbach, it was the capital of the Unterwald, the westernmost zone of Saxon settlement. The German street names have recently been resurrected, but Italian influence is now dominant. In 1438, a Turkish army arrived, demanding the town's surrender; a number of inhabitants barricaded themselves in one of the towers of the **citadel**, which the Turks stormed and burned. The only survivor, a student aged 16, was enslaved, escaping twenty years later to write a best-selling exposé of the bogeymen of fifteenth-century Europe. The **Student's Tower** (also known as the Tailors' Tower), at Str. Traian (or Parkgasse) 6, is thus one of the town's main sights, although it's not actually open. Heading west from Parkgasse brings you to the large **Evangelical Church** (Tues–Sat 10am–1pm & 3–5pm, Sun 3–5pm), built in Romanesque style between 1240 and 1270, with a disproportionately large and grand Gothic choir added by 1382, followed by the upper part of the tower in 1664. The choir boasts Transylvania's best Parleresque statues, and a large polychrome altar dating from 1518. The cemetery chapel, on its north side, was built in 1400 and is now used by the Uniates. In the late fifteenth-century **House of the Voivodes** on the north side of the square is a **museum** (Tues–Fri 8am–5pm, Sat & Sun 10am–4pm) featuring displays on Roma, Saxon and even African ethnography.

The **train** (Sebeş Alba) and **bus stations** are just east, in the new town. From here, a pleasant alternative to the hectic DN1 heads right on Str. Mărăşeşti, crossing the road to Daia Romană – with a view of the dramatic Red Cliffs (Râpa Roşie) to the north – and along Str. Mihai Viteazul to the main square. Should you need to **stay** overnight, the *Clasic* hotel (☎0258/733 016, ⓦwww.hotelsebes .com; ❺), just east on the DN1, has tidy air-conditioned rooms – it's also the best place in town to **eat**. A reasonable spot for a **drink** is the *Café River*, at the end of a jetty on the artificial lake next to Parkgasse. Note that if you're travelling the few kilometres north to Alba Iulia, you're best off catching a bus from Sebeş (2/hr), saving the lengthy wait for a train connection at Vinţu de Jos.

Southwestern Transylvania

Heading west from Mediaş or Sibiu, you soon leave the Saxon part of Transylvania and move into an area where Hungarian influence is more apparent. However, while a Hungarian ruling class lived here for centuries, the peasantry has always been Romanian. Over the millennia, the Stone Age tribes that huddled around the caves and hot springs of the Carpathian foothills developed into a cohesive society, and eventually into the **Dacian kingdom**. The Dacians' strongholds were in the hills south of **Orăştie**, and were ultimately conquered by Roman legions marching up from the Danube through the passes known today as the Eastern Gate (Poarta Orientală) and the Iron Gate (Poarta de Fier) of Transylvania. The conquerors founded their new capital, **Sarmizegetusa**, in the Haţeg depression, and the area became one of the earliest centres of Romanian culture in Transylvania; it's now known for the *haţegana*, a quick dance (and the name of the local beer), and some of Romania's oldest and most charming churches. To the north, Hungarian churches and castles dominate the main route along the Mureş valley to and from Hungary – **Hunedoara** is the site of Romania's greatest medieval fortress. **Alba Iulia**, one of the most important towns in this region, has been a centre of Romania's wine industry since the first century BC. By contrast, the smoggy mining towns at the feet of the Retezat mountains, in the far southwest of Transylvania, belie the beauty of the range, whose peaks feed dozens of alpine lakes, making this one of the most beautiful of the Carpathian ranges and deservedly popular with hikers.

Alba Iulia and around

The tension between the Hungarian and Romanian communities is symbolized in **ALBA IULIA**, 14km north of Sebeş, by the juxtaposition of the Roman Catholic and Orthodox cathedrals in the heart of its citadel. This hill top was fortified by the Romans and then by the Romanians, before the Hungarian ruler, István I, occupied it and created the bishopric of Gyulafehérvár – the city's Magyar name – in the early eleventh century. Only after World War I did the Romanians take power here and build their own cathedral. The town is dominated by its huge **citadel**, in effect the **upper town**, shaped like a wonky star; east of this, the **lower town** has been tidied up since it was partly cleared for "rationalization" in Ceauşescu's last years, and is home to a scattering of low-key Art Deco buildings.

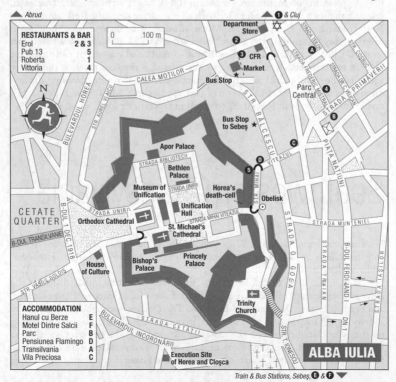

RESTAURANTS & BAR
Erol — 2 & 3
Pub 13 — 5
Roberta — 1
Vittoria — 4

ACCOMMODATION
Hanul cu Berze — E
Motel Dintre Salcii — F
Parc — B
Pensiunea Flamingo — D
Transilvania — A
Vila Preciosa — C

ALBA IULIA

Train & Bus Stations, Sebeş, **E** & **F**

Arrival and information

Alba Iulia's **train** and twin **bus** stations are 1km south of the centre on B-dul Ferdinand I (DN1), reached by buses #3 and #4, looping via the lower town and the Cetate quarter every five to ten minutes, one in each direction. Strada Iaşilor, parallel to the DN1, makes a pleasant walk from the stations into town. Buses for Sebeş leave twice an hour from Str. Bălcescu. The city's **tourist information office** is at B-dul Ferdinand 14 (☎0258/813 736, ✉turism@apulum.ro). **Internet** access is available at a couple of places on B-dul Horea and B-dul Transilvaniei. **Bike** repairs are available at Calea Moţilor 21 (☎0745/880 744).

Accommodation

Accommodation in Alba Iulia is limited and pricey, except for the *Pensiunea Flamingo* and a couple of places by the river 4km south on the DN1 (bus #12 or #13). There's also a small motel to the north at km384.

Hanul cu Berze Str. Republicii 179 ☎0258/810 129. A friendly, family-run place, on the north side of the river 2km south of the bus and train stations. ❷

Motel Dintre Salcii Str. Republicii ☎0258/812 137. Just over the bridge from the *Hanul cu Berze* (and almost as nice), this is a very cheap but pleasant motel. ❷

Parc Str. Primăverii 4 ☎0258/811 723, ⓦwww .hotelparc.ro. Alba's best hotel has a mix of two- and four-star rooms – the former with twin beds only. ❻–❼

Pensiunea Flamingo Str. Mihai Viteazul 6 ☎0258/816 354, ✉pensiunea_flamingo@yahoo .com. The only central budget option, with seven simple rooms (including triples and quads) and a bar serving basic meals. ❸

Transilvania Piaţa Iuliu Maniu 21 ☎0258/812 052. This ugly block hides some perfectly agreeable and modern (if cramped) rooms. ❺

Vila Preciosa Str. Lucian Blaga 10 ☎0258/814 033, ⓦwww.preciosa.ro. A stylish new guesthouse with seven spacious a/c rooms and a fine restaurant and wine bar. ❺

The Town

Between 1715 and 1738, twenty thousand serfs, directed by the Italian architect Giovanni Morandi Visconti, built the Vauban-style **citadel**, named Karlsburg in honour of the reigning Habsburg monarch. Imperial levies on the countryside did much to embitter the Romanian peasants, who turned on their (mainly Hungarian) landlords in the 1784 uprising led by Horea, Cloşca and Crişan. After the uprising had been crushed, Horea and Cloşca were tortured to death, a martyrdom commemorated both at the execution site south of the citadel walls, and by a 22m-high **obelisk** on the east side of the citadel up beyond the newly restored first and second gateways. Above the richly carved Baroque main (third) gateway is Horea's death-cell. Crişan cheated the executioner by committing suicide. To the south of the gateway, the wooden **Trinity church** was built in 1988–92, in traditional Maramureş style.

Within the citadel, the Act of Unification between Romania and Transylvania was signed in the ornate marble **Unification Hall** (Sala Unirii; Tues–Sun 10am–5pm; €2) on December 1, 1918; built in 1898–1900, it served as the officers' mess until 1968, and now holds a small ethnographic collection and temporary exhibits. Facing the hall, a barracks block (1853) houses the exhaustive **Museum of Unification** (Muzeul al Unirii; same hours and ticket), embodying the credo that Romania's history has been a long search for national unity and glorifying the Wallachian prince **Michael the Brave**, who united Wallachia, Transylvania and Moldavia, and made Alba briefly capital of Romania in 1599–1600. In a fit of pique, the Magyars demolished his Coronation Church in 1713, so, unsurprisingly, the Romanians built a vast new

Orthodox Cathedral for the coronation of King Ferdinand and Queen Marie in 1922. Entered under a 58m-high tower, the peach- and cream-coloured, neo-Brâncovenesc cloister belies the medieval style of the cathedral and its neo-Byzantine frescoes, including portraits of Michael and his wife, Stanca. The Catholic **St Michael's Cathedral** to the south of Str. Mihai Viteazul testifies to the Hungarian connection. The foundations of the eleventh-century church have been preserved, as has a superb *Maiestas* carving above a blind door in the south aisle. What you see now was mostly built between 1247 and 1256, in late Romanesque style, with the Gothic choir added in the fourteenth and fifteenth centuries; of the later accretions, the most notable are the Renaissance László and Váraday chapels, built in 1512 and 1524 respectively. The **tomb of Hunyadi**, the greatest of Transylvania's warlords, is the middle of the three to the right of the west door; a century after his death, the tomb was vandalized by the Turks, still bitter at their defeats at his hands. To the south of the Catholic cathedral stands the former **Princely Palace**, where the Transylvanian Diets met between 1542 and 1690. Leaving the citadel to the west, you'll come to the modern **Cetate quarter**, where the liveliest watering holes can be found, as well as the Artists' Union Gallery on B-dul 1 Decembrie 1918.

Eating and drinking

There are pretty slim pickings when it comes to **eating and drinking** in Alba Iulia. In addition to the hotel restaurants, there are three adequate pizza joints: the popular *Roberta*, 150m north of Calea Moţilor at Str. Tudor Vladimirescu 6, with another branch on B-dul Transilvaniei, in Cetate; *Vittoria*, Str. Mistral 3, on the east side of the Parcul Central; and *Erol*, sprawling either side of the pedestrian subway under Calea Moţilor by the market. For drinking, there are several *terasas* on the lively pedestrianized B-dul Transilvaniei; just inside the citadel, across from the obelisk, *Pub 13* makes a pleasant alternative.

Around Alba Iulia

Many of the towns around Alba Iulia, such as **Aiud**, bear witness to the centuries of Hungarian rule, while **Blaj** is of purely historical interest as the cradle of Romanian Nationalism. The area is easily visited on public transport: there are buses more or less hourly from Alba Iulia into the Apuseni highlands and good train and bus links to Sebeş, Blaj and Aiud.

Blaj

The small town of **BLAJ**, 35km northeast of Alba Iulia on the DN14b to Sighişoara, stands at the junction of the main Sighişoara–Cluj rail line and the branch to Sovata and Praid (see p.185). Blaj's main claim to fame is its historical status as the ark of Romanian Nationalism; it is now run-down, but still produces good wine – notably the dry white Feteasca Regală – and Bergenbier is brewed here. The centre is about 1km east of the train station (where buses also pull in); heading east through communist-era blocs you'll come to Str. Republicii, the main drag, with the **History Museum** (Tues–Fri 9am–4pm, Sat & Sun 10am–2pm) to the right in Avram Iancu park. In addition to temporary art shows upstairs, the museum covers Blaj's history as headquarters of the **Uniate Church** (see box opposite) and that of the many intellectuals who taught here at the end of the eighteenth century and beginning of the nineteenth; they are also remembered by numerous plaques around town.

Continuing east on Str. Republicii you'll come to the hotel, and, on Piaţa 1848 behind it, the Uniate (or Greco-Catholic) **cathedral** (1749–79), the first Baroque

The Uniate Church

In 1596, the Austrian government persuaded the Orthodox Church in Galicia (now southern Poland and Ukraine) to accept the authority and protection of the Vatican, hoping to detach them from Russian influence and to tie them more firmly to the western fold. Thus was born the **Uniate Church**, also known as the Catholic Church of the Eastern Rite, or the Greco-Catholic Church, which was introduced to Transylvania in 1700. However, the new Church failed to attract most Romanian Orthodox believers, and was further marginalized when Romania's Orthodox Church gained autonomy in the 1920s. Even so, its leading figures exercised great influence. At the end of the eighteenth century, the **Transylvanian School** (Şcoala Ardeleana), a group of clerics and teachers in Blaj, played a key role in making Romanian a literary language, revitalizing Romanian culture and instilling a sense of nationhood into the Romanian people. The Uniate Church stood for independence of thought and self-reliance, as opposed to the more hierarchical and conformist Orthodox Church, so the communist regime called its million-plus adherents "agents of imperialism" and forcibly merged them with the Orthodox Church. Uniates remained a harassed and often imprisoned minority, with no status under the 1948 and subsequent constitutions (although these recognized the existence of fourteen other denominations or "cults"), until the overthrow of communism.

The Uniates accept four key points of Catholic doctrine: the Filioque clause in the creed (according to which the Holy Spirit proceeds from the Father and the Son, as opposed to the Orthodox doctrine by which the Holy Spirit proceeds only from the Father); the use of wafers instead of bread in the Mass; the doctrine of Purgatory (unknown in the East); and, above all, the supremacy of the pope. In other respects – the marriage of priests, a bearded clergy, the cult of icons, different vestments and rituals – they follow Orthodox practice. In certain areas, such as Maramureş, there is now a considerable revival in the fortunes of the Uniate Church, although hopes that it can again revitalize the country as it did under the Transylvanian School appear misplaced. The Iliescu government also supported, and was supported by, the Orthodox Church, and the Uniates have found it a long, hard struggle to reclaim even their buildings.

building in Transylvania. To its south is the school where classes were taught in the Romanian language from 1754; the great botanist Alexandru Borza (1887–1971) taught here. East of the town centre is the **Field of Liberty**, a famous rallying point in 1848 and 1868 for tens of thousands of Romanians protesting against Hungary's demands to reincorporate Transylvania within the "lands of Stephen". The town's sole **hotel** is the *Târnavele* (☎0258/713 582; ❷), at B-dul Republicii 1, with twin rooms only.

Aiud

The attractive town of **AIUD** (Nagyenyed), almost 30km north of Alba Iulia on the DN1 (E81), and 13km north of Teiuş, the junction of the rail lines from Braşov and Deva towards Cluj, has a reputation for ethnic harmony, despite the grim reputation of its prison. Having held Soviet spies during World War II, and Iron Guardists and other dissidents after the communist takeover, it remains Transylvania's largest prison, housing the country's most serious offenders. The town centre has one of the oldest **fortresses** in Transylvania, dating back to 1302, and still boasting a full ring of walls and eight towers. It shelters two Hungarian churches (the first Lutheran and built in the late nineteenth century on a medieval ground-plan; the second Calvinist and dating from the early fifteenth century) and a **History Museum** (Tues–Fri 8am–4pm, Sat & Sun 8am–noon); there's a display of stuffed animals at the **Natural Sciences Museum** (Tues–Fri 8am–4pm, Sat & Sun 9am–1pm) upstairs in the Bethlen College across the road. Across a footbridge behind the fortress, the landmark, turn-of-the-twentieth-century **Industrial School** rises up like a huge Renaissance palace.

From the **train station**, it's a twenty-minute walk to the centre – head up Str. Coşbuc, just to the left of the station, and after the stadium turn left on to Str. Stadionului and then right through the market to Str. Iuliu Mani. Through-buses stop on Str. Stadionului, while local ones terminate at the station. There's one **hotel**, the *Victoria*, at Str. Iuliu Maniu 8 (℡0258/861 684, ⓔvictoria.aiud @yahoo.com; ❷), and there are various guesthouses just outside the centre, such as *Casa Helvetica*, at Str. Gh. Doja 53A (℡0258/860 867; ❷), with shared bathroom, and the *Mobis* pension at Str. Transilvaniei 120 (℡0258/862 772; ❸), about 1km north of town out on the Cluj road – a smart, fresh place with a pool and the town's best **restaurant**. Otherwise, there's the *Luk* pizzeria by the market at Str. Libertăţii 9, and the *Coroana de Aur*, a stylish modern pizzeria at the junction of Stradas Iuliu Maniu and Băilor.

Orăştie, Deva and Hunedoara

Deep in the mountains south of Alba Iulia are a number of **Dacian citadels**, six of which are UNESCO World Heritage sites; the most interesting, **Sarmizegetusa**, is accessible from **Orăştie**, a quiet town 38km southwest of Sebeş on the main road and railway west towards Deva, Timişoara and Arad. The other citadels are further off the beaten track and you'll have to walk or hitch to reach them. There are also two striking medieval structures in this part of Transylvania: the ruined fortress on the **Hill of the Djinn**, overlooking **Deva**, and the huge, practically undamaged, Gothic castle of the Corvin family at **Hunedoara**, accessible by bus from Deva or by rail from **Simeria**, just east on the main line.

Orăştie and around

ORĂŞTIE, first recorded in 1224 as the Saxon *Stuhl* of Broos, is a pleasant small town in which to break a journey along the Mureş valley. From the **train station**, 3km north of the town, trains are met by buses for the town centre (buses to the station depart from stops along the DN7 and are less predictable – roughly half-hourly – so you'll need to allow a bit of leeway). Heading into town, buses turn right at the Piaţa Europea roundabout; get off here, cross the main road and follow Str. Armatei south to Piaţa Victoriei – marked by a 1930s Orthodox cathedral – and the main street, Str. Bălcescu. The town **museum** (Tues–Sun 9am–5pm), at Piaţa Aurel Vlaicu 1, whose exhibits include textiles, old clocks and Dacian relics, is off Str. Bălcescu to the right, as is the old **citadel** (not open to the public) immediately south, with large German Evangelical and Hungarian Reformed churches crammed close together.

There are three, almost identically priced, **hotels** in town, the best being the *Dacor* at Str. Mureşul 7 (℡0254/244 646, ⓦwww.hoteldacor.ro; ❷), whose clean, sunny rooms are terrific value. There's also the *Mini-Hotel Jorja*, Str. Bălcescu 30 (℡0254/241 574, ⓦwww.pensiunejorja.ro; ❷), a quirky little guesthouse; and the *Şura*, just off Bălcescu at Str. Stadionului 1A (℡0254/247 222, ⓦwww.sura.ro; ❷), which has rooms with and without bathrooms – it also has the town's best **restaurant**. Additionally, there are half a dozen cabins (❶) attached to the *Hanul Margareta* restaurant, just over 1km west of town on the DN7.

Cetatea Costeşti and Sarmizegetusa

Cetatea Costeşti, the first of the Dacian citadels, lies south of Orăştie along the Gradiştie valley. Several buses a day cover the 20km to the village of Costeşti, but from there you'll have to walk about 1km further to a bridge – cross the river and turn right past the sign to the citadel, then left at the junction and sharp left at the farm to reach the three rows of earthworks, grazed by cows and surrounded by birch and cherry trees.

The largest citadel, **Sarmizegetusa**, lies deeper into the mountains. Without your own transport, you'll have to walk or hitch; continue south from Costeşti along the valley road through the hamlet of Grădiştea de Munte and a further 8km over a rougher stretch of road. This was the Dacian capital from the first century BC to 106 AD, though it requires some imagination to conjure up a picture of its grandeur from the weathered walls and stumps of pillars that remain. However, it's clear that Sarmizegetusa was divided into two distinct quarters: the citadel, used as a refuge during times of war; and the sacred area, dominated by the great sanctuary, a stone circle containing a horseshoe of wooden columns where ritual sacrifices were performed. The Romans, always shrewd imperialists, rebuilt Sarmizegetusa after its capture in 106 AD, stationed a detachment of the IV Legion here and appropriated the shrines, rededicating them to members of their pantheon. The Roman capital was southwest of here, near the modern village of Sarmizegetusa – and took its name from the Dacian citadel.

There's **accommodation** at the *Pensiunea Popasul Dacilor*, Costeşti no. 93 (☎0743/089 658, ⓦwww.popasuldacilor.ro; ❶–❷), which has rooms with both shared and private facilities, and at *Pensiunea Sarmizegetusa*, Str. Principala 1, Gradiştea de Munte (☎0722/631 555; ❸).

Deva

The capital of Hunedoara county, **DEVA**, 30km west of Orăştie, lies on the east side of a **citadel** built in the thirteenth century and transformed into one of Transylvania's strongest fortifications on the orders of the warlord, Hunyadi, after 1444. It crowns a volcanic hill in the shape of a truncated cone – supposedly the result of a stupendous battle between the djinns (spirits) of the Retezat mountains and of the plain, hence the nickname **Hill of the Djinn**.

Arrival, information and accommodation

All **trains** on the main line from Arad stop at Deva, making it a good place to pick up services to Budapest or the further corners of Romania; from the station, the town centre is just five minutes south along B-dul Iuliu Maniu. From the **bus stations**, on either side of the **train station**, services leave frequently for Hunedoara, Simeria, Călan and Orăştie, while three a day head for Câmpeni in the Apuseni mountains.

There are a few **hotels** in town; the most pleasant is the *Pensiunea Subcetate*, a homely little guesthouse with a lovely, flower-filled garden, at Str. Delavrancea 6 (☎0254/212 535, ⓔoffice@cazaredeva.ro; ❸). Another option is the *Hostel Elveţia*, hidden among low apartment blocks at Aleea Viitorului 2 (☎0354/101 225, ⓦwww.hotel-elvetia.ro; ❸), with ten businesslike rooms (with hydromassage showers). The pick of the hotels is the slightly dated *Deva* at Str. 22 Decembrie 110 (☎0254/225 920, ⓔdeva.deva@unita-turism.ro; ❸–❹). The *Deer* (or *Căprioara*) **youth hostel** (☎0354/803 494, ⓔturism_hunedoara@yahoo.com; ❶), 4km west of town up in the hills, is clean and well run, but caters largely to groups of young students – the only way to get here is by car (or taxi), though the owners will pick up from the stations upon request.

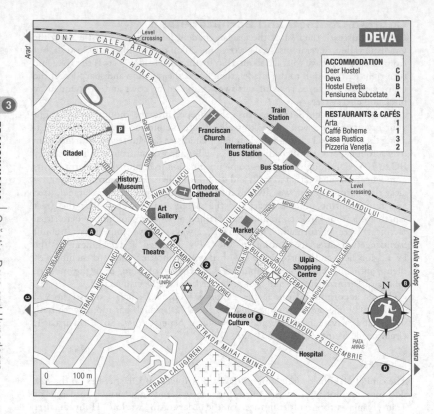

ACCOMMODATION	
Deer Hostel	C
Deva	D
Hostel Elveția	B
Pensiunea Subcetate	A

RESTAURANTS & CAFÉS	
Arta	1
Caffé Boheme	1
Casa Rustica	3
Pizzeria Veneția	2

The Town

Despite the mason charged with building it reputedly immuring his wife in its walls to guarantee his creation's indestructability, Deva's **citadel** was destroyed in 1849 when the magazine blew up, leaving only the ramparts and barracks standing. A sizeable portion remains, including a small cavern, inside which is a memorial to David Ferenc (1520–79), founder of the Unitarian Church (see p.204), who was martyred in the castle's prison. If you don't fancy the stiff 184m climb to the top, you can take Romania's first and only **funicular** (*telecabina*; daily 8am–8pm; €1.50; on the eastern side of the hill by the soccer stadium); the expansive views over the Mureș valley are superb. Facing the lower terminal are busts of world-beating Romanian gymnasts, trained at the *Colegiul National Sportiv Cetate Deva* (Deva Citadel National Sports College), and their equally legendary coaches.

In the park at the bottom of the hill – beneath the Hollywood-style "Deva" sign on the citadel – is the **Magna Curia palace**, rebuilt in 1621 by Voivode Gábor Bethlen, under whom Deva was briefly capital of Transylvania. Since 1882, it has housed a **History Museum** (Tues–Sun 10am–6pm; €1); the medieval galleries reopened after lengthy restoration in 2010 and the Roman exhibits should be in place by 2011, until when you can see some statues from Sarmizegetusa outside. There's also a tiny **art gallery** in the prefecture opposite, on the corner of Str. Avram Iancu. Heading down this street, you'll come to the Orthodox **cathedral of St Nicolae**, dating from 1893. To the north, on Str. Progesului, is the

Franciscan church. Alternatively, head east to the modern centre via the pedestrianized Str. 1 Decembrie, passing the superbly refurbished Secession-style Municipal Theatre, opened in 1911, and the country's only Ecological University in the former *Hanul Mare*, the inn where Alexandru Ioan Cuza slept on his way into exile in 1866.

Eating and drinking

The choice of **restaurants** is limited to pizzerias, notably *Casa Rustica*, on B-dul 22 Decembrie, which offers crispy thin-crust pizzas, and the larger *Pizzeria Veneţia* on B-dul Iuliu Maniu (between B-dul Decebal and Str. 1 Decembrie), which also has a terrace. There's a string of pavement **cafés** along Str. 1 Decembrie, the most appealing of which are *Arta*, with a delectable selection of cakes and ices, and *Caffé Boheme*.

Hunedoara

HUNEDOARA (Vajdahunyad/Eisenmarkt), 16km south of Deva, would be dismissed as an ugly, run-down industrial town were it not also the site of **Corvin Castle** (March & April Mon 9am–3pm, Tues–Sun 9am–5pm; May–Sept Mon 9am–3pm, Tues–Sun 9am–6pm; Oct–Feb Mon 9am–3pm, Tues–Sun 9am–4pm; €2), the greatest fortress in Romania. Patrick Leigh Fermor found its appearance "so fantastic and theatrical that, at first glance, it looks totally unreal". It's moated to a depth of 30m and approached by a narrow bridge upheld by tall stone piers, terminating beneath a mighty barbican, its roof bristling with spikes, overlooked by multitudes of towers. Founded during the fourteenth century and rebuilt in 1441–53 by **Iancu de Hunedoara**, with a Renaissance-style wing added by his son, Mátyás Corvinus, and Baroque additions by Gabriel Bethlen from 1618, it was restored and opened as a museum in 1974. Within is an extravaganza of galleries, spiral stairways and Gothic vaulting, most impressively the Knights' Hall, with its rose-coloured marble pillars. On the second pillar a carved Latin inscription reads "this work has been performed by the great and handsome Iancu de Hunedoara in God's year 1452" – clearly a man not given to modesty. The hall also accommodates a display of weaponry, tacky waxworks and some medallion portraits of the Bethlen family and their acquaintances.

Legend has it that Iancu de Hunedoara, known in Hungarian as Hunyadi János, was the illegitimate son of King Sigismund, who gave the castle to Hunyadi's nominal father Voicu, a Romanian noble, in 1409. Hunyadi, the "White Knight", rose largely by his own efforts, winning victory after victory against the Turks,

---

The Festival of the Călușari

Around the second week of January, Deva hosts the colourful **Festival of the Călușari** (Călușerul Transilvănean). Ensembles from Wallachia and southern Transylvania perform the intricate dances and rituals originally devised to ensure good harvests and dispel the Rusalii – the spirits of departed friends or relations, who, according to Romanian folklore, would take possession of the living should any of the taboos associated with the Week of Rusalii (following Whitsun) be violated. The rite was also intended to promote fertility, and in the old days the dancers (all male) were accompanied by a mute who wore a huge red phallus beneath his robes and muttered lewd invocations. Under communism, such antics were discouraged and the mute carried a more innocuous wand covered in rabbit fur. Contact the Cultural Inspectorate in Deva (Str. 1 Decembrie 28; ☎0254/213 966) to confirm the exact dates of this and other festivals in Hunedoara county.

and routing them at Belgrade in 1456. Appointed *voivode* of Transylvania in 1441, he later became regent of Hungary and a kingmaker (responsible for the overthrow of Vlad Dracul by his son, the Impaler, see p.403), while his own son, Mátyás Corvinus, became one of Hungary's greatest kings. The reserves of iron ore in the hills west of Hunedoara were known in Roman times; they were exploited on an industrial scale from 1884 and then after World War II, when the communists deliberately built a huge and ugly steel plant right in front of the castle. The castle, however, has had the last laugh, as Romania's heavy industry has collapsed in the last two decades.

Practicalities

Buses run every ten minutes between Deva and Hunedoara (every 15min 6pm–midnight, Sat & Sun every 30min; pay on board). There are also **trains** from Simeria and six minibuses a day from Hațeg, 45 minutes to the south (look out for the huge Gypsy palaces on entering Hunedoara from Călan). From the **train** and **bus stations**, it's a twenty-minute walk south to the castle: turn right onto the main road, B-dul Republicii, and right again onto B-dul Libertății, passing the town hall and Ghelari church, until you reach a bridge on the right; cross this and follow the signs for the remaining five-minute walk to the castle.

Once you've seen the castle there's no reason to remain in Hunedoara; if you do get stuck, the much-improved *Rusca* **hotel** at B-dul Dacia 10 (℡0254/717 575, Ⓦwww.hotelrusca.ro; ❹) is a ten-minute walk east of the station; head down Str. Avram Iancu, opposite the station, then turn right along B-dul Dacia. Alternatively, there's the *Maier* at B-dul Republicii 1A (℡0345/417 130, Ⓦwww.hotelmaier.ro; ❸).

Hațeg and around

HAȚEG, 20km southeast of Hunedoara, is the gateway to Transylvania's greatest Roman remains and to the north side of the Retezat mountains. You'll also find a number of interesting **Romanesque churches** in the surrounding area, all of which can, with a little difficulty, be reached by local buses from the terminal at Str. Caragiale 14, off Str. Mihai Viteazul by the market. The area is also known for its dwarf dinosaur fossils and other geological features: the Hațeg Country GeoPark (Ⓦgeopark.go.ro) is an innovative scheme to use these for sustainable tourist development.

For accommodation, the town's two **hotels** are the small but modern *Art Motel*, bang in the centre at B-dul Tudor Vladimirescu 15 (℡0354/409 169, Ⓦwww .geraico.ro; ❹), and the much less appealing, but cheaper, *Belvedere* (℡0254/777 604; ❸), at the Abator bus stop, 1km south on Str. Progesului, the Petroșani road; this is served by buses to Subcetate (Hațeg's rail station). The *Hanul Bucura*, at the northern entrance to town, has no accommodation, but its **restaurant** has great views across the town to the Retezat mountains.

The Romanesque churches

Hidden in the foothills of the Poiana Ruscă mountains, **Prislop Monastery** is 15km northwest of Hațeg at the head of the Silvasului valley. Founded in 1400, this is one of the country's oldest convents but is remarkably little known and very tranquil, and the nuns are happy for you to go in and look around. It lies just off the direct road from Hunedoara to Hațeg, but most traffic goes via **Călan**, on both the rail line and the DN66 (E79) south from Simeria, though the road is terrible in places. Călan itself is quite a sight, its eerily redundant steelworks – closed more than a decade ago now – an appalling spectacle; however, there is a pleasant spa (dating from Roman times) across the river to the east, with the lovely **church of Streisângeorgiu** on its southern fringe. This was built in 1313–14, with frescoes painted at the same time.

Three kilometres south of Hațeg (an easy stroll from where the Subcetate bus turns off the main road), you'll come to **SÂNTĂMĂRIA-ORLEA** (Oraljaboldogfalva), site of another late thirteenth-century church, which marks the transition from the Romanesque to Gothic style and has a fine collection of fourteenth-century frescoes; from the tower, there's a great view of the Retezat range. An eighteenth-century mansion, just across the road from the church and up the path, is now a **hotel**, the *Castell Sântă Măria Orlea* (☎0254/777 768; ❸), a sombre place that provides nothing more than an adequate stopover.

In **DENSUȘ**, 12km west of Hațeg, a very strange little church has been cannibalized from the mausoleum of a fourth-century Roman army officer – most of what you see dates from the early thirteenth century, with frescoes from 1443. Ask at no. 15 on the main road, east of the statue of the etymologist Ovid Densușianu, for someone to let you in.

Roman Sarmizegetusa

SARMIZEGETUSA, 15km southwest of Hațeg, is famous for its **Roman ruins**, whose excavated portions are only part of the original municipality. Just east of the town centre are the remains of the forum, the palace of the Augustales, and the elliptical amphitheatre – it seems unlikely, but this could seat over five thousand spectators. Start by visiting the **museum** (Tues–Sun 9am–5pm; €1) across the road from the ruins, which avoids mentioning the likelihood that most of the Roman colonists believed to have interbred with the Dacians to create the Romanian race were actually of Greek or Semitic origin.

You can get here by **bus** from Hațeg to Caransebeș (four daily). About 500m along the main road, a left turn brings you to some good **pensions**: the very smart *Sarmis* at no. 82 (☎0744/794 051, ⊕www.pensiuneasarmis.ro; ❷), which has an indoor pool, the *Venus* at no. 47A (☎0742/558 510; ❷), and the *Ulpia Traiana* (☎0254/762 153; ❷), a short walk further on.

The Iron Gate of Transylvania

It's only about 6km from Sarmizegetusa to Zeicani at the entrance to the **Iron Gate of Transylvania** (Poarta de Fier a Transilvanei), a narrow pass 700m above sea level. A monumental mace erected near the village commemorates the defeat of 80,000 Turks by 15,000 Transylvanians under Hunyadi's command in 1442. Further up the pass, in 106 AD, the Dacians had their final disastrous clash with the Romans; as recorded by Roman scribes, the Dacians were crushed, and their ruler Decebal committed suicide rather than be ignominiously paraded through the streets of Rome. The pass itself is 10km long, and accessible by road (the DN68).

The Retezat mountains

Road and rail routes southeast from Hațeg skim the northern reaches of the **Retezat mountains**. Access is slightly harder here than in the other Transylvanian mountain ranges, though whereas in the Făgăraș or Piatra Craiului you find yourself for the most part following a ridge walk, with little opportunity to step

③

aside and view the summits from a distance, here you'll find yourself surrounded by well-defined peaks, often reflected in clear alpine lakes. There is a large network of **hiking routes**, so you'll meet fewer walkers and have a better chance of seeing **wildlife** such as chamois and eagles. Note that the northwestern part of the massif is a scientific reserve (Ceauşescu treated it as a private hunting ground) and entry is restricted.

The **Retezat National Park** (☎0372/742 024 or 0254/779 968/9, ⊕ www .retezat.ro) was set up in 1935, becoming a UNESCO Biosphere Reserve in 1980. To enter, you need a permit (€1.50 for a week plus a tent fee of €1/night), available from an entry post or from a patrol; you'll be given a rubbish bag and a ticket with a basic map – it's worth buying a more detailed one in advance. **Visitor centres** are at Ostrovel (entering Râu de Mori) and at the park's headquarters at Nucşoara; boards here and at Câmpu lui Neag give **information** in English and German on the trails and the park's dozen camping sites. **Guides** can be booked through the National Park.

Approaches to the Retezat

There are three main **approaches** to the Retezat: from Râu de Mori, a bus ride from Haţeg and on the west side of the massif; from various points along the Subcetate-Petroşani road and railway to the northeast; and from the West Jiu valley to the south.

From **Râu de Mori** (where there are various guesthouses, it's at least a three-hour walk south along the Râul Mare valley (passing the *Pensuinea Dumbrăviţa* after 5km and the *Pensuinea Anita* 2km further on) to the *Gura Zlata* cabana (see box opposite) and campsite, from where you can strike out for the high peaks. Continuing south, the paved road ends at Lake Gura Apei; 6km to the east, you can stay in Ceauşescu's former Vila Rotunda (☎088216/595 00150, ⊕ www.rotunda.ro; ❹).

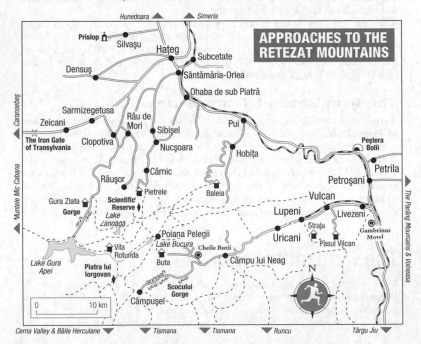

From Gura Zlata

Some popular hikes start from *Gura Zlata* cabana (❶), south of Sarmizegetusa along the Râul Mare valley. A succession of coloured symbols marks successive phases of the trail east from here to the *Pietrele* cabana (❶), going by way of Lake Zănoaga (campsite), Lake Tăul Portii and the Bucura Saddle. This is a nine- to ten-hour hike, which is closed in winter. The road through Gura Zlata continues 12km south to the Lake Gura Apei, from whose western extremity well-equipped hikers can follow a trail west across the mountains to the *Muntele Mic* cabana (❶) in the vicinity of Caransebeş, or south to Băile Herculane; allow two days for each. Heading east along the reservoir and up the Lăpuşnic valley takes you to either the *Buta cabana* (❶) or the Bucura valley in four hours.

From Câmpu lui Neag

Also leading to the cabana at Buta are two of the most popular trails from Câmpu lui Neag and the *Cheile Butii* hotel in the south of the region. Red crosses mark the quickest route to the cabana (6–7hr), which runs through a fir forest and up to the La Fete sheepfold, offering great **views** of the "karst cathedrals" en route. Red triangles indicate the longer trail (10–12hr) to the cabana, which goes via the strange formations of the Scocului gorge, and the plateau of Piatra lui Iorgovan, where you can sometimes spot chamois. A forestry road continues southwest over the watershed from the Jiu valley into the Cerna valley, and on towards **Băile Herculane**, a good two days' walk (see p.331); another path, marked with blue triangles, heads south to Tismana in roughly six hours (see p.114).

Buta lies in the **Little Retezat**, the limestone ridge south of the great glacial trough of the Lăpuşnic valley, which has an almost Mediterranean flora and fauna. However, the best hikes take you into the crystalline **Great Retezat** to the north, past serried peaks and alpine lakes. There are two trails into the Great Retezat from Buta; the first, marked by blue stripes, follows a switchback path to the *Pietrele* cabana (❶; 7hr), dropping into the Lăpuşnic valley, and leading up past the wonderful lakes of the Bucura valley before coming down from a pass of 2206m past the Genţiana club's hut; the second, marked by red stripes then blue triangles, follows a trail to the *Stâne de Râu* cabana (❶), by way of the Barbat springs and the Ciumfu waterfall (9hr; closed in winter).

From the northeast, tracks and roads lead from villages along the rail line between Subcetate and Petroşani. From Ohaba de sub Piatră, it's 18km (a five-hour walk, following blue stripes then blue triangles) to the *Pietrele* cabana (❶), campsite, park information centre and first-aid post. The 2pm bus from Haţeg follows the route via Sălaşu de Sus (where there are guesthouses) as far as Nucşoara, 7km short of the cabana, and summer services, which meet trains at Ohaba, go a few kilometres further to the end of the road at Cârnic; alternatively, an information board at the Ohaba station gives phone numbers for taxis. Two-thirds of the park's visitors arrive this way, so the trail and cabana both get quite crowded. Some hikers therefore prefer to start from either the *Complex Turistic Râuşor* (a two-hour hike from Râu de Mori, following red triangles), with a motel, the *Pensiunea Ancuţa* (☎0256/438 713, ✉adrianpopescu@hotmail.com; ❷), camping and a basic ski-drag; or from the campsite at Pui, east of Ohaba, hiking for six-and-a-half hours up a steep and winding mountain road (marked with red stripes) to the cabanas at Baleia (16km) and Stâne de Râu (6km further) – see the box above for hikes beyond these points.

The final approach to the mountains is from the **mining towns of the West Jiu valley** to the east, but these are grim places with little in the way of accommodation.

From Petroşani to Voineasa

The largest of the mining towns is **PETROŞANI**, served by trains between Simeria and Târgu Jiu; these are desperately slow, and you may prefer to travel by maxitaxi. The only reason to stop here is to stock up on food before hiking in the Retezat mountains, and most people head straight on to the Jiul de Vest (West Jiu) valley by frequent maxitaxis. Five trains a day reach Lupeni, from where buses continue every two hours up the valley to **Câmpu lui Neag**, starting point for some good hikes into the mountains (see box, p.181). In summer, the buses continue about 3km further west to the excellent *Cheile Butii* **hotel** (℡0722/210 278, ⓦwww.cheile-butii.ro; ❸), with various guesthouses nearby.

From Petroşani, the main road and railway follow the Jiu valley south to **Târgu Jiu** (see p.109), cutting through a scenic cleft between the Vâlcan and Parâng mountains and passing **Lainici**, whose motel (℡0253/463 502; ❷) stands near a fine eighteenth-century monastery with a striking new church. The recently paved DN7A heads 83km east from Petroşani to **VOINEASA**, passing the decent *Groapa Seaca* cabana (℡0254/542 246 or 0744/136 555; ❶) at km18; this is very rustic and peaceful, and marks the start of a fabulous day-hike into the Parâng range.

The Székely Land and the eastern Carpathians

In the ethnic patchwork of Transylvania, the eastern Carpathians have long been the home of the **Székely**, a people closely related to the Magyars who speak a distinctive Hungarian dialect and cherish a special historical identity. For a long time it was believed that they were the descendants of Attila's Huns, who had entered the Carpathian basin in the fifth century. However, it's now believed that the Székely either attached themselves to the Magyars during their long migration from the banks of the Don, or are simply the descendants of early Hungarians who pushed ever further east into Transylvania. Whatever their origins, the Székely feel closely akin to the Magyars who, in turn, regard them as somehow embodying the finest aspects of the ancient Magyar race, while also being rather primeval. Today, their traditional costume is close to that of the Romanian peasants, the chief difference being that Székely men tuck their white shirts in while Romanians wear them untucked and belted.

For visitors, the chief attractions of the region are likely to be the **Székely culture** and the scenery. Religion plays an important part in Székely life, as shown by the fervour displayed at the **Whitsun pilgrimage to Miercurea Ciuc**, the continuing existence of Székely mystics, and the prevalence of **walled churches** (less grimly fortified than the Saxon ones). Traditional Székely **architecture** is well represented throughout the Székely Land (Székelyföld); it is epitomized by tiny hilltop chapels and blue-painted houses with carved fences and gateways, incorporating a dovecote above, the best examples being in Corund. The landscape gets increasingly dramatic as you move through the Harghita mountains, particularly around the Tuşnad defile and St Anne's Lake to the south, and Lacu Roşu and the Bicaz gorges just before the borders of Moldavia.

Into the Székely Land

From Sighişoara and **Odorheiu Secuiesc**, the region's western capital, you can either head east to **Miercurea Ciuc**, capital of the eastern Székely Land, or take a shorter loop to **Târgu Mureş** via the spa of **Sovata Băi**. It's possible to approach from Braşov by rail; after passing the showpiece Saxon villages of **Hărman** and **Prejmer**, the route follows the Olt and Mureş valleys through **Sfântu Gheorghe**, Miercurea Ciuc and **Gheorgheni**, looping around to Târgu Mureş. There's a fantastic new online guide to the Székelyföld at ⓦ gototransylvania .ro/index1_en.php.

Odorheiu Secuiesc

ODORHEIU SECUIESC (Székelyudvarhely) lies more or less 50km from Sighişoara, Miercurea Ciuc and Sovata; it's unusually prosperous, thanks to textile companies producing 1.5 million men's suits per year, as well as the furniture, leather and print industries (factory outlets can add a whole new dimension to visits here). The town hosts a series of crafts, food and beer **festivals** throughout the spring and summer, while the excellent Szejke festival is held in mid-June out at the spa of the same name, 4km north by the Sovata road, when folk dance groups put on displays to a picnicking audience. There's also a rock festival at Szejke on the fourth weekend of July, featuring a predominantly Balkan line-up.

Arrival and information

The **bus** and **train stations** are about 1km north of the town centre; trains (run by the private operator RegioTrans) stop first at Odorhei Sud halt (actually on the road north to Sovata), which is nearer the centre. Turning left out of the bus station on Str. Târgului and then right onto Str. Bethlen (with the main train station to the left), it's a couple of minutes to Str. Tompa László, leading south to the citadel. **Information** is available from TourInfo, Piaţa Márton Áron 6 (Mon–Fri 9am–5pm; ☎0266/217 427, ⓦ www.tourinfo.ro), while Robert Roth of Herr Travel (☎0722/201 997, ⓦ www.guide2romania.ro) offers **tours** of the region. There's free **wi-fi** in the town centre, and at several bars and cafés.

Accommodation

The town's best **hotel** is the *Gondüző*, a five-minute walk east of Piaţa Márton Áron at Str. Sântimbru 18 (☎0266/218 372, ⓦ www.gonduzo.ro; ❹), with large, comfortable rooms featuring lovely wood furnishings, thick carpets and corner baths. The *Europa*, at Str. Kossuth Lajos 23 (☎0266/218 228, ⓦ www .europahotel.ro; ❺), is modern and very comfortable, and includes the *Taverna* restaurant. Other central options include the *Târnava* (the *Küküllő* to Magyars) at Piaţa Primăriei 16 (☎0266/213 963/4, ⓦ www.kukullo.ro; ❺), which has decent, if slightly cramped, rooms, gym and sauna facilities, and the simpler *Korona Panzió*, Piaţa Primăriei 12 (☎0266/218 061, ⓔ office@koronapanzio .ro; ❸). There are two classy spa hotels, both with indoor pools: *Septimia*, Str. Orban Balázs 106 (☎0266/217 770, ⓦ www.septimia.ro; ❺); and *Villa Vitae* (Str. Bisericii 15 ☎0266/214 048, ⓦ www.villavitae.ro; ❺), with a restaurant terrace giving great views over the town.

The Town

The busy and attractive town centre is essentially made up of two conjoined squares, **Piaţa Primăriei** (Városháza tér) and **Piaţa Márton Áron**, where three churches stand in a row: to the west, the former Franciscan monastery (1730–79); on the island between the two squares, the Reformed church (1780–81); and, on the hill beyond, the Catholic church of Sf Miklós (1787–93), set between the Jesuits' building of 1651 and the huge Tamasy Aron Gymnasium or high school, established in 1593 and now in a Secession building dating from 1911 to 1912. From Piaţa Primăriei, Str. Cetăţii leads to the fifteenth- and sixteenth-century **citadel**; since 1891 this has housed an agricultural college, but you can go inside to stroll along the walls.

On the Sighişoara road, at Str. Kossuth 29, the town **museum** (Muzeul Haáz Rezsó; Tues–Fri 9am–4pm, Sat & Sun 9am–1pm) has a fine ethnographic collection, with ceramics and Székely funerary posts, which may hark back to the days when a Magyar warrior was buried with his spear thrust into the grave. Used only by Calvinists and Unitarians, these bear carvings of the tools of the deceased's trade and a ring for each decade of life; a man's post is topped with a star and a woman's with a tulip. There's also a superb wooden gate, typical of those found throughout the region. Two kilometres further down the same road is the **Jesus chapel** (Jézus-kápolna), one of the oldest buildings in the area, built in the thirteenth century, with a coffered ceiling fitted in 1667.

Eating and drinking

The town is blessed with several top **restaurants**, the best of which is in the *Gondüző* hotel, a good-looking place with a high-class Hungarian and Romanian menu. Two more fine Hungarian places are the *Gizi Csárda*, Str. József 3, which serves Székely food only, and *Pethö*, south of town beyond Str. Kossuth at Str. Rákóczi 21. Good pizzerias abound, including *Jungle*, in a leafy setting in the park behind the Casa de Cultură (with dark Ciuc beer on tap), *Restaurant-pizzeria Oriente* and *Pizza 21*, facing each other at the junction of Bethlen Gabor and Eötvös Jószef, near the Poliklinika. *Alexsandra*, Piaţa Márton Áron 1, is a fabulous, old-fashioned Hungarian-style *cukrászda* (patisserie) with marvellous coffee and cake, and *Lehel*, Str. Kossuth 56, is a great Székely pastry shop. The town's enjoyable and idiosyncratic **bars** include the mellow *G Café*, with dinky wooden tables and bare-brick walls adorned with prints, the *Udvarhelyi Kávézó-Coffee* with great design and excellent artist shows, both on Str. Sântimbru, and the fancier *Elekes Pub*, just a minute's walk from the *Udvarhelyi* towards the hospital. At the *Hat-Kalapos Pub*, on Str. Kossuth, is a genial little place with two-and-a-half-litre tubes to guzzle beer from, across the road from the elegant *First Floor Pub*. A little further down Str. Kossuth the posh crowd might also visit the *Renaissance* café-restaurant.

Around Odorheiu Secuiesc

The Székely Unitarian village of **DÂRJIU** (Székelyderz), 17km southwest, has a particularly fine fortified church, now on UNESCO's World Heritage list, with frescoes dating from 1419. As in some Saxon villages, ham and grain are still stored inside the church walls, ready for the next siege. The church key is held next door at Str. Principală 163 (☎0266/222 183), where the priest offers accommodation.

MUGENI (Bögöz), 9km west of Odorheiu by road and rail, has a fine fourteenth-century church with wonderful frescoes and a coffered ceiling. There is a fair sprinkling of **accommodation** in the village, such as the *Székelykapu Panzió* at Str. Bisericii 176 (☎0266/245 437, ⓦwww.szekelykapupanzio.com; ❷), which also has space for tents and caravans, and the *Ilyés Panzió* at Str. Principală 383 (☎0266/245 505, ⒲www.ilyespanzio.ro; ❷). Continuing west, you'll eventually reach Sighişoara, via the larger village of **CRISTURU SECUIESC** (Székelykeresztúr), whose excellent **museum** (Tues–Fri 10am–5pm, Sat & Sun 10am–1pm) on the elongated square tells the story of the ceramic industry, established here by 1590, in addition to a natural history display. There are a couple of good restaurants, the *Randevu* and *Bonfini*, while the best place to stay is the *Kúria Vendégház* (Vicarage Guesthouse) just east in Rugonfalva (☎0266/242 927, ⒲www.kuriavendeghaz.ro; ❷). Through-buses stop in the main square, but those terminating here arrive at the bus terminal, which, like the train station, is ten minutes' walk east of the centre.

East of Odorheiu, en route to Miercurea Ciuc, several little resorts with low-key accommodation are handy for breaking your journey. Passing through Satu Mare (Máréfalva), renowned for its carved wooden Székely gates, you'll reach **BĂILE HOMOROD** (Homoródfürdő), which has hot springs that you can bathe in and the good *Lobogo Panzió* (☎0266/247 545, ⒲www.lobogo.ro; ❸). Just east, **VLĂHIŢA** (Szentegyházasfalu) also has mineral springs, as well as a campsite and guesthouses, including *Panzio Harghita* (☎0266/246 335, ⒠info@panzioharghita .com; ❷). About 13km beyond Vlăhiţa, a turning to the north leads 4km up to **HARGHITA BĂI** (Hargitafürdő), in the beautiful, thickly forested Harghita mountains, renowned for their wildlife. Here you'll find ski slopes, and the *UZ Bence* (☎0745/629 337, ⒲www.uzbence.szekelyszallas.hu; ❷) and *Bagolykő* (☎0366/100 148, ⒲www.bagolykomenedekhaz.szekelyszallas.hu; ❷) cabanas. Two buses a day run from Miercurea Ciuc rail station, or it's less than an hour's walk from the turning.

Corund, Praid and Sovata Băi

CORUND (Korond), 25km north of Odorheiu, is famed for its green and brown pottery, as well as the cobalt blue introduced by the Germans in the eighteenth century. You'll see it for sale everywhere, but for the best choice poke around the town's backstreet workshops or visit the colourful market held every year on the weekend closest to August 10.

For a complete change of atmosphere, continue 12km north to **PRAID** (Parajd), a lively little resort where there's a visitable salt mine. It's served by local buses between Odorheiu and Sovata and by the rail branch from Blaj; the helpful **tourist office**, at Str. Principală 211 (daily: mid-May to mid-Sept 9am–6pm; rest of year 9am–3pm; ☎0266/240 272, ⒲www.praid.ro), can arrange **accommodation** in private rooms (❶). The refurbished *Hotel Praid* is at Str. Principală 1098 (☎0266/240 686, ⒲www.hotelpraid.ro; ❷). The hotel has a pizzeria, while the much better *Casa Telegdy* **restaurant**, just north of the centre at no. 1173, serves up mid-priced Székely-influenced food.

Seven kilometres further north by road and rail is **SOVATA** (Szováta), which has the *Ursul Negru* hotel at Str. Principală 152 (☎0265/570 987; ❷), and the *Vasskert* campsite at Str. Principală 129 (☎0265/570 902, ⒲www.szovata.hu). The larger **SOVATA BĂI**, 1km east, is a **bathing resort** amid beautiful forests on the shore of **Lacul Ursu** (Medvetó or Bear Lake). A surface layer of fresh water, 1m deep, acts as an insulator keeping the lower saltwater at a constant temperature of 30–40°C year-round; it rains a lot here, in short showers, but bathing is still pleasant. Its mineral waters are supposedly particularly effective for curing infertility. The resort's most distinctive feature is the array of wooden buildings lining the main street, Str. Trandafirilor: huge, extravagantly balconied villas and twee Hansel and Gretel churches.

Sovata Băi's **bus station** is on Str. Trandafirilor. The resort is dominated by the triumvirate of fine *Danubius*-owned **hotels**: the *Danubius*, Str. Trandafirilor 82 (℡0265/570 151, ⓦwww.danubiushotels.com; ❻), the *Făget* and the *Bradet* (both on Str. Vulturului; same contacts; ❹). Each has a pool and treatment facilities, while the *Danubius* also has an indoor saltwater pool. The *Villa Klein*, Str. Trandafirilor 81 (℡0265/577 686; ❷), is a good guesthouse with pool and sauna. As you continue east along the same road, a left turning, just beyond a strikingly modernist Catholic chapel, takes you onto Str. Tivoli and brings you in about ten minutes to the excellent *Tivoli* hotel (℡0265/570 493; ❹), surrounded by woods with deer foraging outside the windows. Strada Tivoli continues to Lacul Tineretului (Lake of Youth), a five-minute walk, where you can rent pedaloes from the snack kiosks. Another 700m along Str. Trandafirilor, you'll come to the *Stâna de Vale* **campsite** (℡0265/571 048) and, a couple of kilometres further still, the appealing *Edelweiss* hotel (℡0265/577 758, ⓦwww.hoteledelweiss.ro; ❹), set in quiet grounds and with bright, colourful rooms – there's a decent restaurant here too.

Sfântu Gheorghe

SFÂNTU GHEORGHE (Sepsi-Szentgyörgy), 30km northeast of Braşov, is an industrial town which, following Ceauşescu's demise, has become the heart of the Székely cultural revival. The highlight is the **Székely National Museum** (June to mid-Sept Tues–Fri 10am–6pm, Sat & Sun 10am–4pm; winter Tues–Fri 9am–4pm, Sat & Sun 9am–2pm; €1.50) at Str. Kós Károly 10, south of the centre. Built in 1910–12 to the design of **Kós Károly** (see box below), it covers the archeology, history and ethnography of the area, focusing on the revolution of 1848–49 (see p.376).

The museum lies to the south of the town centre, which is focused on the large green space of **Erzsébet Park**, on the west side of which are a technical college designed by Kós (with his bust in front), and a library where the decision was taken in 1848 to fight the Austrians, the local hero Gábor Áron announcing he would cast the necessary cannons. Just north, at Str. Gábor Arón 16, the new Museum of the Eastern Carpathians (Tues–Sat 9am–5pm, Sun 10am–3pm; €0.50) is currently only hosting temporary exhibitions. To the east of the park, the **Arcaded House** is the oldest building in town (1812), and houses the tourist office. At the north

---

Kós Károly

Kós Károly (1883–1977) was the leading architect of the Hungarian National Romantic school, which derived its inspiration from the village architecture of Transylvania and Finland. The Transylvanian style is reflected in the wooden roofs, gables and balconies of his buildings, while the Finnish influence appears in the stone bases and trapezoidal door frames. Fine examples of Kós's work can be seen in Sfântu Gheorghe and Cluj (notably the Cock Church), as well as in Budapest.

After the separation of Transylvania from Hungary, Kós, a native of Timişoara, was one of the few Hungarian intellectuals to accept the new situation, choosing to remain in Cluj (and his country home near Huedin) and to play a leading role in Hungarian society in Transylvania. Continuing his work as an architect, he travelled around Transylvania, recording the most characteristic buildings (of all ethnic groups) in delightful linocuts; these were published in 1929 by the Transylvanian Artists' Guild (co-founded by Kós himself), with Kós's own text outlining the historical influences on Transylvanian architecture. In 1989, an English translation of the book, *Transylvania*, was published by Szépirodalmi Könyvkiadó in Budapest, although the Hungarian edition is well worth having just for the linocuts.

end of the square, the **Art Gallery** (Tues–Fri 9am–4pm, Sat & Sun 10am–2pm) is in a big mustard-yellow block with a clocktower, built in 1870 as a department store and now hosting temporary art shows.

North of the square, beyond the defunct *Bodoc* hotel, Str. Kossuth leads past a Kós Károly house (no. 19) to the cobbled Str. Şoimului and the Old Town, with a fine fifteenth-century walled Reformat **church** at the top of Piaţa Kalvíny. In its cemetery, behind a Székely beamgate raised in 1981, you'll see stone versions of traditional wooden Székely graveposts.

Practicalities

Both the **train** and **bus stations** are 2km east of the centre: take bus #1 (hourly, also #2 and #3 Mon–Fri) or follow Str. 1 Decembrie 1918 to Piaţa Libertăţii. There's a **tourist office** (Mon–Thurs 8am–4pm, Fri 8am–2pm; ℡0267/316 474, ℮sepsinfo @sepsi.ro) in the Arcade House (Casa cu Arcade/Lábasház) on the east side of the park. The town's best **hotel** is the charming little *Sugás*, behind the restaurant of the same name on Str. 1 Decembrie 1918 no. 12 (℡0267/312 171; ℗www.sugaskert .ro; ❹), which has cable internet only; the *Ferdinand Panzió*, off the same dusty car park (℡0740/180 502, ℗ferdinandpension.zoltur.ro; ❹), has simpler rooms but with wi-fi and hair-driers. Alternatively, there's the *Park*, up behind the Museum of the Eastern Carpathians at Str. Gábor Áron 12 (℡0267/311 058, ℗www .hotelrestaurantpark.ro; ❷–❺), with rooms ranging from one to four stars. A cheaper option is the *Consic* (℡0267/310 301; ❶) at B-dul Balan 31 – take bus #2 from the station, or walk north from the BTT travel agency at the junction of B-dul Bălan and Str. 1 Decembrie 1918. Sfântu Gheorghe's BTT branch (B-dul Bălan 16, Bl. 18; ℡0267/351 902) is particularly active in agrotourism, arranging **homestays** in nearby spas and villages; this is also the place to book long-distance buses and flights.

The best **restaurant** in town is at the *Sugás* hotel, serving fine Transylvanian food; the *Rézkakas* (Golden Cockerel), at Str. 1 Decembrie 1918 no. 8, has a similar menu with a lot of pork plus vegetarian choices. Otherwise there are various pizza places, of which the *Tribel* (actually a cafeteria with a self-service counter), at Str. 1 Decembrie 1918 no. 2, is best. The *Tein*, next to the Art Gallery, is a very mellow café. For **drinking**, try the *Di Stefano* jazz pub at Str. Gábor Áron 12, or the *Old Man's Pub*, Str. 1 Decembrie 1918 no. 30. The Zilele Sfântu Gheorghe **festival** covers the week straddling Saint George's Day, April 23.

Covasna and around

Trains east from Sfântu Gheorghe to Târgu Secuiesc and Breţcu pass close to **COVASNA** (Kovászna), 30km away, although the DN11 (E574) lies well to the north. The "spa of the thousand springs", or Valea Zânelor (Fairies' Valley), east of here, is popular with walkers, and there's easy access to the Vrancea and Penteleu mountains. At the east end of the valley a spectacular inclined plane, built in 1886 as part of Romania's first narrow-gauge **forestry rail line**, was listed as a UNESCO World Heritage Monument, but has, disgracefully, been allowed to fall apart. The *mocăniţa* or diesel-hauled **tourist train** that runs along the valley (May– Sept hourly Sat & Sun 9am–4.30pm; €1 return) is a pretty poor substitute.

From the **train station**, buses take you the 2.5km to the modern centre of town, and then continue 5km to the hospital in Valea Zânelor. The **tourist information** office is south of the centre at Str. Unirii 2A (℡0267/340 344, ℗www.info-covasna .ro). In the town centre's park are *mofetas*, emitting health-giving gases, and an art gallery (Tues–Thurs 9am–4pm, Fri 9am–6pm, Sat 9am–2pm; free) on Str. Şcolii, its garden a busy cut-through to the market. The **bus station** is behind the market at Str. Ştefan cel Mare 48, just east of the road to the station; ten buses a day to Sfântu

Gheorghe (seven at weekends) start from opposite the hospital, most continuing to Braşov. For access to the mountains, you're best staying at the spa hotels opposite the hospital, such as the *Hotel Bradul* at Aleea Zânelor 10 (℡0267/340 081; ❸); otherwise try the *Turist* (℡0267/340 573; ❶) at Str. 1 Decembrie 1918 no. 4, a small, friendly place with limited facilities. There are also plenty of guesthouses, such as the *Lux* at Str. Ştefan cel Mare 106 (℡0267/340 758; ❷). A little further up the valley is a **campsite** (℡0267/340 401), which has both cabins (❶) and tent space.

Around Covasna

TÂRGU SECUIESC (Kezdivásárhely), thirty minutes beyond Covasna by train, is something of a backwater – it's a stronghold of Székely culture, with little Romanian spoken – but it was a major trading centre in medieval times and the first Székely town to be granted a charter in 1427 (its Romanian name means Székely Market); people still flock to its Thursday **market** today. Through-buses from Braşov stop on the ring road, Str. Fabricilor, just north of the bus station. From the **train** and **bus stations**, it's about a ten-minute walk north along Str. Gării to the central Piaţa Gábor Arón, lined with nineteenth-century merchants' houses, one of which, at Curtea 10, contains the **Museum of the Guilds** (Tues–Fri 9am–4pm, Sat 9am–1pm, Sun 9am–2pm; €1) – in addition to the history of the guilds, there are surprisingly good displays of costumed dolls, fire engines, and the history of photography, plus temporary art shows. Across the square is the splendid Vigadó House of Culture, with occasional interesting events. If you're looking for somewhere to **stay**, the *Vörös Panzió* (℡0267/360 789, ⓦwww.perlaneagra.ro; ❹), opposite the museum at Piaţa Gábor Arón 19, has charming rooms furnished in traditional Székely style, except for one in Swedish modern style and an apartment with a four-poster bed. Curtea 11 (near the museum) leads to Str. Matko István and then the *Hotel Atrium* at Str. Abatorului 11A (℡0367/412 223, ⓦwww .atrium-hotel.ro; ❹); it has a central courtyard with pleasant rooms opening onto a terrace around it. The *Hotel Christine*, at Str. Gării 3 (℡0267/361 182, ⓦwww .hotel-christine.mlap.hu; ❸), is decent but unexciting. The *Bujdosó*, by the Józsiás park at the southern end of Curtea 33, and the *Székely Vendéglő* on Str. Gábor Arón at Str.Şcolii, both serve **Székely food**, such as goulash and *kohlrabi*.

It's well worth a detour to the **Bod Peter Museum of Székely Life and Culture** (daily 8am–late), 10km down the Braşov road from Târgu Secuiesc at the northern end of **CERNAT DE JOS** (Alsó-csernáton): take the asphalt road signposted to Cernat de Sus, and fork left just beyond the church – the museum is almost 1km along this road, at no. 330. A number of village houses have been moved here and there are excellent collections of wooden implements, cast-iron stoves, painted wooden dowry chests and ceramics; unfortunately, information is in Hungarian only. Five **buses** run from Târgu Secuiesc to Cernat de Sus on weekdays; the last returns at 1.30pm, but if you want to stay over, the museum has a couple of **rooms** (❶). In Zăbala (Zabola), 7km north of Covasna, the **Mikes Estate**, confiscated by the communists, has been returned to the countess and her family, who have opened a six-room boutique hotel (℡0724/003 658 or 0267/375 547, ⓦwww.zabola.com; ❸), as well as self-catering accommodation in a hunting lodge. There's excellent bear-watching in what was one of the largest private forests in Transylvania, and boating on a large lake in a French-style park.

Băile Tuşnad and St Anne's Lake

To the north of Sfântu Gheorghe, the River Olt has carved the beautiful **Tuşnad defile**, at the far end of which is **BĂILE TUŞNAD** (Tusnádfürdó), a spa set amid larch and fir woods, with the *Univers* **campsite** (℡0266/335 087,

ⓔ universtourist@kabelkon.ro; May–Sept) offering bungalows (❶), easily spotted just south of the train station at Lacul Ciucaş.

The road south from the train station joins the main road, Str. Oltului, at Univers Tourist (daily 8am–6pm; ☎0266/335 415, ⓔ universtourist@kabelkon.ro), dispensing **information** and **accommodation** in villas (❷–❹) and at the *Lacul Sfânta Ana* cabana (see below), and excursions. Further down Str. Oltului is the **swimming pool**, with bathing in mesothermal waters (9am–7pm from early May, to 8pm from late June; €2.50), and the *Hotel Tuşnad* at no. 87 (☎0266/335 558, Ⓦ www.tusnad.ro; ❸). Facing the hotel is the *InfoTour* kiosk (summer daily 10am–10pm). North of the station, guesthouses include *Csomad Panzió* at Str. Kovács 64 (☎0266/355 145, Ⓦ www.csomadpanzio.ro; ❷), with a sauna, gym and open salt pool; *Panzió Iris* at Str. Apor 22 (☎0266/335 586, Ⓦ www.irispanzio.ro; ❸), a grander place with a **restaurant**, and *Szurdok Panzió*, Str. Oltului 78 (☎0266/311 217, Ⓦ bailetusnad.ro; ❶–❷), affiliated to Hostelling International.

South of town, a road leads east from the village of Bixad to **St Anne's Lake** (Lacu Sf Ana), a two-hour walk from Băile Tuşnad following blue dot markings. Set in a crater on Mount Ciumatu, the lake is the only intact volcanic lake in Europe. It's run by an NGO that charges a fee to visit; excursions to the lake are run by the Univers Tourist agency (see above) at 3pm Tues–Thurs. The *Lacul Sfânta Ana* cabana is set on the east rim of the crater, near the rare Tinovul Mohoş peat bog (in a secondary crater, with glacial relics such as *Drosera* insectivorous plants viewable from a new boardwalk). A few kilometres beyond, on the Târgu Secuiesc road, the tiny spa of **BĂILE BALVANYOS** (Bálványos-fürdő) makes a good stop, with cabana-type accommodation (❶), pensions (❷) and the upmarket *Hotel Carpaţi* (☎0267/360 310, ⓔ balvanyos@bestwesternhotels.ro; ❼), built as a sanatorium in 1938 and now part of the *Best Western* chain. To the north of Băile Tuşnad, the tiny village of Tuşnad itself is home to a new Mineral Water Museum, at the start of the Mineral Water Trail (Borvízút; Ⓦ www.greenways.ro), a 40m Greenway or cycle route visiting a few of the area's 2,000 mineral springs.

Miercurea Ciuc

MIERCUREA CIUC (Csíksereda/Szeklerburg), 100km north of Braşov, is capital of Harghita county, though it is less charming than Odorheiu Secuiesc. Its main claim to fame these days is as the home of Ciuc, one of Romania's better beers.

Arrival and information

Miercurea Ciuc's **bus** and **train stations** are both west of the centre, south of the Odorheiu road; Ciceu station, one stop north, is the junction for the rail line across the Eastern Carpathians to Adjud (trains between Cluj and Moldavia stop here without passing through Miercurea Ciuc). International bus tickets can be bought from Prestige Tours, Str. Kossuth 22 (Mon–Fri 9am–5pm; ☎0266/317 122, Ⓦ www.prestigetravel.ro). The Zsolt **bike shop** is at the rear of Kossuth 28 (Mon–Fri 8am–6pm, Sat 9am–1pm; ☎0747/220 262). For **tourist information**, Csík-Info is upstairs in the city hall at Vár Tér 1 (Mon–Fri 8am–5.30pm, in theory; ☎0266/317 007, ⓔ csikinfo@szereda.ro); there's free **wi-fi** in front of the prefecture on Piaţa Libertăţii.

Accommodation

The town's most appealing **accommodation** is the *Korona* pension, Str. Coşbuc 40 (☎0266/310 993, Ⓦ www.korona.panzio.ro; ❸), with fifteen large, delightfully coloured rooms. South of the centre, the *Hotel Fenyó* at Str. Bălcescu 11

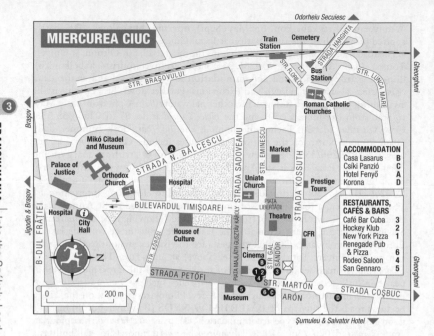

(☎0266/311 493, ⓦwww.hunguest-fenyo.ro; ❺) has adequate yet unspectacular rooms, a gym, sauna and massage room. The *Csíki Panzió*, upstairs at Str. Petőfi 5 (☎0266/314 377, ⓦwww.csikipanzio.ro; ❷), has simple rooms for up to four people, and a kitchen. The excellent *Casa Lasarus* **youth hostel**, at Str. Gál Sándor 9 (☎0266/310 497, ⓦwww.lasarushostel.ro; ❷), has very tidy, en-suite four-bed rooms with TV, plus laundry facilities, internet and a kitchen. There's also a **campsite** and some guesthouses in Băile Jigodin, 2km south on the main road and served by buses #1 (the Red line) and #2 (Yellow); you can walk there by following the blue-dot hiking markings.

The Town

The city centre, with the windswept **Piaţa Libertăţii** at its heart, was extensively rebuilt in communist concrete, a situation made worse by a rash of ugly modern churches, and aside from some Secession and Art Nouveau touches on Str. Petőfi, the **Mikó citadel** south of the centre, and the adjacent 1890s Law Courts and City Hall, there is little of architectural interest here. The citadel itself was built in 1611–21 then rebuilt in 1714 and now contains an excellent county **museum** (Tues–Sun 9am–5pm; Nov 16–March 14 until 4pm), with exhibits on Székely churches. The Museum of the Upper Olt and Mureş at Str. Petőfi 23 (Tues–Sun 9am–5pm; €0.60) has a small ethnographic collection plus temporary shows. Two kilometres south in the suburb of Jigodin (Zsögödfürdó; see above – buses #1 and #2) the **Nagy Imre Gallery** (Tues–Sun 9am–5pm) displays a rotating selection of the forceful paintings of the Székely artist Nagy Imre (1893–1976); his former home, at the rear of the gallery, contains local textiles and Corund ceramics. Near the rail and bus stations, the Roman Catholic **church** on Str. Kossuth was built in 1751–58 in a simple Baroque style; behind it, the utterly weird **Millennium Templom**, also Catholic, is a vision of what the Magyar nomads might have built a millennium ago if they'd had modern materials.

The city's only other attraction is the great Whit Sunday **Székely pilgrimage**, well worth the trip if you're looking for a flavour of the Székely culture. It takes place at Şumuleu (Csiksomlyó), a Franciscan monastery 2km northeast of the city (buses #3, Green, and #4, Purple) and services to Şoimeni from the station). The complex was founded in 1442 by Iancu de Hunedoara in thanks for the Székely victory at Marosszentimre (and rebuilt in Baroque style in 1733–59 and 1804); the festival, however, commemorates the 1567 victory of the Catholic Székely over János Sigismund Báthori, who was attempting to impose Calvinism on them. At least 200,000 black-clad pilgrims attend, singing hymns and queuing up to touch the wooden statue of the Virgin behind the altar, before processing on to the three small chapels on the nearby hill top. From here, there's a good **view** of the plain, dotted with Székely villages.

Eating and drinking

The best **restaurant** in town is at the *Korona Panzió* (see p.189), with Hungarian and Romanian food served in a pleasant courtyard terrace. There are various pizzerias along Str. Petőfi, the best of which is *San Gennaro*, a good-looking place also serving pasta, risotto and fish. Also worth trying along here is the *Renegade Pub & Pizza* and the *New York Pizza*. This being the home of Ciuc beer, you'll be offered little else in the town's **pubs** and **bars**, most of which are also on Str. Petőfi. These include the *Hockey Klub*, with loud music and lots of surprisingly impressive ice hockey memorabilia, and *Rodeo Saloon* close by. Around the corner on Str. Gál, the *Café-Bar Cuba* is stylish but not very Cuban.

The Upper Mureş valley

From Miercurea Ciuc, a semicircular route, by both road and rail, crosses a low pass from the Olt to the Mureş valley and curves around to the city of **Târgu Mureş**. It's a leisurely route taking in the tranquil **Lacu Roşu**, the untamed **Căliman mountains** and a plethora of attractive villages, including Gurghiu and Hodac, both of which hold renowned **festivals**. There are far fewer trains than south of Miercurea Ciuc, and you may need to change at Deda for Târgu Mureş; with your own transport you can take a short cut via Sovata, but there are next to no buses on this route.

Gheorgheni and around

GHEORGHENI (Gyergyószentmiklós) is the jumping-off point for **Lacu Roşu** (see p.192). **Trains** arriving at Gheorgheni are met by buses to spare passengers the twenty-minute hike east into the town centre. Getting back to the station is not so easy, and you'll probably end up having to walk or take a taxi. The **bus station** is immediately south of the train station, but you can also board eastbound buses on B-dul Lacu Roşu, just north of the centre; the only bus west on the DN13B leaves at 10am for Sovata and Târgu Mureş.

The road from the station meets the DN12 at a well-conserved synagogue and continues east as B-dul Lacu Roşu; one block south is Piaţa Libertăţii, ringed with tatty buildings redolent of Austro-Hungarian times. To the north of the square, the pedestrianized Str. Miron Cristea leads to B-dul Lacu Roşu and the splendid high school, completed in 1915; Str. Márton Áron leads east from the square past the Catholic church to Piaţa Petőfi and the **museum** (Tues–Fri 9am–4pm, Sat & Sun 9am–1pm; €1), on the far side of the square at Str. Rácóczi 1. In a former Armenian merchants' inn, it contains some fascinating artefacts, including weatherboards carved with shamanistic motifs brought by the Magyars from Asia.

Practicalities

The town's **tourist office** (Mon–Fri 9am–5pm) is on the south side of the square. The best **hotel** is the *Mureş*, at B-dul Frăţiei 2 (☎0266/364 922, ⓦwww .hotel-mures.ro; ❸), with comfy rooms, gym and swimming pool. At Str. Doua Poduri 2 (opposite the Catholic church) the *Astoria* (☎0266/163 698; ❷) offers simple en-suite rooms above a pizzeria. The *Sport Hotel Avântul* (☎0266/161 270; ❶) at Str. Stadionului 11, off Str. Bălcescu (the Topliţa road), has rooms with shared showers. The *Lázár Panzió*, at Str. Băii 3 (☎0266/362 042; ❸), is a pleasant family guesthouse. There's also a **campsite** (☎0745/810 538) 4km east of town on the Lacu Roşu road, near the newish *Motel Patru* (☎0266/364 213; ❷); this is the start of a fine **cycling trail** along the closed railway to Lacu Roşu. The best **restaurants** are at the *Hotel Mureş* and the *Mukátli*, halfway to the station, while other options are the *Sárkány* Chinese restaurant on Str. Gábor Áron just south of the square, and the pizzeria at the *Astoria* hotel.

Lacu Roşu

In a small depression 25km east of Gheorgheni, **Lacu Roşu**, or the **Red Lake** (Gyilkostó, or Murderers' Lake, in Hungarian), was formed when a landslide dammed the River Bicaz in 1838; you can still see the tips of a few pines protruding from the water, which is rich in trout. Surrounded by lovely scenery and blessed by a yearly average of 1800 hours of sunshine, this is an ideal (and busy) stopover if you're crossing the Carpathians into Moldavia through the wild Bicaz gorges (see p.240). The area is part of the Bicaz Gorges–Haşmaş National Park (ⓦwww .cheilebicazului-hasmas.ro), and the **Eco-Info-Center** (Tues–Sun 10am–6pm), on the main road near the lake at the western end of the resort, offers information on walks. The best hotel is the modern *Lacu Roşu*, Str. Principală 32 (☎0266/380 036, ⓦwww.hotellacurosu.ro; ❸); the more atmospheric *Casa Ranova* (☎0266/364 226; ❷) is right by the lake (next to the boat rental shack), and there are also guesthouses such as the *Floare de Colţ*, Str. Principală 20B (☎0266/380 001, ⓔfloaredecolt @lacu-rosu.com; ❷). The **campsite**, with cabins, is at the eastern end of the resort, although nobody seems to mind if you just pitch a tent anywhere.

Lăzarea

The village of **LĂZAREA** (Szárhegy), 6km north of Gheorgheni on the DN12 (one stop by train), is worth a visit to see **Lazar Castle**, just below the Franciscan monastery whose white tower is visible from passing trains – it's famed as the childhood home of Prince Gabor Bethlen at the end of the sixteenth century. The fifteenth-century castle's fine Renaissance hall and frescoed facade have been gradually restored by artists who hold a summer camp here each year. The **castle gallery** (Tues–Sun 9am–5pm) exhibits the work of artists attending the camp, and there is a well-stocked sculpture park, open all year. The OVR office at Str. Principală 1369 (☎0266/364 695, ⓔemitur@gmail.com) can provide information about their work as well as details of the dozen or more **guesthouses** in the area.

Topliţa and the Căliman mountains

The DN12 and the railway continue north for 30km from Lăzarea to **TOPLIŢA** (Maroshévíz), a third-rate spa and logging town whose only real sights are two wooden churches – Sf Ilie's, 1km north on the main road, built in 1847 and moved here in 1910, and the Doamnei Church in a lovely nunnery 10km further on, dating from 1658 – and a covered bridge south of town. A road cuts through the eastern Carpathians from Topliţa into Moldavia, served by buses to Târgu Neamţ via Borsec and Poiana Largului. The best hotel is the *Mureş*, north of the station at Str. Libertăţii 6 (☎0266/206 890; ❷). There's a campsite in the Bradul spa (which also has a ski slope), west of the centre, as well as guesthouses, such as *Casa Daya* (☎0744/483 438; ❶) and *Pensiunea Harpa* (☎0266/343 304; ❶).

From Topliţa, the road and rail routes head west through the Deda-Topliţa gorge, passing various **places to stay**, such as the *Şoimilor* cabana (❶) 2km west of the Stânceni Neagră train halt, and the lovely *Pensiunea Denisa* (☎0265/264 414, ⓦwww.pensiunea-denisa.ro; ❸) in Sălard, 3km west of Lunca Bradului station – you can rent bikes here, and there's a sauna and jacuzzi. Also in Lunca Bradului is the **Călimani Equestrian Centre** (c/o Transair, Piaţa Trandafirilor 32, ap. 58, Târgu Mureş; ☎0265/268 463, ⓦwww.horseriding.ro), offering great horseback holidays as well as fine meals and accommodation. The wild, unpopulated Căliman mountains rise steeply to the north of this narrow, rugged defile, in which retreating German soldiers made a vain attempt to ambush the Red Army in 1944. Today, the Căliman range – the main volcanic zone of the Carpathians – is a hikers' paradise. The best route in is probably from Răstoliţa, 30km west of Topliţa. There's a road as far as the dam at Secu, from where paths head northeast to the volcanic peaks and the settlements in the huge crater beyond, leading ultimately to Vatra Dornei in Moldavia.

South to Târgu Mureş

From the tiny junction of Deda the railway for Beclean and Cluj heads west, while the road and a minor rail line lead south towards Târgu Mureş. **BRÂNCOVENEŞTI** (Marosvécs), 13km south of Deda and served by slow trains only, was founded on a Roman site and has the fine Kemény castle (visible across the river from the train) dating from the fourteenth century and best known for housing disabled children judged too sick or traumatized to recover during Ceauşescu's regime. **REGHIN** (Szászrégen/Sächsisch Reen), 10km beyond Brâncoveneşti, is ringed by factories, including an amazingly successful violin factory, located here because of the wealth of fine sycamore (also known as flamed maple) in the Gurghiu valley. The main reason to stop here, though, is for bus connections from immediately outside the train station to the traditional shepherding communities **GURGHIU**, 14km east, and **HODAC**, 8km further. Gurghiu is known for its **Girl Fair** (Târgul de fete) on the second Sunday of May, similar to that of Muntele Găina (see box, p.213). At Hodac, there's a **Measurement of the Milk festival** (see p.217) on the first Saturday of May, while the second Sunday in June sees the **Buying Back of the Wives Festival**, reaffirming the economic underpinnings of matrimony. Check event dates at the tourist office in Târgu Mureş (see p.195). During the festivals, special **buses** run from Reghin; at other times, both villages can be reached by buses bound for Dulcea and Toaca, while Gurghiu is also served by buses to Glăjărie and Orşova.

Târgu Mureş

TÂRGU MUREŞ is still at heart **Marosvásárhely**, one of the great Magyar cities of Transylvania, although the Magyar influence has been diluted by recent Romanian and Gypsy immigration – that said, around half of the city's 180,000-strong population is Hungarian. The city was briefly notorious for ethnic riots in 1990, but is better known as a centre of learning – its university is small, but both the medical and drama schools are renowned nationally.

Arrival and information

On a secondary line between Razboieni and Deda, Târgu Mureş is served by several fast trains a day, with extra services in the summer; however, connections south are poor, and you're best off taking a bus or maxitaxi 55km to Sighişoara and catching a train there. The **train station** is a fifteen-minute walk south of the centre, with the **bus station** ten minutes further south on Str. Gheorghe Doja – turn left from the train station or right from the bus station for the city centre; buses to the European Retail Park pass both stations. Note that maxitaxis to Sighişoara and Sovata also call at a stop on B-dul 1 Decembrie 1918, in front of Policlinic no. 2. The I'Velo **free bike-sharing** scheme has sturdy bikes available at the entry to the stadium area on Str. Cuza Vodă (daily 10am–8pm, last rental 7pm).

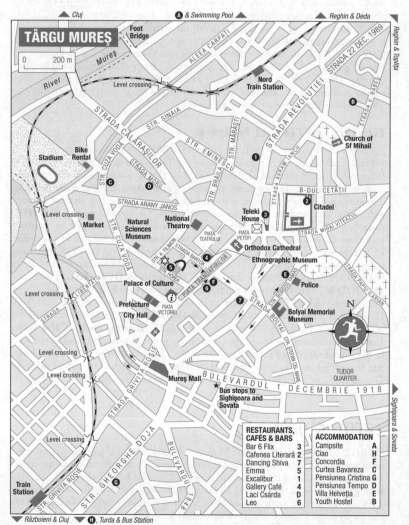

The helpful **tourist office** (May–Sept Mon 8am–4pm, Tues–Fri 8am–8pm, Sat 8–11am; Oct–April Mon 8am–4pm, Tues–Fri 8am–6pm; ⓣ0265/404 934, ⓦwww.mures.ro) is on the corner of Str. Enescu and Piaţa Trandafirilor. **Internet** access is available at Oz, B-dul 1 Decembrie 1918 no. 11 (24hr).

Accommodation

There's plentiful **accommodation** in Târgu Mureş, including several hotels and a clutch of super pensions. The **youth hostel**, within easy walking distance of town at the rear of Str. Victor Babeş 11 (ⓣ0265/218 201, ⓔdjtmures@yahoo.com; ❶–❷), has two- and four-bed rooms; and there's a **campsite** (ⓣ0265/212 009) at the Ştrand on the river at the north end of Aleea Carpaţi, with small, two-person cabins (❷); take bus #14 or #26, or walk from Târgu Mureş Nord train station.

Ciao Str. Gheorghe Doja 143 ⓣ0265/250 750, ⓦwww.hotel-ciao.ro. Modern hotel in the bus station, although it's really only useful if you're planning to leave early or arrive late. ❸
Concordia Piaţa Trandafirilor 45 ⓣ0265/260 602, ⓦwww.hotelconcordia.ro. Top-class hotel with fresh, funky rooms decked out with lush red carpets, zebra-print chairs and big beds. Bathrooms have colourfully tiled walls and flooring, and deep square sinks, and there's a swimming pool, sauna, jacuzzi and Chinese restaurant. ❼
Curtea Bavareza Str. Cuza Vodă 68 ⓣ0265/265 466, ⓦwww.curtea-bavareza.ro. The "Bavarian Court" is a delightful little guesthouse with seven large, superbly equipped rooms (with DVD player),

and immaculate bathrooms with complimentary accessories. Good value. ❺
Pensiunea Cristina Str. Piatra de Moară 1/A ⓣ0265/266 490, ⓔpensiunea.cristina@mureson-line.ro. Nothing fancy, but this welcoming little pension has bright, tidy rooms with a/c – it's also convenient for the bus and train stations. ❸–❹
Pensiunea Tempo Str. Morii 27 ⓣ0265/213 552, ⓦwww.tempo.ro. Upscale yet very affordable pension with eleven simple but stylish, smoothly furnished rooms – terrific restaurant, too. ❸–❹
Villa Helveţia Str. Borsos Tamás 13 ⓣ0265/216 954, ⓦwww.villahelvetia.ro. Extremely cordial, if rather pricey, Swiss-run pension with homely, comfortable a/c rooms. ❹

The Town

Most points of interest are centred on or around the two central squares, Piaţa Victoriei and Piaţa Trandafirilor, with further sights a short walk east.

Piaţa Victoriei and Piaţa Trandafirilor

Both **Piaţa Victoriei** and **Piaţa Trandafirilor** are lined with fine Secession-style edifices, the most grandiose being the adjacent Prefecture and Palace of Culture, dating from 1907 and 1913 respectively and typical of an era when a self-consciously "Hungarian" style of architecture reflected Budapest's policy of "Magyarizing" Transylvania.

The Prefecture's clocktower can be visited at 11am and 2pm (Tues–Sun; book at the Palace of Culture ticket office, Mon–Fri 10am–1pm & 5–7pm); its rooftops blaze with polychromatic tiling, as do those of the **Palace of Culture** (Palatul Culturii; Tues–Sun 9am–4pm; €2), whose facade is richly ornamented with bronze bas-reliefs, ornately carved balconies and a splendid mosaic. Inside, the gloomy corridors are relieved by floral painted walls and stained glass, and 50kg of gilding – working your way up the marble stairs, take a look at the many stained-glass windows illustrating eminent Hungarians, such as the composer Franz Liszt, politician Lajos Kossuth and the poet Sándor Petőfi. One flight up by the right-hand staircase is the most spectacular room of all, the **Hall of Mirrors** (Sala de Oglinzi), with stained-glass windows illustrating local myths. Another flight up is the city's **History Museum**, a dull collection of archeological pieces. Two flights up the left-hand staircase, a door gives you a free glimpse from the gods of the city's concert hall; the huge organ is often used for recitals, and there are classical concerts on Thursdays. Another floor up is the **Art Museum**, focusing on the Hungarian Revival of the late nineteenth and early twentieth centuries. Outside on Str. Enescu, a gallery houses free shows by local artists (Tues–Fri 10am–4pm, Sat & Sun 10am–1pm).

Two blocks north of the Palace of Culture, in the fine Baroque Toldalagy House at Piaţa Trandafirilor 11, is the **Ethnographic Museum** (Muzeul de Etnografie; Tues–Fri 9am–4pm, Sat 9am–2pm, Sun 9am–1pm); it's a rather dry presentation, but the displays on local industry, together with a collection of colourful regional costumes, crafts and icons on glass, are intermittently interesting. Beside the museum stands a tower raised in 1735 – all that remains of the Minorite (Franciscan) monastery – and behind this, the concrete plaza of Piaţa Teatrului, with its undistinguished modern sculptures. A short walk up behind Piaţa Teatrului, beyond the city's synagogue, the **Natural Sciences Museum** (Muzeul de Ştiinţe ale Naturii; same hours) at Str. Horea 24 exhibits a series of large dioramas of stuffed beasts.

The neo-Byzantine **Orthodox Cathedral** (1925–34) marks the northern end of Piaţa Trandafirilor. The Romanian riposte to the imperialistic Magyar administrative buildings dominating the southern end of the square, it pushes aside the more modest Baroque church of the Jesuits (1728–64) on its eastern flank.

East of Piaţa Trandafirilor

Despite its long-standing role as a garrison town, Târgu Mureş also takes pride in its intellectual tradition; the mathematician Farkas Bolyai (1775–1856) and his son János (1802–60), founders of non-Euclidean geometry, receive their due in the **Bolyai Memorial Museum** at Str. Bolyai 17 (Tues–Fri 10am–6pm, Sat & Sun 10am–1pm; free). The museum houses Târgu Mureş's greatest treasure, the **Teleki–Bolyai library** (Biblioteca Bolyai-Teleki). Amassed by the chancellor of Transylvania, Count Samuel Teleki (1739–1822), the collection consists of some 40,000 volumes, including more than 60 incunabula (books printed before 1500), as well as the works of the philosophers of the French Enlightenment, first translations of the Bible in both Hungarian (1590) and Romanian (1688), and the only copy of the first Hungarian encyclopedia. Also on display are paintings by Nagy Imre, the leading Székely artist whose work was heavily influenced by the Transylvanian countryside.

Not far to the north, beyond Str. Mihai Viteazul, stands the **citadel**, sheltering the Calvinist church built for the Dominicans in 1430 and later used by the Transylvanian Diet; there's a small history display in a gate tower (built in 1613). After years of neglect, parts of the citadel have been renovated, including the former barracks lining its eastern side, while the spacious grounds are also becoming a focus for open-air theatre and the like in summer months. Two blocks east of the citadel, along B-dul Cetăţii, Str. Şaguna heads north to the **wooden church** of Sf Mihail (1793–94). Set in a large cemetery, the church has a shingled onion dome, while there are still some traceable frescoes in the largely blackened interior. The porch is a virtual shrine to the national poet, Mihai Eminescu, owing to the fact that he slept in it in 1866 because there was no room at the inn.

Eating, drinking and entertainment

There are two fine Hungarian **restaurants** in town: the *Laci Csárda*, in the *Tempo* pension (see p.195), which replicates a Hungarian-style inn (*csárda*) with lots of rustic trappings and great food, particularly the soups and bread; and *Emma*, Str. Horea 3 (Mon–Sat), a more traditional Hungarian restaurant (*vendéglő*) offering lots of goulash and dumpling dishes. Otherwise, there are a few reasonable options on or just off Piaţa Trandafirilor, such as *Leo* at no. 44, a popular, informal place whose food is solid rather than spectacular, and, north of Piaţa Trandafirilor at Str. Revoluţiei 29, *Excalibur*, a vaguely medieval-themed restaurant specializing in meat-heavy platters.

The best **fast-food** options are the *LactoBar* at Piaţa Trandafirilor 5, which serves big plates of canteen-style grub, and tobacco-free *Panda Pui* at no. 15, which is open round the clock. There are good pastry shops on the north side of Piaţa Trandafirilor, including *Berlin Delicious* (Mon–Sat) on the corner of Str. Horea, and *Cremosa* on the corner of Str. Bartók. Excellent doughnuts (*gogoşi* or *langoş*) are served till 8pm at the rear of the Cinema Arte on the south side of Piaţa Trandafirilor, with another counter selling *covrigi ardelenesti* (Transylvanian bread rings) close by.

By far the most characterful place to **drink** is the *Cafenea Literară 74* (Tues–Sun 5pm–midnight), tucked away in the Butcher's Bastion in the northeastern corner of the citadel – with its bare brick walls, colourful artwork, wicker chairs and leather sofas, it's a relaxing place for a daytime coffee or evening beer, and also stages a cracking programme of music, theatre and comedy. Another arty venue is *Bar 6 Fix*, at the *Ariel* theatre, Str. Poştei 2, where you can listen to jazz, poetry and acoustic music (daily 8am–8pm). Other drinking venues on or near Piaţa Trandafirilor include the *Gallery Café* at no. 17, a cool, somewhat posey cellar with wi-fi, and the *Dancing Shiva* teahouse at Str. Bolyai 16, where you can indulge in a remarkable selection of world teas. The *Félsziget* **rock festival** (Ⓦ www.peninsula .ro), on the last weekend of August, brings 40,000 fans to the Complexul Mureş, east of the city centre between the railway and river.

Cluj and northern Transylvania

Cluj was the great Hungarian capital of Transylvania and remains a natural gateway to the region, just six hours from Budapest by train. There is more buzz to its café life than in other towns, perhaps due to the seventy thousand students resident here.

The area surrounding Cluj, particularly the **Transylvanian Heath** to the east, harbours some of the richest, most varied **folk music** in Europe. Weekends are the best time to investigate villages such as **Sic**, **Cojocna**, **Rimetea** and **Izvoru Crişului**, where almost every street has its own band, and there are rich musical pickings at spring and summer festivals. The city is also a natural base for visiting the **Apuseni massif**, with its wide green pastures, easy walking and caving opportunities, particularly on the **Padiş plateau**.

To the north of the Apuseni is **Sălaj county**, a rural backwater scattered with quaint wooden churches. Further east, the historic town of **Bistriţa**, once centre of an isolated Saxon community (and today more widely known for its Dracula connections), still guards the routes into Maramureş and Bucovina.

Cluj

With its cupolas, Baroque and Secession outcroppings and weathered *fin-de-siècle* backstreets, **CLUJ** (officially known as Cluj-Napoca; Klausenburg in German and Kolozsvár in Hungarian) looks every bit the Hungarian provincial capital it once was. The town was founded by Germans in the twelfth century, on the site of a Roman Municipium, and the modern-day Magyars – now less than a fifth of the city's population – still regret its decline, fondly recalling the Magyar *belle époque* when Cluj's café society and literary reputation surpassed all other Balkan cities. For most Romanians, however, Kolozsvár was the city of the Hungarian landlords until 1920; they consider Ceauşescu's addition of Napoca to its name in 1974 as recognition that their Dacian forebears settled here 1850 years ago, long before the Magyars entered Transylvania. It's rightly said that Romanians live in Cluj and Hungarians still live in Koloszvár, with separate schools, theatre and opera, though relations between the two communities are healthy. Cluj is also the birthplace of the Unitarian creed and its centre in Romania, further adding to the multi-ethnic, multi-faith cocktail.

Under communism, Cluj was industrialized and became Transylvania's largest city, with a population of over 330,000. Nonetheless it retained something of its old languor, as well as a reputation for being anti-Ceauşescu. From 1992 to 2004, the city was run by **Gheorghe Funar**, the "Mad Mayor" of Cluj, former leader of the Romanian National Unity Party, and a man notorious for his anti-Hungarianism – park benches and litter bins were painted in the colours of the Romanian flag, while several absurdly expensive monuments were raised. With a clutch of fine museums, churches and buildings, and buzzing nightlife, Cluj could quite easily detain you for a couple of days.

Arrival and information

From Cluj's **train station**, it's about a twenty-minute walk down Str. Horea, across the Little Someş River, where the road becomes Str. Regele Ferdinand, and into the spacious **Piaţa Unirii**, the focus of the city's life. Across the road from the station, trolley buses #3, #4 and #9 stop on their loop route into the centre, going south on Str. Traian and returning along Str. Horea. The **bus station** is just across the bridge to the north of the train station (bus #31). The airport, 5km east, is reached by bus #8 from Piaţa Mihai Viteazul.

Buses, trolley buses and trams provide frequent and reliable **city transport**, though stops are often far apart; buy tickets at kiosks (€1 for two rides). The most reliable **taxis** are operated by Pritax (℡942), Diesel (℡953), Pro Rapid (℡948), Terra (℡944) and Nova (℡949). **Bikes** can be rented from Umibike, Calea Moţilor 92 (℡0740/074 851 or 0755/092 640, Ⓦwww.umibike.ro), and Downtown Coffee & Something More, Str. D. Ferenc 13 (℡0264/595 529). The **tourist office** at B-dul Eroilor 6 (summer Mon–Fri 8.30am–7pm, Sat & Sun 10am–6pm; winter Mon–Fri 8.30am–5.30pm, Sat 10am–4pm; ℡0264/452 244/9 or 0732/340 669, Ⓔinfo-turism@primariaclujnapoca.ro) is very helpful, with free **internet access**. Excellent **maps** of Cluj (including public transport routes), published by Top-o-Gráf/Freytag & Berndt and Schubert & Franzke, are available from the tourist office, bookshops and kiosks around Piaţa Unirii.

Accommodation

As befits Romania's second-largest city, Cluj has a wide range of accommodation, with a varied selection of **hotels** and **pensions**, terrific **hostels** and, in summer, a range of student accommodation.

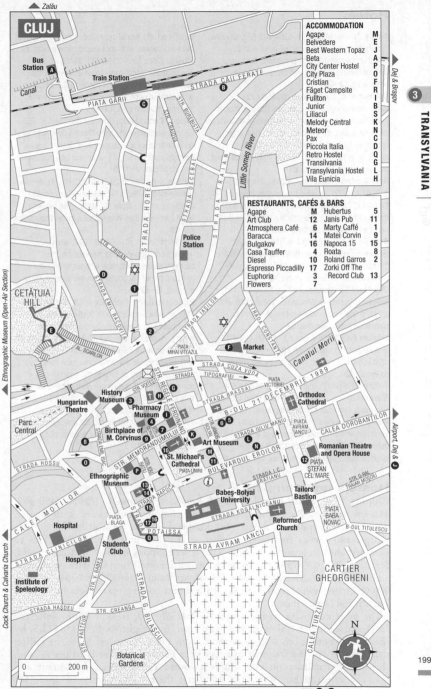

▲ Zalău

CLUJ

Bus Station Ⓐ

Train Station

Ⓑ

Canal

PIATA GĂRII

STRADA CĂII FERATE

PIATA GĂRII

Ⓒ

Dej & Brașov ▶

STR. BUREBISTA

STR. CRAIOVA

Little Someș River

STRADA DECEBAL

STRADA TRAIAN

STRADA HOREA

STR. CHISAN

STRADA EMIL RACOVITA

AL. SCĂRILOR

Police Station

CETĂTUIA HILL

Ⓓ

Ⓔ

Ⓕ Market

STRADA IAȘILOR

STRADA CONSTANTA

Canalul Morii

PIATA MIHAI VITEAZUL

STRADA CUZA VODA

TIPOGRAFIEI

PIATA VICTORIEI

STRADA BRASSAI

B-DUL 21 DECEMBRIE 1989

Orthodox Cathedral

CALEA DOROBANTILOR

Airport, Dej & Ⓙ ▶

History Museum

Hungarian Theatre

Parc Central

Pharmacy Museum

Birthplace of M. Corvinus

Ethnographic Museum

St. Michael's Cathedral

PIATA UNIRII

Art Museum

STR. IANOS BOCHA

STRADA IULIU MANIU

PIATA AVRAM IANCU

Romanian Theatre and Opera House

PIATA ȘTEFAN CEL MARE

STRADA HOSSU

STRADA EMIL ISAC

STR. MEMORANDUMULUI

STR. REGELE FERDINAND

BULEVARDUL EROILOR

STR. NAPOCA

Babeș-Bolyai University

STRADA I.C. GRATIANU

STR. G-RAL TRAIAN MOSOIU

Tailors' Bastion

STRADA AVRAM IANCU

STRADA KOGĂLNICEANU

Reformed Church

PIATA BABA NOVAC

B-DUL TITULESCU

CALEA MOTILOR

Hospital

Hospital

STRADA CLINICILOR

Institute of Speleology

STR. V. BABES

STR. PASTEUR

STRADA HASDEU

STRADA CREANGA

STR. G. BILASCU

Students' Club

PIATA L. BLAGA

STRADA POTAISSA

CARTIER GHEORGHENI

CALEA TURZII

Botanical Gardens

N

0   200 m

◀ Cock Church & Calvaria Church

◀ Ethnographic Museum (Open-Air Section)

▼ Ⓡ, Ⓢ & Turda

Hotels

Agape Str. Iuliu Maniu 6 ☎0264/406 523, ⓦwww
.hotelagape.ro. Peaceful central hotel with big,
colourful rooms with large armchairs, fluffy rugs,
wall lamps and pictures, and gleaming white
bathrooms. ❹–❻

Belvedere Str. Călăraşilor 1 ☎0264/432 071,
ⓔbelvedere.cluj@unita-turism.ro. Upscale modern
place overlooking the town from Cetăţuia hill, with
swimming pool, gym and sauna included. Main
access by foot (up dilapidated steps, not safe at
night), or by taxi – nearest bus is #38, stopping not
too far north at Str. Gruia. ❺

Best Western Topaz Str. Septimiu Albini 10
☎0264/414 021, ⓦwww.bestwesterntopaz.ro. Not
far east of the centre (trolleys #3, #25; bus #33),
this is rather staid and characterless, but its facilities are as good as anything else. ❺

Beta Str. Giordano Bruno 1 ☎0264/455 290,
ⓦwww.hotelbeta-cluj.ro. Refurbished hotel inside
the bus station; rooms are dull and a little poky.
Convenient, if somewhat pricey. ❸

City Plaza Str. Sindecatelor 9 ☎0264/450 101,
ⓦwww.cityhotels.ro. Modern business hotel with
spa, two fine restaurants, and great deals at
weekends and in summer. ❾

Cristian Piaţa Mihai Viteazul 17 ☎0264/434 174,
ⓦwww.hotel-cristian.ro. An affordable new option
right in the city centre, with presentable rooms but
no extras. ❷

Fullton Str. Sextil Puşcariu 10 ☎0264/597 898,
ⓦwww.fullton.ro. Extremely elegant hotel tucked
away near Corvinus's birthplace; the warm rooms
– some with four-poster beds – are smartly
furnished with thick pile carpets and arty decor. ❹

Junior Str. Căii Ferate 12 ☎0264/432 028,
ⓔoffice@pensiune-junior.ro. Clean and quiet, if

slightly scruffy, hostel-type place just 200m east of
the train station, with double and triple rooms. ❷

Liliacul Calea Turzii 251A ☎0264/438 129,
ⓦwww.hotelliliacul.com. South of town on the
DN1, just before the Făget campsite turning, this is
a reasonable option, with well-appointed rooms,
including some triples. ❸–❺

Melody Central Piaţa Unirii 29 ☎0264/597 465,
ⓦwww.centralmelody.com. There's been a hotel of
sorts here for over a century, and despite a great
central location it's quite noisy and now somewhat
lacking in character. ❸

Meteor B-dul Eroilor 29 ☎0264/591 060, ⓦwww
.hotelmeteor.ro. A decent hotel in a very central
location (set back from the street, with parking),
but it can get a little noisy thanks to the downstairs
bar. ❸

Pax Piaţa Gării 1 ☎0264/432 927, ⓦwww
.hotelpax.ro. Opposite the train station, the
fourteen rooms – with and without bathrooms –
here are rather sprightlier than the exterior might
suggest. ❷–❸

Piccola Italia Str. Emil Racoviţă 20 ☎0264/536
110, ⓦwww.piccolaitalia.ro. Well-run little
guesthouse on a quiet residential street, with
breezy, modern rooms, including several triples. ❹

Transilvania Str. Regele Ferdinand 20 ☎0264/594
429, ⓦwww.hoteltransilvaniacluj.ro. A rare city-
centre budget option, though the spartan grey
rooms (some with baths) are pretty dated. ❹

Vila Eunicia Str. Emile Zola 2 ☎0264/594 067,
ⓔoffice@vilaeunicia.ro. This guesthouse's bright
yellow, flower-bedecked facade conceals modern,
slightly cluttered rooms. Very central, but with
free parking. ❸

Hostels and camping

Cluj has a fine **youth hostel** in the ⚑ *Retro*, Str. Potaissa 13 (☎0264/450 452,
ⓦwww.retro.ro; ❷); it's a clean, friendly and well-run place, with singles,
doubles, triples and dorm rooms – breakfast and laundry are available for an extra
charge, and there's free internet/wi-fi access. The hostel sells bus tickets to
Budapest and can organize car hire. Two newer options are the *City Center Hostel*,
Str. Raţiu 2 (☎0264/594 454, ⓦwww.citycenterhostel.com; ❷), with two-, four-
and six-bed rooms; and *Transylvania Hostel*, Str. Iuliu Maniu 26 (☎0264/443 266,
ⓦwww.transylvaniahostel.com; ❷), with rooms holding up to eight beds, and a
kitchen and home cinema.

The *Făget* **campsite** (year-round; ☎0264/596 234) is 4km south along the
DN1 and a further 1.5km off the main road (turn right/south at km472.5, by
the *Liliacul* hotel); bus #40 goes there from Piaţa Ştefan cel Mare, or failing
that, take any of the frequent maxitaxis for Feleacu and Turda to the *Liliacul*,
then walk. Facilities include simple two-bed cabins (❷), a restaurant and
bar, and nonstop hot water (in summer); there's also plenty of space for

tents and caravans. Across the road is the *Silva*, a nice private bar-restaurant, recommended for its tripe soup.

The City

Unlike almost every other Romanian city of comparable size, Cluj avoided the construction of a Civic Centre and the widespread demolition of its old central zone, which remains largely unspoilt within the line of the **city walls**. It is increasingly being pedestrianized, allowing stylish new bars and restaurants to flourish; unfortunately the city's drivers haven't got the message and are trying to cram more and more cars into the remaining space. The focal point of the city is **Piaţa Unirii**, surrounded by shops, cafés and restaurants and dominated by the monumental **St Michael's Cathedral**. Around and close to the square are most of the city's museums, the best being the marvellous **Ethnographic Museum**. South of Piaţa Unirii is the **university area**, sprinkled with several impressive buildings, and a short walk east there's more fine architecture on display, notably the **Romanian National Theatre and Opera House** on Piaţa Ştefan cel Mare.

Piaţa Unirii

Dwarfing **Piaţa Unirii** is the Roman Catholic **cathedral of St Michael**, built between 1349 and 1487 in the German Gothic style of the Saxons who then ruled unchallenged over the city. It's a superb example of a Central European hall-church – not dissimilar to the Black Church in Braşov (see p.138) – comprising three capacious naves separated by mighty pillars that curve into austerely bare vaulting. To this great church the Hungarian aristocracy later added a sacristy – the door of which (dated 1528) encapsulates the Renaissance style introduced under Mátyás Corvinus – a wooden pulpit flush with Baroque carving, and a massive tapering bell tower raised in 1859. Note, too, the fifteenth-century frescoes in the southwestern chapel and on the south wall, to the right as you enter. Free organ recitals are given on Saturdays at 5pm.

South of the cathedral, a clumsy but imposing equestrian **statue of Mátyás Corvinus** (raised in 1902) tramples the crescent banner of the Turks underfoot. His formidable Black Army kept Hungary safe from banditry and foreign invasion for much of his reign (1458–90), but just 36 years later the nation was more or less wiped off the map at the battle of Mohács. A popular lament that justice departed with his death highlights Mátyás's political and military achievements, but his reputation derives equally from his Renaissance attributes, for which his wife, **Beatrix of Naples**, should share the credit. She introduced him to the Renaissance culture of Italy, selecting foreign architects and craftsmen, and humanists like Bonfini to chronicle events and speeches, and personally commissioned many volumes in the Corvin Library. In the southwestern corner of the square stand the **Shot Pillars**, seven elongated bronze cylinders erected in 2003 to commemorate those gunned down in the 1989 revolution, some 26 in total. Across the road, the now defunct **Hotel Continental** was built in 1895 in an eclectic style combining Renaissance, Classical and Baroque elements; it served as the German military headquarters in Transylvania at the end of World War II. Across the road, the University Bookshop is another fine building, bearing two plaques to those killed on December 21 and 22, 1989. On the northern side of the square, on the corner of Str. Regele Ferdinand, the Hintz House housed Cluj's first apothecary from 1573 until 1949. Inside, the **Pharmacy Museum** (Mon–Wed & Fri 10am–4pm, Thurs noon–8pm; €1) displays a beautiful collection of ancient prescriptions, jars and implements, as well as Baroque furnishings and glass cabinets. In the dungeon-like basement is the old laboratory, complete with an assortment of tools, pestles and containers.

East of the cathedral, at Piaţa Unirii 30, stands the **Art Museum** (Wed–Sun 10am–5pm; €1), which, with its counterpart in Bucharest (see p.61), offers the country's best survey of Romanian art. It is housed in the Baroque Bánffy Palace, built in 1774–85 to the design of Johann Eberhardt Blaumann for the Bánffy family. The collection is dominated by works of the largely French-influenced artists of the nineteenth and twentieth centuries, including Romania's foremost painter, Nicolae Grigorescu (1838–1907); as well as his superb landscapes, look out for some wonderful character paintings, such as *Turkish Prisoner* and *Gypsy with Bear*, and a rare self-portrait. Also well represented are Theodor Aman (1831–91) and Theodor Pallady (1871–1956), who spent several decades in Paris and was clearly inspired by Matisse. Some Székely painters, such as Nagy István and Nagy Imre, also get a look-in. In summertime, there's an open-air bar in the courtyard (see p.206), and concerts by anyone from Moldavian Gypsy brass bands to the Cluj Philharmonic.

North of Piaţa Unirii

From the northwest corner of Piaţa Unirii, Str. Matei Corvin leads to the small fifteenth-century mansion at no. 6, the **birthplace of Mátyás Corvinus**, Hungary's greatest king. Born in 1440, he was the son of Iancu de Hunedoara, and thus a Romanian, as a plaque added by Funar (see p.198) proclaims (however, Magyar myth makes his father the illegitimate son of the Hungarian King Sigismund, so this was virtually a place of pilgrimage for Hungarians in Habsburg days). The mansion is now an art college, but it's worth a peek inside to view the entry door and vaulted Gothic ceiling – there are occasional free exhibitions in the basement.

Continuing north, Str. Corvin leads into Piaţa Muzeului. Just to the left of the square, at Str. Daicovici 2, is the **History Museum of Transylvania** (Tues–Sun 10am–4pm; €2). On the first floor, strange skulls and mammoth tusks are succeeded by arrow- and spearheads, charting progress from the Neolithic and Bronze Ages to the rise of the Dacian civilization, which reached its peak between the second century BC and the first century AD. On the floor above, the story continues up to World War I, but overall this is a desperately dull display, and with information in Romanian only. At the east end of the square is the **Franciscan church**, built after the Tatar attack in the thirteenth century and handed over to the Dominicans by Iancu de Hunedoara in 1455; it was transferred to the Franciscans in 1725 and subsequently rebuilt in the Baroque style. Inside, the fanciful main altar features a painting of the Virgin, flanked by statues of the great Hungarian kings, St Joseph and St Stephen.

In the park to the west is a lake with pedaloes, and a casino at its far end; near the river, the Academy of Visual Arts occupies an orange building with a few statues outside. East of here is **Piaţa Mihai Viteazul**, a traffic-laden square dominated by a large statue of Michael the Brave, and an eternal flame. To the east of the square and the busy market (see p.207), a disused synagogue at Str. Croitorilor 13 now houses the university's centres for Jewish Studies, Holocaust Studies, Gender Studies and the like; it's a plain building, almost like a Methodist chapel. Heading north on Str. Horea, across the river and towards the train station, brings you to the Mughal-style Neologue **synagogue**, built in 1886, sacked by the Legionaries in 1927, demolished in 1944 and rebuilt in 1951. Just west, atop Cetăţuia Hill, stand the remains of a fifteenth-century **citadel**, ringing the *Belvedere* hotel. The Securitate used the hotel as its power base, and twelve people were supposedly gunned down on the steps in the 1989 revolution. The plinth of the massive cross, raised here by the Uniate Church in 1993–97 (replacing one demolished in 1948), is the best place to **view** the city. Behind the hotel is a tower that looks something like a dock for airships but was in fact built for testing parachutes.

The university area

From Piața Unirii, Str. Napoca leads west to the **Students' Club** and the old library on Piața Blaga, and Str. Universității heads south past the Baroque church of the Piarist Order (1718–24) to the **Babeș-Bolyai University**. Since its foundation in 1581 as a Jesuit Academy, the university has produced scholars of the calibre of Edmund Bordeaux Székely (translator of the Dead Sea Scrolls), but has also served as an instrument of cultural oppression. Long denied an education in their own language, the Romanians promptly banned teaching in Hungarian once they took over in 1919, only to hurriedly evacuate students and staff when Hitler gave northern Transylvania back to Hungary in 1940. After liberation, separate universities were created to teach in the two languages, but in 1959 the authorities decreed a shotgun merger, enforced by a then little-known cadre called Nicolae Ceaușescu, which led to the suicide of the Bolyai's pro-rector, and, more predictably, a rapid decline in its Hungarian-language teaching. This and a similar running-down of primary and secondary schooling convinced many Magyars that the state was bent on "de-culturizing" them. Since 1989, however, it seems to have found a genuinely multicultural vocation, with teaching in both languages as well as the first Jewish Studies courses in Romania.

Outside the university's main building (1893–1903) stand statues of Samuil Micu, Gheorghe Șincai and Petru Maior, the leaders of the **Transylvanian School** (Școala Ardeleana) whose philological and historical researches in Blaj fuelled the Romanian cultural resurgence of the nineteenth century and the resistance to Magyarization. They inspired the "generation of 1848", including Avram Iancu, who lived as a student in 1841–44 at Str. Avram Iancu 17; nearby, flower and coffin shops mark out the gate of the **cemetery** at no. 26 (daily: March–Oct 6.30am–7.30pm; Nov–Feb 8am–5.30pm); the cave scientist Emil Racoviță and his family lie on the left as you go up to the graves of Kós Károly (see box, p.186) and the writer Emil Isac, both on the right. Cutting across below Kós's resting place to the next avenue east, you'll find the grand tomb of the composer Nicolae Bretan at the junction, and the dramatist Szentgyörgy István on the right just below.

At Str. Bilașcu 42, just south of the university, are the **Botanical Gardens** (daily Sept–March 8am–4pm; April & May 9am–5pm; June–Aug 10am–6pm; €2), with more than 10,000 species. They contain a museum (Mon–Fri 7am–3pm; €1) and herbarium, greenhouses (to 6pm) with desert and tropical plants including Amazon waterlilies 2m across, and a small Japanese garden.

East to Piața Ștefan cel Mare

The tree-lined Str. Kogălniceanu runs east from the university to the Calvinists' **Reformed church**, built in 1486–1516 for Mátyás Corvinus, with a pulpit added in 1646. In front stands a copy of the statue of St George and the Dragon in Prague's Hradčany castle – one of the world's most famous equestrian statues – made in 1373 by the masters Martón and György of Kolozsvár (Martin and George of Cluj). The church's interior features plain late Gothic stonework above the stalls and wooden panels, decorated with the coats of arms of all the leading Hungarian families of Transylvania. The ornate organ (1766) in the gallery, added in 1912 above the west door, is used for recitals. When the church is closed, get the key from Str. Kogălniceanu 21.

Just east of the church, on Piața Baba Novac, is the fifteenth-century **Tailors' Bastion** (Turnul Croitorilor), now housing free exhibits on the city's history (Mon–Fri 9am–7pm, Sat & Sun 10am–6pm) and a pleasant café in the basement. North of the bastion, the elongated square of Piața Ștefan cel Mare is dominated by the **Romanian National Theatre and Opera House**, built in 1906–19 by the

Unitarianism

The **Unitarian Church** was founded in Cluj in 1556 by the hitherto Calvinist minister Dávid Ferenc (1510–79), and by 1568 it was already accepted as one of the four official churches of Transylvania. Unitarianism had its origins among the Italian and Spanish humanists and some of the more extreme Anabaptists, and one of its Italian leaders, Faustus Socinus (1539–1604), came to Cluj in 1578, before moving on to Kraków in 1580.

Unitarianism derives its name from its rejection of the doctrine of the Trinity, as well as other basic doctrines such as the divinity of Christ, his atonement for the sins of the world, and thus the possibility of salvation. However, its significance lies in its undogmatic approach – adherents are conspicuous for their devotion to reason in matters of religion, and to civil and religious liberty, and their exercise of tolerance to all sincere forms of religious faith.

Unitarianism spread worldwide, and by the 1830s had mutated to become the religion, for instance, of the Boston/Harvard establishment, with an emphasis on scientific progress and material success. In Romania there are now around 75,000 Unitarians, almost all among the Hungarian community.

ubiquitous Viennese theatre architects Fellner and Helmer. Inaugurated in 1919, the building has hosted the great and good of Romanian theatre and opera, as testified by the many photos on the lobby walls.

Across the road, in Piaţa Avram Iancu, is the notorious statue of Avram Iancu – leader of the 1848 revolt against the Hungarians – commissioned by Funar in 1993. Looming behind it is the huge and startling **Orthodox Cathedral** (Mon & Sat 6am–1pm & 5–8pm, Tues–Fri & Sun 6am–8pm), built in 1923–33 and looking as if it fell through a time warp from Justinian's Constantinople. It was raised to celebrate the Romanians' triumph in Transylvania, and the neo-Byzantine stone facade hides a concrete structure. Inside, amid the cold, grey concrete and fading frescoes, are many elaborate and colourful adornments. In 2001, the narthex, sections of the nave walls, and a spot just above the interior entrance were decorated with Murano mosaic from Venice – over a hundred hues, including twenty different shades of gold, were used in these beautiful compositions. Meanwhile, the huge iconostasis – bearing the unmistakable stamp of Brâncoveanu – comprises three rows of icons featuring scenes from the life of Christ and images of revered saints. Note, too, the twisted rope motif around the narthex. The enormous chandelier was a gift from King Carol I.

From here, the most direct route back to the centre is along B-dul Eroilor, at the east end of which is another of Funar's absurd erections – the ugly *Memorandum* monument, commonly known as "*The Guillotine*". It commemorates the Romanians imprisoned for protesting in the 1892 *Memorandum* against Hungarian chauvinism.

West of Piaţa Unirii

The city's main east–west axis runs across the northern edge of Piaţa Unirii, continuing eastwards as B-dul 21 Decembrie 1989 and westwards as Str. Memorandumului. At Str. Memorandumului 21, the Reduta Palace, where the Transylvanian Diet met in 1790–91 (and where the 1894 trial of the Memorandumists was held), now houses the main branch of the superb **Ethnographic Museum** (Tues–Sun 9am–5pm; €2), easily the city's finest museum. The exhibition starts with the history of shepherding in the region, featuring finely crafted staffs, cattle horns used for carrying gunpowder, and ferocious bear traps. The importance of traditional crafts is manifest most colourfully in a collection of carved gates from Maramureş, painted Saxon chests and wardrobes, and some exquisite glazed pottery. There's also an outstanding assemblage of musical instruments, such as flutes, alpenhorns and clarions, the latter used throughout the Apuseni region to ward off predators.

Upstairs is probably Romania's finest collection of traditional carpets and folk costumes – from the dark herringbone patterns of the Pădureni region to the bold yellow, black and red stripes of Maramureş. Blouses and leggings are predominantly black or white, but women's apron-skirts, and the waistcoats worn by both sexes for special occasions, are brilliantly coloured. Peacock feathers serve in the Năsăud area as fans or plumes, and the love of complicated designs spills over onto cups, masks, distaffs (used as an application for marriage) and linked spoons (used as a charm against divorce). Afterwards, you can check out the excellent craft shop, then have a drink in the pleasant courtyard café. The museum also has an excellent **open-air section** (Tues–Sun 9am–5pm; €2) on the Hoia hill, northwest of town, with peasant houses and three wooden churches from the surrounding areas; it's a thirty-minute walk from the centre, or take bus #27 from the station, #28 from Piaţa Mihai Viteazul, or #30 from Piaţa Unirii to Piaţa 14 Iulie (Cartier Grigorescu), and then walk ten minutes north up Str. Tăietura Turcului.

Strada Memorandumului continues west from the museum to the splendidly towered city hall, where it becomes Calea Moţilor. At no. 84 is the beautiful Calvinist **Cock Church**, built in 1913 by Kós Károly, who designed everything down to the light fittings, all with a cock motif symbolizing St Peter's threefold denial of Christ before cock's crow; ask for the key at the parish office behind the church. Kós's first house, built for his parents at Str. Breaza 14, north of the train station, now houses the architectural conservation group Utilitas. Further west is the **Mănăştur** quarter, the oldest part of Cluj, although you wouldn't know it from the serried ranks of 1980s apartment blocks – the best **views** are from the Calea Mănăştur flyover, where you can see ancient earthworks to the south and a relatively modern shrine and belfry atop them. Behind these is the **Calvaria Church**, built by the Magyars in the twelfth century and rebuilt by the Benedictines in 1466; it's a Gothic hall-church, simple but surprisingly high, recently restored and with a new belfry.

Eating, drinking and entertainment

Cluj has a reasonable bunch of **restaurants**, including several upmarket, though not expensive, ones, various pizzerias, for instance on B-dul Eroilor, and lots of fast-food options and snack bars, especially on Str. Napoca and Piaţa Blaga. **Café** life in Cluj ranks second only to that of Bucharest, as does the **bar** and **club** scene, thanks to the city's large student population.

Restaurants

Agape Str. Iuliu Maniu 6. Terrific self-service restaurant (Mon–Fri 11am–9pm) offering cheap and cheerful snacks, mains and desserts. There's a regular pizzeria upstairs (noon–midnight).
Baracca Str. Napoca 8A. A place for local yuppies to be seen in, there's good Italian food here, plus a wide range of wines and cocktails with and without alcohol.
Espresso Piccadilly Pies & Wine I.M. Klein 23. This stylish new place really does serve pies (eg Mediterranean chicken, mascarpone chicken

and cheesy zucchini) and imported wines by the glass.
Hubertus B-dul 21 Decembrie 1989 22. The city's most refined dining option, where a well-presented English menu offers the likes of spit-roast game, boar-meat rolls and pheasant ragoût. Dark orange walls, beautifully laid tables and cloth-backed chairs round off the experience superbly.
Marty Caffé Str. Horea 5. Toasted sandwiches, pastas, soups and cooked breakfasts form the mainstay at this bright and breezy restaurant. Two

other branches at Str. Traian Moşoiu 28 and Str. Victor Babeş 39.

Matei Corvin Str. Matei Corvin 3. This relatively small place is one of the city's most elegant restaurants, specializing in Hungarian food (goulash and beef-filled Debrecen pancakes), in addition to, rather oddly, some Mexican options. Terrific wine, too. Closed Sun.

Napoca 15 Str. Napoca 15. A wide-ranging menu features salads, pastas, chicken, beef and filled

pancakes – choose from the formal indoor seating area or the more relaxed terrace.

Roata Str. Alex Ciura 6A. Just off Str. Isac, this cosy, rustically styled restaurant – Transylvanian costumes and textiles draped over the walls – offers some of the city's best Romanian food; add sharp service and a convivial atmosphere, and you've got a most enjoyable place to eat. Closed Mon.

Cafés and bars

Cluj has a nice spread of **cafés**, many of which morph into bars as the hours wear on. Terrace gardens (*gradinas*) are few and far between, but one worth visiting is the *Terasa Muzeu*, in the courtyard of the Art Museum, while *Flowers*, at Piaţa Unirii 25, is a bijou little teahouse. A more bohemian place is the *Art Club*, Piaţa Ştefan cel Mare 14, whose walls are plastered with yellowing posters from past performances at the theatre across the road.

In the evenings, two worthwhile places are the arty *Bulgakov*, Str. Klein 17, and *Atmosphera Café*, at B-dul 21 Decembrie 1918 no. 18, an excellent Hungarian pub. *Euphoria*, Str. Muzeul 4, is a pleasant terrace in the daytime, and becomes a lively cellar-bar after dark. *Casa Tauffer*, at the corner of Str. Goldiş and Str. Puşcariu, hosts live jazz on Friday and Saturday nights. For late-night **music**, there's *Diesel*, Piaţa Unirii 17, a decent, if posey, lounge bar/club; *Janis Pub*, B-dul Eroilor 5; the *Zorki Off The Record Club*, Str. Raţiu 10, playing alt/indie music below, with an arty café and acoustic gigs above; and the pub-like *Roland Garros*, Str. Horea 2, with a riverside balcony and live rock music at weekends.

Entertainment

Cluj has a strong cultural suit, thanks in part to the healthy mix of both Romanian and Hungarian communities. Tickets for the **Romanian Theatre and Opera** can be bought across the road from the theatre at Piaţa Ştefan cel Mare 14 (daily 11am–5pm; ☏0264/595 363). The **Hungarian State Theatre**, Str. Emile Isac 26, is the venue for a prolific number of theatrical and operatic productions, the great majority in Hungarian (box office daily 10am–1pm & 4.30–6.30pm; ☏0264/593

Cinema in Cluj

Cluj is the unofficial capital of Romanian **cinematography** – it was here, in 1905, that the first film studio was inaugurated, and the city has more cinema-goers than any other Romanian city. Moreover, it's one of the few places where city-centre **cinemas** are still flourishing, the best being: Republicii, Piaţa Mihai Viteazul; Arta-Eurimages, Str. Universităţii 3; and Victoria, B-dul Eroilor 51. Cluj is also home to the country's premier film festival, the **Transylvanian International Film Festival** (TIFF), a ten-day jamboree at the beginning of June that features a superb mix of domestic and world films shown at the cinemas listed above.

Romanian **film** is currently on a roll, thanks in part to a clutch of recent award-winners. Three highly acclaimed movies are *The Death of Mr Lazarescu* (2005), a darkly humorous tale of an elderly man's experience of being trawled round Bucharest's hospitals as he faces imminent death; *12:08 East of Bucharest* (2006), a fabulous deadpan comedy surrounding the events of the 1989 revolution; and the Palme d'Or-winning *4 Months, 3 Weeks and 2 Days* (2007), a tragic story of illegal abortion set during the final days of the Ceauşescu regime.

468, ⓦwww.huntheater.ro). The **Cluj Philharmonic** is at Str. Kogălniceanu (box office Mon–Fri 11am–5pm; ☎0264/430 060). For kids, there's the fabulous **Puck Puppet Theatre** at Str. I.C. Brătianu 23 (☎0264/595 992, ⓦwww.teatrulpuck .ro). Note that performances at most of these venues are suspended from around early July to mid-September.

Shopping

Cluj's main **department store**, the Central, is at Str. Regele Ferdinand 22 (Mon–Sat 10am–8pm). The *Mega* supermarket is at the west end of Piaţa Mihai Viteazul, with the daily food **market** hidden behind it; on Thursdays there's also a craft market here selling wood carvings and embroidery from the Apuseni highlands and the Transylvanian Heath. The Napolact shop, Piaţa Mihai Viteazul 8 (Mon–Fri 6am–7pm, Sat 7am–3pm), sells some superb dairy products and other foods.

Three excellent **outdoor gear** shops are Nootka/Trakking Sport, Str. Dacia 1 (Mon–Fri 10am–6pm, Sat 10am–2pm); Alti-Sport, corner of Str. Brassaï and Str. David Ferenc (Mon–Fri 10am–7pm, Sat 10am–2pm); and Polartek Sports, Str. Universităţii 8 (Mon–Fri 10am–6pm). For English-language **books**, try the university bookstore (Mon–Fri 8am–8pm, Sat 9am–4pm) at the corner of Piaţa Unirii and Str. Universităţii, which also has good dictionaries and books on Romanian ethnography and arts, and some French-, German- and Hungarian-language titles. Gaudeamus, Str. Iuliu Maniu 3 (Mon–Fri 10am–6pm, Sat 10am–2pm), and Carturești, in the Iulius Mall, Str. Vaida-Voievod 53 (daily 10am–10pm), also have books and maps in English.

Listings

Airlines TAROM, Piaţa Mihai Viteazul 11 (Mon–Fri 8am–8pm, Sat 9am–2pm; ☎0264/432 669); BlueAir, B-dul Eroilor 4 (☎0264/450 660, ⓦwww.blueairweb.com); Carpatair, at the airport (☎0264/416 016, ⓦwww.carpatair.ro).
Car rental An excellent local company is Pan Travel, Str. Grozăvescu 13 (☎0264/420 516, ⓦwww.pantravel.ro); also Autonom, Str. Universităţii 4 (☎0374/026 092, 0749/151 028, ⓦwww.autonom.ro); Rodna Rentacar, Str. Barbu Lautaru 1 (☎0264/450 711, ⓦwww.rodna-trans.ro).
Internet Intersoft Club Internet, Str. Bariţiu 24; Computer Zone, Str. Cuza Vodă 40; Internet Caffé, Str. David Ferenc 19; Total Net, Str. Isac 2 (24hr); Assault Internet & Games, Str. Brătianu 47.
Left luggage 24 hours at the train station (*bagaj de mâna*).

Libraries British Council Library, Str. Arany Janos 11 (Mon, Wed & Thurs 1–7pm, Tues & Fri 10am–4pm; ☎0264/594 408); American Library, French Cultural Centre, Str. Brătianu 22; American Cultural Centre, Str. Iuliu Maniu 22; German & Italian Cultural Centres, Str. Universităţii 7.
Pharmacy Pharma Net, at the southeast corner of Piaţa Unirii, is open to 11pm daily; Cynara, Calea Floreşti 75 (☎0264/426 272), is open 24hr. Sensiblu, Str. Clinicilor 8 (8am–10pm), is a good modern place by the hospital. For medicinal plants, try Hypericum, Str. Horea 4, or Plante Medicinale, B-dul Eroilor 7.
Train tickets Piaţa Mihai Viteazul 20 (international bookings Mon–Fri 9.30am–5pm).
Travel agents Agrotrip, Str. Câmpului 63 (☎0264/406 363, ⓦwww.agrotrip.ro); Pan Travel, Str. Traian Grozăvescu 13 (☎0264/420 516 or 0722/513 100, ⓦwww.pantravel.ro).

The Apuseni mountains

The **Apuseni mountains** are bordered to the north by the Crişul Repede valley and to the south by the Arieş valley, enabling easy access by public transport. The DN75 follows the Arieş west from **Turda**, with various minor ranges such as the Trascău and Metaliferi (Metal Bearing) mountains to the south, to Câmpeni, where one road heads west into the Bihor, and another runs south to Brad and

Alba. Câmpeni is the capital of the **Moţi highlanders**, who repelled the Roman invaders, then moved from the valleys into the hills in the eighteenth century when the Habsburgs attempted to conscript them into the army. They now live all year round at up to 1400m, some of the highest settlements in Romania, in scattered groups of high-roofed, thatched cottages. **Buses** run east along the valley to Turda and on to Cluj in the early morning, returning west more or less hourly through the afternoon; there are also services from Alba Iulia and Deva to Câmpeni. Along the **Crişul Repede valley**, most Accelerat trains stop only at Huedin, Ciucea and Aleşd, but the infrequent Personal services allow exploration by stopping at every hamlet along the line.

Despite opposition from the forestry and other industries – the uranium mines are now closed, but Europe's largest opencast gold mine is now being planned beneath Roşia Montană (see p.213) – the **Apuseni Nature Park** (Ⓦwww .parcapuseni.ro) was established in 2004, alongside the revival of an excellent network of hiking trails.

Turda

TURDA (Torda), 30km south of Cluj along the DN1 (E60/81), was once one of Transylvania's wealthiest towns, thanks to salt mining. Modern Turda, with its 60,000 mainly Magyar inhabitants, and a large Roma minority, is ringed by defunct factories, but still has a surprisingly elegant centre. The main reasons to come are to visit the salt mine and to explore the spectacular **Turda gorge**, 8km to the west, and the Arieş valley beyond, in the foothills of the Apuseni mountains.

The **Salt Mine** (*Salina Turda*; daily 9am–5pm, last entry 3pm; €4; Ⓦwww .salinaturda.eu) is on the northern edge of town at Aleea Durgaului 7 in Valea Sărată (up Str. Avram Iancu then Str. Vlahuţa); a new entrance has finally allowed access by modern lifts, instead of rickety wooden staircases. Alternatively, maxitaxis from Cluj, or buses #10 or #18 from the centre, can drop you at the leafy park shading the walled Calvinist church of Turda Nouă, built in 1311–40 and the oldest in town; from here, Str. Tunel heads east to the old entrance at Str. Salinelor 54.

Gradually excavated over 250 years, the mine consists of several huge hangar-like chambers, the most impressive being the cavernous **Rudolf Mine**, some 80m long and 50m wide. You'll also pass through the Joseph Mine, known for its twenty or so echoes, and another with an altar sculpted from salt, created for religious services and prayers before miners began their shifts. A glitzy underground theme park has recently been created, with boating on a lake, bowling, minigolf, other sports facilities, and even, at last, toilets. It's under 12°C in the mine, so bring warm clothing. Back in town, on Piaţa Republicii, stand two Gothic churches: the lower, built between 1387 and 1437, is Calvinist, and the upper is Roman Catholic (built in 1478–1504 and rebuilt in 1822 after a fire), with a Baroque interior and facade. It housed meetings of the Transylvanian Diet, including the promulgation of the 1568 **Edict of Turda**, which recognized the equality of four faiths – Calvinist, Lutheran, Roman Catholic and Unitarian – in Transylvania at a time when religious wars were all the rage in Europe. However, it merely tolerated Orthodoxy, the religion of the Vlachs, and contributed to the ethnic and religious discrimination against them. Christianity has a long history in Turda – fifth-century Christian tombs have been found among the remains of the Roman military camp of Potaissa, and some can be seen in the park in front of the fifteenth-century Voivodal Palace at B-dul Haşdeu 2, behind the Calvinist church. This houses the town's **museum**, closed for long-term renovation.

Practicalities

Turda is well served by **buses** from Cluj, picking up at Piața Ștefan cel Mare, and by **maxitaxis** from Piața Ștefan cel Mare 5 (at Str. Brătianu), returning from Str. Avram Iancu 4 at the top of the main drag in Turda. Longer-distance services stop at the Autogară Sens Vest (℡0264/313 431) below the town centre just off Piața Romana, the roundabout where the DN75 (the Arieș valley road) leaves town. **Trains** stop at the town of Câmpia Turzii, 9km east; take bus #20 to Piața Republicii.

At Piața 1 Decembrie 1918 no.1, the friendly staff at the **tourist information office** (Mon–Fri 9am–5pm, Sat 9am–2pm; ℡0264/314 611, Ⓦwww.cit.turda.ro) in the *Finomșaguri arieșene* slow-food deli, have information on tourism across the region, and also run a fine farmers' market in the courtyard on the second Saturday of each month. The town has three **hotels**; the *Hunter Prince Castle*, just off Piața Republicii at Str. Șuluțiu 4 (℡0264/316 850, Ⓦwww.huntercastle.ro; ❹), is pure kitsch, with its jagged roof line and pointy turrets, but the rooms are full of character, their colourful stone walls jutting out at odd angles. The *Centrum* is an excellent modern place just above the maxitaxi station at Str. Avram Iancu 11 (℡0264/315 220, Ⓦwww.hotelturda.ro; ❸). More prosaically, the downbeat *Potaissa*, at Piața Republicii 6 (℡0264/311 691; ❷–❸), has rooms with and without shower. Alternatively, there's the simple *Imperial* (℡0745/259 194; ❷), at the north end of Tureni on the road to Cluj.

The **restaurant** in the *Hunter Prince Castle* is the best in town; despite its overcooked medievalism and the life-size model of Vlad Țepeș in the Dracula Room, both food and service are first class. You can also eat on the terrace overlooking the pretty, flower-strewn garden. Next door, the *Rosalca* café has a fabulous selection of cakes and pastries. There's a large and well-stocked **market** behind Piața Republicii 18, through the arch opposite the church – it may be worth stocking up before heading into the surrounding countryside.

The Turda gorge

The impressive **Turda gorge** (Cheile Turzii) is a two-hour walk (or cycle ride) west from Piața Romană, following red and blue cross markings. Buses can take you most of the way, via Cornești (lined with vegetable stalls) and Moldovenești – get off at the turning 2km beyond Mihai Viteazu and continue north on foot for 5km. There are guesthouses in Cornești and Mihai Viteazul, and the *Hotel Ciprian*, at no. 266 in Moldovenești (℡0264/285 201, Ⓦwww.hotelciprian.ro; ❶–❷), has rooms with shared or private bathrooms. Either way, you'll end up at the *Cheile Turzii* cabana (❶) and campsite (there's also a simple restaurant here) just before the gorge itself. You'll pay a small fee before taking the footpath, marked with red stripes and crosses, up the gorge, overshadowed by 300m-high cliffs containing caves once used as outlaws' hideouts. The unique microclimate provides a habitat for plant species otherwise found only on the shores of the Mediterranean or in Central Asia; there are more than a thousand here, as well as 111 bird species, including golden eagles and rock vultures. After around 3km, the path ends at **Petreștii de Jos**, from where there are occasional buses back to Turda. There's also the *Pensiunea Laura* at no. 36 (℡0732/667 466, Ⓦwww.pensiune-laura.ro; ❷), a modern place with a spa and restaurant. The Rațiu family is currently building a tourist village on the hill to the north, with Maramureș-style houses, a slow-food restaurant and swimming pool, which should open by 2012.

The Turda gorge is also one of the best sites in Romania for **paragliding** (*parapente*) – contact Skyfly (℡0732/870 609, Ⓦwww.skyfly.ro). The Tureni gorge, immediately east, is less popular, but even narrower and more spectacular.

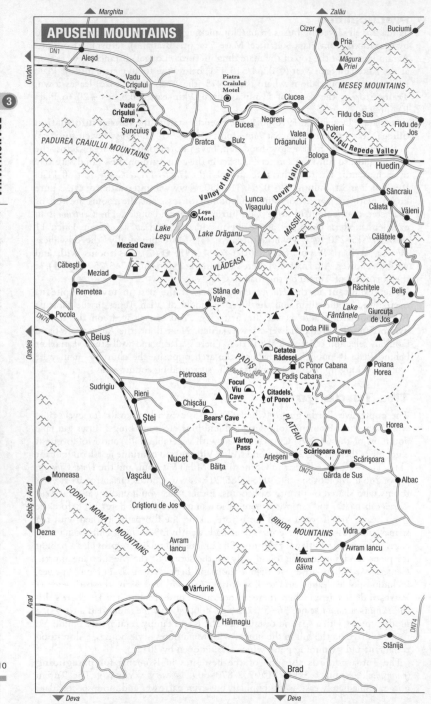

APUSENI MOUNTAINS

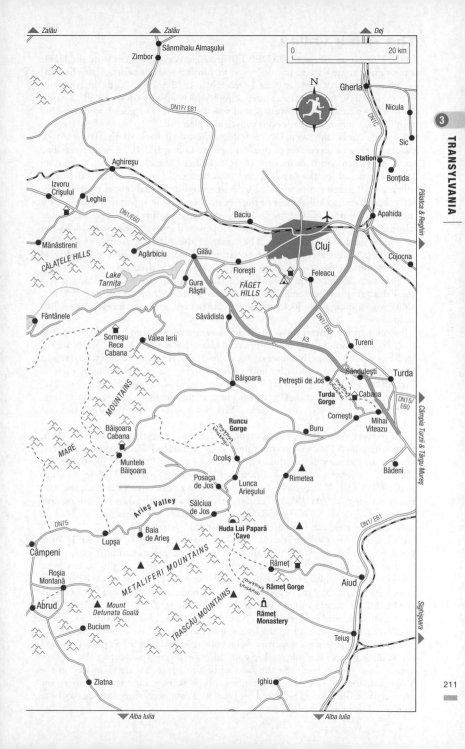

The Arieş valley

In the Hungarian village of **BĂDENI** (Bágyon), a very slow 2km from the DN1, a pilot guesthouse scheme (modelled on that in Rimetea) is being established (❷) – contact the tourist office at Piaţa 1 Decembrie 1918 no. 1 in Turda, or ask at no. 108 or no. 229, next to the former school which now houses a small museum (with a loom, traditional costumes, and wooden tools). The guesthouses here are simpler than some, but the food is superb and plentiful.

West of Turda, the main DN75 follows the north bank of the River Arieş, passing through a succession of small villages including **BURU**. Another very bad road leads 8km south from here to **RIMETEA** (Torockó), famed, at least in Hungary, as one of the loveliest and most authentic of Romania's Hungarian villages – although it was founded by Saxons and inhabited by the Székely only after the Tatars had killed most of the Saxons. Nevertheless the village was rebuilt in Saxon style after a major fire in 1870, and even now furniture is painted in the manner of Sighişoara. The village was prosperous due to its iron mines, allowing its women leisure for craftwork. The centre of the village is now a conservation area, where almost every home has rooms to let, while big modern pensions (and two new monasteries) stand on the outskirts. Traditional dress is worn for festivals on February 22 and the first Sunday of March, and can also be seen on display in the **Ethnographic Museum** (Tues–Sun 9am–5pm; €1), upstairs in the *Primaria*, along with mining tools, locks and keys, women's red boots and an elaborate bridal headdress.

Recommended **guesthouses** include *Aranyos Panzio* at no. 285 (℡0258/768 027; ❷), opposite the eighteenth-century Unitarian church, where prices are for half-board with a superb dinner of typically Transylvanian cuisine (which might include *mămăligă* or goulash, home-baked bread, and local desserts such as "ash-bake" (walnuts in dough); and *Gyopár Panzio-Camping* (℡0258/768 248, Ⓦwww.gyoparpanzio.hu; ❷), a new place at the northern end of the village, with space for camper vans and tents. Five buses a day run from Aiud (just one on Sundays).

Just to the west of Buru, a road turns north to the tiny village of **BĂIŞOARA**, from where it's 14km west to the single-slope **Muntele Băişorii** ski resort; here, you can stay at various guesthouses, the *Băişoara* cabana (℡0264/314 569; ❶), or the *BTT Băişoara hostel* (book through BTT, Piaţa Ştefan cel Mare 5, Cluj; ℡0264/198 067, Ⓔbtt@codec.ro; ❶). Continuing north from Băişoara, the road passes through **SĂVĂDISLA** (Turdaszentlászló), where the *Tamás Bistro* **restaurant** at no. 153 (℡0264/374 455, Ⓦwww.tamasbistro.ro) offers the best Magyar cuisine in the area, and finishes at Luna de Sus, just west of Cluj.

Back in the Arieş valley, it's 14km from Buru to the turn-off for **Ocoliş**, 4km north of the main road (don't confuse this with the Ocolişel turning), and, a little further up from that, the **Runcu gorge**; from the latter, an eight- to ten-hour hike, marked with blue crosses, cuts through the gorge to the Muntele Băişorii ski resort. At km126.5, 4km beyond Ocoliş, an unmarked bridge leads to **LUNCA ARIEŞULUI**, where you can stay at the *Vila Ramona* (℡0264/147 742; ❶). The next stretch of road is lovely, with beech woods, conglomerate boulders, and at km121.5 a small waterfall to the south. After another 2km, a footbridge marks the start of a day-walk south past watermills to the **Huda lui Papară cave** and the **Râmeţ gorge**; the route takes you either on a goat track along the cliff, or through the stream itself. At the far end of the gorge, tourists can stay in the *Râmeţ* cabana (❶), near the fourteenth-century **Râmeţ monastery**, where the festival of St Ghelasie is celebrated on June 30. From here, three buses a day head south to Teiuş and Alba Iulia.

Câmpeni and around

It's another 12km west to **CÂMPENI** (Topánfalva), capital of the Ţara Moţilor and a possible base for forays into the mountains. The town is well served by buses, arriving at the station just east of the centre beyond the market. The best **hotel** is the *Hanul Moţilor* at Str. Horea 2 (℡0258/771 545; ❷), which has a *crama* and pizzeria. The **Avram Iancu Museum**, in his old headquarters by the river on the corner of Str. Revoluţiei 1848, is decrepit but functional, though opening times are erratic. There's a good supermarket opposite, and two simple **restaurants** on the semi-pedestrianized square west of the *Tulnic* hotel.

From Câmpeni, the DN74A leads 10km south to Abrud, passing Gura Roşiei, the turning for **ROŞIA MONTANĂ**, 7km east. Transylvania was a major source of gold throughout history, with the Dacians the first to dig here, then the Romans; others followed more or less continuously until, in the 1970s, Ceauşescu's opencast mining demolished the entire Cetate massif. Now there are plans to create Europe's largest opencast gold mine beneath Roşia Montană, which is to be largely demolished, along with its attractive Baroque houses and historic mining tunnels; however, a campaign against the project has won various legal cases to block the project thus far. Roman lamps, tombstones and wax tablets recording operational details can be seen in the **museum** at Str. Principală 178. The friendly *Hostel La Gruber* is at Str. Principală 229 ℡0741/473 414, ⓦwww.lagruber .rosiamontana.ro; ❷). From here, you can hike south (following red triangles) to **ABRUD** in an hour. The Old Town, whose Baroque buildings incorporate stones from earlier Roman structures and are liberally adorned with plaques commemorating the many notables who visited when Abrud was the Moţi capital, is tatty but far more attractive than Câmpeni. From Piaţa Eroilor, the centre of the Old Town, there are buses to **BUCIUM POIENI**, 13km east and the centre of a *comuna* of six small mining villages; there's a Belgian-owned hostel here, the *Ursita Inn* (℡0723/230 790, ⓦwww.ursita.ro; ❷), and it's also the starting point for an hour's climb to two basalt towers known as the **Detunata**.

Gârda de Sus and Scărişoara

From Câmpeni the DN75 continues for 19km through a gorge to **ALBAC**, where there are plenty of guesthouses; you can hike north to Horea's birthplace in

---

The Girl Fair of Muntele Găina

The **Girl Fair** (Târgul de Fete) of Muntele Găina takes place on the closest Sunday to July 20 on the flat top of Mount Găina, roughly 33km west of Câmpeni, near the village of **Avram Iancu**, named after the leader of the 1848 revolt against the Hungarians who was born here in 1824. The region's largest festival, it was originally a means for young men who were away shepherding for two-thirds of the year to meet young women from other communities and to pursue matrimony. Naturally, prospective spouses made every effort to enhance their appeal, the girls being displayed in their finest attire, surrounded by linen, pottery and other dowry items – even carting along rented furniture. This aspect of the fair has all but disappeared, but thousands still come for the music and spectacle.

Buses bring visitors from Câmpeni to the fair, which is a large and lively event, but the real action is on the hill top, and you should really camp there the night before to catch the dawn chorus on *tulnics* (alphorns). A rough forestry road takes an 8km loop to reach the hill top, but you can find more direct routes on foot. The biggest names in popular traditional Romanian music appear here, with local dance ensembles, and there's plenty of food and drink; there is little drunkenness, however, and everyone behaves well, with unarmed Jandarmaria troops in attendance.

Fericet, and Horea (reached by three buses a day from Câmpeni) where a festival occurs in mid-August. It's another 14km west to **GÂRDA DE SUS**, a pretty village with a part-wooden church built in 1792, with naïve paintings inside; there's accommodation at the *Mama Uța* pension-restaurant-campsite (☏0258/627 901; ❷). More notably, it is the starting point for several excellent hikes, the most popular of which, marked with blue stripes, begins near the **campsite** and leads north through the Ordâncuşa gorges, past a mill and into a forest, reaching the village of **GHEŢARI** after three hours. This is named after the **Scărişoara ice cave** (Peştera gheţarul; daily 9am–6pm; €1), a few minutes west of the village; it contains the world's largest and oldest underground glacier, over 100,000 cubic metres in volume, preserving evidence of climatic change over the last 4000 years. At the back of the main chamber is the "church", so-called because of its pillar formations. You can stay at the excellent *Pensiunea Scărişoara* (☏0744/528 363, ⓦwww.pensiunea-scarisoara.go.ro; ❷), fifteen minutes' walk from the cave, or continue, following blue stripes, to Padiş.

The Padiş plateau

The **Padiş plateau** (Plateul Padiş) is at the heart of a classic **karst** area, with streams vanishing underground and reappearing unexpectedly, and dips and hollows everywhere, all promising access to the huge cave and river systems that lie beneath the plateau. Daily buses (but none at weekends) depart Huedin for Răchiţele and Poiana Horea, where there are many guesthouses (bookable through Green Mountain Holidays – see p.216); from here it's an easy day's hike to the *Padiş* cabana (☏0788/561 223; ❶), the focal point for the region's trails. A quieter (and cleaner) place to stay is the *Vărăşoaia* cabana (☏0788/601 815; ❶), about 2km northwest on the trail (marked with blue stripes) towards Stâna de Vale. Continuing west on the forestry road from the *Padiş* cabana for 2km you'll come to the park's Padiş visitor centre, not far south of Vărăşoaia (by a trail marked with red stripes). The *Sat de Vacanţa IC Ponor* (☏0744/272 465, Ⓔagroturism_icponor @yahoo.com; ❶), with a cabana and eight biggish *casuţe*, is two hours' walk up the road east from Padiş towards Răchiţele.

Hikes on the plateau

Of the various **trails** from the *Padiş* cabana, the most popular, marked with blue dots, is a three-hour hike south to the underground complex of **Cetăţile Ponorului** (Citadels of Ponor), a spectacular series of karst sinkholes up to 150m deep. There's a good camping spot en route at Glavoi, and just south from there the excellent *Cetăţile Ponorului* cabana (☏0259/322 457, ⓦwww.padis.ro; ❶). A trail from the Citadels (marked by yellow dots) leads north for 2km to the **Focul Viu** ice cave (viewed from a wooden balcony) and back to *Padiş*. Alternatively, head south from Ponor to Arieşeni (see p.317) in three hours following red stripes and triangles, or west from Focul Viu to Pietroasa (see p.316) in two and a half hours, following yellow dots and blue crosses.

North of the *Padiş* cabana, you can hike to the **Cetăţea Rădesei** cave; follow red stripes along a track to the forestry road and head north. Ten minutes beyond the Vărăşoaia pass, take another path (red dots) to the right of the citadel itself. Here you follow the stream through a cave – slightly spooky but quite safe, although a flashlight helps – and follow the overground route back (marked by red dots) to see the various skylights from above.

Other hikes simply follow forestry roads, west to Pietroasa (marked by blue crosses), east to Răchiţele or Poiana Horea (unmarked), or northwest to **Stâna de Vale** (red stripes). This last route continues from Vărăşoaia, climbing to the

Cumpănatelu saddle (1640m) and eventually turning right off the main ridge to descend through the forest to the resort (see p.316). Unlike most trails in the area, this six-hour walk is quite safe in winter.

The *Padiş* is also a five-hour hike southeast of Scărişoara (see p.214) along a marked track.

The Crişul Repede valley

From Cluj, the DN1 (E60) heads west along the verdant **Crişul valley**, shadowed for much of the way by the railway. A dozen trains a day run from Cluj to Huedin, eight continuing to Oradea; buses are less frequent. **Cyclists** can take two lovely back roads through the valley that run parallel to the main DN1 to the south: from Leghia to Bologa, and from Bucea to Tileagd.

The Dutch-owned *Camping Eldorado*, just west of Gilău at km496 (☎0264/371 688, ⓦwww.campingeldorado.com; mid-April to mid-Oct), is one of Romania's finest campsites. You'll find a rich choice of other accommodation options along or just off this route, including in **Gura Răştii** (where the *Cabana Lui Pui* offers hiking, kayaking, mountain-biking and tennis), **Valea Ierii** and **Izvoru Crişului** (Körösfó) – this last village is essentially one big bazaar selling Magyar arts and crafts, and also has a seventeenth-century walled Calvinist church with an eighteenth-century painted ceiling.

Huedin and Sâncraiu

HUEDIN (Bánffyhunyad), 46km west of Cluj, is a small town with a largely systematized centre; it's also known for its huge Gypsy palaces lining the main street as you enter from the west. The chief reason for stopping here is to pick up buses to the surrounding valleys. Huedin's **train station** is a five-minute walk

---

The culture of the Kalotaszeg

The area immediately west of Cluj is known to Hungarians as **Kalotaszeg**, and, since the great Hungarian Millennium Exhibition of 1896, it has been revered as the region where authentic Magyar culture has survived uncorrupted. It's common to see local people selling handicrafts by the roadside here – particularly to Hungarian tourists on pilgrimages to the wellsprings of Magyar culture.

The local **embroidery** is particularly famous, usually consisting of stylized leaves and flowers, in one bold colour (usually bright red) on a white background; the style is known as *írásos*, meaning "drawn" or "written", because the designs are drawn onto the cloth (traditionally with a mixture of milk and soot) before being stitched. The Calvinist churches of these villages are noted for their **coffered ceilings**, with square panels (known as "cassettes") beautifully painted in the eighteenth century, along with the pews and galleries, in a naïve style similar to the embroidery. The architects of the National Romantic school, led by Kós Károly, were strongly influenced by Transylvanian village architecture, as well as by that of the Finns, the Magyars' only ancestral relations.

The composers **Béla Bartók and Zoltán Kodály** amassed fine collections of Transylvanian crafts, and Bartók's assortment of carved furniture from Izvoru Crişului (Körösfó) can be seen in his home in Budapest. The composers' main project, however, was to collect the **folk music** of Transylvania. Starting in 1907, they managed to record and catalogue thousands of melodies, despite local suspicion of the "monster" (the apparatus for recording onto phonograph cylinders). They also discovered a rich vein of inspiration for their own compositions; Bartók declared that a genuine peasant melody was "quite as much a masterpiece in miniature as a Bach fugue or a Mozart sonata".

north of the town centre; through-buses stop on the main road while local buses leave from the station. Most of the surrounding villages are served by two or three buses a day during the week, but the service is virtually nonexistent at weekends.

Huedin's only **hotel** is the *Motel Montana* (☎0264/353 090, ⓦwww .motelmontana.ro; ❷) at the eastern edge of town, though **homestays** are a better option, with at least two dozen (❶) available just on the main street of **SÂNCRAIU** (Kalotaszentkirály), only 6km south, and known for its strong Magyar folklore and its thirteenth-century church. These can be booked through Davincze Tours at Sâncraiu no. 291 (☎0264/257 580, ⓔdavincze @clicknet.ro); bikes can also be rented here.

Around Huedin

From Huedin, a minor road heads 9km south to **CĂLATA** (Nagykalota), where on Sundays the Magyar population still wear home-made **folk costumes**, and on to nearby **CĂLĂȚELE** (Kiskalota), where you'll see carved wooden homesteads. Sixteen kilometres beyond (connected to Huedin by three buses on weekdays) is **BELIŞ** (Jósikafalva), a village moved (along with its lovely wooden church) from the valley when the artificial Lake Fântânele was created; there's now a small lakeside resort comprising two identical two-star hotels (both ☎0264/354 183), and various guesthouses.

MĂNĂSTIRENI (Magyargyerómonostor), on a minor road running south from the DN1 east of Huedin, has a lovely thirteenth-century walled Calvinist church whose gallery, pews and ceiling were beautifully painted in the eighteenth century. It's the home of **Green Mountain Holidays**, at no. 277 (☎0264/418 691, ⓦwww.greenmountainholidays.ro), a Belgian-run company that organizes a range of activities (hiking, cycling, kayaking and horseriding) across Romania, and customized trips, such as photo safaris and excursions on steam trains; they can also provide information and arrange homestays throughout the Apuseni. Just west is **Văleni** (Magyarvalkó), where many houses have decorated mouldings. Another thirteenth-century Calvinist church has a wonderful hilltop setting and a collection of carved wooden graveposts, more typical of the Székely Land. In the valleys to the north of Huedin you will find half a dozen villages with striking Gothic-inspired **wooden churches** – typical of those that once reared above peasant settlements from the Tisa to the Carpathians. The most spectacular, and the nearest to Huedin, towers over **Fildu de Sus** (Felsőfüld), a small village reached by a 10km track west from Fildu de Jos (Alsófüld) on the Huedin–Zalău road. Built in 1727, the church was painted in 1860, with scenes of Daniel in the den with some wonderful grinning lions. There's one daily bus from the railway crossing in Huedin to Zalău via Fildu de Jos, where there are guesthouses.

Ciucea

CIUCEA (Csucsa), 20km west of Huedin by road and rail, is notable for a **museum** (Tues–Sun 10am–5pm) dedicated to the poet **Octavian Goga**, prime minister in 1937 for six chaotic weeks. This house belonged to the wife of **Endre Ady**, the great figure of early modernist poetry in Hungary, who lived here until 1917; Goga bought it after his death in 1919 and moved a **wooden church** (built in 1575) here from Galpâiain in order to preserve it – you can still enter through the tiny door to view the faintly traceable frescoes in an otherwise blackened interior. Later still, Goga's own **mausoleum**, an ostentatious piece of work decorated with bright blue mosaics on a silver and gold background, was built in the grounds. The museum is at the east end of the village by the church. There's a faded little **pension**, the *Romanţa* (☎0264/251 585; ❶), by the road and train halt,

The Measurement of the Milk Festival

The practice of shepherds spending summer in the high pastures protecting the flocks from bears and wolves, and making cheese for the community's winter sustenance, gave rise to **Measurement of the Milk Festivals** (Măşurisul Laptelui), the best known of which are held in the villages around Ciucea on the slopes of Măgura Priei, the highest ridge in the Meseş range. At dawn on the first Sunday in May, the flocks are brought to a glade outside the village, where the "measurement" takes place. The nanny-goats are milked by women and the ewes by shepherds – the yield of each family's animals is measured to determine the share of cheese that they will receive that season. The ritual is followed by much feasting and dancing.

Măgura Priei is just 10km or so north of Ciucea, and the festival is reached by buses from Huedin.

and the *Perla Ardealului* (☏0264/258 022, ⓦwww.perlaardealului.ro; ❷) and *Pensiunea Ruta 60* (☏0264/259 051, ⓦwww.route60.ro; ❷) are by the highway just west of town.

Valea Drăganului to Vadu Crişului

Two dramatically named valleys run south into the Apuseni mountains on either side of Ciucea, meeting at Stâna de Vale. To the east, the **Valea Drăganului** (Devil's Valley) runs from the train halt of the same name, passing through Lunca Vişagului, from where you can follow the forestry road south past a reservoir (where there are new guesthouses) before hiking the track marked with blue crosses west to Stâna de Vale (see p.316). The road down the **Valea Iadului** (Valley of Hell) turns off the DN1 at the Piatra Craiului train station, by the wooden church of Bucea, and just east of the *Munţi Piatra Craiului* motel (☏0259/341 756; ❷). Civilization ends after 25km, at the *Leşu Lake guesthouse* (☏0722/468 664; ❸), by the artificial lake of the same name; it's another 20km, past the Iadolina waterfall, to Stâna de Vale.

Local trains stop at **ŞUNCUIUŞ**, 23km west of Ciucea, a short walk from the **Peştera Vântului** (Cave of the Wind), the country's longest cave with 52km of passages discovered so far; this is now being opened to visitors (☏0722/488 585, ⓔalex@telecomenzi.ro). You can walk west along the river and railway to the next halt, Peştera, and the **Vadu Crişului** cave, also open to visitors (Wed–Sun 9.30am–5.30pm; €1). In the village of **VADU CRIŞULUI**, just west, are two fine **places to stay**, *La Contele Dracula* hotel (☏0259/444 493/5, ⓦwww .laconteledracula.ro; ❹), with comfortable rooms plus gym, jacuzzi, sauna and outdoor pool; and a guesthouse at Str. Mică 236 (☏0259/443 216, ⓔlidia_szilagyi@yahoo.com; ❷).

Northern Transylvania

The counties of Sălaj and Bistriţa-Năsăud (and the northernmost part of Cluj county), covering the ranges from the Apuseni mountains to the Eastern Carpathians, are historically referred to as **Northern Transylvania**. Travelling from Cluj to Maramureş, or eastwards over the Carpathians into Moldavia, the roads are fast and direct (the railways a bit less so), but it's well worth considering detours in this little-visited region. To the west, the chief attraction is the idyllic rural scenery of unspoilt Sălaj county, with its many old wooden churches.

Trains into Maramureș run via Jibou to Baia Mare, about two hours from Dej. The quickest road north is the DN1C to Baia Mare. Trains from Cluj into Moldavia run via Năsăud and the Ilva valley to Vatra Dornei and past several of the painted monasteries (see p.259). The DN17 heads east from Dej to Bistrița and through the Bârgău valley to Vatra Dornei. Bistrița and Năsăud, 22km apart, are linked by frequent buses, so it's easy to hop from one route to the other.

Bonțida, Gherla and Sic

From Cluj, the DN1C (E576) and a rail line head north to Gherla and Dej, passing **BONȚIDA** (Bonchida), site of a great Baroque **palace**, barely visible from the road and railway. In 1944 its owner was Miklos Bánffy, a diplomat who was sent to make peace with the advancing Red Army; in revenge, the retreating Germans virtually destroyed the palace. In 2001, two years after the World Monuments Fund placed Bonțida on its list of the world's 100 most endangered monuments, a Built Heritage Conservation Training Centre was established here, whereby craftsmen and architects could be trained while rebuilding the palace. Much progress has since been made, but the main building remains almost totally hollow. There's a small exhibition and visitor reception area in the gatehouse, a community cultural centre in the chapel, and workshops and other facilities in the stables and the Miklós building. One of the first buildings to be renovated was the old kitchen block, now housing a pleasant little **café** (daily 10am–6pm). The **train station** is near the main road at the entrance to the village, from where it's a long (about 2.5km) but pleasant walk to the palace. The palace has no opening times as such, but the entrance – through a small gateway – is usually open (€0.50).

The best time to visit is the last weekend of August, when the **Bonțida Cultural Days** attract up to 6000 people to see craft demonstrations and classical and traditional music and dance from Romanian, Hungarian Jewish and Roma groups. **GHERLA** (Szamosujvár/Neuschloss) has been a centre of Armenian settlement since 1672; many houses have fine gateways topped by carved Armenian family crests, but the population is now assimilated with the local Hungarians. The town is also synonymous with its prison, which, during the communist era, was used for political detainees; in one notorious incident in 1977, the town (and the prison) flooded, but wardens refused to open the cells, resulting in the deaths of some inmates. From the **train station**, it's under five minutes' walk west along Str. Avram Iancu to Piața Libertății and the Baroque Armenian-Catholic **cathedral** on the south side. Built in 1748–98, its greatest treasure is a painting of the *Descent from the Cross*, supposedly by Rubens, in a small chapel to the left of the choir – you may have to ask to see it. The tower, meanwhile, has had a colourful existence, having collapsed no less than three times. Just to the northeast of the square, at Str. Mihai Viteazul 6, the town **museum** (Mon–Fri 9am–4pm) houses its collection of icons on glass and musty Armenian vestments behind the superb gateway of a seminary built in 1859. The only place to **stay** in town is the *Pensiunea Ioana*, a decent, quiet place fifteen minutes' walk south at Str. Clujului 4 (☏0264/243 451, Ⓦwww.pensiuneaioana.ro; ❶–❷), at the petrol station.

One of the best villages to hear **traditional music** in this area is **SIC** (Szék), spread over several hills 20km southeast of Gherla, with a number of churches and municipal buildings testifying to its former importance as a centre of salt mining. The population is largely Magyar, wearing costumes the like of which have long disappeared into museums elsewhere – men in narrow-brimmed, tall straw hats and blue waistcoats, and women in leather waistcoats, red pleated skirts and black headscarves embroidered with flowers. Every street in Sic seems to have its own band (normally consisting of just three musicians – on violin, viola and double bass), typically playing traditional ancient Magyar and Romanian melodies woven in with Gypsy riffs. The village festival is on August 24. Several buses a day come from Gherla, and you can stay at the charming *Sóvirág Panzió*, at the entry to the village, I Str. 504 (☎0264/228 004, ⓦwww.soviragpanzio.ro; ➋).

Dej

DEJ, 46km north of Cluj, lies at the junction of the two branches of the Someş River and the routes from Cluj to Maramureş and Bucovina. The town centre is a good kilometre to the north of the main **train station**, Dej Calatori (bus #2, #3, #8 or #9); maxitaxis leave from the junction of Strada Avram Iancu and 1 Mai, immediately south of the centre. The main square, Piaţa Bobâlna, is an attractive space, its pretty flower-filled park dominated by the **Reformed Church**. The **Municipal Museum** (Tues–Sun 9am–3pm), at Piaţa Bobâlna 2 (entered through a bookshop), has good coverage of the salt mines that drove the medieval economy here, as well as a small ethnographic display. Fifty metres down the road, after a right turn into Str. Petru Rareş, is the **Military Museum** (Tues–Fri 9am–4pm), exhibiting a range of weaponry from the Roman to communist periods.

The better of Dej's two **hotels** is the *Grand Master*, 3km towards Cluj at Str. Vâlcele 1 (☎0264/212 475, ⓦwww.hotel-grandmaster.ro; ➍), with a surprisingly good restaurant.

Năsăud

The small town of **BECLEAN** (Bethlen), 25km east of Dej, was the ancestral seat of the Bethlen family, which provided several distinguished governors of Transylvania. The road and rail routes to Vatra Dornei and Suceava in Moldavia also divide here, drivers heading east to Bistriţa while the train runs further north via Năsăud, also the route to Sighet in Maramureş.

From **Salva**, 24km northeast of Beclean, road and rail routes head north to Maramureş; 9km along this road is the village of **COŞBUC**, named after its most famous son, **George Coşbuc** (1866–1918), poet and activist for Romanian cultural revival. His simple family home is now a **museum** (Tues–Sun 9am–5pm). **NĂSĂUD** (Nussdorf), 6km east of Salva, is at the heart of a region where villagers still wear their traditional embroidered waistcoats and blouses, and hats decorated with peacock feathers. A selection of these is on display in the **museum** at Str. Granicerilor 25. The oddly named *Us – The Locals! Home* (ⓦwww.transylvaniatravel.from.ro; ➋), at Str. Valea Caselor 22a, is a **youth hostel** that offers reductions to HI members and also runs tours. Just 5km south of town along the Bistriţa road is the birthplace of **Liviu Rebreanu** (1885–1944), whose novels *Ion*, *Uprising* and *The Forest of the Hanged* give a panoramic view of Romanian society before World War I.

The Someş Mare valley

Ilva Mică, 20km east of Năsăud, is the junction of a branch line to the shabby spa of **SÂNGEORZ-BĂI**, starting point for hikes north into the Rodna mountains (see p.304). **Guesthouses** such as *Pensiunea Bradul* at Str. Izvoarelor 89A (☎0263/370 441; ➋) are better value than spa hotels such as the large but rather impersonal *Hebe*, Str. Izvoarelor 94 (☎0263/370 521, ⓦwww.hotel-hebe.com; ➌). The branch line ends at the former mining town of **Rodna Veche**, where you can see the ruins of a tenth-century fort and a thirteenth-century church; buses then continue the 7km to **ŞANŢ**, an attractive village of wooden houses with open verandas and shingled roofs. **Homestays** are available at *Pensiunea Grapini*,

Str. Morii 65 (☎0263/379 124; ❶), where there's a kitchen, cable TV and internet access, and *Pensiunea Nechiţa* (☎0263/379 019; ❷).

The main rail line to Vatra Dornei runs to the south of the branch line up the Ilva valley. **LEŞU**, eight minutes up the line from Ilva Mică – from the stop, it's a 4km walk east up the valley to the village – is home to one of the region's best festivals, the **Rhapsody of the Trişcaşi Festival**, bringing together pipers from three counties on the first Sunday of September.

Bistriţa and the Bârgău valley

BISTRIŢA (Bistritz), 40km east of Beclean, and the forested **Bârgău valley** beyond, are the setting for much of Bram Stoker's **Dracula**; it was in Bistriţa that Jonathan Harker received the first hints that something was amiss, on his way to Dracula's castle in the Bârgău valley. Remains of **Neolithic settlements** have been found near Bistriţa, although the earliest record of the town, in 1264, coincided with the arrival of Saxon settlers, who built fine churches in many villages (less fortress-like than those further south). The bulk of the Saxon population left after World War II.

Arrival and information

Trains run from Cluj via Beclean to Bistriţa Nord, but you may have to change trains at Sărăţel, just southwest of Bistriţa on the Dej–Braşov line. Just north of the junction is the small village of **Sărata**; from here, bus #10 runs to Bistriţa. The busy **bus station** is also a major hub for maxitaxis. The Real Bike shop is just north of the centre at B-dul 1 Dec 1918 no. 20 (☎0742/544 877).

The **Tourist Information Centre** in the Centrul Cultural Municipal at Str. Albert Berger 10 (Mon–Fri 9am–5pm; ☎0263/219 919) gives free information (including maps) and can arrange all sorts of outdoor activities. The Clubnet **internet café** (daily 10am–midnight) is on the corner of B-dul Decebal and Str. Ursului, under the external staircase.

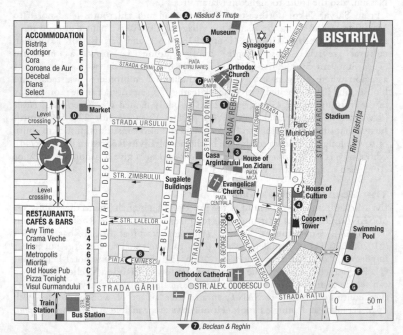

Bistriţa's **International Folklore Festival** is held in the second week of August; there's also a Brass Band Festival in September and **Bistriţa Folk** in late November. The Union of Plastic Artists also has a **gallery** in the Sugălete buildings at Piaţa Centrală 24 (closed Mon & Sun).

Accommodation

There are plenty of **hotels** here, though none is particularly special. Dracula fans should head for the *Coroana de Aur* (Golden Crown) at Piaţa Petru Rareş 4 (℡0263/232 470, ⓦwww.hotel-coroana-de-aur.ro; ❹), where Jonathan Harker stayed en route to the Borgău Pass. Just across the way, the *Bistriţa*, Str. Petru Rareş 2 (℡0263/231 154, ⓦwww.hotel-bistrita.ro; ❹), has renovated rooms far superior (and not that much more expensive) to the older ones, while the very basic *Decebal*, further west at Str. Cuza Vodă 9 (℡0263/212 568; ❷), is reasonable enough. Across the river to the south of town are three lower-profile, cheaper hotels: the *Codrişor* at Str. Codrişor 28 (℡0263/233 814, ⓔhotelcodrisor @coroana.ro; ❸); the *Cora* at no. 23 (℡0263/221 231; ❷), which, though not the most attractive place, is extremely welcoming; and the *Select* next door (℡0263/230 102, ⓦwww.hotel-select.ro; ❷), just about the smartest of these three. With your own transport you may prefer the *Diana*, 1.5km north at Calea Moldovei 80 (℡0263/231 960/1, ⓦwww.dianahotel.ro; ❸), a friendly place with no Dracula tour groups.

The Town

From the train and bus stations, it's about ten minutes' walk to the centre; you'll pass a typically hideous Centru Civic, but then enter a more attractive townscape, with pedestrian alleys linking mostly north–south streets. The main square, **Piaţa Centrală**, is dominated by a great Saxon Evangelical **church** (Tues–Sat 10am– noon & 2–5pm, Sun 3–5pm, service 10am). The fourteenth-century Gothic church was given Renaissance features in 1560–3 by Petrus Italus da Lugano, who introduced the style to Moldavia. A few decades later, a 76m tower was added, the highest stone church tower in Transylvania.

On the northwest side of Piaţa Centrala, the arcaded **Sugălete** buildings (occupied by merchants in the fifteenth century) hint at how the town looked in its medieval heyday. At Str. Dornei 5 the Renaissance **Casa Argintarului** (Silver-smith's House) now houses an art college; continuing northeast, on Piaţa Unirii, there's a church built for the Franciscans in 1270–80 and taken over by the Orthodox church in 1948. Just to the northwest is the synagogue (now a multicul-tural arts centre) and beyond that the **County Museum** (Tues–Sun 10am–6pm), which has a collection of Thracian bronzeware, Celtic artefacts, products of the Saxon guilds, mills and presses, as well as a smallish wooden church at the back of the courtyard. From the museum, you can head back down **Strada Rebreanu**, (Holzgasse), the town's pedestrianized main thoroughfare; with its tree-shaded cafés, and sunny lemon and mint-green coloured townhouses, it's a pleasant place for a stroll, and also contains some interesting buildings, the most notable being the **House of Ion Zidaru**, at the southern end. Built in the fifteenth century in late Gothic style, this was given Renaissance features in the first two decades of the next century by Johannes Murator (John the Mason, or Ion Zidraru in Romanian) – note the fine stone portal and balcony – and is now a restaurant.

Like Braşov and Sibiu, Bistriţa used to be heavily fortified, but successive fires during the nineteenth century have left only vestiges of the citadel along Str. M. Kogălniceanu and Str. Teodoroiu, including the fifteenth-century **Coopers' Tower** (Turnul Dogarilor) – housing the **Galeria de Măşti si Papuşi**, a collection of folklore masks and puppets (ask at the County Museum for admission). Outside the walls is the Municipal Park, which ludicrously claims to have one of just three *Gingko biloba* or maidenhair trees in Europe.

Eating and drinking

There's little to inspire in Bistriţa in terms of dining; the most atmospheric **restaurant**, thanks to its park location and vast terrace surrounded by neatly clipped bushes, is the *Crama Veche*, behind the Cultural Centre – the food, mostly grilled meats, is superb, too, with waitresses scuttling around at optimum speed. Elsewhere, two commendable pizzerias are *Visul Gurmandului*, Str. Rebreanu 45, and the rather more prosaically named *Pizza Tonight*, B-dul Independenţiei 16 – its garden terrace is also a good spot for a draught beer. The *Mioriţa* lacto-vegetarian restaurant, at Str. Rebreanu 8 (Mon–Fri 9am–5pm), is tasteful but unexciting.

For a snack, you can't beat the great *placinte* (pies) filled with cheese, cabbage, apple or plum, sold from a hatch at Str. Şincai 37. There are a couple of interesting and lively **bars** in medieval basements, such as *Any Time*, Piaţa Centrală 1, and *Iris*, Str. Rebreanu 2, as well as the lively *Old House Pub* at the *Coroana de Aur* hotel, open till 3am at least. *Metropolis*, at Piaţa Eminescu (10pm–6am), is one of Transylvania's biggest **clubs**, with dance floors on two levels, as well as bars, pizza and videogames.

The Bârgău valley

Three buses a day head east up the valley to Vatra Dornei in Moldavia (see p.273). Trains follow this route only as far as Prundu Bârgăului, from where it's another 60km to Vatra Dornei, including the 1200m Tihuţa Pass. The Bârgău scenery is dramatic, with huge hills draped in forests of fir trees, and villages that seem living monuments to a way of life unchanged for centuries. In **LIVEZELE**, a long and attractive roadside village 8km from Bistriţa (local bus #3), the **Saxon House Museum** (Muzeul Casa Sasească), at Str. Dorolea 152, demonstrates a way of life that has not vanished further up the valley. Dating from around 1870, the house has two large rooms, kept exactly as they've always been and stuffed with Saxon ceramics, folk dress, furniture, books and photos, and out back there's a large barn with several wine presses – to find the museum, head down the gravel path leading away from the roadside Lutheran church; the key is at Str. Dorolea 197 (☎0263/270 109). There are now only half a dozen Saxon families left in the village.

In **JOSENII BÂRGĂULUI**, 8km beyond Livezele, black pottery is manufactured and old fulling mills and cottages remain in use. **PRUNDU BÂRGĂULUI**, 6km east of Josenii, is the venue for the **Raftsmen's Festival** on the last weekend of March, when unmarried men crown their usual attire of sheepskin jackets with a small hat buried beneath a plume of peacock feathers.

One kilometre beyond Prundu Bârgăului is **TIHA BÂRGĂULUI**, occasional host to the interesting **Festival of Regele Brazilor** (King of the Fir Trees). This is an opportunity to hear traditional songs, and the part-improvised lamentations (*bochet*) of relatives and friends of the deceased, telling of the deceased's deeds in this life; if the festival runs at all, it's on the third Sunday of June. Climbing steadily eastwards, the DN17 (E576) reaches the scattered settlement of **Piatra Fântânele** and at km108 the *Hotel Castel Dracula* (☎0263/265 841; ❺), where staff delight in hiding in a coffin to scare guests; rooms are fine, but the restaurant is less good. Note that the map of hiking trails outside is incorrect; some trails don't exist, while some that do aren't shown. Just beyond, at km113, lies the **Tihuţa Pass**, which may be blocked by snow for the odd day between late October and mid-May. Although the country is relatively densely settled near the main road, the surrounding mountains harbour more **bears** than in any other part of Europe, as well as red deer, boar and **wolves**; the **view** from the pass of the green "crests" of Bucovina to the northeast and the volcanic Căliman mountains to the southeast is marvellous.

Travel details

Trains

Alba Iulia to: Arad (5 daily; 3hr 15min–4hr); Braşov (3 daily; 4hr–4hr 30min); Cluj (7 daily; 2hr 10min–3hr); Deva (9 daily; 1hr 10min–1hr 40min); Hunedoara (1 daily; 2hr); Sibiu (3 daily; 2hr 10min–3hr); Sighişoara (3 daily; 2hr–2hr 30min); Târgu Mureş (3 daily; 2hr–2hr 50min); Timişoara (4 daily; 4hr 40min–5hr 25min).
Bistriţa to: Cluj (3 daily; 2hr 35min–3hr 20min); Sărăţel (9 daily; 15min).
Braşov to: Bucharest (every 1–2hr; 3hr–4hr 40min); Cluj (8 daily; 5hr 30min–7hr 15min); Deva (4 daily; 5h–5hr 35min); Făgăraş (6 daily; 1hr 40min); Miercurea Ciuc (11 daily; 1hr 35min–2hr 30min); Sfântu Gheorghe (13 daily; 30–50min); Sibiu (2 daily; 4hr); Sighişoara (12 daily; 2–3hr); Sinaia (18 daily; 1hr–1hr 30min); Târgu Mureş (3 daily; 5hr 50min–7hr 50min); Zărneşti (hourly; 40min).
Cluj to: Deva (4 daily; 3hr 25min–4hr); Miercurea Ciuc (2 daily; 5hr 50min); Oradea (12 daily; 2hr 35min–5hr); Sfântu Gheorghe (2 daily; 7hr); Sibiu (1 daily; 4hr 25min); Sighişoara (6 daily; 3hr 45min–4hr).
Făgăraş to: Braşov (6 daily; 1hr 40min); Sibiu (8 daily; 1hr 30min–2hr 30min).
Hunedoara to: Simeria (6 daily; 30min).
Miercurea Ciuc to: Baia Mare (1 daily; 8hr 20min); Braşov (11 daily; 1hr 35min–2hr 30min); Dej (3 daily; 4hr 35min–5hr 15min); Gheorgheni (8 daily; 55min–1hr 40min); Sighet (1 daily; 9hr).
Petroşani to: Cluj (3 daily; 4hr 50min–5hr 40min); Craiova (7 daily; 2hr 45min–4hr 35min); Deva (8 daily; 2–3hr); Simeria (8 daily; 1hr 40min–2hr 40min); Târgu Jiu (7 daily; 1hr 10min–1hr 40min).
Sibiu to: Arad (1 daily; 5hr); Braşov (2 daily; 4hr); Cluj (1 daily; 4hr 30min); Deva (3 daily; 2hr 55min); Mediaş (6 daily; 1hr 20min–2hr); Râmnicu Vâlcea (5 daily; 2hr 20min–3hr 20min); Timişoara (2 daily; 6hr 40min).
Sighişoara: to: Alba Iulia (3 daily; 1hr 50min–2hr 15min); Braşov (12 daily; 1hr 55min–2hr 35min); Cluj (6 daily; 3hr 30min).
Sinaia to: Braşov (18 daily; 1hr–1hr 40min); Bucharest (every 1–2hr; 1hr 55min–3hr).

Târgu Mureş to: Deda (7 daily; 1hr 15min–1hr 45min); Deva (2 daily; 3hr 40min); Războieni (8 daily; 1hr–1hr 45min).

Buses & maxitaxis

Abrud to: Alba Iulia (10 daily, Sat & Sun 8 daily); Câmpeni (10 daily); Cluj (3 daily); Oradea (1 daily).
Alba Iulia to: Aiud (11 daily, Sat & Sun 4 daily); Blaj (11 daily); Bucharest (5 daily); Câmpeni (7 daily, Sat & Sun 5 daily); Cluj (18 daily); Deva (5 daily, Sat & Sun 4 daily); Oradea (2 daily); Sebeş (every 30min); Sibiu (12 daily); Târgu Jiu (3 daily); Târgu Mureş (3 daily); Timişoara (3 daily).
Bistriţa to: Baia Mare (2 daily); Braşov (5 daily); Borşa (1 daily); Cluj (5 daily); Iaşi (1 daily); Năsăud (Mon–Fri 11 daily, Sat & Sun 6 daily); Rodna (Mon–Fri 2 daily); Sibiu (3 daily); Sighişoara (4 daily); Suceava (5 daily); Târgu Mureş (6 daily); Vatra Dornei (3 daily).
Braşov (Autogară 1) to: Bacău (7 daily); Bistriţa (5 daily); Bucharest (hourly); Buzău (3 daily); Câmpulung Muscel (1 daily); Covasna (7 daily, Sat & Sun 3 daily); Făgăraş (hourly); Galaţi (6 daily); Hărman (hourly); Iaşi (3 daily); Odorheiu Secuiesc (1 daily); Piatra Neamţ (2 daily); Prejmer (Mon–Fri 7 daily, Sat & Sun 3 daily); Târgovişte (2 daily); Târgu Mureş (8 daily); Târgu Neamţ (1 daily); Târgu Secuiesc (13 daily).
Braşov (Autogară 2) to: Bran (Mon–Fri every 30min, Sat & Sun hourly); Câmpulung Muscel (4 daily); Curtea de Argeş/Râmnicu Vâlcea (1 daily); Piteşti (2 daily); Sibiu (2 daily); Zărneşti (Mon–Fri hourly, Sat 8 daily, Sun 2 daily).
Braşov (Autogară 3) to: Bacău (3 daily); Buzău (Mon–Fri 5 daily, Sat 4 daily, Sun 2 daily).
Câmpeni to: Abrud (10 daily); Alba Iulia (Mon–Fri 7 daily, Sat & Sun 5 daily); Arad (1 daily); Arieşeni (4 daily); Brad (4 daily); Bucharest (1 daily); Cluj (4 daily); Deva (2 daily); Oradea (2 daily); Sebeş (1 daily); Timişoara (2 daily).
Cluj to: Abrud (2 daily); Alba Iulia (18 daily); Baia Mare (10 daily); Bistriţa (7 daily); Braşov (Mon–Fri 2 daily, Sat & Sun 1 daily); Câmpeni (4 daily); Cojocna (3 daily); Deva (4 daily, Sat & Sun 3 daily); Gheorgheni (1 daily Mon–Fri); Huedin (8 daily); Hunedoara (3 daily); Oradea (8 daily); Râmnicu Vâlcea (10 daily); Reghin (1–4 daily); Satu Mare

(5 daily); Sibiu (10 daily); Sighet (3 daily); Târgu Jiu (6 daily); Târgu Lapuş (1 daily); Târgu Mureş (15 daily); Turda (several hourly); Zalău (5 daily, Sat & Sun 2 daily).

Covasna to: Sfântu Gheorghe (9 daily); Târgu Mureş (1 daily); Târgu Secuiesc (4 daily).

Deva to: Brad (16 daily Mon–Fri, 10 daily Sat & Sun); Câmpeni (3 daily); Cluj (Mon–Fri 4 daily, Sat & Sun 3 daily); Hunedoara (every 10–30min); Oradea (2 daily); Sarmizegetusa (2 daily Mon–Fri); Sibiu (6 daily); Târgu Mureş (2 daily); Timişoara (Mon–Fri 9 daily, 8 daily Sat & Sun).

Gheorgheni to: Braşov (2 daily); Cluj (2 daily); Lacu Roşu (3 daily); Odorheiu Secuiesc (1 daily); Piatra Neamţ (3 daily); Târgu Mureş (1 daily); Târgu Neamţ (1 daily).

Haţeg to: Cluj (2 daily); Densuş (2 daily); Hunedoara (6 daily); Reşiţa (2 daily); Sarmizegetusa (3 daily Mon–Fri); Timişoara (1 daily); Târgu Jiu (2 daily).

Hunedoara to: Cluj (3 daily); Craiova (1 daily); Deva (every 10–30min); Drobeta-Turnu Severin (1 daily); Haţeg (6 daily).

Mediaş to: Agnita/Făgăraş (3 daily); Biertan/Richiş (Mon–Fri 5 daily, Sat 2 daily); Braşov (2 daily); Cluj (2 daily); Sibiu (5 daily); Târgu Mureş (4 daily).

Miercurea Ciuc to: Băile Tuşnad (4 daily); Braşov (2 daily); Odorheiu Secuiesc (5–7 daily); Piatra Neamţ (2 daily); Sovata (3 daily); Târgu Mureş (4 daily); Târgu Neamţ (1 daily); Târgu Secuiesc (2–3 daily).

Odorheiu Secuiesc to: Braşov (1 daily); Covasna/ Târgu Secuiesc (1 daily); Gheorgheni (1 daily); Miercurea Ciuc (2 daily); Praid (10 daily); Sf Gheorghe (2 daily); Sovata/Târgu Mureş (6 daily).

Reghin to: Bistriţa (6 daily); Cluj (1–4 daily); Hodac (14 daily); Sighişoara (3 daily); Sovata (2 daily); Târgu Neamţ (1 daily); Vatra Dornei (1 daily).

Sebeş to: Alba Iulia (2 hourly); Câmpeni (1 daily); Cluj (9 daily); Sibiu (12 daily); Timişoara (2 daily).

Sfântu Gheorghe to: Bacău (8 daily); Braşov (5 daily); Covasna (9 daily); Odorheiu Secuiesc (6 daily); Piatra Neamţ (1 daily); Sovata/Târgu Mureş (5 daily); Târgu Secuiesc (11 daily).

Sibiu to: Agnita (4 daily); Bistriţa (3 daily); Braşov (2 daily); Bucharest (3 daily); Cisnădie (every 20–30min Mon–Fri, 10 daily Sat & Sun); Cluj (10 daily); Cristian (hourly Mon–Fri, 5 daily Sat & Sun); Deva (3 daily); Galaţi (2 daily); Gura Râului (11 Mon–Fri, 2 daily Sat & Sun); Mediaş (5 daily); Păltiniş (3 daily); Râmnicu Vâlcea (4 daily);

Sighişoara (4 daily); Slimnic (3 daily); Târgu Jiu (3 daily); Târgu Mureş (6 daily); Timişoara (3 daily).

Sighişoara to: Agnita (4 daily); Bistriţa (3 daily); Braşov (1 daily); Făgăraş (1 daily Mon–Fri); Odorheiu Secuiesc (1 daily); Sibiu (4 daily); Sovata (3 daily); Târgu Mureş (20 daily Mon–Fri, 12 daily Sat & Sun).

Sovata to: Cluj (1 daily); Miercurea Ciuc (3 daily); Odorheiu Secuiesc (5 daily); Reghin (2 daily); Sighişoara (1 daily); Târgu Mureş (8 daily).

Târgu Mureş to: Alba Iulia (2 daily); Bistriţa (6 daily); Braşov (8 daily); Cluj (13 daily); Mediaş (6 daily); Miercurea Ciuc (3 daily); Odorheiu Secuiesc (7 daily); Sibiu (6 daily); Sighişoara (Mon–Fri 20 daily, Sat & Sun 12 daily); Sovata (Mon–Fri hourly, Sat & Sun 8 daily); Târgu Neamţ (4 daily); Vatra Dornei (2 daily).

Târgu Secuiesc to: Bacău (8 daily); Covasna (4 daily); Miercurea Ciuc (2–3 daily).

International trains

Braşov to: Budapest, Hungary (4 daily; 11hr 15min–14hr); Vienna, Austria (1 daily; 15hr 30min).
Cluj to: Budapest (4 daily; 7hr).
Deva to: Budapest (6 daily; 6hr); Vienna (1 daily; 10hr).
Miercurea Ciuc to: Budapest (2 daily; 12hr 45min).
Sighişoara to: Budapest (3 daily; 9hr 10min–9hr 30min); Vienna (1 daily; 13hr).

International buses

Braşov to: Budapest (Tues, Thurs & Fri); Chişinău, Moldova (Mon–Fri); Germany (several daily); Istanbul, Turkey (Thurs & Sun).
Cluj to: Athens, Greece (2 weekly); Budapest (10 daily); Germany (1 daily); Thessaloniki, Greece (2 weekly).
Deva to: Germany (several daily).
Gheorgheni to: Budapest (1 daily).
Miercurea Ciuc to: Budapest (2 daily).
Odorheiu Secuiesc to: Budapest (2 daily).
Reghin to: Budapest (Thurs & Sun).
Sebeş to: Germany (several daily).
Sfântu Gheorghe to: Budapest (1 daily).
Sibiu to: Germany (several daily).
Sighişoara to: Budapest (1 Mon & Fri); Germany (daily).
Târgu Mureş to: Budapest (1 daily).

Moldavia

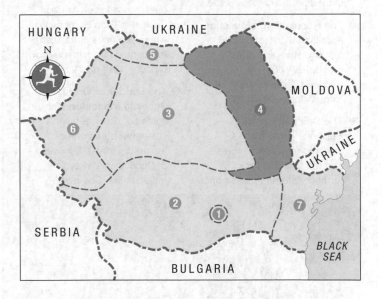

CHAPTER 4　# Highlights

✳ **Ghimeş** An isolated Hungarian enclave perched on the old Habsburg-Ottoman border, this quiet village is surrounded by rolling green hills. **See p.231**

✳ **Agapia Convent** This picture-perfect convent, where over four hundred nuns live in trim cottages, is one of the spiritual centres of the Romanian Orthodox Church. **See p.236**

✳ **The Neculai Popa Museum** A delightful collection of folk sculpture and other curiosities, set in the rugged village of Tărpeşti, south of Târgu Neamţ. **See p.237**

✳ **The Ceahlău massif** Bucovina is the most forested region of Romania, and the hills and rock formations of the massif offer wilderness on an impressive scale. **See p.239**

✳ **Iaşi** The old Moldavian capital is full of surprises, not least some superb religious architecture and a vibrant cultural scene. **See p.241**

✳ **Bucovina pensions** Stay at least a night in one of the dozens of hospitable Bucovina guesthouses such as *Casa Cristian* in Gura Humorului, where you can eat traditional meals made from home-grown produce. **See p.261**

✳ **The Ladder of Virtue, Suceviţa Monastery** This splendid, richly detailed ensemble is just one of the unforgettable frescoes of Bucovina's painted monasteries. **See p.266**

▲ Trams in Iaşi

Moldavia

A large swathe of land covering the easternmost portion of Romania, Moldavia used to be twice its present size, having at various times included Bessarabia (the land beyond the River Prut) and Northern Bucovina (on the edge of the Carpathians). Both territories were annexed by Stalin in 1940, severing cultural and family ties, though these have been revived since the fall of communism, especially between Moldavia and the former Bessarabia (now the sovereign Republic of Moldova). Moldavia's complex **history** is best understood in relation to the cities of **Iaşi** and **Suceava**, the former capitals of the region. The former is one of the country's most appealing destinations, with numerous churches and monasteries retained from its heyday as the Moldavian capital and a strong cultural scene. Suceava, meanwhile, is symptomatic of many towns and cities in Moldavia, a typical new-town development marred by hideous concrete apartment blocks and factories. In contrast, the countryside looks fantastic, with picturesque villages dwarfed by the flanks of the Carpathians. Just over halfway to Suceava, Neamţ county contains the eclectic **Neculai Popa Museum**, as well as Moldavia's largest **convents** – Agapia and Văratec – and the weirdly shaped **Ceahlău massif**, a paradise for hikers and climbers. Backwaters such as **Ghimeş** in the Magyar-speaking **Csángó region** are worth investigating if you're interested in rural life, and there are also numerous local **festivals**.

For travellers, Moldavia gets more interesting the further north you go, and the difficulty of some journeys can, perversely, add to the attraction of your final destination. This is particularly true of the jewels in the Moldavian crown, the **painted monasteries of southern Bucovina**. Secluded in lush valleys near the Ukrainian border, their medieval frescoes of redemption and damnation blaze in polychromatic splendour – Voroneţ and Suceviţa boast peerless examples of the Last Judgement and the Ladder of Virtue, while Moldoviţa is famous for its fresco of the Siege of Constantinople. The unpainted Putna Monastery, final resting place of Stephen the Great, draws visitors interested in Romanian history.

Motorists heading along the DN2 into northern Moldavia should note that although the road is designated on maps as Euro-route 85, it's actually a country road where horse-drawn wagons without lights are a major hazard at night. **Public transport** in the region is fairly good, with decent rail and bus (maxitaxi) links between all the major centres and many of the smaller towns – however, without your own transport, getting to the monasteries will prove difficult.

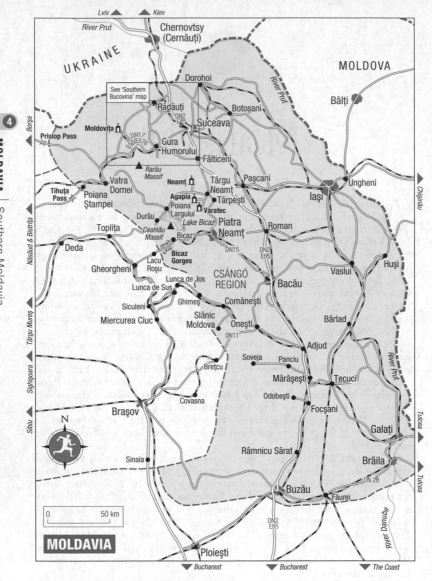

Southern Moldavia

Unlike the northern part of the region, southern Moldavia is almost totally devoid of worthwhile sights. Lying well off the main route through Moldavia, close to the region's southeastern border and the Danube Delta, **Brăila** and **Galaţi** are seldom visited by tourists, and only then while en route to or from Tulcea, the Delta capital. Both were once ports where the Orient and Occident colluded in exporting Romania's agricultural wealth; now they are backwaters and monuments to economic failure, though **Brăila** is certainly worth a visit by dint of its central core of fine buildings. There are no bridges across the Danube in the vicinity, and with no ferries to Tulcea and the Delta, the only way to get to either city from Tulcea is by bus. Fast trains run from Galaţi to Bucharest via Brăila, and slower services, as well as buses and maxitaxis, connect to northern Moldavia.

Brăila

BRĂILA has the air of a restful, pleasantly gone-to-seed Danubian town about it, laid out in concentric streets radiating from the port esplanade. As the region's principal harbour, Brăila shipped the harvests of the Bărăgan Plain to the rest of Europe in the nineteenth century, creating huge fortunes for a few landlords who built elegant villas here, using members of the local Gypsy population – at the time, the largest of any town in Europe – as domestic slaves. Although its docks are now largely silted up, its old town has retained more nineteenth-century architecture than most other Romanian cities and the vestiges of wealth and splendour give the place a romantic, even bohemian, feel.

The old town, rebuilt after being liberated from the Turks in the war of 1828–29, in which it was heavily damaged, is centred on **Piaţa Traian**, a leafy square on which stands the **Church of the Archangel Michael**, built as a mosque by the Turks, probably in the eighteenth century, with a freestanding belfry added later. The town's nicely presented **museum** (Muzeul Brăila; Wed–Sun: May–Sept 11am–7pm; Oct–April 9am–5pm; €1), at Piaţa Traian 3, does a good job of portraying the town in its heyday, with two floors of archeological finds, nineteenth-century furniture, old maps and sepia photos. Leading away from the square, take a walk down pedestrianized Strada Eminescu, showcasing some fine buildings, not least the heavily stuccoed Maria Filotti theatre on the corner with Piaţa Traian. On the opposite side of Piaţa Traian, the lively axis of Calea Călăraşilor leads towards the **Centru Civic**, passing villas variously housing restaurants, shops and banks, as well as a large **Greek Orthodox church** built by the community that dominated the shipping business before World War I. From the bottom of Piaţa Traian, Str. Imperator Traian leads to the **waterfront** with its mournful array of rusting freighters and patrol boats.

Practicalities

Buses from Tulcea terminate at Smârdan, from where regular **ferries** shuttle both foot passengers (€1) and cars (€4, including the driver) across the Danube to Brăila. To reach town from the **train station**, take maxitaxi #4 or walk 1km down Str. E. Grigorescu to B-dul A.I. Cuza; bear right as far as Str. Eminescu, the street which leads left to Piaţa Traian. Brăila's **bus station** is about 200m left of the train station, on Str. Siret. **Maxitaxis** to and from Galaţi call at the intersection of B-dul Dorobanţi and Calea Galaţi, 1km north of the centre.

There's a bunch of **hotels** close to Piaţa Traian, the most satisfactory of which is the oddly named but surprisingly stylish *LMS* at Calea Galaţi 9 (☎0339/110 166, Ⓔlms@braila.astral.ro; ❸). Close by at Str. D. Bolintineanu 4 (the first turning to the right off Calea Galaţi from Piaţa Traian), there's the nondescript but adequate *Hotel Sport* (☎0239/611 346; ❸), and on Piaţa Traian itself, high-rise *Traian* (☎0239/611 404, Ⓦwww.unita-turism.ro; ❸–❹) has a varied mix of older and renovated rooms; breakfast costs extra here. For **eating**, *Crama Veche*, at Str. Eminescu 22, offers the best choice of grilled meats in town, while in summer restaurants and open-air terraces down on the waterfront dispense large portions of *mititei* and draught beer.

From Brăila to Bacău

Heading north from Brăila there's little to get excited about, as one hideously modernized town succeeds another without even the sight of the Carpathians to lift your spirits. Thus there's little reason to stop along the way unless for a detour into one of the wine-growing regions. **Focşani**, around 75km northwest of Brăila, has bus and train links to the **wine-growing regions** of Panciu and Odobeşti, and routes northwest into the hills of Vrancea county. Immediately south of the rail junction of **Mărăşeşti** (20km north of Focşani), a huge mausoleum commemorates the crucial battle in the summer of 1917, when German forces advancing on Iaşi were halted by Romanian troops, determined to preserve the last unoccupied region of their country.

At **Panciu** they make sparkling wines, while **Odobeşti** produces Galbena de Odobeşti, the yellow wine that was Ceauşescu's favourite tipple. Odobeşti is also noted for its **festivals**; the grape harvest is celebrated in late September, and on the third Sunday of November the shepherds of Vrancea county gather to entertain each other with performances on alpine horns and panpipes. Pension **accommodation** in Panciu, Odobeşti and elsewhere can be booked through the Vrancea County Antrec office (℡0237/673 049, ✉vrancea@antrec.ro), located about 50km northwest of Focşani, in the village of Vidra. The large industrial town of **BACĂU**, 65km north of **Focşani**, holds little appeal, though you may find yourself needing to break a journey here, such are the distances between the region's principal towns and villages, and it's also a good base for visiting the **Csángó** region of the Subcarpathians. If you do need to stay, there's the clean and modern *Dumbrava* (℡0234/513 302, ⓦwww.hoteldumbrava.ro; ④), just south of the centre at Str. Dumbrava Roşie 2.

The Csángó region

The name "Csángó" is thought to derive from the Hungarian for "wanderer", referring to those Székely (see p.182) who fled here from religious persecution in Transylvania during the fifteenth century, to be joined by others escaping military conscription in the seventeenth and eighteenth centuries. There is evidence that Hungarians have been present in this area for even longer than that, however; the true origin of the Csángó remains a subject of contentious debate. Once, there were some forty **Csángó villages** in Moldavia, a few as far east as present-day Ukraine, but today their community has contracted into a core of about five thousand people living between Adjud and Bacău, and in **Ghimeş** at the upper end of the Trotuş (Tatros) valley. Most rural Csángó are fervently religious and fiercely conservative, retaining a distinctive folk costume and dialect; their music is harsher and sadder than that of their Magyar kinsfolk in Transylvania, although their dances are almost indistinguishable from those of their Romanian neighbours.

Mutual suspicions and memories of earlier injustices and uprisings made this a sensitive area in communist times. While allowing them to farm and raise sheep outside the collectives, the Party tried to dilute the Csángó and stifle their culture by settling Romanians in new industrial towns like Oneşti. Things are a lot freer now, and the idyllic upper valley is frequently visited during the summer by tour groups from Budapest, as well as a few independent travellers. The tourist infrastructure in these parts, however, remains fairly poor, so bring what supplies and money you're going to need with you.

Practicalities

Adjud is the junction on the main Bucharest–Suceava line for the branch line west to Oneşti, Ghimeş and Transylvania. However, if you're coming to Ghimeş from the north, rather than riding all the way down to Adjud, it may be quicker to disembark at Bacău, catch a bus to Comăneşti, and wait there for the next train up the valley. The first major stop after Adjud is **Oneşti** (Onyest), which can also be reached by bus from Bacău; dominated by the chemical industry, it is notable only as the birthplace of Nadia Comaneci. From here or from **Târgu Ocna** (Aknavásar), a small spa 12km to the west that boasts the largest underground sanatorium in Europe, you can reach the larger spa of **Slănic Moldova** (Szlanikfürdo) which lies 20km southeast of Târgu Ocna.

Accommodation in Târgu Ocna is mainly found near the Saline station, 2km west, which is where the fast trains call; a good choice is *Casa Creangă* at Str. Gălean 33 (℡0234/341 795, ⓦwww.casacreanga.ro; ❷–❸), which has a small indoor spa. In Slănic Moldova, try *Casa Albă*, at Str. Bălcescu 59 (℡0234/348 803; ❸), or *Pensiunea Cristal*, at Str. Bălcescu 70 (℡0234/348 004; ❷). In Comăneşti there's the *Hotel Bradul*, at Str. Republicii 6 (℡0234/374 303; ❸), and in Oneşti the *Hotel Sport*, at B-dul Republicii 43 (℡0234/321 111; ❸).

Ghimeş

The quiet charm that is the real attraction of the beautiful Trotuş valley only begins to reveal itself on the far side of Comăneşti (Cománfalva), a coal-mining settlement that is also the junction for the decrepit oil town of Moineşti, birthplace of Dada founder Tristan Tzara (see box, p.232). Beyond Comăneşti, industry is present only in the form of a few small-scale timber mills, and trains call at one picturesque village after another before finally reaching **Ghimeş** (Ghimeş-Făget or Gyimesbükk), the largest and most rewarding of the Csángó settlements, and the only one that can be visited with any ease. The rail line continues on to Miercurea Ciuc in Transylvania, and daily trains to and from Braşov and Timişoara make this an attractive stopping point en route to Neamţ County, Iaşi or Suceava.

Nearly all of the residents of Ghimeş are Hungarian, though there is a small Gypsy population, which, unusually, is well integrated into village life. This helps to account for the strong musical tradition, most in evidence at the **winter fair** held annually on January 20–21. Ghimeş' appeal lies in its tranquil setting, but the town does have a few modest sights. Its principal monument, at least for those who wish to contemplate the injustices of the Trianon Treaty after World War I, under which Hungary was forced to cede Transylvania to Romania, is the nineteenth-century customs house that marked the old border of Transylvania and Moldavia and, earlier, the Habsburg and Ottoman empires. It's just off the main road, 1.5km east of the station. The steps behind it lead up to the insubstantial ruins of **Rákóczi Castle**, built in 1626 by Prince Gábor Bethlen – more than the ruins, though, it's the **view** of the Trotuş valley from here that makes the climb worthwhile. This is also the beginning of the path that leads up the ridge of Papoj mountain (1271m).

The area's remoteness makes it ideal for **hiking**, and a series of little-used trails, including several longer routes into Transylvania, is delineated on the 1:60,000 DIMAP map of the area, sold at the *Deáky Panzió* (see p.232). The village itself, divided in two by the Trotuş River, is also an inviting place to take a walk – its houses are neat and colourful, with many boasting intricately carved eaves and flower gardens, and its streets are enlivened by the various farm animals wandering about. Opposite the train station, a tiny **museum** (**Gyimesi Házimúseum**; call at the house to the rear) displays a jumble of rural memorabilia, including pottery, textiles and local photographs. The main church, rebuilt in 1976, is 200m up from the station, but more interesting, and a good place to picnic, is the small wooden chapel that overlooks the town from a hilltop meadow across the river. Reaching it entails scaling a few fences, but nobody seems to mind. East towards the head of

My heart belongs to Dada

The magazine *Simbolul* ("The Symbol") was founded in 1912 by three Jewish school-boys in Bucharest: Ion Vinea, Marcel Iancu and Samuel Rosenstock. All three were to play leading roles in the development of avant-garde art, but it was Rosenstock, calling himself **Tristan Tzara** (1896–1963), who was to achieve greatest fame. A poet and playwright, he was a central figure in the absurdist **Dada movement**, founded at Zürich's *Cabaret Voltaire* in 1916; he moved to Paris in 1920 but broke with Dadaism in 1923 when its French leaders, such as André Breton and Louis Aragon, turned to Surrealism. Iancu, better known as **Marcel Janco** (1895–1984), also went to Zürich, returning in 1922 to Bucharest and, with **Ion Vinea** (1895–1964), founding the magazine *Contimperanul* ("The Contemporary") which ran until 1932. Its manifesto (similar to that of the Dutch group De Stijl) was more constructivist than Dadaist. Janco also became the leading architect of Cubist and International Style buildings in Bucharest; after World War II he emigrated to Israel, dying there in 1984.

A younger artist, and perhaps the most important, was **Victor Brauner** (1903–66) who was born in Piatra Neamț and studied briefly at the Bucharest School of Fine Arts; he was involved with the Constructivists before leaving for Paris in 1930. André Breton saw him as "the quintessential magic artist"; a painter of premonitions, as well as a sculptor and print-maker, he was obsessed by blindness, painting figures without eyes, even in a self-portrait. Ironically, at a Surrealist party in 1938 a glass was thrown and smashed, putting out his left eye. He spent World War II in the French Alps, returning to Paris in 1945 and breaking from the Surrealists in 1948.

the valley, Lunca de Jos (Gyimesközeplok) and Lunca de Sus (Gyimesfelsólok) are Csángó villages just across the border in Transylvania.

Practicalities

Ghimeş's handful of commercial establishments are all in the centre of town, opposite the vast **train station**, built in the nineteenth century to handle customs and immigration formalities. The main place to stay here is the *Deáky Panzió* (℡0234/385 621, Ⓔdeakyandras@xnet.ro; May–Sept; ➊–➋), an attractive **pension** 🍴 on a large converted farm by the river. From the station, turn left and follow the main road downhill for about 1km, past the post office until you see the sign on your right. Spead around the grounds are small wooden bungalows, each containing rooms sleeping two or three people. Food and wine, all from local farms, are both excellent and very reasonably priced. If you stay for a few days, your visit is likely to coincide with a group of Hungarian tourists coming for dinner and an evening of wine, dancing and **Csángó and Gypsy music**. The singing, especially, is hauntingly beautiful, if a little overtly patriotic at times. The *Vár* **campsite** (℡0234/385 655), 200m further along, also has small wooden huts (➊). The only place to eat, other than the pension, is a little **restaurant** opposite the train station, with a reasonable Hungarian/Romanian menu.

Neamț county

Neamț county lies to the northwest of Bacău and is the best-known attraction between Bucharest and the old Moldavian capitals of Iaşi and Suceava. Although its towns – **Piatra Neamț** and **Târgu Neamț** – are nothing special, they serve as bases for the **historic convents** of Neamț, Agapia and Văratec, set in wooded foothills that turn gloriously red and gold in autumn, and the delightful collection of naïve art and folk costumes at the **Neculai Popa Museum** in Tărpeşti. Further to the northwest rises the **Ceahlău massif**, whose magnificent views and bizarrely weathered outcrops make this one of Romania's most dramatic hiking spots.

On arrival, you'll be faced with the question of where to base yourself. The pensions around Agapia are best if you're travelling by car, but can be somewhat isolated if you're not. Of the towns, Târgu Neamţ is closer to the sights, but Piatra Neamţ, as the county seat, is livelier and offers a far better choice of places to stay and eat. The two are 40km apart and are linked by frequent **buses** and maxitaxis, almost all of which run via Coşere and Sacalauşeşti, the respective turn-offs for Văratec and Agapia. Buses also link the major towns with Durău, the jumping-off point for the Ceahlău massif.

Piatra Neamţ

Sixty kilometres northwest of Băcau by road and rail, where the River Bistriţa emerges into the Cracau basin, lies **PIATRA NEAMŢ**. Hemmed in by the Carpathian foothills, it is one of Romania's oldest settlements, once inhabited by a string of Neolithic and Bronze Age cultures, and the Dacians, whose citadel has been excavated on a nearby hilltop. The town was first recorded in Roman times as Petrodava, and in 1453 under the name of Piatra lui Craciun (Christmas Rock); its present title may refer to the German ("Neamţ") merchants who once traded here, or may derive from the old Romanian word for an extended family or nation ("Neam"). As one of Moldavia's earliest industrial centres, the town later played a major role in the general strike of 1919, and was one of the few places where the communists were able to sabotage production during World War II.

Arrival, information and accommodation

From the **train** and **bus** stations, it's a ten-minute walk up B-dul Republicii to Piaţa Libertăţii, where you'll find the **tourist information** centre (Mon–Fri 10am–6pm,

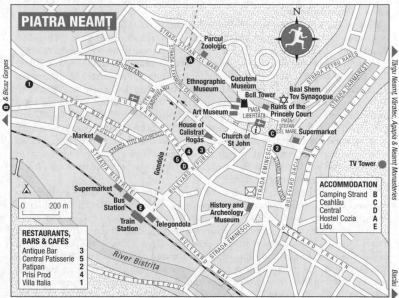

Sat 10am–2pm). **Internet access** is available at the Internet Copy Center inside the Telegondola building in front of the train station. The **gondola** (Tues–Sun 10am–10pm; €4) makes the six-minute ride up to Cozla mountain (657m).

The best of Piatra Neamț's uninspiring **hotels** is the *Central*, a renovated high-rise with modern comforts at Piața Petrodava 1 (☎0233/216 230, ⓦwww .hotelcentral.ro; ②). Otherwise, the choices boil down to the *Ceahlău*, Piața Ștefan cel Mare 3 (☎0233/219 990, ⓦwww.hotelceahlau.ro; ③), another high-rise with ordinary rooms, or the dowdy *Lido*, next to the stations at Piața Gării 5 (☎0233/226 349, Ⓔcontact@pensiune-lido.com; ❶–❷), offering rooms with and without bathrooms. A welcoming alternative is the *Hostel Cozla*, Str. Ștefan cel Mare 31 (☎0233/213 069, Ⓔdjt.neamt@anst.gov.ro; ❶), which has tidy three- to five-bedded dorms with communal bathrooms – breakfast is not available but there is a kitchen for use. There are also wooden cabins at the Camping *Ștrand* site (☎0730/880 926; ❶–❸), across the river on Aleea Tineretului; to get there, head 1km west along Str. Bistriței until you reach the footbridge.

The Town

What's left of the old town is clustered around park-like **Piața Libertății**. The spireless **Church of St John** originally formed part of a Princely Court (Curtea Domnească) founded in 1468, of which only vestiges remain. Erected by Stephen the Great in 1497–98, hard on the heels of his seminal church at Neamț Monastery, it set a pattern for Moldavian church architecture thereafter. The upper part is girdled by niches outlined in coloured brick, in which it was probably intended to paint saintly images. Beside the door, a votive inscription by his son Bogdan the One-Eyed presages a host of tacky modern paintings of Stephen inside the almost blackened interior. A sturdy Gothic **bell tower** with a witch's hat brim, raised in 1499, stands a few paces from the church. Across the road from the church, a large black gate conceals the vaulted ruins of the **Princely Court** (Expoziția Curtea Domneasca; April–Sept 10am–6pm), which have been laid bare by a shaft dug into the slope below the Petru Rares College (a teacher-training college); if it's closed ask at the tourist office.

West of the bell tower, in a building that combines folk architecture with Art Nouveau, is the **Ethnographic Museum** (Muzeul de Etnografie; Tues–Sun 10am–6pm; €1), and beside that a Brâncovenesc mansion, with ceramic studs echoing those on the church, housing the **Art Museum** (Muzeul de Artă; Tues–Sun 10am–6pm; €1), showing work by local painters. Immediately north, at Str. Ștefan cel Mare 3, is the **Cucuteni Museum** (Muzeul de Artă Eneolitică Cucuteni; Tues–Sun 10am–6pm; €1), so named after the Cucuteni culture, one of the most important late Neolithic civilizations, which flourished from 4500–2500 BC and comprised some three thousand settlements scattered throughout eastern Romania, Moldavia and southeast Ukraine. Most characteristic of the Cucuteni is its ceramic work, a superb collection of which is on display here – painted bowls, vases, amphorae and statuettes, though the museum's most celebrated piece is the *Hora de la Frumușcia* (The Frumușcia Dance).

Northeast of the Princely Court, on Str. Dimitrie Ernica, is the eighteenth-century wooden **Baal Shem Tov Synagogue**. Baal Shem Tov, the founder of Hasidism (a branch of Judaism based on the omnipresence of God and man's communion with Him), was for a short time supposed to have lived close to Piatra Neamț, occasionally visiting to pray here. This is almost the only survivor of hundreds of similar buildings that were found across Eastern Europe until World War II. It's generally locked, but there are signs that the site may soon receive funding for restoration from the World Monuments Fund's Jewish Heritage Grant Program. The synagogue is completely surrounded by other buildings, so that you would have no idea of its existence were it not for the stone tablets on the roof. It seems like an annexe to the adjacent newer wing, and both are overshadowed by the late nineteenth-century white-stone **Temple Synagogue** (normally closed), which houses frescoes representing Jerusalem and the Holy Land.

Strada Ştefan cel Mare, dotted with several attractive old villas, heads west out of Piaţa Libertăţii; the **Parcul Zoologic** opposite no. 31 (daily 9am–7pm; €1) is mainly a children's playground – the only animals on show are some goats and sheep. Elena Cuza, widow of the deposed ruler Alexandru Ioan Cuza (see p.376), lived at no. 55 until her death in 1909. One block south of the square, set back from B-dul Republicii, which leads south to the train station, is the small **House of Calistrat Hogaş** (Tues–Sun 10am–4pm), now a memorial museum to the writer (1847–1918), who praised the charms of Piatra Neamţ when it consisted largely of Alpine-style chalets.

Just east of Piaţa Libertăţii is Piaţa Ştefan cel Mare, from where Str. Eminescu heads south to the **History and Archeology Museum** (Muzeul de Istorie şi Arheologie; Tues–Sun 10am–6pm; €1) on the corner of Str. Eminescu and B-dul Decebal. The museum devotes its ground floor to relics from the Bronze Age onwards, including a tomb complete with skeleton. Upstairs, Neamţ county's aptitude for woodcarving is exemplified by a "knitted cable" throne and an exquisite door, with the Moldavian crest entwined in foliage.

Eating and drinking

The town's **dining** possibilities are extremely limited, though the homely, trattoria-like *Villa Italia*, around 1km west of the centre at Str. Burebista 65, has a fine Italian menu and an extensive wine list (closed Mon). There are, though, several agreeable **patisseries** spotted around town, the most enticing of which is *Prisi Prod* opposite the *Hotel Central*, followed by the larger *Central Patisserie*, next to the hotel itself, and *Patipan*, on the corner of Str. Eminescu and Piaţa Ştefan cel Mare. The *Antique Bar*, in an old villa at B-dul Republicii 20, is a good, if smoky, spot for a drink, with live music at weekends in the summer. Across the river, the large and flashy Mix MusicLand leisure park (open 24hr) hosts several restaurants, a disco, and facilities for sports such as football, tennis, basketball, volleyball, handball, skating, skateboarding, swimming and horseriding, with gear to rent, as well as kids' amusements.

Văratec and Agapia

The rolling countryside west of the road between Piatra and Târgu Neamţ provides an idyllic setting for various monasteries and Romania's two largest convents: **Văratec** and **Agapia**, both with over four hundred nuns. Each has its own village – up the road from an agricultural village of the same name – where houses have lovely curvaceous porches, shingled or in metal. The nuns live in cosy houses with blue fretted eaves and glassed-in verandas.

You can get to the convents by **bus** from Piatra Neamţ, Târgu Neamţ or Suceava; services normally wait thirty minutes before starting back. Transportation between the convents is provided by two daily buses between Piatra Neamţ and Agapia, calling at Văratec en route, and one at 8am from Târgu Neamţ to Agapia and Văratec. However, the landscape is so lovely you may prefer to walk from one to the other. If you're staying in Piatra Neamţ and miss the last bus back (which is quite possible if you don't get an early start), walk or hitch the 5km back to the main road, where the last buses between Târgu Neamţ and Piatra Neamţ pass at about 8pm. There are also plenty of charming guesthouses in the villages.

Văratec Convent and around

Hedgerows, alive with sparrows and wagtails, line the narrow road winding through Văratec to the pretty nuns' village and **Văratec Convent**, its whitewashed walls and balconies enclosing a lovely garden shaded by cedars. The novices inhabit two-storey buildings named after saints, while the older nuns live in cottages. Văratec was founded in the eighteenth century, around a church that no longer exists; the site of its altar is marked by a pond with a statue of an angel. The present **church**, built in 1808, is plain and simple, culminating in two bell-shaped domes. To cope with the harsh winters, the nuns have sensibly installed stoves by the columns dividing the narthex from the nave, so that both chambers are heated. The gilt pulpit and the gallery over the entrance to the narthex are unusual, but the interior painting is not great. There's a **museum of icons** to the south, and an **embroidery school** established by Queen Marie in 1934. It's an odd but not unfitting site for the **grave of Veronica Micle**, the poet loved by Eminescu, who couldn't afford to marry her after the death of her despised husband (see box, p.248); she killed herself two months after Eminescu's death.

In fine weather, it's an agreeable **walk** through the woods from Văratec to Agapia; the 7km trail takes about an hour and a half, starting by house no. 219, back down the road from Văratec Convent. It's also possible to walk along the road connecting the two convents (from Văratec, walk about 1km back towards the main road, then turn left; from Agapia take the asphalt road across the bridge at the end of the nunnery village). Picnic tables are provided, but camping is not allowed. The road passes through the pretty village of **Filioara**, where you'll find the *Pensiunea Alina* at no. 282 (℡0233/244 861; ❸ including breakfast and dinner), a friendly place serving excellent meals. Another beech-tree-lined trail from Văratec, marked by blue dots, leads west to **Sihla hermitage** (2hr), built into the cliffs near the cave of St Teodora, and hidden by strange outcrops. A back road turns off the main road from Târgu Neamţ to the Ceahlău Massif, 2km west of the turn-off for Neamţ Monastery (see p.238), and passes the **Sihastria and Secu hermitages** en route to Sihla – an easy 10km hike, if you miss the one daily bus. The Sihastria hermitage was founded in 1655 and subsequently built over with a new stone church in 1734; the Secu hermitage dates from 1602 and has Renaissance-style paintings inside as well as the grave of Bishop Varlaam, who in 1634 printed *Canzania* ("Romania's teaching book"), the first book written in Romanian.

Agapia Convent and around

Agapia Convent actually consists of two convents a few kilometres apart; most visitors are content to visit only the main complex of **Agapia din Vale** ("Agapia in the Valley"), at the end of a village with houses with covered steps. The walls and gate tower aim to conceal rather than to protect; inside is a whitewashed enclosure around a cheerful garden. At prayer times a nun beats an insistent rhythm on a wooden *toaca* while another plays the panpipes; this is followed by a medley of bells, some deep and slow, others high and fast. The convent **church** – much smaller than the one at Văratec – was built in 1644–47 by Prince Basil the Wolf's brother, Gavril Coci. Its helmet-shaped cupola, covered in green shingles, mimics that of the gate tower. After restoration, the interior was repainted between 1858 and 1861 by Nicolae Grigorescu, the country's foremost painter at the time (see box, p.96); he returned to stay at Agapia from 1901 to 1902.

Grigorescu's close attachment to the convent can also be seen in the **museum**, which stars several of the painter's Renaissance-style icons as well as portraits of the Vlahuţă family. Icons, vestments and embroidery from the seventeenth and eighteenth centuries complete a sizeable collection. Beyond the convent walls, and up past the nuns' cottages, is the **Casa Memorial Alexandru Vlahuţă**, the small house where the author (1858–1919) spent summers visiting his mother and sister, who were both nuns here. As well as two traditionally furnished bedrooms, the third room keeps books, photos and mementoes, plus a painting of Vlahuţă's sister Elizabeta by Octav Băncila. Downhill by the Topolniţa stream stands a wooden church with three shingled domes and a modern gate tower. An enticing variety of breads, jams and syrups, all harvested by the nuns, is available from the kiosk outside the convent entrance.

The older **Agapia din Deal** ("Agapia on the Hill"), otherwise known as Agapia Veche ("Old Agapia"), is a smaller, more tranquil convent, high up a wooded slope about half an hour's walk from Agapia din Vale; ten minutes out, turn right at the unmarked junction. Another trail from the main convent leads to Văratec. There are several **pensions** in Agapia; at the far end of the village (and closest to the monastery) the *Pensiunea Maria* (☎0233/245 004; ❷) possesses tidy, pinewood-furnished rooms, a lovely garden and a good restaurant. A further 1km down the road, there's the simple but clean *Pensiunea Andreea* (☎0233/244 760, ✉pens_andreea@yahoo.com; ❷), and 100m away on the opposite side, the *Casa Timofte* (☎0233/244 663; ❷). During the summer, it's also possible to stay in Agapia's theological seminary (❶), 100m down from the convent.

Tărpeşti

Two daily buses from Piatra Neamţ to Târgu Neamţ trace a leisurely semicircle along back roads east of the main route, first taking in the village of **Războieni**, where there is a spireless church (built by Stephen the Great in memory of the soldiers who died here in a 1476 battle with the Ottomans), and then, about 10km southeast of Târgu Neamţ, passing the turn-off to the ramshackle village of **TĂRPEŞTI**, home of the delightful **Neculai Popa Museum** (daily 9am–7pm; €2). It's a pleasant but unshaded 3km walk from the turn-off where the bus leaves you to the village, where signs will direct you to the museum; alternatively, Tărpeşti is served by two direct buses from Târgu Neamţ.

Set in Popa's own yard, the museum's diverse works (all collected by Popa himself) are displayed with care and wit. The main building is devoted to Popa's folk art collections, including paintings by Romanian artists, an unusually good set of icons, and old Moldavian handicrafts such as thick leather belts and painted trousseaux. The colourful masks and folk costumes on display in the second building, many made by Popa's wife Elena, are occasionally used in children's pageants recounting legends such as that of Iancu Jianu, an eighteenth-century forest bandit known as the Robin Hood of Wallachia. In good weather, Popa can be seen in the sculpture garden using a timeworn chisel to fashion a new totem pole or menhir. His son now runs the museum, giving tours in Romanian and French, and there is also a gallery where folk art and icons are sold. There is no accommodation here, and trade is limited to a few basic shops that double as taverns.

Târgu Neamţ and around

TÂRGU NEAMŢ, with its systematized concrete centre, is far smaller and duller than Piatra, and therefore a less attractive stopover. However, it does possess the Neamţ **citadel** (Cetatea Neamţului; daily 9am–7pm; €1), Moldavia's finest ruined castle. Visible from the road to Neamţ Monastery, but far more impressive at close quarters, the citadel is 1km west along Str. Ştefan cel Mare; from the *La Cetate* pension (which is as far as cars can go), it's a stiff fifteen-minute climb to the entrance. Founded by Petru I Muşat in 1359, it was beefed up by Stephen the

Great just in time to withstand a siege by the Turkish Sultan Mohammed II in 1496. Later it was partly demolished on the orders of the Turks, but again saw service in 1691 in the war between Moldavia and Poland. Its military importance waned thereafter, and in 1717 it was almost totally destroyed on the orders of Mihai Racoviţă, erstwhile Prince of Moldavia. Subsequent renovation has quashed much if its historical charm, but it remains a mightily impressive sight. Once at the entrance the approach to the citadel is over a long, curving **wooden bridge** raised on pillars high above a dry moat; the final stretch was originally designed to flip enemies down into an oubliette. Within the **bailey**, a warren of roofless chambers that used to be an arsenal, courthouse and baths surrounds a deep well, ringed by battlements that offer superb views of the Neamţ valley for kilometres around.

Târgu's **bus station** is a few minutes from the centre on Str. Cuza Vodă, and the **train station** is a further twenty minutes east on the same road. The town's one decent place to **stay** is the *Pensiunea La Cetate*, just down from the citadel at Str. Cetăţii 33 (℡0233/660 249, Ⓔlacetateaneamtului.ro; ❹); alongside its beautifully furnished rooms, there is a row of tidy little huts, each with double bed and bathroom (❷). The **restaurant** here is equally accomplished and makes for a lovely spot to eat after viewing the citadel. In the centre of town the *Doina* at Str. Mihail Kogălniceanu 6 (℡0233/790 272, Ⓦwww.hotel-doina.ro; ❸) has dull but cheap rooms; it's behind the main church on B-dul Ştefan cel Mare, 400m east of the central crossroads in the direction of Iaşi. If you're heading to Iaşi by car, consider stopping 15km east of Târgu Neamţ at *Hanul Ancuţei* (℡0233/781 400; ❸), an excellent if slightly kitsch roadside inn and wine cellar, which also has comfortable rooms.

Neamţ Monastery

The twelfth-century **Neamţ Monastery**, 12km northwest of Târgu Neamţ, is the oldest in Moldavia and is the region's chief centre of Orthodox culture; it is also the largest men's monastery in Romania, with seventy monks and dozens of seminary students. It was founded as a hermitage, expanded into a monastery in the late fourteenth century by Petru I Muşat, and then rebuilt in the early fifteenth century by Alexander the Good, with fortifications that protected Neamţ from the Turks. It also had a printing house that spread its influence throughout Moldavia. The new church, founded by Stephen the Great in 1497 to celebrate a victory over the Poles, became a prototype for Moldavian churches throughout the next century, and its school of miniaturists and illuminators led the field.

Outwardly, Neamţ resembles a fortress, with high stone walls and its one remaining octagonal corner tower (there used to be four). On the inside of the gate tower, a painted Eye of the Saviour sternly regards the monks' cells with their verandas wreathed in red and green ivy, and the seminary students in black tunics milling around the garden. The sweeping roof of Stephen's church overhangs blind arches inset with glazed bricks, on a long and otherwise bare facade. Its trefoil windows barely illuminate the interior, where pilgrims kneel amid the smell of mothballs and candlewax. At the back of the compound is a smaller church dating from 1826, containing frescoes of the Nativity and the Resurrection. Outside the monastery stands a large, onion-domed **pavilion** for *Aghiastmatar*, the "blessing of the water", to be taken home in bottles to cure illness. The monastery's main festival is held on May 7.

The monastery can be reached by three daily **buses** from Târgu Neamţ; you could also catch one of the frequent services along the main road to the turn-off at km33 and walk the remaining 4km to the monastery. There are **rooms** (❷) and a summer **campsite** with huts (❶) at the *Hanul Branişte*, 3km east of the turning to

Neamț Monastery. Between here and Târgu Neamț is the delightfully unspoilt village of **Vânători Neamț**, known for its **Reserva de Zimbri** (aurochs or European bison), set up in 1970 when three of the primeval beasts, now extinct in the wild, were brought from Poland. There are also deer, bears and wolves here, though the closest you can get is looking over a fence.

The Ceahlău massif

West of Târgu Neamț, 60km beyond the turning to Neamț Monastery, looms the **Ceahlău massif**. Aptly designated on local maps as a *zona abrupt*, it rises above neighbouring ranges in eroded crags whose fantastic shapes were anthropomorphized in folk tales and inspired Eminescu's poem, *The Ghosts*. The Dacians believed that Ceahlău was the abode of their supreme deity, Zamolxis, and that the gods transformed the daughter of Decebal into the Dochia peak. The massif is composed of Cretaceous sediments – especially conglomerates, which form pillar-like outcrops – and covered with stratified belts of beech, fir and spruce, with dwarf pine and juniper above 1700m. Its **wildlife** includes chamois, lynx, capercaillie, bears and boars, and the majestic Carpathian stag. Ceahlău's isolation is emphasized by the huge, artificial **Lake Bicaz** (Lacul Izvoru Muntelei) that half-encircles its foothills.

A hydroelectric dam, built in 1950, rises at the southern end, 3km beyond the village of **BICAZ**. You can get to the dam from Piatra Neamț by frequent maxitaxis, which terminate halfway between Bicaz and the dam. There are also a few trains (one each from Bucharest and Iași), and buses, mostly turning left here for Gheorgheni, 57km west in Transylvania. Bicaz's **History Museum** (Muzeul de Istorie Bicaz; Tues–Sun 9am–5pm; €1), which has a display on the building of the dam and a small art exhibit, is at Str. Barajului 3, just north of the town's small systematized centre.

Accommodation

Noisy *Pensiunea Ceahlău* (☎0233/254 555; ❶), on the main road just north of town, is cheap and convenient, but it's better to continue the 3km to the *Baraj* cabana (☎0233/254 960; ❷), right below the dam, where you can also camp. A further 3km up, the road reaches the dam, 500m beyond which a cobbled road winds down to the lakefront and the *Bicaz Tourist Complex* (☎0233/254 080, ⓦwww.bicazlac.ro), comprising the *Pescaruş* hotel (❸), the *Lebada* floating hotel (❷; closed in winter), and four-bedded cabins (❷). Pleasure boats sail from here in summer (€2 for 30min).

Midway between here and the village of Potoci you'll find *Motel Cristina* (☎0233/254 456; ❷), with good **cabins** (❶) and rowing boats available at the pontoon jetty. The mountain road north to Vatra Dornei crosses the route from Târgu Neamț to Durău and Transylvania at **Poiana Largului**, at the northern end of the reservoir, where it's feasible to **change buses** if you're prepared to wait a few hours. There are a few shops here, as well as the *Pensiunea Elvi* (☎0233/257 295; ❷) and *Pensiunea Teiul* (☎0233/257 082; ❷), both cheap and adequate if you're stuck. The decent *Popas Petru Vodă* **campsite** is at the Argel Pass, 12km uphill towards Târgu Neamț. In **Fărcaşa**, 10km out of Poiana Largului on the Vatra Dornei road, there's a fine eighteenth-century wooden church, and the small *Pensiunea Orizont* (☎0233/267 029, ⓔpensiuneaorizont@yahoo.com; ❷).

Hiking above Durău

The main base for hiking in the massif is **DURĂU**, on its northwestern side, which can be reached by bus from Piatra Neamț or Târgu Neamț. From the turn-off 7km west of Poiana Largului (and 67km east of Topliţa in Transylvania) it's 12km up a dead-end road to the resort, passing through the village of Ceahlău, where there are various guesthouses. Durău's major draw is the **Ceahlău Feast**, on the second Sunday in August, an opportunity for shepherds to parade their finery and an attraction for many tourists. It also boasts a small **hermitage** built in 1833, overwhelmed by a modern monastery. The *Bradul* (℡0233/256 501; ❸), 300m to the left from the main crossroads, is the largest and best of Durău's several **hotels**.

There's also the *Ursuleţ* campsite (℡0740/470 825), 1km down the road, as well as a dozen or so pensions, of which *Vila Iris* at Str. Releu 1 (℡0233/256 531; ❷) and *Vila Albăstrica* at Str. Releu 3 (℡0722/955 288; ❷) are above-average places with great views, up beyond the TV relay. From December to March, skiing (on a small scale, with just a few drags) replaces hiking as the main activity in the resort. The area is now protected by the Ceahlău National Park (✆www.ceahlaupark.ro) and no motorized vehicles are allowed, so that the road from Durău to the *Izvorul Muntelui* cabana is now closed. You'll pay a fee (€2) for the duration of your stay in Durău and the park at the gate uphill from the resort or in the cabanas. You'll be given a leaflet map (and a garbage bag) at the gate, where they also sell a more detailed map.

From the resort, it's a 45-minute walk to the *Fântânele* cabana (1220m; ℡0233/678 078; ❶), on the steep, red-striped trail starting at the end of the road. A two-hour route (marked by blue crosses, then red crosses and finally yellow triangles) also runs there via the lovely Duruitoarea cascade, 2km from town, which falls a total of 25m in two stages. From Fântânele, the red-striped route (2hr) ascends within sight of the Panaghia rocks and Toaca peak to a plateau with glorious views and, in a further two hours, to the *Dochia* cabana (1750m; ℡0721/179 506; ❶). You can also follow red crosses direct from the cascade to Dochia. The route then continues south via several massive rock pillars, passing Ocolaşu Mare – at 1907m, the massif's highest peak – on its way to Poiana Maicilor, where the red-striped route turns downstream to the *Izvoru Muntelui* cabana (℡0721/179 506; ❶), 7km by road from a turn-off between the Bicaz dam and cabana, while another, less frequented, trail marked with blue crosses runs on to Neagra village, on the road to the Bicaz gorges. Both routes take about two hours from Dochia.

Into Transylvania and north to Vatra Dornei

To the north and south of the massif, narrow valleys enable two routes **into Transylvania**. The northern one crosses the 1112m-high Borsec pass beyond the alpine spa of Borsec, before descending to Topliţa, in the upper Mureş valley (see p.192). It's a scenic route, with buses heading west to Borsec and some continuing to Topliţa. There are also maxitaxis running from Suceava to Târgu Mureş. A better route runs through the **Bicaz gorges** (Cheile Bicazului), 25km upriver from Bicaz, past the lovely village of **Bicaz Ardelean**, which has a wooden church dating from 1829. Sheer limestone cliffs rise as high as 300m above the river, pressing so close around the Gâtul Iadului ("Neck of Hell") that the road is hewn directly into the rockface. The Cheile Bicazului cabana, amid the gorges, marks the start of several **hiking** trails, and a longer one ascends from Lacu Roşu (see p.192) to the *Piatra Singuratică* ("Lonely Rock") cabana. **Buses** from Piatra Neamţ, Târgu Neamţ and Bicaz travel this way en route to Gheorgheni (see p.191).

Alternatively, you can head north from Târgu Neamţ via Poiana Largului to **Vatra Dornei** (see p.273). By bus the 136km journey takes four hours, following the River Bistriţa through a narrow, twisting valley hemmed in by fir-covered peaks. About 20km before Vatra Dornei, you'll see the well-signposted *Zugreni* cabana (℡0230/574 548) across the river, from where a trail leads to the heart of the Rarău massif (see p.272).

Iaşi

IAŞI (pronounced "yash"), in the northeast of Moldavia, is the region's cultural capital and by far its most attractive city, the only one where you're likely to want to stay a while. Its university, theatre and resident orchestra rival those of Bucharest – which was merely a crude market town when Iaşi became a princely seat – and give it an air of sophistication enhanced by a large contingent of foreign students. Cementing its place in the nation's heart, Romanians associate Iaşi with the poet Eminescu, Moldavians also esteem it as the burial place of St Paraschiva, and several million smokers remember it as the home of Carpaţi, the country's cheapest and roughest brand of cigarettes under communism. Despite lying east of the main route northwards through Moldavia, Iaşi is accessible by direct **trains** from Bucharest, Cluj and several other major cities across the country, by **buses** and **maxitaxis** from most towns in Moldavia (and some in Transylvania), and by **flights** from Bucharest and Timişoara.

Some history

Iaşi's ascendancy dates from the sixteenth century, when the Moldavian princes (*hospodars*) gave up the practice of maintaining courts in several towns, and settled permanently in Iaşi. This coincided with Moldavia's gradual decline into a Turkish satellite, ruled by despots who endowed Iaşi with churches and monasteries to trumpet their earthly glory and ensure their eternal salvation. **Basil the Wolf** (Vasile Lupu, 1634–53) promulgated a penal code whereby rapists were raped and arsonists burned alive; he also founded a printing press and school, which led to the flowering of Moldavian literature during the brief reign, from 1710–11, of the enlightened **Dimitrie Cantemir**.

After Cantemir's death, Moldavia fell under the control of **Greek Phanariots**, originally from the Phanar district of Constantinople (Fener in modern Istanbul), who administered the region on behalf of the Ottoman Empire, chose and deposed the nominally ruling princes (of whom there were 36 between 1711 and 1821), and eventually usurped the throne for themselves. The boyars adopted Turkish dress and competed to win the favour of the Phanariots, the sole group that advised the sultan whom of the boyars he should promote. As Ottoman power weakened, this dismal saga was interrupted by the surprise election of **Prince Alexandru Ioan Cuza**, who clinched the unification of Moldavia and Wallachia in 1859 with the diplomatic support of France. In the new Romania, Cuza founded universities at Iaşi and Bucharest, introduced compulsory schooling for both sexes, and secularized monastic property, which at the time accounted for one-fifth of Moldavia. Finally, his emancipation of the serfs so enraged landowners and military circles that in 1866 they overthrew Cuza and restored the status quo ante – but kept the union.

The latter half of the nineteenth century was a fertile time for intellectual life in Iaşi, where the Junimea literary circle attracted such talents as the poet **Mihai Eminescu** and the writer **Ion Creangă**, who, like the historian **Nicolae Iorga**, became national figures. This was also the heyday of Jewish culture in Iaşi (or Jassy, as it was called in Yiddish), and in 1876 local impresario **Avrom Goldfadn** staged the world's first Yiddish theatre performance at the Pumul Verde ("Green Tree") wine garden, facing the present National Theatre. The Junimea brand of nationalism was more romantic than chauvinist, but unwittingly paved the way for a deadlier version in the Greater Romania that was created to reward the Old Kingdom (Regat) for its sacrifices in World War I, when most of the country was occupied by the Germans, and the government was evacuated to Iaşi. With its borders enlarged to include Bessarabia and Bucovina, Moldavia inherited large minorities of Jews, Ukrainians and Gypsies, aggravating ethnic and class tensions in a region devastated by war.

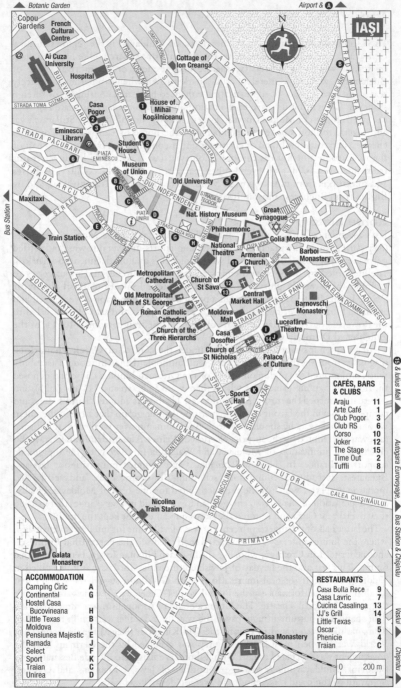

Copou Gardens

French Cultural Centre

Ai Cuza University

Hospital

1 House of Mihai Kogălniceanu

Casa Pogor **2** **3**

Eminescu Library

Student House **4** **5**

Museum of Union

8 **10** C

Cottage of Ion Creangă

STRADA TOMA COZMA

STRADA PACURARI

STRADA ARCU

Maxitaxi

Train Station

Old University **9** **7**

Nat. History Museum

Great Synagogue

Philharmonic

Golia Monastery

Barboi Monastery

National Theatre

Armenian Church

Metropolitan Cathedral

Church of St Sava

11

12

13

Old Metropolitan Church of St. George

Roman Catholic Cathedral

Central Market Hall

Barnovschi Monastery

Church of the Three Hierarchs

Moldova Mall

Casa Dosoftei

Luceafărul Theatre

14 J

Church of St Nicholas

Palace of Culture

Sports Hall

TICĂU

MOLDAVIA

Bus Station

NICOLINA

Nicolina Train Station

Galata Monastery

Frumoasa Monastery

Cetăţuia Monastery

CAFÉS, BARS & CLUBS

Araju	11
Arte Café	1
Club Pogor	3
Club RS	6
Corso	10
Joker	12
The Stage	15
Time Out	2
Tuffli	8

ACCOMMODATION

Camping Ciric	A
Continental	G
Hostel Casa Bucovineana	H
Little Texas	B
Moldova	I
Pensiunea Majestic	E
Ramada	J
Select	F
Sport	K
Traian	C
Unirea	D

RESTAURANTS

Casa Bulla Rece	9
Casa Lavric	7
Cucina Casalinga	13
JJ's Grill	14
Little Texas	B
Oscar	5
Phenicie	4
Traian	C

0   200 m

The Iron Guard and România Mare

Moldavia and Iaşi have long been associated with the far right of Romanian politics. The most ardent member of Iaşi's League of Christian National Defence was **Corneliu Codreanu**, who went on, in the early 1930s, to found the Legion of the Archangel St Michael, better known as the **Iron Guard**. Wearing green shirts with bags of Romanian soil around their necks, the Legionari chased away village bailiffs to the delight of the peasantry, and murdered politicians deemed to be insufficiently nationalistic, until Marshal Antonescu jailed its leaders and Codreanu was shot "trying to escape". His followers fled to Berlin, returning with the Nazis to help carry out their genocidal "Final Solution" in Romania.

After the war, the communists employed ex-Legionari as thugs against the socialists and the National Peasant Party, whom they regarded as their real enemies. Following the 1989 revolution, fascism has been making a comeback with the **România Mare** ("Greater Romania") party of **Corneliu Vadim Tudor**, which ascribes all the nation's problems to a conspiracy of Jews, Magyars, Gypsies and everyone else who isn't a "pure" Romanian. Their headquarters in Iaşi is rather bizarrely shared with the Ecology Party.

During the 1920s, Iaşi became notorious for **anti-Semitism**, spearheaded by a professor whose League of Christian National Defence virtually closed the university to Jews, then over a third of the population, and later spawned the Iron Guard (see box above). Their chief scapegoat was **Magda Lupescu**, Carol II's locally born Jewish mistress, widely hated for amassing a fortune by shady speculations; in 1940 she fled abroad with Carol in a train stuffed with loot.

Arrival, transport and information

Arriving at Iaşi's main **train station** on Str. Silvestru, or the large **maxitaxi station** across the street (both of which have left luggage facilities), you can either catch tram #3, #6 or #7 (buy a ticket from the driver or at one of the kiosks marked RATI), take a taxi or walk in ten to fifteen minutes to the central Piaţa Unirii. Trains from Chişinău (in Moldova) arrive at the Gara Internaţională in Nicolina, south of the centre. By **bus** you might also arrive at the basic Autogara Iaşi Vest, behind the Autocenter, 1km northwest of the train station on Şoseaua Moara de Foc (tram #2 or bus #30 to Iaşi centre), or the Autogara Eurovoyage, at Str. O. Teodoreanu 49, 100m south of Calea Chişinăului in an industrial wasteland to the southeast of the centre (trams #2, #7, #15). Iaşi's tiny **airport** (☎0232/271 590) is 7km northeast of the centre, and the only way to get to or from it is by taxi (around €8).

Buses and **trams** rock and roll their way to most parts of the city every ten to fifteen minutes (5am–10pm); fares are €0.40 for a single ride, €0.80 for two, €1.50 for a day or €3 for ten rides. In general, **taxis** in Iaşi are metered and reliable, charging around €0.40/km (€0.50/km after 10pm). Delta Taxi (☎0232/222 222) and Pro-Taxi (☎0232/218 584) are two good companies. The city's helpful **tourist information office**, at Piaţa Unirii 12 (Mon–Fri 9am–5pm, Sat 9am–noon; ☎0232/261 990; Ⓦwww.turism-iasi.ro), has a good stock of information as well as a free city map.

Accommodation

Iaşi has a healthy stock of **hotels**, with some decent mid-range options alongside the typically more expensive business-like establishments. Budget possibilities are few, though you might find a bed in one of the many student dorms (*camin de studenţi*) located around the university on B-dul Copou, 1km northwest of the centre (☎0232/201 000; ❶). The wooded *Camping Ciric* (☎0232/219 000; tents ❶, cabins ❷), by a lake 2km north of town on the airport road, is only open in summer; buses run there hourly at weekends (and less frequently during the week) from the Târgul Cocului interchange, outside the Golia Monastery. The city's Antrec's representative, at Str. Sf. Lazar 24 (☎0232/211 060, ✉iasi@antrec.ro), can arrange **homestay** accommodation outside the city.

Continental Str. Cuza Vodă 4 ☎0232/211 846, ✉hotelcontinental@clicknet.ro. Cheapest of the central hotels; the rooms here are a little old-fashioned and rather clumsily furnished, but they're clean enough and all have bathrooms. Air-conditioned rooms cost a little extra. ❸–❹

Hostel Casa Bucovineana Str. Cuza Vodă 30 ☎0232/222 913. A quirky budget place right in the centre offering clean little rooms with TV and shared showers, or with shower but no toilet. With trams rattling by, however, it can get a little noisy. Breakfast not available. ❷–❸

🏃 **Little Texas** Stradela Moara de Vânt 31 ☎0232/272 545, ⓦwww.littletexas.org. Beautifully set on a hilltop out on the road towards the airport, this small and gracious American-run hotel is a cut above anything else in Iaşi. The well-appointed rooms incorporate custom-made US furniture and offer great views from the balconies, while you'll also receive a typically hearty American breakfast in the superb restaurant (see p.250). ❻–❼

Moldova Str. Anastasie Panu 31 ☎0232/260 240, ⓦwww.unita-turism.ro. A high-rise communist-era tower whose smartly designed rooms are much nicer than the exterior suggests, and it's decently priced too; sauna, gym and indoor swimming pool. ❺

Pensiunea Majestic Str. Petru Rareş 7 ☎0232/255 557, ⓦwww.pensiuneamajestic.ro. Close to the main train station but on a quiet street, this large and peaceful guesthouse offers two dozen double rooms mostly furnished in oak, bronze and burgundy, and some have balconies. ❻

Ramada Str. Grigore Ureche 27 ☎0232/256 070, ⓦwww.ramadaiasi.ro. Hidden behind the *Moldova*, this is one of the city's classiest outfits; supremely comfortable rooms with high beds and thick duvets, plush red carpets and glassed-in bathrooms. The adjoining coffee house is lovely too. ❼

Select Piaţa 14 Decembrie 1989 no. 2 ☎0232/216 440, ⓦwww.selectgrup.ro. This handsome building sports wonderfully cool rooms, combining smooth wood furnishings, soft grey carpets and bright, crisp drapes. Good-sized, sparkling bathrooms too. ❽

Sport Str. Sfântu Lazăr 76 ☎0232/232 800. A few hundred metres downhill from the Palace of Culture near the Pod' Ros transit interchange. Passable rooms with bathrooms, hot water and cable TV, but often filled by athletic groups in summer. ❷

🏃 **Traian** Piaţa Unirii 1 ☎0232/266 666, ⓦwww.grandhoteltraian.ro. Atmospheric establishment designed by the Eiffel company in 1882 featuring sky-blue and cream coloured rooms furnished in classic French period style; there are some neat touches too, such as wrought-iron wall lamps, old-style phones, and tea-and-coffee making facilities. ❼–❽

Unirea Piaţa Unirii 5 ☎0232/205 006, ⓦwww .hotelunirea.ro. Although somewhat less glamorous than the adjacent *Traian*, this large 1960s high-rise conceals very modern, sunny and solidly furnished rooms. ❻

The Town

The majority of Iaşi's sights are strung along a north-south axis through the city, with the main square, **Piaţa Unirii**, joining the two halves. To the north of the square, beyond the excellent Museum of the Union, lie the university district of **Copou**, with its parks and gardens, and the residential district of **Ţicău**, location for a couple of memorial houses. South of the square, along B-dul Ştefan cel Mare, stand the city's most important religious buildings, not least the magnificent **Church of the Three Hierarchs**, which in turn leads down to the huge **Palace of Culture**, housing several museums. Beyond here is the Nicolina quarter, where you'll find the hilltop **monasteries**.

Piaţa Unirii and the Museum of the Union

A large, surprisingly lifeless concrete square, **Piaţa Unirii** merits little attention save for a couple of big hotels. Northwest of the square, at Str. Lăpuşneanu 14, you'll find Cuza's mansion, which now houses the absorbing **Museum of the**

Union (mid-April to Oct Tues–Sun 10am–8pm; €3). Cuza actually rented the property between 1859 and 1862, after which time the building served as the headquarters for King Ferdinand during World War I. Whilst the ground floor is largely given over to the history of the union, the first floor reveals more about Cuza himself; the richly furnished rooms where he and his wife, Elena, lived, worked and entertained contain many personal items, such as Cuza's oak bureau, pipe and briefcase in the cabinet office, and a pristine billiard table alongside his cue in the games room. Look out, too, for the many Grigorescu paintings, as well as a coffee set emblazoned with an imperial "N", indicating Napoleon III's support for unification between Wallachia and Moldavia.

The rather comic tale of Cuza's downfall in 1866 is glossed over. Bursting into his bedroom, soldiers found Cuza making love to the King of Serbia's daughter-in-law; when pressed to sign a decree of abdication, he objected, "But I haven't got a pen." "We have thought of that," they said, producing a pen and ink, whereupon Cuza complained of the lack of a table. "I will offer myself," said a colonel, presenting his back to forestall further procrastination, and so Cuza signed and went into exile. He died in Heidelberg in 1873.

South along Bulevardul Ştefan cel Mare

Iaşi's traditional interplay of civil and religious authority is symbolized by a parade of edifices along B-dul Ştefan cel Mare şi Sfânt (simply Ştefan cel Mare on most addresses), where florid public buildings face grandiose churches. Midway along the street is the huge, colonnaded **Metropolitan Cathedral** (Catedrala Mitropolitana), begun in 1833 and completed in 1887, and now being refurbished. Still the largest Orthodox church in Romania, it dwarfs worshippers with its cavernous interior, painted by Tattarescu, and dominates the neighbouring Metropolitan's Palace and Theological College. In 1641, Basil the Wolf spent the country's entire budget for the next year and a half to acquire the **relics of St Paraschiva** of Epivat (c.980–1050), which were moved to the cathedral in 1889. Venerated as the patron saint of Moldavia, households, harvests, traders and travellers, St Paraschiva seems to be a conflation of four Orthodox martyrs of that name. There are pilgrims here throughout the year (some crawling the last 100m or so), but on October 14 (the saint's day) the cathedral overflows with thousands of worshippers who come to kneel before the blue and gold bier containing the relics. Immediately to the south stands the **Old Metropolitan Church of St George** (Biserica Sf. Gheorghe), built in 1761; the pillars of its glassed-in porch are carved with symbolic animal reliefs, in the post-Brâncoveanu style of Wallachia. Inside it's like a mini-Sistine chapel, the large nave painted in a neo-Byzantine style and enhanced by effective uplighting. From 1999–2000 neo-Byzantine mosaics were added in the porch, with four scenes of paradise and one of the arrival of the relics of St Andrew the Apostle in Iaşi in 1996. Just south, the circular **Roman Catholic cathedral** was completed in 2005; the white interior is set off by a lovely mosaic of the Virgin and angels behind the altar, and there's rich stained glass set into the roof on the upper level.

Across the road, and east of the elegant Pumul Verde Park, is the French-eclectic-style **National Theatre**, built by the Viennese architects Fellner and Helmer in the 1890s, with one of the most beautiful auditoriums in the country. The theatre is named after Vasile Alecsandri (1821–90) who co-founded the company in 1840 and, owing to a lack of plays in Romanian, had to write much of its initial repertory.

A few minutes further south along B-dul Ştefan cel Mare from the Church of St George, you arrive at the famous **Church of the Three Hierarchs** (Biserica Trei Ierarhi; daily 9.30am–noon & 3–5pm; €1), its exterior carved all over with chevrons, meanders and rosettes as intricate as lace. When it was completed in

1639 – perhaps by the Armenian master builder Ianache Etisi – Basil the Wolf had the exterior gilded, desiring it to surpass all other churches in splendour. Aside from its unique carvings, the church follows the classic Byzantine trilobate plan, with two octagonal drums mounted above the *naos* and *pronaos* in the Moldavian fashion. Over the following two centuries, the church was damaged by fire and six earthquakes, but was rebuilt by the French architect Lecomte de Noüy from 1882–87. Inside the formidably dark interior you can just make out the **sarcophagi** of its founder Basil the Wolf, Dimitrie Cantemir and Alexandru Ioan Cuza. Since 1990 this has once more been a working monastery. The adjacent abbot's house, in which Basil the Wolf set up Moldavia's first printing press in 1644, contains a display of religious icons (officially Tues–Sun 10am–4pm; ask in the church if the door is locked).

From the Church of the Three Hierarchs, Str. Costache Negri heads east to the **Church of St Sava**, a contemporary yet quite different building whose red pantiles and massive, squat bell tower give it the look of an Andean village church. The tower is doubly impressive for being devoid of ornamentation.

The Palace of Culture and around

At the southern end of Ştefan cel Mare, an equestrian **statue of Stephen the Great** and a cross commemorating the martyrs of the revolution are overshadowed by the stupendous **Palace of Culture** – a neo-Gothic pile built between 1906 and 1925 as a government centre, which now houses four of the city's **museums**. The palace's spired tower and pinnacled wings presage a vast lobby awash with mosaics, stained glass and armorial reliefs, dominated by a magnificent double staircase. However, at the time of writing the entire building was undergoing extensive renovation, with work likely to continue into 2012.

It is anticipated that the museums will be retained within the palace, in which case you can expect to find the **Museum of Science and Technology**, displaying music boxes, symphonia and orchestrions; the **Moldavian History Museum**, which is strong on local archeology; and an **Ethnographic Museum**, whose collection includes a small windmill, 2m-long Moldavian alpine horns, hollow trunks used as beehives, and oil-presses the size of trees. Best of all is the **Museum of Art**, which is divided into Romanian and European galleries, has over two dozen paintings by Grigorescu, and a fine collection by the post-1919 Colourist painters, such as Luchian and Pallady. Portraits of bearded boyars in Turkish fur hats, and scenes of Jewish life by Octav Băncila (1872–1944), give more local colour. In the European section, Ludovic Starski's *The City of Iaşi in 1842* presents an unrecognizable vision of church spires not hemmed in by concrete. There's also a *Pietà* by Murillo and a Rubens of *Caesar Receiving Pompey's Head*. The vaulted Hall of Voivodes (*Sala Voievozilor*), containing the portraits of dozens of rulers, is used for temporary art shows.

Two much-restored relics of Iaşi's past stand between the Palace and the Centru Civic. The arcaded **Casa Dosoftei**, built between 1677 and 1679, is a fitting home for the dull **Museum of Old Moldavian Literature** (Tues–Sun 10am–5pm; €1) – it once housed a press that spread the words of the cleric and scholar Metropolitan Dosoftei, a statue of whom sits outside. The Phanariot policy of using Iaşi's presses to spread Greek as the language of Orthodox ritual had the unintended result of displacing the ossified Old Slavonic tongue from this position, clearing the way for intellectuals to agitate for the use of their own language, Romanian. Close by is the **Courtly Church of St Nicholas**, in theory the oldest building in Iaşi, erected by Stephen the Great in 1492 but pulled down and rebuilt by Lecomte de Noüy from 1885–97; its svelte facade now masks a hermetic world of carved pews and gilded frescoes.

From the Centru Civic to Golia Monastery

From the south end of B-dul Ştefan cel Mare, Str. Anastasie Panu leads east through the typically grey and austere **Centru Civic**, though there are a couple of shopping malls to brighten things up here. Further east, opposite the World Trade Center and next to an open park at Str. Ghica Vodă 26, you can catch a glimpse of the former **Barnovschi Monastery**, founded by Prince Miron Barnovschi in 1627; it's now reduced to a white church with a Baroque porch and two onion-shaped spires, flanked by a gate tower through which you enter the church. The **Bărboi Monastery**, at the far end of the main road, has fared better. Housed in a tranquil walled garden with a tall neo-Byzantine gate tower, it still bears the name of Urşu Bărboi, who founded it in 1613, although the present Church of Peter and Paul, with an overhead gallery for the choir, was built from 1841–44 by Dimitrie Sturdza, who is buried in the *pronaos* in a tomb covered with Greek inscriptions. It's a large open church, painted throughout, with a gilt iconostasis.

A little to the north, beyond the busy Str. Sărărie, you can see the Star of David atop the **Great Synagogue** – a sad misnomer for this low-domed edifice built between 1659 and 1671 and restored after an earthquake in 1977, shortly before most of its congregation left for Israel. Outside is an obelisk to the victims of the pogrom of June 28–29, 1941.

Just west, beyond the Târgul Cucu bus and tram interchange, is the **Golia Monastery**, a peaceful haven in the heart of Iaşi whose dozen monks enjoy a rose garden dotted with shrines and protected by a 30m-tall gate tower and rounded corner bastions. Founded in the 1560s by Chancellor Ion Golia, when the capital was moved from Suceava, the monastery was rebuilt and fortified by Basil the Wolf, who began a new **Church of the Ascension** within the monastery's grounds, completed by his son Ştefăniţa in 1660. The walls and towers were built in 1668 (with the gate tower added in 1855); it was burnt three times and damaged by an earthquake, but survived to become the Metropolitan Cathedral in 1786; however, by 1863 it was a ruin, being rebuilt only in 1947. A striking mixture of Byzantine, Classical and Russian architecture, with the traditional Moldavian domed plan but Corinthian capitals on the exterior, the church boasts of its associations with Tsarist Russia, since it was visited by Peter the Great in 1711, and serves as the burial place for the **viscera of Prince Potemkin**, Catherine the Great's favourite. These were removed so that the rest of his body could be preserved and returned home after he died in 1791, after catching a fever in Iaşi and defying doctors' orders by wolfing huge meals, starting at breakfast with smoked goose and wine. He actually died across the border in present-day Moldova. The interior was painted in 1838 and is being filled with wooden platforms as these are slowly restored; the arcaded eighteenth-century house to the east of the church was home to dean Ion Creangă from 1866 to 1871.

West along Bulevardul Independenţei

Bulevardul Independenţei, a drab thoroughfare linking the Golia Monastery with Piaţa Eminescu, has a few sights worth noting. Midway along the boulevard stands the **old university**, a Baroque edifice that was constructed between 1795 and 1806 as the Callamachi family palace, and given to the university in 1860; now overshadowed by newer wings, it is the centrepiece of the University of Medicine and Pharmacology. On the university's west side rises the **gate tower** of the Sf. Spiridion Monastery of 1786, which now houses a hospital. The monastery's old **church** contains the tomb of its founder, Grigore III Ghica, whose head was sent giftwrapped to the sultan in 1777, for harbouring treasonous thoughts. Opposite the university, at no. 16, the **Natural History Museum** (Muzeul de Istorie Naturală; closed Aug; Tues, Thurs & Sat 9am–3pm, Wed, Fri

& Sun till 4pm; €1) occupies the eighteenth-century Ruset House, in whose Elephant Hall Cuza was elected Prince of Moldavia in 1859. At that time, the house belonged to the Society of Physicians and Naturalists, who had opened their collections to the public in 1834, making this one of the first such museums in Romania. From the street it now seems very run-down, but the entrance is in fact around the corner to the east; there are the usual dead birds and animals, fossils, shells, and a conservation exhibit.

The boulevard leads to the **Independence Monument**, a statuesque woman striding forth ahead of billowing drapery, sculpted by Gabriela and Gheorghe Adoc in 1980, and finally to Piaţa Eminescu. From here, you can head towards the university district or return to Piaţa Unirii via the shopping precinct behind the *Hotel Unirea*.

The university district

Copou, the university district, lies northwest of the centre, out along the B-dul Carol I, where trams (#1, #11 and #13) and buses (#28 and #41) toil uphill. The foot of the hill is distinguished by a Stalinesque **Student House** to the right, with bas-reliefs of musical youths, alongside a small park overlooked by statues of Moldavian princes, and the colonnaded **Eminescu Library** on the opposite side of B-dul Carol I. Working as a librarian in an earlier incarnation of this building, Eminescu could nip across the road (just where a statue of him now stands sage-like in a cloak) for meetings of the Junimea literary society (1863–85) in the **Casa Pogor**, just north of the Student House at Str. Vasile Pogor 4. Casa Pogor was built in 1850 by Vasile Pogor, a co-founder of the Junimea society, and now houses the **Museum of Romanian Literature** (Tues–Sun 10am–5pm; €2). In re-creating the atmosphere of Iaşi's literary world at that time, the ground floor is laid out with furnishings belonging to both the Pogor family and the former prime minister, Mihail Kogălniceanu; take a close look at the wonderful ceramic stoves in each room. The second floor is largely devoted to the activities of the society itself, though the star exhibits are Eminescu's death mask and his gold ring and watch – indeed, Eminescu (see box below) lived here for a very brief period in 1874.

It's a few minutes' walk further uphill to the **A.I. Cuza University**, an Empire-style edifice built in the 1890s, which acts as an umbrella for 26 faculties and eight research institutes of the Romanian Academy. Just to the north are the Titu Maiorescu Dendrological Park, then fine 1880s villas housing the Goethe Zentrum and Chamber of Commerce. Also here are the tranquil **Copou Gardens**, where Eminescu meditated under a favourite lime tree, now squat and ugly and boxed in by a low hedge. In the centre of the park a small cultural centre houses the dreadfully dull **Eminescu Museum** (Tues–Sun 10am–5pm; €1).

Mihai Eminescu

Mihai Eminescu, Romania's national poet, was born in 1850 in Botoşani, east of Suceava, and schooled in Cernăuţi, the capital of Habsburg Bucovina. At the age of 16, he gave his surname, Eminovici, the characteristic Romanian ending -escu and became a prompter for a troupe of actors, until his parents packed him off to study law in Vienna and Berlin. Returning to Iaşi in 1874, he found a job as a librarian, joined the Junimea literary society, and had a tortured affair with Veronica Micle, a poet and wife of the university rector. After the rector's demise, Eminescu decided that he was too poor to marry her and took an editorial job in Bucharest to escape his grief. Overwork led to a mental breakdown in 1883, and from then on, until his death from syphilis six years later, periods of madness alternated with lucid intervals. He is best remembered for *Luceafărul* (*The Evening Star*), a 96-stanza ballad of love.

Further out on B-dul Carol I is Romania's oldest **Botanic Garden**, at Str. Dumbrava Roşie 7 (mid-April–Oct 9am–8pm, Nov–mid-April 9am–5pm), founded in 1856 and moved in 1963 to this site, with a lake and a seventeenth-century church. The rose garden and the tropical greenhouses are particularly attractive.

Ticău

Ţicău is a pretty, hilly, old residential quarter, east of the university area, with lime trees, some modernist houses (from the 1930s–50s), and two memorial museums that provide an excuse for a ramble. At no. 11 on the street that now bears his name, the **house of Mihail Kogălniceanu** (Wed–Sun 10am–5pm; €1) commemorates the orator and journalist who was banned from lecturing for lambasting "oppression by an ignorant aristocracy". He fled to Habsburg Bucovina in 1848, returning in the 1850s to help secure Cuza's election and serve as foreign minister. More entertaining is the **cottage of Ion Creangă** (Bojdeuca), dating from 1850 at the latest, at Str. Simion Bărnuţiu 4 (Tues–Sun 10am–5pm; €1), which displays first editions and prints of his works, including stills from films based on them. A defrocked priest and failed teacher, Creangă (1837–89) wrote *Recollections of Childhood* and fairy tales such as the *Giants of Irunica*, finally achieving success just before he died. The pretty, stepped garden in front of the house is used as an amphitheatre for local productions.

The southern monasteries

A more ambitious way to stretch your legs is to visit the **monasteries** in the Nicolina district, south of the city centre. Catch bus #9 or a southbound maxitaxi downhill past the Palace of Culture and out along Str. Nicolina; cresting the flyover, you'll see the Cetăţuia and Galata monasteries on separate hilltops to the east and west, and a modern Roman Catholic church with a prow-like spire in the valley, which is where you should alight. From here, either follow Str. Tudor Neculai west up the hill and past a cemetery to Galata Monastery, or cross the main road and head east through apartment buildings and under the tracks to find Frumoasa Monastery and the trail south to Cetăţuia. If you're intending to visit all three, it's best to see Cetăţuia first and work your way back to the others, as the hike to Cetăţuia requires the most effort.

The **Galata Monastery** stands on Miroslavei hill and is entered by a fortified gate tower. To the right of the gateway, beside a newer building in use today, are the ruins of the original monks' quarters and a Turkish bath. The monastery's church was built between 1579 and 1584 to a typically Moldavian plan, with an enclosed porch and narthex preceding the nave, which was painted in 1811. Its founder, Prince Petru Şchiopul, is buried in the nave with his daughter, Despina.

Frumoasa Monastery, on a hillock surrounded by low walls, was derelict for decades, but after restoration is close to living up to its name, meaning "beautiful", once more. Largely built by Grigore II Ghica from 1726 to 1733, Frumoasa differs from the other monasteries thanks to the ponderous form of Neoclassicism in favour when the complex was reconstructed in the 1830s. On the north side are Ghica's summer garden and court, beyond a grand marble Neoclassical tomb built in 1842 by Francesco Vernetta for the family of Prince Mihail Sturdza.

For the **Cetăţuia Monastery**, turn left out of the gate onto Str. Cetăţuia and (after five minutes) cross B-dul Poitiers, along which runs bus #43; on the far side the road climbs through woods for 1.5km to a hilltop. You can turn off onto a short-cut path, which is more of a slog. It's well worth the hike, especially if you're not going to Bucovina. Here, the monastery (whose name means "citadel") seems remote from Iaşi; on misty days, the city is blotted out, and all you can see are the surrounding ridges. Its high walls conceal a harmonious ensemble of white stone buildings with rakish black roofs, interspersed by low conifers and centred on a church that's similar to the Church of the Three Hierarchs in town, but hardly carved, except for a cable moulding and Renaissance window frames. Prince Gheorghe Duca and his wife, now buried in the *pronaos*, founded the monastery in 1669, with a royal palace that served as a refuge for the ruling family in time of war.

Eating, drinking and entertainment

Although increasingly sophisticated, Iaşi's **restaurant** scene is steady rather than spectacular. That said, there are now a number of stylish places offering Romanian interpretations of various world cuisines, in addition to the many traditional establishments where you can try Moldavian cooking. Thanks in part to its large student population, Iaşi's reputation for its diverse **nightlife** is well deserved, though it's cool and laid-back rather than particularly energetic. Most of the cafés listed here double as bars, and so are as good for an evening beer as they are for a daytime coffee. In addition to the ones listed below, there are several flashy clubs 2km east of the centre, in the vicinity of the Iulius Mall. To get there, take tram #8, trolley-buses #42 or #43, or any maxitaxi marked *Tudor*.

Restaurants

Casa Bolta Rece Str. Rece 10. Secreted away in a quiet residential area, this legendary and still popular restaurant and wine garden dates back over two centuries. The food is decent traditional Romanian, while the kitsch peasant decor, allied to live folk music most evenings, draws the tourist groups.

Casa Lavric Stradela Sf. Atanasie 21. Handsome three-floored establishment in lime-green and rust-brown, with beautifully set tables and musical instruments dangling from the walls; the adventurous menu concentrates mainly on Moldavian specialities such as *tochitură moldovenească*, though there's plenty of international fare on offer. Unusually, there are well-defined smoking and no-smoking areas.

Cucina Casalinga Str. Costache Negri 6. Unassuming backstreet pizzeria across from the Moldova Mall serving up decent thin crusts on large wooden boards; good lunchtime offers available.

JJ's Grill Str. Grigore Ureche 27. Attached to the *Ramada* hotel, this relaxing grill garden is one of the most enjoyable places to eat in the city. Take your pick from a long list of meats (thin and spicy *Plescoi* sausages, steaks, ribs, wings), soups and salads, or even even fish and chips. Warm and attentive service too.

Little Texas Stradela Moara de Vânt 31. At the hotel of the same name (see p.244), this American establishment offers exemplary burgers, steaks, chicken platters and Tex-Mex, after which you can round it off with apple pie and vanilla ice cream.

Either dine inside, amid the more or less tasteful Wild West decor (smoking downstairs only, on the way to the toilets), or on the fabulous terrace. Impeccable service to boot.

Oscar Str. Lascăr Catargiu 12. Take a seat on the elevated outdoor terrace with its smartly laid wooden tables, brown suede cushioned seats and cool overhead drapes. The food is high-class international fare, though with some Romanian dishes thrown in too. They have the best wine list in town.

Phenicie Str. Sulfinei 13. Although not as refined as *Oscar* immediately next door, and with a much smaller terrace, this colourful Lebanese restaurant has a wide selection of mezze dishes (*tabouleh, fattoush, hummus*), *kofte* and *shawarma* (marinated meats on skewers).

Traian Piaţa Unirii 1. Cavernous echoing place from the days when waiters eavesdropped for the Securitate. The ambience is lovely and the food is on a par with anything else in the city, with prices remarkably low for such a posh place.

Cafés, bars and clubs

Araju Str. Sf. Sava 15. If you want a serious chill-out, this delightful café/bar is perfect, sup a beer or take tea inside the two artily painted rooms, furnished with low wooden bench seating and wicker chairs, red cushions and floor lamps. They occasionally stage low-key concerts.

Arte Café Str. M. Kogălniceanu 11. Just behind the Kogălniceanu memorial house, this classy coffee bar attracts a laid-back crowd to its comfy outdoor sofas and wicker chairs, while the interior is cosy enough for cooler evenings.

Club Pogor Str. Vasile Pogor 4. A small, agreeably tatty concrete terrace, pleasant for an afternoon drink, when you can feel at least vaguely in tune with Eminescu and his pals who held their literary meetings here.

Club RS Str. Fătu 2A. Greek-owned restaurant, bar and cocktail bar whose Mediterranean-style garden plays host to a wired mix of occasional live music and tone-deaf lounge singers. Surprisingly good fun.

Corso Str. Lăpuşneanu 11. Massive semicircular terrace bar set around lush lawns that looks like an MTV dance set; relaxing by day, it becomes a somewhat more invigorating venue at sundown.

Joker Str. Sf. Sava 2. Very popular summer beer garden located a short walk down from *Araju*,

between the National Theatre and the Central Market Hall.

The Stage B-dul Mangeron 71A. Large bar-restaurant near the Chemistry Faculty that has a regular programme of live music focusing mainly on house and electronic, but also with jazz and other events.

Time Out B-dul Copou 4. Wide-open, well-shaded terrace with comfortable wicker furniture to watch the traffic on the boulevard; the funkily designed interior does the job in cooler weather, though it can get smoky.

Tuffli Str. Lăpuşneanu 7. A fixture on this lively pedestrianized street for years, this excellent coffee house and patisserie offers a wide range of beverages, cakes and pastries. Park yourself inside or on one of the terrace's squidgy sofas.

Entertainment

Lovers of classical music should try to attend a performance of the **Moldavian Philharmonic**, the country's best orchestra outside Bucharest. Its own venue, at Str. Cuza Vodă 29, was damaged in a recent fire, and for the next few years performances will be held in either the Luceafărul Youth Theatre, Str. Grigore Ureche 5 (☎0332/407 218, ⓦwww.luceafarul-theatre.ro), the Ateneu Tătăraşi (Str. Pictorului 4) or the Sala Studio Teofil Vâlcu of the **National Theatre**, Str. Agatha Bârsescu 18 (ⓦwww.teatrulnationaliasi.ro). The same venues are all also used by the **Opera Naţională Romana Iaşi**. Tickets are available from the ticket agency (Agenţia Teatrală; Mon–Sat 10am–5pm; ☎0232/255 999) at B-dul Ştefan cel Mare 4, near Piaţa Unirii.

Iaşi's big annual event is the **St Paraschiva festival week** (Sarbatorile Iaşului) starting on October 14, when people from all over Moldavia flood into town to pay homage to the saint buried in the Metropolitan Church. The **Festival of the Three Hierarchs** is celebrated on January 30, when literally a million pilgrims come to worship in the presence of the church's relics. Traditional folklore festivals include the **Folk Music Festival** in mid-December, and a week-long **Ceramics Fair** (Târgul de Ceramicâ "Cucuteni 5000") in mid-June.

Shopping

Iaşi has a decent variety of **shops**, including some of the best **bookstores** and **antique** retailers in the region. The Galeriile Anticariat at Str. Lăpuşneanu 24 (Mon–Sat 9am–9pm, Sun 11am–6pm), selling antiques, icons and secondhand books in several languages, is easily the best shop of its kind in Moldavia, whilst the Galeriile de Artâ at no. 7 is one of the few places where you can purchase genuine pieces of work by Iaşi's finest artists. There are outdoor Anticariat bookstalls along the same street and on Piaţa Unirii, while the secondhand bookshop at Str. Cuza Vodă 15 is also worth a look. The best place for new books in English is the small Librăria Humanitas (Mon–Sat 10am–8pm, Sun 10am–5pm) directly opposite the *Hotel Traian* on Piaţa Unirii; nearby, through the underpass, the Librăria Junimea (Mon–Fri 8.30am–8pm, Sat 9am–5pm, Sun 9am–4pm) stocks books and maps.

On the ground floor of the **Hala Centrala** (Central Market), on Str. Anastasie Panu, you'll find G'Market, the most central of the modern **supermarkets** (daily

9am–10pm), while the smaller, old-style Unic supermarket (Mon–Sat 7am–8pm, Sun 8am–noon) is on Piaţa Unirii. The city's main shopping centre is the **Iulius Mall** (daily 10am–10pm), 1.5km east of the city centre, though far more convenient is the modern Moldova Mall (same times) across from the Palace of Culture.

Listings

Car rental Avis, at the airport (☎0232/228 923, ✇www.avis.ro); Autonom, B-dul Ştefan cel Mare 8 (☎0232/220 504, airport ☎0748/110 557, ✇www .autonom.com); Sixt, Str. Păcurari 4 (☎0232/245 690, ✇www.sixt.ro); and Total Car, Str. Pallady 8 (☎0232/277 210, ✇www.totalcargrup.ro).

Flights TAROM, Str. Arcu 3–5 (Mon–Fri 9am–5pm; ☎0232/217 027, ✇www.tarom.ro), has 2–4 flights a day to Bucharest. Carpatair, Str. Cuza Vodă 2 (Mon–Fri 9am–7pm, Sat 9am–1pm; ☎0232/215 295, ✇www.carpatair.com), has a daily flight (except Sun) to Timişoara for international connections. Austrian Airlines, at the airport (☎0232/241 144), has a flight to Vienna daily except on Sat.

Hospital Urgenţe (emergency) admission is on the corner of Str. L. Catargiu and Str. G. Berthelot (☎0232/216 584).

Internet The British Council library, Str. Păcurari 4 (☎0232/316 159, ✇www.britishcouncil.ro/iasi; Mon & Tues 1–7pm, Wed–Fri 10am–4pm, closed Aug), is the best place to log on; the entrance is actually on B-dul Carol I. There's also the French Cultural Centre, B-dul Carol I no. 26 (☎0232/267 637; Mon,

Tues & Fri 11am–6pm, Wed & Thurs 11am–7pm), and OK Internet, Str. Maiorescu 3.

Pharmacy Iaşi has three 24hr pharmacies: Centrofarm, B-dul Ştefan cel Mare 3 (☎0232/214 428); Farmacia Sf. Parascheva next to the Kodak shop at Piaţa Unirii 3 (☎0232/220 549); and Rosmarin, Str. Tudor Vladimirescu 44 (☎0232/263 365).

Post office Str. Cuza Vodă 3 (Mon–Fri 8am–7pm, Sat 8am–1pm). There's a smaller branch in the arcade on Str. Muzicescu (Mon–Fri 10am–5pm) immediately south of Piaţa Eminescu.

Sports facilities The Ştrand athletic club, below the Palace of Culture on B-dul Ştefan cel Mare (daily 8am–7pm), has a swimming pool and tennis courts. The Piscina Moldova covered pool is in the *Hotel Moldova* at Str. A. Panu 29.

Train tickets The CFR office is at Piaţa Unirii 10 (☎0232/147 673; Mon–Fri 7.30am–8.30pm); upstairs, you can make international bookings, including for the overnight *Prietenia* to Chişinău in Republica Moldova, for which some foreigners may need a visa, obtainable from the Moldovan embassy in Bucharest (see p.84).

Suceava and around

Crossing the industrial sprawl between the stations and the city centre, it's difficult to imagine **SUCEAVA**, 150km northwest of Iaşi, as an old princely capital. The city's heyday more or less coincided with the reign of **Stephen the Great** (1457–1504), who warred ceaselessly against Moldavia's invaders – principally the Turks – and won all but two of the 36 battles he fought. This record prompted Pope Sixtus IV to dub him the "Athlete of Christ" – a rare accolade for a non-Catholic, which wasn't extended to Stephen's cousin Vlad the Impaler (see p.403), even though he massacred 45,000 Turks during one year alone.

While Stephen's successors, **Bogdan the One-Eyed** and **Petru Rareş**, maintained the tradition of building a new church or monastery after every victory, they proved less successful against the Turks and Tatars, who ravaged Suceava several times. Eclipsed when Iaşi became the Moldavian capital in 1565, Suceava missed its last chance of glory in 1600, when **Michael the Brave** (Mihai Viteazul) completed his campaign to unite Wallachia, Moldavia and Transylvania by marching unopposed into Suceava's Princely Citadel. In terms of national pride, Suceava's nadir was the long period from 1775 to 1918, when the **Habsburgs** ruled northern Moldavia from Czernowitz (Cernăuţi), although Suceava was able to prosper as a trading centre between the highland and lowland areas.

Under communism, this role was deemed backward and remedied by hasty **industrialization** – the consequences of which long blighted the town. Its

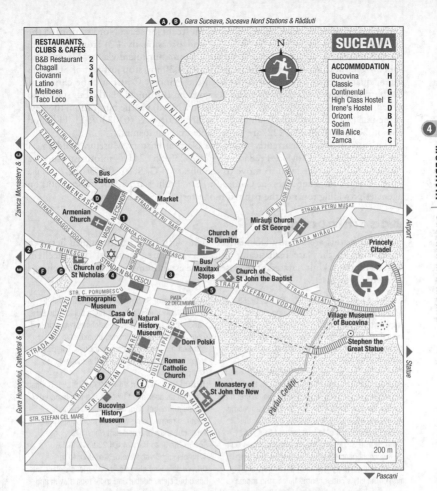

Pascani ▼

wood-processing and tanning plants poisoned the Suceava River for kilometres, while the "Suceava Syndrome" of malformed babies was linked to air pollution from the artificial fibres factory. The paper mill, one factory that has seen some success in recent years, is responsible for the distinctive odours with which Suceava is too often enveloped. For visitors, Suceava is primarily a base for excursions to the **painted monasteries** (see p.259), although the town itself has several worthwhile sights, not least the superb Bucovina village museum.

Arrival, transport and information

The Suceava River and adjoining industrial areas separate the city's three train stations from the city centre and from each other. **Suceava Nord** (in the Iţcani suburb, 6km northwest) is the most useful and the one where most trains stop. The other useful station is Gara Suceava in Burdujeni, a similar distance north. The **bus station** is just northwest of the town centre on Str. V. Alecsandri. Suceava's **airport**, 12km east of town, is accessible only by taxi (around €15). Public transport is provided by buses on key routes (notably to the train stations) and private **maxitaxis**. Buses #1 and #5 run from Ițcani (Suceava Nord station) to the southwestern suburb of Obcini; bus #2 (and occasionally #3) from Burdujeni (Gara Suceava) to Obcini; and bus #4 from Cinema Burdujeni via Str. Marașești to Obcini. All these buses (every 10min, 4.15am–10.30pm) stop just east of Suceava's main square, Piața 22 Decembrie, between the Princely Court and the church of St John the Baptist. Maxitaxis #6 and #9 go from Burdujeni via the bus station to Obcini; maxitaxi #12 runs from Ițcani (Suceava Nord) via the bus station, the new cathedral (Str. Enescu) and Zamca to Obcini. Eurotaxi (T0230/511 111) and Canon Taxi (T0230/522 222) are respectable taxi companies.

The **tourist office** is currently inside the Natural History Museum building, at Str. Ștefan cel Mare 23 (Mon–Fri 8am–4pm; T0230/551 241, Einfoturist@suceava .rdsnet.ro), but is scheduled to move to the library (I.G. Sbierea) near the *Bucovina* hotel. There's **internet** access at Games Pit, Str. Eminescu 13. For information on agencies providing tours of the painted monasteries, see the box on p.263.

Accommodation

Suceava's **hotels** are a really lacklustre bunch, with little to distinguish between them, though they are realistically priced. There are, however, two excellent hostels in town. Unless stated otherwise, all the establishments listed below charge extra for breakfast.

Bucovina B-dul A. Ipătescu 5 T0230/520 250, Wwww.hotelbucovina.ro. Still bearing all the trappings of the communist era, this ugly high-rise on the centre's southern fringe is a bit shabby, though all rooms have shower and a/c; it's very cheap too. ❷–❸

Classic Str. Universității 32 T0230/510 000, Wwww.classic.ro. Run-of-the-mill hotel in the university district, 700m southwest of the centre; the rooms are drab and a little tatty, and the bathrooms are on the small side, though there's always the decent Swedish buffet to look forward to. ❸–❹

Continental Str. Mihai Viteazul 4 T0230/304 904, Wwww.continentalhotels.ro. Cheek by jowl with the fifteenth-century church of St Nicolas, this is one of the city's better central hotels; the rooms are painted in the slightly dull blue colour that is the trademark of the chain, but they're comfortable and reasonably sized. Breakfast included. ❹

🏃 **High Class Hostel** Str. Eminescu 19 T0723/782 328, Wwww.classhostel.ro. On a quiet street (fork left at *B&B Restaurant*), this friendly and sweet little hostel offers bunk-bed dorms with glassed-in balconies, one double room, bathrooms upstairs and down, and a kitchen. A simple breakfast and unlimited coffee and tea all day are included in the price. The owner leads excellent trips to the monasteries (see p.263). ❶

Irene's Hostel Str. Armenească 4 T0744/292 588, Wwww.ireneshostel.ro. Right behind the bus station, this small and tidy hostel has two four-bed rooms as well as one double; breakfast is not included but there is a kitchen for use. The owners of this hostel also offer trips to the monasteries (see p.263). ❶

Orizont Str. Jean Bart 24 T0230/518 851. Budget option in an apartment block just a few hundred metres in front of Gara Suceava, the hideously coloured rooms come with bathroom and TV. It's a small cut above the adjacent *Socim*. ❷

Socim Str. Jean Bart 24 T0230/516 901, Ehotelsocim@yahoo.com. Next door to the *Orizont*, this very cheap and very friendly place has basic but clean double and triple rooms, with and without bathrooms and TV. ❶

Villa Alice Str. Simion Florea Marian 1 bis T0230/522 254, Wwww.villaalice.ro. Centrally located but very peaceful pension with a variety of differently priced rooms; the more expensive ones have a/c, DVD player and balcony. Good value. ❷–❹

Zamca Str. Zamca 28 T0230/521 008, Wwww .hotelzamca.ro. Named after the monastery which it stands next to, this bright hotel has the most modern rooms of any in town. It's a twenty-minute walk from the bus station, from where you can also take a taxi. ❸–❹

The Town

Suceava's principal sights are a good twenty minutes' walk from the centre, namely the **Princely Citadel** and **Village Museum** to the east, and the **Zamca**

Monastery to the west. The city's remaining attractions, including a cluster of fine churches, are close to the main square, **Piaţa 22 Decembrie**.

Piaţa 22 Decembrie and around

Immediately north of the main square is the **Church of St Dumitru**; built by Petru Rareş from 1534–35, it is typical of Moldavian churches of the period, with a double row of niche-bound saints under its eaves, and coloured tiles ornamenting its drum. The interior frescoes of gruesome martyrdoms date from the sixteenth to the nineteenth centuries and have recently been restored. The freestanding bell tower, added in 1561, bears the Moldavian crest (see box, p.256). A short walk west from the church, along Str. Petru Rareş, will bring you to Suceava's hectic **market**, which is busiest on Thursdays, when cartloads of peasants roll into town to sell their produce. Some wear traditional dress, such as leather or sheepskin waistcoats lined with polecat fur, wraparound skirts or white woollen pantaloons.

The **Church of St John the Baptist**, built as his court chapel by Basil the Wolf in 1643, is just east of Piaţa 22 Decembrie, on the far side of the main B-dul Ana Ipătescu. It's simple yet attractive, with a tiny dark interior and a small bell tower linked only by its roof to the church. At weekends, visitors may witness funerals here, where the deceased is laid out in an open coffin, amid candles and loaves of bread, while a horse-drawn hearse waits outside. Northeast of the square along Str. Mirăuţi is the **Mirăuţi Church of St George**, the oldest in Suceava. Founded by Petru I Muşat in about 1390, this was the Metropolitan cathedral, where the early princes of Moldavia were crowned. Its facade is decorated with blind arches and a sawtoothed cornice sandwiched between thick cable mouldings, while below the eaves are frescoes of saints, added when it was heavily over-restored between 1898 and 1903 by Emperor Franz Jozef I.

Fine embroideries and crafts are exhibited in the **Ethnographic Museum** at Str. Ciprian Porumbescu 5 (Tues–Sun 10am–6pm; €1), one block west of Piaţa 22 Decembrie via Str. Bălcescu. The museum is housed in a half-timbered building, the oldest civil edifice in Suceava county, which served as the court guesthouse in the seventeenth century. Immediately south of Piaţa 22 Decembrie, in between Str. Ştefan cel Mare runs parallel to and B-dul Ana Ipătescu, the drab **Natural History Museum** (Muzeul de Ştiinţele Naturii; Mon 8am–3pm, Tues–Sun 9am–5pm; €1.50) possesses the usual stuffed species, as well as a modest aquarium and vivarium. Alongside it, the Roman Catholic church, built in 1836, is a plain Neoclassical building now shared by Greco-Catholic and Armenian-Catholic congregations. Further down, at no. 33, the **Bucovina History Museum** (Tues–Sun 10am–6pm; €1) begins with an array of Neolithic shards, and works stolidly on through medieval times and the independence struggles. There's better coverage of World War II here than in most Romanian museums, plus some portraits by local artists. The main attractions are the treasury, full of gold ornaments, and a life-size model of Stephen's throne room, occupied by richly costumed figures. Continuing west on Str. Ştefan cel Mare you'll come to the big half-built **Orthodox cathedral** (at the junction of Str. Mârăşeşti and Str. Enescu), which will be the seat of the new archbishopric of Suceava and Rădăuţi, which was only created in 1991.

Midway between the two museums, Str. Mitropoliei heads east to the **Monastery of St John the New** (Mănăsteria Sf. Ioan cel Nou), easily identified by its colourful steeple striped with blue, black and yellow chevrons. Started by Bogdan the One-Eyed in 1514 and finished by his son Ştefăniţă in 1522, its monumental **Church of St George** was intended to replace the Mirăuţi Church as Suceava's Metropolitan cathedral, so no expense was spared. In 1534 it was painted inside and out with frescoes like those of the painted monasteries of Bucovina, but only the *Tree of Jesse* on the south wall (the far side) and a fragment of the *Last Judgement* on the west end remain, both in very poor condition. The interior frescoes are now being restored. The relics of St John the New rest here, to the right of the nave, and are taken on a grand procession through the city each year on June 24, the feast of St John the Baptist (the feast of Sânziene). St John the New's martyrdom is depicted inside a small chapel near the church, where nuns now run a shop selling religious paraphernalia. Arrested for preaching in Turkish-occupied Moldavia in 1332, he was dragged through the streets of Cetății Alba behind a horse, and slashed to death by enraged Muslims. There's also a pavilion housing a 230-litre drum of holy water, for the faithful to take away in bottles.

The Princely Citadel and the Village Museum of Bucovina

Suceava's most impressive monument is the **Princely Citadel** (Tues–Sun 10am–6pm; €1), which overlooks the city from a hill to its east. Also known as the Throne Citadel of Moldavia (Cetatea de Scaun a Moldovei), it was built by Petru I Mușat (reigned 1375–91), who moved the Moldavian capital from Siret to Suceava; it was subsequently strengthened in the fifteenth century by Alexander the Good. Stephen the Great added the moat, curtain walls and bastions that enabled it to defy the artillery of Mohammed II, conqueror of Constantinople, in 1476. Although blown up by Dumitrascu Cantacuzino (as ordered by the Turks) in 1675, much of the three-storey keep and the outlying chambers remain; unfortunately, the view towards the town is now largely obscured owing to the thicket of trees standing in the way.

In a former pasture opposite the citadel, you'll find the superb **Village Museum of Bucovina** (Muzeul Satului Bucovinean; mid-March to mid-Oct Tues–Fri 10am–6pm, Sat & Sun 10am–8pm; €1.50), a work in progress currently displaying some two dozen wooden buildings, all removed from Bucovina villages and reassembled on the site. Most are late nineteenth- or early twentieth-century structures, uniformly constructed from fir beams and reinforced with whitewashed clay, then topped off with shingled roofs. Some buildings, including a family house from Roșu (near Vatra Dornei) and a sizeable tavern from Șaru Dornei, have been furnished with colourful textiles, handmade furniture and housewares, while many of the region's traditional crafts and industries are also represented – a potter's workshop from Marginea and a flour mill from Humor. There's also a wooden church from Vama, a chunky stone and wood edifice dating from 1783 and which is still used for services – alongside it stands an octagonal bell tower. Throughout the summer various shows are

Prince Dragoș and the aurochs

Throughout Moldavia, churches display the emblem of the medieval principality, often over the main gateway: an aurochs' head and a sun, moon and star. This symbolizes the legend of **Prince Dragoș**, who is said to have hunted a giant **aurochs** (the *zimbru* or European bison) all the way across the mountains from Poland, until he cornered it by a river and slew the beast after a fight lasting from dawn to dusk – hence the inclusion of the Sun, Moon and Morning Star in the emblem. Dragoș's favourite hunting dog, **Molda**, was killed in the fight, and the prince named the River Moldova in her honour, adopting the aurochs, the mightiest animal in the Carpathians, as his totem. The last wild aurochs in Romania was killed in 1852 near Borșa, although captive-breeding populations survive, notably at Vânători Neamț, just west of Târgu Neamț.

performed on the open-air stage just inside the entrance; the main event is the **Folk Handicraftsman Fair** taking place in August.

To reach the citadel and the museum, head east from Piaţa 22 Decembrie through the park and across the bridge into the woods, where rather steep steps lead up to a giant equestrian **statue of Stephen the Great**, unveiled in 1977; the bas-reliefs on the pedestal depict his victory over the Turks at Vaslui in 1475. From here a road leads around the Village Museum to the car park and cafés between it and the citadel.

Zamca Monastery

The neglected ruins of the Armenian **Zamca Monastery** straddle a plateau on the northwest edge of town, twenty minutes' walk from the centre along Str. Armenească or a short walk from Str. Mărăşeşti. The Armenian diaspora had reached Moldavia by 1350, and Alexander the Good founded the Armenian bishopric of Suceava in 1401; in 1551, they fell foul of the Rareş family, leading to a pogrom, but in 1572 an Armenian actually became ruler of Moldavia. The buildings here, which combine Gothic and classical elements with oriental motifs, were founded in 1606 and later fortified with ramparts and a gate tower. The three-storey gatetower and guesthouse, where dignitaries were once accommodated, is currently closed as part of the long and slow restoration project, though you can view the plain white church, which is home to a few lovely **frescoes**. Though not much from a monumental standpoint, the site has a desolate grandeur, particularly at dusk, when you can walk around the earthworks. Also worth seeing are the simple sixteenth-century **Armenian church of the Holy Cross** (Sfânta Cruce; daily 9am–2pm), immediately south of the bus station, and the active **Hagigadar Monastery**, dating from 1513, 15km south of Suceava.

Eating, drinking and entertainment

Suceava's **nightlife** is scarce, though one place that does pull in large crowds is *Café Giovanni*, a sizeable venue at Str. Nicolae Bălcescu 1; popular with early morning coffee drinkers (light breakfasts are available too), it's transformed into a heaving lounge bar by nightfall, with DJs, live music and themed parties. Otherwise, *Chagall* (see below) is as good a place as any for a beer. The excellent **Ciprian Porumbescu Dance Ensemble** (Ansamblul Artistic Ciprian Porumbescu; ℡0230/531 280), a folk dance troupe named after the Romanian composer, performs in the Dom Polski, at B-dul Ana Ipătescu 5, beside the Sfânta Înviere Church. The ensemble is often away on tour, but is sure to appear at the **folklore festival** at Ilişeşti, in July (see box, p.258).

Though there are one or two good **restaurants** in town, the selection is rather limited – if you want to sample Bucovina's indigenous cuisine, you'll be much better off in village guesthouses near the monasteries.

B&B Restaurant Str. Eminescu 18B. Despite the strange name (don't be fooled by the "Pensiunea" sign, there's no accommodation here) and unassuming appearance, the food at this little corner establishment is fresh and very tasty, and the staff do their best to please.
Chagall Str. Ştefan cel Mare 19. A lively pizzeria/pub in the courtyard east of the pedestrian plaza and south of the church of Sf. Dumitru. The lunch menu (€4) is a bargain.
Latino Str. Curtea Domnească 9. Opposite the bus station, this cool Italian place is the best restaurant

in town, with superb pasta and pizza, German beer, and professional and friendly service.
Melibeea Piaţa 22, Decembrie. Next to *McDonalds*, this always busy outfit doles out excellent breads, sweet and savoury bites, and coffee – sit down or takeaway.
Taco Loco Str. Vasile Bumbac 5. Although this place casts itself as a Mexican, the emphasis is most definitely on Romanian food, with Moldavian specialities such as *tochitură bucovineană* and *tochitură moldovenească* forming the mainstay of a lengthy and varied menu.

Festivals at Ilişeşti

Many villages in northern Moldavia, including Ilişeşti, 15km along the main road west from Suceava, still hold **winter festivities** that mingle pagan and Christian rites. Preparations for Christmas begin in earnest on St Nicholas's Day (December 6), when people butcher pigs for the feast beside the roads – not a sight for the squeamish. Women get to work baking pies and the special *turte* pastries, which symbolize Christ's swaddling clothes, while the men rehearse songs and dances. On Christmas Eve (Ajun), boys go from house to house, singing carols that combine felicitations with risqué innuendo, accompanied by an instrument that mimics the bellowing of a bull. After days of feasting and dancing, the climax comes on the day of New Year's Eve, when a dancer, garbed in black and red, dons a goat's-head mask with wooden jaws, which he clacks to the music of drums and flutes, and whips another dancer, dressed as a bear, through the streets. It's a rather bizarre twist on the new year driving out the old, apparently. Ilişeşti also hosts the **From the Rarău Mountain Folklore Festival** (De sub montele Rarău), on the second Sunday of July. Ensembles from three counties – Bacău, Neamţ and Maramureş – participate, and it's a chance to experience a round dance (*horă*), shepherds' dances, fiddles, flutes and alpine horns, plus a panoply of costumes. Ilişeşti is easily reached from Suceava by buses and maxitaxis towards Gura Humorului, which will also drop you at the Motel Han Ilişeşti (☏0788/404 290, 0722/345 221, ⊛www.hanulilisesti.ro) to the west at km232 (although this will be full at festival times).

Dragomirna Monastery and Pătrăuţi Church

The nearest of the Bucovina monasteries to Suceava is the (unpainted) Drago-mirna Convent, 3km beyond the village of **Mitocul Dragomirnei**, which is 12km north of Suceava. As there is almost no public transport to the monastery, the best way to get there without taking a taxi is to get a ride, in a minibus or private car, from the Dragomirna turn-off on the outskirts of Suceava. Take bus #1 to Iţcani, get off under the road bridge by the railway, and walk across the tracks to the right-hand or east side of the main road, Str. G.A. Ghica. The turn-off is on the right, 50m ahead, from where it's 4km to the start of the village and 4.5km more to the monastery, which is hidden from view by rolling plains until the last moment. You may have to walk from the village, but you'll pass a couple of sheepfolds along the way.

Massively walled like a fortress, the **Dragomirna Monastery** was founded in 1602 by Metropolitan Anastasie Crimca, who designed its **church**, which is dramatically proportioned at 42m high but only 9.6m wide. There's a cable moulding around the exterior, and Renaissance windows. The octagonal tower, set on two star-shaped pedestals, is carved with meanders and rosettes, like the Church of the Three Hierarchs in Iaşi. Inside, it doesn't seem so high and thin, gradually rising by steps to the *pronaos* and *naos*, with an unusual star-vault and a very ornate Baroque iconostasis. Crimca himself is buried in the *pronaos*; his portrait is visible on the pillar to the left as you walk through.

The complex's solid walls and towers were added in 1627 owing to the threat of foreign invasions. These were so frequent that wooden village churches were sometimes mounted on wheels so that they could be towed away to safety. The complex is in excellent condition, with living quarters on two sides for the nuns who farm much of the surrounding land, and a **museum** harbouring five of the surviving 26 manuscripts of the school of illuminators founded here by Crimca, himself a talented artist. One 1602 manuscript features Crimca's self-portrait, the earliest known by a Romanian. Also on display is an enormous candle first lit for the monastery's consecration in 1609. The tiny original church is in the cemetery, to the left as you leave by the gateway, but it is usually locked. **Accommodation** in the convent is for women only, and only up to four of them at a time. The lodgings are comfortable (but lacking hot water), and the ambience is tranquil. Opposite the convent, and open to both sexes, is a complex of cabins (❶) with a snackbar.

A few kilometres further north on the main DN2/E85 is the turning to **Pătrăuți**, the first church founded by Stephen the Great, in 1487. After the turning it's 3km east through Pătrăuți village to the church at the far end, facing a museum about the church, where you should ask for entry if the church itself is locked. The prototype for subsequent Moldavian churches, it also contains the oldest paintings in Moldavia, and is on UNESCO's World Heritage list. Alas, only fragments of a *Last Judgement* are visible on the exterior.

From the church, signs show that it's just 6km to Dragomirna Monastery; the road is closed to cars, but it makes a lovely easy **hike**, once you're past the Gypsy area on the edge of the village and into the state forest. An easier option is to start from Dragomirna and then fork left to return via Lipoveni to Mitocul Dragomirnei, a loop of about 5km.

Southern Bucovina

The **painted monasteries of Southern Bucovina**, in the northwest corner of Moldavia, are rightfully acclaimed as masterpieces of art and architecture, steeped in history and perfectly in harmony with their surroundings. Founded in the fifteenth and sixteenth centuries, they were citadels of orthodoxy in an era overshadowed by the threat of infidel invaders. **Grigore Roșca**, Metropolitan of Moldavia in the mid-fifteenth century, is credited with the idea of covering the churches' outer walls with paintings of biblical events and apocrypha, for the benefit of the illiterate faithful. These **frescoes**, billboards from the late medieval world, are essentially Byzantine, but infused with the vitality of the local folk art and mythology. Though little is known about the artists, their skills were such that the paintings are still fresh after 450 years of exposure. Remarkably, the layer of colour is only 0.25mm thick, in contrast to Italian frescoes, where the paint is absorbed deep into the plaster.

Perhaps the best of these are to be found at **Voroneț**, whose *Last Judgement* surpasses any of the other examples of this subject, and **Sucevița**, with its unique *Ladder of Virtue* and splendid *Tree of Jesse*. **Moldovița** has a better all-round collection, though, and **Humor** has the most tranquil atmosphere of them all. Nearby **Putna Monastery**, though lacking the visual impact of the painted monasteries, is worth a visit for its rich historical associations.

The monasteries are scattered across a region divided by **rolling hills** – the *obcine* or "crests" which branch off the Carpathians – and by the legacy of history. Although settlers from Maramureș arrived here in the mid-fourteenth century, the area remained barely populated for two centuries until Huțul shepherds moved south from the Ukrainian mountains. They lived in scattered houses in the hills, and the region was a sort of free republic until the Habsburgs annexed northern Moldavia in 1774, calling it Bucovina, a Romanized version of their description of this beech-covered land (Büchenwald). Soon the place was organized and the Huțuls moved into villages such as Argel, Rașca, Moldovița and Ciocănești, where they could better be taxed and drafted into the army. Bucovina remained

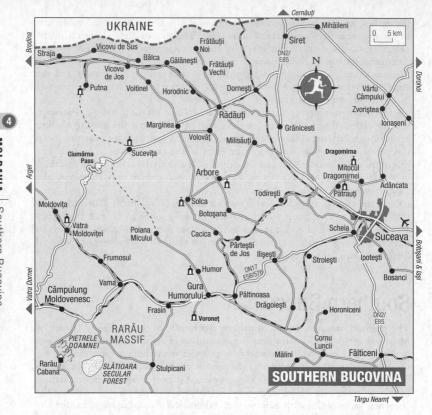

Târgu Neamţ ▼

under Habsburg rule until the end of World War I, when it was returned to Romania, only to be split in half in 1940 – the northern half being occupied by the Soviet Union and incorporated into Ukraine, where it remains today. Thus, Romanians speak of **Southern Bucovina** to describe what is actually the far north of Moldavia – implying that Bucovina might be reunited one day. Names aside, the scenery is wonderful, with misty valleys and rivers spilling down from rocky shoulders heaving up beneath a cloak of beech and fir. The woods are at their loveliest in May and autumn.

Gura Humorului

The monasteries of Voroneţ and Humor lie a few kilometres either side of **GURA HUMORULUI**, a small logging town an hour west of Suceava by bus or train that has more than enough facilities to make a satisfactory base. In the nineteenth century its population was seventy to eighty percent Zipser German and twenty percent Jewish; the Germans left after 1945 and the last Jew died in 2006, so the population is now all ethnic Romanian.

Be sure to leave the **train** at Gura Humorului Oraş station, adjacent to the **bus** station ten minutes' walk west of the town centre, and not Gura Humorului station amid the fields to the east. Humor Monastery is serviced by maxitaxis that shuttle to and from Gura Humorului every twenty to thirty minutes, but there are none to Voroneţ. Both monasteries, however, are within walking distance of Gura

Humorului; there are also plenty of taxis. In the small park across from the *Best Western Bucovina* hotel, you'll find the **tourist information hut** (☎0330/100 394), where you can pick up information on the region, arrange accommodation in Humor, Voroneţ and elsewhere, and organize monastery tours.

The **Bucovina Museum of Folk Customs** (Muzeul Obiceiurilor Populare din Bucovina; Tues–Sun 8am–4pm; €1), by the huge new Orthodox church at Piaţa Republicii 2, displays temporary shows of art, usually by émigré Romanians, on the ground floor, and ethnographic displays upstairs. These are built around tableaux of Christmas, New Year and Easter scenes, showing carol singers, masque costumes (such as the king and queen, bears, witches and Gypsies), fish traps, beehives, a smithy and a sheepfold.

Accommodation

Best Western Bucovina Piaţa Republicii 18 ☎0230/207 000, ⊛www.bestwesternbucovina.ro. A ten-storey block towering over the roundabout at the centre of town, this is the finest large hotel in this part of Romania. The rooms are well appointed and there are lots of good facilities including sauna, Jacuzzi and Turkish bath. ➐

🏃 **Casa Cristian** Str. Victoriei 22 ☎0230/230 864, ⊛www.cristianhouse.com. Just off the road to Humor, 1.5km north of the centre, this magnificent four-star pension is a class above anything else in town, with individually designed rooms and Austrian-style glassed-in balconies. Cristian's top-class facilities are complemented by gracious hospitality, scrumptious organic meals, and a manicured garden with over a hundred varieties each of roses and tulips. The house also hosts regular Sunday morning concerts by some of Europe's finest classical musicians. ➏

🏃 **Hilde's Residence** Str. Şipotului 2 ☎0230/233 484, ⊛www.lucy.ro. Fabulous boutique guesthouse just off the main road to Voroneţ, with smooth, crisp rooms of varying degrees of comfort. A lovely flower garden with

gazebo and a top-notch restaurant round things off superbly. ➍–➏

Pensiunea Lions Str. Ştefan cel Mare 39 ☎0230/235 226, ℮pensiunea.lions@yahoo.com. Situated at the turning to the train station, this vaguely alpine-looking place possesses eight cosy and quirkily designed rooms, furnished with lovely hand-carved wooden beds. Breakfast is extra but this is still terrific value. ➌

Pensiunea Renate Str. Ştefan cel Mare 43 bis ☎0230/235 039. It looks pretty uninviting from the outside, and the reception (the bar) is slightly off-putting, but the en-suite rooms are perfectly clean and tidy, not to mention ridiculously cheap. Breakfast not available. ➊

Simeria Str. Mihail Kogălniceanu 2 ☎0230/230 227. ⊛www.hotelsimeria.ro. Centrally positioned, this is the only other conventional hotel in town, a low-key place with distinctly average, but very cheap, rooms. Breakfast is extra. ➌

Vila Fabian Str. Câmpului 30 ☎0230/232 387. Out on the road towards Voroneţ, this is a clean and friendly mid-range option, offering good food, saunas and massages, plus billiards and other games. ➋

Eating and drinking

The only decent **restaurant** in Gura Humorului, though you wouldn't know it from outside, is the *Moldova* at Str. Ştefan cel Mare 16. The English menu features a variety of delicious and inexpensive local specialities; the *sarmale* are good, as are *pârjoale moldoveneşti* (lightly fried meatballs in a rich tomato sauce). Otherwise, the restaurants in the *Hilde and Best Western Bucovina* hotels offer excellent international cuisine. For self-catering, there are various minimarkets along Str. Ştefan cel Mare, all stocking more or less the same range of products.

Voroneţ Monastery

Ion Neculce's chronicle records that Stephen the Great founded **Voroneţ Monastery** in 1488 to fulfil a pledge to his confessor, the hermit Daniil, who had previously assured the despondent *hospodar* that, should he undertake a campaign against the Turks, he would be successful. The Turks were duly forced back across the Danube, and Voroneţ was erected in three months; chronologically, it comes between Putna and Neamţ monasteries. Its superb **frescoes** – added at the behest of Metropolitan Roşca between 1547 and 1550 – have led to Voroneţ being dubbed the "Oriental Sistine Chapel", and put "Voroneţ blue" into the lexicon of art alongside Titian red and Veronese green. Obtained from lapis lazuli, this colour appears at its most intense on a rainy day, just before sunset.

The church was designed to be entered via a door in the southern wall, with a closed exonarthex replacing the usual open porch, thus creating an unbroken surface on the western wall (at the far end). Here is painted a magnificent *Last Judgement*, probably the finest single composition among the painted monasteries. Fish-tailed bulls, unicorns and other zodiacal symbols form a frieze below the eaves, beneath which Christ sits in majesty above a chair symbolizing the "Toll Gates of the Air", where the deceased are judged and prayers for their souls counted. On either side are those in limbo, the Turks and Tatars destined for perdition. Beneath them, devils and angels push sinners into the flaming river that sweeps them down to hell. In response, graves open, a sunken ship is returned from the deep, and wild animals come bearing the limbs of those they have devoured – all except the deer (a symbol of innocence) and the elephant (no threat in Romania). Amusingly, there's a crush of righteous souls at the gates of the Garden of Heaven.

The south wall, seen as you enter, is covered by three compositions: comic-strip scenes from the lives of St Nicholas and St John on the buttress; a *Tree of Jesse*; and a register of saints and philosophers where Plato is depicted with a coffin-load of bones. There are more saints and philosophers on the curved east end. Weather has largely effaced the frescoes along the north-facing wall, but you can still distinguish Adam and Eve (clothed in the Garden of Eden, semi-naked and ashamed thereafter), the first childbirth, the discovery of fire and the invention of ploughing and writing. Also notice *Adam's Deed*, illustrating the myth that Adam made a pact with Satan.

Inside, the walls and ceiling of the exonarthex are painted with martyrdoms and miracles. The second row from the bottom on the left depicts Elijah in his "chariot of fire" (like a standard Romanian *caruţa*), intent on zapping devils with his God-given powers. According to local folklore, God promptly had second thoughts and restricted Elijah's activities to his name day. On the right-hand sides of the narthex and star-vaulted sanctuary are the **tomb of Daniil** the hermit, and, facing the altar, a fresco of Stephen, his wife Maria Voichiţa and their son Bogdan presenting the monastery to Christ. After 1786, the monastery was dissolved and

Visiting the painted monasteries

Tours

Given that almost everyone comes to Southern Bucovina to visit the **painted monasteries** but public transport to them is limited, it's not surprising that many visitors opt for organized **tours**, which can be arranged either in Suceava or Gura Humorului. In **Suceava**, tourist agencies will provide a comfortable car with a driver for between €60 and €80, depending on the number of sights, and an additional €5–10 for an English-speaking guide. The fee is generally for the car (or minibus), not per person; the best agency in Suceava is Gigi Turism (☏0330/102 680, ✉travel@gigiturism .com), which offers a rate of €20–30 per person for those willing to share a car with others. Ciprian Slemcho, at *Irene's Hostel* (see p.254), and Monica Zavoianu, at Suceava's *High Class Hostel* (see p.254), are both knowledgeable independent guides who offer day tours of the main four monasteries for around €25 per person (minimum three). Another option, which may be a bit cheaper if you bargain well, is to hire a taxi driver for the day, though the majority of nuns who give tours do not speak English (usually just French or German). You'll have more time to see the monasteries if you choose to stay in **Gura Humorului**, where *Vila Fabian* (see p.261) runs. tours for between €50 and €80, and there are plenty of private taxis for hire. The higher prices for tours from both Suceava and Gura Humorului include Putna Monastery, which is out of the way and thus more expensive to visit (and also makes for a long, rushed day).

On your own

By making the trip independently, you'll be able to spend more time at each monastery and stay in Bucovina's charming **pensions**, many of which serve terrific home-cooked, organic meals. There's not much choice at Moldovița, but plenty at and around the other monasteries. The route entails striking out from Suceava and following a circular course that requires some backtracking, although this can be avoided by hiking across the hills at certain points. It can be done in reverse, but it's most convenient to head first to **Gura Humorului**, the jumping-off point for Voroneț and Humor. From Gura Humorului, it's relatively easy to reach Vatra Moldoviței, site of Moldovița Monastery, but from here travel becomes more difficult; the road that leads from here to Sucevița Monastery is traversed only by two buses a day, and light traffic makes hitching uncertain. The road continues from Sucevița Monastery to Rădăuți, where you're likely to have a long wait for a train to Putna; otherwise there are hourly maxitaxis back to Suceava. A good compromise is to make Gura Humorului your base, see Voroneț and Humor on your own, and then either book a tour to the rest with *Vila Fabian* or commandeer a taxi for the day.

Though the monasteries have no set **visiting hours**, you can assume they'll be open daily from 9am to 6pm (8pm in summer). There is a modest **admission charge** (€1), which includes entrance to the **museums** (all closed Mon) attached to the monasteries, plus a surcharge (€2) for cameras or videos (which are not allowed inside the churches anyway). As working convents or monasteries, they prohibit smoking and ask that visitors dress appropriately; a few robes are kept on hand for those who arrive in shorts. The small markets set up outside the monastery entrances in summer are among the best places in the country to buy **traditional handicrafts**.

---

the surrounding monks' cells disappeared, but are now being rebuilt; the **bell tower** also survives. More information about the iconography of the frescoes can be found in *The Sacred Monastery of Voroneț*, a passionate and intelligent (though awkwardly translated) guide to the monastery by resident nun Elena Simionovici, on sale at the entrance for about €3.

A **taxi** from Gura Humorului to Voroneţ shouldn't cost more than €2, but on a fine day it's no hardship to walk the 4km; from the train station (where you can leave baggage), head left along the main road, Str. Ştefan cel Mare, for 750m to the clearly signposted turn-off. There's no chance of going astray on the valley road – fork right after 3.5km to the monastery, entered by a gate near the cemetery. Of all the monasteries, Voroneţ is the busiest with tourists and, being the smallest, can feel very crowded if you come at the wrong moment. Larger groups, however, rarely stay long; wait a bit and you may have the place to yourself.

With Gura Humorului so close, you'll probably not need to **stay** the night, but there are some good options if you do: turning left after the bridge (1.3km from the main road), the *Voroneţ Residence* (☎0230/231 024, ⓦwww.voronet-residence.ro) has rooms in both a newer building (❸) and an older, cabana-style building (❶); you can **camp** here too, in the wide-open field between the hotel and the river. Somewhat more impersonal is the *Casa Elena* (☎0230/235 326, ⓦwww.casaelena .ro; ❺), at the entrance to the village (the north end), a large complex of villas with smart double rooms. Across the road is the simple and comfortable *Pensiunea Căprioara* (☎0230/232 542, ⓔvoronet_turism@yahoo.com; ❷). You'll also find plenty of houses offering rooms (*cazare*) throughout the village.

Humor Monastery

In another valley 4km north of Gura Humorului, passing the Jewish cemetery, the tranquil village of **Mănăstirea Humor** straggles towards its namesake, the sixteenth-century **Humor Monastery**.

Unlike the other complexes, Humor is protected by a wooden stockade rather than a stone rampart (although the ruins of the stone wall can be seen), and lacks a spire over the *naos* – indicating that it was founded by a boyar, in this case Teodor Bubuiog, Chancellor of Petru Rareş, in 1530; he is now buried here with his wife Anastasia. The **frescoes** were painted by Toma of Suceava; the prevailing hues are reddish brown (from oriental madder pigment), but rich blues and greens also appear.

The *Last Judgement* on the wall beneath the unusual open porch is similar to that at Voroneţ, with the significant difference that the Devil is portrayed as the Scarlet Woman, though this patch is now so faint that you can't actually tell. Such misogyny had its counterpart in the peasant conception of hell, which was said to be a cavern upheld by seven old women who had surpassed Satan in wickedness during their lifetimes. Since the women are mortal, the legend goes, the Devil (Dracul) must constantly search the world for replacements – and he never fails to find them. The *Tree of Jesse* along the northern wall has been virtually effaced by weathering, but restorers have touched up the *Hymn to the Virgin* on the south front (with a wonderful *Adoration of the Virgin and Child* in the middle). As at Voroneţ, this depicts her miraculous intervention at the siege of Constantinople by the Persians – although the enemy was changed into Turks for propaganda purposes. Morale may have been stiffened, but neither murals nor the stone watchtower added by Basil the Wolf could save Humor from marauding Turks, and the monastery was eventually declared derelict in the eighteenth century. The interior is also fully painted with the usual calendar of saints and martyrdoms, as well as St Luke painting the Virgin and Child. It is now a small convent – the villagers use another church, on a nearby hillock.

Twelve kilometres further up the Humor valley, three **trails to Suceviţa Monastery** have their starting point at the long strung-out, Slovak-populated village of **Poiana Micului**; the easiest (marked by blue stripes) follows a forestry track and takes about five hours.

Practicalities

Maxitaxis leave for Humor from Gura Humorului's Piaţa Republicii, next to the *Best Western Bucovina* hotel, though it's a pleasant walk in warm weather. If you don't want to walk back, wait for a maxitaxi at the bench just below the fork in the road. The monastery is 200m to the left of the cemetery.

The village is awash with **pensions** (all ❷), all of which are close to the monastery. French is spoken at most places, though owners' children are likely to speak English. Two especially welcoming, family-run places are the *Marion* guesthouse, next to the village church at Str. M. Sadoveanu 3 (✆0230/572 829), with two rooms and two apartments, and *Casa Ancuţa* (✆0744/638 749), 150m north of the monastery at Str. Ştefan cel Mare 154, which has eight homely rooms with and without bathroom; both of these places serve delicious meals. Also lovely is *Casa Buburuzan*, just down from the monastery (✆0230/572 861), which has five rooms with shared bathrooms. *Casa Gheorgiţa* (✆0230/572 784), across the road and 100m north of *Casa Ancuţa*, has upstairs rooms giving a lovely panorama of the valley; it's also possible to **camp** here.

Moldoviţa Monastery and Vatra Moldoviţei

Approaching from Gura Humorului, you'll find the **Moldoviţa Monastery**, a couple of hundred metres to the right shortly after entering the village of **Vatra Moldoviţei**. The monastery is a smaller complex than Suceviţa but equally well defended, its ivy-clad walls enclosing white stone buildings with lustrous black-shingled roofs. It was founded in 1532 by Stephen the Great's illegitimate son, Petru Rareş, during whose reign the Turks finally compelled Moldavia to pay tribute and acknowledge Ottoman suzerainty. The monastery was painted (inside and out) by Toma of Suceava in 1537, at a time when Petru Rareş still hoped to resist the Turks, despite the inexorability of their advance since the fall of Constantinople in 1453.

To raise morale, the Turkish siege was conflated with an earlier, failed attempt by the Persians in 626 AD. A delightfully revisionist *Siege of Constantinople* along the bottom of the south wall depicts Christians routing the infidel with arrows and cannons, and miraculous icons being paraded around the ramparts. Illustrated above this is the *Hymn to the Virgin*, composed by Metropolitan Sergius in thanksgiving for her intervention, while to the right is a lovely *Tree of Jesse*, with dozens of figures entwined in foliage. All the compositions are set on an intense blue background. There's a parade of saints and philosophers on the east end, but little remains on the north wall.

The open porch contains a fine *Last Judgement*, showing a crowd of dignitaries growing agitated as a demon drags one of their number, said to be Herod, by his beard towards the fires below, where Satan sits on a scaly creature – defaced with oddly formal German graffiti, left during the years 1786 to 1931 when the monastery was closed down by the Austrians. Within the church, saints and martyrs are decapitated en masse around the narthex, nave and the intervening tomb chamber, whose doorway bears an expressive *Virgin and Child*. Although built on a Byzantine plan, the church has Gothic windows and Renaissance internal doors. Note the charming mural of Petru Rareş with his wife and sons, dutifully presenting the monastery to Jesus, on the right as you enter the nave, and the superb Crucifixion and Pentecost in the conches (virtually side apses) of the nave.

Nuns' cells line the south side of the compound, while in the northwest corner rises an imposing two-storey *clisarniţa*, a guesthouse for passing dignitaries, with a circular tower. Built in 1612, this contains a **museum** of monastic treasures including a silver-chased Evangelistry presented by Catherine the Great and the wooden throne of Petru Rareş, a bust of whom stands outside.

There are no other important sights here, but of all the monastery villages Vatra Moldoviţei is the most isolated and picturesque. It's also the highest, and the air here feels cleaner than elsewhere in Bucovina. Shepherds' trails in the surrounding hills offer ample opportunities for **walking**, with the added incentive of a view of the monastery from above.

Practicalities

Vatra Moldoviţei can be reached by a limited number of bus and train services, only two of which continue to Suceviţa Monastery. Even hitching is likely to take a while, as there's not much traffic over the Ciumârna Pass, which separates the two monasteries. This is a very scenic route, built only in the 1950s by the army, with a viewpoint at the pass over the low, parallel Obcinele Bucoviniei ridges.

Trains to Vatra Moldoviţei run from Câmpulung Moldovenesc via Vama (see below), heading up a branch line that runs through Vatra Moldoviţei's main street, en route, confusingly, to Moldoviţa proper. Trains depart from Vama at 7.10am, 3.35pm and 11.24pm; the 14km trip takes 45 minutes. Returning, they pass through Vatra Moldoviţei at 1pm and 7.15pm. A few buses and maxitaxis from Câmpulung Moldovenesc pass through Vama and Vatra Moldoviţei on the way to Moldoviţa and the obscure Huţul hamlet of Argel. The two daily **buses** from Câmpulung to Rădăuţi that cross the Ciumârna Pass leave Vatra Moldoviţei at 7.45am and 3.30pm, reaching Suceviţa Monastery at 8.30am and 4.30pm. In the other direction they leave Rădăuţi at 6.30am and 3pm, passing Suceviţa about half an hour later and Vatra Moldoviţei about an hour after that.

There's not much **accommodation** in Vatra Moldoviţei, and the best of it is the charming *Vila Crizantema* at Str. Mănăstirii 204 (☎0230/336 116, Ⓔvilacrizantema @yahoo.com; ❷), just off the main road on the way to the monastery. It's an attractive and comfortable pension with small and well-furnished en-suite doubles and simple, delicious meals. Another good choice is *Vila Lulu* (☎0744/396 685, Ⓔvilalulu @yahoo.com; ❷), a chalet-style pension/campsite with swimming pool, tennis court and trout pond, as well as the only restaurant in the area. It's 1.5km north of Moldoviţa Monastery on the road to Suceviţa. For self-catering, there are a few basic shops on the main street, as well as a Sunday market that stretches for 1km through the village.

VAMA, the next village west of Gura Humorului on the Suceava–Câmpulung highway and railway, is the jumping-off point for Vatra Moldoviţei and offers more opportunities for staying overnight. It's pretty enough, but less remote and tranquil than Vatra Moldoviţei. *Casa Lucreţia*, set on a hillside 400m west of the Moldoviţa road at Str. Caragiale 18 (☎0230/239 100, Ⓦwww.casa-lucretia .ro; ❸), is a superb pension with huge double and triple rooms in a stylish modern building. In the centre you can stay at *Pensiunea Letiţia*, just south of the main road at Str. Gării 20 (☎0230/239 212; ❷), or *Casa Iasmina* at Str. Cuza Vodă 10 (☎0724/835 106; ❷).

Suceviţa Monastery

Suceviţa Monastery – the last and grandest of the monastic complexes to be built in Bucovina – is a monument to Ieremia Movilă, Prince of Moldavia, his brother and successor Simion, and his widow, Elisabeta, who poisoned Simion so that her own sons might inherit the throne. The family first founded the village church in 1581, followed by the monastery church in 1584, and its

4

walls, towers and belfry in stages thereafter. The fortified church's massive, whitewashed walls and steep grey roofs radiate an air of grandeur; its **frescoes** – painted in 1596 by two brothers – offset brilliant reds and blues with an undercoat of emerald green.

Entering the monastery through the formidable gate tower, you're confronted by a glorious *Ladder of Virtue* covering the northern wall, which has been largely protected from erosion by the building's colossal eaves. Flights of angels assist the righteous to paradise, while sinners fall through the rungs into the arms of a grinning demon. The message is reiterated in the *Last Judgement* inside the unusual fully closed porch – reputedly left unfinished because the artist fell to his death from the scaffolding – where angels sound the last trumpet and smite heathens with swords, Turks and Jews can be seen lamenting, and the Devil gloats in the bottom right-hand corner. Outside the south porch, you'll see the two-headed Beast of the Apocalypse, and angels pouring rivers of fire and treading the grapes of wrath. The iron ox-collar hanging by the north doorway is a *toaca*, beaten to summon the nuns to prayer.

The *Tree of Jesse* on the south wall symbolizes the continuity between the Old Testament and the New Testament, being a literal depiction of the prophecy in Isaiah that the Messiah will spring "from the stem of Jesse". This lush composition on a dark blue background amounts to a biblical Who's Who, with an ancestral tree of prophets culminating in the Holy Family. *The Veil* represents Mary as a Byzantine empress, beneath a red veil held by angels, while the *Hymn to the Virgin* is illustrated with Italianate buildings and people in oriental dress. Along the bottom is a frieze of ancient philosophers clad in Byzantine cloaks – Plato bears a coffin and a pile of bones on his head, in tribute to his meditations on life and death.

Inside the narthex, the lives of the saints end in burning, boiling, spit-roasting, dismemberment or decapitation – a gory catalogue relieved somewhat by paintings of rams, suns and other zodiacal symbols. Ieremia and Simion are buried in the small tomb chamber (*camera mormintelor*) between narthex and *naos*, in marble tombs carved with floral motifs. The frescoes in the tomb chamber are blackened by candle smoke, but those in the nave have mostly been restored and you can clearly see a votive picture of Elisabeta and her children on the wall to the right. Ironically, her ambitions for them came to naught as she died in a Sultan's harem – "by God's will", a chronicler noted sanctimoniously.

Sucevița's **museum**, to the east in what was once the council chamber, displays a collection of richly coloured tapestries, including sixteenth-century tomb covers featuring the portraits of founder Ieremia Movilă and his brother Simion, as well as icons, an ancient wooden lectern and illuminated manuscripts bound in silver. By climbing the **hill** behind the village church's graveyard, you can see the complex as a whole, and appreciate its magnificent setting at the foot of the surrounding hills, carpeted with firs and lush pastures. The **trail to Humor** starts next to the *Pensiunea Memory*, about 1km north of the village. It's not well marked, but heading southeast from here it should take about five hours to reach **Poiana Marului**, 12km north of Humor along a logging road that's busy enough to make hitching feasible. Opposite the monastery a forestry road leads north, continuing over the watershed (as a trail marked with blue crosses) to Putna.

Practicalities

Sucevița lies midway between Moldovița Monastery, 30km to the west beyond the Ciumârna Pass, and Rădăuți, 17km to the east. The two daily **buses** from

Rădăuți to Câmpulung that cross the Ciumârna Pass leave at 9.30am and 3pm, passing Sucevița about half an hour later and Vatra Moldoviței about an hour after that. In the other direction, they leave Vatra Moldoviței at 7.45am and 3.30pm, reaching Sucevița at 8.30am and 4.30pm. There are more to the east of Sucevița, with half a dozen a day heading for Rădăuți and three turning south at Marginea (known for its black pottery) for Solca, Gura Humorului and Câmpulung.

There are plenty of **places to stay** in Sucevița. A short walk east of the monastery, set back from the main road at no. 478, ⚲ *Casa Felicia* (☎0230/417 083 or 0745/560 253, ⊜cazac_dama@yahoo.co.uk; ❷) has six gorgeous bedrooms decked out wall to floor with local textiles; if you can, try and bag one of the two rooms in the traditional wooden house. The owners of the house also run the *Reteaua Verde* ("Green Network") information centre, and can provide assistance on local crafts, architecture and **walking trails**, for instance to Putna or Humor. The neighbouring *Motel Han* (☎0745/796 754; ❷) doesn't look great from the outside, but it's perfectly acceptable.

Heading in the opposite direction, 1.5km southwest of the monastery, the *Popas Turistic Bucovina* (☎0230/417 000, ⓦwww.popas.ro) has rooms in four charming wood-panelled houses (❹), each with a communal area, and a range of modern villas (❹–❺). There's space here for camper vans (with electrical hook-ups) but not for tents, and facilities for tennis and horseriding, as well as a good restaurant.

Putna Monastery

Putna Monastery lacks the external murals of the painted monasteries, but as the first of the great religious monuments of Southern Bucovina and the burial place of Stephen the Great, it is rich in historical associations and is as important to Romanian patriots as to the Orthodox faithful. The slow train ride past meandering rivers and fir-clad hills whets your appetite for **PUTNA** village, a wonderful jigsaw of wooden houses with carved gables and shingled roofs. Head west from the station to the main road and bear left for the monastery, which is at the end of a tree-lined drive, 1km further on, beyond a cemetery and a garish new church. Behind this church is the **wooden church** (Biserica de Lemn) of Dragoș-Vodă, supposed to be the oldest in Romania, built by Dragoș in 1346 and moved to its present location by Stephen in 1468. It's very picturesque, with no tower.

In 1466, Stephen chose the site of **Putna Monastery** by firing an arrow from the steep hill that now bears a white cross. The monastery was burnt down and rebuilt in 1484, 1536 and 1691, ravaged by war three times in the seventeenth century, and repaired in the eighteenth (by Metropolitan Iacob Putneanu, who was born here and is buried in the porch), only to be damaged by an earthquake and restored again in 1902 and from 1955 to 1988. Its walls and bell tower were plainly intended for defence; in these less troubled times, they emphasize Putna's status as a patriotic reliquary. The bust of Eminescu inside the entrance identifies the national poet with Moldavia's national hero Stephen the Great, and commemorates the speech he gave here in August 1871, on the occasion of the monastery's quadricentennial: "Let us make Putna the Jerusalem of the Romanian people, and let us also make Stephen's grave the altar of our national conscience". The Pan-Romanian Festival he organized in 1871 was followed by others in 1904 and 2004.

The **church** itself is plain and strong, its facade defined by cable mouldings, blind arcades and trefoil windows, while the interior follows the usual configuration of three chambers: the sanctuary, containing the altar, at its eastern end, separated by the iconostasis from the nave, and the narthex, just inside the *pridvor* or porch – although at Putna this has also been enclosed to form an exonarthex. Prince Bogdan the One-Eyed, the wife of Petru Rareș, and Stephen's daughter and nephew are buried in the narthex, which is separated from the nave by two thick, cable-moulded columns. Here, a graceful arch and a hanging votive lamp distinguish the **tomb of Stephen the Great** from those of his two wives, both called Maria, and two sons. In the narthex lie *voievodes* Bogdan and Petru and their family members. The frescoes, illuminated by stained-glass windows, are now being repainted with gold leaf.

Outside, under the western eaves, stand three **bells**, the largest of which, cast in 1484, was only used to herald events such as royal deaths, and was last rung in 1918, when it was heard as far away as Suceava. Hidden from the communists for almost fifty years, it only reappeared after the 1989 revolution. The middle bell traditionally served for everyday use, while the end one was the gift of an archimandrite who repaired its sixteenth-century precursor. At the rear of the yard stands the **Treasury Tower**, the only building surviving intact from Stephen's time; it kept safe one of the world's most important collections of Byzantine embroidery, now in the Abbot's House to its north. The Abbot's House was converted in 1976 to a museum and displays a wealth of icons, antique embroidery and illuminated manuscripts, as well as a fourteenth-century carved chest that once held the relics of St John the New. The monks' cells along the wall date from 1856 (the other Bucovina monasteries now house nuns, but Putna is still all male). Uphill and slightly to the east of the monastery, there's a curious hollowed-out rock with a door and window, reputedly once the **cell of Daniil the Hermit** – Stephen's confessor, whose prediction led to the foundation of Voroneț Monastery.

Practicalities

Putna is accessible by **train** from Suceava via Rădăuți, but services on this route are few and very slow. There are four or five **maxitaxis** a day from Rădăuți, where you need to change to a bus or maxitaxi to reach Sucevița and the other monasteries. Alternatively, you could **hike to Sucevița** in about five hours, a route now dubbed "the Prince Charles hike" after he walked it. Pick up the route (marked by blue crosses) from Putna station and follow the main valley for about an hour; ignore the turn-off to the left near a hut and a bridge, but take the next turning right, cross another bridge and carry on round to the left, which will bring you out at a forestry hut, called Canton Silvic 13. From here, stick to the track up to another forestry hut, Strulinoasa Sud, which deteriorates into a pony trail as it approaches the watershed, but improves once it descends into an open valley. You should reach the monastery about an hour and a half after crossing the watershed. If in doubt, take the major route at every junction, turning left at the only really ambiguous one.

The best **place to stay** is *Pensiunea Mușatini*, at Str. Mănăstirii 513A (☎0230/414 444, ⓦwww.pensiuneamusatini.ro; ❸), a big modern place on the main road near the station. Rooms have a balcony, big TV and a good bathroom, while there are cheaper rooms with shared bathroom in the attic. On the left just before the monastery, friendly *Pensiunea Isidora* at Str. Mănăstirii 228A (☎0740/776 017, ⓦwww .pensiunea-isidora.ro; ❷) has simple, clean rooms with shared/private bathrooms. Otherwise, try the good-value pensions *Carola* (☎0230/414 188, 0745/295 149; ❶), near the station, or *Aga* at Str. Mănăstirii 165 (☎0230/414 223; ❶), on the right just before the monastery gates. The monastery itself has a guesthouse as well as a summer **campsite** with cabins.

Rădăuți

Going to and from Putna you're obliged to pass through the market town of **RĂDĂUȚI**, which plays a key role in the local transport network as the junction for roads to Suceava, Putna and the painted monasteries of Sucevița and Moldovița. If you find yourself with a wait between connections, there are a few sights of interest in the town centre, including the **Bogdana Church**, facing the roundabout just south of the centre of town, which makes a welcome refuge on a hot day. It's the oldest stone church in Moldavia, built between 1359 and 1365 and in its original state except for the addition of a closed porch in 1559 and a semi-fortified bell tower in 1781. Unlike the monasteries, it has aisles alongside the nave. A few blocks northwest at Piața Unirii 63, on the corner of Str. Republicii (the Sucevița road), the **Ethnographic Museum** (Muzeul Etnografic; daily 9am–5pm; €1) has a fine collection of local costumes and artefacts. It also displays **black pottery** made in Marginea and houses a studio which makes the painted ceramics of birds and flowers that are also typical of the region; items can be bought from their workshop. On the north side of the central plaza, Piața Unirii, the town's large synagogue faces down Str. Putnei. There's also a stud (*herghelia*), known for its Arabian horses, on Str. Bogdan Vodă, on the southern edge of town, where you can ride (☎0230/561 524).

Rădăuți's **bus and train stations** are opposite each other, some 750m west of the centre on Str. Gării. Exiting the train station, turn right (turn left if exiting the bus station) and walk for 100m, round the bend in the road, and up to the main road, Str. Ștefan cel Mare; turning right here will bring you into town. If you need **accommodation**, two very good value places in the vicinity of the stations are the accomplished *Motel La Vatră*, right next to the train station at Str. Gării 9 (☎0230/561 783; ❸), and the *Hotel Fast*, at Str. Ștefan cel Mare 80 (☎0230/560 060, ✉rezervari@fast-radauti.ro; ❸), which also has a decent bistro. A more central alternative is the polished *Hotel Maria*, Piața Unirii 4 (☎0744/637 699, ✉hotelmaria@radauti.info; ❸).

Arbore and Solca

Though **ARBORE** is often grouped together with the painted monasteries by virtue of its external frescoes, it is in fact merely a village church. This quibble aside, however, its kinship in form and spirit is undeniable. Arbore lies on a back road about 35km northwest of Suceava, and **public transport** from the city is intermittent, so that you'll be lucky to get any further than Sucevița or Gura Humorului the same day. **Buses** leave Suceava for Arbore on weekdays at 6.30am, noon and 6.30pm, and at 6.30am on Saturdays; alternatively, the church is 9km west from the village of Milisăuți (populated by Ukrainians who are known for making pickle barrels), served by maxitaxis from Rădăuți.

Opposite the cemetery, 1km east of Arbore's central crossroads, stands the **church**, built in 1503 by Luca Arbore, lord of the village and Marshal of Moldavia, who defended Suceava for forty years before he was treacherously killed in 1523. While its wooden stockade and stone bell tower are rustic enough, its frescoed walls and sweeping roof are as majestic as any monastic edifice. Like the painted monasteries, its **murals**, dating from 1541, follow iconic conventions inherited from Byzantium, which designated subjects for each wall, arranged in rows according to their hierarchical significance. This is obvious on the apses, where the angels and seraphim appear at the top, archangels and biblical saints below, then martyrs, and lastly a row of cultural propagators or military saints.

The best-preserved **frescoes** are found on the relatively sheltered south and west walls. The west wall has eight rows of scenes from Genesis and the lives of the saints, while the eaves and buttresses have protected half of the battered *Last Judgement* at the east end of the south wall, which consigns "heathens" awaiting hell to the top right-hand corner. In the courtyard lie two heavy, hollowed-out stone slabs used for mixing dyes to paint the walls, after they had been rendered with charcoal and lampblack. The founder now lies in the *pronaos*, under a Gothic baldachino with his wife and family members. The **iconostasis**, brought here in 1777 and blackened by centuries of smoke and incense, is at last being cleaned, together with the frescoes of the *naos*.

From Arbore, it's 7km west to a road junction 2km north of the centre of **SOLCA**, where a road leads 500m west to a **church** founded in 1614 by Ştefan Tomşa II. It's also possible to get here by occasional maxitaxis from Rădăuţi. The church was a monastery until 1785 and like other Bucovina monasteries was fortified and used as a garrison in times of crisis. It is tall and heavily buttressed, with the characteristically Moldavian octagonal belfry on a double star-shaped base. The exterior is plain except for its Renaissance doors and windows; the church is unpainted but there are strong cable mouldings inside and a score of processional crosses and banners, as well as a horse-drawn hearse and bier outside. Just before the monastery you'll pass the *Han Solca* (☎0230/477 508; ❷), a friendly local inn with six three/four-bed rooms and one double, all en suite.

Cacica

The old salt mine of **CACICA**, 12km south of Solca, was founded in the late eighteenth century by Austrian emperor Franz Josef II. The first miners to be settled here were Polish, and they named the village after wild ducks (*kaczki* in Polish) found nesting in nearby swamps. Workers of other nationalities followed, and by the mid-nineteenth century Cacica was known for its ethnic mix and nicknamed "little Austria". The Czechs, Germans and Slovenes who once laboured here are long gone, but there is still a sizeable Polish community and lots of Polish visitors to the church (a Minor Basilica) and summer events.

The **old mine** (daily 10am–4pm; €1.50) is in the centre of town, adjacent to the modern mine. Inside, a moderately treacherous staircase descends to a large chamber 25m below the surface, where there is a chapel featuring salt reliefs. Stairs from the chapel open into the next cavern, which is adorned with biblical sculptures, also carved from salt. From here, a long hallway leads to a swimming pool and a tennis court. The rest of the more than 50km of underground passages are off limits to the public. The Cacica air is said to be beneficial for those suffering from respiratory diseases. However, the salt vein here is mixed with clay and needs to be heated to the point of evaporation to crystallize: for many years, fuel oil was used in this process, and today a strong odour of petroleum acts as a deterrent to would-be convalescents.

Câmpulung Moldovenesc

The logging town of **CÂMPULUNG MOLDOVENESC**, 70km west of Suceava on the main road and rail line to Cluj, is chiefly of interest as a base for **hiking** in the Rarău and Giumalău massifs, and as a way-station en route to Transylvania or Maramureş. Being strung out along the valley, it has two **train stations** – alight at Câmpulung Est only if you want to hike straight off up Rarău (or are staying at the *Hotel Eden*). To reach the centre from Câmpulung

Moldovenesc station, exit left and walk along Str. Viitorului for 100m, whereupon you reach the **bus station**; turn right here, past the market (with a small Ukrainian bazaar) and up to the main street, Calea Transilvaniei (which becomes Calea Bucovinei east of the town centre). Another longish block east by the tracks brings you to memorials to the Red Army soldiers killed in 1944 and to political prisoners under communism (a telling conjunction) at Str. D. Cantemir. Left of here is a **riverside park** with embankment paths and decent footbridges east and west; right is the main pedestrianized plaza on Calea Bucovinei – don't miss the impressively kitsch bronze **statue of Prince Dragoş** and the aurochs (see box, p.256).

The **Museum of Wooden Art** (Muzeul Artei Lemnului; Tues–Sun 9am–5pm; €1), beside the gaudy pseudo-Byzantine church at Calea Transilvaniei 10, demonstrates the absolute ubiquity of wooden products in traditional life here. The displays upstairs include fish traps, log beehives, a honey centrifuge, a butter churn and mould, wooden ploughs, hayforks, ceremonial hatchets, carved shepherds' staves, musical instruments, plates, spoons and mugs, and everything else from limebark sandals up to oil and fruit presses and carts and sleighs, with black-and-white photos of them in use. Many are intricately carved, but all have the beauty of functionality and some are very imaginative. There are also some sculptures inside the front door, as well as portrait plaques and modern abstract sculptures; in the yard at the rear are a few wooden houses and gateways. There are captions in English, French and German, but sadly no mention of which kinds of wood are used.

Câmpulung also boasts the late Professor Tugui's vast **collection of wooden spoons** (Colecţia de Linguri din Lemn), a bizarre delight that's said to be the only one of its kind in Europe, just west of the centre (and near the station) at Str. Gheorghe Popovici 1. Look for the numerous colourful plates affixed to the exterior.

Practicalities

Buses leave at 11.30am, 12.45pm and 5.30pm for Rădăuţi via Vatra Moldoviţei (for Moldoviţa Monastery) and Suceviţa Monastery. The best **hotel** in Câmpulung Moldovenesc is the three-star *Eden* (℡0230/314 733, @www.hotel-eden.ro; ❹), with pool, sauna and fitness facilities, at Calea Bucovinei 148, on the edge of town 1km west of the Câmpulung Est station. There's also a tightly packed row of bungalows here (❷). In the centre the high-rise *Zimbrul*, Calea Bucovinei 1–3 (℡0230/314 356, @www.rarau-turism.ro; ❸), is dingy looking but has fairly modern rooms, while the *Pensiune Bucovina*, in a communist apartment block at Calea Transilvaniei 13 (℡0230/311 883, @www.pensiunebucovina.ro; ❹), is in fact pretty nicely presented, with clean tidy rooms. You'll not find anywhere cheaper in the country than the *Pensiunea Incom*, an old-style workers' guesthouse with shared bathrooms, set back to the north at Calea Bucovinei 43 (℡0740/831 065; ❶). The large and lively **restaurant** in the *Bucovina* is comfortably the best place to eat.

The Rarău massif

The **Rarău massif** to the south of Câmpulung is a popular **hiking** spot, with its dense spruce forests harbouring lynx, bears, roebuck and other **wildlife**. Most visitors base themselves at the *Rarău* cabana (❷), 14km and three to four hours' walk up the road from Câmpulung Est station. Reservations can be made through the Rarău tourist agency in Câmpulung. From the cabana, a four-hour trail marked by red triangles leads past the **Pietrele Doamnei** ("Princess's Rocks"), three huge Mesozoic limestone towers, to reach the ancient **Slătioara Secular**

Forest of 50m-high firs and spruces. Another route (red-striped) runs southwest from *Rarău* to the *Giumalău* cabana (3–4hr), from where you can hike on to Vatra Dornei via the Obcina Mică peak (5–6hr). None of these trails is feasible in winter.

The road **to Vatra Dornei** crosses the Mestecăniș Pass (1096m), by way of two villages with Ukrainian-style **wooden churches**, to enter the Bistriţa valley. The *Mestecăniș* cabana (❶) is here, 8km east of the large village of Iacobeni, the site of a murder by poison recounted in Gregor von Rezzori's *The Snows of Yesteryear*, and where trains usually halt after emerging from a tunnel below the pass. Accommodation is available at the *Roşan* cabana in the village of Mestecăniş (☎0742/469 589; ❶) and the good *Pensiunea Braduţul* in Iacobeni (☎0745/357 891; ❷).

Vatra Dornei

Forty kilometres west of Câmpulung Moldovenesc, the former logging town of **VATRA DORNEI** has been better known as a spa since Habsburg times, and has dabbled in skiing and other outdoor activities since the 1970s. The skiing facilities in particular have developed in recent years, and though the slopes themselves are not challenging, Vatra Dornei is an increasingly popular winter destination for Romanians and Ukrainians, and is rich in hotels and pensions, if not sights. Across the river by a footbridge from Vatra Dornei Băi train station (more useful than the Vatra Dornei station, east of the centre), you'll see the ochre and white Baroque casino, once the focal point for visitors but now derelict. Behind this is the spa's large and lovely **park**, home to a few red squirrels, a mineral spring piped through a mock-Gothic tower, a neo-Byzantine church and a small restaurant opposite an onion-domed bandstand. Turning left at the casino and following the river east, you'll come to a junction: to the right is Str. Unirii (the Piatra Neamţ road), with a small **Museum of Natural Science and Hunting** (Muzeul de Ştiinţe Naturale şi Cinegetica; Tues–Sun 10am–6pm; €1) at no. 3. The **Ethnographic Museum** (same hours) is back in the town proper on the corner of Str. Eminescu and Str. Gării, in the Florentine-Renaissance town hall built in 1897; from the train station head along pedestrianized Str. Luceafărului and turn right.

Arrival, information and accommodation

Vatra Dornei's **bus station** and **market** are both 200m east of the casino, although a few long-distance maxitaxis call at the train station instead. The **tourist information office**, across from Vatra Dornei Băi station at Str.Gării 2 (Mon–Fri 9am–5pm; ☎0230/372 767), has town **maps** as well as a map of local **hiking trails**.

Most of Vatra Dornei's many **hotels** are located on the spa side of the river, with a cluster pensions located in the maze of side streets between the ski lifts. Most appealing of the hotels is the *Alpin*, by the Parc ski-drag at Str. Tudor Vladimirescu 5a (☎0230/370 038, ⓦwww.hotel-alpin.ro; ❹), whose facilities include spa (indoor pool, dry and wet saunas), jacuzzi and solarium. Alternatively, the *Carol*, just to the right of the casino at Str. Republicii 3 (☎0230/374 690, ⓦwww.hotelcarol.ro; ❸), is a reasonably elegant establishment. The only hotel on the train station side of the river is the quiet and competent *Silva*, at Str. Dornelor 10 (☎0230/371 033, Ⓔchirutavalentina@yahoo.com; ❸).

On the opposite side of the river, up the hill at Str. Runc 6, *Camping Autoturist* (☎0230/371 829), also has cabins (❶) available in summer. One excellent agrotourism pension, easily accessible only if you're travelling by car, is *Poiana* (☎0745/809 234; ❷), located in the mountain village of Poiana Negri, 15km southwest of Vatra Dornei.

There are fine **hikes** on all sides of Vatra Dornei, as shown on maps available at the tourist office and in hotels such as the *Silva*. One of these (which takes approximately 22hr), to the Rotunda Pass in the Rodna mountains (marked by blue stripes), begins at the Băi station. It then runs up Str. Luceafărului and west along Str. Eminescu, past an abandoned Moorish-style synagogue, and leaves town past a self-styled motel (actually a bar full of hunting trophies) and the **campsite**; you'll need your own camping gear for this hike as there are no cabanas along the route. A shorter trail (marked with blue then red stripes), with more dramatic scenery and a choice of mountain cabanas, heads east from the Băi station to Giumalău (5.5hr), Rarău (9–10hr from Băi station) and Câmpulung Moldovenesc (11–13hr from Băi station). The **chairlift** at the top of Str. Negreşti is open year-round (daily 10am–5pm but sometimes closed from 1–3pm; €4 return); from Str. Republicii, walk up Str. G. Coşbuc or Str. Negreşti, following the *telescaun* signs. The lift takes 25min to ascend to the peak of Dealul Negrii (1300m), where ravens circle over alpine meadows. Bring provisions as the café at the top of the lift is frequently closed. There's also a shorter ski-drag, the Teleschi Parc, immediately west of the park, that operates only in winter, with ski rental shacks and a bar at its foot. An Olympic cross-country ski centre is near the campsite at the top of Str. Runc.

The headquarters of the Căliman National Park are at Str. 22 Decembrie 5 (☎0230/371 104, ⊛www.calimani.ro). The local Salvamont mountain rescue group can arrange guided hiking, ice-climbing, cross-country skiing and mountain biking, and rafting is a particular speciality. Contact Petru Ariciuc at Str. Eminescu 17 (☎0230/372 767, ⊜salvamontdorna@yahoo.com).

Eating and drinking

Hotel **restaurants** aside, the pick of what few places there are to eat in town is the *Londinu* pizzeria at Str. Eminescu 32, where you can chomp on *mici* on the big open terrace. Next door is the fabulous *Bristena* patisserie and coffee house with a delectable selection of cakes and pastries. Other restaurants worth a try are *Camy Lact* on Str. Coşbuc, which also has a small shop where local cheeses are sold, and the Italian-themed *Les Amis* at Str. Luceafărului 15.

Routes to Maramureş and Transylvania

From Vatra Dornei, you can head southeast towards **Neamţ county**, northwest into **Maramureş**, or west into **Transylvania**. Seven buses a day follow the scenic Bistriţa valley down to Poiana Largului, at the northern end of Lake Bicaz and in the vicinity of the Ceahlău massif (see p.239); three of them carry on to Piatra or to Târgu Neamţ.

The route to Maramureş heads up the valley past such lovely villages as **Ciocăneşti**, where Huţul houses with decorated facades are perched on hillocks. There are ski-drags here and newish hiking trails on both sides of the valley, and facilities for equestrian tours. The various guesthouses have a central booking system (☎07739/189 396, ⊜accommodation@ciocanesti.com; ②–③). The village holds a Painted Egg Festival before Easter and a trout fishing festival in July or August. Just north, **Botos** has a new **wooden church** in the Ukrainian style: very broad and square, with one large and four small cupolas. *Hotel Mario & Ema* (☎0230/575 879, ⊛www.hotelmario-ema.ro; ②), with cabins (①), is north of the centre of **Cârlibaba**, founded by Zipser German foresters in the late eighteenth century. Eight kilometres north of the village the road forks towards the Rotunda Pass into Transylvania, and the Prislop Pass into Maramureş, where the **Horă at Prislop Festival** occurs on the second Sunday in August. One bus daily (leaving Vatra Dornei at 1.30pm) crosses the mountains to Vişeu de Sus in Maramureş, while two others run as far as Cârlibaba, from where you could probably hitch over the pass. Heading north instead of west from Cârlibaba, a battered road that ends at the Ukrainian border passes through the tiny Huţul hamlet of Moldova Suliţa. From there it's 7km up a dirt path to the **Lucina Stud**, where the famous Hutzul horses, used for cavalry in Austrian times, are bred. It's possible to ride here for around €10 per hour, although the stud's hotel is semi-derelict.

Of the three routes into Transylvania, the most dramatic is via the **Tihuţa Pass** – otherwise known as the Bârgău Pass, where Bram Stoker located Dracula's castle. Along the way, you'll find accommodation in **Poiana Ştampei**, at the *Vila din Carpaţi* (☎0230/379 312; ❺), located high up beside the main road. There are also a few **pensions** here. Three buses a day from Vatra Dornei run through the pass en route to Bistriţa. Travelling **by train**, you'll take a more northerly route via Ilva Mică; the Leşu Ilvei halt, one stop before Ilva Mică, is within walking distance of Leşu (see p.220). The third route, only possible if you're driving, crosses the 1271m-high **Rotunda Pass**, which is prone to blizzards.

MOLDAVIA | Travel details

Travel details

Trains

Bacău to: Bicaz (3 daily; 1hr 40min–2hr 20min); Iaşi (5 daily; 2hr 15min–3hr 20min); Piatra Neamţ (8 daily; 1hr 10min–1hr 40min); Suceava (9 daily; 1hr 50min–2hr 10min).

Galaţi to: Braşov (1 daily; 5hr 40min); Bucharest (6 daily; 3hr 30min–4hr 15min); Constanţa (1 daily; 5hr 30min); Iaşi (2 daily; 4hr 20min); Mărăşeşti (5 daily; 2hr–2hr 55min); Târgu Mureş (1 daily; 10hr).

Ghimeş to: Adjud (7 daily; 2hr–3hr 15min); Braşov (1 daily; 3hr); Galaţi (1 daily; 4hr 55min); Miercurea Ciuc (4 daily; 1hr 20min–1hr 45min); Siculeni (5 daily; 1hr–1hr 30min); Suceava (1 nightly; 5hr 25min); Târgu Mureş (1 daily; 5hr 25min).

Gura Humorului to: Câmpulung Moldovenesc (4 daily; 1hr); Suceava (4 daily; 55min); Vama (4 daily; 30min); Vatra Dornei (2 daily; 2hr 10min).

Iaşi to: Bucharest (6 daily; 6hr 30min–7hr 20min); Cluj (4 daily; 8hr 40min); Constanţa (1 daily; 8hr 15min); Suceava (7 daily; 2hr–2hr 50min); Timişoara (3 daily; 14hr 30min–16hr).

Piatra Neamţ to: Bacău (8 daily; 1hr 10min–1hr 35min); Bicaz (3 daily; 30–45min); Bucharest (2 daily; 6hr).

Suceava to: Bucharest (6 daily; 6hr 30min–7hr 20min); Câmpulung Moldovenesc (10 daily; 1hr 30min–2hr); Cluj (5 daily; 6hr 30min–7hr 10min); Gura Humorului (4 daily; 55min); Iaşi (8 daily; 1hr 50min–2hr 45min); Putna (4 daily; 2hr 45min–3hr);

Rădăuţi (5 daily; 1hr 30min–2hr); Timişoara (5 daily; 12hr 30min–14hr); Vama (10 daily; 1hr 10min–1hr 50min); Vatra Dornei (9 daily; 2hr 30min–3hr 20min).

Vama to: Moldoviţa (3 daily; 48min).

Vatra Dornei to: Cluj (4 daily; 4hr); Iaşi (4 daily; 4hr 40min–5hr); Ilva Mica (8 daily; 1hr 30min–2hr 15min); Suceava (5 daily; 2hr 35min–3hr 15min).

Buses and maxitaxis

Brăila to: Bucharest (3 daily; Constanţa (1 daily); Focşani (2 daily); Galaţi (every 20min); Tulcea (2 daily).

Câmpulung Moldovenesc to: Cluj (2 daily); Gura Humorului (8 daily); Iaşi (3 daily); Moldoviţa (3 daily); Piatra Neamţ (1 daily); Rădăuţi (4 daily); Suceava (6 daily); Târgu Mureş (1 daily); Vatra Dornei (5 daily).

Galaţi to: Brăila (every 20min); Braşov (3 daily); Bucharest (15 daily); Constanţa (13 daily); Focşani (5 daily); Iaşi (4 daily); Piatra Neamţ (5 daily); Sibiu (2 daily); Soveja (1 daily).

Gura Humorului to: Câmpulung Moldovenesc (10 daily); Iaşi (4 daily); Moldoviţa (1 daily); Piatra Neamţ (1 daily); Rădăuţi (4 daily); Solca (1 daily); Suceava (12 daily); Târgu Mureş (1 daily); Vatra Dornei (3 daily).

Iaşi to: Bacău (every 30–45min); Bicaz (3 daily); Bistriţa (1 daily); Bucharest (hourly); Câmpulung Moldovenesc (2 daily); Cluj (1 daily); Comăneşti

275

(2 daily); Durău (4 daily); Galaţi (3 daily); Gura Humorului (2 daily); Piatra Neamţ (hourly); Rădăuţi (6 daily); Slănic Moldova (1 daily); Suceava (12 daily); Târgu Mureş (2 daily); Târgu Neamţ (hourly).
Piatra Neamţ to: Agapia (2 daily); Bacău (hourly); Bicaz (every 30min); Braşov (2 daily); Bucharest (10 daily); Câmpulung Moldovenesc (1 daily); Cluj (1 daily); Comăneşti (1 daily); Durău (Mon–Sat 2 daily); Gheorgheni (3 daily); Gura Humorului (1 daily); Iaşi (15 daily); Oneşti (2 daily); Rădăuţi (2 daily); Sibiu (1 daily); Suceava (4 daily); Târgu Mureş (1 daily); Târgu Neamţ (hourly); Topliţa (1 daily); Văratec (2 daily); Vatra Dornei (2 daily).
Rădăuţi to: Arbore (3 daily); Câmpulung Moldovenesc (3 daily); Iaşi (5 daily); Putna (5 daily); Solca (6 daily); Suceava (hourly); Suceviţa (8 daily); Târgu Neamţ (1 daily); Vatra Dornei (1 daily).
Suceava to: Bistriţa (4 daily); Braşov (2 daily); Bucharest (3 daily); Câmpulung Moldovenesc (10 daily); Cluj (2 daily); Constanţa (2 daily); Gura Humorului (12 daily); Iaşi (14 daily); Pătrăuţi (Mon–Fri 7 daily, Sat–Sun 5 daily); Piatra Neamţ (2 daily); Rădăuţi (hourly); Solca (Mon–Fri 2 daily); Târgu Mureş (2 daily); Târgu Neamţ (2 daily); Văratec (Mon–Fri 4 daily, Sat–Sun 2 daily); Vatra Dornei (6 daily).
Târgu Neamţ to: Agapia (4 daily); Bacău (1 daily); Bicaz (1 daily); Braşov (1 daily); Câmpulung

Moldovenesc (1 daily); Durău (6 daily); Gura Humorului (2 daily); Iaşi (5 daily); Neamţ Monastery (3 daily); Piatra Neamţ (13 daily); Rădăuţi (2 daily); Sihistria (1 daily); Suceava (4 daily); Târgu Mureş (3 daily); Văratec (3 daily); Vatra Dornei (2 daily).
Vatra Dornei to: Bistriţa (4 daily); Cârlibaba (3 daily); Cluj (2 daily); Gura Humorului (3 daily); Iaşi (1 daily); Piatra Neamţ (2 daily); Poiana Largului (4 daily); Rădăuţi (2 daily); Suceava (7 daily); Târgu Mureş (2 daily); Târgu Neamţ (2 daily); Vişeu (1 daily).

International trains

Iaşi (Nicolina) to: Chişinău, Moldova (1 daily; 5hr 10min).
Suceava Nord to: Cernăuţi, Ukraine (1 daily; 5hr 30min); Kiev, Ukraine (1 daily; 20hr); Moscow, Russia (1 daily; 32hr); Sofia, Bulgaria (1 daily; 18hr).

International buses

Iaşi to: Bălţi, Moldova (2 daily); Chişinău, Moldova (2 daily); Istanbul, Turkey (1 daily).
Suceava to: Cernăuţi, Ukraine (5 daily); Chişinău, Moldova (1 daily); Balţi, Moldova (1 daily); Istanbul, Turkey (1 daily).

Maramureş

CHAPTER 5 **Highlights**

✳ **Wooden churches** With their magnificent spires, wooden churches, such as the finely crafted structure at Şurdeşti, are an integral part of the Maramureş landscape. See p.286 & p.287

✳ **Prison Museum, Sighet** Illuminating and moving tributes to the victims of communism in Sighet's notorious prison. See p.294

✳ **Winter Customs Festival, Sighet** Lively Christmas spectacle featuring folk music, wacky costumes and traditional customs. See p.295

✳ **Merry Cemetery, Săpânţa** Exuberantly coloured and beautifully crafted wooden grave markers in one of Romania's most unusual attractions. See p.295

✳ **Logging train, Vişeu de Sus** Jump aboard the early-morning *mocăniţa* for a picturesque ride up the Vaser valley. See p.303

✳ **Rodna mountains** Beautifully unspoilt mountain range offering some of the country's most enjoyable and secluded hiking. See p.304

▲ Logging train in the Vaser valley

Maramureş

R omania has been described as a country with one foot in the industrial future and the other in the Middle Ages – still true enough of **Maramureş**, crammed up against the borders with Hungary and Ukraine and little changed since Dacian times. Within 30km of industrial Baia Mare, forested mountains and rough roads maintain scores of villages in almost medieval isolation, amid rolling hills with clumps of oak and beech and scattered flocks of sheep.

The historic county of Maramureş, north of the Gutâi Pass, was merged in 1968 with parts of Someş and Satu Mare counties to form present-day Maramureş, though for convenience this chapter also includes the town of Satu Mare and the Oaş region, both in Satu Mare county. The county's main attraction is its **villages**, with their superb wooden houses and churches, and traditional way of life. Every family occupies a compound with its livestock, fenced with timber, brush or latticework, and entered via a beamed gateway (*poarta*), the size of which indicates the family's status and prosperity. Nowhere else in Europe do **folk costumes** persist so strongly, men wearing tiny *clop* straw hats and medieval rawhide galoshes (*opinchi*) or archaic felt boots bound with thongs, and women weaving boldly striped *catriniţa* aprons of cloth from the water-powered fulling mills. They embroider the wide-sleeved cotton blouses worn by both sexes – most conspicuously during markets and **festivals**. On Sunday afternoons people promenade, and there may be a public dance, in the street or on a purpose-built wooden platform. Villagers have retained their traditional **religion** (the Uniate rite alloyed with pagan beliefs), myths and codes of behaviour.

Most interesting of all is the marvellous **woodwork** of Maramureş: the gateways, many elaborately carved with symbols such as the Tree of Life, sun, rope and snake, continue to be produced today, and are rivalled only by the *biserici de lemn* or **wooden churches**, mostly built during the eighteenth century when this Gothic-inspired architecture reached its height. Crouching beneath humpbacked roofs, they rear up into fairy-tale spires, and are generally sited on the highest ground in the village. While some wooden churches are in a poor state, around twenty of the most valuable have been restored in recent years, and eight are on UNESCO's World Heritage List. In recent years many new monasteries have also been constructed, in a modern version of the traditional style. Wooden houses, on the other hand, are vanishing from Maramureş's villages, as modern homes are built and old timbers sold off to panel bars across Western Europe.

It's particularly worth making the effort to see the towering wooden church at **Şurdeşti**, the beautiful church paintings at **Bârsana**, **Rogoz** and **Deseşti**, the frescoes and icons of **Călineşti** and **Budeşti**, the superb prison museum in **Sighet** and the quirky "Merry Cemetery" at **Săpânţa**. Further afield in the Iza Valley, the

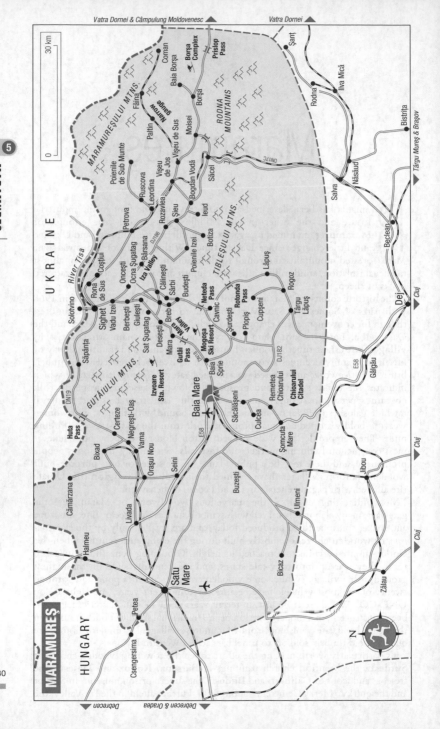

MARAMUREŞ

HUNGARY

UKRAINE

River Tisa

GUTÂIULUI MTNS.

MARAMUREŞULUI MTNS.

RODNA MOUNTAINS

TIBLEŞULUI MTNS.

Vatra Dornei & Câmpulung Moldovenesc

Vatra Dornei

Debrecen

Debrecen & Oradea

Târgu Mureş & Braşov

Cluj

Cluj

Cluj

30 km

0

N

Borşa Complex

Prislop Pass

Coman

Baia Borşa

Borşa

Moisei

Săcel

Şanţ

Rodna

Ilva Mică

Bistriţa

Năsăud

Salva

Beclean

Dej

Gâlgău

Jibou

Zalău

Bicaz

Ulmeni

Buzeşti

Şomcuta Mare

Culcea

Săcălăşeni

Baia Mare

Baia Sprie

Remetea Chioarului

Chioarului Citadel

Cupşeni

Rogoz

Târgu Lăpuş

Lăpuş

Surdeşti

Plopiş

Cavnic

Rotonda Pass

Neteda Pass

Budeşti

Sârbi

Breb

Desești

Mara

Gutâi Pass

Mogoşa Ski Resort

Izvoare Sta. Resort

Seini

Oraşul Nou

Vama

Negreşti-Oaş

Certeze

Huta Pass

Bixad

Cămârzana

Livada

Halmeu

Petea

Csengersima

Satu Mare

Sat Şugatag

Giuleşti

Berbeşti

Vadu Izei

Sighet

Sâpânţa

Solotvino

Rona de Sus

Onceşti

Ocna Şugatag

Coştiul

Petrova

Poienile de Sub Munte

Ruscova

Leordina

Rozavlea

Şieu

Ieud

Bârsana

Călineşti

Iza Valley

Poienile Izei

Botiza

Bogdan Vodă

Vişeu de Jos

Vişeu de Sus

Paltin

Făina

Narrow Gauge

Mara Valley

The Maramureş Pass

The **Maramureş Pass** is a card that gives tourists discounts of between 5 and 50 percent at a range of tourist attractions (including museums and the *mocăniţa* steam train), hotels and pensions, restaurants and bars, travel agencies, car and bike rental agencies and an outdoor equipment shop, all of which display a Maramureş Pass sticker – it won't take long to recover the outlay of around €2.50.

The best place to buy the pass is Maramureş InfoTurism in Baia Mare, either in person or by email (©office@visitmaramures.ro); see ®www.visitmaramures.ro for details of discounts. Other outlets include Maramont Sport in Baia Mare; the Popasul din Deal in Ocna Şugatag; the Maramureş Microregion Association information office; the Maramureş Ethnographic Museum in Sighet; and the CFF (*mocăniţa*) station in Vişeu de Sus.

visions of hell painted inside the church at **Poienile Izei** are the most striking images you'll see in Maramureş, while the frescoes at **Ieud** are the most famous. There's also good hiking in the peaceful **Rodna and Maramureş mountains** on the borders with Bucovina and Ukraine.

Getting around can be tricky, as side roads are rough and **public transport** is patchy, especially at weekends. The alternatives to renting a car are cycling – a great way to see the region, especially given the short distances between villages – or hitching, though be prepared for intermittent lifts or rides in the back of carts or vans. **Hotel accommodation** is generally limited to towns, but there are many **village guesthouses**. In fact Maramureş is leading the way in developing rural tourism, with homestay schemes and cycle circuits (including a Greenway trail south and west from Ocna Şugatag to Budeşti and Deseşti, over half of its 88km on forestry roads) – **bikes** can be rented in Sighet, Breb, Deseşti and Ocna Şugatag.

Baia Mare

To the south of the Gutâi and Igniş mountains, **BAIA MARE**, the largest town in Maramureş, makes a good base for forays into the surrounding countryside. Mining has been important here since the fourteenth century when, under its Magyar name of Nagybánya, it was the Hungarian monarchs' chief source of gold, but it remained a small town until the Communists turned it into a major non-ferrous metals centre in the 1950s, diluting its largely Hungarian population to just fourteen percent of the total. The town has an attractive old core, now largely restored, and a couple of worthwhile museums, in particular the **Art Gallery** and **Village Museum**.

Arrival and information

The **train** and **bus stations**, some 2km west of town on Str. Gării, are linked to the centre by buses. The **airport** lies 9km west on the Satu Mare road, and is best reached by taxi. Local **car rental** companies include Rent a Car Maramureş, Str. Bogdan Vodă bl.3 sc. E (℡0744/705 873, ®www.rentacarbaiamare.ro), and CCA Motors, B-dul Independenţei 48 (℡0262/349 221, ®www.ccamotors.ro). Bikes can be rented from Boneshaker, Str. Valea Roşie 13C (℡0362/407 134, 0745/573 138, ©szollosyszabolcs@gmail.com; Mon–Fri noon–7pm). Your first stop for **information** should be Maramureş InfoTurism, in the Prefectura

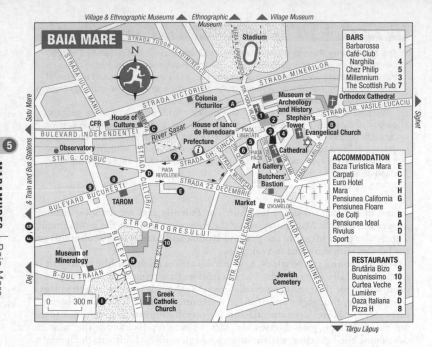

Village & Ethnographic Museums ▲▲ Ethnographic ▲▲ ▲ Village Museum
Museum

BAIA MARE

BARS
Barbarossa 1
Café-Club
Narghila 4
Chez Philip 5
Millennium 3
The Scottish Pub 7

ACCOMMODATION
Baza Turistica Mara E
Carpați C
Euro Hotel F
Mara H
Pensiunea California G
Pensiunea Floare
de Colți B
Pensiunea Ideal A
Rivulus D
Sport I

RESTAURANTS
Brutăria Bizo 9
Buonissimo 10
Curtea Veche 2
Lumière 6
Oaza Italiana D
Pizza H 8

(County Hall) at Str. Șincai 46 (☎0262/206 113, ⓦwww.visitmaramures.ro;
Mon–Thurs 9am–4.30pm, Fri 9am–2pm). **Hiking maps** and gear can be bought
at Maramont, Piața Păcii 1.

Accommodation

Baia Mare has a good selection of **hotels**, mostly affordable; alternatively, there's a
campsite just beyond the Firiza dam, 10km north of town and served by bus #18
eight times a day from the IMMUM stop, out east on Str.Vasile Lucaciu (last at
10.30pm). It's part of the *Complex Căprioara* (☎0262/270 049, ⓦwww
.complexcaprioara.ro), which also includes a guesthouse (❷ with shared showers, ❸
in new building), restaurant and swimming pool. Beyond Firiza, at a trout farm
18km from town, the *Complex Lostrita*, Str. Blidari 13B (☎0262/270 216, ⓦwww
.complexlostrita.ro; ❷), is a good modern **guesthouse**.

Baza Turistica Mara Str. Culturii 7a ☎0262/217
123, ⓦwww.e-tineretemm.ro. Down an alley on
the south side of Piața Revoluției, between a
pharmacy and Constructiv Grup, this student hostel
has large, clean, shared rooms with basin, toilet
and TV but shared showers. ❶
Carpați Str. Minerva 16 ☎0262/214 812 or 3 or 4,
ⓦwww.hotelcarpati.ro. A pricey little hotel with
smallish rooms and bathrooms, but nicely located
by the river. ❻
Euro Hotel B-dul București 23 ☎0262/222 405,
ⓦwww. bestwesterneurohotel.ro. Decent modern

hotel towards the station, with gym, spa, sauna,
bowling and the city's only indoor swimming pool.
Some rooms are a/c. ❹–❺
Mara B-dul Unirii 11 ☎&ⓕ0262/226 656,
ⓦwww.hotelmara.ro. This big, white
block southwest of the centre conceals
comfortable rooms, and features a glitzy spa
and restaurant. ❺
Pensiunea California Str. Lăpușului 5
☎0262/250 005, ⓦwww.pensiuneacalifornia.ro.
Out towards the station, this chalet-style
guesthouse has comfortable rooms with TV. ❷

Pensiunea Floare de Colți Str. Vasile Lucaciu 48 ☎0262/250216, ⊕www.floaredecolti.ro. Pretty central and with free parking, this new guesthouse has twelve simple en-suite rooms and a decent restaurant. ❷
Pensiunea Ideal Str. Steampului 6 ☎0362/411 411, ⊕www.pensiuneaideal.ro. A new pension with large frilly rooms, wi-fi, a restaurant-bar and car park. ❷

Rivulus Str. Culturii 3 ☎&Ⓕ0262/216 302, ⊕www.hotelrivulus.ro. Well refurbished, with stylish design, a lift, and a/c and wi-fi in all rooms; it's not huge but it's right in the city centre. ❹
Sport B-dul Unirii 14a, but actually one block west on Str. Transilvaniei ☎0262/226 869. A classic (that is very basic and very cheap) sport hotel intended for visiting teams but open to all. Plenty of space, unless there's a big tournament on. ❶

The Town

Baia Mare's main attraction is its **Village Museum** (Muzeul Satului; Tues–Sun 10am–6pm; €1), ten minutes' walk north of the centre on Florilor hill, where many peasant houses, wine presses, watermills and other structures from the surrounding region are preserved. In particular look out for the wooden church – raised in 1630 in Chechiş, just south of Baia Mare – and, close by, the homestead from Berbeşti, with its fine carved gate with the Tree of Life motif. Just west on Str. Dealul Florilor, the **Museum of Ethnography and Folk Art** (Muzeul de Etnografie şi Artă Populară; May–Sept Tues–Sun 10am–8pm; Oct–April 10am–4pm; €1) presents a neat array of agricultural and viticultural implements, ceramics, textiles and garments.

The heart of Baia Mare's **old town** is **Piaţa Libertăţii**, a beautifully restored square lined with sixteenth- to eighteenth-century houses; its eastern half, and parts of the neighbouring streets, are pedestrianized. At no. 18, the thick-walled **Casa Elisabeta** (now a hotel) was begun by **Iancu de Hunedoara**, fifteenth-century Regent of Hungary, for his wife, and completed by their son, Matei Corvin; next door is the house where the great Hungarian actor Lendvay Márton was born in 1807. To the south of the square rises the 50m-high **Stephen's Tower**, built in 1442–46 and all that remains of a cathedral that burnt down in 1769; the adjacent Baroque pile, built by the Jesuits in 1717–20, then became the city's Roman Catholic cathedral. Behind the cathedral at Str. 1 Mai 8, the **Art Gallery** (Mon–Fri 8am–3pm; €1) contains eighteenth- and nineteenth-century paintings on wood and glass, and a number of canvases by artists of the **Nagybánya School** (see box, p.284). Much of the work is now in Hungary, however, and the stuff here is attributed to the "Baia Mare School". There are also temporary art shows north of the river at the **Colonia Picturilor** at Str. Victoriei 21 (a villa that housed the Nagybánya School in 1910–12; Mon–Fri 8am–3pm); the modern library next to the House of Culture; and the **Galeria Millennium** (Tues–Sun 10am–4pm) on the east side of Piaţa Liberţătii, which focuses on photography.

The **Reformat church** at the junction of Str. Monetăriei and Str. Podul Viilor, just north of Piaţa Libertăţii, is a landmark, built in 1809 and topped by what seems to be a giant red diver's helmet, which appears in many works of the Nagybánya School. Nearby, in the old mint (1738–42) at Str. Monetăriei 1, is the **Museum of History and Archeology** (Muzeul de Istorie şi Arheologie; Tues–Sun 9.30am–4.30pm; €1), whose exhibits include coverage of the local mining industry, with Bronze Age metalwork and coins, some produced in this very mint, as well as around 300 clocks, sixteenth- to nineteenth-century religious books and an impressive collection of medieval ceramics. The **Museum of Mineralogy**, towards the stations at B-dul Traian 8 (Muzeul de Mineralogie; Tues–Sat 9am–5pm, Wed to 8pm, Sun 9am–2pm; €1), displays a myriad varieties of rocks, crystals and ore deposits extracted from the region's mines.

The Nagybánya School

The **Nagybánya (or Baia Mare) School** was responsible for transforming Hungarian art at the close of the nineteenth century. Its founder was **Simon Hollósy** (1857–1918), born of Armenian stock in Sighet and trained in Munich, where he was influenced by the refined naturalism of Jules Bastien-Lepage. In 1886 he set up his own school in Munich, and from 1896 brought his students to a summer school in Baia Mare, where he painted *en plein air* for the first time. An exhibition in 1897 of the school's paintings was seen as marking the start of a new era in Hungarian art and the school became known as the "Hungarian Barbizon", although the area's motifs and colours were closer to those of Provence.

In 1902, Hollósy suffered a creative crisis, and the leadership of the school was taken over by **Károly Ferenczy**; tuition fees were abolished, and the embittered and jealous Hollósy left to set up a rival school in Técső, now the Ukrainian town of Tyachiv, just downstream of Sighet. Ferenczy suffered a similar crisis in 1910, and did little work thereafter. Of the second generation of artists, the most gifted was Cavnic-born Jenő Maticska (1885–1906). After his untimely death, Béla Czóbel, Csába Vilmos Perlrott, Sándor Ziffer and others revolted against creeping stagnation; their 1906 exhibition, influenced by German Expressionism and by Cézanne and Matisse, again marked the start of a new era in Hungarian art. After World War I the school was opened to both Hungarian and Romanian students – up to 150 a year – but interest faded in the 1930s and the school closed its doors.

Other renowned artists associated with the school include Eugen Pascu (1895–1948), Tibor Boromisza (1880–1960), János Krizsán (1886–1948) and Krizsán's wife Antónia Csikos (1887–1987).

Running east from Piaţa Libertăţii, **Strada Dr Vasile Lucaciu** has some interesting old buildings whose cellars are entered from the street, and an attractive Hungarian Lutheran church. At the early twentieth-century Orthodox Cathedral, head south along Str. Olarilor (following the line of the old city walls) to reach Piaţa Izvoarelor, where the fifteenth-century **Butchers' Bastion** (Bastionul Măcelarilor) overlooks the market place in which Robin Hood-style outlaw Pintea Viteazul (Pintea the Brave) was shot in 1703.

Eating, drinking and entertainment

The choice of **restaurants** in Baia Mare is improving fast. In addition to the places reviewed below, the restaurant in the *Mara* hotel is perfectly agreeable, serving very reasonably priced Romanian and international dishes.

For **drinking**, try *Chez Philip*, Piaţa Libertăţii 4, on the south side of the square, a fashionable café-bar specializing in bottled beers; the nearby *Millennium Pub*, and *Barbarossa*, on the north side of the square, have big *terasas* and free wi-fi. The *Scottish Pub*, on the northeast corner of Piaţa Revoluţiei, is, of course, totally Romanian. Move on to the *Café-Club Narghila*, Str. Vasile Lucaciu 4 (daily till 3am).

The **Chestnut Festival** (Sărbătoarea Castenelor), held over the last weekend of September, celebrates – naturally – the chestnut season, with exhibitions, a riotous beer festival and traditional music on the Sunday.

Restaurants

Brutăria Bizo B-dul Bucureşti 8. A fine patisserie that also serves sandwiches and hot and cold drinks.
Buonissimo Str. Şcolii 3A. Very stylish joint for coffee, ices and pizza.

Curtea Veche Piaţa Libertăţii 16. Hearty Romanian dishes, including game, in a fine historic Hungarian Renaissance building.
Lumière Piaţa Libertăţii 3. Very stylish restaurant-café-gelateria appealing to the city's affluent youth.

Oaza Italiana Str. Culturii 3. In the *Hotel Rivulus*, this is less an Italian oasis than a pleasant Romanian restaurant that also serves pizza.

Pizza H B-dul Bucureşti 6. Bright and breezy, better-than-average pizzeria that also dabbles in pasta and chicken dishes.

Southern Maramureş

The area south of the Oaş-Gutâi-Tibleş mountains was part of Someş county until it was dismembered in the 1968 reforms. The southwestern corner of the present Maramureş county, beyond the River Someş, is known as **Codrul**; the area immediately south of Baia Mare is **Chioarul**; and further east lies **Lăpuş**. Whilst the green and rolling landscape is not as dramatic as in the north, it is unremittingly lovely, and you could easily spend a couple of days pottering around the region's fine wooden churches, at settlements such as **Şurdeşti**, **Plopiş** and **Rogoz**. Folk costumes here are similar to those of historic Maramureş, although the tall straw hats are unique to the region.

Codrul and Chioarul

The most accessible village in Codrul is **BUZEŞTI**, 30km west of Baia Mare. Its wooden church, built in 1739, has a bulbous steeple that bears witness to the penetration of Baroque influences into this area, while its four corner pinnacles echo the Gothic towers of both Transylvania and Hungary. Far remoter, at the county's western extremity (though served by two or three buses a day from Baia Mare), is **BICAZ**, whose Orthodox church and wall paintings both date from the early eighteenth century. As in Buzeşti, a new church has been built and the old one, though repaired, is disused.

Many of the villages of Chioarul have old churches, but the most interesting is at **SĂCĂLĂŞENI**, just 10km south of Baia Mare. Rebuilt at the end of the seventeenth century, the church dates from 1442, with a carved doorway and paintings from 1865. There's a good **motel** here: the simple, but clean and modern, *Moara Veche* at no. 137 (☏0262/289 353; ❷), which has two-, three- and four-bed rooms and a swimming pool. Just 2km southwest, in **CULCEA**, is an early eighteenth-century wooden church with plastered walls, hidden on a small rise just beyond the ugly modern church. A further 5km south is the larger village of **REMETEA CHIOARULUI**, also with a fine church, dating from 1800 – for entry, find the caretaker of the adjacent modern church. The village is also the starting point for a great hike south through the gorge of the River Lăpuş to the ruins of the sixteenth- to eighteenth-century **Chioarului citadel** (6km each way; 3hr return); in fact you can continue through the gorge for 25km to Groape. Five buses a day run from Baia Mare to Şomcuta Mare, via Săcălăşeni and Remetea.

Lăpuş

Your natural base in the centre of the Lăpuş area, the small, nondescript town of **TÂRGU LĂPUŞ** has various pensions and houses offering **private rooms**, including *Pensiunea Aurica*, Str. Tibleşului 54 (☏0262/385 082, ⓦwww .pensiunea-aurica.ro; ❷). Buses run from the station (a 5min walk east of the centre across the bridge) to Baia Mare (7 daily) and the surrounding villages, many of which boast fine wooden churches.

The best examples are the two in **ROGOZ**, 5km east of Târgu Lăpuş, which, despite the arrival of a large modern church, remain well maintained: the Uniate church, built around 1695 in Suciu de Sus and moved here in 1893, stands in the grounds of the Orthodox church, built of elm in about 1663. The latter is

There is a strong tradition of building **wooden churches** right across Eastern Europe, from northern Russia to the Adriatic, but in terms of both quality and quantity the richest examples are in Maramureş. From 1278, the Orthodox Romanians were forbidden by their Catholic Hungarian overlords to build churches in stone, and so used wood to ape Gothic developments. It was long thought that most were rebuilt after the last Tatar raid in 1717, acquiring large porches and tall towers, often with four corner-pinnacles, clearly derived from the masonry architecture of the Transylvanian cities. However in 1996–7 a tree-ring study showed that the wood used in many churches (notably those of Corneşti, Breb and Onceşti) was far older, the oldest dating from 1367.

In general, the walls are built of blockwork (squared-off logs laid horizontally) with intricate joints, cantilevered out in places to form brackets or consoles, supporting the eaves. However, in Maramureş, Western techniques such as raftering and timber framing enabled the development of the area's characteristic high roofs and steeples, rather than the tent roofs or stepped cupolas used further north. Following the **standard Orthodox ground plan**, the main roof covers the narthex and *naos* and a lower one the sanctuary; the *naos* usually has a barrel vault, while the narthex has a low-planked ceiling under the tower, its weight transmitted by rafters to the walls and thus avoiding the need for pillars. The main roof is always shingled and in many cases double, allowing clerestory windows high in the nave walls, while the lower roof may be extended to the west to form a porch (exonarthex or *pridvor*).

Inside, almost every church has a choir gallery above the west part of the *naos*, always a later addition, as shown by the way it is superimposed on the **wall paintings**. These extraordinary works of art were produced by local artists in the eighteenth and early nineteenth centuries, combining the icon tradition with pagan motifs and topical propaganda. They broadly follow the standard Orthodox layout, with the *Incarnation* and *Eucharist* in the sanctuary (for the priest's edification), the *Last Judgement* and moralistic parables such as the *Wise and Foolish Virgins* in the narthex (where the women stand), and the *Passion* in the *naos*; the treatment of the last, however, changed in the nineteenth century as the Uniate Church gained in strength, with more emphasis on the *Ascension* and the *Evangelists*.

The first of the major painters was **Alexandru Ponehalski**, who worked from the 1750s to the 1770s in Călineşti and Budeşti, in a naïve post-Byzantine style with blocks of colour in black outlines. From 1767 to the 1780s, **Radu Munteanu** worked around his native Lăpuş and in Botiza, Glod and Deseşti, painting in a freer and more imaginative manner. A far more Baroque style developed in the first decade of the nineteenth century, with **Toader Hodor** and **Ion Plohod** working in Bârsana, Corneşti, Văleni, Năneşti and Rozavlea.

Since 1989, there has been a renaissance of the **Uniate** or Greco-Catholic faith, repressed under communism and forcibly merged with the Romanian Orthodox Church: many parishes have reverted to Greco-Catholicism, reclaiming their churches; in others, one church is now Orthodox and the other Uniate, while in some villages the congregations even manage to share one building. Many villages have built large, new churches, making it more likely that you'll find the wooden churches locked – even on a Sunday. Finding the key-holder can be problematic, but ask around long enough and someone is bound to help out. Remember that people **dress conservatively** here, and wearing shorts is not appropriate for visiting churches.

Of about a hundred wooden churches in Maramureş, 35 are left in the north of the county and thirty in the south. Eight were placed on UNESCO's World Heritage List in 1999: Bârsana, Budeşti (Josani), Deseşti, Ieud (Deal), Siseşti, Plopiş, Poienile Izei and Rogoz.

unique thanks to its naturalistic horse-head cantilevers supporting the roof at the west end, and its asymmetric roof, with a larger overhang to the north sheltering a table where paupers were fed. It's one of the most beautifully decorated churches in Maramureş, with paintings by Radu Munteanu, notably a *Last Judgement*, to the left inside the door, and the *Creation* and the *Good Samaritan*, on the *naos* ceiling.

There are four buses a day from Baia Mare heading for Băiuţ or Grosii Tibleşului via Rogoz, as well as local services from Târgu Lăpuş. Buses to Baiuţ also pass through **LĂPUŞ**, 7km east of Rogoz, which boasts a village museum and a seventeenth-century wooden church with carved and painted walls. The church's oldest murals date from the early eighteenth century, and its icons include the first works of Radu Munteanu (see box opposite). **CUPŞENI**, 11km north of Rogoz (just one bus a day from Târgu Lăpuş), is one of the region's most idyllic villages and home to some of its best carpenters. Here, the upper church, built in 1600, has a fine tower but badly damaged paintings, and the tiny lower church, moved here from Peteritea in 1847, was beautifully painted in 1848 by Radu Munteanu. A new cycle trail, marked with a blue "C", makes a fine 46km loop from Târgu Lăpuş via Cupşeni and Rogoz.

Baia Sprie, Şurdeşti and Plopiş

The small town of **BAIA SPRIE** lies 10km east of Baie Mare along the Sighet road (served by city bus #8), and, like most Romanian mining towns, is highly multi-ethnic, something reflected in its multiplicity of churches. On Piaţa Libertăţii, just north of the modern centre (at the Cavnic junction), you'll find the massive Neoclassical Roman Catholic church (1846–58) and Calvinist church; down a lane to the right is the wooden-roofed Orthodox church, built in 1793. From here there are two roads into the historic county of Maramureş; the one via Cavnic, to the right/east, gives access to some dramatic wooden churches on the fringes of the Chioar district.

The magnificent Uniate wooden church at **ŞURDEŞTI**, 10km south of Baia Sprie, stands just beyond the village on a hill overlooking a stream. Built in 1721, it's clad in thousands of oak shingles, and boasts a 54m-high tower, three times the length of the church itself, which was the tallest wooden structure in Europe until the new monasteries at Bârsana and then Săpânţa (see p.300 & p.296) topped it. Inside the church, which someone from the house three doors back up the road will unlock for you, there are remarkable wall paintings dating from 1810, and some interesting late eighteenth-century icons. **Rooms** are available at *Pensiunea Amethyst* at Str. Cavnic 455 (☎0262/289 530, ✉costin_gavrila@yahoo.com; ❷), and also at *Secret Garden* in Dăneşti, on the Baia Sprie road (☎0262/298 036, ⓦwww.secret-garden.ro; ❹), a modern resort with swimming pools, gym and a stylish restaurant.

PLOPIŞ, 1km or so south across the fields, has a similar though slightly smaller church, built between 1798 and 1811, with four corner turrets on its spire, a characteristic of many wooden churches here and in the Erdehát region of Hungary. Continuing north, you'll pass through the former mining town of Cavnic (now reinventing itself as a ski resort – stay at the *Hotel Roata*, Str. Maramureşului 3; ☎0262/295 142, ⓦwww.hotelroata.com; ❸), over the **Neteda Pass** (1039m) and down to **Budeşti** (see p.290). There are five buses a day from Baia Mare to Cavnic via Şurdeşti, of which one continues to Budeşti and Sighet; otherwise, you'll have to hitch.

Four kilometres northeast of Baia Sprie, on the DN18 towards Sighet, a road breaks off to the **Mogoşa ski complex**, 3km east, which has the best ski facilities in Maramureş; there's **accommodation** at the simple *Motel Mogoşa*

(☎0262/260 800; ❷) and the very comfortable *Şuior Hotel* (☎0262/261 485, ⓦwww.suior.ro; ❹). Beyond the Gutâi Pass a paved road heads left to the **Izvoare ski resort** (☎0262/222 339, ⓦwww.statiuneaizvoare.ro), 27km from Baia Mare, with **accommodation** at the *Cabana Izvoare* (❷) and the three-star *Ignis* and *Merişor* hotels (both ☎0262/276 984; ❸).

Northern Maramureş

The historic county of Maramureş – the heart of the present-day county – lies north of Baia Sprie, beyond the Gutâi Pass. Here, you'll find idyllic rolling countryside, still farmed in the traditional manner, together with some of the region's finest **churches**, set in picturesque villages where customs have remained virtually unchanged for centuries. The main town is **Sighet**, worth visiting for a couple of splendid museums, and a good base for touring the villages.

The Mara valley

From Baia Sprie the DN18 zigzags up to the 987m-high **Gutâi Pass** and the *Hanul lui Pintea*, a basic **restaurant with rooms** (❶) for hikers. There follow 15km of winding descent into the Mara valley, past the excellent *Alex* trout farm and restaurant (☎0726/254 276) and the splendidly carved gateways of **Mara** village. In the village of **DESEŞTI**, 1km beyond Mara, a lovely wooden church is hidden among trees to the left, above the trackbed of an old forestry railway now used as a cycle path. Built in 1770, it's a fine example of the "double roof" or clerestory style, with windows high up inside the nave to increase the illumination; nowadays electric lighting allows you to fully appreciate the marvellous **wall paintings**. Executed by Radu Munteanu in 1780, these seem more primitive and less stylized than those in the Moldavian monasteries, which were painted two centuries earlier. Boldly coloured in red, yellow and white, saints and martyrs are contrasted with shady-looking Jews, Turks, Germans, Tatars and Franks. There are also folk-style geometric and floral motifs, and inscriptions in the Cyrillic alphabet – Old Church Slavonic remained the liturgical language of Romanian Orthodoxy until the nineteenth century. **Accommodation** (❷) is available at *pensiuneas* including *Irina*, no. 259 (☎0262/372 603), with bike rental; *Crisart*, no. 187 (☎0262/372 694); and *Anca*, no. 286 (☎0262/372 635, ✉floaredecrin87@yahoo.com).

Some 2km along the road, in **HĂRNICEŞTI**, the church, built in 1770, houses some fine icons; the apse was widened in 1942 and a porch added in 1952, so that now the tower seems disproportionately short. The **Casa Iurca** at Str. Principală 8, at the exit north to Sighet, is a museum house, built in 1792 and supposedly the only remaining eighteenth-century noble home in Maramureş; they provide fairly primitive **accommodation** (*Pensiunea Casa Nobilă Iurca*; ☎0262/372 933; ❷). The church stands just north of a turning east towards Ocna Şugatag and Budeşti; two buses a day from Baia Mare to Ocna Şugatag take this road via **HOTENI**, 2km east of Hărniceşti. Hoteni has its day in the spotlight on the first or second Sunday of May. This is a celebration of the **First Ploughman**, a fertility rite dating back at least to Roman times: a dozen youths adorn bulls and lead them to the house of the chosen First Ploughman, the hardest-working farmer in the village, for him to plough the first field of the season, before dunking him in water and commencing the feasting and dancing. Hoteni also has a wooden church, built in 1657 and brought here in 1788.

A couple of kilometres further north is **SAT-ŞUGATAG**, where a wooden church is set, unusually, on flat land beside the road. Accessed via a finely carved wooden gate, this beautifully compact church was built in 1642 and painted internally in 1783, and features a twisted rope motif just below the eaves. The graveyard contains beautiful stout wooden crosses and the village itself has some picturesque cottages. A minor road heads east from here to Ocna Şugatag, Călineşti, Sârbi and Budeşti, with another right turn 2km north leading to **MĂNĂSTIREA**, a tiny village with a tiny church, founded in 1653 and now shared by Orthodox and Uniate congregations; it boasts fine paintings from 1653 and 1783, as well as late eighteenth-century icons by Alexandru Ponehalski.

The main road continues northwards to **GIULEŞTI**, a larger village which has a stone church and, like many of these villages, an ancient **watermill**: its two mill wheels grind wheat and corn, the miller traditionally taking one cupful of each hopper-load. Everything is made of wood, right down to the little water channels lubricating the spindles of the wheels, and it doubles as a fulling mill, its large wooden mallets beating the cloth clean.

On the northern edge of **BERBEŞTI**, a 300-year-old carved wooden crucifix (*troiţa*), adorned with four mourning figures and symbols of the sun and moon, stands beside the road, a reminder of a time when travel was considered dangerous; no journeys were made on Tuesdays, deemed unlucky, and it was believed that after dark ghosts and vampires roamed the highways, seeking victims. From Berbeşti, the DN18 continues to Vadu Izei, the mouth of the Iza valley (see p.291), and beyond to Sighet (see p.291).

The Cosău valley

From **Fereşti** (2km south of Berbeşti), where the wooden church dates from the 1790s, a road leads southeast up the **Cosău valley** – the most interesting of all in Maramureş – to several picturesque villages where traditional costume is still worn. These villages can also be approached from the west via Hoteni; from the south over the Neteda Pass (see p.287); or from Bârsana, to the east.

Across the river from Fereşti is small, tranquil **CORNEŞTI**, where the church (painted in 1775) dates in part from 1406, making it the second oldest in Maramureş; there's another **watermill** here, which also serves as a laundry. Here, women beat clothes with carved wooden laundry bats beside the river, often improvising songs and verses as they work, using a distinctive local technique called singing "with knots" (*cu noduri*), in which the voice is modulated by tapping the glottis while the singer doesn't breathe for lengthy periods.

Continuing south, you come to three villages about 4km apart, with two **wooden churches** apiece. At sprawling **CĂLINEŞTI**, the beautiful Susani (Upper) or Băndreni church, high above the road just north of the junction, was built and painted in the 1780s. Its companion, the Josani (Lower) or Caieni church, built in 1628, is one of the loveliest in Maramureş, with its huge nineteenth-century porch and beautiful internal paintings by Ponehalski. It's best reached by taking a path across the fields next to house no. 385, on the road east to Bârsana. There are also wooden *vâltoare* or whirlpools (used for giving woollen blankets back their loft) and *horincă* stills at nos. 96 and 129. **SÂRBI** has two unassuming little wooden churches – the Susani to the north, built in 1638 and painted by Ponehalski in 1760, with icons by Radu Munteanu and a beautifully carved door frame, and the Josani, to the south, built in 1703 – and some fine watermills, notably at no. 181, along with *vâltoare*, two fulling mills and a *horinca* still, as well as various workshops.

Maramureş funerals

The **Cult of the Dead**, central to Romanian culture, is particularly well developed in Maramureş, where the rituals are fixed and elaborate; if anything is omitted, it's believed that the soul will return as a ghost or even a vampire. There are several phases, covering the separation from the world of the living, preparation for the journey, and entry into the other world. A dying person asks forgiveness of his family and neighbours, who must obey his last wishes. Black flags are hung outside the house where the deceased lies for three days, during which period the church bells are rung thrice daily, neighbours pay their respects and women (but not men) lament the deceased in improvised rhyming couplets.

When the priest arrives at the house on the third day, the wailing and lamenting reach a climax before he blesses a pail of water, extinguishes a candle in it, and consecrates the house with a cross left etched on the wall for a year. The coffin is carried by six married men, stopping for prayers (the priest being paid for each stop) at crossroads, bridges and any other feature along the way, and then at the church for absolution. The funeral itself is relatively swift, with everyone present throwing soil into the grave and being given a small loaf with a candle and a red-painted egg, as at Easter; these must also be given to passers-by, including tourists (if offered one, be aware it would give great offence if you refused it). The knot-shaped loaves or *colaci* bear the inscription NI KA ("Jesus Christ is victorious"), stamped in the dough by a widow or some other "clean woman" using a special seal called a *pecetar*. The seal's handle, usually wooden, is often elaborately carved with motifs such as the Endless Column, the Tree of Life, wolf's teeth or a crucifix.

Three days later there is another *pomană* or memorial meal, when bread is again given to all present. After nine days, nine widows spend the day fasting and praying around the deceased's shirt; six weeks and then six months after the funeral, the absolution is repeated with another meal, as the dead must be given food and drink, and after a year a feast is given for all the family's dead. Mourning lasts a year, during which time the close family may not attend weddings or dances and women wear black. As elsewhere in Romania, *ýergare* (embroidered napkins) are hung over icons in the church or over plates on house walls in memory of the dead. The Uniates also remember their dead on All Souls' Day.

Marriage is seen as essential, so much so that if a person of marriageable age (in fact from 8 years old, the age of first confession) dies unmarried, a **Marriage of the Dead** (Nunta Mortului) is held. A black flag is carried, while the deceased, a stand-in bride or groom (as appropriate), and a bridesmaid or best man dress in wedding costume, although everyone else wears mourning garb.

Budeşti and around

BUDEŞTI, 4km south, is a large village but remarkably unspoilt, with even its new houses largely built in the traditional style. The Josani church, in the centre of the village, was built in 1643 and contains a chain-mail coat that belonged to the outlaw Pintea the Brave (see p.284). Its frescoes are amongst Alexandru Ponehalski's finest works, especially the *Last Judgement*. The Susani church, dating from 1586, has particularly fine paintings from the 1760s, also by Ponehalski, and has been gradually extended westwards, so that the tower is now almost central. Budeşti's **guesthouses** include *Pensiune Mara* at no. 449 (☎0262/373 634 or 0743/887 951; ❶); *Borodi Ileana*, no. 829 (☎0262/373 683; ❶); *Cupcea Ioana*, no. 214 (☎0262/373 639; ❶); and *Pensiunea Poieniţa*, to the south at Str. Poieniţei 258 (☎0262/373 725, ⓦwww.pensiuneapoienita.com; ❷).

The village is reached by four **buses** a day from Sighet, taking the high road via **OCNA ŞUGATAG**, a former salt-mining centre that is now a booming spa. It's also the commercial centre for the surrounding villages, with a post office, bank,

ATMs and some shops, and a market on Thursday mornings. By the lake, just west from the central crossroads, the *Lacul Sarat* (☎0764/013 067, ⓦwww.laculsarat .ro) is a bar and restaurant with a salt-water pool (8am–8pm daily) and pedalos (€7/hr); the owners speak English and also offer rooms (❷). There's a group of modern pensions at the south end of the main street, Strada Unirii, including *Pensiunea Miller* at no. 94 (☎0262/374 049, ⓦwww.casa-miller.com; ❷), with rooms with shared or private bathroom, while for something simpler and more traditional, also with tent space in the orchard, go to Str. Unirii 9 (☎0744/951 554; ❶), to the north near the public pools. You can **rent bikes** and buy the Maramureş Pass at the rather sterile *Popasul din Deal* at the far north end of the village (☎0262/374 133, ⓦwww.popasul.ro; ❹).

From Budeşti, there's a particularly fine 10km walk through idyllic countryside to **Hoteni** (see p.288) via **BREB**, a small village with a very lovely and tranquil Uniate wooden church dating from 1531 hidden away in the valley. It's becoming known as something of a **museum village**, due to wooden houses threatened with collapse elsewhere being rebuilt here (one is traditionally furnished – ask for Maria alui Gheorghe din Zavoia, who has the key). A British family also offers **accommodation**, in both the village and the hills (ⓦwww.somewheredifferent .com; ❷), as well as tours. It's a great place to visit craftsmen, such as woodcarver Petru Pop at no. 370. There are two **guesthouses**: *Pensiunea Mărioara* at no. 346 (☎0262/374 593, ⓦwww.marioara.ro; ❷), offering bike rental and minibus tours/transfers (ask for the rooms in the traditional house); and *Pensiunea Lucica*, at no. 285 (☎0262/374 584; ❷).

Vadu Izei and around

At the junction of the Iza and Mara valleys, **VADU IZEI** has plenty of guest-houses, making it an alternative base to Sighet; these include *Casa Teleptean*, 1km south of the centre at Str. Principală 320 (☎0262/330 341 or 0744/828 898; ❷), with a couple of other decent options nearby, as well as a similar group near the bridge at the northern end of the village, and *Pensiunea Dumbrava Minunata*, with good views across the river at Str. Dumbrava 534 (☎0262/330 038 or 0740/493 516; ❷). You could also stay 1.5km east of Vadu Izei on the Bârsana road at the excellent *Casa Muntean*, Str. Dumbrava 505 (☎0262/330 091 or 0744/664 955, ⓦwww.casamuntean.ro; ❷), which gives discounts for Hostelling International members (and only charges by the bed); there are seven twin rooms, plus meals, internet access, *horincă*, free pick-ups in Sighet and excursions. **Bikes** can be rented at *Pensiunea Doina*, 3km west at Str. Şugău 75 (☎0262/330 602, ⓦwww .pensiune-doina.ro; ❹), where you can stay either in a modern or a traditional house. Right at the heart of the village, at the road junction, *La Petre* **restaurant** provides a simple alternative to **home cooking**.

Though almost a suburb of Sighet, the tiny hamlet of **VALEA STEJARULUI**, 5km east on a rough road (cart and sleigh rides available), remains remarkably unspoilt, with many fine wooden beam gates and a wooden church dating from 1620 and painted in 1809.

Sighet

Sighetu Marmatiei, or **SIGHET** as it's generally known, is just 1km from the Ukrainian border and was a famous smuggling centre before World War I when the territory to the north was called Ruthenia. History is repeating itself today; the bridge to Solotvino (Slatina to Romanians), destroyed in World War II and reopened in 2006, is now clogged with traffic crossing into Ukraine to buy cigarettes and petrol for resale on Romania's black market. A peaceful town of

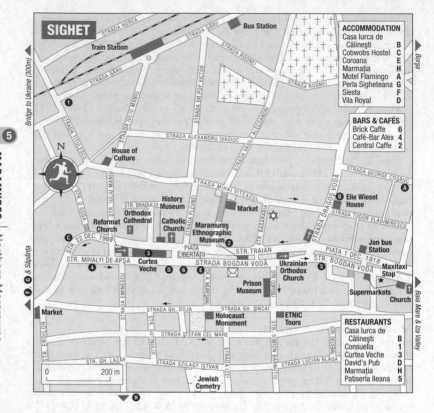

SIGHET

Bus Station

Train Station

ACCOMMODATION
Casa Iurca de	
Călineşti	B
Cobwobs Hostel	C
Coroana	E
Marmaţia	H
Motel Flamingo	A
Perla Sigheteana	G
Siesta	F
Vila Royal	D

BARS & CAFÉS
Brick Caffe	6
Café-Bar Alex	4
Central Caffe	2

House of Culture

STRADA HOREA · STRADA GĂRII · STRADA RODNEI · STRADA VASILE ALECSANDRI · STRADA GĂRII · STRADA IULIU MANIU · STRADA DR POP VICTOR · STRADA RODNEI

STRADA ALEXANDRU IVASIUC

STR. IULIU MANIU · STR. O GOGA · STR. 22 DEC. 1989 · STR. TITULESCU

STRADA MIHAI VITEAZUL · STRADA GEORGE COŞBUC

History Museum

Market

Elie Wiesel House

STRADA TUDOR VLADIMIRESCU

Orthodox Cathedral · STR. BRADULUI · STRADA PLEVNEI

Reformat Church

Catholic Church

Maramureş Ethnographic Museum

STR. BASARABIA · STRADA DRAGOŞ VODĂ

Jan bus Station

PIAŢA LIBERTĂŢII · STR. TRAIAN · PIAŢA 1 DEC. 1918

STR. MIHALYI DE APŞA · STRADA BOGDAN VODĂ · STR. BOGDAN VODĂ

Curtea Veche

Ukrainian Orthodox Church

Maxitaxi Stop

STR. A. MUREŞANU · STR. COPŞU

Prison Museum

Supermarkets · Church

STRADA EMINESCU

Market

STRADA GH. DOJA · STRADA GH. ŞINCAI

Holocaust Monument

ETNIC Tours

RESTAURANTS
Casa Iurca de	
Călineşti	B
Consuella	1
Curtea Veche	3
David's Pub	D
Marmaţia	H
Patiseria Ileana	5

STR. EROILOR · STR. GH. LAZĂR · STRADA ŞTEFAN CEL MARE · STRADA SZILAGY ISTVAN · STRADA IZEI · STR. GHINŢULUI · STR. SIMION BĂRNUŢIU · STRADA LUCIAN BLAGA · STR. DECEBAL

0   200 m

Jewish Cemetery

N

around 42,000 inhabitants, it has always been highly multi-ethnic, with a plethora of churches and schools catering for Ukrainians, Hungarians and others. You can see residents of the surrounding villages in local costume, on Wednesdays and especially on the first Monday of the month, when a livestock market is held 1km out on the Baia Mare road. The key attractions are the superb **Prison Museum** – one of Romania's best – the Village Museum and the **memorial house** dedicated to Holocaust survivor Elie Wiesel. The town is also famed for its **winter carnival** on December 27 (see box, p.295), when many of the participants wear extraordinary shamanistic costumes and masks.

Arrival and information

The **train and bus stations** are ten minutes' walk north of town on Str. Gării; there's also the private Autogara Jan on Str. Bogdan Vodă, opposite the supermarkets where buses and maxitaxis to Baia Mare and most villages also pick up passengers. The Maramureş Microregion Association at Piaţa Libertăţii 21 (☎0262/312 552, ⓦwww.mtmm.ro), is a good source of **information**, especially on the surrounding villages. Etnic Tours, Str. Şincai 20 (Mon–Fri 9am–5pm; ☎&ⓕ0262/315 011, ⓦwww.etnictours.ro) also has information on the region; they can book you into village guesthouses (with bikes available, as well as cart rides and music) and arrange accommodation and tours in Solotvino, across the river in Ukraine. Look out also for Teo Ivanciuc's English/Romanian map of

Maramureş, sold at major bookshops, the Memorial Museum and the Merry Cemetery in Sapânţa.

Internet access is available at Naroma, on the north side of the Curtea Veche. **Bikes** can be rented at Yellow Sheep Rent a Bike, above a bar at Str. Eminescu 18 (☎0740/021 091). A local **car rental** firm is Rent A Car Sighet, Str. Bogdan Vodă 5, ap. 18 (☎0742/732 911, ⓦwww.rentacarsighet.ro). **Moving on**, there are good, if sporadic, bus connections to the surrounding villages – the remotest are reached by a single departure at about 4pm.

Accommodation

Sighet has a good selection of reasonably priced **hotels**, though none really excels; alternatively, **homestays** are available in nearby villages such as Vadu Izei or Rona de Jos, from where you can easily visit Sighet.

Casa Iurca de Călineşti Str. Dragoş Vodă 14 ☎0262/318 882, Ⓔriurca@casaiurca.com. A good restaurant with rooms, all in "new Maramureş style" and a bit pretentious. Rooms have a/c, internet, hairdrier and minibar. ❺

Cobwobs Hostel Str. 22 Decembrie 1989 42 ☎0745/615 173 or 0740/635 673, Ⓔcahul1 @yahoo.com. British-run, this is a genuine backpackers' hostel, in a modern house with very spacious dorms (with lockers, proper duvets and big towels) and good showers, as well as bikes, wi-fi and a kitchen. If in doubt, ask at The Loom shop in front. They also organize village tours and evenings camping at a farm. ❶

Coroana Piaţa Libertăţii 21 ☎0262/312 645 or 315 484. The most central of Sighet's hotels, now partially renovated; some rooms are big, and there are lots of small ones with single beds. ❷

Marmaţia Str. M Eminescu 97 ☎0262/721 210, ⓦwww.hotelmarmatia.ro. The classiest place in town, a beautifully refurbished 1940s building in

the Gradina Morii park, with a lovely restaurant/bar, craft shop and a terrace bar and barbecue. However there's wi-fi only in the lobby, and the tiny lift doesn't reach the top floor. ❺

Motel Flamingo Str. George Coşbuc 36 ☎0262/317 265. Despite the unprepossessing exterior, this has comfortable rooms, though the downstairs bar can be noisy. ❷

Perla Sigheteană Str. Avram Iancu 65 ☎0262/310 613, ⓦwww.perlasigheteana.ro. A little way out of town, on the road to Sapânţa, this motel has a pool, sauna and gym, plus a pretty decent restaurant. ❸

Siesta Str. Avram Iancu 42 ☎0262/311 468, Ⓔmotelsiesta@yahoo.com. To the west, 300m beyond the *Perla Sigheteană*, this is marginally more enticing, with slightly better facilities. ❸

Vila Royal Str. Mihaly de Apşa 1 ☎0262/311 004, ⓦwww.vilaroyal.ro. Although little more than rooms above a bar (with entry from the side alley), *Vila Royal* is nicely designed, with parking at the rear. ❸

The Town

From the train and bus stations, it's a ten-minute walk south down Str. Iuliu Maniu to the **Reformat church**, a fourteenth-century structure rebuilt just before World War I on an unusual ground plan. The town centre, to the east, comprises two one-way streets, both of which change their names and are linked by several squares, so it can be hard to make sense of addresses.

Immediately east of the Reformat church is the **Curtea Veche**, the Baroque county hall of 1691, now housing a restaurant and shops. Beyond here is Piaţa Libertăţii, with the Baroque **Roman Catholic church**, built by the Piarist order in 1730–34, on its northern side. On the east side of the church at Piaţa Libertăţii 22, the **Ukrainian high school** is a splendid piece of Art Noodle, as some jokingly refer to the Hungarian version of Art Nouveau. The **Museum of History, Archeology and Natural Sciences** (Muzeul de Istorie, Arheologie şi Ştiinţele Naturii; Mon–Fri 9am–3.30pm; €0.50), on the west side of the church at Piaţa Libertăţii 16, has dull displays of Stone Age axes and hunting trophies. To the east of the square, the far more enticing **Maramureş Ethnographic Museum** (Muzeul Etnografic Maramureşului; Tues–Sun 10am–6pm; €1) has an above-average collection of local pottery and woodwork – including some beautifully

The prison of the ministers

Sighet prison operated from 1898 until 1977, achieving a notoriety gained by few others. Its nadir was between 1950 and 1955, when political prisoners (former government ministers, generals, academics and bishops) were held here so that they could be "protected" by the Red Army or rapidly spirited away into the Soviet Union if the communist regime was threatened. The 72 cells held 180 members of the prewar establishment, at least two-thirds of them aged over 60; they were appallingly treated and, not surprisingly, many died. The most important figure to perish here was **Iuliu Maniu**, regarded as the greatest living Romanian when he was arrested in 1947 (at the age of 73) and now seen as a secular martyr – the only uncorrupt politician of the prewar period, organizer of the 1944 coup, and notably reluctant to pursue revenge against Transylvania's Hungarians after the war.

The leading Hungarian victim was **Árón Márton**, Roman Catholic bishop of Alba Iulia, who opposed the persecution of the Jews in 1944 and of the Uniates in 1949, and was imprisoned from 1950 to 1955, surviving until 1980. Others who died in Sighet included two of the three members of the Brătianu family imprisoned here – Dinu, president of the National Liberal Party and Finance Minister (1933–34), and Gheorghe, historian and second-division politician – as well as Mihail Manoilescu, theoretician of Romanian fascism, and Foreign Minister in 1940. Their graves can be seen at the rear of the Cimitrul Săracilor or Paupers' Cemetery, just off the main road to the west of town, by a new Pentecostal chapel.

carved gates and gateposts – as well as a selection of costumes and masks worn by participants during the town's winter carnival (see box opposite). A little further east, between the two carriageways, sits a tiny **Ukrainian Orthodox church**, built in 1803–4 and totally rebuilt in the 1990s.

At Str. Coposu 4, to the south of the Ethnographic Museum, stands the former **prison** (see box above), which opened in 1997 as the **Memorial Museum of the Victims of Communism and of the Resistance** (Memorial Victimelor Comunismului şi Rezistenţei; mid-April to mid-Oct daily 9.30am–6.30pm; mid-Oct to mid-April Tues–Sun 10am–4pm; €1; ⓦwww.memorialsighet.ro). The cells have been converted into exhibition spaces, covering the oppression of the communist era; little is in English but the general outlines are clear enough. In addition to memorials to Iuliu Maniu and Gheorghe Brătianu, the prison's two most famous inmates, there are displays on collectivization, forced labour on the Danube–Black Sea Canal, the deportations to the Bărăgan, and the demolition of the heart of Bucharest during the 1980s. There's also fascinating coverage of the feared Securitate, and another cell-full of Ceauşescu-oriented memorabilia (aptly entitled "Communist Kitsch"), including paintings, busts, lists of the Romanian leader's honorary doctorates, and photos of him lording it with world leaders such as Castro and Nixon. In the courtyard is an underground memorial hall, its walls inscribed with the names of some 8000 people imprisoned under communism, and a dozen or so uninspiring bronze statues.

One block west of the museum along Str. Şincai you'll find a **monument** to the 38,000 Maramureş Jews rounded up by Hungarian gendarmes and deported in 1944. The synagogue, dating from 1904, survives at Str. Basarabia 10, on the far side of Piaţa Libertăţii. A plain house a block east at Str. Tudor Vladimirescu 1, at the corner of Str. Dragoş Vodă, was the childhood home of **Elie Wiesel**, Auschwitz survivor and winner of the 1986 Nobel Peace Prize for his work in helping to understand and remember the Holocaust. It's now an impressive **memorial house** and Museum of Jewish Culture in Maramureş (Tues–Sun 10am–6pm; €1), with books, furniture and religious items donated by local Jewish families; there are documents on the Jewish and other communities in Sighet before World War II, along with photos of the deportation of the Jews, Wiesel's liberation from Buchenwald, and his many visits to Sighet, including one in 2002 to open the house. Photo captions are in English and French, but otherwise the texts, including quotations from Wiesel, are in Romanian only.

Set on Dobăieş hill on the town's eastern outskirts, the **Village Museum** (Muzeul Satului; Tues–Sun 10am–6pm; €1) presents dozens of houses, farm buildings and churches from the surrounding valleys – worth viewing if you'll miss the real thing. It's a half-hour walk, or take bus #1 to the bridge and School no. 5, then walk northeast for five minutes up Str. Muzeului.

Eating and drinking

There are few options for **eating out** in Sighet. The best restaurant, with excellent service, is at the *Hotel Marmaţia*; the *Casa Iurca de Călineşti* is also good, although a bit touristy in feel, serving Western dishes like Chateaubriand, schnitzel and "roast beef anglaise" as well as traditional Maramureş food. *Consuella*, at the corner of Stradas Titulescu and Gării, is also excellent, and rather cheaper; the soups are particularly good, and it also does decent pizza. You could also try *Curtea Veche*, Str. Mihalyi de Apşa 2, which serves solid Romanian food (to 9pm), or *David's Pub* across the road at no. 1 (next to painter Simon Hollósy's birthplace), offering Romanian/international cuisine and with one smoke-free room. *Patiseria Ileana* on Str. Bogdan Vodă serves fine pastries and coffee; good coffee and juices (and wi-fi) are also available at the *Central Caffe*, Piaţa Libertăţii 24.

For a beer or two, try the *Café-bar Alex*, at Str. Milahy de Apşa 35, or, for something a bit classier, *Brick Caffe* at Piaţa Libertăţii 11. **Picnic food** is provided by the Carrefour Express or (less good) Unicarm supermarkets, on Str. Bogdan Vodă just east of the centre.

Săpânţa and the Oaş depression

Eighteen kilometres northwest of Sighet (via the Hungarian village of Câmpulung la Tisa, known for its cabbages), and served by six buses a day, **SĂPÂNŢA** has achieved widespread fame thanks to the work of the woodcarver Stan Ion Pătraş (1908–77). Its **Merry Cemetery** (Cimitir Vesel; €1), 1km south of the main road, is a forest of beautifully worked, colourfully painted wooden grave markers carved

Winter Customs Festival

Held in Sighet on December 27, the **Winter Customs Festival** (Festivalul Datinilor de Iarna) is a vibrant display of music, and winter costumes and customs, illustrating the dual influences of ancient pagan and Christian beliefs. The festival is heralded by brightly decorated horses galloping down the main street, followed by up to fifty groups from villages all over Maramureş, Bucovina, Transylvania and Ukraine slowly making their way down the street to present their song or skit to the mayor.

Thereafter, a rather mishmash play begins with soldiers arriving to tell King Herod about the rumour of a saviour, while bears roll around the ground to raise the earth spirits. Horsemen are called to find the infant child and men bring heavy iron cowbells to drive away evil spirits, represented by multicoloured, animist-style *dracus*. Present throughout is the clapping wooden goat (*capra*), warding off evil spirits to ensure that spring will return. In the afternoon, a full-length concert takes place both on the streets and in a nearby theatre, lasting until early evening when more impromptu celebrations take over.

with portraits of the deceased or scenes from their lives, inscribed with witty doggerel (in Romanian) composed by Pătraş as he saw fit. Some are terse – "who sought money to amass, could not Death escape, alas!" – while a surprising number recall violent deaths, like that of the villager killed by a "bloody Hungarian" during World War II, or a mother's final message to her son: "Griga, may you pardoned be, even though you did stab me." Pătraş himself is buried right in front of the church door, his carved portrait flanked by two white doves ("Ever since I was a lad, I have been Stan Ion Pătraş…"). The grave markers are now carved and painted by Dumitru ("Tincu") Pop, whom you may be lucky enough to see going about his work in the cemetery. You can find more of Pătraş' artistry in his modest wooden cottage some 250m along the dusty road behind the cemetery (it's signposted). The barn where he worked is adorned with some spectacularly colourful fixtures and fittings, as well as highly unusual wood-carved portraits of the Ceauşescus. The village, also known for its traditional *cergi* or woollen blankets, is lined with handicraft stalls and has become rather too accustomed to busloads of tourists making a thirty-minute stop before rushing on.

Săpânţa's most recent claim to fame, the world's highest wooden tower, is at the **Peri monastery**, which has been under construction since 1995; follow the main road east from the Merry Cemetery for 200m across the Râul Săpânţa bridge then (at an ATM) turn left/north for 500m (if you're on foot, take the path diagonally through the Pădurea Parc Livada forest reserve). The church, though wooden, is not at all traditional in detail, set on a very high concrete base and with a 38m tree trunk inside its tower, which soars to a height of 75m.

Săpânţa practicalities

There's plenty of **accommodation** here, including four basic rooms in Ileana Şteţca's pension (☎0262/372 137 or 0745/491 756; ❸) opposite the cemetery at no. 656; the nearby *Pensiunea Maryuka* (☎0262/372591 or 0745/469480; ❷); *Pensiunea Miuţa* (☎0262/372 355; ❷), on the road to the Peri monastery; and, just off the main road to the east at no. 106, *Pensiunea Anca* (☎0262/372 148, ✆ion .braicu@yahoo.com; ❷). There's also the simple Poieni **campsite** (☎0262/372 228), with a handful of two-bed **cabins** (❶), at a trout farm 2.5km south of the cemetery, together with a **restaurant** and the *Pensiunea Săpânţa* (☎0728/629 282, ✆pensiuneasapanta@yahoo.com; ❸). Otherwise, the only places to eat are the guesthouses.

The Oaş depression

Beyond Săpânţa, the road turns south towards Satu Mare, winding up to the **Huta Pass** (587m) to enter the **Oaş depression**. Oaş was once billed as "undiscovered Maramureş", but so many local men now work abroad that the roads are lined with new bungalows and imported Mercedes, and traditional costume is little worn except at festivals and in the remotest villages such as Cămârzana, where you'll find just about the only wooden houses left in Oaş. The region's shepherds assemble on the first or second Sunday of May for the **festival of Sâmbra Oilor**, when the milk yield of each family's sheep is measured. Whether this process – known as *Ruptul Sterpelor* – occurs in May (as here) or June or early July (as it does further south), the participants dress for the occasion in waist-length sheepskin jackets (*cojoc*) covered in embroidery and tassels, or fluffy woollen overcoats called *guba*, and heartily consume fiery *horinca* (double-distilled plum brandy) and sweet whey cheese.

NEGREŞTI-OAŞ, some 35km southwest of Săpânţa, is the largest settlement in the region. Here, the **Oaş Museum** has a display of local landscapes (Tues–Fri 9am–4pm, Sat & Sun 10am–4pm), at Str. Victoriei 17, just north of the systematized centre, and a more worthwhile open-air **ethnographic display** (Tues–Fri 9am–5pm, Sat & Sun 9am–2pm) on Str. Livezilor, to the south beyond the bridge. Here there are half a dozen blue-painted houses, mostly from the nineteenth century, and a wooden church, built in 1600, from Lechința; its interior was painted in 2006. Negrești's **festival** is on September 1.

In addition to local **buses** and hourly **maxitaxis** from Satu Mare, Negrești can be reached by **trains** on the Satu Mare–Bixad line: get off at the Negrești halt, rather than at the station, which is a couple of kilometres west of town. **Accommodation** is available at the dated *Oșanul Hotel*, 400m south of the museum at Str. Victoriei 89 (☎0261/854 162, ℻851 163; ❸); the adequate *Regal* and *Orizont* **restaurants** are on the square just north of the hotel.

Other **places to stay** in Oaș include the *Complex Pintea*, Str. Valea Mariei 224 (☎0261/857 155, ⓦwww.complex-pintea.ro), with swimming pool and Jacuzzi, 4km north of Vama; the *Călinești* (☎0261/851 400; ❷) in Călinești-Oaș, by a reservoir 15km west of Negrești; and the *Motel Mujdeni* (Orașul Nou, ☎0261/830 077; ❷), just north of the pass into Satu Mare county.

Satu Mare

When the diplomats at Versailles signed the Trianon Treaty, they dismembered Hungary's Szabolcs-Szatmár county, handing its capital Szatmárnémeti to Romania, since when its Hungarian population has fallen from about 75 percent of the total to about 30 percent. Renamed **SATU MARE** (meaning "Big Village" in Romanian) and shorn of its historic links with the Great Plain, the town lost its role as a trading post on the River Someș, shipping salt downstream from Ocna Dejului; today, it's relatively prosperous, largely due to its position near the

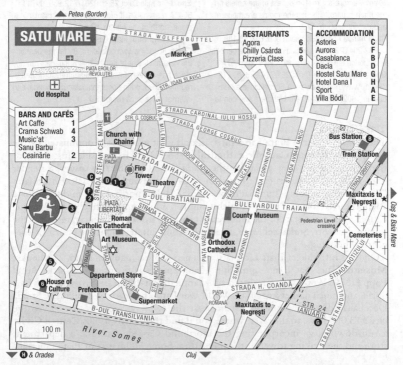

border. Although there's little to detain you, it's a useful spot to break a journey to or from Oradea or Hungary.

Arrival and information

The **bus and train stations** are 1km east of the centre on Str. Griviței (a continuation of B-dul Traian, running east from Piața Libertății), and are connected to town by bus #1 (every 15–20min). Bus #9 links the **airport** (10km south towards Zalău; €3 by taxi) with Piața Libertății. Hourly **maxitaxis to Negrești** leave from Piața Romană and head north on Str. Botizului.

The hotels can provide limited **tourist information**. **Internet access** is available at Computer Service, Str. Corvinilor 22, just south of B-dul Traian (daily 10am–9pm), and the *Rambo Net Café*, Str. Gheorghe Lazăr 3, while the *Agora* restaurant (see below) has free wi-fi.

Accommodation

There's plenty of **accommodation** in Satu Mare, whether you want to stay in the heart of things around Piața Libertății or out by the station. In the Centrul de Vacanța Ştrand at Str. 24 Ianuarie 17, the HI-affiliated *Hostel Satu Mare* (☎ 0261/750 472 or 0741/190 544, ✉ djtsatumare@gmail.com; ❶) has comfortable rooms with hot water and large TVs, as well as cheaper *căsuțe*.

Astoria Str. Kogălniceanu 1 ☎ 0261/806 185, ⓦ www.hotel-astoria.ro. At the northwestern corner of Piața Libertății, this new hotel has large rooms, good bathrooms and wi-fi – but no lift. ❺

Aurora Piața Libertății 11 ☎ 0261/714 946, ⓦ www.aurora-sm.ro. The ugliest of the hotels on the main square, although the rooms are modern and decent enough. ❹

Casablanca At the bus station ☎ 0261/768 188, Ⓕ 768 204. The rooms (including triples) are perfectly fine, though the downstairs bar is very noisy. ❸

Dacia Piața Libertății 8 ☎ 0261/714 276, Ⓕ 715 774, ⓦ www.hoteldacia.ro. A Secession-era gem built in 1902, closed for refurbishment and due to reopen as a four-star hotel in 2012, with swimming pool and gym.

Hotel Dana 1 Drum Carei 128 ☎ 0261/768 465, ⓦ www.dana-hotel.ro. Peaceful, newish hotel, 2km west of town towards Oradea. ❹

Sport Str. Mileniului 25 ☎ 0261/712 959, Ⓕ 711 604. A reasonable, if predictably unspectacular place, north of the centre. ❷

🏃 **Villa Bódi** Piața Libertății 5 ☎ 0261/710 861, ⓦ www.villabodi.ro. By far the best of the central cluster of hotels, this Hungarian-run place has a lovely foyer and beautifully furnished rooms with wooden floors, plus Jacuzzi, sauna, and internet ports in all rooms. ❻

The Town

The centre of town, **Piața Libertății**, is a pleasant green space dominated by the Neoclassical **Roman Catholic cathedral** (1785–93) on its east side. Just north of the square, off the alley alongside the *Dacia*, you'll see the **fire tower**, a slender 45m-high red brick structure raised in 1904 and resembling a Turkish minaret (Tues–Fri & Sun noon–7pm, Sat noon–4pm; €1). Just north, in the middle of Piața Păcii, is the Reformat **"Church with Chains"**, a long and relatively low Baroque church built at the start of the nineteenth century; from here you can return to the square along Str. Ştefan cel Mare, lined with some interesting if tatty turn-of-the-century buildings.

On the south side of Piața Libertății, in a neo-Gothic mansion at no. 21, the **Art Museum** (Tues–Sat 10am–6pm, Sun 10am–2pm; €1) features local artist Aurel Popp (1879–1960), who produced sun-dappled post-Impressionist views of Baia Sprie, and much darker images of World War I and the death of capitalism. Strada Decebal leads south from the square, past the twin synagogues that served the city's 13,000 Jews, to the river, where you'll find the ghastly 1980s **Centru Civic**, a run-down plaza incorporating the moribund Casa de Cultura, a department store and the striking tower of the prefecture. Some 500m east of Piața Libertății along B-dul Brațianu, at Piața Vasile Lucaciu 21, the **County Museum** (Tues–Sat 10am–6pm, Sun 10am–2pm; €1) has both ethnographic and archeological exhibitions. The former contains standard rural implements and folk costumes, as well as brightly coloured ceramics from Hollóháza in Hungary and Vama in Oaș, while the beautifully presented archeological exhibitions feature fine Daco-Roman remains, clay vessels and grave goods, including some intricate jewellery kept in the treasury (Tues–Sun 11am–2pm).

Eating and drinking

There are few decent **places to eat** in Satu Mare other than in the hotels, of which the *Villa Bódi* is the best. There's fiery Hungarian food at *Chilly Csárda*, Str. Petőfi 30. Just west of the Centru Civic is a cluster of **Italian bar-pizzerias**, of which *Agora* and, below it, *Pizzeria Class* are acceptable. For **coffee and cakes**, head to the stylish *Art Caffe* on the alley west of the fire tower, or *Sanu Barbu Ceainărie* at Str. Tiblești 2 (off Piața Libertății), a dark teahouse and café, also serving cocktails with and without alcohol.

For a **drink**, try the terrace bars on the north and south sides of Piața Libertății, the *Music'at* café and music pub at the corner of Petőfi and Hám János, or the *Crama Schwab* Bierkeller, courtesy of the town's Swabian (German) minority, at Piața Lucaciu 9 (Mon–Fri 9am–5pm, Sun 9am–2pm), which also puts on German films and choir recitals.

The Iza valley

Some of the loveliest villages and wooden churches in Maramureș are in the **Iza valley**, extending roughly 60km from Sighet to the Rodna mountains, on the frontier with Bucovina. There are regular buses to Vișeu de Sus and Borșa – most following the DJ186 along the Iza valley, although some take the DN18 along the Rona and Vișeu valleys – and a daily bus to most of the villages in the Iza's side valleys.

Oncești

Despite being on a main road, **ONCEȘTI**, 11km from Sighet, is perhaps the village that has best preserved its folk customs, with many people wearing traditional dress on Sundays. It still boasts two fine groups of wooden houses, one by Str. Principală 241 (just east of the school), but the old wooden church is now in Sighet's Village Museum. There are some fine **guesthouses** here, including *Pensiunea Bud Mariana* (☏0262/348 448, ✉budmariana@yahoo.com, ❶www .agrotur.ro/bud; ❶) at no. 360, and ⚿*Pensiunea Sub Cetate la Matei* (☏0262/348 498 or 0742/342 328, ❶www.oncesti.rdsor.ro; ❷), at the west end of the village at no. 480, a small museum including tools saved from a blacksmith's forge, which has rooms with TV, friendly service, good home-grown food and traditional furnishings.

Bârsana and Rozavlea

The wooden church of **BÂRSANA**, 19km southeast of Sighet on the DJ186, is small and neat and perfectly positioned atop a hillock to the west of the village centre. Built in 1711, its florid **paintings**, among the best in Maramureș, date from 1720 and 1806. Hodor Toador and Ion Plohod were responsible for the later set of paintings, with icons on wood by the former artist – the narthex is adorned with saints and processional images, while the *naos* is painted with Old and New Testament scenes, each in a decorative medallion. Look in particular for the images of angels covered in eyes. At the east end of the village, 4km from the centre, stands the new **Bârsana Monastery**, a large complex of wooden buildings, all in traditional style, including the wooden church which, unusually, has a pentagonal *privdor* and two apses, as well as a 57m steeple, briefly the highest in the world but now overtaken by that at Săpânţa (see p.296). The original monastery was closed down by the Austrians in 1791; construction of a new one (in fact a nunnery) began in 1993, and it has expanded steadily since.

The monastery attracts many visitors, some staying in its **guesthouse** (☎0262/331 101; ❶); however, non-pilgrims may be happier in a **homestay** such as *Pensiunea Paşcă*, Uliţa Pietriş (☎0262/331 165; ❷), or *Pensiunea Dumbrava*, Str. Principală 332 (☎0262/331 187; ❷). *Pensiunea Pop*, Str.Principală 442 (☎0262/331 064, ✉ghpop1@yahoo.fr; ❷), is affiliated to Hostelling International. Just east of the Călineşti junction, you can visit the splendid woodworker Teodor Bârsan, with carvings big and small for sale.

As a border region, Maramureş remained vulnerable to attacks by nomadic tribes until the eighteenth century, and the wooden church just east of the centre of **ROZAVLEA**, 20km further along the valley, was one of many rebuilt after the last Tatar invasion in 1717 and painted by Ion Plohod. Its magnificent double roof, recently restored, is now weathering nicely. There are **homestays** (❷) here – including *Casa Tomşa* at no. 961 (☎0262/333 155) and *Pensiunea Vanessa*, just west of the centre at Str. Ţipţarai 825 (☎0262/333 288) – and in **ŞIEU**, 2km east, which has another wooden church (500m south on the Botiza road) built in 1760.

Botiza, Poienile Izei and Glod

BOTIZA, 10km south of Şieu, is a growing centre for **agrotourism**, with many good guesthouses. Victoria Berbecaru (☎0262/334 107; ❷), renowned for her carpet-making using natural dyes, has a modern house just south of the church at no. 743, but she also has rooms, and her weaving studio, in the charming wooden house (built c.1790) right in front of the church. Other good options (❷) include *Casa Maria Poienar*, south at no. 429 (☎0262/334 149, 0727/165 434); *Pensiunea Ancuţa*, west at Valea Sasului 222 (☎0262/334 079); and *Pensiunea Adriana*, Valea Sasului 333 (☎0262/334 012).

The **wooden church**, beautifully set on a hillside, was built in 1699 in Vişeu de Jos and moved here two hundred years later. Beyond a few blackened frescoes of the Apostles and some floral motifs, there's little to see inside, but if you want a look, ask for the key at no. 743. There are several **mineral springs** along the road to Poienile Izei, notably a sulphurous well at a ruined spa by the bridge about 1km from the village centre. The "For my Darling from Botiza" **folk festival** takes place over the fourth weekend of August. From the second bridge below the church there's a delightful (but unmarked) hike to Ieud; turning right onto a lovely path across fields, it takes half an hour to a low pass, after which you need to keep to the right.

Although there's a good road from Şieu, from Botiza only a rough sidetrack leads into the hills to the village of **POIENILE IZEI** (The Meadows of the Iza), 6km northeast and famous for its old wooden church (1604–32) filled with nightmarish **paintings of hell**. The red walls depict dozens of demons (*draci*) with goat-like heads and clawed feet, torturing sinners and driving them into the mouth of hell – an enormous bird's head with fiery nostrils. These pictures constitute an illustrated rulebook too terrifying to disobey, a huge pair of bellows, for instance, being used to punish farting in church, while a woman guilty of burning the priest's robes while ironing them is herself pressed with a hot iron. Adultresses are courted by loathsome demons and a woman who aborted children is forced to eat them. These hell scenes presumably formed the nasty part of a huge *Day of Judgement* in the narthex, the other half of which has, ironically, not been saved.

Opposite are paintings of gardens and distant cityscapes in a sort of Gothic Book of Hours style, executed around 1793–4. The nave's murals are badly damaged and soot-blackened, but from the gallery you can recognize *Adam and Eve*, *The Fall* and episodes from the lives of Christ and John the Baptist. If the church is locked, anyone in the house above the new church will unlock it for you. **Homestays** include *Pensiunea Domniţa* at Str. Dubului 135 (☎0262/334 383 or 0724/764 036, ✉domnitailies@yahoo.com; ❷).

An even worse road leads on to the tiny and unspoilt village of **GLOD** (more easily reached by a 7km road from the Iza valley just east of Bârsana), which is known for its folk beliefs – for instance in werewolves and spirits of the night – and associations with the outlaw Pintea Viteazul; tales tell of his treasure buried under a spring and protected by a curse. There's also a wooden church, dating from 1784. The *Pensiunea In Poiana* (☎0262/332 367 or 0720/071 787, ⓌWwww.pensiunea-inpoiana.ro; ❷) is an excellent **guesthouse**.

Ieud and beyond

Back in the Iza valley, a turn-off at Gura Ieudului, about 6km east along the valley road, leads upstream to the village of **IEUD**, 2.5km south. It was Ieud artisans, supervised by master carpenter Ion Ţâplea, who restored Manuc's Inn in Bucharest (see p.72), and master carpenter Gavrilă Hotico is currently building new wooden churches all over Maramureş and beyond; the tradition of woodworking has been maintained since the superb Orthodox **Hill Church** (Biserica din Deal; summer Mon–Sat 9am–2pm & 3–8pm, Sun 1–4pm & 5–8pm; winter Sun 1–4pm & 5–8pm; €0.50) was first raised here in 1364. Long thought to be the oldest church in Maramureş (though largely rebuilt in the eighteenth century), with a double roof and tiny windows, it once housed the Ieud Codex (1391–92, now in the Romanian Academy in Bucharest), the earliest-known document in the Romanian language. It has perhaps the most renowned paintings of any Maramureş church, executed by Alexandru Ponehalski in 1782; look out for Abraham, Isaac and Jacob welcoming people in their arms, in the *pronaos*. And don't miss the ingenious removable ratchet used to open the bolt in the main door. No less splendid than the Orthodox church is the Uniate **lower church** (the Val or Şes church), built by 1718 and featuring a magnificently high roofline, though, unusually, no porch; few wall paintings survive, but the icons on glass and the iconostasis are artistically valuable. The **Muzeul Pleş** (daily 8am–noon, 1–8pm; €1), 150m before the Hill Church, consists of a couple of traditional buildings stocked by the Pleş family with old wooden tools and home-made clothing.

Homestay accommodation (❷) is available in the village: contact Dumitru Chindriş at no. 233 (☎0262/336 100); Vasile Chindris at no. 201 (☎0262/336 197, ✉vasilechindris@personal.ro); or *Pensiunea Ilea*, no. 333 (☎0262/336 039, ⓌWwww.pensiuneailea.ro), which has wi-fi.

BOGDAN VODĂ, stretching east along the valley road from Gura Ieudului, is one of the valley's main villages, on the road leading to Moldavia and with long-standing ties to that region. The village was known as Cuhea until the late 1960s, when it was renamed in honour of the local *voivode*, Bogdan, who left in 1359 supposedly to hunt bison, but ended up founding the Moldavian state (see p.373). The influence of Stephen and other Moldavian rulers imparted a semi-Byzantine style to the frescoes inside Bogdan Vodă's wooden church, though the materials used in 1718 were typical of eastern Maramureş – thick fir beams rather than the stone used at Putna and other Moldavian monasteries, or the oak of western Maramureş. Unfortunately, the church is now dwarfed by a huge modern successor erected far too close to it.

From Bogdan Vodă's churches, a rough road leads 14km north to Vişeu de Jos (see below), while the main road continues east to **DRAGOMIREŞTI**, where the **Muzeul Tarancii** (daily 9am–7pm; €0.50), just west of the centre, displays a wide range of domestic and agricultural implements, almost all wooden; just west of this is a Uniate wooden church (on a concrete base), completed in 2000 to replace the village's original church, now in Bucharest's Village Museum (see p.76). The next village is **SĂLIŞTEA DE SUS**, 4km east, which boasts two old wooden churches, one built in 1680 and the other in 1724 – the latter painted by Radu Munteanu in 1775. There are also two new churches, an ATM and various guesthouses, including *Pensiunea Vasilica Buleasa* at no. 250 (℡0742/243 308, ✉i_dominc56@yahoo.com; ❷). The road ends, 53km from Vadu Izei, at **SĂCEL**, known for its unglazed red ceramics, from where the DN17C heads for Moisei (11km north) or Salva and Bistriţa (44km and 71km south, in Transylvania). You can **stay** at *Pensiunea Maria*, just east of the centre at Str. Centru 235 (℡0262/339 064, ⓦwww.pensiuneamaria.ro; ❷), or the hotel-like *Pensiunea Lăcrămioara* at no. 755 to the north (℡0262/339 071, ⓦwww.cazarevaleaizei.ro; ❷ – rates include breakfast out of peak season only).

The Vişeu valley and the Rodna mountains

The railway east from Sighet follows the River Tisza for 25km before heading up the beautiful **Vişeu valley**; the DN18 runs just to the south of the railway, and local buses from Sighet pass through the villages of Rona de Jos and Rona de Sus before terminating at the tiny spa of **COŞTIUI**, 22km from Sighet, which has a motel and *căsuţe*. **RONA DE JOS** has few obvious sights, beyond a cave and mineral springs, and a wooden church built in 1720, which was taken over by the Uniates in 2001 and restored, but the proactive guesthouse-owners' association organizes cart rides and bike hire, and there's a new festival, Fii Satului (Sons of the Village), on the last Sunday of August or the first of September.

At the west end of the village, 11km from Sighet, the excellent *Pensiunea Rusucu* (℡0262/361 148 or 0724/063 143, ⓦwww.rusucu.com; ❷) has a minibus for tours and transfers, while *Pensiunea Marin* (℡0262/361 048; ❷) provides rooms for up to five people. Beyond the Ukrainian village of Rona de Sus (and the turning to Coştiui) the road climbs to a pass in lovely beech forest and meets the railway again after 16km at **PETROVA**. From **Leordina** (once home to Harvey Keitel's parents), 7km southeast of Petrova, a rough side road follows the River Ruscova north into an enclave of Huţul or Ruthenian people, the archetypal inhabitants of the Carpathians, who speak a dialect of Ukrainian incorporating many Romanian words. There's still a synagogue in **RUSCOVA**, once home to British politician Michael Howard's father. The centre of the area is the village of **POIENILE DE SUB MUNTE**, where there's a Ukrainian-style wooden church dating from 1788 and a couple of guesthouses. Back in the Vişeu valley, trains continue 10km east from Leordina to **VIŞEU DE JOS**, then turn south through Săcel and Salva en route to Beclean; passenger trains no longer run up the branch line from Vişeu de Jos to Borşa, but there are regular buses as far as Vişeu de Sus, and fewer on to Borşa.

Vişeu de Sus and the logging train

Just east of Vişeu de Jos is **VIŞEU DE SUS**, a fair-sized town that's the starting point for the logging train up the steep Vaser valley. A **Museum of History and Ethnography** (Muzeul de Istorie şi Etnografie; Mon–Fri 9am–5pm; €1) opened in 2003 at Str. Libertăţii 7; it's far from finished, but there's a display on the ethnography of the Romanian, Ruthenian, Jewish and Zipser communities. The

Zipsers (Ţipţerai in Romanian) were German foresters who until World War II lived here in some numbers, trading mainly with Jewish timber merchants. On the far side of Str. 22 Decembrie is the very attractive town hall, and just to its west a wooden Uniate church built in 1993–5 by Gavrilă Hotico of Ieud. Across the river, by Str. Republicii, the market stands on the edge of the ţipţerai Quarter.

The narrow-gauge railway up the wild Vaser valley, towards the Ukrainian border, is still used by logging trains, usually hauled by a diesel engine; in addition a tourist train, usually hauled by a small steam locomotive known as the **mocăniţa** or coffee machine (restored by Swiss enthusiasts) runs as far as Paltin, 21km up the valley, returning by about 3pm. It leaves at 8.30am (July to mid-Sept daily, €10 round trip, 10 percent less with Maramureş Pass; May/June & mid-Sept to mid-Oct Thurs–Sun €8; ☎0262/353 381 or 0744/686 716, ⓦwww.cffviseu .com, ⓦwww.mocanita.ro) from the yard about 1km north of the centre on Str. A.I. Cuza – head up Str. Carpaţi, opposite Str. I. Maniu. There's also a huge standard-gauge steam locomotive (a 2-10-0) near the *mocăniţa* station, which may be properly displayed soon.

Along the route, you may see bears and deer drinking from the river, unperturbed by the trains. The River Vaser, rich in trout and umber, descends rapidly through the 50km-long valley; its whirling waters have begun to attract kayakers to logging settlements like **MĂCIRLĂU**, the start of a very rugged trail over the Jupania ridge of the Maramureş mountains to the former mining centre of Baia Borşa, just north of Borşa.

Practicalities

Fundaţia ProVişeu (ⓦwww.turismviseu.ro), on a corner with the main road, Str. 22 Decembrie, at Str. Libertăţii 1 (Mon–Sat 9am–5pm; ☎0262/352 285), offers tourist information and public internet access, and can organize private **rooms** here and in the surrounding area.

The *Hotel Brad* (☎0262/352 999; ❷), at Str. 22 Decembrie 50 (at the junction of Str. Iuliu Maniu), is perfectly decent but often full; *Hotel Gabriela* (☎0262/354 380, ⓦwww.hotel-gabriela.ro; ❷), at Str. Rândunelelor 1, about 1km east on the road to Moisei, is a better bet. There are various guesthouses, such as *Pensiunea Sanda* (☎0262/352 032; ❶) and *Pensiunea Ancuţa* (☎0262/352 528; ❶), both on Str. Moldova, almost opposite the *mocăniţa* station, as well as the better *Pensiunea Casa Alba* (☎0745/297 457; ❷) at Str. Iuliu Maniu 10, and the grand *Pensiunea Nagy*, north of the river in the Ţipţerai Quarter at Str. Prislop 82 (☎0262/354 681, ⓦwww.pensiunea-nagy.ro; ❷), which has sauna, Jacuzzi and solarium. Rail enthusiasts may want to stay with one of the engine drivers at *Pensiunea Bârsan* (☎0262/355 653, ⓔpensiunea_barsan@yahoo.com; ❷), 600m beyond the station at Str. A.I. Cuza 69B.

For **eating**, *Café Maya* and *Pizzeria Andra*, both on Str. 22 Decembrie, are nothing special but decent enough, and convenient for the *Hotel Brad*, across the road; there are **ATMs** nearby. There's also the *Café-Museum Elefant* at the station. **Buses** depart from the dusty yard about 300m south of the tourist office at the bottom of Str. Libertăţii and Str. Iuliu Maniu, but local maxitaxis for Moisei (continuing to Borşa Mon–Fri) start from km125, on the main road just east of the centre.

Beyond Vişeu de Sus

The straggling village of **MOISEI**, 12km west of Vişeu de Sus, lies beneath the foothills of the Rodna massif, whose peaks are often still snowy while fruit is ripening in the village's orchards. Though today it seems tranquil, in October 1944 Moisei suffered a tragedy that's become a symbol of atrocity and martyred innocence throughout Romania, when retreating Hungarian troops machine-gunned 29 villagers and set Moisei ablaze – a massacre commemorated by a circle of twelve stone figures by Vida Geza, with faces modelled on two of the victims and on the masks worn during Maramureş festivals. The memorial is 5km east of the centre, opposite a small museum at km141. A couple of kilometres along a side valley south of the village (off the Săcel road) stands a **monastery** that on August 15, the Feast of the Assumption, is the scene of a major pilgrimage. **Accommodation** in Moisei includes the pleasant *Motel Lido* (T0262/347 622; ❷) at Str. Principală 410, just east of the village centre at km137, and the *Pensiunea Călina* (T0262/347 602; ❶) at no. 380, at the west end of the village, half a kilometre east of the Săcel turning.

Most of the valley's amenities, including several cheap **hotels**, lie in BORŞA, a grubby town 5km east of Moisei – naturally, there's also a wooden church here, hidden away north of Str. Libertăţii, west of the centre; it was rebuilt in 1718 and painted internally by Zaharia Zugrav in 1765. At km143, 3km west of the centre, is the clean and tidy *Pension Rominvest* (T0745/275 910; ❷), while the *Motel Rodna* (T0262/344 961, Wwww.borsa.ro/rodna; ❷), down an alley opposite Str. Libertăţii 197, just 300m west of the centre, has small but neat and good-value rooms. Right in the centre, the dilapidated *Hotel Iezer* (T0262/343 430 or 0740/141 156; ❶) offers very cheap rooms without hot water or breakfast. Just east, there's the overly rustic *Perla Maramureşului*, opposite the hospital at Str. Victoriei 37 (T0262/342 539; ❷). For **food**, the *Motel Rodna* houses an *autoservire* restaurant and pizzeria, and there's a Unicarm supermarket just west of the *Perla Maramureşului*, with **internet** and video games just beyond. **Hiking maps** (in French and Hungarian) are available in shops and tourist agencies. **Maxitaxis** west to Moisei (continuing to Vişeu de Sus Mon–Fri) leave from the west end of the bridge (just west of the centre); those to the east leave from the hospital, opposite the *Perla Maramureşului*.

It's 10km (maxitaxis every 40min) to the **Borşa Complex ski resort** (beginners and intermediates only), where there's also plenty of **accommodation**, mostly open year-round: the best is the modern *Hotel AS* (T0262/342 333, Wwww .hotel.as.borsa.ro; ❸) by the main road at the bottom of the complex, but it's more convenient to stay near the chairlift (daily 9am–5pm), just above the maxitaxi terminal. Here you'll find the *Cerbul* (T0262/344 199; ❸) and the slightly nicer *Focus* (T0262/344 038; ❸), which also houses a ski school (T0744/154 933). There are several friendly little **pensions** (❷), with two- to five-bed rooms, such as *Pensiunea Calin* (T0262/344 263, Wwww.pensiuneacalin.eborsa.ro), 300m beyond the *Cerbul* at Str. Bradet 9B; *Pensiunea Favorit* (T0722/621 649) and *Pensiunea Mihali* (T0740/490 397), both just below the maxitaxi terminal; and *Pensiunea Hantig-Lucian* (T0262/343 663), at Str. Cascada 6. The last is 1km up the track to the **Cascada Cailor** (Horses' Waterfall), Romania's highest. There's also a **camping** spot at the start of Str. Cascada. A new wooden church has been built in the resort, in traditional style except for its massive stone plinth. From Borşa Complex, a hairpin road heads up to the **Prislop Pass** – 2km away as the crow flies, but a dozen kilometres by this tightly twisting road.

There are four buses a day to Borşa from Baia Mare via the Iza valley, one each from Bistriţa and Vatra Dornei, and three daily Sighet–Cluj services at Săcel. **Buses** from Borşa to Baia Mare and elsewhere usually set off from either Borşa Complex or Baia Borşa (and vice versa).

Hiking in the Rodna mountains

The **Rodnas** are one of Romania's best **hiking** areas, largely because you're sure to have them virtually to yourself. The easiest way into the mountains is either by the chairlift from Borşa Complex (you may have to wait until a dozen or so people have gathered) or from the 1416m **Prislop Pass**; from the pass you can head either north into the Maramureş mountains, wild and largely unvisited, although scarred by mining and forestry, or south into the Rodnas. Following red triangles, then blue stripes, it should take you two hours at most to reach the main crest at the Gărgălău saddle, from where you can follow red stripes east to the Rotunda Pass and ultimately to Vatra Dornei (see p.273), or west into the highest part of the massif. The route west will get you to La Cruce in four-and-a-half hours, from where you can turn right to follow blue stripes up to the weather station on the summit of **Mount Pietrosul** (2303m), ninety minutes away. There are great views in all directions, particularly deep into Ukraine to the north. Borşa is 1600m below, and it takes another two-and-a-half hours to get back there. Alternatively, you can just follow red stripes from the Complex to the Cascada Cailor (see opposite), which takes ninety minutes.

The **Rodna National Park** is based on the south side of the mountains (℡0263/377 175, Ⓔparcrodna@email.ro), but there's an office in Borşa at Str. Zorilor 2B (℡0740/002 125, Ⓔpnmrborsa@ddcnet.ro); the Maramureş Mountains became a Natural Park in 2005, with its headquarters in Vişeu de Sus, at Str. 22 Decembrie 20 (℡0262/352 216, Ⓦwww.muntiimaramuresului .ro). Apart from camping, the only place to **stay** in the mountains is the *Puzdrele cabana* – two to three hours' trek from the hamlet of Poiana Borşa (east of Borşa), following the route marked by blue triangles, which continues to the main ridge in another couple of hours. With a map, you can hike on south and down towards the Someş Mare valley and Năsăud (see p.219) in two days, camping wild en route.

Routes on to Moldavia and Transylvania

Just before the Prislop Pass, at the border of Maramureş with **Bucovina**, you'll see a monument marking the site where the last Tatar raid was finally driven off in 1717. At the pass, close to the Hanul Prişlop bar, the *Cabana Alpina*, and a new (stone) monastery, the **Horă at Prislop festival** takes place on the nearest Sunday to August 1, attracting thousands of participants and spectators. On the far side of the pass, the road runs down the lovely Bistriţa Aurie Valley to Câmpulung Moldovenesc (see p.271), from where you can reach Suceava and several of the painted monasteries by rail. A daily bus runs from Vişeu (at 7am) to Vatra Dornei; you can change either there or at Iacobeni for trains to Câmpulung Moldovenesc. Travelling to **Transylvania**, four trains a day link Vişeu de Jos with Salva, 61km to the south and a junction on the busier line from Cluj to Vatra Dornei and Suceava; there's also a daily bus from Borşa to Bistriţa, and three from Sighet to Cluj via the Iza Valley and Săcel.

Travel details

Trains

Baia Mare to: Beclean (2 daily; 3hr); Brasov (3–4 daily; 7hr 45min–9hr 35min); Bucharest (3 daily; 10hr 30min–12hr 10min); Cluj (4 daily; 2hr 45min–5hr 20min); Dej (8 daily; 1hr 55min–3hr 50min); Satu Mare (10 daily; 1hr 10min–2hr); Timişoara (1 daily; 6hr).

Satu Mare to: Baia Mare (10 daily; 1hr 10min–1hr 50min); Brasov (2–3 daily; 9hr–11hr 10min); Bucharest (2 daily; 12hr–13hr 30min); Cluj (2 daily; 4–5hr); Negreşti-Oas (5 daily; 1hr 35min–2hr); Oradea (6 daily; 1hr 55min–3hr 10min); Timişoara (1 daily; 4hr 45min).

Sighet to: Beclean (3 daily; 4hr 15min); Brasov (1 daily; 10hr 20min); Bucharest (1 daily; 13hr

30min); Cluj (2 daily; 5hr 40min–6hr); Salva (4 daily; 3hr 35min–4hr); Timişoara (1 daily; 12hr 35min); Vişeu de Jos (6 daily; 1hr 50min).

Buses and maxitaxis

Baia Mare to: Bicaz (3 daily); Bistrita (3 daily); Borsa (4 daily); Bucharest (2 daily); Cavnic (4–5 daily); Cluj (7 daily); Hoteni (1 daily); Negreşti-Oas (3 daily); Oradea (2 daily); Satu Mare (8 daily); Sighet (7 daily); Târgu Lăpuş (7–9 daily); Vişeu (4–5 daily); Zalau (2 daily).

Borşa to: Baia Mare (4 daily); Bistrita (1 daily); Sighet (3 daily); Vatra Dornei (1 daily).

Satu Mare to: Baia Mare (8 daily); Bistrita (3 daily); Cluj (2 daily); Negreşti-Oas (4 daily); Oradea (7 daily); Sighet (3 daily Mon–Fri, 1 daily Sat & Sun); Timişoara (1 daily).

Sighet to: Baia Mare (7 daily); Borsa (4 daily); Botiza (2 daily Mon–Fri); Budeşti (5 daily Mon–Fri); Cluj (3 daily); Costiui (7 daily); Ieud (1 daily); Mara (10 daily); Satu Mare (3 daily Mon–Fri, 1 daily Sat & Sun); Sapânta (10 daily); Târgu Lăpuş (1 daily); Oradea/Timişoara (2 daily); Poienile de sub Munte (2 daily Mon–Fri, 1 daily Sat & Sun); Poienile Izei (1 daily Mon–Fri); Vişeu (2 daily).

Târgu Lapuş to: Baia Mare (7 daily); Baiut (2 daily); Cluj (1 daily); Cupseni (1 daily); Sighet (1 daily).

Vişeu to: Baia Mare (2–3 daily); Borsa (4 daily Mon–Fri); Botiza (1 daily); Sighet (2 daily).

International buses

Baia Mare to: Budapest, Hungary (Tues & Fri).
Satu Mare to: Budapest (1 daily Mon–Sat).

The Banat

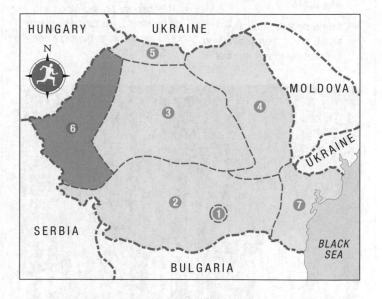

CHAPTER 6 # Highlights

✳ **Oradea** Charming town, rampant with Secession architecture and near a couple of small spa resorts. See p.309

✳ **Chişcău and Meziad Caves** Take a tour through these atmospheric caves, featuring stunning stalactite and stalagmite formations. See p.316

✳ **Stâna de Vale** Attractive alpine resort, from where you can partake in any number of hikes along the western spur of the Apuseni mountains. See p.316

✳ **Timişoara** Birthplace of the 1989 revolution, this vibrant, engaging city is characterized by colourful squares, green parks and lively nightlife. See p.323

✳ **Băile Herculane** Elegant Habsburg-era buildings and bathing opportunities aplenty in this once fashionable spa. See p.331

▲ Piaţa Unirii, Oradea

The Banat

The **Banat** (Bánság) is the historical term for the western marches of Romania between the Timiş and Mureş rivers, but it has also come to include the Crişana, to the north between the Apuseni massif and the Hungarian border. With its largely featureless scenery, great rivers, historical sites and intermingled ethnic groups, the Banat has much in common with its neighbours, Hungary's Great Plain and Serbia's Vojvodina region. The frontiers were supposedly settled according to the principle of national self-determination at the Versailles conference of 1918–20, each country's delegates bringing reams of demographic maps and statistics to support their claims, but in truth the region's ethnic tangle could not be unpicked. Communist policies towards minorities were comparatively fair until the 1960s, when an increasingly hard line led to a haemorrhaging of the Banat's population, particularly of Magyars. In both 1988 and 1989, around 80,000 left, as liberalization gained pace in Hungary but things went downhill fast in Romania. The Schwab Germans, who colonized this area when the marshes were drained after the expulsion of the Turks, have now almost all emigrated to Germany. Nevertheless, many Slovaks, Serbs, Magyars and other minority groups remain.

Key attractions are the cities of **Oradea**, **Arad** and **Timişoara**, each of which also dominates a route between Transylvania and Hungary or Serbia, and gives access to most other places of interest in the region. Timişoara, in particular, is hugely enjoyable, and the city not to miss should you have to choose just one in the region. There are also rural temptations aplenty, such as the western ranges of the **Apuseni mountains**, with their stalactite caves and wooden churches, and the spas at **Băile Herculane** and **Băile Felix**; moreover, there are some terrific **festivals** in the smaller villages.

Oradea and around

The congenial city of **ORADEA**, on the banks of the River Crişul Repede, is the capital of Crişana. It's close to the site of Biharea – the capital of the Vlach *voivode*, Menumorut, who resisted Hungarian claims on the region during the tenth century. Founded around a monastery, the medieval town of Nagyvarad (as the Magyars still call it) prospered during the reign of **Mátyás Corvinus**, who was raised at the Bishop's Palace here, and later acquired a mammoth Vauban-style citadel and the wealth of charming Secession buildings (built in the decade before World War I) which are today Oradea's most characteristic feature. Aside from being a useful place to break a journey to or from Hungary, Oradea is just a short bus ride away from the spas at **Băile Felix** and **Băile 1 Mai**.

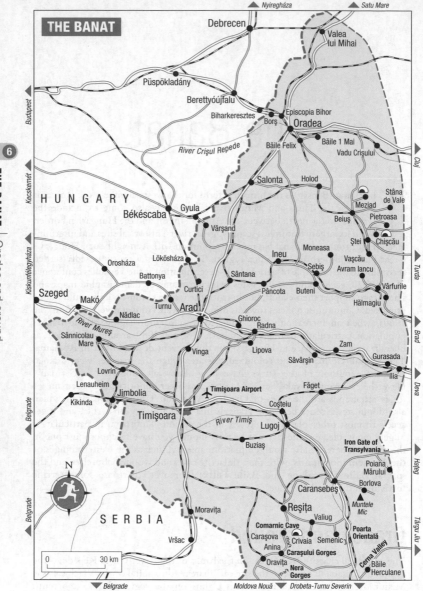

THE BANAT

Nyireghaza   Satu Mare

Debrecen

Valea
lui Mihai

Püspökladány

Berettyóújfalu

Biharkeresztes   Borş   Episcopia Bihor
                                Oradea

River Crişul Repede   Băile Felix   Băile 1 Mai
                                        Vadu Crişului

Salonta   Holod

Stâna
de Vale

H U N G A R Y   Gyula   Meziad   Pietroasa

Békéscaba   Beiuş

Vărşand   Ştei   Chişcău

Ineu   Moneasa

Orosháza   Vaşcău
Lökösháza   Sebiş   Avram Iancu
Battonya   Sântana
Curtici   Pâncota   Buteni   Vârfurile
Szeged   Makó   Turnu   Arad   Hălmagiu
Nădlac   Ghioroc
River Mureş   Radna
Sânnicolau   Vinga   Lipova   Zam
Mare   Săvârşin   Gurasada
Lovrin   Ilia
Lenauheim   Timişoara Airport   Făget
Kikinda   Jimbolia   Costeiu
Timişoara   River Timiş   Lugoj
Buziaş   Iron Gate of
Transylvania
Poiana
Mărului
Borlova
Caransebeş
Moraviţa   Reşiţa   Muntele
Mic
Valiug
Comarnic Cave   Poarta
Caraşova   Crivaia   Semenic   Orientală
Vršac   Anina   Caraşului Gorges
Oraviţa   Băile
Nera   Herculane
Gorges

N

0   30 km

S E R B I A

Belgrade   Moldova Nouă   Drobeta-Turnu Severin

Budapest
Kecskemét
Kiskunfélegyháza
Belgrade
Belgrade
Cluj
Turda
Brad
Deva
Hateg
Târgu Jiu
Cerna Valley

Arrival and information

From the **train station** on Piaţa Bucureşti, trams run south along Calea
Republicii towards the city centre (those with black numbers #1N and #3N run
from the station and those with red numbers #1R and #3R run north to it), past
the Crişul department store and southeast along Str. Gen. Magheru. To reach
the city centre proper, alight at the department store stop and walk on along

Str. Republicii. The **bus station** is southeast of the centre at Str. Războieni 81, 200m east of the Oradea Est train halt; take bus #10 into town, or it's a thirty-minute walk. C&I maxitaxis run from the station forecourt. The **airport** is on the southern edge of Oradea, on the Arad road; buses leave from the TAROM office, Piaţa Regele Ferdinand 2, seventy minutes before each flight. A taxi to or from the airport should cost no more than €5.

A tourist office may appear just north of the *Hotel Astoria*, opposite the theatre, but until then the best source of information is Apuseni Experience, at Piaţa 1 Decembrie 4–6 (Mon–Fri 9am–5pm; ☎0259/472 434, Ⓦwww .apuseniexperience.ro); they can arrange visits to the Chişcău and Meziad caves (see p.316), as well as organize a range of hiking, biking and ski-touring trips in the Apuseni, and cultural tours. There's **internet access** at the Internet Club Andeznet, Str. A. Edy 2 (daily 10am–2am); opposite the Military Museum on Str. Armatei Române; Computer House, Str. Iuliu Maniu 6 (daily 8am–9pm); Internet Café, Str. Enescu 24 (daily 9am–10/11pm); Gamester, Str. Eminescu 6; and Club Internet, Str.Chitu 1.

Accommodation

Oradea's **hotels** tend to be either budget or high-end, with little in between. The Posticum cultural and youth centre, south of the fortress at Str. Teiului 26 (☎0259/431 398, Ⓔinfo@posticum.ro), has **dorm beds** for just €3 with your own sleeping bag or €5 without, or rooms with two to four beds (❸). The HI-affiliated *Hostel Felix*, Str. Eminescu 11 (☎0259/437 011, Ⓔtineret_bh @yahoo.com), has beds in spacious four-bed rooms (with or without bathroom) from €10. Otherwise, there are possibilities in **Băile Felix** and **Băile 1 Mai**, two resorts a short distance southeast of town (see p.315). The latter also has a **campsite**.

Astoria Str. Teatrului 1 ☎0259/430 508.
A pleasant Secession building with a range of rather tired, but clean and cheap, one- to three-bed rooms, with or without baths or showers. ❷

Atlantic Str. Iosif Vulcan 9 ☎0359/172 263, Ⓦwww.hotelatlantic.ro. Decent new four-star place with a/c rooms decorated in different primary colours; there's a restaurant and spa, and good weekend rates. ❸–❹

Atrium Str. Republicii 38 ☎0259/414 421, Ⓦwww.hotelatrium.ro. Exceptional, very good-value hotel with windows opening onto an airy atrium. The rooms are very stylish, while the bathrooms come with cute little corner tubs. Home to a quality restaurant, too. ❺

Continental Aleea Ştrandului 1 ☎0259/418 655, Ⓦwww.continentalhotels.ro. Part of the *Continental* chain, this thoroughly modern and efficient hotel is frequented almost exclusively by businesspeople and tour groups. ❻–❽

Elite Parcul I.C. Brătianu 26 ☎0259/414 924, Ⓦwww.hotelelite.ro. A far classier and less expensive option than the nearby *Continental*, this small hotel has sumptuous rooms full of character; facilities include private parking, sauna and

Jacuzzi, not to mention an enchanting little restaurant. ❺–❼

Gala Str. B. P. Haşdeu 20 ☎0259/467 177, Ⓦwww.hotelgala.ro. Reasonable-value hotel with comfortable, if slightly colourless, rooms; facilities include sauna, massage, private parking and an inviting cellar bar. ❹

Góbé Pension Str. D. Gherea 26 ☎0259/413 513, Ⓦwww.gobe.ro. Just south of the citadel, this is a little gem of a guesthouse, with fittings in the style of a Hungarian *csarda*, such as brightly coloured hand-woven duvets and wooden furniture painted with Hungarian peasant motifs. Friendly owners and very reasonably priced, too. ❹

Parc Calea Republicii 5 ☎0259/411 699. Another pleasant if slightly shabby Secession building on the city's main pedestrianized street. The rooms – singles, doubles and triples with and without shower – are perfectly clean and spacious. ❷

Scorilo Parcul Petőfi 16 ☎0259/470 910, Ⓦwww.hotelscorilo.ro. Comfortable if functional rooms with balconies over a courtyard, but there's a fine (non-smoking) restaurant as well as courtyard/cellar bar (depending on season), and well-trained staff. ❹

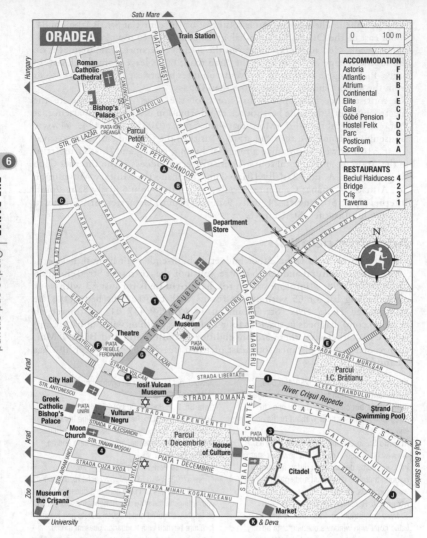

The City

Oradea sits astride the **Crişul Repede River**, north of which are the main shopping area and a couple of small museums, while to the south are the city's most interesting buildings and the citadel.

North of the river

In the large leafy park just west of the train station, the **Roman Catholic Cathedral**, reputedly the largest Baroque building in Romania, was built in 1752–80 by countless serfs. Ordinary enough on the outside, its interior is decorated with gold leaf and marble and accommodates a huge organ – posters advertise regular concerts. The serfs' labour was also doubtless exploited to construct the vast U-shaped **Bishop's Palace** adjacent to the cathedral; built by

The great outdoors

Romania's abundant mountains, forests, hills, rivers and lakes offer unlimited potential to indulge in a wide range of outdoor pursuits, from hiking the dramatic peaks of the country's many mountain ranges and hitting the pistes in Poiana Brașov, to tracking an astonishing range of birds in the Danube Delta or wildlife in the Carpathians. Moreover, adventure sports such as kayaking and canoeing are beginning to make their mark.

Scaling the peaks

Crisscrossed by an intricate nexus of forestry tracks and waymarked paths, the beautiful and unspoilt Romanian countryside offers some of the most enjoyable **hiking** anywhere in Europe, with trails to suit all abilities. Cutting across the country are the sinuous **Carpathian mountains** – a continuation of the Alps – whose best-known range is the **Făgăraş** (see p.146), between Braşov and Sibiu in the south of Transylvania, harbouring more than seventy lakes and Romania's most elevated peaks, the highest of which is Moldoveanu (2544m). However, it's the **Retezat** and **Piatra Craiului** mountains (see p.181 & p.144) which present Romania's most challenging and scenically rewarding hikes, the former spotted with dozens of glacial lakes, and the latter a small but stunning limestone ridge. Nearby, just south of Braşov, the **Bucegi massif** (see p.126) offers shorter and easier walks among dramatic crags, caves and waterfalls. Less well known, and consequently less visited, options include the remote and lovely **Rodna** mountains (see p.304), near the Ukrainian border in Maramureş; the more modest **Bucovina** hills (see p.259) – studded with glorious painted monasteries – immediately east; and, closing off the western end of the Transylvanian plateau, the **Apuseni** mountains (see p.207), which offer comparatively undemanding hikes and great karstic phenomena such as limestone caves, potholes and gorges. Scattered around all these ranges are cabanas, convivial places offering basic accommodation and sometimes meals. Green Mountain Holidays (see p.216) offer an exciting range of guided hikes.

Hikers in the Făgăraş mountains ▲

Mountain stream in the Retezat range ▼

Hitting the slopes

Although the skiing is nowhere near as advanced as in many other European countries, Romania's ten or so small, rapidly developing **ski resorts** are well equipped, efficient, safe and inexpensive. The most popular ski centre is **Poiana Braşov** (see p.141), thanks to its superior slopes and facilities; it also has the longest season (Nov–March/April). Elsewhere, there's good skiing at Predeal, Buşteni and Sinaia, a chain of resorts along the lovely Prahova Valley (see p.126); Borşa in Maramureş (for beginners); Păltiniş south of Sibiu; Semenic in southwestern Transylvania; and Durău/Ceahlău on the edge of Moldavia. Most of Romania's **pistes** are rated "medium" (red) or "easy" (blue), but the major resorts have at least one "difficult" (black) run each.

▲ Snowboarder in Poiana Braşov

▼ Mountain cabin, Buşteni

Wildlife-watching

As Europe's most extensive wetland, and the world's largest continuous reedbed, the Danube Delta (see p.338) is heaven for **birdwatchers**. Millions of birds winter here, or stop over during the spring (March–May) and autumn (Aug–Oct) migrations a unique and colourful concentration of different **species**, including heron, little egrets, red-breasted geese, the endangered pygmy cormorant and Europe's largest pelican colonies. The best times for viewing are April to early June and August to early October, but you'll be rewarded with a fantastic birding experience at any time of year. Agencies arrange **boat tours** down the main Delta channels, and their Tulcea offices may sometimes rent small boats, which are the only means of penetrating the backwaters where most of the birds nest. Canoes, kayaks or rowing boats are

Little egret in the Danube Delta ▲

Tourist cave ▼

best for **exploration**, and it's also fun to negotiate with a local fisherman for a boat (*Pot s'închiriez o barcă?*) – he'll probably act as rower and guide.

No less exhilarating is **wildlife-tracking** in the Carpathian mountains, which typically entails exploration of the forests looking for markings and tracks made by large carnivores. Specially designed forest hideouts are used for **bear watching**, and there's a reasonable chance of catching sight of these captivating animals, though you're unlikely to have the same degree of success with the magnificent grey **wolf**. A couple of excellent agencies specializing in wildlife trips are Transylvanian Wolf (see p.145) and Roving Romania (see p.135).

Caving

Romania has some marvellous **large caves** (*peşteri*), replete with magnificent stalactites and stalagmites, and many **mountain caves** known only to a dedicated band of potholers. Indeed, the science and practice of caving owes much to a Romanian, Emil Racoviţă, who founded the world's first speleological institute at Cluj University, near the karst zone of the Apuseni mountains (see p.214). This region offers fabulous possibilities, from easy strolling passages to vertical shafts and flooded tunnels: the most renowned **tourist caves** are Meziad and the even more spectacular "Bears' Cave" at Chişcău (see p.316); there are also big **river caves** such as Humpleu, Magura and Cetăţile Ponorului. The other main areas are the Mehedinţi massif in the southern Banat, which has river caves such as Topolniţa, Cloşani and Comarnic, and the Piatra Craiului, where you'll find the Dâmbovicioara cave. Serious potholers should contact the Racoviţa Institute in Bucharest or Cluj (Ⓦ www.iser.ro).

Franz Anton Hillebrandt in 1762–77, it was modelled on Lucas von Hildebrandt's Belvedere Palace in Vienna. The composer Michael Haydn, brother of the more famous Joseph, worked here as the bishop's music director from 1760–62.

Turning south towards the river, **Calea Republicii** becomes a pedestrianized promenade, lined with shops, cafés, fast-food joints and many ostentatious Secession buildings in various states of decay. Of particular interest are the buildings at the intersection of Calea Republicii and Str. Eminescu; although missing much of their original plasterwork, the buildings at no. 10 and no. 12 (the former Apollo Palace) have retained some outstanding features, notably heavily stuccoed facades and corner turrets.

Calea Republicii leads to **Piața Regele Ferdinand**, dominated by the State Theatre, a typically pompous design by the Viennese duo Helmer and Fellner completed in 1900. Just behind the theatre stand two fine Secession buildings: the Adorján tenement houses at Str. Patrioților 4 and 6, built in 1903 and 1904, and each sporting a flurry of rosettes.

Just to the east of Str. Republicii are two small memorial houses: the lovely **Muller building** (Wed, Fri & Sat 10am–2pm & 4–6pm, Tues, Thurs & Sun 10am–3pm) in the tiny Traian Park commemorates the Magyar poet **Endre Ady** (1877–1919) who lived in Oradea for four years and, unusually for his era, opposed Hungarian chauvinism towards the Romanians. Formerly a society café where Ady and his pals would gather for evenings of drinks and bonhomie, it now keeps a handful of personal effects and Ady-era furnishings, including a neatly arranged editorial suite complete with beautiful oak bureau – to the rear is a cool, shaded terrace café and basement bar (see p.314).

The other memorial house, at Str. Vulcan 16 (same times), remembers the poet and novelist **Iosif Vulcan** (1841–1907), who lived here from 1880 to 1906. Vulcan gathered the works of key literary players of his day in the literary journal *Familia*, which survives to this day – it was in this magazine that Mihai Eminescu made his debut in 1866 with the poem *De-aș avea* (*If I Had*), a copy of which is on display. The house contains a few items of furniture, including Vulcan's Biedermeier desk, though it largely seeks to re-create the atmosphere of a late nineteenth-century literary salon. Across the road at Str. Vulcan 11, the Darvas-La Roche house (1909–10) is the best example of a Secession-style private house in Oradea.

South of the river

Across the Crișul Repede from Piața Regele Ferdinand is **Piața Unirii**, a vast open space which, beyond the nondescript Catholic church (1720–41) half-blocking the square's north side, is replete with fanciful Secession buildings. The **City Hall** in the northwestern corner is, however, a monumental restatement of well-worn classical themes to which the architects added a fun touch: chimes that play the *March of Avram Iancu* every hour. Given that the Habsburgs were still in control when the building was raised in 1902–03, it seems odd that they allowed this commemoration of Iancu, a Romanian revolutionary who inspired the protest on the "Field of Liberty" at Blaj in 1848 (see p.173), and who then took to the hills with a guerrilla band, harassing Magyar troops and landlords and urging the serfs to revolt. Just south of City Hall is the **Greek Catholic Episcopal Palace** (1905), a spectacular pile spotted with all manner of protrusions and jutting towers.

Facing these across Piața Unirii is the splendidly named **Vulturul Negru** (Black Eagle), an ornate Secession-style edifice dating from 1908. Running through it is an arcade, notable for its beautiful stained-glass roof connecting three streets; recently renovated, the arcade is now lined with cafés and bars, making it one of the most enjoyable places in town for a drink. Part of the complex is occupied by a hotel – once an ill-lit labyrinth of rooms and corridors inhabited by brooding staff and a furtive clientele, it reopened as a luxury hotel, but alas soon closed again.

To the south of the hotel, on the corner of Piaţa Unirii and Str. Alecsandri, the **Moskovits Palace** (1911) is another enduring Secession edifice – cut into the brickwork on the upper half of the green-and-yellow checked facade are several fine reliefs of men and women tackling their daily chores. Beyond here, Oradea's main Orthodox church, built in 1784–92, marks the stylistic transition from Baroque to Neoclassical; it is better known as the **Moon Church** after the large sphere mounted beneath its clock, which rotates to indicate the lunar phases in a 28-day cycle.

A short walk east of here, along Str. Traian Moşoiu, is the city's small Jewish quarter. There are no fewer than three imposing **synagogues** nearby (there were once eleven in the city), testament to Oradea's role as a major Jewish settlement prior to World War II: on Str. Independenţei near the Vulturul Negru; on Piaţa Rahovei; and the only one still functioning, just east of Piaţa Unirii at Str. Mihai Viteazul 2. In 1927 Codreanu's League of the Archangel Michael, soon to become the Iron Guard (see box, p.243), held a congress here – they wrecked four synagogues before leaving.

To the east of Piaţa Unirii rises the imposing bulk of Oradea's **citadel**, built in the fourteenth century on the site of an earlier wooden fort – rebuilt by Italian engineers in 1569–98, and given its final shape in 1775–6, it has survived at least eight sieges. The Gothic cathedral, in which five Hungarian kings were buried, was destroyed in 1565, while the present Fortress Church was built in 1775–6 by Lodovico Marini.

The pentagonal citadel, with bastions guarding each corner, was additionally protected by a moat filled from the River Peţea, which runs around the southern edge of the town. Refurbishment of its dilapidated walls and buildings such as the bakery and officers' barracks, both dating from 1692, and the food store and administration block, built in 1775, is finally under way. Part of the old Princely Palace (built in 1620–9 by the Italian Giacomo Resti) now houses the university's art faculty – you can enter the courtyard to view some interesting pieces of sculpture. There's also a summer craft school, and an open-air theatre in the sixteenth-century Ciunt Bastion; a bread museum should open soon.

Heading south from Piaţa Unirii, Str. Avram Iancu becomes Calea Armatei Romăne, where at no. 1A is the **Museum of the Crişana**, which should reopen in 2011. Previously in the Bishop's Palace, the collection comprises fairly standard history, natural history and ethnographic displays, as well as a good selection of nineteenth- and twentieth-century art. On the left at no. 24, the **Military Museum** (Mon–Fri 10am–4pm; €0.50), contains a dusty collection of costumes, weaponry and medals through the ages. Opposite it is the garrison's modern **wooden church**; under 1km south is another one, built in Letca in 1762 and moved here in 1991 to be the chapel of the university's theological faculty. With its new porch, radiators and spick-and-span pine pews, it no longer has the authentic atmosphere of a village church, but it is usually open and you can climb up into the tower.

Eating, drinking and entertainment

The town has a smattering of fairly lively **drinking** venues, the most popular being *The Bridge* (see opposite) and the cool *Chanson Café* in the basement of the Endre Ady memorial house – it has live music on selected weekdays. *Kelly's*, at the corner of Str. Republicii and Str. Moscovei, is a poor imitation of an Irish pub, but it has a pleasant enough terrace and limited bar meals. Otherwise, there is a cluster of cafés and bars inside the revamped Vulturul Negru arcade.

Theatrical and operatic performances (in both Romanian and Hungarian) at the State Theatre on Piaţa Regele Ferdinand (Ⓦwww.teatruloradea.ro) are well regarded, as are concerts by the town's **Philharmonic Orchestra** at Piaţa 1 Decembrie 10 (tickets from Str. Republicii 6). There's often live jazz at the Posticum Centre (see p.311). Children will enjoy performances (often puppet shows) at the Arcadia **Children's Theatre**, at the Str. Alecsandri end of the Vulturul Negru arcade.

There's scant choice when it comes to **eating in Oradea**; the best of the hotel restaurants is at the *Scorilo*, but the *Atrium* and *Elite* also have smart and affordable restaurants, both with accomplished international menus.

Beciul Haiducesc Str. Traian Moşoiu 5. With its pine benches and wooden partitions draped with sheepskins, this makes a cosy venue to tuck into above-average Romanian food (closed Sun).

The Bridge Aleea Gojdu 2. At the southern end of the footbridge, this is a convivial pub-restaurant serving pizza and pasta.

Criş Piaţa Independenţei 51. One of Romania's few vegetarian restaurants, and it's a surprisingly pleasant venue. Mon–Thurs & Sun 9am–8pm, Fri 9am–5pm.

Taverna Str. Eminescu 2. With traditional Romanian fare and waitresses in local costume, plus a no-smoking section, this is a reliable choice.

Băile Felix and Băile 1 Mai

Within easy reach of Oradea are the **spas** of Băile Felix and Băile 1 Mai. Neither is especially attractive, but they're enjoyable places to spend an afternoon relaxing; treatments (available at hotels) include healing baths in sapropelic fossil mud, and dips in pools fed by the warm and slightly radioactive River Peţea, in which the **thermal lotus**, otherwise found only in the Nile Delta, has survived several ice ages.

Just 8km southeast of Oradea along the DN76, **BĂILE FELIX** is a compact town whose atmospheric residential core has been swamped by an ugly jumble of concrete high-rise hotels. Its central attractions are a large **thermal pool** (daily 8am–7pm; €3) surrounded by mock-rustic buildings, and a park containing a **wooden church**. Most of the dozen or so hotels are bland and not particularly good value, though there are one or two reasonable choices: the best upper-end places are the *Termal* (☎0259/318 214, @hotel.termal@turismfelix.ro; ❺), which has pool, sauna and solarium, and *Nufărul* (☎0259/318 142 ❺). Decent-value two-stars include the *Lotus* (☎0259/318 361; ❸) and the very basic *Felix* (☎0259/318 421, ☏318 422; ❷). Much more homely is the bright little *Pension Sebastian* (☎0745/048 367; ❶), near the market stalls, and, nearby, the *Bungalow Monaco* complex (☎0722/318 180, Ⓦwww.hotelmonacofelix.com; ❸), with hotel rooms (some a/c) and bungalows in its own little compound – and **bikes** for rent.

You'll also find many houses advertising private rooms (*cazare* or *camera*), not to mention proprietors hanging about the streets with signs – expect to pay around €25 for a double with bathroom. At the entry to Felix the small *Apollo* **campsite** is open all year (☎0743/189 898, Ⓦwww.campingapollo.ro; ❶). As for **restaurants**, take your pick from any number of identical places. The resort is served by tram #3N from Oradea's train station or bus #12 from Piaţa Unirii to the Nufărul terminal on the city outskirts, and then a minibus (€0.50); alternatively, eight trains a day head for Felix.

The much smaller and less developed spa of **BĂILE 1 MAI** (Ântâi Mai) is also reached by minibus from Nufărul, turning off the DN76 just before Băile Felix. The *Perla* (☎0259/318 230, Ⓦwww.perla1mai.ro; ❹) is the best hotel here, with various pools, hot tubs and sauna; there are also some excellent pensions, such as *Catalin* at no. 15a (☎0259/319 848; ❸) and, a few paces along at no. 87, *Chrisland* (☎0259/319 048; ❸).

The western Apuseni mountains

The **Apuseni mountains** lie predominantly in Transylvania (see p.207), but a few attractions along its **western approaches** are within easy reach of Oradea. Most are close to the DN76, but trains to Beiuş and Vaşcău now take a very roundabout route, following the main Arad line through **SALONTA**, birthplace of the Hungarian poet Arany János (1817–82). In a seventeenth-century tower on the main square, Str. Libertăţii, a small **museum** (April–Oct Tues–Fri & Sun 10am–2pm & 4–6pm; Nov–March daily 10am–4pm) exhibits a few of his personal effects.

Beiuş and the caves

The small town of **BEIUŞ**, 55km southeast of Oradea, is the main jumping-off point for the impressive stalactite **caves of Meziad and Chişcău**, excursions to which are organized by Apuseni Experience in Oradea (see p.311).

Travelling independently from Beiuş, take one of four daily buses from the station on the southern edge of town to **MEZIAD**, some 10km northeast. The famous Meziad cave, with its huge entrance arch, is a further 3km beyond the village. The cave was first explored in 1859, and after a road was built in the 1960s it was visited by some 25,000 people a year until its popularity was usurped by the opening of the even more spectacular cave at Chişcău in 1980. Hour-long **tours** (Tues–Sun 9–11am & 2–4pm; €2) start whenever enough people gather; guides point out the stalactites and other features of this warren, whose total length is almost 5km. The excellent *Turul Panzío* (℡0259/325 243, 🅦www.remeteturul .ro; ❶) is 6km from the cave in the village of Remetea.

There are also bus services (Mon–Sat 2 daily) from Beiuş to **CHIŞCĂU**, some 25km southeast, where in 1975 quarry workers discovered a cave containing dozens of Neolithic bear skeletons – hence its name, **"Bears' Cave"** (Peştera Urşilor). Unlike other Romanian caves, this is atmospherically lit, making the one-hour tour (Tues–Sun 10am–5pm; €4) an unmissable experience. The rock formations of the 488m-long upper gallery – shaped like castles, wraiths and beasts – are accompanied by the sound of water crashing into subterranean pools.

Roşia, 20km north of Beiuş on a newly surfaced road to Bratca and Bucea (with daily buses from Beiuş to Roşia via Remetea), is the base for hiking in the unspoilt Padurea Craiului; *Tradiţional Casa* (℡0745/602 203, 🅦www.traditionalcasa.ro; ❺) is a tourist village with accommodation in beautifully restored houses, and other unusual features such as a climbing wall and furniture workshop, as well as horseriding, mountain bikes and great sunsets. **STÂNA DE VALE**, 30km east of Beiuş, is a modest alpine resort, where there's an excellent three-star hotel, the *Iadolina* (℡0259/322 583; ❸), plus cabins and a campsite serving hikers in summer and skiers in winter. The resort's three ski pistes are usually open from November to April, with lessons available for beginners. From here, it's about six hours' walk to the *Padiş* cabana (see p.214), taking a path marked with red stripes via the Poieni peak, the Cumpănăţelu saddle and the Vărăşoaia clearing. Experienced hikers might prefer the more challenging trail to Meziad (6–8hr, marked by blue triangles, not recommended in winter or bad weather); with many twists and turns around karstic features, this follows the ridge above the Iad valley, surmounting the Piatra Tisei peak.

East into the mountains

Buses run from Beiuş as far as **PIETROASA**, a picturesque village on the upper reaches of the River Crişul Pietros, where water-powered sawmills remain operational and older residents still wear traditional Bihor costume. Each year, on a Sunday in August, the villagers troop 8km north up the Aleu valley for the **festival** of Bulciugul de Valea Aleu. A forest road up to the Padiş plateau (see p.214) can be covered on foot or by car, and the hiking trail to the *Padiş* cabana, marked with blue crosses, follows the road for the most part, with a path diverging south after about 5km (marked by yellow triangles) to the Focul Viu cave and Cetăţile Ponorului. If you plan extensive hiking in the mountains, arm yourself with either the 1:200,000 *Munţii Apuseni* or the 1:35,000 *Valea Arieşului* **map**.

Just south of the turning to Pietroasa is Sudrigiu, where you'll find the headquarters of the Apuseni Nature Park; a couple of kilometres further south, **RIENI** is worth a look for its **wooden church**, just west of the village by the train halt. Built in 1753, this is now slightly run-down, with lots of woodpecker damage, but interesting for its doorway and its spire, typical of this area. However, the best part of the journey to Scarişoara comes once you leave the DN76 and the rail line beyond the grimy industrial town of **Ştei** – known as Dr Petru Groza under communism (see box) – and head eastwards along the sinuous DN75, where the scenery becomes more dramatic. The village of **BĂIŢA**, 10km east along the DN75, has several caves nearby and holds a lively **fair** on the last Sunday in September. On the far side of the Vârtop Pass (1160m) lie **Arieşeni** and **Gârda de Sus**, southern entry points to Padiş (see p.214).

Trains from Oradea terminate at **Vaşcău**, but the DN76 continues through the mountains for 32km to meet the Arad–Brad road and railway at the village of **Vârfurile**.

Arad and around

One of the Banat's oldest towns, **ARAD** has fewer sights than Oradea or Timişoara, and lacks their vibrancy. However, it can showcase an impressive number of Habsburg-era buildings as well as an eighteenth-century citadel, while its position on the road and rail routes between these two cities, and from Transylvania into Hungary, makes it a convenient place to stop off for an afternoon. It's also a good base from which to strike out towards **villages** in the foothills of the Apuseni mountains.

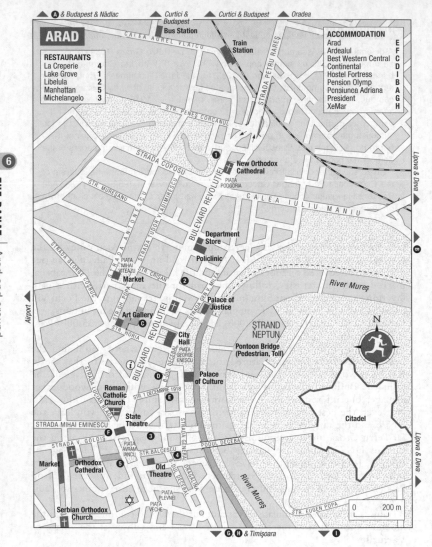

ARAD

A & Budapest & Nădlac   Curtici & Budapest   Curtici & Budapest   Oradea

Bus Station

Train Station

RESTAURANTS
La Creperie	4
Lake Grove	1
Libelula	2
Manhattan	5
Michelangelo	3

ACCOMMODATION
Arad	E
Ardealul	F
Best Western Central	C
Continental	D
Hostel Fortress	I
Pension Olymp	B
Pensiunea Adriana	A
President	G
XeMar	H

CALEA AUREL VLAICU

STRADA PETRU RAREŞ

STR. PENEŞ CORCANUL

STRADA COPOSU

New Orthodox Cathedral

PIAŢA PODGORIA

CALEA IULIU MANIU

STR. MUREŞANU

STRADA ANTONESCU

BULEVARD REVOLUŢIEI

STRADA TUDOR VLADIMIRESCU

Department Store

Policlinic

STR. CRIŞAN

PIAŢA MIHAI VITEAZU

Market

STRADA GEORGE COSBUC

STRADA DENY MICA

Palace of Justice

River Mureş

STR. GH. POPA

Art Gallery

STR. HORIA

City Hall

PIAŢA GEORGE ENESCU

ŞTRAND NEPTUN

Pontoon Bridge (Pedestrian, Toll)

BULEVARD REVOLUŢIEI

N

Roman Catholic Church

STR. 1 DECEMBRIE 1918

Palace of Culture

B-DUL DECEBAL

STRADA LUCIAN BLAGA

STRADA MIHAI EMINESCU

State Theatre

STRADA V. GOLDIŞ

PIAŢA AVRAM IANCU

STR. BĂLCESCU

Market

Orthodox Cathedral

Old Theatre

B-DUL DECEBAL

STRADA GENERAL

PODUL DECEBAL

Citadel

PIAŢA PLEVNEI

PIAŢA VECHE

Serbian Orthodox Church

STR. EUGEN POPA

River Mureş

0   200 m

Airport

Lipova & Deva

Lipova & Deva

G, H & Timişoara

Arrival and information

The **train and bus stations** lie 500m apart in the north of the city on Calea Aurel Vlaicu; take tram #1 or #6 for the city centre. Some trains from Timişoara halt only in the southern suburb of Arad Nou, from where tram #3 and bus #19 head into the centre. Arad's tiny **airport** (☎0257/254 440) is only 3km west of town, though you'll have to rely on taxis (around €5) as there's no public transport. The **tourist office** is at B-dul Revoluţiei 84 (Mon–Fri 9am–5pm, Sat 10am–2pm; ☎0257/270 277, ✉turism@primariaarad.ro).

Accommodation

There's plenty of accommodation here, with **hotels** and **pensions** both in the centre and the suburbs. The *Hostel Fortress*, south of the citadel at Str. Cetății 34 (☎0745/357 989, ✉fortress_arad@yahoo.com; ❶), is more like a youth hotel, with en-suite rooms rather than dorms, plus breakfast. There are also two reasonable **motels** within reach of the city: the *Hanul de la Răscruce* (☎0257/254 665; ❷), 8km west along the Nădlac road; and the *Vinga* (☎0257/460 630; ❷), in the village of the same name some 20km south of Arad on the road and railway to Timișoara.

Arad B-dul Decebal 9 ☎0257/280 894, ✉hotel_arad@yahoo.com. This decent place, in a fairly quiet central location, has large, high-ceilinged rooms, with and without bathroom. Good value. ❷–❸

Ardealul B-dul Revoluției 98 ☎0257/280 840, ⓦwww.hotelardealul.ro. Arad's most characterful hotel is a former coaching inn where Brahms, Liszt, Johann Strauss and Casals all once performed. The grand, spiralling staircase rather belies the faded, soulless rooms (triples and quads available, too), but it's reasonably cheap and there's a hearty breakfast included. ❸–❺

Best Western Central Str. Horia 8 ☎0257/256 636, ⓦwww.bestwesternarad.ro. This modern, central hotel has well-furnished rooms, plus sauna and gym; the welcoming staff also makes this one of the better places to stay. ❻

Continental Forum B-dul Revoluției 79 ☎0257/281 700, ⓦwww.continentalhotels.ro. The town's most expensive hotel is much like others in the Continental chain, a slick but ultimately charmless place aimed at business visitors and offering great online deals. ❹–❽

Pension Olymp Str. Vrancei 36 ☎0257/279 443, ⓦwww.pensiuneaolimp.ro. A sweet little pension in the eastern suburbs with fifteen clean and inviting rooms (with up to six beds), all with TV and bath; laundry facilities too. ❸

Pensiunea Adriana Str. Frații Neumann 7 ☎0257/289 120, ⓦwww.pensiuneaadriana.ro. Immediately west of the UTA Stadium, this simple but cosy option is handy for the bus and rail stations. ❷

President Calea Timișorii 164 ☎0257/278 804, ⓦwww.hotel-president.ro. This classy place, 2km south in Aradul Nou, has neat, colourful and airy rooms; there's also a decent restaurant. Tram #3 or #5. ❺

Hotel XeMar Calea Timișorii 1 ☎0257/287 485, ✉office@xemar.ro. Just across the bridge 1.5km south of town, this smart hotel has lovely, warmly decorated rooms; they've also got a simple, homely little pension 200m down the road at no. 13 (same tel. no). ❷–❹

The Town

Spearing southwards from the train station is **Bulevardul Revoluției**, its wooded central park bisected by busy tram lines. Of the many impressive buildings lining the boulevard, the standout is the brilliant white **City Hall** at no. 75, a wedding-cake-like edifice raised in 1872–74. Directly in front of it a plaque commemorates those who died during the 1989 revolution, while opposite, in the middle of the road, is a simple monument to the same martyrs. Closing off the street's southern end is the **State Theatre**, dating from 1872–74, while close by is the massive **Roman Catholic church** (1902–04), with an impressive domed entrance hall.

Immediately behind the theatre sits **Piața Avram Iancu**, a large green square fringed by numerous two- and three-storey Secession buildings, many adorned with interesting stucco work and motifs. East of the square, at Str. Gheorghe Lazăr 2, is the semi-derelict **Old Theatre**, built in 1817 – Eminescu and many famous actors worked here – while to the west lies the main **market** and the Baroque Romanian Orthodox cathedral (1862–65). The jumble of dusty streets south of the square once comprised Old Arad, and was also home to a large Serb minority, served by the **Serbian Orthodox church** (1698–1702), a standard Habsburg structure on Piața Sârbească.

Commanding a loop of the River Mureş, Arad's huge **citadel** faces the town on the west bank. A six-pointed star with ramparts and bastions angled to provide overlapping fields of fire, it was the state of the art in fortifications when it was constructed, in the style of Vauban, between 1762 and 1783. The Turks, against whom it was ostensibly raised, had already been pushed out of the Pannonian basin in 1718, but its underground casements provided the Habsburgs with a ready-made prison following the suppression of the 1784–85 and 1848–49 rebellions, as well as for Napoleonic prisoners of war, and for Gavrilo Princip after triggering World War I. The army has only recently moved out, and the citadel will become a museum complex before long.

After 1718, the Habsburgs drained the marshy southern Banat, an area known as the Partium, and colonized it with Swabians, Slovaks, Serbs and Romanians, excluding Magyars so as to facilitate the assimilation of this strategic region into their empire; despite this, Arad's population rose up against Habsburg rule in 1848–49. The revolt was finally crushed with the help of Tsarist Russia, and the Habsburgs made an example of the ringleaders by executing thirteen generals, mostly Hungarian, outside the fortress walls – a monument was placed there, but was moved after World War I to a less conspicuous site. In 2000 Iliescu (needing Hungarian votes) promised to move it back to the city centre, but dragged his feet, and failed to show up in 2004 for the inauguration of the **Plaza of Romanian–Hungarian Reconciliation** (just west from the market on Strada Goldiş), shared by a Statue of Liberty with the generals' busts around the base, and a monument to the Romanian heroes of 1848, a mini-Arch of Triumph with Avram Iancu, Bălcescu and a crowd of others marching through.

The executions feature prominently in the **County History Museum** (Tues–Sun 9am–5pm; €0.50) housed in the eclectic **Palace of Culture** (1913) behind the City Hall on Piaţa George Enescu; there are also decent archeological, ethnographical and natural history displays here, though the absence of English captions will leave you none the wiser. Far more engrossing is an exhibition on the **1989 revolution** – there are some moving exhibits – such as a blood-soaked jacket and a trainer with a bullet hole through it (and the offending bullet) – in addition to some superb photos. Officially, nineteen people died here, relatively few compared to other cities.

On the opposite side of B-dul Revoluţiei, in the library building (1913) at Str. Gheorghe Popa 2, the Art Gallery (Tues–Sun 9am–5pm) features furniture from the seventeenth century on, as well as the odd painting by the likes of Grigorescu and Aman.

Eating and drinking

The main food **markets** are on Piaţa Catedralei and Piaţa Mihai Viteazu. In summer, most townsfolk head to the Neptun Ştrand Park (May to mid-Oct; €1), across the river by the citadel, which is rammed with swimming pools, cafés, bars and open-air discos. Otherwise, there are decent **bars** on the south side of Piaţa Avram Iancu.

La Creperie On the corner of Str. Bălcescu and Str. Dragalina. A terrific selection of sweet and savoury pancakes to eat in or take away. Mon–Fri 10am–8pm, Sat & Sun 4–10pm.

Lake Grove B-dul Revoluţiei 20B. With a large terrace overlooking an artificial lake, this is a pleasant spot for a bite or a beer. Closed Sun.

Libelula B-dul Revoluţiei 51. The place to indulge in cakes and ices.

Manhattan Piaţa Avram Iancu. On the west side of the square, *Manhattan* offers good solid food such as beef and goulash (closed Sun).

Michaelangelo Str. Unirii 12. The best of Arad's few restaurants, this is a cosy little pizza and pasta house – though with just half a dozen tables, you'd do well to get in early. Mon–Sat noon–midnight, Sun 6pm–midnight.

West of Arad

The area to the west of the Arad–Timişoara route is the quintessence of the Banat – originally marshy plains drained after the expulsion of the Turks and settled with a patchwork of diverse ethnic groups, some of whom still remain. One of the largest towns here is **SÂNNICOLAU MARE** (Nagyszentmiklós), known for the Nagyszentmiklós Hoard; 23 golden vessels, made for an Avar chieftain and buried at the time of the Magyar invasion of 896, were found here in 1799 and removed to Vienna, where they still reside in the Imperial collection. The town is also famed as the birthplace of the Hungarian composer **Béla Bartók** (1881–1945), some of whose personal effects can be seen inside the House of Culture, at the start of the main pedestrianized street (Tues–Sun 9am–5pm). His birthplace, a simple dwelling marked by a plaque, is a good walk north of town at Str. Cerbului 3.

It's a long trudge north into town from the **train station** – exit right, turn left past the petrol station and continue for about 2km along the main road, where a church marks the centre. If you need to stay here, there are two decent modern **hotels**, the *Malvina* (℡0256/370 867, Ⓦwww.hotelmalvina.ro; ❸), not far south of the church at Str. Republicii 18; and the *Timişoara* (℡0356/108 790, Ⓦwww.hotelsannicolaumare.ro; ❸) at Piaţa 1 Mai 6.

Immediately west of Arad, the **Parcul Natural Lunca Mureşului** (Mureş Floodplain Natural Park; Ⓦwww.luncamuresului.ro) protects an area of backwaters with islands covered in luxuriant vegetation, home to around 200 species of birds – a sort of miniature Danube Delta. It's best seen by kayak, which can be rented (€2/hour, €12/day) from the Ceala visitor centre, just west of town, and returned at Pecica, 25km downstream.

Moving on into Hungary and Germany

Arad, like Oradea, 117km north, lies just inside the border from Hungary. The crossing at Nădlac on the E68, some 50km away, is now mainly frequented by trucks; **cars** and buses are encouraged to use a new, quieter route off the DN7 (E68) to Turnu, 17km from Arad, to Battonya in Hungary. Travelling **by train**, you'll cross over from Curtici, 12km north of Arad, to Lőkösháza in Hungary. All international **bus services** to Budapest and most of those to Germany run from the station forecourt. Tickets for Budapest can usually be bought on the bus, but travel to Germany should be booked in advance from Adriana, inside the station (℡0746/399 074), AtlasSib, B-dul Revoluţiei 35 (℡0257/251 871, Ⓔromania .arad@atlassib.ro), or Andronic, Calea Victoriei 104 (℡0257/230 005).

Northeast of Arad

From Arad, it's possible to reach a number of villages noted for their **festivals**, either by road, or by branch rail lines. The formerly Schwab village of **SÂNTANA**, 7km east of the Arad–Oradea highway (30min by train from Arad towards Oradea or Brad, then a 15min walk), hosts the Sărbătoarea Iorgovanului festival on the last Sunday of May, a Schwab Kirchweih (church fair) on August 1, and a Pumpkin Festival (Festivalul Dovleacului) at the end of October. Although nowadays little more than an excuse for dancing, music and dressing up in traditional costumes, the Sărbătoarea originated as a parish fair, like the one on February 1 at **PÂNCOTA**, 15km east and another 25 minutes by train towards Brad. In **INEU**, 20km northeast of Pâncota (and another 30min by train), there's nothing except an abandoned castle (1645–52) which once held one of Romania's notorious orphanages, but **BÂRSA**, a further 18km east (and 30min by train), is noted for its pottery and its fete, Sărbătoarea Drustelor, held on the first Sunday in April.

Continuing southeast towards Brad, you'll come to **Vârfurile** at the junction with the DN76 from Oradea. Just west, a minor road runs 6km north to the small village of **AVRAM IANCU** (not to be confused with the other village of the same name just over the mountains), where people from thirty mountain villages gather on the second Sunday of June for the **Nedeia of Tăcaşele mountain festival**. In addition to trading and socializing, this large fair is an excellent opportunity to hear musicians playing *cetera* (fiddles), *nai* (panpipes) and *buciume* or *tulnic* (alpine horns). The connection between new life and stirring lust probably underlies a good many spring festivals, and it is one that the delightfully named **Kiss Fair** (Târgul Sărutului) at **HĂLMAGIU**, 10km and two stops by train to the south of Vârfurile, acknowledges. Traditionally, the event enabled young people to cast around for a spouse while their elders discussed the fecundity of livestock and crops; it takes place in March, but the exact date varies from year to year so check with the tourist office in Arad first. Continuing towards Transylvania, trains terminate at **Brad**, but around a dozen buses a day plug the 32km gap to Deva; there are also daily services to Cluj, Oradea and Timişoara.

From Bârsa, another road branches off to the east, through the villages of Sebiş and Dezna, and up to **MONEASA**, a small spa resort in the Codru-Moma mountains. There's a fair amount of **accommodation** here, including the very average *Hotel Moneasa* (☎0257/313 151, ⓦwww.hotelmoneasa.ro; ❷–❹), which has two- and three-star rooms, a thermal pool and various treatments; the similarly unspectacular *Hotel Parc* (☎0257/313 231; ❸); and, facing it, colourful *Pensiunea Ana* (☎0257/499 737; ❻), which has four sumptuous rooms, a pool, sauna and Jacuzzi. Cheaper alternatives include the *Dallas* cabana (☎0257/313 202; ❶), serenely set beneath wooded slopes north of the village, and the many private rooms advertised all around. Seven buses a day come here from Arad, and there are also local buses from Sebiş train station.

East of Arad

In 1934, the future travel writer Patrick Leigh Fermor walked from Arad into Transylvania, staying with Magyar aristocrats whose run-down mansions spoke eloquently of the decline in their fortunes since the Trianon Treaty. Nowadays, you're more likely to make the journey by road or train, but be warned that fast services stop at few places of interest. At **SÂMBĂTENI**, 17km from Arad, you'll see huge Gypsy palaces with colonnaded and pedimented fronts, built with the proceeds of sanction-busting trade with former Yugoslavia.

The first major stop is **RADNA**, 35km from Arad, where Leigh Fermor played skittles with a Franciscan monk, until "we were both in a muck-sweat when the bell for vespers put an end to play". The Abbey of Maria-Radna is an old pilgrimage site, where many churches were built, then destroyed by the Turks; the current Baroque edifice was begun in 1756, but only consecrated in 1820. The corridor to the left of the church is lined with sacred hearts and images of bloody crashes in which Mary supposedly helped make things less bloody; it opens onto the courtyard of the abbey, now a hospital.

Radna station, served by slow trains from both Arad and Timişoara, is actually nearer to **LIPOVA**, a quaint little town on the south bank of the Mureş. Its main sight is the lovely Orthodox Church of the Annunciation, with its classical facade and rather eccentric spire; these belie the interior, which dates from 1338 and contains the most important murals in the Banat – in pure Byzantine style, though painted in the early fifteenth century. Fragments of old murals are also visible on the exterior of the north wall. Having served as a mosque from 1552 to 1718, the church was rebuilt in 1732 in the Baroque style. Ask at the parish house, immediately north, for access. The **museum** (Tues–Sun 9am–5pm; €0.50) at Str. Bălcescu 21 is identified by casts of Trajan's Column over the door and cast-iron lanterns either side, and holds a painting apiece by Grigorescu and Aman, and old Bibles and bits of sculpture and furniture. The *Pensiunea Faleza*, at Str. P. Maior 13 (☎0257/561 702; ❷), is a perfectly decent guesthouse by the river northeast of town. There's little at the spa of Lipova Băile, 4km south and reached by eight buses a day from Radna station, save for the pool and a campsite with two-bed huts (☎0257/563 139, ✉sbc@dntar.ro; ❶), a restaurant and terrace bar. There's also the *Bistro* campsite, just west of Radna on the DN7.

The Mureş defile

Just 3km east of Radna lies the ruined castle of **Şoimoş**. Built in the thirteenth century, and beefed up by Iancu de Hunedoara and his son Mátyás Corvinus in the fifteenth century, it guards the entry to the **Mureş defile** between the Zărand and Poiana Ruscă mountains. At the narrowest point of the defile is **SĂVÂRŞIN**, which hosts fairs on January 30 and November 27; a small castle in the centre of the village, rebuilt in Neoclassical style in the nineteenth century, has been restituted to the royal family – it currently houses the comfortable *Hotel Castel Regal* (☎0257 557 447; ❹). Slow trains make half a dozen more stops before they reach **ILIA**, scene of fairs on July 1 and March 25. If you want to break the journey, there are several homestays in **LESNIC**, 10km east (contact Dorinel Ilea, no. 174, ☎0254/623 160), plus the usual roadside motels. From here, the railway and the DN7 continue eastward towards Deva, Cluj and Sibiu, a route described more or less in reverse order in Chapter 3. Alternatively, you can head southwest towards Lugoj (see p.329), on the DN68A or the secondary railway (one slow and three fast trains daily).

Timişoara

The engaging city of **TIMIŞOARA** has long been the most prosperous and advanced of the Banat's cities, claiming to be the first place in Romania to have a public water supply, the first in Europe to have electric street lighting and one of the first in the world to have horse-drawn trams. It still boasts Romania's premier technical university.

From the fourteenth century on, Timişoara was the capital of the Banat, playing a crucial role during the 1514 uprising and Hunyadi's campaigns against the Turks, who occupied the city from 1552 until 1716. The Habsburgs who ejected them proved relatively benign masters over the next two centuries, when Temeschwar, as they called it, acquired many of its current features. These days, Timişoara is best known as the **birthplace of the 1989 revolution**, and still sees itself as the true guardian of the revolution's spirit, swiftly hijacked by the neo-communists of Bucharest.

Close to the borders with Serbia and Hungary, and with flights from all over Europe and Romania, Timişoara is also a major transport hub.

Arrival and information

From the main **train station**, Timişoara Nord, it's a twenty-minute walk east to the centre along B-dul Republicii (or express buses #E1 or #E3, trolley buses #11, #14 or #18). The grubby **bus station** is across the canal from the train station and one block west, at Str. Iuliu Maniu 54, next to the main market. Normandia buses to Târgu Jiu and Bucharest leave from near the former abattoir on B-dul Eroilor

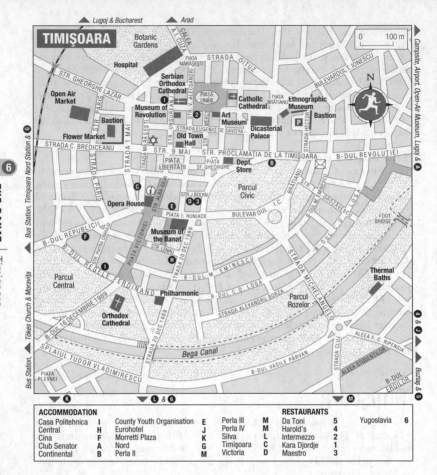

Lugoj & Bucharest ▲ Arad

Bus Station, Timișoara Nord Station & ⑤

Bus Station, Tőkés Church & Moravita

Campsite, Airport, Open-Air Museum, Lugoj & ⓐ

④ & ⓙ

Buziaș & ⑤

TIMIȘOARA

0   100 m

N

Botanic Gardens

Hospital

Open Air Market

Serbian Orthodox Cathedral

Museum of Revolution

Bastion

Flower Market

Catholic Cathedral

Ethnographic Museum

Art Museum

Old Town Hall

Dicasterial Palace

Bastion

Dept. Store

Parcul Civic

Opera House

Museum of the Banat

Parcul Central

Thermal Baths

Philharmonic

Parcul Rozelor

Orthodox Cathedral

Bega Canal

FOOT BRIDGE

ACCOMMODATION						RESTAURANTS			
Casa Politehnica	I	County Youth Organisation	E	Perla III	M	Da Toni	5	Yugoslavia	6
Central	H	Eurohotel		Perla IV	M	Harold's	4		
Cina	F	Morretti Plaza	J	Silva	L	Intermezzo	2		
Club Senator	A	Nord	G	Timișoara	C	Kara Djordje	1		
Continental	B	Perla II	M	Victoria	D	Maestro	3		

de la Tisa. The **airport** (☎0256/493 123) is 12km east of the city; it's reached hourly by express bus #E4, while a taxi should cost no more than €8 (call ☎940, ☎942, ☎945 or ☎949).

The very helpful **tourist office** at Str. Alba Iulia 2 (Apri–Sept Mon–Fri 9am–8pm, Sat 9am–5pm; Oct–March Mon–Fri 9am–6pm, Sat 10am–3pm; ☎0256/437 973, ⓔinfoturism@primariatm.ro) has **maps and leaflets**, as well as the useful English-language listings magazine, *Timișoara What, Where, When*. The websites ⓦwww.e-timisoara.info and ⓦwww.timisoreni.ro are also useful.

Accommodation

Timișoara has plenty of **hotels**, most of which are optimistically aimed at the business traveller. The very good all-year **campsite** (☎0256/208 925, ⓦwww .campinginternational.ro), has well-equipped cabins (③–⑤) sleeping one to four people, on Aleea Pădurea Verde, 4km east of the city in the Green Forest. Take trolley bus #11, which terminates opposite the campsite on Calea Dorobanților (the DN6).

Hotels

Central Str. Lenau 6 ☎0256/490 091, ⓦwww
.hotel-central.ro. Simple but clean, modern and a/c
rooms, a great central location and extremely
welcoming staff. ❹

Cina B-dul Republicii 7 ☎0256/491 903. One of
the cheapest city-centre options, this completely
renovated hotel has rather gloomy rooms and small
bathrooms, but it's perfectly acceptable. Breakfast
is extra; no internet. ❸

Club Senator Calea Lugojului 7 ☎0256/225 463,
ⓦwww.hotelclubsenator.ro. This bright and breezy
three-star hotel, 6km east of town towards the
airport, has a swimming pool, sauna and smart
restaurant. ❹

Continental B-dul Revoluției 3 ☎0256/494 145,
ⓦwww.hotelcontinental.ro. Used mainly by
business visitors and tour groups, this ugly white
high-rise is as charmless and expensive as the
others in this chain. ❼

Eurohotel Str. Mehadia 5 ☎0256/201 251,
ⓦwww.eurohotelsite.com. High-standard hotel
with plush, a/c rooms, although it's somewhat out
of place amongst a jumble of apartment blocks;
it's a 15min walk east of the centre across the
canal. ❸

Nord B-dul Gen. Dragalina 47 ☎0256/497 504,
ⓦwww.hotelnord.ro. Cheerless, functional but very
cheap and right outside the station; some rooms
without toilets. No food, wi-fi in the lobby only. ❷

Perla II Str. Dragomir 7 ☎0256/495 203; ❹;
Perla III Str. Celebi 14 ☎0256/497 858; ❹–❺;
Perla IV Str. Dragomir 9 ☎0256/203 100; ❻;

ⓦwww.hotelperla.ro. Three excellent hotels:
modern, chic and comfortable.

Silva B-dul V. Babeș 25 ☎0256/201 406, ⓦwww
.hotel-silva.ro. One of the city's best small hotels;
nicer in than out, with comfortable, bright, and very
spacious rooms. ❹

Timișoara Str. Mărășești 3 ☎0256/498 854,
ⓦwww.hoteltimisoara.ro. In a plum location
overlooking Piața Victoriei, this grand hotel has
recently been refurbished, with modern lifts, gym,
sauna and car park. ❻

Victoria Str. Lucian Blaga 3 ☎0256/431 602,
ⓦwww.victoria-hotel.ro. Renovated hotel in a
lovely old building with large if fairly bare rooms
but no lift. ❺

Hostels and guesthouses

Casa Politehnica B-dul Ferdinand 2 ☎0256/496
850. A student residence – through the black door
– with decent double rooms and breakfast
included. ❸

Direcția Județeana pentru Tineret Timiș Piața
Huniade 3 ☎0256/490 469, ✉djt.timis@yahoo
.com. The County Youth Organization has clean
and simple three-bed rooms right in the city
centre. ❶–❷

Morretti Plaza Str. Romulus 32 ☎0356/105 837,
ⓦwww.morretiplaza.ro. A three-star guesthouse
that also puts up backpackers in shared six-bed
rooms. It's cheap and clean, but there's no kitchen
and you have to pay for virtually all extras,
including baggage storage and use of the
refrigerator or a hair-drier. ❷–❸

The City

Timișoara grew up around a Magyar fortress in the marshes between the Timiș and
Bega rivers, the draining of which created the **Bega Canal**, which now separates
the old town, to the north, from the newer quarters. The city's sights are clustered
around the two large main squares, **Piața Victoriei** and **Piața Unirii**.

Piața Victoriei and around

A wide, pedestrianized boulevard flanked on either side by shops and cafés and
sliced down the middle by an attractive strip of greenery, **Piața Victoriei** was
where, in December 1989, the Romanian **revolution** gathered momentum;
demonstrators came out in force and the tanks rolled in for a series of bloody and
tragic battles. There's now little sign of those events, save for the odd memorial
or pockmarked building, such as the one above *McDonald's* at the square's
northern end. At the square's southern end, near the Bega Canal, is the
monumental **Romanian Orthodox Cathedral**, constructed between 1936 and
1946. The cathedral, which blends neo-Byzantine and Moldavian styles, houses a
fine collection of eighteenth-century Banat icons in its basement, but is best
known as the site where many protesters were gunned down in the 1989
uprising; there are memorials and candles to the victims outside. With its
83m-high middle dome, it can be a startling sight when lit up at night.

Beyond the cathedral, across the canal, the **Tökes Reformed Church** is where Lászlo Tökés ignited the 1989 revolution (see box below). A plaque marks the plain apartment building at Str. Timotei Ciprariu 1 (left off B-dul 16 Decembrie 1989), where his eviction took place – Tökés's church was on the first floor and its stained-glass windows can just about be seen from the street.

A few paces to the west of the square, the **Museum of the Banat** (Tues–Sun 10am–4pm; €1) occupies the Huniade Castle, raised for the Hungarian monarch Charles Robert in 1307–15 and extended by Hunyadi in 1443–47. Alas, no effort has been spared to make the voluminous display of historical exhibits as dull as possible. Outside, two street lamps boast that Timişoara was the first city in Europe to have electric street lighting, in 1884.

Leaving the square to the north, you'll pass the **Opera House**, built in 1872–75 by the Viennese duo Helmer and Fellner, with a charmless neo-Byzantine facade added in 1923–28, and enter **Piaţa Libertăţii**, with a substantial Baroque pile on its north side; built in 1734 as the **Town Hall** and now the university's music faculty, it stands on the site of the Turkish baths. The square was the setting for the gruesome execution of György Dózsa (Gheorghe Doja), leader of the peasant uprising that swept across Hungary and Transylvania in 1514; an iron throne and crown for the "King of the Serfs" were heated until red-hot, then Dózsa was

László Tökés and the Revolution of 1989

Despite doubts about the authenticity of the events of **December 1989** in Bucharest, Timişoara's popular uprising is still regarded as the catalyst of the revolution. The spark was lit to the southwest of the centre, when crowds gathered to prevent the internal exile of the Reformat pastor **László Tökés**.

Tökés came from a distinguished dynasty of Reformed (Calvinist) churchmen in Cluj. Born in 1952, he followed his father into the priesthood, but was soon in trouble for teaching Hungarian culture and history to his parishioners in Dej; after two years without a job, he was posted to Timişoara in 1986. Here, he became increasingly outspoken in his criticism of the government and the church authorities, while stressing that he spoke not only for Hungarians but also for the equally oppressed Romanians. In particular, he protested against the systematization programme, denouncing it on Hungarian television in July 1989. This led to an increasingly vicious campaign against him by the Securitate, who spread slanderous rumours about him, smashed his windows and harassed his family and friends, culminating in the murder in September 1989 of one of the church elders.

László Papp, Bishop of Oradea, a government placeman, agreed that he should be transferred to the tiny village of Mineu, north of Zalău, but he refused to leave his parish and resisted legal moves to evict him. Being officially deemed unemployed, he lost his ration book, but his parishioners brought him food despite continuing harassment. Eventually, he was removed to Mineu on December 17, and stayed there until the 22nd; the fact that it took so long for a police state to shift him, and that the eviction was so clearly signalled and then delayed for a day or two, is cited as evidence that plotters against Ceauşescu were deliberately trying to incite an uprising. After Tökés's removal, **riots** erupted on the streets of Timişoara, culminating in Ceauşescu's ordering the army to open fire.

The new National Salvation Front (FSN) tried to co-opt Tökés onto its council, along with other dissidents, but he soon asserted his independence; appropriately, in 1990 he took over the job of Bishop Papp, who fled to France. Romanian nationalists have accused him of being an agent of the Hungarian government and of the CIA, and he continues to be a hardliner, pushing for autonomy for the Magyar-dominated areas. Having co-founded the National Council of Transylvanian Hungarians, he was elected to the European Parliament in 2007.

seated and "crowned" before his body was torn asunder by pincers. Some of his followers were starved, compelled to watch his torture and then force-fed parts of the charred corpse, before themselves being executed, while others were hanged above the gates of Oradea, Alba Iulia and Buda as a deterrent.

Piaţa Unirii and around

Two blocks north and east of Piaţa Libertăţii is the vast **Piaţa Unirii**, a splendid traffic-free showpiece of Baroque urban design lined with delightful yellow, green and red buildings, though a few could still do with sprucing up. At the heart of the square is the Trinity or **Plague Column**, with carvings of plague victims, which was raised in 1740 following a particularly virulent attack of the disease. On opposing sides of the square are two monumental churches: the **Roman Catholic Cathedral**, on the eastern side, was built between 1736 and 1754 to the design of the younger Fischer von Erlach and is a fine example of the Viennese Baroque style; the **Serbian Orthodox Cathedral** was built at the same time (1744–48), with beautiful paintings completed by local artist Constantin Daniel.

The **Art Museum** (Tues–Sun 10am–6pm; €2), on the south side of the square at no. 1, features work by several eminent Romanian artists, such as Cornelia Baba – notably three portraits of George Enescu – as well as by lesser-known Italian, German and Flemish masters. There's some decorative art here, too, but of more interest are the rotating temporary exhibitions – often photographic. To the east of Piaţa Unirii, the huge but dull **Dicasterial Palace** (1855–60), built for the Habsburg bureaucracy, is hard to overlook. One block west, on the corner of Str. Eugeniu de Savoya and Str. Augustin Pacha, a plaque marks the house in which Cuza apparently spent his last two nights in Romania on his way to exile (see p.376) – as the Banat was not part of Romania until 1918, he was presumably under the impression that he was already in exile.

To the west of Piaţa Unirii, at Str. Ungureanu 8, sits the marvellous **Museum of the Revolution** (Tues–Sun 9am–4pm; free), part of the National Centre of Research into the 1989 Romanian Revolution. A tiny chapel remembers the hundred or so (the actual number is unknown) martyrs gunned down in the city, while photos, newspaper cuttings and a moving set of paintings by local school children illustrate vividly those extraordinary few days. Equally gripping is a documentary film (subtitled in English; 25min) containing some remarkable footage, such as Ceauşescu's final, fatal, speech on the balcony of the Communist Party Headquarters building, and the moment when he and his wife Elena were informed of their impending execution.

In 1868, the city purchased the redundant citadel from the Habsburg government, and demolished all but two sections, loosely known as the **Bastions**, to the west and east of Piaţa Unirii. Today, the western section contains a market, named Timişoara 700, in honour of the city's 700th anniversary in 1969, and the eastern section – now being refurbished – houses a beer and wine bar (entrance at Str. Hector 2). Just west of here, at Str. Popa Şapcă 4, is the **Ethnographic Museum** (Tues–Sun 10am–4.30pm; €1), with nicely presented displays of textiles and folk costumes, icons on glass, and beautifully carved staffs and musical instruments. Disappointingly, though, there's little mention of the region's ethnic diversity, or of the 40,000 Serbs exiled to the Dobrogea in 1951, which radically altered the Banat's ethnic make-up. There's also the **open-air Village Museum,** about 5km east of town, where old Banat homesteads and workshops have been reassembled in the **Pădurea Verde** (Green Forest) – take trolley bus #11 to the end of the line. Just beyond is the city's **zoo** (Tues–Sun: mid-April to Sept 10am–8pm; Oct to mid-April 10am–5pm; €1), which has been transformed into a spacious and attractive home for animals from around the world, including wallabies, guanacos, maras, bears, monkeys and many kinds of birds.

Eating and drinking

For such a large and cosmopolitan city, Timişoara has a surprisingly slim selection of **restaurants**, although there are fine Italian and Serbian places. Conversely, there's no shortage of **drinking** venues, particularly down by the canal in the summer, and, during term-time, around the lively student area – principally Aleea Studenţilor, where there's also plenty of fast food.

Restaurants

Da Toni Str. Daliei 14. Genuinely excellent and extremely popular Italian place near the student quarter, just behind the OMV station off B-dul Eroilor de la Tisa; non-smoking area and terrace.

Harold's Aleea Studenţilor 17. A touch of class amid the fast-food joints dominating the student quarter, this neat Chinese place also offers Mexican and Romanian dishes and is one of the best places in town for vegetarians.

Intermezzo Piaţa Unirii 3. A genuine, and genuinely good, Italian restaurant-pizzeria, at the top of Str. Vasile Alecsandri.

Kara Djordje Str. Lazăr 2. A full-blooded Serbian place serving lashings of meat, such as schnitzels, lamb and carp; closed Sun.

Maestro Str. János Bolyai 3. Stylish establishment with a wide international menu. Choose between the cosy interior or the small but convivial outdoor terrace. Live music some nights.

Yugoslavia Str. G. Dragomir 10. Hugely enjoyable, and typically hospitable, Serbian restaurant in the south of town, opposite the *Perla III/IV* hotel, serving specialities such as *Čevapi* (minced spiced meat rolls) and *sarma* (cabbage leaves wrapped around rice and meat). Vegetarians need not bother.

Cafés and bars

In summer, there are two main venues for outdoor **drinking**: along the canal behind the Orthodox cathedral, and on Piaţa Unirii, where numerous – almost identical – terraced **cafés** vie for custom. The best is *Timi's Ice Café*, just south of the square at Str. V. Alecsandri 7, a fresh and funky place with a delectable range of Italian-style panini, gelati, coffees, cakes and desserts. The hectic student quarter also offers some good possibilities, such as *Café Olli*, next door to *Da Toni's* restaurant at Str. Daliei 14, which is worth venturing to for its fabulous **ice cream** (till 10pm daily).

The best of the bars are *Café Colţ*, at the corner of Stradas Ungureanu and Lazăr, a vibrant café-cum-bar on two floors, open around the clock; *Komodo*, Str. Lazăr 5, a cool lounge-bar with big leather sofas and large windows opening onto the street; and *Celso Club*, a banging bar with DJ nights at Str. Mehadia 10.

Entertainment

The city's main concert venue is the **Opera House** on Piaţa Victoriei, also housing two theatres staging plays in German and Hungarian; the box office is at Str. Mărăşeşti 2 (daily 10am–1pm & 5–7pm; ☎0256/433 020). The Banat **Philharmonic** performs at B-dul C.D. Loga 2 (box office 9am–1pm and 1hr before concerts; ☎0256/492 521).

The *Anpura Music Arena*, at Calea Aradului 48, is a huge new **dance** venue, mainly for electronica and techno music; **Setup Venue**, at Str. Pestalozzi 22, is the place for drum and bass, jungle and dance music. Otherwise, there's *Club 30*, at Piaţa Victoriei 7 (the southern end), for Seventies and Eighties retro-style gigs and parties.

The city stages several terrific **festivals**, and there's plenty going on over the summer; in early May there's the **Timişoara Muzicală Festival**, a series of classical concerts and opera at the Opera House. **Little Venice** is a programme of concerts and plays on Piaţa Unirii every weekend (weather permitting) between May and September. The **Plai** world music festival, held at the Village Museum in mid-September, attracts some of the best performers from around the globe. In mid-October, **TM-Base** is a festival of dance and electronic music, based at the Setup Venue but mainly in disused buildings around town.

Listings

Airlines Austrian, Timişoara airport (☎0256/490 320); British Airways, Timişoara airport (☎0256/303 222); Carpatair, Timişoara airport (☎0256/300 970) & City Business Center, Str. Brediceanu 10 (☎0256/300 903); Lufthansa, Timişoara airport (☎0256/490 397); Malev, Timişoara airport (☎0256/493 194); TAROM, B-dul Revoluţiei 3 (☎0256/494 182); Wizzair, Timişoara airport (☎0903/760 100).

International buses Services to Germany are run by Andronic Reisen, Str. Ion Slavici 75 (☎0256/218 063); AtlasSib, Piaţa Victoriei 7 (☎0256/201 040, ✆romania.timisoaracentru@atlassib.ro); Eurolines, Str. Kogălniceanu 20 (☎0256/288 132, ✆timisoara.ag@eurolines.ro) & Str. Bocşa 4 (in the Bega department store; ☎0256/435 799,

✆timisoara@eurolines.ro); and Priamus, Str. Brâncoveanu 79 (☎0256/490 202). There are also services to Istanbul with Oz Murat (☎0256/497 868).

Internet access Club Internet, Eminescu 5 (24hr); also wi-fi at cafés (daily to midnight) such as *Java*, Str. A. Pacha 6, and *Café Colţ*, Str, Ungureanu 9.

Pharmacy Open 24hr: Vlad, B-dul 16 Decembrie 53; and Vladarmed, Str. Brâncuşi 13.

Shopping For Romanian books in English, try Humanitas, Str. Blaga 2 (Mon–Sat 10am–7pm, Sun 1–7pm); Cartureşti, Str. Mercy 7 (Mon–Fri 10am–9pm, Sat 11am–8pm); and Librărie Noi, Str. Hector 2–4 (Mon–Fri 9am–8pm, Sat 10am–6pm, Sun 11am–5pm), with a particularly good arts section.

The Timiş valley

The main rail line and the DN6 follow the River Timiş southeast from Timişoara towards Băile Herculane and Wallachia, passing through the small Habsburg towns of **Lugoj** and **Caransebeş**. Caransebeş offers easy access into the mountains, either west into the Semenic massif, or east to Muntele Mic, Ţarcu, Godeanu and, ultimately, the Retezat range.

Wine has been made in **RECAŞ**, 23km east of Timişoara, since at least the fifteenth century; privatized in 2000 and now a Romanian-British business, the Cramele Recaş winery, 3km from Recaş station, produces excellent vintages in a Schwab German style. Visits are welcome, and well organized, but should be booked in advance (☎0256/330 100, ⊛www.recaswine.ro); they range from a one-hour tasting of seven wines (€8) to seven samples and a full meal of goulash accompanied by an unlimited supply of your preferred wine.

Lugoj

LUGOJ, 63km east of Timişoara, is notable as the birthplace of several Romanian musicians, including the operatic tenor Traian Grozăvescu (1895–1927), and the composers Tiberiu Brediceanu (1877–1968), Filaret Barbu (1903–84) and Ion Vidu (1836–1931). Its non-Romanian sons are less likely to be remembered by plaques, but Béla Ferenc Blasko (1882–1956) immortalized his birthplace's Hungarian name when he became Béla Lugosi, Hollywood's most famous Dracula and the nearest yet to a genuinely Transylvanian Count.

Exit left from the **train station** and head up Str. Al. Mocioni – soon pedestrianized – towards the Iron Bridge, thrown across the Timiş in 1902 to link the formerly Schwab town to the Romanian quarter. To the right at Str. Bălcescu 2, the dusty old **town museum** (Tues–Sun 9am–5pm; €0.50) has displays of weapons, ceramics and local costumes. Cross the river to Piaţa Republicii, where the **Uniate Cathedral** (1843–54) has some fine neo-Byzantine paintings. Nearby, on Piaţa Victoriei, is the **Orthodox Church of the Assumption**, a hall-church built in 1759–66 by the younger Fischer von Erlach, which is one of the most important Baroque buildings of the Banat. The tower of the church of St Nicholas (1726) stands alongside.

There are two **hotels** in Lugoj: the rather pricey *Dacia*, at Strada Mocioni 7 (☎0256/352 740, ✆turismdacialugoj@yahoo.com; ❹–❻) and a hotel of sorts since 1835, has individually (and tastefully) designed rooms. Rather better is the sleek *Tivoli*, across the bridge at Str. A. Popovici 3 (☎0256/355 233, ✆hotel .tivoli@yahoo.com; ❸), which has seven air-conditioned, designer-furnished rooms. Its restaurant is also the classiest **place to eat** in town. In addition to these places, there's the *Pensiunea Domacris*, Str. Filaret Barbu 12 (☎0256/357 981, ✆domacrisparc@yahoo.com; ❶), and the very cheap but perfectly acceptable *Tirol*, 3km out along the DN68A to Făget and Deva at Str. Salcâmului 15 (☎0256/353 832; ❷).

Caransebeş and the Muntele Mic

CARANSEBEŞ lies beneath the mountains at the confluence of the Timiş and Sebeş rivers, where Gypsies of the Zlatari tribe used to pan for gold. Having been the Banat's judicial centre in medieval times and commanding communications through the Eastern Gate, Caransebeş inevitably became a Habsburg garrison town – hence, the outcrops of *belle époque* buildings among the prefabricated structures of the socialist era. There's little to detain you today, other than the **County Museum of Ethnography and the Border Regiment** (Tues–Fri 10am–6pm, Sat–Sun 10am–4pm; €1), in the eighteenth-century barracks on Piaţa Dragolina, with some impressive artefacts from central and south Banat, but you may well pass through en route to the mountains.

The main **train station** is well north of town, from where maxitaxis run into the centre; otherwise, it's at least twenty minutes' walk. Some local services also stop 2km further south at the Caransebeş halt, west of the centre. Caransebeş is on the railway line from Timişoara to Orşova and Turnu Severin on the Danube (see p.114) and onwards into Wallachia, but there's also a branch line west to Reşiţa (see p.332). There's a small private **bus terminal** at the north end of the bridge on Calea Severinului, south of the centre, from where maxitaxis run to Reşiţa and Borlova; otherwise, through buses stop at the station and south of the bridge.

There are several **hotels**, all on the main road from the main train station and just west of the centre of town: exiting right at the station, walk 300m and cross the road for the cheap, though not particularly cheerful, *Vila Natalia* (☎0255/517 645; ❷), where there's no breakfast. Continuing over the bridge, the modern *Gea* at Str. Crişan 1A (☎0255/511 637; ❸) has a gym and sauna but no internet access, and a superior sister hotel across the road (same phone; ❹). Easily the best of the bunch is the 🌲 *Armando*, at Str. Libertăţii 35 (☎0255/517 308, ⓦwww .hotelarmando.ro; ❹), whose beautifully furnished rooms are tremendous value – its **restaurant** is pretty fine, too. There are also three or four adequate pizzerias.

Borlova and the Muntele Mic

BORLOVA, 13km east of Caransebeş, is noted for its embroideries and peasant weddings, and holds a **Measurement of the Milk festival** around April 23 every year. Most visitors, however, pass straight through en route to the **Muntele Mic** (Little Mountain) resort, where you can sleep in a range of guesthouses and cabanas. You can hitch a ride to the resort on the staff bus or hike the 10km from Borlova, followed by a chairlift ride. Heavy snowfalls mean you can **ski** from late autumn until late spring; there are also good **hiking** trails. You can walk north to the Muntele Mic itself in an hour, or south to the weather station (2190m) atop Mount Țarcu in three hours. Well-equipped hikers can take trails eastwards towards Lake Gura Apei and the Retezat mountains in four hours (following red stripes), or southwards to Godeanu and the Cerna valley in six hours (red dots). From Muntele Mic, there's also a route (following blue stripes) to Poiana Marului, to the east, from where three buses a day head back to Caransebeş via Otelu Roşu.

The Cerna valley

The road and rail routes south from Caransebeş pass through the **Poarta Orientalis** or Eastern Gate of Transylvania before reaching **Băile Herculane** and its spa at the bottom of the **Cerna valley**. The middle and upper reaches of the valley itself, now protected by the **Domogled–Valea Cernei National Park**, are much as Patrick Leigh Fermor described them in the 1930s: "a wilderness of green moss and grey creepers with ivy-clad water-mills rotting along the banks and streams tumbling through the shadows [illuminated by] shafts of lemon-coloured light". Among the butterflies and birds that proliferate here are bright blue rollers, which the Romanians call *dumbrăveancă*, "one who loves oakwoods".

Băile Herculane and around

BĂILE HERCULANE gets its name from the Roman legend that Hercules cured the wounds inflicted by the Hydra by bathing here, and the nine springs, with their varied mineral content and temperature (38–60°C), are used to treat a wide range of disorders. The Roman baths were rediscovered in the nineteenth century, and royal patronage made Herkulesbad, as it was then known, one of Europe's most fashionable watering holes. Today, Băile Herculane is split between the old spa, run-down but once elegant, centred on Piața Hercules, and the ugly but livelier satellite spa of **PECINISČA**, 2km towards the train station and dominated by half a dozen or so grim high-rise hotels.

Other than a wallow in the renowned **baths**, Băile Herculane's chief attraction is its surroundings – soaring limestone peaks clothed in lush vegetation and riddled with caves. You can bathe in the **Seven Hot Springs** (Şapte Izvoare Calde) just beyond the Cerna rapids about 35 minutes' walk upstream from Piața Hercules, while another two hours' hiking up the valley brings you to **Gisella's Cross**, from where there are magnificent views. From here, an unmarked path leads in thirty minutes to a forest of black pines, dotted with boulders, and a spectacular 300m precipice. Other paths provide access to the vaporous **Steam Cave** on Ciorci Hill (1hr 30min), the **Outlaws' Cave** where Stone Age tribes once sheltered (30min), and **Mount Domogled**, which has trees and flowers of Mediterranean origin and more than 1300 varieties of butterfly (4hr).

It's roughly 40km from Băile Herculane to the watershed of the River Cerna, on a forestry road that continues to Câmpuşel and the Jiu valley. A path marked with red stripes runs parallel along the ridge to the north to Piatra lui Iorgovan in the **Retezat mountains** (see p.181) – allow one or two days.

Practicalities

From Băile Herculane's lovely turn-of-the-century **train station**, 5km from the spa, buses run on the hour and half-hour to Piața Hercules. There are just a few **hotels** here in the old spa: the best-value is the recently renovated *Cerna* (℡0255/560 436, ℻560 440; ❶–❷), next to the open-air thermal baths, which has rooms with and without bathroom. The *Ferdinand* at Piața Hercules 1

(☎0255/561 121, ⓦ www.hotel-ferdinand.ro; ④) is the classiest place around and has its own baths. Beyond the little octagonal Catholic church at the end of Piaţa Hercules a one-way road continues a few hundred metres to the *Hotel Roman* (☎0255/560 390; ②), straddling the road, and the **Imperial Roman Baths** (daily 8am–6pm; €2.50).

None of the big and unsightly hotels in Pecinişca differs much from each other, but they're all pretty cheap, and there should be rooms aplenty. There are also numerous new **pensions** (①–②) between the station and Pecinişca, as well as signs advertising cheaper **private rooms**. There are a couple of **campsites**, the better of which is *Camping Hercules* (☎0255/523 458), hidden beside a bright green motel about 800m north of the train station on the Timişoara road: this excellent little site also has a handful of rooms available, as well as a **restaurant**. The other site is the *Flora* (☎0255/560 929), just north of the new part of the resort, which also has some very basic huts (①). The best **restaurant** is in the *Hotel Ferdinand*, followed by the *Grota Haiducilor*, on the road to the Hotel Roman; you could also try the Greek *Pizza Dimitrios*, on Piaţa 1 Mai near the Hotel Cerna.

Reşiţa and the Semenic range

People have been beating iron into shape around **REŞIŢA**, 40km southwest of Caransebeş, since Dacian times. The foundry can trace its history back to 1771, and steam locomotives were manufactured here from 1872 until 1964. The iron works, and the ropeway across town, are still active, but the town is largely communist concrete and has a depressed feel to it. Arriving at the grubby **bus station** on Str. Lalescu, walk west past the post office and theatre, over the footbridge and under the ropeway, and you'll come to the windswept central plaza, Piaţa 1 Decembrie 1918, with a massive rotating fountain. **Trains** terminate at Reşiţa Sud station, just across from the plaza by a footbridge.

The only sights are a collection of Reşiţa-built steam locomotives at the first station to the north, Reşiţa Nouă (on B-dul Revoluţiei din Decembrie, the main road north), and the **Museum of Mountainous Banat**, at B-dul Republicii 10 (Tues–Sat 9am–5pm; free), not far from the next station, Reşiţa Nord, which only hosts temporary shows by local artists and the like, due to lack of funds. Ancient trams link the two halves of town, 4km apart. However, the town does stage a couple of festivals: steelworkers take pride of place in the **Spring Parade** (Alaiul Primăverii), normally in the first week of April, while there's also the **Bârzava Song Festival** in August. At other times you may as well continue straight on to the mountains.

The best **hotel** is the *Rogge*, Str. Caragiale 12 (☎0355/411 111, ⓦ www .hotelrogge.ro; ⑤), whose fine rooms come with comfortable, wood-framed beds and large plasma TVs. Nearby is the *Semenic*, an ugly, squat hotel on Piaţa 1 Decembrie 1918 (☎0355/213 481; ③), whose rooms are actually quite smart. The *Intim*, Str. Republicii 2 (☎0255/252 595, ⓦ www.intimhotel.ro; ③), is handy for the museum, and perfectly comfortable. There's cheaper accommodation outside town at Semenic or Crivaia (see opposite) or at one of the guesthouses 13km east on Lake Secu, such as the *Pensiunea Flavia* (☎0726/621 443, ⓔ modogcezar@yahoo.com.au; ①) or *Pensiunea Brânduşa* (☎0744/300 120, ⓔ rezervari@ghidcazareromania.ro; ①). If you're planning to hike in the Semenic mountains, Reşiţa is the last chance to stock up on food; there's a good covered **market** just east of the Sud train station.

Into the Semenic mountains

Occasional buses run on summer weekends to Văliug, 12km southeast of Reşiţa and starting point for excursions into the Semenic mountains, but otherwise you'll have to hitch or take a taxi. From here one road leads 3km south to **CRIVAIA**, where there are guesthouses, such as *Pensiunea Daniels* (T 0371/368 922, W www .pensiunea-daniels.ro; ❷), and a **campsite**, while another leads up to **SEMENIC**, also accessible by chairlift from Văliug, which has chalet-style **accommodation** and two hotels, the *Central* (T 0255/214 450; ❸) and *Gozna* (T 0255/223 599; ❸). **Skiing** is possible here from November to April – pistes are graded from very easy to difficult.

Although the massif is lower and less rugged than others in the Carpathians, it still offers good hiking. One of the most popular trails heads west from Semenic through Crivaia to the Comarnic Cave and on to the Caraşului Gorges (10–11hr; blue stripe markings). Just before the eastern entrance to the gorges, the Comarnic Cave is the Banat's largest grotto, with a spectacular array of rock "veils" and calcite crystals distributed around its four hundred metres of galleries on two levels (guided tours Sat & Sun 10am–5pm, Mon–Fri call T 0763/276 349; €2). The gorges themselves are wild and muddy and harbour several more caves. If you don't fancy hiking here from Semenic or Crivaia, the gorges can also be entered near **CARAŞOVA**, on the main road 16km south of Reşiţa. However, they may occasionally be impassable due to flooding, in which case you should follow the blue stripes onwards from Comarnic to the hamlet of **PROLAZ**, and pick up the route through the gorges there.

Travel details

Trains

Arad to: Brad (2 daily; 4hr 30min); Braşov (4 daily; 7hr–7hr 35min); Bucharest (4 daily; 10hr–11hr 15min); Deva (14 daily; 2hr–3hr 25min); Hălmagiu (2 daily; 3hr 40min); Oradea (8 daily; 2hr–3hr 25min); Radna (10 daily; 30–45min); Sânnicolau Mare (5 daily; 1hr 30min–2hr); Sântana (12 daily; 35min); Satu Mare (1 daily; 4hr 25min); Sibiu (1 daily; 5hr); Sighişoara (4 daily; 5hr–5hr 35min); Timişoara (13 daily; 50min–1hr 30min); Vârfurile (2 daily; 3hr 30min).
Caransebeş to: Băile Herculane (11 daily; 1hr 20min–2hr 30min); Bucharest (7 daily; 6hr 45min–7hr 20min); Drobeta-Turnu Severin (8 daily; 2hr 10min–3hr 50min); Lugoj (12 daily; 30–55min); Orşova (10 daily; 1hr 45min–3hr); Reşiţa (9 daily; 55min–1hr 20min); Timişoara (16 daily; 1hr 10min–2hr 30min).
Oradea to: Arad (8 daily; 2hr–3hr 15min); Baia Mare (1 daily; 3hr 40min); Bucharest (4 daily; 12hr); Ciucea (8 daily; 1hr 20min–2hr 30min); Cluj (14 daily; 2hr 40min–4hr 10min); Iaşi (1 daily; 11hr 50min); Satu Mare (5 daily; 2hr 15min–3hr 20min); Suceava (1 daily; 9hr 40min); Timişoara (5 daily; 2hr 50min–4hr 45min).

Timişoara to: Arad (15 daily; 50min–1hr 25min); Bucharest (7 daily; 8–9hr); Buziaş (8 daily; 45min–1hr 25min); Caransebeş (14 daily; 1hr 10min–2hr 20min); Lugoj (20 daily; 45min–2hr 30min); Oradea (5 daily; 3–5hr); Reşiţa (5 daily; 2hr 30min); Sânnicolau Mare (4 daily; 2hr 10min).

Buses and maxitaxis

Arad to: Abrud (2 daily); Câmpeni (4 daily); Deva (2 daily); Lipova (5 daily); Moneasa (7 daily); Oradea (10 daily); Satu Mare (2 daily); Timişoara (10 daily).
Băile Herculane to: Craiova (3 daily).
Caransebeş to: Borlova (7 daily).
Oradea to: Alba Iulia (1 daily); Arad (10 daily); Cluj (8 daily); Deva (2 daily); Sighet (1 daily); Târgu Lăpuş (1 daily); Timişoara (10 daily).
Reşiţa to: Băile Herculane (1 daily); Caransebeş (8 daily); Deva (Mon–Sat 1 daily); Drobeta (4 daily); Lugoj (Mon–Fri 1 daily); Târgu Jiu (2 daily); Timişoara (3 daily Mon–Sat, 1 daily Sun).
Timişoara to: Anina (1 daily); Arad (10 daily); Băile Herculane (1 daily); Caransebeş (1 daily); Câmpeni (1 daily); Lipova (3 daily); Lugoj (1 daily); Moneasa (1 daily); Oradea (10 daily); Oraviţa (5 daily Mon–Fri, 4 daily Sat, 2 daily Sun); Sibiu (2 daily).

International trains

Arad to: Budapest, Hungary (8 daily; 4hr); Vienna, Austria (1 daily; 8hr).
Oradea to: Budapest (2 daily; 4hr 10min).
Timişoara to: Belgrade, Serbia (1 daily; 4hr 10min); Budapest (2 daily; 5hr).

International buses

Arad to: Budapest (several daily), Germany (several daily).
Oradea to: Budapest (several daily); Debrecen, Hungary (1 daily); Kecskemet, Hungary (1 daily).

The Delta and
the coast

CHAPTER 7

Highlights

✳ **Bird life in the Delta** Even visitors without a special interest in winged fauna will be taken aback by the abundance and diversity of bird life on view in the Danube Delta. See p.339

✳ **Fresh fish** All over the Delta, meals consist of the day's haul: carp, pike or catfish, usually served with juicy tomatoes from local gardens. See p.339

✳ **Sfântu Gheorghe** This cluster of brightly painted houses of mud and reed is one of the prettiest of the Delta's fishing villages and a perfect base for exploring the surrounding wetlands. See p.348

✳ **Halmyris** The ancient Roman city of Halmyris is an archeological work in progress that recently saw the discovery of the remains of legendary martyrs Epictet and Astion. See p.350

✳ **Constanţa** Romania's principal port is rich in historical associations, and offers an attractive mix of places to stay and eat. See p.354

✳ **Mamaia** The epicentre of Black Sea tourism, brash Mamaia might not be sophisticated, but it has fine beaches and vigorous nightlife. See p.360

✳ **Vama Veche** This charming small retreat on the Bulgarian border remains the most untouched and free-spirited of the Black Sea resorts. See p.367

▲ Casino on the seafront, Constanţa

The Delta and
the coast

Nearly 3000km downstream from the Black Forest, the **Danube Delta** is a vast network of reeds and shifting land clinging to the far eastern side of Romania. Rich in **wildlife**, the Delta provides a unique habitat for 330 species of bird, many of which are found nowhere else in Europe. Most visitors head for the main arm (*braţ*) of the Danube that flows from the Delta capital of **Tulcea** down to **Crişan** and **Sulina**, and it can feel very crowded in July and August; the southern arm, which terminates at the fishing village of **Sfântu Gheorghe**, is an attractive alternative. To really appreciate the diversity of bird life, however, you're best off taking a tour or paying one of the local fishermen to row or motor you into the backwaters and lakes; travel in the Delta can be time-consuming, so if you're seriously bent on birdwatching, be prepared to spend at least a week here.

To the south, Romania's **Black Sea coast** is blessed with abundant sunshine, warm water and sandy beaches, but due to the popularity of summer resorts such as **Mamaia**, **Neptun** and **Venus** it's best to book a package holiday from home, or head to one of the prettier former fishing villages near the Bulgarian border: **Doi Mai** is quiet and family-oriented, while the more independent-minded resort of **Vama Veche** grows more fashionable by the year. For a drop of culture amidst all this sea and sand, the port city of **Constanţa** offers a splendid array of museums and historical riches in both its old quarter and elsewhere, as well as some of the best restaurants on the coast. There are further Roman remains inland, notably at **Adamclisi** and **Histria**.

Transport to the region is fairly simple. **Trains** to Constanţa are reasonably fast and frequent, but very overcrowded in season, when many services continue to Mangalia. In addition, quick (but cramped) **maxitaxis** regularly run between Bucharest and Constanţa, and between Constanţa's train station and the various resorts. **Driving** from Bucharest, you can take one of Romania's two motorways, though at present this only goes as far as Cernavodă.

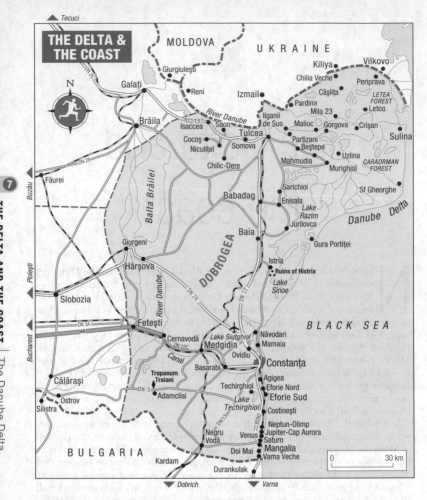

The Danube Delta

Every year, the River Danube dumps forty million tonnes of alluvium into the **Danube Delta** (Delta Dunării), the youngest, least stable landscape in Europe, abutting the oldest, the heavily eroded Hercynian hills immediately south. Near **Tulcea**, the river splits into three branches (named after their respective ports, Chilia, Sulina and Sfântu Gheorghe), dividing the Delta into more than 4000 square kilometres of reeds and marsh, half of which is flooded in spring and autumn. The **grinduri**, tongues of accumulated silt supporting oak trees, willows and poplars, account for the five percent of the Delta that remains permanently above the water. The distinction between these and the **plauri** (floating reed islands) is a fine one, since flooding continually splits, merges and often destroys these patches of land, making any detailed map of the delta outdated almost as soon as it's drawn. Although fishing communities have lived here for centuries, it's an inhospitable environment for humans: a Siberian wind howls all winter long, while in summer the area is inundated with mosquitoes.

Yet it's a paradise for wildlife, and after years of environmental neglect culminating in Ceauşescu's plan to drain the Delta for agricultural use, it was declared a **Biosphere Reserve** in 1990, with over 500 square kilometres strictly protected, and a UNESCO World Heritage Site the following year. Today the area is under threat once again, this time from the new Bystroye Canal, dug by Ukraine despite international protests, which is expected to cut the water to Letea and Rosca-Buhaiova lakes. The area is particularly important for **birds**, which pass through during the spring and autumn migrations, or come from Siberia to winter here or from Africa to breed in summer. Besides herons, glossy ibis, golden eagles, avocets, shelduck and other Mediterranean breeds, the Delta is visited by reed buntings, white-tailed eagles and various European songbirds, as well as whooper swans, arctic grebes and half-snipes from Siberia, saker falcons from Mongolia, and egrets, mute swans and mandarin ducks from China. Its lakes support Europe's largest pelican colonies, which come from Africa to breed. The best time to see birds is from April to early June (the latter being the wettest month of the year), and September. Some 135 species of **fish** have also been catalogued in the Delta, with healthy stocks of carp and pike, as well as a resurgence in sturgeon; the best time to fish is May, September and October. The Delta is also home to otters, mink, boars, wolves and other **animals**, while at night streets in the Delta villages are alive with frogs, beetles and hawk moths.

Tulcea and around

Clustered around the south bank of a bend in the Danube, **TULCEA** has been tagged the "Threshold of the Delta" ever since ancient Greek traders established a **port** here. Its maritime significance was slight until the closing stages of the period of Ottoman domination (1420–1878), when other powers suddenly perceived it as commercially and strategically important. Nowadays, the outskirts of the town are heavily industri-alized, and the port is too shallow for large modern freighters, but it's still the chief access point for passenger vessels entering the Delta. The uninspiring town centre has enough attractions to fill a day, and there's plenty of accommodation here, but your time will be better spent in the Delta; it's worth arriving early enough to catch one of the ferries that depart at 1.30pm. Tulcea is busiest in August and December, when its regular **festivals** take place: the International Folk Festival of the Danubian Countries, held in odd-numbered years, and an annual winter carnival.

Arrival and information

Tulcea's futuristic **train station** is on the western edge of town, from where it's an easy walk along the waterfront to Piaţa Republicii, passing the NAVROM-Delta **ferry terminal** (Gara Fluviala; tickets daily 11am–1.30pm) and office and the **bus station** on the way.

The **tourist information office** is on the waterfront at Str. Gării 26 (Mon–Fri 8am–4pm; ℡0240/519 130, @tourisminfo_tulcea@yahoo.com), though it actually faces Str. Portului, next to the Port Captain's headquarters (Căpitănia Portului). However, for everything pertaining to travel within the Delta head to the well-informed **Danube Delta Biosphere Reserve Administration** (ARBDD), located between the ferry terminal and the tourist office at Str. Portului 3 (Mon–Thurs 8am–4.30pm, Fri 8am–2pm; ℡0240/518 945, ⓦwww .ddbra.ro); they've got good maps of the Delta, as well as information on

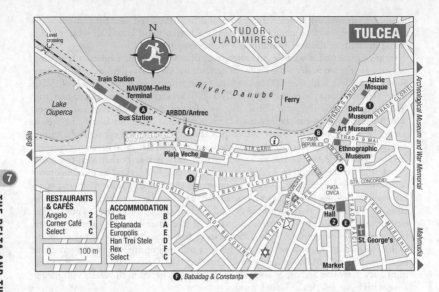

F, Babadag & Constanța ▼

accommodation, trips and **permits**. Indeed, this is the only place where you can obtain permits, if required.

In the same buidling you'll also find the Antrec office (Mon–Fri 8am–5pm, Sat & Sun 9am–4pm; ☎0764/501 690, ✉antrec@tulcea.ro), where you can make reservations for **homestay** and **pension accommodation** in the Delta. Most **travel agencies** are concerned with Delta trips (see box opposite). There's **internet access** at Future Games, Str. Isaccei 12.

Moving on, Tulcea is linked to Bucharest and Constanța by train, but it's a slow journey down to the junction at Medgidia. Travelling onwards to Brăila and Galați in Moldavia, you'll have to take a bus or maxitaxi to Smârdan and I.C. Brătianu respectively, from where ferries shuttle back and forth across the Danube.

Accommodation

Tulcea has several decent **hotels** spread across town, the best of which are located along the waterfront.

Delta Str. Isaccei 2 ☎0240/514 720, ⓦwww
.hoteldelta.eu. Sprawling place overlooking the
Danube, which has both three- and four- star rooms,
though it's worth paying the extra for the much
smarter four-star ones; either way, try to bag a room
with river view. There's an indoor pool too. ❻–❽
Esplanada Str. Portului 1 ☎0240/516 607,
ⓦwww.hotelesplanada.ro. In a plum location on
the waterfront, opposite the ferry departure point,
this impressive large hotel has good-sized, airy and
colourfully decorated rooms, in addition to a very
accomplished restaurant. ❼
Europolis Str. Păcii 20 ☎0240/512 443, ⓦwww
.europolis.ro. Slightly bland and colourless hotel
just south of Piața Civică, but there's a range of
different rooms available, including some cheaper

ones without bathroom. ❸–❹
Han Trei Stele Str. Carpați 16 ☎0756/933 515.
Up on the right by the steps behind the chaotic
Piața Veche market, this rock bottom budget option
has antiquated rooms with communal showers.
Breakfast not available. ❶
Rex Str. Toamnei 1 ☎0240/511 351, ⓦwww
.hotelrex.ro. Upmarket though not expensive hotel,
just beyond the synagogue on Str. Babadag,
providing decently furnished rooms with coffee-
making facilities. ❺
Select Piața Civică 1 ☎0240/506 180, ⓦwww
.calypsosrl.ro. Unmissable bright red building
concealing solid, as opposed to inspiring, rooms,
though there's a pretty decent restaurant attached.
Breakfast costs extra. ❹

Travel agencies in Tulcea mostly offer packages to **floating hotels** (*hotel plutitoare*) in the heart of the Delta, and even then these are usually aimed at groups; expect to pay around €75 per night, including all meals, on most hotels. Note that their tours generally stick to the main axes, from which most of the wildlife has been scared off. The best agency is Ibis Tours, at Str. D. Sturza 6 (℡0240/512 787, Ⓦwww.ibis-tours .ro), who have two four-star floating hotels, both with ten cabins sleeping two people each: they also specialize in birdwatching and other wildlife tours. Also reliable are Sincron Delta, Str. Isaccei 29 (℡0240/534 155, Ⓦwww.sincrondelta.ro), whose four-star vessel accommodates nine a/c rooms, and Europolis, in the *Hotel Europolis*, Str. Păcii 20 (℡0240/512 443, Ⓦwww.europolis.ro), whose ship has six doubles and two apartments. Some agencies also have tourist complexes on dry land; Simpa Tourism (℡0240/519 618, Ⓦwww.simpaturism.ro), at the *Hotel Delta*, charges around €65 per night for two people at its *Complex Cormoran* in Uzlina, while Europolis has the *Europolis Tourist Complex* on Lake Casla, just 2km west of Tulcea. Both these options offer high standards of accommodation, but are isolated from the Delta's fascinating village life.

A host of agencies also offer **day-trips** into the Delta – typically up the Sulina channel to Crişan and Mila 23 – for around €40–45 per person, including lunch; outfits worth trying here are Amatour (℡0240/518 894, Ⓦwww.amatour.ro), on the waterfront near the *Hotel Delta*, and Escape Travel (℡0240/516 649 or 0743/609 626, Ⓦwww.deltaescapetravel.ro), inside the *Hotel Europolis*. Two-, three- and four-day trips are also available. Smaller and less formal outfits along the Tulcea waterfront charge anywhere between €20 and €50 per group per hour, depending on the size of the boat.

The Town

Although systematized Piaţa Civica is the heart of town, Piaţa Republicii is where you'll find the main sights, and in particular a cluster of enjoyable museums. Chief amongst these is the **Danube Delta Eco-tourism Museum Centre**, at Str. 14 Noiembrie 1 (Centrul Muzeul Ecoturistic Delta Dunării; Tues–Sun 10am–6pm; €3.50). With extensive use of interactive maps and some thoughtfully presented dioramas, the bulk of the museum is given over to the formation and evolution – both natural and man-made – of the Biosphere Reserve. Among the many fascinating items on display is a *Gheţărie*, a subterranean ice house made of reeds which was traditionally used in winter months for the storing of fish. Down in the basement is a better than average aquarium, featuring local aquatic species as well as a smaller collection of tropical fish, including sharks.

Diagonally across from here, at Str. 9 Mai 2, the **Museum of Ethnography and Folk Art** (Muzeul de Etnografie şi Artă Populară; Tues–Sun: May–Oct 10am–6pm; Nov–April 8am–4pm; €1) has displays on the multifarious groups that have long inhabited the region. In a large L-shaped barn to the rear of the building is a sizeable collection of equipment and tools representing the various crafts and trades that have long been prominent in Dobrogea, not least the agricultural and viticultural industries.

Just around the corner from the Delta Museum, at Str. G. Antipa 2, is the **Art Museum** (Muzeul de Artă; Tues–Sun: May–Oct 10am–6pm; Nov–April 8am–4pm; €1), built by Ismail Pasha in 1870; its fine collection of paintings includes Impressionistic female nudes by Pallady, Delta landscapes by Sirbu and Stavrov, and a selection of avant-garde works, including the country's best collection of paintings by the Romanian Surrealist Victor Brauner (1903–66). You'll also see Igolesco's *Balchik*, a depiction of the thriving artistic community in southern

Dobrogea, a village so loved by Queen Marie that she asked for her heart to be buried there. When the area was handed over to Bulgaria, the queen's heart was brought back in a casket that now rests in the National History Museum in Bucharest (see p.68).

Strada 14 Noiembrie heads north to the nondescript nineteenth-century **Azizie Mosque**; having been fairly inconspicuous under communism, the local Turkish women are now much more visible, dressed in bright colours and baggy trousers. Beyond the mosque, Str. Gloriei runs through a pretty area of small white houses with gardens, ending at the **Parcul Monumentului Independenţei**, where you'll find an **obelisk** to the dead of the 1877–78 war, some **Roman remains** and the **Museum of History and Archeology** (Muzeul de Istorie şi Arheologie; Tues–Sun: May–Oct 10am–6pm; Nov–April 8am–4pm; €1), noted for its collection of Roman, Greek, Byzantine and medieval coins. A newer building houses prehistoric remains and temporary exhibitions.

Back on the waterfront, **ferries** (every 15min from dawn to dusk) shuttle across the river to the largely Russian suburb of **Tudor Vladimirescu**, where there's a sandy bank for sunbathing.

Eating and drinking

There's nothing to get excited about when it comes to **eating** in Tulcea. Your best bet, therefore, is to head to the upscale restaurant in the *Esplanada* hotel, which also possesses a downstairs trattoria serving pizza and pasta. Not bad either is the **restaurant** in the *Hotel Select*, whose menu (presented in five languages) includes dozens of schnitzel dishes alongside a bit of pasta and fish. The classiest places for a drink are the **bars** in the *Delta* and *Esplanada* hotels, both of which have floor-to-ceiling windows looking out on the Danube, perfect for watching passing bird life. The *Corner Café*, opposite the Delta museum at Str. 14 Noiembrie 10, is a modern glassed-in lounge bar, while *Angelo*, next door to the *Europolis* hotel, does the job for all things sweet and sticky.

If you need to buy snacks and provisions for trips into the Delta, head to the main **market**, just south of the centre down Str. Păcii, beyond St George's. The smaller Piaţa Veche, off Str. Isaccei, is handier for the stations and NAVROM terminal. The **supermarket** at Str. Unirii 2 (between the Piaţa Civică and Piaţa Republicii) has Tulcea's best selection of imported foods, as well as decent bread and fruit.

Upstream from Tulcea

West of Tulcea, the Danube is up to 1km wide, with a **floodplain** of almost 100 square kilometres that is inundated every spring as nature intended. The area near **Rotundu**, 25km west of Tulcea, is especially rich in plankton and fish, and although it's a closed reserve there are plenty of birds to be seen in the vicinity, such as swans, little bittern and white-tailed eagles (Romania's largest raptor). The *Delta Nature Resort*, 3km north of the DN22 on the road to Parcheş (0212/304 301, ⓦwww.deltaresort.com; ⑧), is a luxury eco-centre in a superb location overlooking the wetlands; thirty well-heeled villas are complemented by a fine restaurant, a library and extensive sporting and leisure facilities (tennis and volleyball courts, rowing boats and kayaks). A range of excursions is also offered, including a sunset cruise (€35 including drinks) and a fishing/nature safari in the Delta (€100/boat).

Three kilometres south of the main road, the village of **NICULIŢEL** boasts a church dating from around 1300, which, according to legend, was found buried underground by a shepherd – evidently, the church was influenced by the Turkish restrictions on the height of such buildings, which led to them being built half-underground in places. There are also the remains of a **paleo-Christian church** (Bazilica paleocreștină; Tues–Sun: May–Sept 10am–6pm; Oct–April 8am–4pm; €1), dating from the fourth century, with a triple nave and a crypt built to house the relics of four martyrs. The village is also known for its wine flavoured with wormwood. There are two simple **pensions** here, *Nichy* (☎0722/522 955; ❷) and *Dascalu Stere* (☎0240/542 308; ❷). Inland is a beautiful **open forest**, more typical of the Dobrogean steppes than the Delta, which was established as a nature reserve in 1927 by the botanist King Ferdinand, thanks to its rare species of peonies; bird life includes buzzards, nightingales, ortolan buntings, tawny pipits and woodpeckers. Three famous **monasteries** are nearby: at Cocos, 7km south of Niculițel (founded in 1833, although the present church dates from 1916, and much visited due to the relics of four martyrs held there); Chilic-Dere (1840, where there's a wooden windmill), 8km south of the main road; and Saon (1846), 3km north of the main road. It's possible to sleep at these monasteries, and the monks (or, at Saon, nuns) may even feed you.

Into the Delta

The following sections cover each arm of the Delta in turn, starting from Tulcea, and then the Lake Razim region. If you just want to take a trip down to the sea and back, **Sfântu Gheorghe** is probably the best choice; it's prettier than Sulina, has a more tranquil beach, and is within easy reach of several good birdwatching spots. **Sulina** is more crowded and built-up, but richer in historical associations. Of the numerous ancient ruins in the vicinity of the Delta, the Roman city of **Halmyris**, near Murighiol, is easily accessible.

Brațul Chilia

The **Chilia arm** of the river (Brațul Chilia), which branches off upstream from Tulcea and marks the border with Ukraine, carries more than half of the Danube's water, but very little tourist traffic, mainly because boats will only carry you as far as the largely Lipovani village of **PERIPRAVA** (100km from Tulcea but still 30km from the Black Sea), where there's a total lack of tourist facilities. In the days when the entire Delta was part of Moldavia, **CHILIA VECHE**, 35km from Periprava, was merely a suburb of Chilia (now Ukrainian Kiliya) across the river. When the town repelled a Turkish invasion in 1476, Chilia was just 5km from the coast – today, it's 40km away. There are several **pensions** in Chilia Veche: *Mariuța* (☎0744/557 671; ❷); *Sirby Villa* (☎0744/615 518; ❷); and the cheaper *Vital* (0744/276 435, ✉vital_delta@yahoo.com; ❷). There's also the 40-site *Camping Chilia* (☎0240/519 090 or 0744/336 685).

Lake Roșca, roughly 10km south of Babina on the Cernovca tributary between Chilia Veche and Periprava, is one of the larger strictly protected reserves, harbouring geese, egrets, storks and Europe's largest **white pelican colony**. Immediately to the east is **Periprava**, south of which lies the **Pădurea Letea**, a forest of oaks tangled with lianas, now a haven for falcons, white-tailed eagles, boar and wildcats. Surrounding the forest are **sand dunes** inhabited by tortoises, lizards and the horned viper.

One way of seeing a little of the Brațul Chilia route is to travel as far as **Ceatalchioi**, 20km north of Tulcea, where the reeds (*stuf*) that are used to build Delta houses are gathered in winter, when it's possible to drive tractors on the ice. Not far beyond Ceatalchioi (due north as the river flows), boats pass **Izmail**, the main Ukrainian city in the Delta, whose bloody recapture from the Turks in 1790 is described in Byron's *Don Juan*.

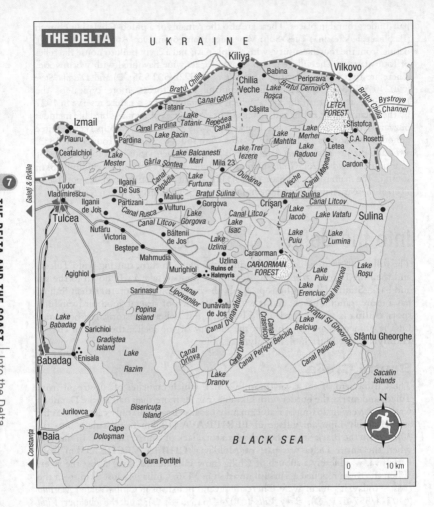

THE DELTA

UKRAINE

Kiliya

Chilia
Veche

Babina

Periprava

Vilkovo

Bratul Chilia

Canal Gotca

Lake
Roşca

Bratul Cernovca

Bratul Chilia

Bystroye
Channel

Tatanir

Câşlita

LETEA
FOREST

Sfistofca

Izmail

Canal Pardina

Lake
Tatanir

Repedea
Canal

Lake
Mahtita

Lake
Merhei

C.A. Rosetti

Plauru

Pardina

Lake Bacin

Lake Trei
Iezere

Lake
Raduou

Letea

Cardon

Ceatalchioi

Lake
Mester

Gârla Sontea

Lake Balcanesti
Mari

Mila 23

Dunărea

Veche

Canal Magearu

Tudor
Vladimirescu

Ilganii
De Sus

Canal
Papadia

Lake
Furtuna

Bratul Sulina

Bratul Sulina

Crişan

Canal Litcov

Sulina

Tulcea

Ilganii
de Jos

Partizani

Maliuc

Gorgova

Canal Litcov

Lake
Iacob

Lake Vatafu

Nufăru

Canal Rusca

Vulturu

Lake
Gorgova

Lake
Isac

Lake
Puiu

Lake
Lumina

Victoria

Canal Litcov

Beştepe

Bâltenii
de Jos

Lake
Uzlina

Mahmudia

Uzlina

Caraorman

CARAORMAN
FOREST

Lake
Puiu

Lake
Roşu

Agighiol

Murighiol

Ruins of
Halmyris

Canal Invancea

Sarinasuf

Canal
Lipovanilor

Dunăvatu
de Jos

Canal Dunăvătului

Canal
Crasnicol

Lake
Erenciuc

Bratul Sf Gheorghe

Lake
Belciug

Sfântu Gheorghe

Lake
Babadag

Sarichioi

Popina
Island

Canal Dranov

Canal Perişor Belciug

Canal Palade

Gradiştea
Island

Lake
Razim

Canal
Orlova

Sacalin
Islands

Babadag

Enisala

Lake
Dranov

Jurilovca

Bisericuţa
Island

Baia

Cape
Doloşman

BLACK SEA

Gura Portiţei

N

0   10 km

Braţul Sulina

Between 1862 and 1902, the **Sulina arm** (Braţul Sulina) was shortened from
84km to 63km by the digging of long straight sections, now paralleled by a
communist-era power line. Distances from the sea were marked in **nautical
miles**, as opposed to the kilometres later used on the other arms. Constant
dredging and groynes running 10km out to sea still enable 7000-tonne freighters
to take this route from Tulcea; with the additional tourist traffic, this is the
busiest and least serene of the Danube's branches. However, it does have a tourist
infrastructure and several settlements that offer a fair chance of renting boats to
visit a variety of wildlife habitats. **Sulina** itself has seen something of a revitali-
zation in recent years and is now the Delta's most popular tourist destination. It's
also the most built-up, and the only one with streets and cars. There are a few
interesting sights in Sulina, but the fishing villages along the way make much
better bases for seeing wildlife and exploring the wetlands. The journey from

To enter the **Danube Delta Biosphere Reserve (RBDD)**, you need a **permit**, which gives access to everywhere except the strictly protected reserves. If you're taking a tour, this will be handled by the company; independent travellers can get permits (€1.50 for a day, €4 for a week) from the ARBDD in Tulcea. The ARBDD recommends electric boats and a 10km/hr speed limit, both generally ignored. Expensive organized tours are limited to seven routes; if you're planning to explore further, take a compass and a detailed **map** – the best is the *Danube Delta in Europe* map (free from the ARBDD information centre in Tulcea). Another comprehensive one is the Amco Delta map. There are very few **hotels** in the Delta, though this is compensated for by **resort complexes** and **pensions** (most open May–Sept). If these are full, try **B&B** accommodation in a cheaper **private home**, though some may not have hot water. Antrec, in Tulcea, can help you find a pension. Wherever you stay, expect generous fish dinners and tomato salads. Most pensions offer full board, but our price codes reflect the B&B equivalent. **Camping** is possible in Crişan, Maliuc, Murighiol, Partizani, Sulina, Sfântu Gheorghe and on the shore of Lake Roşu, but buy **essential supplies** like canned food, fruit and cheese in Tulcea; candles and mosquito repellent are also useful. Most Delta villages have a bakery, but fresh bread sells quickly.

There are three weekly **ferries** (Nava Clasica) operated by NAVROM-Delta (ⓦwww .navrom.x3m.ro) to Sulina (from Tulcea Mon, Wed & Fri; returning Tues, Thurs & Sun), two to Sfântu Gheorghe (from Tulcea Wed & Fri, returning Thurs & Sun) and two to Periprava (from Tulcea Mon & Fri; returning Tues & Sun). They leave Tulcea at 1.30pm and take 4hr 30min to Sulina or Sf. Gheorghe and 5hr 30min to Periprava. Ferries return early: from Sulina and Sf. Gheorghe at 7am and from Periprava at 6am. NAVROM-Delta also operates a pair of **fast catamarans**, Delta Expres 1 and 2, which traverse all three branches of the Delta (to Sulina Tues, Thurs & Sat, returning Mon, Wed & Fri; to Sf. Gheorghe Mon & Thurs, returning Tues & Fri; to Periprava Wed, returning Thurs). These also leave Tulcea at 1.30pm and take 2hr to Sulina and 3hr to Sf. Gheorghe or Periprava; returns are at 7am from Sulina and Sf. Gheorghe and 6am from Periprava. On the **winter schedule**, from October to June, Sulina is reached by ferries (Mon, Wed & Fri) and *rapids* (Tues & Thurs); Sfântu Gheorghe by a ferry (Wed) and *rapids* (Mon & Fri); and Periprava by a ferry (Fri) and *rapids* (Mon & Wed). The Sageaţa (Arrow) **hydrofoils**, once state-owned, are now operated by private companies from Tulcea's Gara Fluviala to Sulina only, leaving daily at noon and 3.30pm and returning at 7am and noon. These are businesslike craft with opaque windows, taking just 90min for the journey. In Tulcea the **ticket office** for all the services outlined above (open sailing days only 11am–1.30pm) is in the Gara Fluviala on the waterfront; **tickets** (€7.50 by ferry to Sulina, €9 by fast cat, around €12 by hydrofoil) can only be bought on the day you're travelling, up to 2hr before departure. There's a 30kg baggage limit.

Tulcea to Sulina takes ninety minutes by hydrofoil, two hours by fast catamaran, or four-and-a-half by ferry.

Travellers attempting to explore the Delta **by canoe** will face turbulence from the wakes of passing ships on the main waterway, but **beyond Ilganii de Sus** you can escape into calmer backwaters leading to the inland lakes. Just east of Ilgani, on the north bank where the Sulina and Sfântu Gheorghe arms split (and just 6km from Tulcea), the *Complex Mila 35* (ⓣ0744/688 404, ⓦwww.mila35 .ro; ⓺) is a reed-thatched three-star resort that's less grandiose than most of the Delta's new resorts.

Maliuc

Fishermen in **MALIUC**, on the left bank of the river 27km from Tulcea, can row you to see the pelicans and marsh terns nesting on **Lake Furtuna**. The reeds in this

area provide a home for pike, great-crested grebes, the solitary red-necked grebes,
bearded reedlings – which nest in piles of cut reeds – and herons and little egrets,
which favour nesting in overhanging willow trees. Maliuc has the *Salcia* **hotel**
(℡0240/546 539; ❹) and a **campsite**. From Lake Meşter or the Păpădia channel,
canoeists can try following the Gârla Şontea to reach the original Dunărea Veche
course of the river near Mila 23 (see below); be warned, though, that submerged
roots and aquatic plants may block the way. Nearby **Lake Gorgova** hosts a large
colony of glossy ibis, and has a small cabana (❶).

Crişan

CRIŞAN, a fishing settlement that consists of a single dirt path, lined with houses
and straggling along the south bank of the shoreline for 7km, is the main tourist
centre in this part of the Delta, and a good place to see the region's most common
bird species; the ditch that runs behind the houses shelters herons, egrets and other
waders, and you're likely to find hoopoes, rollers and goldfinches in the brushland at
the west end of the village. Pelicans glide high overhead in long formations
throughout the day, making their way from Lake Merhei to Lake Iacob. Across the
river at Mila 13, there is a **monument** unveiled by Carol I in 1894 to inaugurate the
new short-cut sections. Also on the north bank, before Mila 14 near the *Lebăda* hotel,
is the ARBDD's **information centre** (May–Oct Tues–Fri 10am–5pm, Sat & Sun
10am–2pm; Nov–April Mon–Fri 8am–4pm; ℡0728/281 466), with plenty of
materials and advice on travelling around the Delta, plus an excellent viewing tower.

Ferries stop on the south bank, in the centre of Crişan; both the best shop and
the bakery are by the ferry pier. There's stacks of **accommodation** here, starting
with the moderately luxurious *Sunrise* hotel at Str. Babadag 140 (℡0240/547 191,
Ⓦwww.hotelsunrise.ro; ❼), which also has villas. The best of the many **pensions**
are the *Nufărul* (℡0744/294 217; ❷), a few hundred metres east of the ferry
landing, which can arrange day-trips to remoter parts of the Delta; and, in the
other direction, 500m west of the landing, the much larger *Delia* (℡0745/116
186, Ⓦwww.deltadelia.ro; ❷), also offering camping space. *Oprişan Andrei*
(℡0240/547 034; ❷), 200m east of the ferry landing, is also recommended.
Crişan's **campsite** (℡0745/832 293) is at the far west end of the village.

Around Crişan

Boats meet the ferry (but not the hydrofoil or fast catamaran) at Crişan to take you
across to the north bank, and continue on to **MILA 23**, 10km northwest on the
"old" branch of the Danube; this is the starting point for excursions to most of the
surrounding lakes. Mila 23 is a large Lipovani village of thatched cottages (rebuilt
after a flood in the 1960s), where the men fish and the women tend to gardens of

vegetables, plums, pears, grapes and quinces, and look after the poultry, pigs and beehives. Golden orioles – which nest high in deciduous trees – and bladder frogs are widespread around here. **Pensions** include *Cristina* (☎0240/546 430; ❷) and the slightly classier *La Grig* (☎0240/517 476; ❸).

South of Crişan, the forest of **Pădurea Caraorman**, now a strict reserve, is the best area of dunes in the Delta, striped with unusual linear forests of ancient oaks, poplar, ash and willow and protecting wildlife such as Ural owls, white-tailed eagles, wildcats, boars and wolves. The dyke that runs south from Crişan leads to a dead end; to get to the forest, catch the boat that meets ferries at Crişan to take passengers to the predominantly Ukrainian village of **CARAORMAN**, where there are a couple of **pensions**: *Grindul Verde* (☎0722/732 076; ❷), which has English-speaking staff, and the small but slightly more upmarket *Purda Nicoara* (☎0744/381 528; ❷). Half-a-dozen unfinished skeletal apartment blocks are testament to plans, under Ceauşescu, to remove the dunes en masse; the 1989 revolution intervened.

Three remote and very different settlements lie to the north of Crişan, on the south side of the Letea forest: **LETEA**, a village of Lipovani/Ukrainian fisherfolk, where there's a rangers' house and birdwatching tower; neighbouring **C.A. ROSETTI**, home to Romanian cattle breeders and the Delta's last windmill; and **SFISTOFCA**, an even smaller Lipovani village. You may get a room in these places on the spot, but it's best to check with the ARBDD or Antrec in Tulcea (see p.339) before setting out. The **Letea forest**, just north of Rosetti and Letea, is strictly off-limits, but the **Sfistofca forest**, to the south, is almost as good, a maze of trees up to two hundred years old, tangled with lianas and orchids.

Sulina

Ever since it was recorded as a port by a Byzantine scribe in 950, **SULINA** has depended on shipping. Genoese vessels used to call here during the fourteenth century, while throughout the Ottoman period it was not so much a trading port as a nest of pirates who preyed on traffic in the Black Sea. Devastated during the Crimean War – only the church and lighthouse survived after the British, driving out the Russians, burnt the place down – Sulina was rebuilt and went on to prosper as the headquarters of the European Commission of the Danube, established in 1856 to regulate free passage along the waterway. In 1900 it became a free port, and its freewheeling multinational life was captured in the novel *Europolis* by Jean Bart (pseudonym of the Romanian sea captain Eugeniu Botez, 1874–1933). Within a decade, however, larger vessels and worldwide recession had emptied Sulina, so that by 1940 the writer John Lehmann found "a hopeless, sinking feeling" in a place where "people get stranded, feel themselves abandoned by civilization, take to drink, and waste into a half-animal existence". Today, expensive annual dredging is required to enable even small-capacity ships to enter, while larger freighters can now bypass the Delta altogether by taking the Danube–Black Sea Canal. Tourism is succeeding where trade failed, and, drawn by the long sandy beach 2km from the port, a small but growing contingent of Romanians has chosen Sulina as an alternative to the more established resorts further south.

A taste of the ambience of Sulina's golden days survives in the nineteenth-century houses along the waterfront, and at the **Old Lighthouse** (Farul Vechi; Tues–Sun: May–Sept 10am–6pm; Oct–April 8am–4pm; €1); built in 1870, it is now a history museum, with a room dedicated to Jean Bart and the conductor George Georgescu (born in Sulina in 1887), and another to the European Commission of the Danube. The lighthouse is two blocks south of the ferry landing at Str.II 15; 500m further to the southeast, between the town and the sea, is the **cemetery**, which provides an evocative record of all the nationalities who lived and died here in the town's days as a free port. Greeks dominated business, but there was also a large British contingent, some now resting beneath dignified Victorian tombstones in the Anglican plot, directly behind the chapel. Like so much of the Delta, the cemetery is full of birds – this is one of the best places to see hoopoes, and possibly cuckoos and orioles. From the cemetery, it's a 1km walk to the **beach** (maxitaxis also run this route). Also look for two **churches** from the nineteenth century: the Greek Church of Saint Nicholas on the waterfront, and the Russian church near the west end of town.

Practicalities

The ARBDD **information centre** is near the dock in the centre of town on Str. I (May–Oct Tues–Fri 8am–3pm, Sat & Sun 8am–noon; Nov–April Mon–Fri 8am–4pm; ☎0728/281 467). There are plenty of **pensions** in Sulina, many of which send touts to meet the ferries. *Casa Coral*, on the waterfront at Str. I 195 (☎0742/974 016, ⓦwww.casacoralsulina.ro; ❸), is a colourful establishment with smart rooms and a restaurant. Shabbier, but more atmospheric, is the *Jean Bart*, Str. I 190 (☎0240/543 128, ⓦwww.pensiuneajeanbart.ro; ❷); the fish **restaurant** here is the best place to eat in Sulina. Around the corner from the *Jean Bart* is the reasonable *Vâlcu* (☎0240/543 403; ❷), and a few blocks further in, at Str. IV 144, the modest but friendly *Ana* (☎0230/543 252; ❷). You'll find the *Hostel Danube Delta*, also known as *Cazare Camping Sulina*, at Str. II 1 (☎0745/327 805, ⓦhttp://holiday-danube-delta.ro; ❶); it has two-, four- and six-bed rooms and **camping** space. There are a few **bars** in Sulina, but the principal evening activity is strolling on the promenade, where the shops do a brisk trade in ice cream.

Brațul Sfântu Gheorghe

The Delta's oldest, most winding arm, **Brațul Sfântu Gheorghe**, is the least used by freighters and fishing boats; it's wider but shallower than the Sulina arm. It carries a fair amount of tourist traffic and, unlike other parts of the Delta, some of its settlements can be reached by bus from Tulcea. If you plan to visit these, it's easiest to go direct to **Sfântu Gheorghe**, then head by boat to **Murighiol**, from where you can make a boat trip to the fishing village of **Uzlina** or visit the ruins of **Halmyris**. There's plenty of parking in Murighiol; if you've come by car, it's better to leave it there rather than in Tulcea.

Sfântu Gheorghe

SFÂNTU GHEORGHE, 75km downriver from Murighiol, is a small village of brightly painted Lipovani and Ukrainian cottages that has subsisted on fishing since the fourteenth century. Most prized is the **sturgeon**, whose eggs, *icre negre* or black caviar, once drew thousands of Romanian tourists here on shopping trips. The catch is not what it used to be, though you still might find some caviar if you come in late August or early September. The **reed and mud houses**, most of which support colonies of swallows, are the main attraction of the village itself, but most tourists come for the relatively untouched **beach** (stretching 38km north to Sulina) or to make trips into the surrounding **marshes**. A large tractor, one of the two or three motorized land vehicles in the village, carries tourists the 2km to and from the beach in a trailer, departing every hour or so from the centre – the schedule should be posted on one of the information boards near the main square.

The best **place to stay** in Sfântu Gheorghe is the *Delfinul Tourist Village* (☎0749/187 551, ⓦwww.deltasfantugheorghe.ro; ❻), 700m east on the road to the beach; it includes high-class villas (some actually in the village), cabins and a **campsite**. The best of the dozen or so pensions in town is the *Mareea* (☎0744/306 384, ⓦwww .mareea.go.ro; ❸), which has attractively furnished rooms and offers superb meals – there's a good chance of finding sturgeon on the menu. The owner, who speaks English, can arrange fishing and birdwatching excursions. Less exclusive, and without air conditioning, is the *Pensiunea Sperante*, at Str. I 30 (☎0744/197 042; ❸); locals know it as *casa galben*, the yellow house. Dora Dumitru has a summer home (☎0240/540 219; ❷) one block north of the *Sperante*, with four bedrooms; she also prepares fish in a mouthwatering variety of ways. *Casa Ichim* (☎0745/600 650; ❷) has three rooms and an open porch for dining, plus a boat that is available for excursions. There are half a dozen simple guesthouses rated with one daisy (all ❷); their owners and other villagers with private rooms (❶) will meet your ferry.

Sfântu Gheorghe's **shops** are in the centre near the dock, as is the bakery. The *Delfinul Tourist Village* has three cinemas used for the excellent **Anonimul Film Festival** in mid-August, a celebration of independent films from around the world (🖰www.festival-anonimul.ro).

Around Sfântu Gheorghe

During July and August, the Sfântu Gheorghe tractor makes occasional day excursions to **Sulina** (1hr 30min) – look for a sign in the town centre or ask around if you're interested. Otherwise you can take **boat trips** north to **Lake Roşu**, or south down the Gârla de Mijloc canal to **Lesser Sacalin Island** (Insula Sacalinu Mic) at the river's mouth, which is inhabited by all three species of marsh tern, stilts, ibis and other waders, as well as goosanders, red-breasted geese, and goldeneyes. This is one of the oldest parts of the Delta and a strictly protected reserve, so boats are not allowed to moor: to get to the beach on the island, you'll have to wade through the ankle-deep mud at the canal's end. Depending on the wind, the trip takes an hour or more; the motorboat is faster but, at €10 per hour, at least twice as expensive. Look for kingfishers along the way. Further south still is **Greater Sacalin Island** (Insula Sacalinu Mare), while to the west, on Lake Lejai and near the Crasnicol sand bank, is the remote area where the Delta's three hundred or so Dalmatian pelicans breed. The trip to **Lacul Roşu** (Pink Lake) is longer than that to Lesser Sacalin Island, but you're likely to see white pelicans. There's an isolated **campsite** on the canal between Roşu and Puiu lakes.

Murighiol

Returning towards Tulcea, the main settlement en route is **MURIGHIOL**, which, though connected to the outside world by road as well as water, still has some of the isolated feeling of an interior Delta village. Murighiol has its natural attractions – namely black-winged stilts, red- and black-necked grebe, Kentish plover, avocets, and red-crested pochards, and Romania's only colony of Mediterranean gulls, all nesting around the late-freezing **salt lakes** (Sărături Murighiol) nearby, but the principal reason to come here is to visit the ruin at **Halmyris**, or the fishing village of **Uzlina**. Six buses a day run to and from Tulcea, on a circular route via either Mahmudia or Sarinasuf. Be warned that the buses don't go anywhere near the ferry landing, which is 5km northeast from the centre of the village – if you're on your way to or from Sfântu Gheorghe, you'll have to walk or hitch.

The best of Murighiol's **accommodation** is at the entrance to the village (coming from Tulcea); *Pensiunea La Tavi* (☎0742/058 447, 🖰www.pensiunealatavi.ro; ❷), almost the first house, is not a pension at all but instead eight handsomely constructed and well-equipped two-bed huts pitched amongst trim lawns. If you wish to **camp**, walk 200m along to the private *Camping Lac Murighiol* (☎0744/175 581; ❶) – the bus from Tulcea can set you down at either of these places. Buses continue into the centre of Murighiol, where you'll find a handful of shops and loads of places offering boat trips.

Some 3km out of the village (turning left at the fork in the road), and just beyond the defunct *Halmyris* hotel, is a boat-rental kiosk, where staff can arrange day-trips or transportation to their *Complex Cormoran* at Lake Uzlina (see box, p.341). For **ferries** to Sfântu Gheorghe, follow the forested road that begins next to the *Halmyris*; it's 1.5km on to the ferry landing, where there's also a large car park.

Halmyris

Two kilometres out from Murighiol, on the road to Dunavatu de Jos, lies the ruined Roman city of **HALMYRIS**. One of the most important ancient sites in Romania, Halmyris was continuously inhabited from the sixth century BC to the seventh century AD, when a combination of marauding barbarians, climatic changes and dwindling imperial support led to its demise. Originally a small seafront fort – in ancient times, a Danube channel met the Black Sea only a few hundred metres to the east – it grew in size and importance until it became the permanent home to Roman troops and a station for the Danube fleet *Classis Flavia Moesica*, serving as a stopping point on the road that connected the major Roman settlements of the Delta.

Today, Halmyris is best known for the **tomb of Epictet and Astion**, two Christians from Asia Minor who were tortured and executed here on July 8, 290, after refusing to renounce Christianity, thus becoming the earliest Romanian martyrs (and earning a place on the Romanian Orthodox calendar). One of their judges was said to have been converted by the resolve with which Epictet and Astion met their fates, and to have secretly buried their remains, which were then kept hidden until the conversion of Constantine, when they were interred in Halmyris's **basilica**. The story seemed to be the stuff of legend until 2001, when a **crypt** containing two skeletons was discovered beneath the basilica's altar, along with a **fresco** (currently under restoration) bearing the name "Astion".

In addition to the basilica and the crypt, the two-hectare site also features extensive remains of an L-shaped private **bathhouse**. The Western Gate, which dates from the sixth century AD, was constructed largely of stones carved with honorary inscriptions that had in earlier times adorned the homes of the town's more prominent citizens. Much of Halmyris, as well as the surrounding cornfields that cover its harbour, remains unexcavated (digging only began here in 1981), and its greatest attraction is not the ruins themselves, or the tombs of Epictet and Astion, but the chance to see an ancient city still in the process of being uncovered.

Uzlina, Dunavatu de Jos and Mahmudia

Murighiol is also the jumping-off point for the tiny fishing village of **UZLINA**, the site of the scientific centre of the Biosphere Reserve and the Cousteau Foundation, and an **EcoInfoCenter** in what was Ceaușescu's lodge. North of Uzlina, the Isac and Uzlina lakes are home to a protected **pelican colony**, which you can see from a respectful distance. Heading downstream, the new channel is edged by high levees, but the meanders of the old channel are tree-lined and populated by deer, boar, foxes, water snakes, black ibis and egrets. **Lake Belciug**, roughly halfway back towards Sfântu Gheorghe, is one of those least affected by algal blooms and deoxygenation, and retains the submerged vegetation once typical of the Delta, as well as a colony of glossy ibis.

To the southeast, 8km beyond Murighiol, the road ends at **DUNAVATU DE JOS**, on a channel between the Sfântu Gheorghe arm and Lake Razim, where you can stay at the warm and comfortable *Hotel Egreta* (☎0742/828 831, ⓦwww .hotelegreta.ro; ⊙), as well as half a dozen pensions around the village. Ferries also call at **MAHMUDIA**, on the Tulcea road 7km west of Murighiol; there's accommodation here in the shape of two classy waterfront **hotels**, namely *Mon Jardin*

(☎0240/545 511, ⓦwww.hotelmonjardin.ro; ❻), a dazzling white building with immaculate rooms, and, 150m further along, the wood- and glass-built *Casa Teo* (☎0240/545 550, ⓦwww.pensiuneacasateo.ro; ❺), which is almost as appealing.

Around Lake Razim

South of the Delta proper, **Lake Razim** is separated from the Black Sea by two long, tongue-like *grinds*. Like other parts of the Delta, Razim has been adversely affected by development: the western shores were reclaimed in 1969 for fish farming, and in 1974 a sluice at Gura Portiței cut the lake off from the sea, causing it to fill with fresh water, which has led to frequent algal blooms, deoxygenation, and a steady decline in fish yields and biodiversity. It's still a good spot for birdwatchers, however, particularly in November and December, when the western shoreline is invaded by a million white-fronted and red-breasted geese from arctic Russia, which stay here and on Lake Sinoe just south until the reed beds freeze. In the north of the lake, Popina island is now a closed reserve.

Babadag and Enisala

From Tulcea, the DN22 and the rail line head south to **BABADAG**, home to the **Ali Ghazi Mosque**, Romania's oldest, dating from 1522. There's a visible Turkish minority here, present since 1263, but the mosque is little used. Just down the street though, the **Museum of Oriental Art** (Muzeul de Artă Orientală; Tues–Sun 10am–6pm) has a small but engaging display of the folk art of the Dobrogean Turks, including embroidered robes and copper vessels. Maxitaxis between Tulcea and Constanța, as well as the less frequent services to Enisala and Jurilovca, call at the **bus station** across the street from the mosque. There's fairly modern **accommodation** at the *Hotel Parmac*, along from the bus station at Str. Republicii 91 (☎0240/562 235; ❷), while its flower bedecked terrace is a pleasant place to lunch. The *Popas Doi Iepurași* (☎0240/562 035; ❷) offers a peaceful night in the oak forest a couple of kilometres south of Babadag. Babadag is the base for Romania's elite Marine Battalion, forcibly disbanded after World War II but then re-established in 1971 as Ceaușescu increasingly defied Moscow; since 2007 US Marines have also been stationed here and at Constanța's Mihail Kogălniceanu airport.

A quiet village of reed-thatched cottages, **ENISALA** lies 8km east of Babadag. In the centre of town, a traditional peasant home has been preserved as a **museum** (Punct Muzeal Gospodăria Țărănească; Wed–Mon 10am–6pm) displaying colourful tapestries, painted carts and a wealth of implements. About 1km north, overlooking the lake, is the **ruined citadel of Heracleia**, built by Genoese merchants late in the thirteenth century at the behest of the Byzantine emperor, on the site of a seventh-century Byzantine fort. Taken by Sultan Mehmet I in 1417, it was held by the Ottomans until they abandoned it around the sixteenth century. This area is one of Europe's prime birdwatching sites, thanks to a mix of habitats: a vast area of reedbeds along the shoreline, stretching back to open land and the Babadag forest. You're likely to spot white-fronted and red-breasted geese, terns, waders, pelicans, herons and warblers. If you're coming from Tulcea, watch the left side of the road: shortly before passing the citadel, you'll see an apiary that supports a sizeable colony of bee-eaters. Around half a dozen buses from Tulcea take the rough back road through Enisala en route to Babadag.

Jurilovca and Gura Portiței

The tiny fishing village of **JURILOVCA**, 17km further down the coast and served by three daily buses from Tulcea, is of interest mainly for its access to Lake Razim's outer rim. It also has a small **Ethnographic Museum**, which bears witness to the village's population of Romanians, Lipovani and a few Muslim

Turks and Tatars: unlike Transylvania, the Delta has never really been noted for ethnic rivalry, since all groups are relatively recent colonists. Around 5km east of Jurilovca, on Cape Doloşman, lie the remains of the second- to sixth-century Greek citadel of **Arganum**, which faces **Isla Bisericuţa (Chapel Island)**, itself the site of some medieval ruins. The only **place to stay** in Jurilovca is *Pensiunea Milica* (book through Antrec ℡0240/519 214; ❷).

From Jurilovca (where there's guarded parking), three boats (departing 9am, 2pm & 6pm; €6) sail daily to **GURA PORTIŢEI**, on a spit of land between Lake Razim and the sea. Before 1989, this was one of the few remote corners of Romania where it was possible to escape the Securitate for a week or two; today, it consists of a few Lipovani huts and the *Eden Complex* (May to mid-Oct; ℡0724/214 224, ⓦwww.guraportitei.ro), a large holiday village accommodating a variety of rooms in villas (❸–❺) as well as cabins (❶) and space to camp. Both rowing and motor boats are available, in addition to fishing and birdwatching excursions to the **Periteaşca-Leahova reserve**, just north, where 20,000 red-breasted geese (half the world population) spend the winter. Continuing towards Constanţa, you'll rejoin the main DN22 at the north end of **BAIA**, better known as **Hamangia**, site of Romania's most famous Neolithic finds.

Istria

Heading south from Babadag and Baia and turning left at Mihai Viteazul, you'll pass through **ISTRIA**. Eight kilometres east of the village (and 35km north of Constanţa), on the shores of Lake Sinoe, is the **ruined city of Histria** (Cetatea Histria) with its shattered Greek temples to diverse deities, as well as Roman baths and other Romano-Byzantine edifices. The **ruins** (Wed–Sun: June–Sept 9am–8pm; Oct–May 9am–5pm; €3) cover a fairly small area, despite the fact that this was long the most important of the ancient Greek settlements along the coast. It was founded in 657 BC, though none of the remains dates from before 300 BC. Istria's decline began soon after that, but it was inhabited until early in the seventh century AD, when the port was smothered in silt and the town abandoned after attacks by Avar-Slavic tribes. The **museum**, in an ugly glass building next to the entrance, holds a substantial assemblage of Greek and Roman finds, the first of which were unearthed in 1914 by the eminent historian Vasile Pârvan; prominent amongst the display are dozens of pillars, altars and funereal stones (*steles*), with marble friezes, sculptural fragments, terracotta statuettes and ceramics comprising the remainder of this exceptional hoard. Today, this strictly protected zone is one of Europe's best areas for birdwatching, with more than 200 species making an appearance in the winter months. A handful of **maxitaxis** a day run from Constanţa to Istria village, though you've still got 7km to the site to negotiate; the Istria train stop is on the DN22, too far west to be of use.

The coast

Romania's **Black Sea coast** (the *litoral*) holds the promise of white beaches, dazzling water and an average of ten to twelve hours of sunshine a day between May and October. Under communism, over a million people flocked to the resorts during the season; visitor numbers then halved but have since recovered to close to a million again, with far better conditions than previously. Travelling from Bucharest or the Delta, your first stop on the coast will almost certainly be **Constanța**, a relaxed seaport-cum-riviera town, dotted with Turkish, Byzantine and Roman remains, which has always seemed to keep a discreet distance from the surrounding resorts.

North of Constanța, **Mamaia** is indisputably the coastal hotspot, swarming with hotels and buzzing with nightlife, while the resorts to the south, merging imperceptibly with one another, are more uniform. Beyond **Mangalia**, the only town of any real size south of Constanța, the twin resorts of **Doi Mai** and **Vama Veche**, just a few kilometres from the Bulgarian border, offer a more relaxed vibe and a welcome escape from the crowds. If you're not part of a **package tour**, then finding accommodation along the coast in July and August may be tricky, though there are plenty of agencies (*Dispecerat de Cazare*) which can help out. You'll also find plenty of places advertising rooms (*cazare*), while many people wait at stations and at the entrance to resorts touting rooms. Note that most resorts pretty much close down by mid-September.

The Dobrogea and the Danube–Black Sea Canal

The overland approaches to Constanța cross one part or another of the bleak northern **Dobrogea**, a poor area where donkeys still haul metal-wheeled carts. While there's no reason to break your journey here, the changes wrought over the last forty years certainly merit some explanation. Driving on the DN2A, you'll cross the Danube at **Giurgeni** and see orchards and fields planted on what used to be pestilential marshland; this transformation is nothing compared to the great works further to the south, starting at **Cernavodă**, where the Danube is spanned by what was, when it opened in 1895, Europe's longest bridge (4037m, with a main span of 1662m); trains now run alongside on a bridge built in 1987. A road bridge was added in the same year, linking the DN3A and the DN22C to provide the most direct road route to Constanța, parallel to the rail line and the **Danube–Black Sea Canal**. The motorway bridge, opened in 2006, passes diagonally under the 1895 rail bridge, with its carriageways continuing on either side of the railway.

Cernavodă and the canal

CERNAVODĂ, whose name rather ominously translates as "Black Water", was chosen in the late 1970s to be the site of Romania's first nuclear power station, but it's better known as the western entrance to the **Danube–Black Sea Canal**. Opened to shipping in 1984, the canal put Cernavodă a mere 60km from the Black Sea, offering obvious savings in time and fuel. However, realizing a profit on such a huge investment remains dependent on European economic revival and on the success of the Rhein–Main and Nürnberg–Regensburg canals. Charlemagne's vision of a 3000km-long waterway linking Rotterdam with the Black Sea finally came to fruition in 1993, although environmental protests in Bavaria and soaring costs had stalled the final stage of the project for ten years.

Along the canal

Most trains through the Dobrogea stop at the town of **MEDGIDIA** (the junction for Tulcea and Negru Vodă, the crossing point to Bulgaria) on the canal, 24km east of Cernavodă, while slow trains also halt at the canal-side town of **BASARABI** and its eastern suburb of **MURFATLAR**, which gives its name to the surrounding wine-growing region. Three million bottles a year are produced here, seventy percent white, although the full fruity reds are more distinctive. You can only visit on **tours** organized by travel agencies in the beach resorts; these take in the wine cellars at Calea Bucureşti 10, and the nearby **Vine and Wine Museum** (Muzeul Viei şi Vinului), displaying Greek and Roman amphorae and more recent presses.

Adamclisi and crossing into Bulgaria

Just north of the DN3 and the village of **ADAMCLISI** stands an arresting marble structure, a reconstruction of the **Tropaeum Traiani** (Wed–Sun: June–Sept 9am–8pm; Oct–May 9am–5pm; €1). An armoured, faceless warrior gazing over the plateau from a height of 30m, the trophy-statue was erected here in 109 AD to celebrate Trajan's conquest of the Dacians, every facet reflecting unabashed militarism, not least the dedication to Mars Ultor. Carved around the side of its 32m base are 49 bas-reliefs or **metopes** portraying the Roman campaign. Each of the six groups of metopes comprises a marching scene, a battle, and a tableau representing victory over the enemy, an arrangement identical to the one that underlies scenes XXXVI–XLII of Trajan's Column in Rome, a copy of which is in Bucharest's National History Museum (see p.68). Around the statue are **ruins** of buildings once inhabited by the legionary garrison or serving religious or funerary purposes. **Buses** run from Cernavodă and Medgidia (heading for Băneasa and Ostrov), and a few daily maxitaxis from Constanţa via Băneasa stop here on their way to Oltina.

Into Bulgaria

Sixty kilometres west of Adamclisi along the DN3 is the small border town of **OSTROV**, where you can cross over to the Bulgarian town of **Silistra** (also accessible on a ferry across the Danube from Călăraşi). Although the **Vama Veche** crossing (see p.367) is more suitable if you're driving down the coast to Varna, it's also possible to enter Bulgaria from **NEGRU VODĂ** at the south end of the DN38 (57km southwest of Constanţa), a crossing that's also used by three local trains a day from Medgidia. All three crossings are open 24 hours a day; if you need a visa, make sure you get it either before leaving home or in Bucharest (see "Listings", p.84).

Constanţa

Most visitors first encounter the Black Sea coast at **CONSTANŢA**, a busy riviera town and Romania's principal port. Its ancient precursor, Tomis, was supposedly founded by survivors of a battle with the Argonauts, following the capture of the Golden Fleece; centuries later, the great Roman poet Ovid was exiled here for nine years until his death in 17 AD. These days, the town is an attractive mix of Greco-Roman remains, Turkish mosques and crisp modern boulevards, home to several interesting **museums** and a lively restaurant scene. Pilot cutters mounted by the road at its northern and southern entries attest to its status as a maritime town, as does its biggest festival, **Navy Day** on August 15, when up to 10,000 people watch the parade.

Arrival, transport and information

The modern **train station** is 2km west of the centre at the southern end of B-dul Ferdinand, with the grotty main **bus station** (*Autogară Sud*) 200m north of here on Str. Theodor Burada. Constanţa is served by **Mihail Kogălniceanu airport** (℡0241/258 378), 25km northwest of town, from where it's a half-hour journey into the centre; a taxi should cost no more than €10. There are also hourly **maxitaxis** on the main road outside the airport, heading for the train and bus stations.

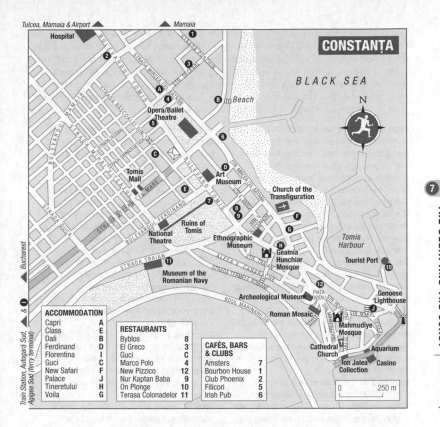

Tulcea, Mamaia & Airport ▲   ▲ Mamaia

Hospital

CONSTANȚA

BLACK SEA

Beach

Opera/Ballet
Theatre

Tomis
Mall

Art
Museum

Church of the
Transfiguration

Tomis
Harbour

Ruins of
Tomis

National
Theatre

Ethnographic
Museum

Geamia
Hunchiar
Mosque

Tourist Port

Museum of the
Romanian Navy

Archeological Museum

Genoese
Lighthouse

Roman Mosaic

Mahmudiye
Mosque

Cathedral
Church

Ion Jalea
Collection

Aquarium

Casino

Bucharest ◀

Train Station, Autogară Sud,
Agigea Sud (ferry terminal) ▲ & ❶

ACCOMMODATION	
Capri	A
Class	E
Dali	B
Ferdinand	D
Florentina	I
Guci	C
New Safari	F
Palace	J
Tineretului	H
Voila	G

RESTAURANTS	
Byblos	8
El Greco	3
Guci	C
Marco Polo	4
New Pizzico	12
Nur Kaptan Baba	9
On Plonge	10
Terasa Colonadelor	11

CAFÉS, BARS & CLUBS	
Amsters	7
Bourbon House	1
Club Phoenix	2
Filicori	5
Irish Pub	6

0 _____ 250 m

From the train station, **trolley buses** #40 and (in summer) #41 run along B-dul Ferdinand to the centre and then swing north. Buses run from 5.15am (5.45am at weekends) to 11pm, and tickets, each good for two rides within Constanța or one if you're going all the way to Mamaia, are available from most kiosks. There are also tickets valid for three hours (€1.50), six hours (€2) and twelve hours (€3). Remember to punch your ticket on the bus (both ends if you're going to Mamaia) – inspectors are especially vigilant here, with a stiff fine for riding without a ticket. General Taxi (☎0241/617 844) and Romaris (☎0241/690 000) are trustworthy **taxi** companies.

Trolley bus #40 runs from the train station to the southern edge of **Mamaia**; in summer #41 runs all the way through the resort. Buses #32 and #100 run frequently to the **Sat de Vacanță** (holiday village) just south of Mamaia, passing the **Autogară Nord** (Str. Soveja 35), from which maxitaxis head north to destinations along the coast, including **Tulcea** and **Galați**; maxitaxi #23 takes the same route from just north of the train station to Mamaia. Özlem Tur (☎0241/662 626) runs the overnight **bus to Istanbul**, departing daily at 3pm; its office is in the bus station.

There's no **tourist information office** in Constanța, but there is one in Mamaia (see p.360).

Accommodation

The city has a large stock of central **hotels**, and whilst there's little to differentiate between many of them, there are enough places for those on a lesser budget. If you're looking for something very cheap, take bus #32 or #100 from the station to the far end of **Lake Tăbăcărie**, or #40 to **Pescărie**, where you'll find the **Sat de Vacanţă** (holiday village); its eastern half is all funfair rides and fast food, but across a stream to the west is an area of restaurants named after *judeţs* (counties), some of which have remarkably cheap rooms too. However, it can be very noisy and crowded during the summer. Otherwise, locals with **private rooms** sometimes wait by the train station, holding signs reading *cazare*.

Capri Str. Mircea cel Bătrân 109 ☎0241/553 090, ⓦwww.capri.ro. Well insulated from the busy main road, this mid-sized hotel has comfortable rooms with big beds, in addition to some decent amenities, including indoor swimming pool, sauna, jacuzzi and billiards room. ❻

Class Str. Răscoalei 1907 1 ☎0241/660 766, ⓦwww.hotelclass.ro. Neat, quiet hotel located just across from the Art Museum, harbouring good-sized rooms with low beds and leather armchairs. Good value. ❺

Dali Str. Smărdan 6A ☎0241/619 717, ⓦwww .hotel-dali.ro. Popular and well-appointed four-star hotel with pastel facade and comfortable, spacious rooms, including some with a sea view. ❻

Ferdinand B-dul Ferdinand 12 ☎0241/407 761, ⓦwww.hotelferdinand.ro. A classic mid-twentieth-century Deco-style building concealing fifteen well-furnished burgundy-coloured rooms, some of which have balconies. Try to avoid those facing the noisy road. ❻

Florentina Str. I. C. Brătianu 24 ☎0241/512 535, ⓕ510 202. Perfectly acceptable budget place, though the rooms, all with shower, TV and a/c, are a little careworn. Triples available too. Exiting the train station, turn left, walk past the bus station, then left again on to Brătianu – the hotel is 150m up on the right. ❸

Guci Str. Răscoalei din 1907 23 ☎0241/695 500, ⓦwww.hotel-guci.ro. Classy, compact hotel, just off the main pedestrianized area, with smoothly furnished rooms, laminate flooring and attractive wall lamps and pictures.The rooftop restaurant is worth a try too. ❺

New Safari Str. Karatzali 1 ☎0241/555 571, ⓦwww.newsafari.ro. Oddly named seven-room pension in a very favourable position overlooking the harbour; comfortable, Mediterranean-style rooms and a lovely breakfast terrace make this a good choice. ❺

🏃 **Palace** Str. Remus Opreanu 5-7 ☎0241/614 696, ⓦwww.rrt.ro. The only hotel on the Peninsula, this fabulous early twentieth-century pile offers an array of differently priced rooms, though all are finished to a high standard and some have tremendous sea views. ❹–❽

Tineretului B-dul Tomis 20–26 ☎&ⓕ0241/613 590. Constanţa's youth hotel is not a particularly pretty sight – small beds, old carpets and antiquated bathrooms – but it's clean, well located and very cheap. Breakfast is included in the price. ❷

Voila Str. Callatis 22 ☎0241/508 002, ⓦwww .voilahotel.ro. A relatively small four-star hotel, idiosyncratically decorated with pseudo-Roman mosaics; the pretty rooms are furnished in deep burgundy, with big cast-iron beds and an amazing array of trinkets. There's a small restaurant on top with great views. ❼

The Town

The oldest area of Constanţa, centred on **Piaţa Ovidiu**, stands on a headland between what is now the tourist port and the huge area of the modern docks to the south and west, and is home to the excellent **Archeological and National History Museum**. Walking up the shore from the tourist port, you'll find Constanţa's passable **beach**, and inland, beyond the remains of the walls of ancient Tomis, the modern **commercial area**, along boulevards Ferdinand and Tomis. Further north, nearing the resort of **Mamaia**, are various sights designed to appeal to children (but perhaps more likely to frighten them), including a **funfair** and **planetarium**

Piaţa Ovidiu

Piaţa Ovidiu, the central square of the old quarter, is dominated by a mournful statue of Ovid, exiled here from Rome by Emperor Augustus in 8 AD. Marooned in backwater Tomis, the poet spent his last years unsuccessfully petitioning emperors for his return, and composing his melancholy *Tristia*.

On the southern side of the square, Constanţa's **Archeological and National History Museum** (Muzeul de Istorie Naţională şi Arheologie; Wed–Sun: June–Sept 9am–8pm; Oct–May 9am–5pm; €3) harbours a quite brilliant collection of marble and limestone friezes, reliefs, miniature busts and ceramic figurines. The museum's signature piece, however, is the extraordinary **Glykon Serpent**, a unique creation about the size of a squatting toddler, with an antelope's head, human hair and eyes, and a gracefully coiled serpentine body ending in a lion's tail, which dates from the second or third century BC. There are more similarly dazzling treasures up on the first floor, while the top floor is devoted to a largely forgettable history section. That said, do look out for the pipe room, in which several cabinets hold an array of exquisitely carved and painted porcelain pipes.

To the rear of the museum, an ugly glass and concrete structure encloses extensive remains of the fine **Roman mosaic** (Edificiul Roman cu Mozaic; same times as museum; €1), close to 800 square metres in area and featuring some remarkably well-preserved geometrical and floral motifs. Discovered 5m below street level in 1959, it may have once graced the upper hall of the Roman baths, whose outer walls can be seen from Aleea Canarache. Built in the late fourth century AD, this was part of a three-storey structure linking the upper town to the port, which also incorporated warehouses and shops. Outside, in front of the mosaic building, is an array of funerary stelae from the second to fourth centuries AD, their touching inscriptions translated into Romanian and English.

South of Piaţa Ovidiu

From **Piaţa Ovidiu**, it's a short walk south to the **Mahmudiye Mosque** (daily 9am–6pm; €1), also called the Carol Mosque after it was rebuilt upon the orders of King Carol in 1910 – the original dated from 1834. It's now the seat of the Mufti, the spiritual head of Romania's 55,000 Muslims (Turks and Tatars by origin), who live along the coast of the Dobrogea. Climbing the 140 steps leading up through the 47m-high minaret is worth it for the great **view** of the town and harbour.

South from the mosque along Str. Arhiepiscopei (look for the fine Art Nouveau ironwork gates) is the fancy **Orthodox Cathedral of St Peter and St Paul**, an early (1884) neo-Byzantine design by Ion Mincu, and, at the street's end, opposite more ruins of ancient Tomis, the **Ion Jalea collection** (Muzeul Ion Jalea; Wed–Sun: May–Sept 10am–6pm; Oct–April 9am–5pm; €1), an assortment of conventional and academic sculptures in a nice neo-Brâncovenesc villa.

On the pedestrianized **waterfront**, the former **casino** stands on a jutting promenade. Originally erected as an Art Nouveau pavilion for Queen Elisabeta (Carmen Sylva) in 1904–10, it's now a forlorn site, with its broken windows and graffitied facade. During a visit in 1914 by the Russian Imperial family, it was the venue for a disastrous gala performance that ended in smashed scenery and broken limbs; the Russians sailed away the next day, Grand Duchess Olga having refused a proposed marriage to Prince Carol and thus sealed her fate at the hands of the Bolsheviks three years later. Opposite it is a small **aquarium** (daily 9am–8pm; €3). Just beyond, you can see the so-called **Genoese Lighthouse**, a squat structure erected in 1860 in memory of the thirteenth- and fourteenth-century mariners who tried to revive the port.

Around boulevards Ferdinand and Tomis

The focal point of the new town is the junction of **Bulevardul Ferdinand and Bulevardul Tomis**. Here, you'll find an archeological park displaying sections of ancient walls, serried amphorae and **ruins of Tomis**. Tomis was settled by Greeks from Miletus in the sixth century BC as an annex to Histria, which it later superseded before being incorporated within the Roman empire at the beginning of the Christian era. The most prominent remains are those of the defensive wall, created in the third and fourth centuries, and the Butchers' Tower, raised in the sixth century by Byzantine colonists who revived the city and renamed it to honour the emperor's sister Constantia.

South of the archeological park, Str. Traian overlooks the north end of the commercial *port maritim*, and provides an appropriate setting for the **Museum of the Romanian Navy** at no. 53 (Muzeul Marinei Române; Wed–Sun 9am–5pm; €2). Despite its name, the museum includes models of Greek triremes that sailed long before Romania existed, and photographs recording the unexpected visit of the battleship *Potemkin*, whose mutinous sailors disembarked at Constanţa in July 1905 and scattered. Little is said about the role of Romania's own navy during World War II, when it supported the occupation of Odessa and aided the Nazi fleet. Amongst the many fascinating items on show is a model of the supertanker, MT *Independenţa*, sunk by a Greek freighter in 1979; standing next to it is the champagne bottle used by Elena Ceauşescu to launch the vessel in 1977, leading many to suggest that because the bottle had not broken the ship was inevitably doomed. Today's Romanian navy counts around 6500 servicemen and women, with three frigates, one of which, *Regele Ferdinand*, was formerly HMS *Coventry*.

Back on B-dul Tomis, north of B-dul Ferdinand, the **Art Museum** at no. 82 (Muzeul de Artă; Wed–Sun: June–Sept 9am–8pm; Oct–May 9am–5pm; €1) has some interesting canvases by Iosif Iser, Ştefan Dumitrescu and other painters of the Dobrogean landscape. Much of the top floor is devoted to the abstract artist Ion Gheorgiu; his paintings are less engaging than the collections of seashells, beetles and primitive icons decorating his *atelier*, which is preserved intact. South of here, at no. 32, the **Ethnographic Museum** (Muzeul de Artă Populară; Wed–Sun: June–Sept 9am–8pm; Oct–May 9am–5pm; €1) has a fine display of beautifully woven Dobrogean rugs, pewter vessels and eighteenth- and nineteenth-century Lipovani and Greek icons, some of which were painted by naive artists. Immediately south of the museum, fast-food joints and coffee houses sprawl across a scruffy pedestrianized section of the road, with the **Geamia Hunchiar**, a small mosque built in 1869, overlooking them to the south.

The beach and Lake Tăbăcăriei

Visitors with children or a low tolerance for provincial museums head straight for the **beach** north of the tourist port, spread beneath a terraced cliff behind the art museum, or the park at **Lake Tăbăcăriei**, between Constanţa and Mamaia, where there's a huge wooden church, built by carpenters from Maramureş. Bus #32 heads up B-dul Alexandru Lapuşneanu on the west side of the lake, while buses #40 and #41 (from the train station) run along B-dul Mamaia, to the east of the park, passing a **dolphinarium** (daily: July & Aug 8am–9pm; Sept–June 8am–4pm; shows at 11am, 3pm and 7pm; adults €8, children €4) at the southeastern corner of the park, at B-dul Mamaia 255. There's also a **planetarium here** (same hours, with shows roughly every 90 minutes starting at 10am; tickets are included with the dolphinarium) and a collection of **exotic birds**. From the nearby **Tăbăcăriei Wharf**, a **miniature train** carries children around the lake, which due to algal bloom may be a toxic-looking hue of green. On the other side is the **Sat de Vacanţă**, and just to the north, at the entrance to Mamaia, the noisy **Luna Park** (Parc Distracţii), with various decrepit rides and games. There's a **bowling alley** here, and an **ice-skating rink** on the edge of the Pioneers' Park.

Eating, drinking and entertainment

Whilst it may not be flush with great **restaurants**, Constanţa can certainly boast the most appealing and diverse range of places to eat anywhere along the coast.

Conversely, the city's **nightlife** can't match that of many of the coastal resorts, particularly Mamaia, but that's no bad thing here. The city's main **theatre** is at B-dul Ferdinand 11, and the Teatrul Liric (putting on opera, ballet and symphonic concerts) at Str. Mircea cel Bătrân 97; buy tickets at the agency at B-dul Tomis 97. The city's **International Festival of Music and Dance** takes place in late May and early June.

Restaurants

Byblos B-dul Tomis 48. Noisy location and kitschy decor aside, this lively restaurant is certainly worth visiting for its food; a strong Middle-Eastern menu with tasty, well cooked and colourfully presented staples such as *tabouleh*, falafel and lamb kebabs. Round off the evening with a hookah pipe.

El Greco Str. Decebal 18. Located in a residential street, *El Greco* is a fairly anonymous, orange-brick building, but its comprehensive ostensibly Greek menu features marinated lamb and pork, spit-roasted chicken and a fair few fish dishes.

Marco Polo Str. Sarmisegetuza 2. Above-average Italian restaurant, as impressive for its decor – cool chocolate-brown tables and chairs and crisp white tablecloths – as it is for its food. There is also a no-smoking room, while the wood-decked, tree-shaded terrace is rather fine too.

New Pizzico Piața Ovidiu 7. Just about the only worthwhile place to eat down in the old quarter, this large, fashionable restaurant offers a lot more besides pizza; the vast menu also incorporates fish soup, seafood pasta, grilled octopus and baked bream. Alternatively, park yourself down on the sunny terrace with a coffee after visiting the Archeological Museum opposite.

Nur Kaptan Baba B-dul Tomis 48. Next door to *Byblos*, an ordinary-looking but very agreeable Turkish restaurant serving oriental salads, soups, *lahmacun* and *shaworma* (kebab) as well as baklava and coffee.

On Plonge Portul Turistic Tomis. Constanța's best restaurant, not only because of its lovely harbourside setting, but also for the array of both fresh and saltwater items on the menu – carp, trout, crab, cuttlefish, mussels and mackerel, to name just a few.

Terasa Colonadelor Str. Traian 57. Vast beer garden serving up grilled sausages, pizza and pasta, as well as more adventurous dishes such as fried brain or testicles. Good three-course daily menus for €5.

Cafés, bars and clubs

Amsters B-dul Tomis 55. A small and dark, vaguely Dutch-themed pub spread over three narrow floors, with good lagers on tap and reasonable food.

Bourbon House Str. Pușchin 36. Close to the intersection of boulevards Tomis and Mamaia, this pleasantly chaotic bar offers a long list of cocktails in its buzzing terrace garden, while the music is a mix of house and R&B.

Club Phoenix Str. Capitan Dobrila Eugeniu 1, near the Ciresica complex in the suburb of Tomis Nord (bus #42 or #43). Constanța's main live music venue hosts jazz, blues and rock on a regular basis; its sister club, *Phoenix 2*, at B-dul Mamaia 67, is a relaxing café.

Filicori B-dul Tomis 101. Sprightly pavement café on the main boulevard, with top-drawer beverages, including coffees, teas, fresh juices and Belgian beers. The sleek, modern interior is ideal for cooler weather, or if you just want to escape the traffic.

Irish Pub Str. Ștefan cel Mare 1. Massively popular pub-restaurant with a large wood interior and a fine terrace offering lovely views across the port; ideal for both a daytime coffee or a bout of more serious evening drinking, when there's also often a DJ.

Listings

Car rental Autonom, at the airport and B-dul Mamaia 1B (☎0241/550 177, ⓦwww .autonom.ro); Avis c/o TAROM, at the airport and Str. Ștefan cel Mare 15 (☎0241/616 733); Budget c/o Latina, B-dul Ferdinand 70 (☎0241/639 713, ⓦwww.budget.com); Europcar, at the airport (☎0722/211 518, ⓦwww.europcar.com.ro) and in the *Hotel Dobrogea*, B-dul A. Lapușneanu 194 (☎0241/543 311); Hertz, at the airport and B-dul Tomis 213 (☎0241/661 100 or 0744/338 776, ⓦwww.hertz.com.ro); Rodna, at the airport (☎0748/210 382, ⓦwww.rodna-trans.ro).

Consulates Turkey, B-dul Ferdinand 82 (Mon–Fri 9am–noon; ☎0241/611 135).

Flights TAROM is at Str. Ștefan cel Mare 15 (Mon–Fri 9am–6pm, Sat 9am–1pm; ☎0241/662 632, ⓦwww.tarom.ro). Carpatair (at the airport; ☎0241/555 422, ⓦwww.carpatair.com).

Hospital B-dul Tomis 145 (☎0241/516 800 or 961).

Internet *Planet Games*, at the intersection of Str. Ștefan cel Mare and Str. Răscoalei din 1907, is open 24hr, as is *Café-bar R9* at B-dul Tomis 31 (south of the mosque).

Left luggage At the train station, in the subway under the tracks (daily 6.30am–10pm).

Pharmacy Constanţa has four 24hr pharmacies: Eurosantis, Str. Ecaterina Varga 55 (at B-dul Ferdinand); Minifarm, B-dul Tomis 133; Dumifarm, in the Tomis Mall at Str. Ştefan cel Mare 49 (at Str. Mihai Viteazul); and one inside the train station building.

Post office B-dul Tomis 79 (Mon–Fri 7am–8pm, Sat 8am–1pm) and Str. 22 Decembrie 1989 (Mon–Fri 7.30am–7.30pm).

Shopping The largest shopping mall in Constanţa is City Park (daily 10am–10pm), out by Lake Tăbăcăriei on the road to Mamaia. In the centre, Str. Ştefan cel Mare is the main shopping street – especially the pedestrianized stretch from Str. Răscoalei din 1907 to Str. Duca – with the Tomis Mall (daily 8am–10pm) opposite the Eminescu bookshop. The Mega Image supermarket in the basement (same hours) is the best in the centre. Supermarket Grand, below B-dul Tomis 57 (at B-dul Ferdinand; open 24hr), suffices for most supplies. Anticvariat, at Str. Mircea cel Bătrân 4, has used books in English and French.

Mamaia

MAMAIA, 6km north of Constanţa, is Romania's best-known coastal resort, and the place where the majority of package tourists end up. Legend has it that the gods created the **beach** to reunite a kidnapped princess with her daughter, who was abandoned on the seashore wailing "Mamaia, Mamaia!"; its fine, almost white sand, fringed with wild pear trees, is the resort's greatest asset, especially since its gentle gradient and the absence of currents and strong tides make it particularly safe for children.

Arrival and information

In summer, **buses** #32 and #41 run from **Constanţa's train station** to the far end of Mamaia; out of season, you'll have to take the #40, which claims to go to Mamaia but in fact terminates at Pescărie, one stop south of the beginning of the resort, where you'll have to change to the #47 or the frequent yellow midibuses heading north to Năvodari. Alternatively, you could walk the short distance to the **telegondola** (see p.362), a cable car that can carry you the 2km to the heart of Mamaia, near the casino. Arriving by car in high summer, you'll find tollbooths operating immediately north of Pescărie.

Located by the telegondola is the Romanian Riviera Association (☏0241/831 321, ⓦwww.infolitoral.ro), which, although primarily concerned with marketing, can provide useful **tourist information** on the Black Sea coast. If you arrive without a **room reservation**, look for a Dispecerat de Cazare (room allocation) office, such as the **Agenţia de Turism Mamaia**, just west of the *Hotel Condor* (☏0241/831 517, ⊜travelagency@sc-mamaia-sa.ro).

Mamaia's main **shopping centre** is the Bazar (daily 9am–9pm), at the northern end of the resort, where you'll find a small supermarket and a **pharmacy**; otherwise, there is a string of shops near the casino, where you can buy sunscreen, beachballs and clothing. There are **post offices** in the Bazar and just south of the casino and a summer-only **internet café** in the *Hotel Unirea*.

Accommodation

Most of Mamaia's seventy-odd **hotels** (all but a handful of which are ageing concrete-block structures) are clustered around, and just north of, the casino, and many of these are within 100m of the beach. Unless otherwise stated, the hotels listed here are only open between May and September.

At the northern end of the resort is the very basic *Tăbăra* **campsite** (☏0241/831 144), which also has *casuţe* (cabins). A few hundred metres further north, beyond

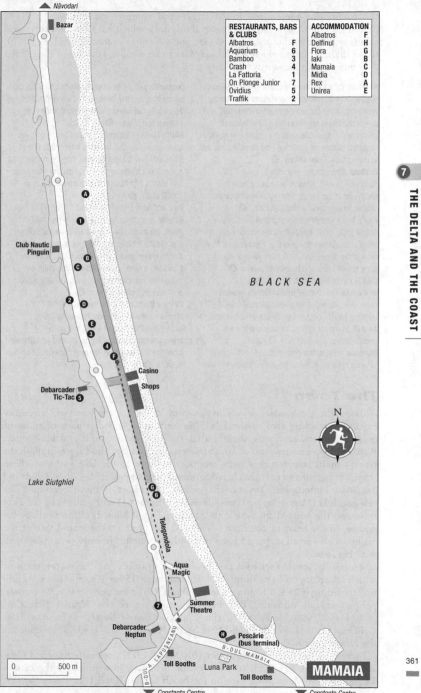

Năvodari

■ Bazar

RESTAURANTS, BARS & CLUBS
Albatros	F
Aquarium	6
Bamboo	3
Crash	4
La Fattoria	1
On Plonge Junior	7
Ovidius	5
Traffik	2

ACCOMMODATION
Albatros	F
Delfinul	H
Flora	G
Iaki	B
Mamaia	C
Midia	D
Rex	A
Unirea	E

BLACK SEA

Club Nautic
Pinguin

Casino

Shops

Debarcader
Tic-Tac ⑤

Lake Siutghiol

Telegondola

N

Aqua
Magic

Summer
Theatre

Debarcader
Neptun

Pescărie
(bus terminal)

0 ___ 500 m

Toll Booths

Luna Park

Toll Booths

MAMAIA

Constanța Centre

Constanța Centre

the tollbooths, there's the much larger and comprehensive *Camping GPM* (☎0241/831 002, ✉gpm_camping@yahoo.com), which has two- and three-bed cabins with and without shower (❷–❺), and *Camping Pescăresc* (☎0241/831 170); to get to these places, which are all open May to September, take one of the regular #23 buses heading towards Năvodari.

Albatros By the northern terminal of the telegondola ☎0241/831 381, ⓦwww.hotelalbatros.ro. Warm, welcoming hotel right in the heart of the resort, and one of the few in Mamaia with a semblance of character; comfortable, colourful rooms and quirkily designed bathrooms featuring little steps leading up to corner tubs. Open all year. ❼

Delfinul Opposite the entrance to Luna Park ☎0241/831 640. Basic, cheap place near the south end of the resort, with somewhat cramped rooms, though they're clean and tidy. ❹

Flora Two hundred metres north of the *Delfinul* ☎0241/831 059, ✉hotelflora98@yahoo.com. A brute of a building, the two-star *Flora* is a bit frayed around the edges, though it does have a mix of fairly priced older and renovated rooms. ❹

Iaki North of the casino ☎0241/831 025, ⓦwww.iaki.ro. Owned by Romania's greatest footballer, Gheorghe Hagi, this palatial-looking building boasts cool, superbly appointed rooms, as well as indoor and outdoor pools and an excellent spa. Open all year. ❾

Mamaia North of the casino ☎0241/831 100, ⓦwww.mamaia-hotel.ro. Small, exclusive five-star hotel with just 24 bedrooms, which gives it a more personable air; the large, high-ceilinged rooms are beautifully furnished and decorated in striking yellows and blacks. ❾

Midia North of the casino ☎0241/831 940. As basic as it gets, this roadside low-rise is one of Mamaia's few budget options, offering rooms with and without bathroom and TV. Ideal for stumbling into after a night out at the nearby *Bamboo* or *Traffik* clubs. ❸

Rex Northern end of the resort ☎0241/831 520, ⓦwww.grandhotelrex.ro. A stately pile built in 1936, the hacienda-style *Rex* is Mamaia's oldest and swishest hotel, the only one to achieve anything like grandeur. Immaculate, classically furnished rooms (many with commanding sea views) are complemented by a gorgeous outdoor pool and first-class service. ❾

Unirea North of the casino ☎0241/831 064. Similar to the *Midia*, though slightly more expensive, this budget hotel has perfectly adequate rooms, though it is located just across from the *Bamboo* club, so expect noise. Breakfast is extra. ❹

The Town

As late as the 1930s, Mamaia was, in the words of Gregor von Rezzori, "an empty expanse, excepting two or three bathing huts and a wooden pier, of miles of golden sand and tiny pink shells"; a far cry from what you'll find here today. Ranged along a narrow spit of land between the Black Sea and Lake Siutghiol, the resort's **main street** curves away around the shore of the lake – the southern stretch of beachfront promenade is dominated by unappealing fast-food stands and *autoservire* buffets, but, beyond the casino, the resort is more peaceful. The **telegondola** (Mon 4–6pm, Tues–Sun 10am–10pm; €3) will whisk you the 2km from near the Aqua Magic park at the southern end of Mamaia to just north of the **casino**, in the heart of the resort. There's a big plaza on the inland side of the casino, with a small stage and rows of family restaurants (mostly pizza places, all with big *terasas*).

Mamaia has ample **facilities** for those wanting to play on the **water**, most of which take place on Lake Siutghiol – waterskiing (€15 for 10min), jet-skiing and wakeboarding (€25 for 10min), and kayaking (€5/hr for one person, €8 for two people) are all possible. The best facilities are at the *Nautica Blue Club* (☎0241/607 000), attached to the *Club Scandinavia* hotel, the nearby *Club California* (☎0241/879 063), and *Club Nautic Pinguin* (☎0241/831 050), opposite the *Hotel Majestic*.

There are also two tennis clubs, *Sen* (☎0241/831 025), opposite the *Hotel Flora*, and *Idu* (☎0241/831 225), to the west of the main road south of the casino. There's free two-hour **bike hire** on the beach behind Hotel Iaki. Easily the best place in Mamaia to take **children** is the gleaming **Aqua Magic waterpark** (May–Sept daily 8am–8pm; €10 adults, €5 children, after 2pm €7 and €3), near the southern end of Mamaia, which has all the requisite slides and chutes.

From Mamaia, regular **motorboat trips** (every 30min 10am–midnight; €5) run from the Tic-Tac dock opposite the casino to **Ovid's Island** – where there's a suitably rustic restaurant, the *Insula Ovidiu* (☎0241/252 494) – at the northern end of **Lake Siutghiol**. Also known as Lake Mamaia, **Lake Siutghiol** was formed when a river's outlet silted up, and for many centuries it was a watering hole for herds of sheep and cows brought down from the Carpathians – hence the name, meaning "Lake of Milk" in Turkish.

Eating, drinking and nightlife

The majority of Mamaia's **restaurants** are predictably samey: big terraces serving grilled meats and pizzas, a slew of which line the promenade either side of the casino. Avoiding these, head a little north to *La Fattoria*, next to the *Majestic* hotel, a decent Italian place with a classy interior and fresh, tasty food. Nearby is the *Albatros*, a jolly family restaurant and terrace, serving pizza, steak and fish. Alternatively, *Aquarium* is an upscale **seafood** place near the *Flora* hotel whose menu features swordfish, sturgeon and Portuguese carp. If you fancy spending a bit more, the restaurants in the five-star *Rex* and *Mamaia* **hotels** are excellent. *On Plonge Junior*, at the Debarcader Neptun dock at the south end of Mamaia, has little in common with the fine *On Plonge* in Constanţa, but serves Romanian and Italian food and has a lovely lakeside terrace.

Evening **entertainment** is pretty much centred around the casino, with open-air beach bars both north and south of here. Of the bars along the promenade, *Crash*, an enormous tented venue situated by the casino, packs them in on a nightly basis. Mamaia is home to the coast's most vibrant **clubs**, two of which, *Traffik*, at B-dul Mamaia 218, and *Bamboo,* 100m further down the road, are the most popular; both stage live concerts and theme parties most weekends in summer. Alternatives consist of glitzy **cabaret** most nights at the *Melody* near the casino, or the *Nunta la Romani* (Wedding in Romania) **folklore show** at the *Majestic*. The *Ovidius* **floating restaurant-bar** is just west of the casino, and there's the open-air Cinema Albatros just north of the *Hotel Hefaistos*. The kitschy **Mamaia Pop Music Festival** is held over the last weekend of August, in the open-air Summer Theatre.

Agigea to Vama Veche

Just south of Constanţa, the road and rail line cross the Danube–Black Sea Canal where it meets the coast at the **Agigea** port complex. Beyond this, the array of **resorts** extending to **Mangalia** is another facet of Romania's development over the last quarter century – modern complexes created where only scrubland or run-down villages existed before. Except for the fact that most are situated along a cliff top overlooking the beach, they are fairly similar to their prototype, Mamaia, to the north, although they have a shorter season. The exceptions are Mangalia, which is not dependent on tourism and is thus more alive off season, and **Doi Mai** and **Vama Veche**, neither of which saw any development until after the fall of communism.

From Constanţa, the resorts down to Mangalia are best reached by **maxitaxis** and **private buses**; these leave several times per hour, from early morning to around 8pm, from a spot 100m to the right of the railway station as you exit. For Doi Mai and Vama Veche, you'll have to change at Mangalia.

Eforie Nord and Lake Techirghiol

Trains, buses and maxitaxis run 14km south along a decent dual carriageway from Constanța to **EFORIE NORD**. Founded in 1899 by Bucharest's Eforia hospital as a spa for convalescent patients, Eforie Nord extends along a cliff top above the rather narrow beach. The resort is, however, best known for the therapeutic **black mud** scooped from the shores of **Lake Techirghiol**, whose mineral-saturated waters gave the lake its name, derived from *tekir*, Turkish for "salt" or "bitter". **Baths** by the lake (a few minutes' walk south of the train station) specialize in treating rheumatic disorders and the after-effects of polio, while on the lake's single-sex nudist beaches, people plaster themselves with mud, wait until it cracks (happily exposing themselves to passing trains), and then jostle good humouredly beneath the showers.

The resort itself comprises two parallel streets; along the cliff top, B-dul Tudor Vladimirescu is where most of the town's **hotels** are congregated, and B-dul Republicii is where you'll find more hotels as well as the **bus stop**, shops and restaurants. The *Europa*, at B-dul Republicii 13 (☎0241/702 801, ⓦwww .anahotels.ro; ❾), is a towering, steel-blue four-star and incorporates one of the top spas in the country, the *Ana Aslan Health Spa*. Just up the road, at no. 42, the *Hotel Vera* (☎0241/742 200, ⓦwww.hotelvera.ro; ❺) is a modern three-star with air-conditioned rooms and jacuzzi showers.

Closer to the beach, at B-dul Tudor Vladimirescu 9, is the *Astoria* (☎0241/742 475, ⓦwww.anahotels.ro; June–Sept; ❽), a smaller and more compact facility under the same management as the *Europa*. Just south of the central bus stop, the *Villa Ad-Ella*, an attractive Brâncovenesc villa at Str. Mureșanu 11 (☎0241/743 473; ❺), has pleasant rooms and also houses an art gallery/tea shop/tea garden. The *Hotel Decebal* (☎0241/741 023; ❷), adjacent to the train station and run by Romanian Railways, is old but ridiculously cheap, while another budget possibility is the *Cristal* (☎0241/742 828; open June–Sept; ❷), behind the bus stop.

The nicer of the resort's two **campsites** is the *Meduza*, just inland at the northern end of B-dul Tudor Vladimirescu. There are numerous self-service *autoservires* around town, with a particularly large and modern one opposite the *Vera* hotel. For a **drink**, walk a couple of blocks north from the bus stop to *333*, a friendly Guinness-themed pub that also serves good espresso.

From Eforie Nord, it's a pleasant 2km trip around the lake to **TECHIRGHIOL** (terminus of bus #11), where you can stay at the *Baze de Tratament* at Str. Ovidiu 4 (☎0241/735 614, ⓦwww.sbtghiol.ro; ❷), a clean and friendly spa run by the Romanian Orthodox Church. Bizarrely, in this historically Muslim area, there's a wooden village **church** (moved here from Transylvania in 1951) in front of the spa.

South to Mangalia

A fast four-lane highway runs a few kilometres inland from Eforie Nord to **Mangalia**; buses loop through the resorts, but the more frequent maxitaxis from Constanța to Mangalia will only drop you off at the junctions to the resorts – it's usually best to go to Mangalia and return on the local maxitaxi from there. Express trains slow to a crawl between Constanța and Mangalia, taking an hour to cover 43km; from mid-June to mid-September extra services run, providing a fairly frequent service along the coast, with reservations required only west of Constanța.

Neptun and Olimp

Sixteen kilometres south of Eforie Nord, **NEPTUN** was built in 1960 between the Comorova forest and the sea, ensuring a lush setting for the artificial lakes and dispersed villas. Originally enclaves for the communist *nomenklatura*, today

Neptun and its classier satellite of **OLIMP**, just north, are patronized by relatively affluent Romanian families and some Western tourists.

Fast trains stop only at the *halta* by the *Hotel Albert*; if travelling to or from Constanța by road, note that it's a walk of nearly 3km from Neptun to the highway. The resort itself is strung out along Aleea Trandafirilor; about halfway along, near the main complex of shops, Aleea Steagurilor leads down between a couple of lakes to the **beach**, with waterslides, beach bars and restaurants, and paths leading around the lakes; to the north are government-owned and private villas – from the path you can see albino peacocks in one garden.

Most rooms are still assigned to those on **package tours**, however, so if you're without **accommodation** and need somewhere to stay, try Rainbow Travel (May–Sept daily 10am–10pm; ☎0241/701 300, ✉anatravel@xnet.ro), in Neptun Park Gardens, midway along Aleea Trandafirilor. The best **hotel** in Neptun-Olimp, and one of the most appealing anywhere along the coast, is the *Cocor* spa hotel at the southern edge of Olimp (☎0241/701 042, ⒲www.cocorspahotel.ro; ➑); first-class rooms and facilities are complemented by two cool clamshell bars by the swimming pool. Decent alternatives comprise the *Majestic*, in the centre of Olimp (☎0241/701 130; ➐); on the northern fringe of Neptun, the *Albert* (☎0241/731 514, ⒲www.hotelalbert-neptun.ro; ➐); and the *Doina* (☎0241/701 012, ⒲www.complexdoina.ro; ➏), which is open from March to November thanks to its sea-water pool and treatment centre.

There are stacks of **restaurants** along the main drag, the best of which are *Pizza Antik*, nicely pitched amongst the greenery of Neptun Park Gardens, and, close by, the *Rosemarie* grill with its western-themed decor. *Insula*, on a lake island behind the *Hotel Neptun*, is worth trying for its fish, while it's also worth checking out the *Café-Bar Efendi*, also north of the post office, possibly the only Tatar hostelry you'll ever experience. The resort's top nightspot is the *Club Why Not* **disco**, in the Neptun Park Gardens. Aside from the beach there's plenty to keep the kids entertained, including mini-golf near the *Cocor* hotel, and a fairground near the Bazar at the southern end of the resort. There's **internet** access at Telefonet, in the Neptun Park Gardens.

Jupiter, Aurora, Venus and Saturn

The four resorts to the south of Neptun are more uniform, less lively and likely to have fewer hotels open outside July and August. The first, immediately abutting Neptun, is **JUPITER**, between the forest and the artificial Lake Tismana, beyond which is a gently sloping beach with fine sand.

The most appealing **place to stay** is *Complex Hercules* (☎0341/566 905, ⒲www .hercules-jupiter.ro; ➎), a nautically themed hotel right on the beachfront. Other good options are *Sat Vacanță Liliacul* (☎0241/731 169; ➏), a comfortable villa complex and, directly opposite here, budget *Violeta* (☎0241/731 115; ➌). The best of several **campsites** hereabouts is *Zodiac* camping (☎0241/731 404, ⒲www .campingzodiac.ro), which is as close to Neptun as it is to Jupiter; there are bungalows here too. *The Four Seasons* pizza and grill is the standout **restaurant**, though ship-shaped *Hercules* is a fun place and has the added bonus of sea views. **Nightlife** focuses on *Captain Mondy's*, opposite the Liliacul, which has some extremely slick mixologists.

Imagine Maya architects called upon to redesign Palm Beach and you'll get some idea of the pyramidal multi-hotel complexes that characterize **Aurora**, the most recent resort, set on the cape of the same name immediately southeast of Jupiter. There's a minimal gap before you hit **VENUS** – broadly similar to Jupiter, but quieter and more family-oriented. There are several upmarket **hotels** here, notably the *Dana* (☎0241/731 638, ⒲www.hotel-dana.ro; ➐), a sprawling low-rise with smart villas, a delightful kidney-shaped swimming pool and an open-air restaurant set in gorgeous gardens. Two superbly located beachfront hotels are the *Afrodita* (☎0241/706 271, ⓦwww.hotelafrodita.ro; ⑥), with open and indoor swimming pools, and the *Palace* (☎0241/732 065, ⓦwww.palacehotel .ro; ⑧), boasting a fabulous double pool. In between these two, the down-at-heel but very cheap *Silvia* (☎0757/013 161; ②) attracts a young crowd, while the *Orlando* (☎0241/731 605; ⑤) is a decent mid-range hotel. **Camping** *Palace-Venus* (☎0241/731 148), to the south of the resort, is a good-sized, well-shaded site with decent facilities. *Calipso*, opposite *Orlando* hotel, is the best of the resort's **discos**. Also to the south are a sulphurous **spa** and, just inland, the Herghelia Mangalia **stables** (☎0241/751 325) where you can **hire horses** to explore the forest, inhabited by roe deer, grouse and pheasants.

A reed-fringed lake lies between Venus and **Saturn**, a small resort with half a dozen low-rent, high-rise **hotels**. Water from mineral springs is piped through showers on the beach, and there's a small waterpark, **Aqua Park Balada** (summer daily 8am–7pm), with three pools, slides, snack bars and a stage for entertainment.

Mangalia

The modern suburbs of **MANGALIA** are close to swallowing up Saturn, and in fact Mangalia's train station is nearer to Saturn than to the centre of town. As with Constanţa, Mangalia's appearance of modernity belies its ancient origin – the Greeks founded their city of **Callatis** here during the sixth century BC, when population pressure impelled them to colonize the Black Sea coast. In Byzantine times it was renamed **Pangalia**, meaning "most beautiful". The **ruins of Callatis**, which include sarcophagi and the vestiges of a Christian basilica, are in Parc Stadionului, with the **Archeological Museum** (Muzeul de Arheologie Callatis; May–Sept daily 9am–8pm; Oct–April Tues–Sun 9am–6pm; €1), near the main roundabout at Şoseaua Constanţei 23, displaying a rich collection of grave goods. Elegantly preserved within the *Hotel President*, in the town centre, are sections of wall from Callatis as well as other finds uncovered during the hotel's construction in 1993–94. Other sights of note include the **Sultan Esmahan Mosque** just south of the small town centre at Str. Oituz 1. Founded in 1525, the mosque is surrounded by a Muslim graveyard.

Practicalities

Heading south from the **train station** and left at the roundabout, you'll reach the hulking *Hotel Paradiso*, Str. Matei Basarab 3 (☎0241/752 052, ⓦwww .hotelparadiso.ro; ⑥), an upmarket spa **hotel** with an outdoor swimming pool and treatment centre. At Str. Teilor 6, just south by the town centre, rises the *Hotel President* (☎0241/755 861, ⓦwww.hpresident.com; ⑥), which relies more on business conferences than bikinis and is the most appealing **place to stay**, with all the facilities you'd expect of a four-star – it also has the added attraction of the ancient ruins. The one budget option in town is the *Pensiunea Oituz*, west of the mosque at Str. Oituz 11 (☎0241/740 770; ③), whose bright and modern rooms represent great value; reception is in the Anna travel agency below. The nearest **campsite**, *MHT Camping* (☎0723/946 850, ⓦwww .camping-mht.ro; ③), is actually in Saturn – from the train station, turn left, then right after ten minutes at the *Saturn* sign; it's a further 400m down on your right, beyond the grubby Dunarea complex. A small, neat site, it's got a few pitches plus excellent two- and three-bed huts with showers (②).

The best **restaurants** are in the *President* hotel (overlooking the archeological site) and, immediately across the street, the *Café del Mar*, which has an ambitious menu and is open 24 hours in the summer. The *Peach-Pit Patisserie*, at the top of the pedestrianized section of Şos. Constanţei, is a cracking little place for a sweet or savoury snack, while for drinking, two lively **bars** just north of here are the *Christopher Pub* and *Lavrion*; the latter also has **internet** access.

Doi Mai and Vama Veche

The laidback villages of **Doi Mai** and **Vama Veche**, traditionally the haunts of artists, intellectuals and nonconformists, lie between Mangalia and the Bulgarian border, 10km south along the coast. Tourist facilities in both villages have grown rapidly in recent years, but fortunately the new developments have been planned with consideration for their surroundings and are on a reasonably modest scale. Doi Mai (2 May), despite lying in the shadow of the massive yellow cranes of Mangalia's shipyard, is peaceful and relaxed, and popular with families; Vama Veche (Old Customs Post) has a better beach and retains an air of bohemian sophistication not found elsewhere on the coast.

Maxitaxis shuttle from Mangalia to the Bulgarian border every twenty minutes or so during the summer and hourly out of season, with additional services every fifteen minutes to Doi Mai. There are no **ATMs** in either village, so bring what money you'll need with you.

Doi Mai

Coming from Mangalia, you'll be dropped off midway along Str. Mihail Kogălniceanu, **DOI MAI**'s main street. There's a fair bit of accommodation in the village, most of it along Str. Falezi, the narrow street running along the cliff top above the beach. One such place is the small and quiet *Casa Vizante* at no. 8 (☎0722/805 125; ❸). Back on Str. Mihail Kogălniceanu, at no. 501, *Casa Margo* (☎0723/249 405; ❸) is a clean **pension** offering thirteen air-conditioned rooms with bath and TV. Three hundred metres further inland, at the far end of Str. Scolii, the pleasantly bohemian, Greek-owned *Hellios Inn* (☎0241/732 929, Ⓦwww.hellios-inn.ro; May–Sept; ❸) has simple, attractive en-suite rooms, some with bare-brick walls. Here, too, is a lovely green garden with small outdoor pool, as well as a rustic seafood **restaurant** (the best in the village).

The **Doi Mai–Vama Veche Marine Reserve** begins just south of the Mangalia port and extends to the border. Loggerhead turtles can be seen here, as well as sea horses, two species of dolphin, and corals. **Diving** trips can be arranged through the *Hellios Inn*.

Vama Veche

Under communism, **VAMA VECHE**, just short of the border with Bulgaria, was closed to all but staff of Cluj University or those who could claim some vague affiliation with it; it became a haven for nonconformists looking for an escape from the surveillance of the Securitate. In recent years, locals and investors have begun to capitalize on Vama Veche's countercultural reputation, and there's now an attractive assortment of **accommodation** on offer, ranging from three-star hotels and pensions to wild camping on the beach. There are still, however, plenty of chickens and sheep wandering about, and the **Save Vama Veche** organization has thus far succeeded in keeping the ravages of mass tourism at arm's length.

This spirit is most obviously manifest in **Stufstock** (Ⓦwww.stufstock.com), a five-day arts festival put on by the organization. Once a free event protesting against environmental threats to the area, it's now a more sophisticated happening, with jazz, blues, rock and folk, alongside film and theatre, taking place on several stages on the beach. Passes cost around €80.

Most things are on, or just off, Str. Ion Creangă, the main street leading down to the beachfront. Towards the bottom of the street, you'll pass Bibi Vama Veche

(April–Sept daily 8am–10pm; ℡0241/858 009 or 0722/889 087, ⓔvamaveche @bibi.ro), a private **tourist office** which can help you find a place to stay; it also acts as the reception for the terrific 🏕 *BazArt* youth hostel (℡0241/858 009, ⓦwww.bazarthostel.ro; ❸), which features sweet, hut-like double rooms (with and without bathrooms) arranged around a pretty courtyard. Continuing down to the beach, two good-value **hotels** are *La John* (℡0720/806 450; ❺), with two storeys of wooden galleries containing en-suite rooms with balconies, and just to the south, *Sunset Beach* (℡0752/037 148, ⓦwww.sunsetbeach.ro; ❹), whose rooms are slightly smaller. Further south, set back from the beachfront in a grubby field, the *Hotel Laguna* (℡0241/858 030, ⓦwww.corsarulvamaveche.ro; ❺), with Daliesque mosaics on its exterior and an Arabian-style interior, has smart rooms situated around a clean and attractive swimming pool.

Heading south out of the resort, and just 500m shy of the Bulgarian border, *Cortina Gate Camping* (℡0744/380 861, ⓦwww.cortinagate.ro) is a neat, if somewhat exposed, site with good facilities and bikes for hire. At the north end of the village, *Camping Vama Veche* (℡0745/629 157) has a ten-room motel, with rooms with (❸) and without bathroom (❷) and bungalows (❷). **Camping** wild is easiest south of the main part of the beach, where you'll also find the naturist area, although it's also possible to camp to the north.

Most of the hotels have reasonable **restaurants**, the best of which is *Lyana*, behind *La John*, with good fish, and lively *Bibi Bistro*, next to to the *BazArt* hostel. There are *shaworma* (kebab) and burrito stands on Str. Ion Creangă, while Bibi Market (the village's general store) stocks enough provisions for a beachfront **picnic**. Vama Veche's **nightlife** is some of the best along the coast, with open-air dancing till dawn and live music in some great little **bars** on the beach, most wooden-walled and thatch-roofed. Prominent here is *Expirat*, a thumping party place at the southern end of the beach, though *Club Goblin*, *Stuf* and *Gulag* near the centre of the beach are similarly vibrant venues.

Travel details

Trains

Constanţa to: Bucharest (6–9 daily; 3hr 40min–5hr 15min); Galaţi (1 daily; 5hr 45min); Iaşi (1 daily; 8hr 40min); Mangalia (5–7 daily; 1hr 10min–1hr 30min); Medgidia (6–10 daily; 25–50min); Suceava (1 daily; 9hr 30min).
Medgidia to: Babadag (4 daily; 1hr 40min–2hr 5min); Bucharest (6–8 daily; 3hr 15min); Constanţa (7–11 daily; 30–45min); Negru Vodă (3 daily; 1hr 30min); Tulcea (2 daily; 2hr 50min).
Tulcea to: Medgidia (2 daily; 2hr 50min).

Buses and maxitaxis

Constanţa to: Brăila (5 daily); Bucharest (every 45min); Cernavodă (every 30min); Galaţi (10 daily); Hârşova (4 daily); Iaşi (2 daily); Istria (4 daily);

Jurilovca (5 daily); Mangalia (every 20min); Medgidia (every 30min); Oltina (for Adamclisi, 3 daily); Suceava (2 daily); Tulcea (every 30min).
Mangalia to: Doi Mai and Vama Veche (May–Aug every 20min, Sept–April every 90min); Saturn-Olimp (frequent).
Tulcea to: Brăila (6 daily); Bucharest (7 daily); Cocoş monastery (4 daily); Constanţa (every 30min); Enisala (9 daily); Focşani (2 daily); Galaţi (15 daily); Iaşi (2 daily); Jurilovca (1 daily); Mahmudia (5 daily); Murighiol (6 daily); Niculiţel (6 daily); Parcheş (9 daily).

International buses

Constanţa to: Athens, Greece (Tues, Thurs & Sat, 1 daily); Chişinău, Moldova (2 daily); Istanbul, Turkey (3 daily); Varna, Bulgaria (1 daily).

Contexts

Contexts

History

Although inhabited since prehistoric times, Romania achieved statehood only in the nineteenth century, and Transylvania, one-third of its present territory, was acquired as recently as 1920. Hence, much of Romania's history is that of its disparate parts – Dobrogea, the Banat, Bessarabia, Maramureş and, above all, the principalities of Moldavia, Wallachia and Transylvania.

Greeks, Dacians and Romans

Despite the discovery of bones, weapons and implements in Carpathian caves, very little is known about the nomadic hunter-gatherers of the early **Stone Age**. With the retreat of the glaciers, humans seem to have settled first in Dobrogea, where a people known to archeologists as the **Hamangia Culture** probably had a matriarchal society, worshipping fertility goddesses. Other societies developed in the Bronze and Iron Ages, followed by Celts who arrived from Asia in the last millennium BC.

During the sixth and seventh centuries BC, **Greek traders** established ports along the Black Sea coast, the ruins of which can still be seen at Istria (Histria), Constanţa (Tomis), Mangalia (Callatis) and other sites, but the interior remained virtually unknown to the Greeks until 512 BC, when the Persian emperor Darius attempted to expel the Scythians, another Asiatic people newly settled along the Danube. In 335 BC, Alexander the Great occupied Dobrogea and crossed the Danube, defeating the Getae but failing to subdue them.

The chronicler Herodotus had reported in the sixth century BC that of the numerous and disunited **Thracian** tribes inhabiting the mountains on both sides of the Danube, the "bravest and most righteous" were those subsequently known as the "Geto-Dacians". Nowadays "Thracian" refers to all the tribes then occupying this area, including the Getae on the Danube, the Dacians to their north, the Thracians proper to the south, and the Illyrians in present-day Albania. Over time these tribes gradually coalesced until a single leader, Burebista (82–44 BC), ruled a short-lived **Dacian empire**, occupying the territory of modern-day Romania and beyond, with its capital at **Sarmizegetusa**, in the Orăştie mountains. Archeological digs have revealed Dacian settlements from the Black Sea to Slovakia, and the sheer size of the kingdom contributed to its fragmentation after Burebista's demise.

A Roman colony

Decebal (87–106 AD) managed to reunite this kingdom, but the **Romans** had already occupied the lower reaches of the Danube and soon began expanding northwards. Decebal defeated a Roman army but was then driven back; a stalemate followed until two campaigns (in 101–102 and 105–106 AD) by the Emperor Trajan (98–117 AD) led to the conquest of Dacia. Although the Apuseni mountains, Maramureş and Moldavia were never subdued, most regions fell under Roman rule, maintained by the building of roads and garrison posts. The province of **Dacia** grew so rich and important that it was known as Dacia Felix or Happy Dacia, but with increasing incursions by nomadic Asian tribes such as the Goths in the third century, the defence of Dacia became too costly, and in 271 AD, Emperor Aurelian withdrew Rome's presence from the region.

The Age of Migrations and Daco-Romanian Continuity

The **Age of Migrations** was defined by the arrival of nomadic peoples sweeping out of Asia, including the Huns (4th and 5th centuries), Avars (6th century), Slavs (7th century) and Bulgars (7th century, along the coast en route to Bulgaria). The mountains protected the area now called Transylvania, where coins have been found whose dates show continuing trade with the empire despite Roman withdrawal; the **Daco–Romanian Continuity theory** holds that the Romanians are descendants of the Roman settlers and indigenous Dacians, and Romanian philologists point to numerous Latin-derived words in their language. Yet while some Romanians boast about their Roman heritage, many of the settlers would have been not free Romans but former slaves and soldiers, many of them Greeks and Arabs.

The theory would be of academic interest only were it not entwined with the centuries-old dispute between Magyars and Romanians over the **occupation of Transylvania**. By claiming uninterrupted residence, Romanians assert their rightful ownership of Transylvania. Conversely, the Magyars (who had first passed through around 896 as just another Asiatic horde before settling Hungary) claim that their occupation, from about 997 to the thirteenth century, met little resistance, and that the indigenous people were of Slavic stock. According to some Magyar historians, **Vlachs** (Romanians) are first mentioned in Transylvania around 1222 as nomadic pastoralists crossing the Carpathians, having wandered over the centuries from their original "homeland" in Macedonia and Illyria.

The medieval principalities

Whatever the indigenous population's identity, the Árpád dynasty gradually extended Hungarian rule over **Transylvania**, using foreigners to bolster their own settlements. Besides subduing local Cumans, Bulgars and Vlachs, the colonists had to withstand frequent invasions by the **Tatars** (or Mongols), nomadic warriors who devastated much of Eastern Europe in 1241–42 and continued to wreak havoc over the next five centuries.

The Teutonic Knights colonized the Bârsa Land (around Braşov) in 1211 but were evicted in 1225; however, other groups of Germans – subsequently known as **Saxons** – built up powerful market towns like Hermannstadt (Sibiu) and Kronstadt (Braşov), which were granted self-government as "seats" (Sedes, or Stühle). Another ethnic group, the **Székely**, colonized the eastern marches, also enjoying relative autonomy.

Hungarians, however, were either classed as plebs liable to all manner of taxes, or as nobles and thus tax-exempt. This group dominated the **feudal system**, being represented alongside the Saxon and Székely "nations" on the Diet that advised the **Voivode**, who governed for the Hungarian king. Under the Árpád dynasty, Diets included Romanian-speaking Vlachs who even then may have constituted the majority of Transylvania's population. From the mid-fourteenth century onwards, however, Vlachs faced increasing **discrimination**. Besides the mistrust sown by Bogdan Vodă's revolt in Maramureş (see opposite), **religion** played an important part in this process. Whereas the Vlachs were Orthodox (barring a few apostate nobles), the other communities adhered to the Catholic Church.

Wallachia and Dobrogea

On the far side of the Carpathians, fully fledged principalities emerged somewhat later. Chronicles attribute the foundation of **Wallachia** (Vlahia or the Ţara Românească) to Negru Vodă (the Black Prince), who made Câmpulung its first capital in 1290, though they may instead refer to his son Radu Negru (1310–52), usually credited as the first of the Basarab dynasty. The shift in Wallachia's capitals over the centuries – from Câmpulung in the highlands down to Curtea de Argeş and Târgovişte in the foothills and then Bucharest on the plain – expressed a cautious move from the safety of the mountains to the financial opportunities of the trade routes with Turkey. Tithes and labour squeezed from the enserfed masses allowed the landowning **boyars** to endow Orthodox churches and plot against the ruling *voivodes*, although commerce was entirely in the hands of Germans, Poles, Greeks and Jews.

Moldavia and Bessarabia

Attempts to enforce Hungarian rule in Maramureş provoked some of the indigenous population to follow **Bogdan Vodă** over the Carpathians in 1359 to the cradle of a new principality, **Moldavia**, but the process of occupying the hills and steppes beyond the Carpathians had begun centuries earlier. Groups of Romanian-speaking pastoralists and farmers gradually moved to the Dnestr where they encountered Ukrainians who named them Volokhi. The Moldavian capital shifted southeastwards from Rădăuţi to Suceava and then to Iaşi. **Alexander the Good** (Alexandru cel Bun) may have gained his honorary title by ousting Turks from the eastern marches, though it could well have been bestowed by the Basarab family, whom he made feudal lords of the region, subsequently known as **Bessarabia**. Besides Tatar and Turkish invasions and rebellious boyars, Moldavia faced threats from Hungary, Poland and the Turks.

Ottomans, Nationes and Phanariots

From the mid-fourteenth century the **Ottoman empire** of the Seljuk Turks spread inexorably northwards, finally subjugating Bulgaria in 1393. The Turks were briefly halted by **Mircea the Old** (Mircea cel Bătrân; 1386–1418) at the battle of Rovine in 1394, but subsequent defeats compelled Mircea to acknowledge Ottoman suzerainty in 1417. By surrendering the fertile **Dobrogea** region and paying tribute, outright occupation was avoided and Wallachia's ruling class retained their positions; henceforth, both rulers and ruled were confronted with the alternatives of submission or resistance to an overwhelming force.

Even before the fall of Constantinople in 1453, Wallachia, Moldavia and Transylvania had become Christendom's front line of resistance to the Turks – and indeed, with Russia, the only Orthodox Christian land remaining free. Throughout the fifteenth century, the principalities' history is overshadowed by this struggle and the names of four remarkable military leaders. First was Transylvanian *voivode* **Iancu de Hunedoara** (Hunyadi János), who defeated the Turks near Alba Iulia and Sibiu in 1441–43 and led multinational armies to victory at Niş and Belgrade. Iancu's son **Mátyás Corvinus** (1440–90, also known as Hunyadi Mátyás or Matei Corvin), Hungary's great Renaissance king, continued to resist the Turks, who were dislodged from southern Bessarabia by **Stephen the Great** (Ștefan cel Mare) of Moldavia and temporarily checked by the fortresses of Chilia and Cetatea Alba (now in Ukraine). However, their resurgence under Bajazid II, and treaties signed by the Turks with Poland, Hungary and Venice in the 1470s and 1480s, presaged the demise of Moldavian independence, as was apparent to Stephen by the end of his embattled reign (1457–1504). Meanwhile, due to Wallachia's greater vulnerablity, its rulers generally preferred to pay off the Turks rather than resist them – **Vlad Țepeș** (Vlad the Impaler – see p.403) being a notable exception from 1456 to 1476.

In **Transylvania**, the least exposed region, the **Bobâlna peasant uprising** of 1437–38 rocked the feudal order. To safeguard their privileges, the Magyar nobility concluded a pact known as the **Union of Three Nations** with the Saxon and Székely leaders, whereby each of these three ethnic groups (Nationes) agreed to recognize and defend the rights of the others. As a consequence, Vlachs were relegated to the position of "those who do not possess the right of citizenship... but are merely tolerated by grace", effectively prohibited from holding public office or residing in Saxon and Magyar towns. The increasing exploitation of the Magyar peasantry led in 1514 to an uprising under György Dózsa (Gheorghe Doja), savagely repressed by governor **János Zápolyai** (Johann Zapolya, 1510–40), who imposed the onerous Werbőczy Code, or Tripartium, a feudal version of apartheid, in 1517.

The crushing defeat of Hungary by Suleyman the Magnificent at **Mohács** (1526) and the Turkish occupation of Buda (1541) exacerbated the isolation of the principalities. Although Austria's Habsburg dynasty laid claim to what was left of Hungary after Mohács, Zápolyai won Ottoman support to maintain a precarious autonomy for Transylvania, even gaining control of Hungary east of the River Tisza (the Partium) in 1538. Successors such as István Báthori (1571–81, who was elected King of Poland from 1575 and drove back Ivan the Terrible) and Zsigmond Báthori (1581–97) maintained this independence; in Moldavia, however, **Petru Rareș** could only hold his throne (1527–38 and 1541–56) by breathtaking duplicity and improvisations, while his successors plumbed even further depths.

Short-lived unification

Understandably, Romanian historiography prefers to highlight more successful leaders such as **Michael the Brave** (Mihai Viteazul, often known in Wallachia as Mihai Bravul). Ruler of Wallachia from 1593, his triumph against the Turks in 1595 was followed by the overthrow of Andrew Báthori in Transylvania in 1599 and a lightning campaign across the Carpathians in 1600 to secure the Moldavian throne. This opportunist **union of the principalities** – which fragmented immediately following his murder in 1601 – has since been presented as a triumph of Romanian nationalism, but it was only between 1604 and 1657 that Transylvania enjoyed genuine independence from both Habsburgs and Ottomans.

From the 1630s on, Moldavia and Wallachia avoided direct occupation as Turkish *pashaliks* by accepting Ottoman "advisers", known as **Phanariots**. In Moldavia, they encouraged the Orthodox Church to abandon the Old Slavonic language in favour of Greek, but this had the unintended result of stimulating a move towards the Romanian language. This presaged a minor cultural renaissance – particularly in the field of architecture – during a period of relative stability from 1633 to 1711 in Moldavia and to 1714 in Wallachia. Thereafter, the Turks dispensed with native rule and instead appointed Phanariot princes; their greed, combined with more than seventy changes of ruler in Moldavia and Wallachia until 1821, crippled both regions.

The struggle for independence and unification

Habsburg power grew after the failure of the Turkish siege of Vienna in 1683; after the collapse of a Hungarian revolt led by Ferenc II Rákóczi, in 1704–11, Austrian governors were imposed on Transylvania rather than local princes. As Catholics and imperialists, the Habsburg monarchy persuaded some Orthodox clergy to accept papal authority, promising that Vlachs who joined the **Uniate Church** (see p.173) would be granted equality with the Nationes. Although this promise was retracted in 1701, Bishop Inocenţiu Micu and the intellectuals of the Transylvanian School agitated for equal rights and articulated the Vlachs' growing consciousness of being **Romanians**. Thus Joseph II's edict of religious toleration in 1781, his dissolution of the monasteries and embarkation upon the abolition of serfdom all came too late to prevent the great peasant rebellion led by **Horea**, **Crişan** and **Cloşca** in 1784–85. Its crushing only stimulated efforts to attain liberation by constitutional means, however.

The gradual development of liberal and nationalist factions in **Moldavia and Wallachia** had a variety of causes, including the ideals of the Romantic movement and the French Revolution, the success of Serbian and Greek independence movements, and the emergence of capitalism in the principalities, showing that Turkish dominance and feudalism were in decline. The upshot was a major uprising in Wallachia in 1821, led by **Tudor Vladimirescu**. Although defeated, it persuaded the Turks that it was time to end Phanariot rule, and power was restored to native boyars in 1822.

The rise of Russia and World War I

As the Ottoman empire declined, **Russia** grew in power. Fired by imperialist and Pan-Slavist ideals and a fear of Habsburg encroachment (manifest in 1774, when Austria annexed the region henceforth known as **Bucovina**), Russia expanded its territories towards the Balkans as well as into the Caucasus and Central Asia, presenting itself as guardian of the Ottomans' Christian subjects. In 1792, Russian forces reached the River Dnestr; one Russo-Turkish war led to the annexation of Bessarabia in 1812, and another to the Treaty of Adrianople (1829), by which Moldavia and Wallachia became Russian protectorates, allowing Western European trade and ideas free access at last. The Tsarist governor **General Paul Kiseleff** was in no sense a revolutionary, but introduced liberal reforms and assemblies in both principalities, which remained in force after the Russians withdrew in 1834, having selected two rulers. Of these, Michael Sturdza in Moldavia was the more despotic but also the more energetic, levying heavy taxes to construct roads, dykes, hospitals and schools.

Given the boyars' dominance of the assemblies, economic development took precedence over the political and social reforms demanded by bourgeois liberals such as Nicolae Golescu, Ion Brătianu, Nicolae Bălcescu and Mihail Kogălniceanu. The **democratic movement** they led campaigned for the unification of Moldavia and Wallachia and briefly came to power in 1848, the **Year of Revolutions** (see p.376).

Russia intervened militarily to restore the status quo, while the build-up to the Crimean War saw Russia also occupying Moldavia and Wallachia and fighting the Turks along the Danube. The Congress of Paris, ending the war in 1856, reaffirmed Turkish rule (although with increased autonomy for the boyars), and the nationalist cause was thwarted until 1859, when the assemblies of Moldavia and Wallachia proclaimed their **unification** under a single ruler, **Alexander Ioan Cuza**. The reformist Cuza abolished serfdom and introduced agrarian reform, provoking landowners and other conservatives to overthrow him in 1866, inviting a German prince, Karl von Hohenzollern, to rule in his place as **Carol I**. Yet another Russo-Turkish war led to Rumania (as the United Provinces had renamed themselves in 1862) declaring independence on May 9, 1877, recognized the next year by the Treaty of Berlin.

Events in **Transylvania** followed a different course, with popular support for Hungary's 1848 revolution split along ethnic lines. While the peasants all welcomed the abolition of serfdom, the Romanian population opposed Transylvania's unification with Hungary, which Magyars greeted with enthusiasm; the Saxons were lukewarm on both issues. Following protest meetings at Blaj, **Avram Iancu** formed Romanian guerrilla bands to oppose the Hungarians; attempts by Kossuth and Bălcescu to compromise over Romanian rights came too late to create a united front against the Tsarist armies which invaded Transylvania on behalf of the Habsburgs. As in Hungary, there was widespread repression following the failed revolution.

In 1867, the Ausgleich (Compromise) established the Dual Monarchy of the Austro-Hungarian Empire; Transylvania became part of Greater Hungary, ruled directly from Budapest, with a policy of **Magyarization** making Hungarian the official language and undermining Romanian culture (Bucovina and Maramureş remained under Austrian rule and avoided the worst of this). The cultural association **ASTRA**, founded in 1861, and the **National Party**, founded in 1881, defended the Romanians, maintaining close links with kindred groups across the Carpathians.

The influence of foreign capital increased enormously around the turn of the century, as Rumania's mineral wealth – particularly its oil – inspired competition among the great powers. While the Liberal and Conservative parties squabbled ritualistically and alternated in power, nothing was done about the worsening impoverishment of the people. Peasant grievances exploded in the **răscoala** of 1907 – a nationwide uprising that was savagely crushed (with around 11,000 deaths) and followed by ineffectual agrarian reforms.

Rumania's acquisition of territory south of the Danube in 1878 was one of the many causes of the **Balkan Wars** that embroiled Rumania, Bulgaria, Serbia, Macedonia and Greece. Rumania sat out the first Balkan War (1912–13), but joined the alliance against Bulgaria in 1913, thus gaining southern Dobrogea. King Ferdinand, who succeeded Carol in 1914, was married to Marie, granddaughter of both Queen Victoria and Tsar Alexander II; thus, when Rumania entered **World War I** in 1916, it joined Britain, France and Russia and attacked the Austro-Hungarian forces in Transylvania. This was a total fiasco, and only desperate defence at Mărăşeşti prevented the loss of the whole of Rumania. An onerous peace treaty was imposed in May 1918, but by October the disintegration of the Central Powers reversed this situation entirely, and Rumanian armies advanced into Transylvania, and then on into Hungary to overthrow the short-lived communist regime of Béla Kun in August 1919. On December 1, 1918, the assembly of Alba Iulia declared **Transylvania's union with Rumania** to scenes of wild acclaim. The Romanian population of Bessarabia, freed by the Russian Revolution, had already declared their union with Rumania in March 1918, followed in November by Bucovina. The **Treaty of Trianon** in 1920 upheld Rumania's gains and the nation doubled both in population and territory, while Hungary lost half of its populace and two-thirds of its land – the source of great resentment ever since.

Greater Romania

The country's enlarged territory was dignified by the adoption of the name **Greater Romania**, but the lives of the masses hardly improved. Hungarian estates and farms in Transylvania were expropriated, but much of the land was grabbed by speculators. Similarly, Hungarian employees were dismissed on a huge scale, with Romanian immigrants brought in to replace them.

Romania was governed from 1920 by the **National Liberal Party**, favoured by the king but pursuing damaging nationalist and populist policies. On Ferdinand's death in 1927, it was dismissed and replaced by the **National Peasants Party**, led by **Iuliu Maniu**, which in 1928 won the only remotely fair election of this period. Despite a parliamentary majority and genuinely reforming policies, Maniu took a conservative line, constrained by the world economic crisis of 1929, vested interests and entrenched corruption.

However, it was a bizarre moral issue that led to the government's fall: in 1930, after a three-year regency, **Carol II** took the throne on condition he leave his divorced Jewish mistress, Magda Lupescu. He broke the promise, the puritan Maniu resigned and the government fell apart. Carol then exploited his right to dissolve parliament and call elections at will; a corrupt system soon developed whereby the government would fix elections by every means possible, only to be dismissed and replaced by the opposition when the king had tired of them. Between 1930 and 1940, there were no less than 25 separate governments, leading ultimately to the collapse of the political parties themselves. Strikes in the oil and rail industries in 1933 were put down by armed force; Carol set up his own "youth movement", and soon began routine phone-tapping by the **Siguranța**, the Securitate's predecessor, enabling him to blackmail the entire political establishment except for Maniu.

The Iron Guard and World War II

A **fascist movement** also established itself, particularly in Bessarabia, which had a long tradition of anti-Semitism. The main fascist party, taking much of the National Peasant Party's rural support, was the Legion of the Archangel Michael, founded in 1927; its green-shirted paramilitary wing, the **Iron Guard** (see box, p.243), extolled the soil, death, and a mystical form of Orthodoxy; it also fought street battles against Jews and followers of other political parties, and murdered four current and former prime ministers. In 1937, the anti-Semitic National League of Christian Defence and National Christian Party were installed in power by the king, but the prime minister, the poet Octavian Goga, insulted Lupescu and was dismissed in February 1938, after just six weeks in power. This at last provoked Carol to ban all political parties (other than his own National Rebirth Front) and set up a royal dictatorship.

In February 1939, Germany demanded a monopoly of Romanian exports in return for a guarantee of its borders, and in March agreed an oil-for-arms deal. Carol obtained feeble guarantees from Britain and France, but in August the equilibrium was shattered by the Nazi–Soviet Non-Aggression Pact. In June 1940, the Soviet Union annexed Bessarabia and northern Bucovina, and, two months later, Hitler forced Carol to cede Northern Transylvania to Germany's ally Hungary, and southern Dobrogea to Bulgaria. Unable to maintain his position after giving away such huge portions of Romanian territory, Carol fled with Lupescu and his spoils in September, leaving his son **Mihai**, then 19 years old, to take over the throne.

Mihai accepted the formation of a government led by **Marshal Ion Antonescu**, who styled himself Conducator ("leader", equivalent to Führer) but had little

The Holocaust in Romania

In 1939, Romania had the third-largest **Jewish population** in Europe after Poland and the Soviet Union. Most lived in Bessarabia, Bucovina and parts of northern Moldavia. In June 1940, Bessarabia and northern Bucovina were ceded to the Soviet Union, as demanded by Hitler, and at least fifty Jews were killed in Dorohoi by retreating Romanian troops. A year later troops carried out an awful pogrom in Iaşi, killing about 8000 Jews, leading the Germans to comment, "we always act scientifically... we use surgeons, not butchers". As the army (and the German Einsatzgruppe D) advanced, there were many more massacres; at least 33,000 Jews died in Bessarabia and Bucovina between June 22 and September 1, 1941, and, in fact, the worst single massacre of the Holocaust was committed by Romanians whilst they took Odessa.

Deportations to Transnistria, the conquered territory beyond the River Dnestr, began in earnest on September 16; around 150,000 Jews were taken, of whom 18,000 to 22,000 died in transit. Up to 90,000 more died from starvation, disease and general mistreatment. Between November 21 and 29, 1941, all 48,000 Jews in the Bogdanovka camp in southern Transnistria were killed; another 18,000 were killed in the Dumanovka camp.

In July 1942, the Germans began to press for the Jews of Wallachia, Moldavia and southern Transylvania to be deported to the camps, following the 120,000 already taken to Auschwitz from Hungarian-controlled Northern Transylvania. This was agreed but then refused after lobbying by neutral diplomats and the Papal Nuncio, although it was probably more due to the fact that the Jews were still vital to the functioning of the economy. In November 1942, it was decided that Romanian Jews in Germany should be sent to the death camps.

When Romania was thinking of changing sides, the **World Jewish Congress** in Geneva proposed a plan to save 70,000 Romanian Jews, and possibly 1.3 million more in Eastern Europe, by paying the Romanian government twelve shillings per head to allow them to leave by ship for Palestine. This plan was blocked by opposition from anti-Semites in the US State Department and Britain, worried about the reaction of Arabs to further Jewish immigration to Palestine, as well as by the practical implications of sending money to a Nazi ally. Thirteen ships did leave, with 13,000 refugees, but two sank (with 1163 on board) and others were stopped by Turkey, under pressure from both Britain and Germany.

In 1944, Antonescu began a **limited repatriation** from the camps of Transnistria, bringing back 1500 in December 1943 and 1846 orphans by March 1944. He warned the Germans not to kill Jews as they retreated; nevertheless, a final thousand were killed in Tiraspol jail. On March 20, 1944, the Red Army reached the Dnestr, and the worst of the nightmare ended. In Antonescu's trial in 1946 he claimed to have saved about 275,000 Jews by his policy of keeping them for extermination at home; however, this did not save him from execution. Overall, between 264,900 and 470,000 Romanian Jews, and 36,000 Gypsies, died in the war; 428,000 Jews survived or returned alive. In 2003, a row erupted with Israel when Iliescu appeared to claim that the Holocaust hadn't occurred in Romania and hadn't just affected the Jews, and compared it to the suffering of prewar communists. Since 2004, **Holocaust Day** in October has been officially marked in Romania.

influence over local legionary groups who unleashed an orgy of violence against Jews and liberals. To ensure himself a stable and productive ally, Hitler forced Antonescu to disarm the Iron Guard; this provoked an armed uprising (and the savage butchery of 124 Jews in Bucharest) in January 1941, only suppressed by the army after a fierce struggle.

Romania entered **World War II** in June 1941, joining the Nazi invasion of Russia with the objective of regaining Bessarabia and northern Bucovina. Romanian troops took Odessa and participated in the battles of Sevastopol and Stalingrad, taking heavy casualties. Jews and Gypsies in Bessarabia, Bucovina and the Hungarian-controlled area of Transylvania were rounded up and deported for slave labour and then on to extermination camps. By 1943, however, the Red Army was advancing fast, and Antonescu began to look for a way to abandon Hitler and change sides. Opposition to the war mounted as the Russians drew nearer, and, as they crossed the border, a **royal/military coup** on August 23, 1944 overthrew the Antonescu regime – a date commemorated until 1989 as **Liberation Day**, although it took a further two months to clear the Germans from the country.

The People's Republic

The first postwar government was a broad coalition, with **communists** only playing a minor role. Gradually, however, they increased their influence, and, in March 1945, the Soviets forced the king to accept a new coalition led by **Dr Petru Groza** (leader of the Ploughmen's Front), with the key posts occupied by communists. Land reform in 1945 benefited millions of peasants at the expense of the Saxons and Swabians of Transylvania and the Banat, while women voted for the first time in 1946, supposedly contributing to the election of another ostensibly balanced government. In fact, virtually every device ever used to rig an election was brought into play and the takeover steamed ahead.

Like Groza's first administration, this included leading capitalists and former Guardists, whom the communists initially wooed, since their first aim was to eliminate the left and centre parties, who were often forcibly merged with the communists. On December 30, 1947, King Mihai was forced to abdicate and Romania was declared a **People's Republic**. Antonescu and up to 60,000 were executed after highly irregular trials in 1946 and 1947. Eighty thousand arrests followed in an effort to overcome peasant resistance to **collectivization** (a reversal of the earlier agrarian reform), with around 180,000 more from 1948 in the campaign to "liquidate" the Uniate Church. Also in 1948, the **nationalization** of industries, banks and utilities placed the main economic levers in the hands of the Communist Party, which openly aimed to reshape society on Stalinist lines. **Police terror** was used against real or potential opponents, with victims imprisoned or sent to work on the Danube–Black Sea Canal, the "Canal Mortii" (see p.353) that claimed over 100,000 lives.

The Communist Party itself was split by bitter conflicts between the Muscovites (those who had spent the war in Moscow, led by Ana Pauker and Vasile Luca) and the nationalists, themselves divided between the prison-communists and the secretariat-communists who had remained free and in hiding. In 1952, the prison-communists emerged victorious, under **Gheorghe Gheorghiu-Dej**, General Secretary of the party's Central Committee since 1945, who had retained Stalin's confidence largely because the secretariat group was too ideologically flexible, while Pauker and her group were simply too Jewish. She and 192,000 other members were purged from the Party, and Lucrețiu Pătrășcanu (Minister of Justice 1944–48) was executed in 1954.

Stalin had died in 1953, but Gheorghiu-Dej took great exception to reformist trends in the USSR, and stuck grimly to the Stalinist true faith, developing heavy industry and claiming the impossible growth rate of 13 percent per year.

The USSR, having annexed Bessarabia once more, had given some of it to Ukraine and created the puppet **Republic of Moldova** from the rest. Therefore, Gheorghiu-Dej's increasing refusal to follow the Moscow line was a great success domestically, tapping into a vein of popular nationalism. By arresting the leadership of the left-wing Hungarian People's Alliance and establishing an "Autonomous Hungarian Region" in the Székely Land in 1952, he simultaneously decapitated the Magyar political organization in Transylvania while erecting a facade of minority rights.

Gheorghiu-Dej died in 1965 and was succeeded by a collective leadership, but by 1969 **Nicolae Ceauşescu**, until then a little-known party hack, had outmanoeuvred his rivals and established undisputed power.

The Ceauşescu era

There seems little doubt that for the first few years of his rule, **Ceauşescu** was genuinely popular: he encouraged a cultural thaw, put food and consumer goods into the shops, denounced security police excesses (blaming them on Gheorghiu-Dej), and above all condemned the Warsaw Pact invasion of Czechoslovakia in 1968. His independent **foreign policy** gained Romania the reputation of being the "maverick" state of the Eastern bloc, building links with the West and maintaining ties with countries with which the USSR had severed contact.

However, he soon reverted to tried and tested methods of control as his **economic failure** became obvious. Ceauşescu stuck throughout to a Stalinist belief in heavy industry, and during the 1970s the country's **industrialization programme** absorbed thirty percent of GNP and $10.2 billion in foreign loans. Living standards plummeted as all but a minimal amount of food was exported, and the population was obliged to work harder and harder for less and less. Amazingly, all the foreign debt was repaid by 1989, although there was no prospect of any improvement in living standards thereafter.

Ceauşescu was convinced that the key to industrial growth lay in building a larger workforce, and in 1966 banned abortions and contraception for any married woman under 40 with fewer than four children (in 1972, the limits were raised to 45 and five); by 1989 11,000 women had died due to illegal abortions. In 1984, when his developing paranoia and personality cult was putting him increasingly out of touch, he introduced the **Baby Police** and compulsory monthly gynaecological examinations, and higher taxation for the childless. Ceauşescu also **discriminated against the minorities**: it became increasingly hard to get an education or to buy books in Hungarian or German, or to communicate with relatives abroad; and families were persuaded to give their children Romanian names.

The two million-plus **Magyars** (including the Székely and Csángós) bore the brunt of this chauvinism, damaging diplomatic relations with Hungary. Neither this, nor criticism of the treatment of the **Gypsy** population, worried Ceauşescu, but he tried to keep on the right side of the German and Israeli governments, who purchased exit visas for ethnic Germans and Jews in Romania for substantial sums.

Human rights abuses worsened through the 1980s, including the **systematization** programme for rural redevelopment (see p.85) and constant repression by the **Securitate** (secret police), which produced an atmosphere of fear and distrust even between family members, as up to one in four of the population was rumoured to

The result of Ceauşescu's scheme to increase the workforce was that many women had children that they could not possibly afford to bring up and these were abandoned in dire **state orphanages**, grossly under-staffed and underfunded. With desensitized staff and no mental stimulation, it's not surprising that many orphans were diagnosed (at 3 years old) as mentally handicapped and left without education in "Institutes for the Irrecuperable".

After the 1989 revolution, the Western media was saturated with distressing images of these orphanages, and emergency aid and volunteers flooded into Romania. Today, relief agencies focus on long-term strategies with emphasis on training and helping the Romanians to help themselves. Increasingly, orphanages are being replaced by family-home-type units, and family support centres have opened in some towns. In 2001, a shocking EU report linked adoptions to the organ trade and child pornography, and a moratorium was imposed on adoption, which continues, to the approval of the EU; however, there's pressure from the US for adoptable children to be made available.

The problem of unwanted children remains, and will do so until there is comprehensive family planning, now the object of a huge programme, but official funds for charities have dried up and donations are welcome. Some Romanian families are now adopting, but most orphans are Gypsies and therefore not wanted. However, social security money is now reaching the Roma, so the numbers of children being abandoned has fallen greatly.

Charity contacts

Cleaford Christian Trust UK ☎0845/124 9402, ⓦwww.cleafordchristiantrust.org.uk, ⓦwww.riac.org.uk

FARA UK ☎01328/821 444, ⓦwww.faracharity.org

Medical Support for Romania UK ☎01223/276 504, ⓦwww.msr.org.uk

Peace Corps US ☎1800/424 8580, ⓦwww.peacecorps.org

Regional Environmental Centre Romania ☎021/314 0433, ⓦwww.recromania.ro

Relief Fund for Romania UK ☎020/7733 7018, ⓦwww.relieffundforromania.co.uk

Romanian Angel Appeal Romania ☎021/323 6868, ⓦwww.raa.ro

Romanian Challenge Appeal UK ☎0121/744 2828, ⓦwww.romanian-challenge.org

be an informer. Increasingly, key posts were allocated to relatives of the Ceauşescus, while all other senior figures were rotated every few years between jobs to prevent anyone building up an independent power base.

In the **1980s**, everything went downhill rapidly, as the truth about the country's economic collapse was hidden from Ceauşescu by his wife and subordinates. Absolutely everything was in short supply, but Nicolae and Elena pushed on with megalomaniac projects such as the Palace of the People in Bucharest, the Danube–Black Sea Canal (again) and the village systematization programme. Ceauşescu also made plain his opposition to *glasnost*.

The Revolution

By **1989**, the situation was so desperate that it seemed impossible for Ceauşescu not to bow to the wave of change sweeping over the whole of Eastern Europe. A series of strikes and riots in December that year culminated with a mass demonstration of 100,000 people in Timişoara on December 20 demanding Ceauşescu's resignation; despite his orders to fire, the army withdrew rather than launch a massacre. The very next day, another crowd of 100,000, brought from their workplaces to show support, gathered in Piaţa Republicii (now Piaţa Revoluţiei) in Bucharest to hear him speak, but he was soon interrupted by heckling. The police and Securitate opened fire but were unable to drive the crowds away, partly because the Minister of Defence, **General Vasile Milea**, ordered the army not to fire. On the morning of December 22, Ceauşescu had Milea shot, but this merely precipitated the defection of many army units to the side of the protestors. By noon, the crowds had broken into the Party's Central Committee building, and the Ceauşescus fled by helicopter from the roof. After going to their villa at Snagov and on to a military airfield near Titu, they hijacked a car before being arrested in Târgovişte. When the news of their capture proved insufficient to stop loyal Securitate units firing on the crowds, they were summarily tried and **executed** on Christmas Day.

Meanwhile, there was street fighting in many cities, with army and police units changing sides; it's unclear at what point their leadership had decided to abandon Ceauşescu, but evidence suggests that it was earlier rather than later. Nor is it clear at what stage the **National Salvation Front** (Frontul Salvării Naţionale or FSN), which emerged to take power from December 22, had been formed; supposedly shaped in the Central Committee building that very afternoon by people who had gathered there independently, it's now clear many of them were already in contact. The key figures were Party members who had been sidelined by Ceauşescu, and **Ion Iliescu** was soon named president; his prime minister was **Petre Roman**, an up-and-coming member of the younger generation of communists.

Around a thousand people died in the revolution and the "terrorist" phase that lasted until January 18, although, initially, both the new government and the Hungarian media published inflated death tolls of 10,000 or more.

Free Romania

It didn't take long after the Ceauşescus' execution for the FSN to consolidate its power; within a month it reversed its pledge not to run as a party in May's elections, and it was evident that the former governing elite had no intention of losing power. **Protests** in Bucharest even saw the government shipping in around 10,000 miners to deal (violently) with the crowds, leaving seven dead and 296 injured. The nation went into shock, remaining cowed for the next year while the economy collapsed.

In the meantime, the FSN easily won Romania's **first free election**, while Iliescu won the vote for president. The whole process was deemed fair enough by international observers, even though a million more votes were cast than were on the register, supposedly "due to the enthusiasm of the people for democracy". Most intellectuals soon took to referring to December 1989 as the "so-called revolution", and it was increasingly taken for granted that nothing much had changed.

Economic reform got under way slowly, but hardship was unavoidable as the country was rocked by its opening up to Western imports and by world recession. Food subsidies were cut in November 1990, and **prices** increased steadily from then on, while **inflation** reached almost 300 percent in 1993. In 1991 the miners were brought back to force Roman to resign; he was replaced by **Teodor Stolojan**, and the FSN soon split.

A **second general election** was held in 1992, after the adoption of a new constitution establishing a **presidential democracy**, in which the prime minister has little autonomy. Iliescu won the presidency, and a coalition government under the PSD's **Nicolae Văcăroiu**, with support from the ultra-nationalists, was installed. The need for aid and fear of international isolation kept it on a seemingly reformist course. In 1992 Romania was granted Most Favoured Nation status by the US and Associate status by the EU; in 1993 it became the last Eastern Bloc state to join the Council of Europe, and in January 1994, it was the first to sign the Partnership for Peace.

Particularly welcome (and rewarded by substantial loans) was Iliescu's support for the tight **fiscal policies** of the National Bank's governor Mugur Isărescu, which halved inflation to 6 percent per month. In 1995 taxes were cut to the lowest levels in Central or Eastern Europe and the economy continued to improve, with unemployment falling and real wages rising 16 percent in 1995. However, this wasn't enough to win Iliescu the 1996 general elections as a series of **scandals** alienated voters.

Constantinescu and the return of Iliescu

The 1996 election was won by the Democratic Convention of Romania (CDR), a coalition of four main parties and a dozen smaller ones. **Emil Constantinescu**, a professor of geology and former rector of Bucharest University, became president and appointed the youthful mayor of Bucharest, Victor Ciorbea, as prime minister. Their government was genuinely liberal-democratic and Western-oriented; its priorities were accelerated privatization, the slashing of the budget deficit and elimination of almost all price controls, introduction of a transparent tax system, and an attack on corruption, all with increased social protection. They soon found the coffers were empty due to Iliescu's attempts to buy re-election, and the result was the most radical "shock therapy" campaign anywhere in East Central Europe. In January 1997 alone, fuel and phone prices doubled, the cost of electricity rose five times, and rail fares rose by eighty percent, as subsidies were

The King of Romania

In the 1990s, many people looked to **the King** for an escape from the intrigues of the politicians. **Mihai** was born in 1921 and reigned from 1940 to 1947; he earned his people's respect by his role in the coup of August 23, 1944, when he dismissed Antonescu, and by his attempts to resist communism thereafter. When forced to abdicate by the communists, he and his wife went into exile in England and then Switzerland. He was refused re-entry to his country, being expelled after twelve hours in 1990, until a brief visit in 1992, which drew large crowds. The situation changed totally with the election of Constantinescu; Mihai began to visit Romania frequently and in 2001 returned to live. From 1997 he was an active ambassador for Romanian entry to NATO and gained in stature, with even Iliescu calling him "Majesty" for the first time. Nevertheless, royalism has faded as a political force, although his daughter Princess Margarita is popular.

A castle at **Săvârşin** and the **Elisabeta Palace** in Bucharest have been restored to Mihai; the issue of Peleş was more difficult, but in 2005 parliament voted to pay him €30m for the main castle while handing him Pelişor (both remain open as museums).

removed, so that real wages fell by twenty percent in that month; fuel prices rose by half again in February.

Ciorbea was unable to control the coalition members, busily scheming for their own interests; he was forced to resign early in 1998 and was replaced first by **Radu Vasile**, who was better at politicking but less good at pushing ahead with reform, and then by the central bank governor **Mugur Isărescu**. However, in 1999 an attempt by striking miners to march on Bucharest and overthrow the government only narrowly failed, and increasingly, the government was perceived as failing to deliver, in particular in the war against corruption and in reforming and reviving the economy, and became particularly unpopular.

In the **general elections of 2000**, an angry electorate returned to power Iliescu and his Social Democratic Party (PSD; the latest incarnation of the FSN), with a huge vote for the ultra-nationalist Greater Romania Party (PRM); compared to their candidate, the rabid Corneliu Vadim Tudor, Iliescu suddenly seemed relatively benign to the West. **Adrian Năstase**, who had been successful as foreign minister, became prime minister of another coalition government, also supposedly committed to continuing the move towards a market economy and integration with the West; although various scandals led to resignations, the government proved remarkably stable, and in 2002 the **EU** announced that Romania could join in 2007. Romania also joined **NATO** in 2004. The PSD saw that it only had to make a show of fighting corruption, and did all it could to entrench its position by patronage and abuse of power. By 2004, around 300 people closely tied to the PSD controlled approximately a quarter of Romania's economy; nevertheless, the EU decided the country had a functioning market economy, even as evidence to the contrary mounted.

Băsescu vs. Tariceanu – and the future

A new opposition alliance, **Justice and Truth** (DA), was formed in 2003 by the PNL and PD, and in November's general election won 31 percent of the vote, while the PSD and allies won 37 percent; however, there was widespread outrage at blatant vote-rigging and the run-off for the presidency was relatively clean. It was narrowly won by PD leader and mayor of Bucharest **Traian Băsescu**, who asked PNL leader **Calin Popescu-Tariceanu** to become prime minister. He was able to form a coalition government, but not before the smaller parties had allowed the PSD to install its former prime ministers Adrian Năstase and Nicolae Văcăroiu as speakers of the House of Deputies and the Senate respectively. A lower flat rate of tax was swiftly introduced and many PSD figures were indicted for corruption; however, judicial reform (urgently required by the EU) was blocked by the Constitutional Court (stuffed with Iliescu's cronies).

In 2005 Dinu Patriciu, one of the richest men in Romania, was indicted for **corruption** in the privatization of the oil industry; his close friend the prime minister (himself very wealthy) was alleged to have phoned the prosecutor-general to have the case dropped. The oligarchs, entrenched in all the major parties (and controlling the previously fairly free media), realized that Băsescu was the first Romanian leader to be serious about tackling corruption; once the country was safely in the European Union (which was promising up to €1.2 billion per year in badly supervised aid, perhaps €32 billion in all), on January 1 2007, they forced the removal of Justice Minister Monica Macovei and then went for the president himself.

With president and prime minister now openly at war, the Liberal/Democratic alliance dead, and accusations of corruption flying on all sides, the PSD applied to the Constitutional Court for Băsescu's impeachment on grounds of abusing his office by interfering with cabinet government and criticizing the judiciary. The court ruled that he was guilty only of minor infringements, to which PSD leader Mircea Geoana responded by accusing Băsescu of blackmailing the judges. In any case parliament voted by 322 to 108 the next day (just three and a half months after Romania joined the EU) to **suspend Băsescu** pending a referendum on impeachment.

Efforts by Băsescu's opponents to fix the referendum rules failed, meaning that the president, by far the country's most popular politician, was always going to win, despite being largely banished from television. After a vicious campaign, on May 19 2007 a clear majority voted **against impeachment**. Tariceanu and his government of course refused to resign, meaning that the stand-off continued. The EU was appalled by how thoroughly it had been hoodwinked, but despite talk of safeguard clauses there was little it could do – as Tariceanu plainly stated. In June 2007 the European Commission merely extended the monitoring period for legal reform and the anti-corruption campaign.

The constant infighting and fragmentation of Romania's political parties continues, with defectors from the PNL forming a **Liberal Democrat** party which merged in 2008 with the Democrats as the Democrat-Liberal Party (PD-L), and the Berlusconi-esque owner of the Steaua football club, **Gigi Becali**, forming the New Generation Party and at once becoming the country's second most popular politician. The 2008 elections led to a government led by the PD-L's **Emil Boc** in coalition with the PSD, but now it was the PSD's Geoana who pursued a frenzied feud against Băsescu, pulling his party out of the government a month ahead of the November 2009 presidential elections. Băsescu just managed to beat Geoana, who responded with bizarre accusations of parapsychological mind control, and Boc remained prime minister.

There's no doubt that Băsescu, a bluff former sea captain, is often tactless and impulsive, while his opponents are far suaver, but he has widespread popular support. Parliament has very little credibility, with deputies jumping opportunistically from party to party and buying their place on a party's list with a view to profit. Until the EU makes a serious effort to convince the elite that it's in their best interests to comply with European standards, it's hard to see how things will improve. Even then, the tens of billions of euros already looted from the national economy are likely to persuade them to carry on as they are.

An economic boom began in 2001, with an average 6 percent annual GDP growth from 2004 to 2008, until halted by the global crisis. The economy shrank by 7 percent in 2009 and inflation rose to 6 percent (the highest in the EU); IMF loans kept the economy afloat, but only with steep tax rises and cuts in pensions and public sector salaries and jobs. Nevertheless, Romania's **economy** remains sound, helped by billions in Foreign Direct Investment and in earnings remitted by up to two million Romanians working in Western Europe. There's no doubt, however, that ongoing **extreme weather** – and the long-term effects of the country's recent disastrous floods (see p.386) – will take their economic toll.

Wildlife and environmental issues

Thanks to its antiquated agriculture and extensive areas of untouched native forest and wetland, Romania is uniquely important for **wildlife** in Europe. While the image of the country abroad is of industrial pollution, the reality is that it is far more pristine than much of Europe. Climbing into the hills, you enter a world where pesticides and fertilizers have never been used and where meadows are full of an amazing variety of birds and wild flowers – a landscape representative of Europe two or three centuries ago.

That said, the country has suffered, and there are numerous **industrial plants** that cause immense local damage. While the bulk of the damage occurred under communism, some of the worst offenders, such as Copşa Mică's carbon-black plant and the Valea Călugărească fertilizer plant (east of Ploieşti), were built in the capitalist period, while the Reşiţa and Hunedoara steelworks and the Zlatna copper smelter date back to the eighteenth century.

With the end of communism, new problems have appeared, due mainly to the return of woodland to the families of the pre-communist owners and the subsequent felling of more than half a million hectares of forest. Coupled with extreme weather, this has led to disastrous **flooding and landslides**. In 2005 floods caused more than a billion euros of damage, with at least seventy deaths. In January 2006 temperatures fell to -30°C, causing 45 deaths, while heatwaves killed 56 in 2005 and at least 35 in 2007, when temperatures were over 40°C nationwide, and up to 45°C in Bucharest.

Habitat

One-third of Romania is mountain, largely forested, and this is where most of the more interesting flora and fauna are to be found. One-third of the country is hill and plateau, and one third is plain, mostly intensively farmed.

The **Carpathian mountains** form an arc sweeping south from Ukraine and around Transylvania to end on the Danube at the Iron Gates. At lower levels (up to around 800m) the natural vegetation is forest of oak, hornbeam, lime and ash, a kind of forest that has largely disappeared elsewhere in Europe. Even the hill farmland at this height – largely grazing and hay meadowss – is comparatively rich in wildlife, with an abundance of butterflies. Above 800m, beech becomes increasingly common, and at around 1400m it forms an association with silver fir and sycamore known as Carpathian Beech Forest (*Fagetum carpaticum*). Spruce is dominant above this, and above 1700m comes the lower alpine zone, characterized by dwarf pine, juniper and low-growing goat willow, and then, from 1900m upwards, the higher alpine zone of grass, creeping shrubs, lichen, moss and ultimately bare rock.

Elsewhere, particularly on the **Transylvanian plateau**, there is much more oak and beech forest, although much has been cleared for farming. Until the twentieth century, large areas of eastern Romania – particularly southern Moldavia and Dobrogea – were covered by grassy steppes, the majority of which went under the plough after World War II, though remnant areas can still be found, some (such as Cheia Dobrogea, 38km northwest of Constanţa) protected as nature reserves.

In the **southwest** of the country, near the Iron Gates of the Danube, the spectacular Cerna Valley is notable for its more Mediterranean climate, with Turkey and downy oaks, Banat pine and sun-loving plant species on limestone rocks.

The **Danube Delta** is a unique habitat. Formed from the massive quantity of sediments brought down the river, it is Europe's most extensive wetland and the world's largest continuous reedbed. It is a uniquely important breeding area for birds, as well as a wintering area and a key stepping stone on one of the most important migration routes from northern Europe via the eastern Mediterranean to Africa.

Nature reserves have existed in Romania since the 1930s, and some 6.6 percent of the country is now protected. These reserves range from vast uninhabited areas to relatively modest, but still valuable, sites, including caves, rocks and even individual trees. The Retezat and Rodna mountains and the Danube Delta have been named as part of UNESCO's worldwide network of Biosphere Reserves, and at least ten other national parks are yet to be designated. These include the Bicaz and Nera gorges, the Cerna valley, and the Apuseni, Piatra Craiului and Căliman mountains.

Flora

In springtime, the **mountain meadows** of Romania are a riot of wild flowers, 12 percent of which are endemic to the Carpathians. Between April and July, depending on altitude, you should be able to find spectacular scenes of clover, hawkweed, burdock, fritillary and ox-eye daisy covered in butterflies and, at higher levels, gentians, white false helleborine, globeflower and crocus. **Alpine plants** include campanulas, saxifrage, orchids, alpine buttercup, pinks and, in a few places, edelweiss. The **hay meadows** lying below the mountain forest are also extremely rich in flowers.

In the warmer **southwest** of the country, the Turda, Cerna and Nera gorges and the Retezat mountains are home to sun-loving rarities. One of the most accessible flower-rich sites is the wonderful Zanoaga Gorge in the Bucegi mountains.

The **Danube Delta** is home to more than 1600 plant species, of three main groups. The floating islets (*plaur*) that occupy much of the Delta's area are largely composed of reeds (80 percent *Phragmites australis*), with mace reed, sedge, Dutch rush, yellow water-flag, water fern, water dock, water forget-me-not, water hemlock and brook mint. In the still backwaters, wholly submerged waterweeds include water-milfoil, hornwort and water-thyme; while floating on the surface you'll find water plantain, arrowhead, duckweed, water soldier, white and yellow waterlily, frog bit, marsh thistle and épi d'eau. The river banks are home to white willow and poplar, with isolated strands of alder and ash, while the more mature forests of Letea and Caraorman also contain oaks, elm, aspen and shrubs such as blackthorn, hawthorn and dog rose. The Romanian peony can be found in woodlands such as Babadag Forest, just to the south.

Birds

Europe's most important wetland, the **Danube Delta**, serves as a breeding area for summer visitors, a stopping-off point for migrants and a wintering ground for wildfowl; permanent residents are relatively few. Dedicated birders come from the end of March to early June, and from late July to October – but the Delta and the more accessible lakes and reedbeds to the south are worth a visit with binoculars at any season. The Delta lies on the major migration route from Africa via the eastern Mediterranean and northwards along the rivers of Russia to the Arctic.

The **spring period**, especially May, is an excellent time to visit, with the rare breeding species – black-winged pratincole, pygmy cormorant, glossy ibis, white and Dalmatian pelicans, and warblers – all arriving. The reedbeds are alive with the returned songbirds, most obviously the very noisy great reed warbler. These are accompanied by large numbers of waders on passage to wetlands far to the north, such as little stints, five species of sandpipers and vast flocks of ruff. By this time, the great colonies – of herons (night, grey and squacco herons, great white and little egrets), and of both species of cormorant – are at a peak of activity; the lower Danube holds most of the world population of the endangered pygmy cormorant. The wader colonies are also very active, and you will be scolded loudly when near the nests of avocets and black-winged stilts.

High summer is a good time to see the first of the returning waders, and the population of summer visitors peaks immediately after breeding. This is an excellent time to see formation-flying white pelicans (and the rare Dalmatian pelican), as well as birds of prey such as the colonial red-footed falcon, lesser spotted eagle, marsh harrier and long-legged buzzard.

In **winter**, the number of visiting birds in the Delta area is reduced but still impressive. Main visitors include most of the European population of great white herons (or egrets), at times the entire world population of red-breasted geese (around 70,000 birds) and up to a third of a million white-fronted geese; there are significant populations of other wildfowl including the exotic-looking red-crested pochard, as well as pintail, goldeneye, wigeon, teal, smew and red- and black-throated divers; just offshore the sea can teem with wintering black-necked grebes, and rough-legged buzzards are a common sight on roadside wires in open country.

On the **inland plains**, some species indicative of steppe country still persist, such as short-toed and calandra larks (the largest European lark), while summer visitors include the exotic-looking hoopoe, lesser-spotted and booted eagles, red-footed falcons, European rollers, bee-eaters and lesser grey shrikes – the last three often seen on roadside wires in Dobrogea and the lowlands.

Away from the Delta, the most worthwhile nature reserves are inevitably in the **mountains**; golden eagles are now rare, but ravens are common. On the tree line, black and three-toed woodpeckers can be found, together with ring ouzels in summer, while on the highest crags there are alpine accentors and wallcreepers, together with the common black redstart, water pipits and alpine swifts and, in some lower crags, crag martins and rock buntings. There are also birds usually associated with more northerly regions, such as shore larks and dotterel (breeding only in the Cindrel mountains).

Mountain forests are home to the very shy capercaillie, as well as the (slightly easier to see) hazel grouse and (in the north, around dwarf pine areas) black grouse. Restricted to the vast forests, mainly of spruce, is the nutcracker, as well as the crested, willow and coal tits and the crossbill. The forests are also home to raptors, including buzzards, honey buzzards, sparrowhawks and goshawks, and a number of owls, including the Ural owl, eagle owl, pygmy owl and Tengmalm's owl. The relatively healthy state of Romania's conifer forests favours some birds now rare elsewhere (for example in Scandinavia), notably the white-backed woodpecker.

Romania's extensive **lowland deciduous forests** harbour huge numbers of common European woodland birds – chaffinches, hawfinches, nuthatches, song thrushes, treecreepers and great, marsh and blue tits. Oak woods are home to the middle-spotted woodpecker, joined in summer by nightingales, wood warblers, chiffchaffs and common redstarts.

Romania is also a refuge for the white stork, whose large nests are characteristically built in the heart of human habitations, on telephone poles and chimneys. The much shyer and rarer black stork breeds in extensive areas of forest near water, for example along the Olt in southern Transylvania.

Animals

Romania has the most important national populations of **large carnivore species** – bear, wolf and lynx – in Europe. Having been protected under Ceauşescu for his own personal hunting, there are now five or six thousand **brown bear** in Romania, particularly in the eastern Carpathians. Although they do raid garbage bins on the outskirts of Braşov and in Poiana Braşov – as well as any mountain hut near or below the tree line – they are generally afraid of humans and will keep well clear unless you come between a female and her cubs in April or May. Whilst they will take prey as large as red deer (not to mention sheep, cattle and horses), they are by diet omnivorous, famously raiding wild bees' and wasps' nests not only for honey but also for the larvae. They will also eat carrion, especially wolf-kill, large amounts of wild fruit (occasionally raiding apple orchards), and beech mast. Bears are hunted, but in a strictly controlled way, and the population is at a healthy level.

There are currently around three thousand **wolves** in Romania, generally restricted to forests. Their prey consists almost entirely of deer, occasionally boar and chamois, and the odd sheep, and they pose no danger to humans. They are hunted, especially in winter, when their tracks can be followed in the snow. **Lynx** are fairly widespread (but very hard to spot) in hill forests and are the most specialized large predator of all; they take roe deer in forest areas and chamois above the tree line.

Red deer can be found in some lowland forests but are most common in spruce forest in hill areas. The stags' mating cries echo through the valleys in September and October, and it's sometimes possible to observe their ritual conflicts from a distance. Above the tree line in the Transylvanian Alps and the Rodna, the most visible mammal is the **chamois**, seen grazing in flocks with a lone male perched on the skyline to keep watch. **Wild boar** are also widespread, from the Delta and lowland forests all the way up to and beyond the tree line in the mountains. They appear mostly at night, and can leave a clearing looking as if it has been badly ploughed when they have finished digging for roots. Weighing up to 200kg, they have a reputation for aggression when protecting their young in the springtime.

Other mammals include the European bison, kept in a semi-wild state in several areas; the golden jackal, now spreading from its stronghold in the south, especially in Dobrogea; the wild cat, which occurs commonly in lowland forests as well as up to the highest mountain forests; the red fox, which is even more widespread, from the forests of the Delta to the highest mountain summits; and the badger, which is widespread but very uncommon. There are three species of polecat, all very shy, and in the mountain forests pine martens are common, as are beech martens in lower-altitude woods.

The Danube Delta is one of the last refuges of the European mink (still thriving there), and also home to enot (or raccoon dog), coypu and muskrat, all North American species that have escaped from fur farms in the former Soviet Union. European beaver was native to Transylvania and has recently been reintroduced there. Romania's predators depend to a large extent on rodents for their prey; in steppe areas (especially in Dobrogea) it is impossible to miss the charming European souslik, Romania's very own gopher. Three kinds of hamster occur, including the endemic Romanian hamster, and hikers in the Făgăraş, Retezat, Rodna and a few other areas will encounter the alpine marmot, living in colonies well above the tree line. In forest areas there are no fewer than four kinds of dormouse. Stoats and weasels are also widespread, as are bats.

The most frequently seen **amphibians** are the abundant little bombina toads: yellow-bellied toads in the hills and fire-bellied toads in the lowlands. More unusual amphibians include two species of spadefoot toad, the moor frog and the agile frog. The amazingly loud frog chorus of the Danube Delta and other lakes and reedbeds is produced by male marsh frogs. Newt fanciers find heaven in Romania's myriad ponds and watercourses; as well as the familiar warty, smooth and alpine newts there is the endemic Montandon's newt, restricted to the Eastern Carpathians. Fire salamanders with their vivid black and orange colouring are easily seen in the woods during or just after rain, while the exotic-looking green toad (with its trilling call) is frequently seen under village street lights as it hunts for bugs that are attracted by the light.

There is a healthy population of **snakes** – the commonest being the grass snake, found in the Danube Delta and up to some altitude in the mountains. In coastal areas is the more aquatic, fish-hunting dice snake; other non-venomous species include the smooth snake, four-lined snake and the impressively large whip snake. Europe's most venomous and fastest-moving snake, the horned viper, occurs near Băile Herculane, and the common viper (or adder) is more widespread, particularly in hill areas. The steppe viper (or Orsini's viper) survives in the Delta, for example in the woods north of Sfântu Gheorghe.

The warmer climate of the southern Banat and Dobrogea is especially suitable for **other reptiles** – not just snakes but also some exotic-looking lizards, such as the Balkan green lizard, the green lizard and the Balkan wall lizard. More everyday species, such as the sand lizard and viviparous lizard, are widespread. The aquatic European pond terrapin is common around the edge of lowland lakes and in the Danube Delta, and there are two species of tortoise: the rare Hermann's tortoise, found only in areas of the southwest such as the Cerna valley, and the more widespread spur-thighed tortoise, fairly common in woods in Dobrogea.

With little in the way of industry and an absence of fertilizers and pesticides in almost all hill areas, the river systems have impressive populations of **fish**, for instance grayling, in Carpathian hill streams. Six species of sturgeon occur in the Danube, and the picture for these is less rosy, as the Iron Gates dam prevents migration upstream. Rainbow trout have been less widely introduced than in western Europe, so that the native brown trout is much more common; the endemic Danube salmon or huchen is now very rare.

It is scarcely possible to avoid fish when in the Danube Delta; the common species caught are common carp, crucian carp, pike (especially in autumn), pikeperch or zander, and catfish or wels. In fact, the Delta is a remarkable place for fish, with catfish around 2m long often caught and confirmed accounts of even larger specimens showing some interest in taking village women fetching water from channel banks. Sturgeon migrate through the Delta, as do Danube mackerel. Several fairly rare goby species also occur, especially in lakes and lagoons south of the Delta. Most of these species have declined to some extent due to pollution, overfishing and eutrophication of the water due to algal blooms. For this reason, several areas of the Delta have become strictly protected reserves, with great efforts made to preserve the water quality.

Wildlife section by: James Roberts, a true friend of Romania, who died far too young

The environment

Communist Romania's mammoth increase in industrial output – particularly of steel and fertilizer – was achieved by a total disregard for any considerations other than maximizing production. Thus, industrial injuries were commonplace, while **energy consumption** was shockingly wasteful; **pollution** is calculated to affect 10 percent of the population (5 percent severely), and 20 percent of the country's territory. **Rubbish**, too, is a developing problem, as Western-style packaging takes over.

The most polluted sites are Copşa Mică, Zlatna and Baia Mare, where smelters produced acid rain and a cocktail of heavy metals that ran straight into the water system; life expectancy remains up to ten years below average in all three places. In **Baia Mare**, for example, the industrial zone was built upwind of the residential area, and in a valley subject to thermal inversions that trap the pollution. Almost as bad were the artificial fibre factories of **Brăila** and **Suceava** and the fertilizer and petrochemical plants in Arad, Dej, Făgăraş, Piteşti, Ploieşti and Târgu Mureş. Emissions halved after 1989, due to industrial recession; nowadays, while both air and water are far cleaner than they were, emissions are rising again, due to increasing prosperity. It will cost between €20 billion and €30 billion over the next two decades to bring Romania up to EU standards.

Additionally, the use of **fertilizers**, **pesticides** and **insecticides** has caused problems, damaging 900,000 hectares of agricultural land and leaving 200,000 hectares totally unproductive; agricultural nitrates, too, entered the drinking water supply, putting millions of people at risk, and many of the country's rivers are now dead. In January 2000, a dam at the Aurul goldmine near Baia Mare gave way, releasing water containing a hundred tonnes of cyanide, which made its way into Hungary, killing everything in the Someş and Tisa rivers – the situation wasn't helped by the chairman of Aurul's Australian owners claiming the fish had died of cold. In March that year, there was also a spill of sludge contaminated with heavy metals from a mine at Baia Borşa, which also made its way into the Tisa.

Furthermore, the damming of the Iron Gates and the dyking of the Danube flood plain has led to a dramatic cut in the **Danube's flow** through the Delta, leading to algal blooms and lower fish yields; unless flows can be speeded up, the Delta may die. The Black Sea is one of the most polluted areas in the world – toxic wastes, overfishing, and a one-fifth fall in freshwater inputs combining to disastrous effect. Surfeits of nutrients cause plankton blooms (red tides), leading to loss of light and dissolved oxygen, and thus decimating fish stocks.

Ceauşescu was determined to have his own **nuclear power station** at Cernavodă, on the Danube. However, construction standards were so appalling that it had to be almost totally rebuilt. The second reactor entered service in 2007, and the complex now produces eighteen percent of Romania's power. Thirty percent of power comes from hydroelectric dams, a wind power project is to be developed in Constanţa harbour, and the Austrian government is sponsoring a scheme in Călimăneşti to provide domestic hot water from geothermal energy.

The protection of **historical monuments** was upheld until 1977, when the Historical Monuments Administration was disbanded for daring to oppose Ceauşescu's plans for Bucharest's Civic Centre. There was no effective protection from then until 1989, and many towns have simply been gutted. In 1990, the bureau was re-established but without financial support, and the required legislation got stuck in parliament. In 2001, a law was at last passed to end the demolition of listed buildings, but most conservation to date has been achieved with funding from the Church, or, in the case of Saxon monuments, from Germany. **Biertan**, the **Bucovina** and **Horez monasteries**, and a group of wooden **Maramureş churches** have all become UNESCO World Heritage sites.

Music

The Carpathian mountains trace the cultural fault line separating Central Europe from the Balkans, sharply dividing the musical styles on either side. Of course such borders are rarely impermeable; the Romanian language is spoken on either side and there is plenty of cultural and musical cross-fertilization. Romanian music preserves almost archeological layers of development, from the "medieval" music of Ghimeş and Maramureş, to the "Renaissance" sounds of Mezőség and the more sophisticated music of Kalotaszeg.

Tours to study Romanian folk dance are organized by the Doina Foundation, Aarhuispad 22, 3067 PR Rotterdam, Netherlands (℡10/421 8622, Ⓦwww .stichtingdoina.nl), which also helps organize an annual Balkan festival in Zetten and sells flutes, boots, costumes and icons.

Transylvania

With its age-old ethnic mix, Transylvania's music is extraordinary, with wild melodies and dances lasting all night. While recognizably part of a Central European tradition, it also springs from a distinctly Transylvanian culture – the composers Bartók and Kodály found this the most fertile area for their folk-song

---

Classical music

Classical music was lavishly funded by the communist state and still has far less elitist connotations than in the West. Main cities have a philharmonic orchestra and/or an opera house, and tickets (available through the local Agenţia Teatrale) are cheap. Additionally, the Saxon communities have maintained a Germanic tradition of singing chorales by Bach and his contemporaries.

Romanian classical music remains virtually synonymous with **George Enescu**, born near Dorohoi in 1881. His *Romanian Rhapsodies* were first performed in 1903 and remain his most popular works; his *Third Violin Sonata* is his best chamber work and also has a Romanian flavour. Later works also showed experimental features, such as the use of a musical saw in his masterpiece, the opera *Oedipe*, the most comprehensive treatment of the myth, covering Oedipus's entire life from birth to death. There is a good modern recording (1989) featuring José van Dam. Romania's greatest pianist was **Dinu Lipatti** (Enescu's godson), who died aged just 33 from leukaemia in 1950. In his lifetime he was referred to as "God's chosen instrument". His recordings (just five CDs) have never been deleted; one of them, made in Besançon just months before his death, is particularly highly regarded. **Sergiu Ceilibidache** (1912–96) studied in Berlin and conducted the Berlin Philharmonic, the Swedish Radio Symphony Orchestra, the Stuttgart Radio Orchestra, and from 1980 the Munich Philharmonic, making his US debut only in 1984. Described as "transcendentally endowed", although not very interested in music outside the mainstream Germanic repertoire, he was also a perfectionist, demanding up to eighteen rehearsals for some concerts.

The most prominent **contemporary Romanian musicians** are soprano **Angela Gheorghiu** (born in 1965) – a true diva and regular performer at the world's greatest opera houses – and violinist Alex Bălanescu, founder of the **Bălanescu Quartet**, who has worked with David Byrne, Kraftwerk, Spiritualized, Gavin Bryars and Michael Nyman amongst others.

collecting trips in the early twentieth century. Music serves a social function, with regular weekly dances in some places, but everywhere music is played around Christmas, at weddings, sometimes at funerals and at other occasions.

The **Romanians** and **Hungarians** share many melodies and dances and it takes a very experienced ear to tell the difference (and even then, a tune may be described as Hungarian in one village and Romanian in another just over the hill). Romanian dances may have a slightly less regular rhythm than the Hungarian, but often the only difference between one tune and another is the language in which it is sung. There's even a unique recording of an old man from the village of Dimbău (Küküllődombó) singing a song with the first half of each line in Hungarian and the second half in Romanian.

The music of Transylvania sounds much less Balkan than that from over the Carpathians. The traditional ensemble is a **string trio** – a violin, playing the melody, and a rhythm section of viola (*contra*) and double bass, plus in certain parts of Transylvania, a cimbalom. The *contra* has just three strings and a flat bridge so it only plays chords, and it's the deep sawing of the bass and the rhythmic spring of the *contra* that gives Transylvanian music its particular sound. Often an extra violin or *contra* is added to give more volume.

Wedding parties

Wedding parties last a couple of days and often take place in a specially constructed wedding "tent", strung with ribbons and fir branches. Tables are piled high with garish cakes and bottles of *ţuică*, and fresh courses are served at regular intervals.

Wedding **customs** vary slightly from region to region but generally the band starts things off at the bride's or groom's house, accompanying the processions to the church and possibly playing for one of the real emotional high spots – the bride's farewell song (*cântecul miresei*) to her family and friends, and to her maiden life. While the marriage takes place in the church, the band plays for the young people, or those not invited to the feast, to dance in the street outside. Then there's another procession to the wedding feast where the musicians will play all night, alternating dances with songs to accompany feasting; there are even particular pieces for certain courses of the banquet.

Late in the evening comes the bride's dance (*jocul miresei*) when, in some villages, the guests dance with the bride in turn and offer money. Dances are strung together in sets up to twenty minutes long, starting with slow tunes and picking up speed. Things usually wind down by dawn on Sunday; people wander off home or collapse in a field somewhere, and then around lunchtime the music starts up again for another session until the late evening.

With the trend towards larger weddings, all sorts of **instruments** have started to find their way into bands. Most common is the piano-accordion, which, like the *contra*, plays chords, though lacking its rhythmic spring. You'll often hear a clarinet or the slightly deeper and reedier *taragot*, which sounds wonderful in the open air. Unfortunately, young people often demand guitars, drums and electric keyboards – along with appalling amplification, which is increasingly used, too, by traditional acoustic bands. Groups that stick unswervingly to the traditional line-up include the marvellous **Pălatca** band, recognized as one of the finest in Transylvania.

Gypsy bands

The band from Pălatca (Magyarpalatka), like most village musicians in Romania, are **Gypsies**. Gypsy communities all tend to live along one particular street in the village outskirts, often called Strada Muzicanţilor or Strada Lăutari – both meaning "Musicians' Street". Gypsy musicians will play for Romanian, Hungarian and Gypsy weddings alike and they know almost instinctively the repertoire required. Children grow up with the music in their blood, often playing alongside their parents from an early age.

It's difficult to highlight the **best bands** – there are dozens of them – but in addition to Pălatca, the following central Transylvanian villages have excellent bands (the names are given in their Romanian form with the Hungarian in brackets): Vaida-Cămăraş (Vajdakamarás), Suatu (Magyarszovát), Sopuru de Câmpie (Mezőszopor), Sângeorz-Băi (Oláhszentgyorgy) and Sic (Szék), one of the great treasure houses of Hungarian music.

For many, however, at least those outside Romania, Gypsy music is synonymous with two bands in particular, both of which have gone on to achieve world acclaim. The **Taraf de Haidouks**, from the village of Clejani near Bucharest, was formed in 1989, with a fairly fluid line-up, though it usually comprises between seven and a dozen musicians playing violins, flutes, double bass and cimbalom. Their recordings are extraordinary, packed with virtuoso performances, while their live shows – they tour relentlessly throughout Europe – are fantastically entertaining. Since 2002 several of the band's founders have died, and things will never be quite the same again. **Fanfare Ciocărlia**, from the tiny village of Zece Prăjini in Moldavia, is one of the finest Gypsy brass bands in the Balkans, a twelve-piece ensemble featuring tenor and baritone horns, trumpet, tubas, clarinets, saxophones and bass drum. Their extremely fast, high-energy sound is thrilling live.

The Hungarians

The music of the Hungarian minority has made most impact outside Transylvania, as the Hungarians consciously promoted the culture of their brethren in the region. Hungaroton, the state label, produced many excellent recordings, while Budapest-based groups such as **Muzsikás** and the **Ardealul Ensemble** are splendid ambassadors for the music.

Transylvania has always held a special place in Hungarian culture as it preserves archaic traditions and medieval settlement patterns that have disappeared in Hungary itself. Communist repression led the Hungarians to wear their traditional costumes, sing their songs and play their music as a statement of identity, even protest. National costume and dances are still more visible among the Hungarian minority than the majority Romanians (other than in Maramureş).

Regional styles

Within the overall Transylvanian musical language, there are hundreds of local dialects: the style of playing a particular dance can vary literally from village to village. But there are some broad musical regions where the styles are distinct and recognizable.

Bartók gathered much material around **Hunedoara**. The area is still musically very rich, though, strangely enough, a recent survey found that virtually the entire repertoire had changed. Further north is the area the Hungarians call **Kalotaszeg**, home to some of the region's most beautiful music. It straddles the main route from Cluj (Kolozsvár) to Hungary and Central Europe, and the influence of Western-style harmony shows itself in sophisticated minor-key accompaniment – a development of the last thirty or forty years. Kalotaszeg is famous for its men's dance, the *legényes*, and the slow *hajnali* songs performed in the early morning as a wedding feast dies down, which have a sad and melancholy character all their own.

One of the best of all recordings of Transylvanian music includes both these forms, featuring the Gypsy *primás* **Sándor Fodor** from Baciu (Kisbács), just west of Cluj.

Probably the richest area for music is known to the Romanians as **Câmpia Transilvanei** and to the Hungarians as **Mezőség**. This is the Transylvanian Heath, north and east of Cluj – a poor, isolated region whose music preserves a much more primitive feel with strong major chords moving in idiosyncratic harmony.

Further east is the most densely populated Hungarian region, the **Székelyföld** (Székely Land), a wild and mountainous land where the music is different once again, with eccentric ornamentation and very often a cimbalom in the band.

For Hungarian-speakers, the songs are fascinating as they preserve old-style elements that survive nowhere else. One village ballad about a terrible massacre of the Székelys by the Habsburgs in 1764, often sung as if it had happened yesterday, recounts their flight over the Carpathians into Moldavia, where they preserved music and customs that are no longer found in the Székelyföld itself. In those outer reaches, the string bands of Transylvania have given way to a solo violin or flute accompanying the dances.

Moldavia and Maramureş

The **music of Moldavia** – with its archaic pipe and drum style – sounds wild and otherworldly, split across the divide between Transylvania and the Balkans. The music of the Csángós (Hungarians living in the Ghimeş (Gyimes) valley) often features peculiar duos of violin (or flute) and *gardon* – a sort of cello played (usually by the fiddler's wife) by hitting its strings with a stick. The fiddle playing is highly ornamented and the rhythms complex and irregular. The extraordinary Csángó singer **Ilona Nyisztor** from Oneşti (in Bacău county) has a growing reputation.

The music of **Maramureş** and **Oaş**, in the northwestern corner of Romania, includes magic songs and spells of incantation against sickness and the evil eye. You can still find Sunday-afternoon village dances, and a *băută* or musical party can be arranged on the slightest pretext. From birth, through courtship and marriage to death, life has a musical accompaniment.

The music of Maramureş, while recognizably Transylvanian, is reminiscent of Carpathian Ukraine. As often in the highlands, the music is played predominantly by Romanians, not Gypsies. With violin (*cetera*), guitar (*zongora*) and drum (*doba*), it has a fairly primitive sound, lacking beguiling harmonies and with a repeated drone chord on the *zongora* (with only four or five strings, often played vertically and back to front). Hundreds of years ago, much of the music of Europe sounded much like this. Probably in the 1930s a strange hybrid instrument appeared here and in Bihor (around Oradea), the *higheghe* or *vioară cu goarnă*, a violin with an old gramophone horn for amplification.

The music of Oaş is even odder, with just a *zongora* accompanying a high-pitched fiddle, playing the melody on two strings at once; singing is in a similarly harsh, high-pitched style.

A *zăcală de băut* or drinking song is an instrumental piece during which people call out improvised couplets, usually men teasing women and vice versa; a *zăcală de jucat* is a dance, of which the most popular are the *bărbătesc* (men's dance), a circle dance for men with similar improvised lyrics, and the *învârtita*, a quick couple dance.

Wallachia

Most village bands in **Wallachia** are comprised of **Gypsies**: the group is generally named **Taraf** followed by the name of their village or their lead fiddler (*primás*). These musicians (*lăutari*) are professionals who play a vital function in village life, yet their music sounds altogether different from that of their Transylvanian counterparts. The word *taraf* comes from the Arabic and suggests the more oriental flavour of this music. Songs are often preceded by an instrumental improvisation called *taksim*, another name borrowed from the Middle East.

The lead instrument is the fiddle, played in a highly ornamented style. The middle parts are taken by the *ţambal* (cimbalom), which fills out the harmony and adds a rippling texture. At the bottom is the double bass, ferociously plucked rather than bowed Transylvanian style. In the old days, you'd always find a *cobză* (lute) in such bands, but it has given way to the *ţambal*, guitar and accordion. The staple dances are the *horă*, *sârbă* and *brâu* – all danced in a circle.

In Romanian, the word *cânta* means both "to sing" and "to play an instrument", and the *lăutari* of Wallachia usually do both. Whereas in Transylvania the bands play exclusively dance music, the musicians in southern Romania have an impressive repertoire of **epic songs and ballads**, including specific marriage songs and legendary tales like *Şarpele* (*The Snake*) or exploits of brigands. One tune you hear played by *lăutari* all over Romania, and in concerts worldwide, is *Ciocărlia* (*The Lark*).

The region's most renowned Gypsy music comes from **Clejani**, a ramshackle village southwest of Bucharest (see p.87); many of its five hundred or so Gypsies are professional musicians, much in demand throughout the area, and it's also where the Taraf de Haidouks, and a flashier spin-off called Clejani Express, hail from.

The doină

The **doină** is a free-form, semi-improvised ancient song tradition. With poetic texts of grief, bitterness, separation and longing, it might be called the Romanian blues. It is essentially private music, sung to oneself at moments of grief or reflection, although nowadays the songs are often performed by professional singers or in instrumental versions. Traditional *doinăs* can still be found in Oltenia, between the Olt and Danube rivers in the south of the country.

Flutes and pipes

The pastoral way of life is fast disappearing in Romania, and with it the traditional instrumental repertoire of the *fluier* (shepherd's flute). But there is one form – a sort of folk tone poem – that is still regularly played all over the country: the **shepherd who lost his sheep**. Referred to as early as the sixteenth century by the Hungarian poet Bálint Balassi, it begins with a sad, *doină*-like tune as a shepherd laments his lost flock. Then he sees his sheep in the distance and a merry dance tune takes over, only to return to the sad lament when he realizes it's just a group of stones. Finally the sheep are found and the whole thing ends with a lively celebratory dance.

For years, Romania's best-known musician on the international stage was **Gheorghe Zamfir**, composer of the film soundtrack for *Picnic at Hanging Rock*. He plays *nai*, or **panpipes**, which have existed in Romania since ancient times. In the eighteenth century "Wallachian" musicians were renowned abroad and the typical ensemble consisted of violin, *nai* and *cobză*. But by the end of the next century the *nai* had begun to disappear and after World War I only a handful of players were left. One of these was the legendary **Fanica Luca** (1894–1968), who taught Zamfir his traditional repertoire. Nowadays, Zamfir plays material from all over the place, often accompanied by the organ of Marcel Cellier; **Radu Simion** is another fine player.

The Banat

The **Banat**, Romania's western corner, is ethnically very mixed, with communities of Hungarians, Serbs, Slovaks, Germans and Gypsies living alongside the Romanians. Its music is fast, furious and relatively new, having absorbed a lot from the *novokomponovana* or turbofolk music of neighbouring Serbia. Exemplified by the Taraf de Carancebeş, it's extremely popular, played all the time on national radio and by Gypsy bands everywhere. Probably its attraction is its fast, modern, urban sound, with saxophones and frequently erotic lyrics.

The Ceauşescu legacy

Nicolae Ceauşescu's legacy covers even folk music, which was manipulated into a sort of "fakelore" to glorify the dictator and present the rich past of the Romanian peasantry. Huge sanitized displays called **Cântarea Romaniei** (Song of Romania) were held in regional centres around the country with thousands of folk-costumed peasants bussed out to picturesque hillsides to sing and dance. This was shown on television every Sunday (indeed, programmes of this kind may still be used to fill the odd half-hour gap in the TV schedule). The words of songs were often changed – removing anything deemed to be religious or questioning the peasants' love of their labours, and replacing it with bland patriotic sentiments or hymns to peace.

This gave folklore a pretty bad name among the educated classes, though the peasants were hardly bothered by it. They just did what they were told for Cântarea Romaniei and got on with their real music in the villages. The fact is that traditional music still flourishes throughout Romania – probably more than anywhere else in Europe – not thanks to Ceauşescu, but despite him.

Discography

Many of these recordings can be bought from Passion Music in the UK (☏01256/770 747, ⓦwww.passiondiscs.co.uk); see also ⓦwww.hungaroton.hu, www.fono.hu, www.etnofon.hu, www.crammed.be, www.cdroots.com and www.bbc.co.uk/radio3.

General compilations

Romania: Musical Travelogue (Auvidis/Silex, France). An excellent disc with music from the Banat, Maramureş and Wallachia, including good music by ethnic minorities and beautiful *cobză* playing by Dan Voinicu.

Romania: Wild Sounds from Transylvania, Wallachia & Moldavia (World Network, Germany). The best overall anthology of Romanian music, with great ensembles including the Taraf de Haidouks and the Fanfare Ciocărlia.

Transylvanian music

Romanian, Hungarian and Gypsy village bands, as well as *táncház* groups from Budapest.

Ardealul Ensemble *Gypsy Music From Transylvania* (Ethnophonie, Romania). Instrumental music led by Emil Mihaiu, perhaps the best fiddler in Transylvania. Excellent notes. Also Emil Mihaiu Ensemble, *Romanian and Hungarian Music from Transylvania* (Ethnophonie).

Budatelke Band *Budatelke /Szászszantgyörgy* (Fonó, Hungary). The village band of Budatelke in northern Mezőség, playing mainly Romanian repertoire plus Hungarian, Gypsy and Saxon tracks.

Sándor Fodor *Hungarian Folk Music from Transylvania* (Hungaroton, Hungary). From the Kalotaszeg region's most respected Gypsy fiddler, this compelling disc of both Hungarian and Romanian music has fantastic energy and bite. One of the essential Transylvanian records. Also *The Blues at Dawn* (Fonó, Hungary), a beautifully produced CD of the slow, melancholy *hajnali* (morning songs).

The Mácsingó Family *Báré – Magyarpalatka* (Fonó, Hungary). One of the important musical Gypsy families from the villages of Báré and Déva in central Transylvania. This may be too raw for some tastes – the bass saws, grates and often slides onto its notes and the lead fiddle is heavily ornamented, drawing energy and emotion out of every note – but it is the real thing.

 Muzsikás *Máramaros* (Hannibal/ Ryko, UK). A fascinating CD

The End of the Millennium in the Romanian Village (Ethnophonie, Germany). A fine Romanian-produced collection of traditional bands from all over the country.

from the top Hungarian *táncház* group joined by two veteran Gypsy musicians on fiddle and cimbalom to explore the lost Jewish repertory of Transylvania, distinguishable by the Oriental-sounding augmented intervals in the melody. Also *Blues for Transylvania* and *Morning Star*, fine selections of Hungarian music from Transylvania, and *The Bartók Album*, re-creating the music collected by Bartók (all Hannibal/Ryko, UK).

Ökrös Ensemble *Transylvanian Portraits* (Koch, US). Comprehensive guide to the various Transylvanian styles by one of the best Budapest *táncház* groups. Stunning fiddle-playing by Csaba Ökrös on the last track.

Palatca Band *Magyarpalatka – Hungarian Folk Music from the Transylvanian Heath* (Hungaroton, Hungary). Probably the most celebrated band of central Transylvania, led by members of the Codoba family in the village of Magyarpalatka and typically comprising two fiddles, two contras and bass. A beautiful selection of traditional dance sets – one CD from the archives, the other recent.

Katalin Szvorák, Márton Balogh, Márta Sebestyén and the Hegedos Ensemble *Tündérkert (Fairyland) – Hungarian and Romanian Folk Music from Transylvania* (Hungaroton, Hungary). Released in 1988 and something of a classic, a cross section of tunes from the various regions of Transylvania.

Various *Prímások – Musicians from Transylvania and Moldavia* (Etnofon, Hungary). A great selection of

Hungarian bands, plus a few Csángó musicians.

Szászcsávás Band *Transylvanian Folk Music* (Thermal Comfort, Hungary). Szászcsávás (Ceuaş in Romanian) is a predominantly Hungarian village in the Kis-Küküllő region with one of the area's best Gypsy bands. They have a wide dance repertoire, including Hungarian, Romanian, Saxon and Gypsy tunes.

Váralmási Band *Váralmási Pici Aladárés Bandája* (Fonó, Budapest). One of the last old-time Kalotaszeg groups, whose *primás* (leader) died shortly after the recording in 1997. Includes a bizarre Jewish tango.

Various *Musiques de Transylvanie* (Fonti Musicale, Belgium). One of the best introductions to Transylvanian music, featuring mainly Hungarian repertoire from Kalotaszeg, Mezőség and Ghimeş plus Romanian dances from Bihor and Moldavia.

Various *Romania – Music for Strings from Transylvania* (Chant du Monde, France). A great collection of dance music played by village bands from the Câmpia Transilvaniei, Maramureş and Oaş. Excellent notes and photos, too.

Various *Visa – Traditional Hungarian Music from the Transylvanian Heath* (Fonó, Hungary). From the Zoltán Kallós Archive, recorded in the Mezőség village of Visa in 1964–65 and 1987.

Various *La Vraie Tradition de Transylvanie* (Ocora, France). A pioneering disc from the 1970s that highlighted real peasant music from Maramureş and Transylvania when sanitized folklore was prevalent. It features some excellent ensembles, bagpipes and a violin with a horn, and from Maramureş there's Gheorghe Covaci, son of a fiddler recorded by Bartók in 1913.

Hungarian music from Ghimeş and Moldavia

Mihály Halmágyi *Hungarian Music from Gyimes* (Hungaroton, Hungary). Halmágyi, a veteran Csángó fiddler from Ghimeş, played a violin with a resonating fifth string, producing strange and wild music. Dances, laments, and a great performance of "the shepherd and his lost sheep", with running commentary.

Ilona Nyisztor *To The Fat Of The Earth, To The Sun's Little Sister* (Fonó, Hungary), *The Little Bird Has Gone Away* and *Pusztinai Nagy Hegy Alatt – Csángó Hungarian Songs from Moldavia*

(both Etnofon, Hungary). Ilona Nyisztor sings Csángó songs handed down through the generations.

Various *Moldavia Csángómagyar "Síposok" – Csango-Hungarian Bagpipers of Moldavia* (Fonó, Hungary). Field recordings (1973–2001) of the unearthly Csángó bagpipe music.

János Zerkula *János Zerkula and the Szigony Ensemble* (Folk Europa, Hungary). János Zerkula, a renowned Csángó fiddler from Ghimeş, performs laments, songs and dances accompanied by gardon and flute.

Maramureş

Iza *Craciun in Maramureş* (*Christmas in Maramureş*) (Buda/Musique du Monde, France). *Zongoră*-player Ioan Pop, with various fiddlers and drummer Ioan Petreuş, is trying to keep the traditional

style intact. Excellent notes and translations.

Pitigoi Ensemble *Musiques de Mariage et de Fêtes Roumaines* (Arion,

France). The best selection of the extraordinary music of Oaş, played by the Pitigoi brothers. Also a good selection of music from Maramureş and Bihor.

Ioan "Popicu" Pop and Ensemble *Romanian, Ukrainian and Jewish Music from Maramureş* (Ethnophonie, Romania). Exploring links between the music of Maramureş, Carpathian Ukraine, and the region's Jewish heritage: the *hori* are sung individually or in groups, with or without accompaniment; the *zicali* (instrumental pieces) are performed on fiddles, guitars and drums.

Various *The Edge of the Forest: Romanian Music from Transylvania* (Music of the World, US). Dances from Codru and Chioar (southern Maramureş), part of the central Transylvanian tradition, and a few tracks from Maramureş proper and Oaş.

Various *Fiddle Music from Maramureş* (Steel Carpet, UK). Peasant fiddlers recorded in their homes in the Mara Valley.

Various *Musiques de Mariage de Maramureş* (Ocora, France). Maramureş wedding music, performed by three village bands.

Lowland music compilations

Romania: Wedding Music from Wallachia (Auvidis/Ethnic, France). Songs and dance tunes from various bands including members of the Taraf de Haidouks and more urban repertoire from Ion Albeşteanu.

Taraf: Romanian Gypsy Music (Music of the World, US). A very

good selection of tracks from various Wallachian *tarafuri* including members of the Taraf de Haidouks. Mostly small ensembles of a brace of violins, *ţambal* and bass, with *cobză* lute on a couple of tracks.

Specific artists

Ion Albeşteanu *The Districts of Yesteryears* (Buda/Musique du Monde, France). Albeşteanu, who died in 1998, was an expressive violinist and singer. Here he is accompanied by a good band with beautifully textured *ţambal*, accordion and *cobză* playing. "At the Reed House", sung in an intimate "head voice", is quite lovely. Good notes.

Alexander Bălanescu *Possessed* (Mute), a fusion of classical, pop and jazz; *Luminitza* and *Angels and Insects* (Mute), scores to the films of the same name; and *Lume Lume* (Mute), a live festival soundtrack, all serve to demonstrate Bălanescu's diverse range. His most recent recording, *Maria T* (Mute), is a gorgeous reworking of the songs of the legendary Romanian singer Maria Tănase.

Fanfare Ciocărlia *Radio Paşcani* and *Iag Bari* (Piranha, Germany). Frenetic romps, punchily recorded, with some fearsomely fast dance numbers, the pace occasionally breaks for a *doină*. Their most recent release, *Queens and Kings* (Asphalt Tango, Germany), is superb, featuring collaborations with other Gypsy legends such as Šaban Bajramovič, Esma Redzepova and Ljiljana Butler. There's also a terrific live concert DVD, *Gypsy Brass Legends* (Asphalt Tango, Germany).

Panseluţa Feraru *Lautar Songs from Bucharest* (Long Distance, France). A live recording by the veteran "restaurant singer" (indicating that she's a cut above other Gypsy singers), with great backing from a band led by husband Gheorghe Stephane.

Nicolae Gutsa *The Greatest Living Gypsy Voice* (Auvidis/Silex, France). Nicolae Gutsa is a very popular singer, performing traditional music in a contemporary style. Despite the absurd title, this is a great disc.

Trio Pandelescu *Trio Pandelescu* (Auvidis/Silex, France). Virtuoso accordionist Vasile Pandelescu played for many years with Gheorghe Zamfir. Recorded live with high-quality, intimate playing, delicate moments of real poetry, and all the requisite fire; including a couple of beautiful *ţambal* solos by his son Costel.

Maria Tănase *Malediction d'Amour* (Oriente, Germany). A versatile talent, Tănase distinguished herself as an actress, an operetta singer, a music-hall star, but mainly as the finest interpreter of Romanian folk songs.

Taraf de Carancebeş *Musiciens du Banat* (Silex, France). A five-piece band of saxophone, trumpet, clarinet, accordion and bass. Stunning virtuoso playing, explaining the popularity of the Banat style.

🏃 Taraf de Haidouks *Honourable Brigands, Magic Horses and Evil Eye, Dumbala Dumbala* (Crammed, Belgium). Romania's most recorded Gypsy band allows you to trace the dynamic development of Gypsy music in Wallachia as new styles are absorbed without diluting the distinctive flavour of the *taraf*. *Honourable Brigands* is the best starting point, while 2001's live set, *Band of Gypsies*, is probably their best-known recording in the West. 2007's *Maşkaradă* is altogether different, featuring classical interpretations. There's also a marvellous DVD, *The Continuing Adventures of the Taraf de Haidouks*, comprising an entire UK concert, documentaries, interviews and rare archive footage of the band.

Other recordings

Dumitru Fărcaş & Marcel Cellier *The Art of the Romanian Taragot* (ARC Music Production, UK) and *Taragot et Orgue* (Pierre Verany Records, France). One of the leading players of the clarinet-like *taragot*, here with Zamfir's accompanist on church organ.

Toni Iordache *A Virtuoso of the Cimbalom 2* (Electrecord, Romania). One of the great virtuosi of the cimbalom (dulcimer), accompanied by small folk orchestras.

Luca Novac accompanied by the Orchestras of Radu Simon and Paraschiv Oprea *A Virtuoso of the Taragot* and Petrica Pasca accompanied by the Rapsozii Zarandului Band *Un Virtuose du Taragote* (both Electrecord, Romania). Two of the Banat's numerous *taragot* virtuosi.

The Rough Guide to the Music of Romanian Gypsies A fantastic introduction to the irrepressible sounds of Gypsy music, with twenty tracks plus enhanced data and links.

The Rough Guide to Music of the Gypsies and The Rough Guide to Music of the Balkan Gypsies Romania is represented on both these CDs by the Taraf de Haidouks and Fanfare Ciocărlia.

Radu Simion *Pan pipe concert* (Electrecord, Romania). Simion is one of the most gifted interpreters of the *nai* (panpipe), here accompanied by various folk orchestras.

Gheorghe Zamfir *Folksongs from Romania* (Delta, US). Born in Bucharest in 1941, *nai* player Zamfir must be Romania's most recorded musician, with albums of easy-listening arrangements of anything from Vivaldi to Andrew Lloyd-Webber. Zamfir's music has little to do with the traditional music of Romania, but his arrangements of *doinas* and folk tunes have an ethereal beauty.

Various *Roumanie: polyphonie vocale des Aroumains* (Le Chant du Monde, France). CNRS/Musée de l'Homme recordings of the Romanians living in Dobrogea, Bulgaria and elsewhere in the Balkans. Hard-core ethnic stuff.

Various *YIKHES: Klezmer recordings from 1907–1939* (Trikont, Germany). Remastered 78s, including a couple of 1910 tracks by Belf's Romanian Orchestra, virtually the only European Klezmer band of the period to have been recorded.

Music section by Simon Broughton

Dracula and vampires

Truth, legends and fiction swirl around the figure of **Dracula** like a cloak, and perceptions of him differ sharply. In Romania today, schoolbooks and historians extol him as a patriot and a champion of order in lawless times, while the outside world knows him as the vampire count of a thousand cinematic fantasies derived from Bram Stoker's novel of 1897 – a spoof-figure or a ghoul.

The disparity in images is easily explained, for while vampires feature in native folklore, Romanians make no associations between them and the historical figure of Dracula, the Wallachian prince Vlad III, known in his homeland as Vlad Țepeș – **Vlad the Impaler**. During his lifetime (c.1431–76) Vlad achieved renown beyond Wallachia's borders as a successful fighter against the Turks and a ruthless ruler; his reputation for cruelty spread throughout Europe via the newly invented printing presses and the word of his political enemies – notably the Transylvanian Saxons. At this time, Vlad was not known as a vampire, although some charged that he was in league with the Devil – or (almost as bad) that he had converted to Catholicism.

The historical Dracula

He was not very tall, but very stocky and strong, with a cold and terrible appearance, a strong and aquiline nose, swollen nostrils, a thin reddish face in which very long eyelashes framed large wide-open green eyes; the bushy black eyebrows made them appear threatening. ... The swollen temples increased the bulk of his head. A bull's neck connected his head to his body from which black curly locks hung on his wide-shouldered person.

Such was the papal legate's impression of **Vlad Țepeș** – then in his thirties and a prisoner at the court of Visegrád in Hungary. Born in Sighișoara, he was raised at Târgoviște after his father, Vlad Dracul, became Voivode of Wallachia in 1436. Vlad's privileged childhood effectively ended in 1442, when he and his brother Radu were sent by their father as hostages to Anatolia, to curry favour with the Turkish Sultan. Vlad Dracul incurred the enmity of Iancu de Hunedoara, prince of Transylvania, who arranged his murder in 1447; his sons were released to be pawns in the struggle between the expanding Turkish empire, Iancu and the new ruler of Wallachia. The experience of five years of Turkish captivity and years of exile in Moldavia and Transylvania shaped Vlad's personality irrevocably, and educated him in guile and terrorism.

Seeking a vassal, Iancu helped Vlad to become **ruler of Wallachia** in 1456 but promptly died, leaving him dangerously exposed. Signing a defence and trade pact with the Saxons of Brașov, Vlad quickly decided that it was also prudent to pay an annual tribute of 10,000 gold ducats to the Sultan while he consolidated his power in Wallachia. For generations the boyar families had defied and frequently deposed their own rulers, including Vlad's father and his elder brother Mircea, whom they buried alive.

His method of law enforcement was simple: practically all crimes and individuals offending him were punished by death, and Vlad's customary means of execution was **impalement**. Victims were bound spread-eagled while a stake was hammered up their rectum, and then were raised aloft and left to die in agony, for all to see.

Vlad moved among his subjects in disguise, testing their honesty by leaving coins in shops and slaying all who kept them; foreigners reported the demise of theft, and Vlad symbolically placed a golden cup by a lonely fountain for anyone to drink from.

On Easter Day in 1459, Vlad eliminated the potentially rebellious boyars en masse by inviting them and their families to dine at his palace; guards then entered and seized them, impaling many forthwith, while the remainder were marched off to labour at Poienari. In a similar vein, he invited Wallachia's disabled, unemployed and work-shy to feast with him at Târgovişte, and asked if they wished to be free of life's sufferings. Receiving an affirmative reply, Vlad had them all burnt, justifying his action as a measure to ensure that none of his subjects should ever suffer from poverty or disability.

All this was but a ramp for Vlad's ambition to be the acknowledged ruler of a mighty power, which caused much feuding with the Saxons of Braşov, Sibiu and the Bârsa Land. It began in 1457, when he accused them of supporting claimants to his throne, and decided to end the Saxon merchants' practice of trading freely throughout Wallachia. When they persisted, Vlad had them impaled, and led his army through the Red Tower Pass to burn Saxon villages. In 1460 he annihilated the forces of his rival, Dan III, who invaded with the support of Braşov; and on this occasion dined in a garden among the impaled bodies of his enemies, using a holy icon as a dish, according to the *Chronicon Mellicense*. A month later, he attacked the Bârsa Land, and impaled hundreds of townsfolk on Sprenghi Hill within sight of Braşov's defenders before marching off to ravage the Făgăraş region.

At the same time, Vlad plotted to turn **against the Turks** in alliance with his cousin Stephen of Moldavia and the Hungarian monarchy. Having defaulted on tribute payments for two years, and nailed the turbans of two emissaries to their heads when they refused to doff them, Vlad **declared war** by raiding Turkish garrisons from Vidin to Giurgiu. A massive army led by Sultan Mehmet II crossed the Danube into Wallachia in 1462, but found itself advancing through countryside denuded of inhabitants, food and water, "with the sun burning so that the armour of the ghazzis could well be used to cook kebabs". As the invaders approached the capital, Târgovişte, they found 20,000 Turkish and Bulgarian captives impaled on a forest of stakes 1km by 3km wide, and retreated in disorder.

Vlad's downfall has been attributed in part to the Saxons, who defamed him throughout Europe after he had raised customs duties to pay for his army. They probably forged the implausible "treason note" (in which Vlad purportedly offered to help the Sultan capture Transylvania) – the pretext for Mátyás Corvinus to order Vlad's arrest in 1462, after a fresh Turkish attack had forced him to flee over the Făgăraş mountains from Poienari. Until 1475 he was a "guest" at Visegrád, where Mátyás would introduce him to Turkish ambassadors to disconcert them; Wallachia's throne was occupied by Vlad's pliable brother Radu "The Handsome", who had once served as the Sultan's catamite. Having married a relative of Mátyás, Vlad was released to continue the anti-Turkish struggle, spending a year in Sibiu (the townsfolk deeming it politic to be hospitable) and regaining his throne in 1476. His triumph was short-lived, however, for Radu offered the boyars an alternative to "rule by the stake" and a chance to placate the Turks, which they seized gratefully. In circumstances that remain unclear (some say that a servant was bribed to slay him), Vlad was betrayed and killed. His head disappeared – supposedly sent to the Sultan as a present – while his decapitated body was reputedly buried at Snagov Monastery, where it's said to remain today.

The lack of an inscription on Vlad's tomb or of portraits of him in medieval church frescoes suggests that attempts were made for some time to erase his memory in Romania, although he was remembered in the nineteenth century, and also in the Ceaușescu epoch, as a fighter for national independence.

Vampires

Horrible though his deeds were, Vlad was not accused of **vampirism** during his lifetime. However, vampires were an integral part of folklore in Eastern and Southeastern Europe, known as *vámpír* in Hungarian and *strigoi* in Romanian. In essence, a vampire is an **undead corpse** that fails to decay, no matter how long in the grave. Vampirism can be contagious, or people might occasionally be born as vampires, bearing stigmata such as a dark-coloured spot on the head or a rudimentary tail. However, a vampire is usually created when a person dies and the soul is unable to enter heaven or hell. The reason may be that the person has died in a "state of sin" – by suicide, for example, or holding heretical beliefs – or because the soul has been prevented from leaving the body. Hanging was a form of death dreaded by Romanians, who believed that tying the neck "forces the soul down outward"; while the Orthodox custom of shrouding mirrors in the home of the deceased was intended to prevent the soul from being "trapped" by seeing its reflection. As Catholicism and Orthodoxy competed for adherents in the wake of the Ottoman withdrawal from the Balkans, priests also claimed that the cemetery of the opposing church was unconsecrated land, thereby raising the fear of vampires rising from the grave.

Once created, a vampire is almost immortal, and becomes a menace to the living. In Romanian folklore, vampires frequently return to their former homes at night, where they can be excluded by smearing garlic around the doors and windows, or propitiated with offerings of food and drink. A newborn baby must be guarded until it is christened, lest a vampire sneak in and transform it into another vampire. Two nights of the year are especially perilous: **April 23**, St George's Day (when, as Jonathan Harker was warned in Bram Stoker's novel, "all the evil things in the world will have full sway"), and **November 29**, St Andrew's Eve. On that night, vampires rise with their coffins on their heads, lurk about their former homes, and then gather to fight each other with hempen whips at crossroads. In Gypsy folklore, *mulé* (vampires) control the roads, trees and everything else at the exact moment of midday, when the sun casts no shadow. Interestingly, Gypsies only fear their own *mulé* – the ghosts and vampires of *gadjé* (non-Gypsies) are of no account.

The greatest danger was presented by **vampire epidemics**, which began in the seventeenth century, perhaps due to the influence of Gypsy folklore. Although in Stoker's novel and later films vampires must bite their victims and suck blood to cause contagion, in Eastern European folklore the vampire's look or touch can suffice. A classic account refers to the Austro-Hungarian village of Haidam in the 1720s, where, before witnesses, a man dead ten years returned to his son's cottage, touched him on the shoulder and then departed. The man died the next morning. Alarmed by this report and others relating how long-dead villagers were returning to suck their children's blood, the local military commander ordered several graves to be exhumed, revealing corpses showing no signs of decay. All were burnt to ashes – one of the classic methods of exterminating vampires. Another epidemic occurred from 1727 in the Serbian village of Medvegia. A soldier claimed to have been attacked by a vampire in Greece (where vampire legends also abound), and died upon his return home. Thereafter, many villagers swore they had seen him at night, or had dreamt about him, and ten weeks later complained of inexplicable weakness. The body was exhumed, was found to have blood in its mouth, and so had a stake driven through its heart. Despite this precaution, there was an outbreak of vampirism a few years later, and of the fourteen corpses examined by a medical commission in 1732, twelve were found to be "unmistakably in the vampire condition" (undecayed).

This was the catalyst for an explosion of interest across Europe, until Pope Benedict XIV and the Austrian and Prussian governments declared vampirism a fraud and made it a crime to dig up dead bodies. But in 1899 Romanian peasants in Caraşova dug up thirty corpses and tore them to pieces to stop a diphtheria epidemic, and in 1909 a Transylvanian castle was burned down by locals who believed that a vampire emanating from it was causing the deaths of their children. As recently as 1988, near Niş in Serbia, a 13-year-old girl was killed by her family, who believed her to be a vampire.

Sceptics may dismiss vampires and vampirism entirely, but some of the related phenomena have rational or scientific explanations. The "return of the dead" can be explained by premature burial, which happened frequently in the past. Nor is the drinking of blood confined to legendary, supernatural creatures – numerous examples can be found in the annals of criminology and psychopathology.

Bram Stoker's Dracula

The first respectable **literary work** to arise out of the European vampire craze was Goethe's *The Bride of Corinth* (1797), soon followed by Polidori's *The Vampyre*, which arose out of the same blood-curdling holiday on Lake Geneva in 1816 that produced Mary Shelley's *Frankenstein*. Other variations followed, by Kleist, E.T.A. Hoffmann, Mérimée, Gogol, Dumas, Baudelaire, Arminius Vambery, and Sheridan Le Fanu, whose *Carmilla* features a lesbian vampire in Styria.

These fired the imagination of **Bram Stoker** (1847–1912), an Anglo-Irish civil servant who became manager to the great actor Sir Henry Irving in 1878 and wrote a few other novels, now being rediscovered. In 1890 he conceived the suitably *fin-de-siècle* idea of a vampire novel set in Styria, with an antihero called "Count Wampyr"; but after detailed research in Whitby Public Library and the British Museum's Reading Room, the setting moved east to Transylvania, and **Count Dracula** was born. Stoker was possibly influenced by the "Jack the Ripper" murders a decade earlier in Whitechapel; he lived there for a time while writing his book. The author delved deep into Romanian folklore, history and geography, and the book is masterly in its mixing of fantasy and precise settings.

Other books on the same theme followed, but it was the advent of cinema and the horror **film** that ensured the fame of Dracula. The silent *Nosferatu* (1922) is perhaps the greatest vampire film, followed by Béla Lugosi's 1931 *Dracula*, while Hammer's 1958 classic *Dracula* boasted the dream coupling of Christopher Lee as the Count and Peter Cushing as Van Helsing. The BBC's *Count Dracula* (1978) is the most faithful to Stoker's novel, while Coppola's *Bram Stoker's Dracula* (1992) confuses things by including the historic Vlad Ţepeş in a prelude. There is also a fine tradition of **spoofs** such as *Love at First Bite* (1979), which opens with the communists expelling Dracula from his castle, not to mention *Count Duckula* (1988–93), the vegetarian vampire duck.

Books

The surge in interest in Eastern Europe since 1989, and the particularly dramatic nature of Romania's revolution and its problems since then, have led to several excellent writers visiting in quick succession. In addition, there is a wealth of nineteenth-century and early twentieth-century travellers' accounts, although many are out of print. Romanian literature is still under-represented in translation.

The **Center for Romanian Studies**, based in Iaşi (Ⓦ www.romanianstudies.ro), publishes many books on Romanian history and literature. Out-of-print titles are indicated as (o/p).

Specialized guides

John Akeroyd *The Historic Countryside of the Saxon Villages of Southeast Transylvania*. A detailed account of the human and natural ecology of a wonderfully unspoilt medieval landscape.

Dave Gosney *Finding Birds in Romania*. This covers the Danube Delta only.

Informative, but strangely it does not include a checklist of possible species.

James Roberts *Romania – a Birdwatching and Wildlife Guide*; and *The Mountains of Romania*. Detailed guides to the fauna and habitats of Romania, and information for hiking.

Travellers' tales

Many of the out-of-print accounts listed below may be found online, in second-hand bookshops or at Marijana Dworski Books, 21 The Meadows, Hay-on-Wye HR3 5LF, UK (Ⓣ&Ⓕ01497/820 200, Ⓦ www.dworskibooks.com).

Recent accounts

William Blacker *Along The Enchanted Way*. An intimate account of rural life in Maramureş and with Gypsies in a Saxon village, which feelingly describes both a magical way of life, and its inevitable demise in the modern world.

Helena Drysdale *Looking for Gheorghe*. A search for a lost friend leads to unsavoury insights into life with the Securitate and finally to a hellish "mental hospital". The picture of Romanian life both before and after the revolution is spot-on.

Jason Goodwin *On Foot to the Golden Horn*. An engaging and well-informed

writer walking from Gdansk to Istanbul in 1990 – almost half the book is, in fact, set in Transylvania. Very thoughtful, but it's annoyingly hard to work out which are the author's opinions and which those of the characters he meets.

Brian Hall *Stealing from a Deep Place*. Hall cycled through Hungary, Romania and Bulgaria in 1982 and produced a beautifully defined picture of the nonsense that communism had become.

Georgina Harding *In Another Europe*. Another cycle tour, this one in 1988. Slimmer than Hall's book but concentrating far more on Romania, with a more emotional response to Ceaușescu's follies.

Eva Hoffman *Exit into History*. Not a patch on *Lost in Translation*, her superb account of being uprooted from Jewish Kraków to North America, but this tour of East-Central Europe in 1990 still yields seventy insightful pages on Romania.

Caroline Juler *Searching for Sarmizegetusa*. A captivating glimpse of traditional life and the pressures that are undermining it.

Rory MacLean *Stalin's Nose*. With its wonderfully surreal humour, this is not exactly a factual account, but it is fundamentally serious about the effects of World War II and communism all over Eastern Europe.

Dervla Murphy *Transylvania and Beyond*. A serious, analytical book that

tussles with the problems that Transylvania faced immediately post-revolution, and its ethnic tensions in particular.

Alan Ogden *Romania Revisited*. An anthology and bibliography of English travellers to Romania between 1602 and 1941, interwoven with the author's own journeys in 1998.

Bronwen Riley *Transylvania*. Evocative account of the vanishing rural lifestyle of Transylvania and Maramureș, with superb photos.

Julian Ross *Travels in an Unknown Country*. A summer-long horseride across Transylvania and Moldavia, witnessing a fast-disappearing rural world.

Sophie Thurnham *Sophie's Journey*. Heart-warming story of work in the orphanages.

Older classics

Henry Baerlein (ed). *Romanian Scene* and *Romanian Oasis* (o/p). Two fine anthologies of travellers' tales in which most of the prewar authors listed below are featured.

Emily Gerard *The Land Beyond the Forest* (o/p). One of the classic nineteenth-century accounts of Transylvania – rambling, but highly informative on folk customs, superstitions, proverbs and the like.

Donald Hall *Romanian Furrow*. Newly republished, the definitive account of 1930s Romanian rural life, clearly threatened by the modern world even then.

Patrick Leigh Fermor *Between the Woods and the Water*. Transylvania provides the setting for the second volume in this unfolding trilogy, based on Leigh Fermor's diaries for 1933–34, when he walked from Holland to Constantinople. His

precocious zest for history and cultural diversity rose to the challenge of Transylvania's striking contrasts and obscurely turbulent past; the richness of his jewelled prose is impressive.

Peter O'Conner *Walking Good: Travels to Music in Hungary and Romania* (o/p). An Irish fiddler in search of Gypsy music, forty years after Starkie (see below). O'Conner's quest took him to Slobozia, Cojocna and Făgăraș, staying with local people a few years before this became illegal. Entertaining.

Lion Phillimore *In the Carpathians* (o/p). A fascinating account of a journey by horsecart through the Maramureș and Székelyföld just before World War I, by a proto-hippy who wants only to commune with the mountains and the trees.

Sacheverell Sitwell *Romanian Journey*. Motoring around, the

Sitwells were both politely appalled, and vaguely charmed, by Romania, but most of all seem to have been relieved that their gastronomic fortunes didn't suffer unduly.

Walter Starkie *Raggle Taggle* (o/p). Starkie tramped through Transylvania to Bucharest, where his encounters with Gypsies and lowlife are recounted in a florid but quite amusing style.

History and politics

Mark Almond *The Rise and Fall of Nicolae and Elena Ceauşescu* (o/p). Very readable account by one of the best academics writing on Romania, though too kind to the sinister Silviu Brucan. Rather wayward footnotes and accents.

Dan Antal *Out of Romania*. An insider's version of the dreadful oppression under Ceauşescu and even worse disillusion after the revolution. Well enough told by a sympathetic character.

Ed Behr *Kiss the Hand You Cannot Bite*. A good, populist account of the Ceauşescus' rise and fall.

Burton Y. Berry *Romanian Diaries 1944–47*; and **Donald Dunham** *Assignment: Bucharest*. The communist takeover of Romania, as seen by senior US diplomats.

Dennis Deletant *Communist Terror in Romania: Gheorghiu-Dej and the Police State, 1948–65*; *Ceauşescu and the Securitate: Coercion and Dissent in Romania 1965–89*; *Romania under Communist Rule*. Fascinating coverage of many hidden aspects of communist Romania.

Terence Elsberry *Marie of Romania*. A colourful biography of Queen Marie.

Mary Ellen Fischer *Nicolae Ceauşescu: A Study in Political Leadership*. Academic, detailed and readable description of the system created by Ceauşescu that was soon to drag him down.

Stephen Fischer-Galati *Twentieth Century Rumania*. An easy read with good illustrations, basically

sympathetic to many changes that happened under communism.

Tom Gallagher *Theft of a Nation: Romania since Communism*. A fine analysis of the continuing crisis of Romanian politics, including its historical roots and the IMF and EU's blindness; also *Romania After Ceauşescu*, focusing on the cynical exploitation of nationalism.

Vlad Georgescu *The Romanians: A History*. The best modern history in translation, although the importance of dissidents under Ceauşescu seems overstated. Georgescu, head of the Romanian Service of Radio Free Europe, died in 1988, but an epilogue covers the events of 1989.

Sheilah Kast & Jim Rosapepe *Dracula is Dead*. A former US ambassador to Romania and his wife give snapshots of Romania just before EU accession – rather rosy-eyed, but with some revealing interviews.

Nicolae Klepper *Romania: An Illustrated History*. Paperback history giving the standard view of the progress of the Romanian people towards nationhood.

Alan Ogden *Fortresses of Faith*. A history of the Saxon churches with fine black-and-white photos. He also wrote *Revelations of Byzantium*, on the painted churches of Bucovina, plus *Winds of Sorrow* and *Moons and Aurochs*, two historical tours.

Ion Pacepa *Red Horizons*. A lurid, rambling "exposé" of the Ceauşescu regime, written by its former intelligence chief (who defected in

1978), describing disinformation and espionage abroad, corruption and perversions among the elite, and much else. Pacepa was deeply involved but reveals little about himself.

Prince Paul of Hohenzollern-Roumania *King Carol II: A Life of my Grandfather* (o/p). The nephew of King Mihai, Paul doesn't deny his grandfather's dreadful personal life, but attempts to rehabilitate him as a statesman placed in an impossible position.

Ioan Aurel Pop *Romanians and Romania – A Brief History*. Romanian history and civilization from the first century BC to the present.

Ivor Porter *Michael of Romania – the King and the Country*. A careful account of Mihai's life and of his role in history.

Martyn Rady *Romania in Turmoil*. Wonderfully clear account of Ceauşescu's rise and fall, continuing to the end of 1991.

Nestor Ratesh *Romania: The Entangled Revolution*. A careful account of the revolution, laying out all the confusion that still surrounds it.

Ion Ratiu *Contemporary Romania*. A generally negative portrayal of the communist system by an émigré who made a million in Britain and returned after Ceauşescu's downfall to lead an opposition party.

R.W. Seton-Watson *A History of the Roumanians*. Although it largely ignores social history and eschews atmospherics, and even the author admits his despair at the welter of dynastic details, this remains the classic work in English on Romanian history before 1920.

Christine Sutherland *Enchantress: Marthe Bibesco and her World*. A brilliant snapshot of both Romanian and French society and politics in the first half of the twentieth century, and of one of its most charismatic figures, Queen Marie's rival.

Marcus Tanner *The Raven King: Matthias Corvinus and the Fate of his Lost Library*. A new account of the great Renaissance king of Hungary (and Transylvania), including his ambivalent relationship with Vlad the Impaler.

Vladimir Tismăneanu *Stalinism for All Seasons: A Political History of Romanian Communism*. By Romania's leading political scientist, a full and detailed history of the Romanian Communist Party.

Lászlo Tökes *With God, for the People*. The autobiography of the man who lit the spark of the revolution and continues to be a thorn in the establishment's side, even as a bishop.

Kurt Treptow (ed) *A History of Romania*. From ancient times to the 1996 elections; with accompanying CD-ROM.

Richard Wurmbrand *In God's Underground*. The memoirs of a Lutheran priest who spent many years incarcerated at Jilava, Piteşti and other notorious prisons.

Folklore

David Buxton *Wooden Churches of Eastern Europe* (o/p). A learned and thorough tome.

Garth Cartwright *Princes Among Men – Journeys with Gypsy Musicians*. A heady musical tour of Southeastern Europe, with 68 pages on Romania.

Nicolae Klepper *Taste of Romania; its Cookery and Glimpses of its History, Folklore, Art and Poetry*. Cookery and cultural asides.

Gail Kligman *The Wedding of the Dead;
Calus: Symbolic Transformation in
Romanian Ritual; The Politics of
Duplicity – Controlling Reproduction in
Ceaușescu's Romania.* The first is a
wonderful book if you want to know
everything about the anthropology
and rituals of one Maramureș village,
Ieud; the second is a slim but interesting anthropological study of the
Whitsun Căluș rite, which still lingers
in parts of southern Romania; and the
third is a similar study of Ceaușescu's
efforts to boost the birth rate.

Karsten D McNulty *Romanian Folk
Art: A Guide to Living Traditions.* A
paperback overview of Romania's
many types of crafts, with colour
photos.

Katherine Verdery *Transylvanian
Villagers: Three Centuries of Political,
Economic and Ethnic change.* Based on
field work west of Sebeș – a duller
area than Maramureș, but therefore
more broadly applicable than
Kligman's book, though not as
readable.

Dracula

Paul Barber *Vampires, Burial and
Death: Folklore and Reality.* Proclaims
itself as "a scholarly work on human
decomposition and historical attitudes
to it", which says it all.

Barbara Belford *Bram Stoker: A
Biography of the Author of Dracula.* A more
rigorous biography than Farson's,
though marred by cod psychology.

Daniel Farson *The Man who wrote
Dracula: A Biography of Bram Stoker.*
Entertaining account of the life of the
fictional Dracula's creator.

Radu Florescu and Raymond
McNally *In Search of Dracula; Dracula: A
Biography; Dracula, Prince of Many Faces,
His Life and Times.* Founts of knowledge
on the Impaler but overstating his
connection with Dracula.

🏃 Christopher Frayling *Vampyres.*
Primarily a study of the vampire
theme in literature and broader
culture, but also a near-definitive
review of the phenomenon itself.

Clive Leatherdale *Dracula: The Novel
and the Legend.* More concerned with

the novel than with its Romanian
background.

Elizabeth Miller *A Dracula Handbook*
All you need to know, from the queen
of Dracula studies; also *Reflections on
Dracula*, and *Sense & Nonsense*, essays
that entertainingly debunk many of
the myths surrounding Stoker and his
most famous book.

Jamie Poole *Vampire in our Midst.* A
lively voyage through the bewildering
multiplicity of vampires in contemporary culture – films, TV, computer
games, comics and even books.

🏃 Bram Stoker *Dracula.* The
Gothic horror original that
launched a thousand movies. From a
promising start with undertones of
fetishism and menace in Dracula's
Transylvanian castle, the tale
degenerates into pathos before
returning to Romania, and ending in a
not too effective chase.

Kurt Treptow *Vlad III Dracula.* A
balanced biography of the historical
Vlad.

Romanian prose

Miklós Bánffy *They Were Counted,*
They Were Found Wanting and *They*
Were Divided. The *Transylvanian*
Trilogy, written in the 1930s, is a tale
of two Transylvanian cousins that has
been compared to Proust, Dostoevsky
and Trollope. Also *The Phoenix Land,* a
memoir of Hungary after the Trianon
Treaty dismembered it.

Emil Cioran *On the Heights of Despair.*
A key early work (1934, reissued in
1992) by this nihilist anti-philosopher.
Also *A Short History of Decay,* published
in 1949 and recently reissued.

Mircea Eliade *Shamanism; Youth*
without Youth; Fantastic Tales. The first
is the most interesting and informative
example of the academic work for
which he is internationally known.
The latter two are fiction, which don't
quite match his reputation as a magical
realist in the South American
tradition, although this is partly due to
the translation.

Herta Müller *The Passport; The Land*
of Green Plums; Everything I Possess I
Carry With Me; The Appointment.
Müller is a Schwab who left Romania
in 1987 and won the Nobel Prize for
Literature in 2009. *The Passport* is a
tale, in a distinctive staccato style, of
the quest for permission to leave for
Germany; *The Land of Green Plums*
deals more with repression under
Ceauşescu and is more accessible.
Everything I Possess I Carry With Me is
the story of a Transylvanian-German
youth deported to a labour camp in
the Soviet Union; and *The Appointment*
is an allegory of the struggle to remain
human under communist repression.

Liviu Rebreanu *Uprising; Ion; The*
Forest of the Hanged. This trilogy
comprises a panoramic picture of
Romanian social life from the late
nineteenth century to World War I.
Uprising, which deals with the 1907
peasant rebellion, shocked Romanian
readers with its violent descriptions
when it first appeared in 1933.

Elie Wiesel *Night.* Wiesel was born in
Sighet in 1928 and was deported to
Auschwitz, where his family died, in
1944. After the war, he pursued an
academic career in the US and was
awarded the Nobel Peace Prize in
1986. This slim book opens in the
ghetto of Sighet, but soon moves to
the death camps.

Romanian poetry

George Bacovia *Plumb/Lead.* Along
with Arghezi (none of whose work is
available in translation), Bacovia is the
leading prewar Romanian poet.
Exquisitely melancholy.

Maria Banuş *Demon in Brackets.* Born in
1914, Banuş was a leftist activist
through the 1930s and 1940s, but her
intimate lyricism remains popular today.

Lucian Blaga *Complete Poetical Works.*
At last, one of Romania's finest and
most popular poets available in English
translation.

Ion Caraion *The Error of Being.* A
leading poet of the older generation,
who composed many of his poems in
the camps of World War II.

Petru Cârdu *The Trapped Strawberry.* A
Romanian-Yugoslav, Cârdu writes
ironic poems in both Romanian and
Serbo-Croat.

Nina Cassian *Call Yourself Alive?*
Cheerleader for a Funeral. Savagely
sensual and wickedly funny work from
one of Romania's best poets.

Paul Celan *Selected Poems*. Romania's greatest poet – although all his work is in German – and one of the best of the twentieth century. Born in Bucovina in 1920, Celan survived the camps of Transnistria and emigrated to Paris, killing himself in 1970.

Mihai Eminescu *Poems and Prose*. The national poet – it's a scandal that there isn't a paperback in English of his greatest works.

John Farleigh (ed) *When the Tunnels Meet*. A great idea – contemporary Romanian poems in versions by contemporary Irish poets, with a corresponding volume published in Romania: Dinescu, Sorescu and, most notably, Blandiana interpreted by Seamus Heaney.

Ioana Ieronim *The Triumph of the Water Witch*. Prose poems about the destruction of a Saxon community by Ceauşescu, written before 1989 and only published (and shortlisted for the Weidenfeld Prize) ten years later.

Oskar Pastior *Many Glove Compartments: Selected Poems*. A Saxon, Pastior spent five years in a Soviet labour camp after World War II, and has since been obsessed by themes of freedom and determinism.

Marin Sorescu *Let's Talk About the Weather*; *Selected Poems 1965–73*; *The Biggest Egg in the World*; *Censored Poems*;

The Bridge. Hugely popular and respected both before 1989 and after (when he was briefly Minister of Culture), Sorescu died in 1996. His style is more ironic and accessible than that of many of his contemporaries.

Adam Sorkin (trans & ed) *Transylvanian Voices*; *City of Dreams and Whispers*. Anthologies of contemporary poets from Cluj and Iaşi respectively. Sorkin has also translated Magda Carneci, Ioan Flora, Saviana Stănescu and Daniela Crasnaru.

Nichita Stănescu *Bas-Relief with Heroes*. Stănescu died aged 50 in 1982, but is still very influential.

Ion Stoica *As I Came to London one Midsummer's Day*; *Gates of the Moment*. A poet of the older generation, blending old and new influences.

Grete Tartler *Orient Express*. An excellent Schwab writer, translated by Fleur Adcock.

Liliana Ursu *The Sky Behind the Forest*. "Carnivorous and tender, majestic and human", a clear insight into her country and its people.

Brenda Walker (ed) *Anthology of Contemporary Romanian Poetry*. Features the work of Romania's two best living poets, Nina Cassian and Ana Blandiana. Also *Young Poets of a New Romania*.

Foreign prose

Paul Bailey *Kitty and Virgil*. A fine novel of survival in Ceauşescu's Romania and love found and lost in Britain.

Saul Bellow *The Dean's December*. The repression and poverty of Ceauşescu's Romania is contrasted with the hypocrisy and decadence of 1980s America.

Alan Brownjohn *The Long Shadows*. By a poet whose work has been

intimately involved with Romania for decades, this novel is the story of Tim Harker-Jones (a tip of the hat to Bram Stoker there), who travels to Romania while writing a friend's biography, and has some extraordinary adventures.

Olivia Manning *The Balkan Trilogy*. This epic story of thoroughly exasperating characters renders the atmosphere of wartime Bucharest well, but as an extended study of human relationships it's weakly constructed.

Bel Mooney *Cascades: The Voices of Silence*. A 13-year-old's experience of Ceauşescu's overthrow; written for the same age group, studying themes such as the individual and society.

🏃 **Gregor von Rezzori** *Memoirs of an Anti-Semite*; *The Snows of Yesteryear*. Two evocative accounts of growing up in the largely Romanian city of Czernowitz (Cernăuţi, now in Ukraine).

Jules Verne *The Castle of the Carpathians*. A Gothic adventure tale, long loved by French children and now in English too.

Barbara Wilson *Trouble in Transylvania*. Inveterate traveller Cassandra Reilly goes to Sovata to investigate a murder, and gets the hots for most of the women she meets. Pretty strong on local colour in other respects.

Language

Language

Romanian

Romanian is basically a **Romance language** with a grammar similar to Latin, making it easy for anyone who speaks French, Italian or (to a lesser extent) Spanish to recognize words and phrases in Romanian. Its vocabulary also contains words of Dacian, Slav, Greek and Turkish origin, with more recent additions from French, German and English.

German may be understood – if not spoken – in the areas of Transylvania and the Banat traditionally inhabited by Saxons and Swabians, and many educated Romanians have learned the language for professional reasons, although the tendency nowadays is increasingly towards English. Foreigners who can muster any scrap of **Hungarian** will find it appreciated in the Magyar enclaves of Transylvania, but its use elsewhere invites hassle rather than sympathy, which is even more the case with **Russian** – a language greeted with derision by almost everyone except the Lipovani communities of the Delta.

Romanian **nouns** have three genders – masculine, feminine and neuter. **Adjectives** (usually placed after the word they describe) and **pronouns** always "agree" with the gender of the noun. *Mai* and *cel mai* are generally used to make comparatives and superlatives: eg. *ieftin* (cheap); *mai ieftin* (cheaper); *cel mai ieftin* (the cheapest). Romanian **verbs** are conjugated, so do not require pronouns such as "I" or "you", although these may be added for emphasis. Nor are **articles** always needed: the indefinite article "a" comes before the noun and is *un* for masculine and neuter words, *o* for feminine ones; the definite article "the" is added to the end of the noun: *-a* for feminine words, *-ul* or *-le* for masculine or neuter ones. The plural forms of nouns are slightly more complicated, but tend to end in *-i* or *-le*.

Pronunciation is also fairly straightforward. Words are usually stressed on the syllable before last, and all letters are pronounced except for the terminal "–i". Romanians tend to slur words together when speaking.

Elementary Hungarian

Yes	**Igen**	Cheap	**Olcsó**
No	**Nem**	Expensive	**Drága**
Please	**Kárem**	Good	**Jó**
Thanks	**Köszönöm**	Bad	**Rossz**
Hello	**Jó napot, servus, csokolom**	Open	**Nyitva**
		Closed	**Zárva**
Goodbye	**Viszontlá tósra**	Station	**Palyaudvar, vasú, allomas**
Cheers!	**Egeszegedre!**		
I don't understand	**Nem értem**	Hotel	**Szálloda**
Where is...?	**Hol van...?**	Restaurant	**Étterem**
When?	**Mikor?**	Bar	**Pince**
Today	**Ma**	Bread	**Kenyér**
Tomorrow	**Holnap**	(No) meat	**(Nem) hús**
How much is it?	**Mennyibe kerül?**		

Elementary German

Yes	**Ja**	How much is it?	**Wieviel kostet es?**
No	**Nein**	Cheap	**Billig**
Please	**Bitte**	Expensive	**Teuer**
Thanks	**Danke**	Good	**Gut**
Hello	**Guten Tag, Grüss Gott**	Bad	**Schlecht**
		Open	**Offen**
Goodbye	**Auf Wiedersehen**	Closed	**Geschlossen**
Cheers!	**Prost!**	Station	**Bahnhof**
I don't understand	**Ich verstehe nicht**	Hotel	**Gasthaus**
		Restaurant	**Restaurant**
Where is...?	**Wo ist...?**	Bar	**Kneipe**
When?	**Wann?**	Bread	**Brot**
Today	**Heute**	(No) meat	**(Kein) Fleisch**
Tomorrow	**Morgen**		

A "**o**" sound as in done.
 (or Î) is pronounced "**uh**", midway between the O in lesson and the O in sort.
Ä "**er**" sound as in mother; the combinations AU and ĂU resemble the sounds in how and go.
C and Ch are hard, like "**k**" or as in country, except when C precedes E or I, when it sounds like "**ch**".
E sounds as in ten; but at the start of a word it's pronounced as in year; while the combined EI sounds like bay or ray.
G is hard as in gust, except in the diphthong EG (like sledge), or preceding E or I when it is soft as in gesture; GHI is hard (as in gear).

I is as in feet; except for the vowel combinations IU as in you; IA as in yap; and IE as in yes.
J is like the "**s**" in pleasure.
K only occurs in imported words like kilometre.
O is as in soft; except for OI, which is like boy, and OA as in quark.
R is always rolled.
Ş is slurred as in shop.
Ţ is a "**ts**" sound as in bits.
U sounds like book or good; but UA is pronounced as in quark.
W occurs in such foreign words as whisky and western.

Words and phrases

Basics and greetings

Yes	**Da**	Do you speak English?	**Vorbiţi englezeste?**
No	**Nu**	I don't understand	**Nu ânţeleg**
And	**Şi**	Please speak slowly	**Vă rog să vorbiţi mai rar**
Please	**Vă rog**		
Thank you	**Mulţumesc**	Please write it down	**Scrieţi, vă rog**
Sorry, excuse me	**Îmi pare rău, permiteţi-mi**	Say that again, please	**Vreţi să repetaţi, vă rog**
Good	**Bun**	I, we, you	**Eu, noi, dumneaţa (tu is informal)**
Bad	**Rău**		
		Hello	**Salut**

Good morning	Bună dimineața
Good day	Bună ziua (or Servus)
Good evening	Bună seară
Goodnight	Noapte bună
How are you?	Ce mai faceți?
What's your name?	Cum vă numiți?
Cheers! (literally good luck!)	Noroc!

Good, that's fine	Bun, minunat
Goodbye Bon voyage (literally "Good road")	La revedere (or ciao, pa) Drum bun
Leave me alone!	Lăsați-ma ân pace!

Directions and accommodation

Where?/When?	Unde?/Când?
The nearest	Cel mai aproape
A (cheap) hotel	Un hotel (ieftin)
Campsite	Loc de campare, popas
Toilet	Toaletă, WC (pronounced vay-say-oo)
Is it far?	Este departe?
What bus must I take?	Ce autobuz trebuie să iau?
Is there a footpath to...?	Există potecă spre...?
Right, left, straight on	Dreapta, stânga, dreapt ânainte
North, south, east, west	Nord, sud, est, vest
Have you a room?	Aveți o cameră?
With, without	Cu, fără

Twin beds	Două paturi
Double bed	Un pat dublu
For one person (alone)	Pentru o persoană (singura)
Shower, bathroom	Duș, baie
Hot	Cald/fierbinte,
Cold	Frig/rece
How much per night?	Cât costa pentru o noapte?
Is breakfast included?	Micul dejun este inclus în preț?
Have you got anything cheaper?	Nu aveți altceva mai ieftin?
Can you suggest another (a cheaper) hotel?	Puteți să-mi recomandați un alt hotel (un hotel mai ieftin)?

Signs

Arrival	Sosire
Departure	Plecare
Entrance	Intrare
Exit	Ieșire
Vacant	Liber
Occupied	Ocupat
No vacancies	Nu mai sânt locuri
Open	Deschis
Closed	Închis

Admission free	Intrare gratuită
Ladies' (Gents') WC	WC femei (bărbați)
Waiting room	Sală de așteptare
Operating, cancelled (for transport services)	Circulă, anulat
No smoking	Fumatul oprit (Nefumatori)
No entry, danger	Intrare interzisa, pericol

Requests and buying

I want (would like)...	(Aș) vreau...
I don't want...	Nu vreau...
How much?	Cât costă?
A little (less)	(Mai) puțin
Is there...?	Există...?

Have you/do you sell...?	Aveți...?
Where can I buy...?	Unde pot să cumpăr...?
Too expensive	Prea scump

What do you recommend?	Ce îmi recomandați?	Bill, receipt	Notă, chitanță
Waiter, waitress	Chelner, Chelnerița	When will it be ready?	Când este gata?
Two glasses (bottles) of beer	Două pahare (sticle) de bere	At once, we're in a hurry	Imediat, noi grăbim
Same again, please	Încă un rând, vă rog	What's the rate for the pound/dollar?	Care este cursul lirei sterling/dolarului?
Is it any good?	Merita?	Will you refund my money?	Vă rog să-mi dați banii ânapoi?
Bon appétit	Poftă bună		

Getting around

Does this bus go to the train station?	Autobuzul acesta merge la gară?	When does the train leave?	Le ce ora pleacă trenul?
To the bus terminal	La autogară	Two seats for… (tomorrow)	Două locuri pentru... (mâine)
To the beach	La plajă		
Into the centre	În centru	I want to reserve a sleeper (couchette)	Vreau să rezerva loc de vagon de dormit (cu cușete)
Does it stop at …?	Oprește la ...?		
Has the last bus gone?	A trecut ultimul autobuz?	I want to change my reservation to…	Aș vreau să schimba rezervă pentru...
I (want to) go to…	(Vreau să) merg la...	Is this the train for…?	Acesta este trenul
Where are you going?	Unde mergeți?	Where do I change?	de...? Unde schimb trenul?
Stop here (at…)	Opriți aici (la...)		
Is it a good road?	Drumul este bun?	arrival time	sosire (sos.)
It isn't far	Nu este departe	departure time	plecare (pl.)
Crossroads	Intersecție, răscruce	Is there a boat from here to…?	Există curse de vapor de aici la...?
Bridge	Pod		
Which platform does the train to… leave from?	De la ce peron pleacă trenul catre...?	How much do you charge by the hour/ for the day?	Cât costa ora/ziua?

Time and dates

What's the time?	Ce oră este?	Sunday	Duminică
This morning	Azi dimineață	Monday	Luni
Day	Zi	Tuesday	Marți
Afternoon	După masă	Wednesday	Miercuri
Midday	Amiază	Thursday	Joi
Midnight	Miezul nopții	Friday	Vineri
Evening	Seară	Saturday	Sâmbătă
Night	Noapte	Every day	În fiecare zi
Week	Săptămână	January	Ianuarie
Month	Lună	February	Februarie
Today	Azi/astăzi	March	Martie
Yesterday	Ieri	April	Aprilie
(Day after) tomorrow	(Poi) mâine	May	Mai
Soon	Curând	June	Iunie
Never	Niciodată	July	Iulie

August	August	December	Decembrie
September	Septembrie	New Year	Anul Nou
October	Octombrie	Easter	Paşte
November	Noiembrie	Christmas	Crăciun

Numbers

0	zero	20	douăzece
1	un, una	21	douăzeci şi un(a)
2	doi, doua	30	treizeci
3	trei	40	patruzeci
4	patru	50	cincizeci
5	cinci	60	şaizeci
6	şase	70	şaptzeci
7	şapte	80	optzeci
8	opt	90	nouăzeci
9	nouă	100	o sută
10	zece	500	cinci sute
11	unsprezece	1000	o mie
12	doisprezece	first	întâi
13	treisprezece	second	al doilea
14	paisprezece	1 kilo	un kilo
15	cincisprezece	a half	jumatăte
16	şaisprezece	a third	o treime
17	şaptsprezece	a quarter	un sfert
18	optsprezece	three quarters	trei sferturi
19	nouăsprezece		

Food and drink glossary

Basic foods

brânză	cheese
iaurt	yoghurt
lapte	milk
omletă	omelette
orez	rice
oţet	vinegar
ouă	eggs
pâine/pîine	bread
piper	pepper
sandvici/tartină	sandwiches
sare	salt
smântâna	sour cream
ulei	oil
unt	butter
zahăr	sugar

Soups (supe)

ciorbă	mixed soup, with sour cream
ciorbă de burtă	tripe soup
ciorbă de cartofi	potato soup
ciorbă de fasole	dried or green bean soup
ciorbă de miel	lamb broth
ciorbă de perişoare	soup with meatballs
ciorbă de peşte	fish soup
ciorbă ţaranească	soup with meat and mixed vegetables

supă	soup with one main component
supă de carne	consommé
supă de găină	chicken soup
supă de găluşti	dumpling soup
supă de roşii	tomato soup
supă cu tăiţei	noodle soup
supă de zarzavat	vegetable soup

Salads (salate)

salată de cartofi cu ceapă	potato and onion salad
salată de fasole verde	green bean salad
salată de icre de crap	carp roe salad
salată de roşii şi castraveţi	tomato and cucumber salad
salată de sfeclă roşie	beetroot salad
salată verde	green salad

Meat and poultry (carne şi pasăre)

babic (ghiudem)	smoked (goat's meat) sausage
berbec/oaie	mutton
biftec	steak
chiftele	fried meatballs
crenwurst	hot dog
curcan	turkey
ficat	liver
gâscă	goose
ghiveci cu carne	meat and vegetable hotpot
miel	lamb
mititei	spicy sausages
parizer	mortadella-type sausage
(pastramă de) porc	(salted and smoked) pork
patricieni	sausages (skinless)
pui	chicken
raţă (pe varză)	duck (with sauerkraut)
rinichi	kidneys
salam	salami
slănină	bacon fat
şniţel pane	wiener schnitzel
şuncă	ham
tocană de carne/de purcel	meat/pork stew
vacă	beef

varză acră cu costiţă afumată	sauerkraut with smoked pork chops

Vegetables (legume)

ardei (gras/iute)	(green/chilli) pepper
cartofi	potatoes
ceapă (verde)	(spring) onion
ciuperci	mushrooms
conopidă	cauliflower
dovlecei	courgettes/zucchini
dovleci	marrows
fasole	beans
ghiveci	mixed fried vegetables, (may be eaten cold)
gogoşari	red peppers
lăptucă	lettuce
mazăre verde	peas
morcovi	carrots
roşii	tomatoes
sfeclă roşie	beetroot
spanac	spinach
usturoi	garlic
varză	cabbage
vinete	aubergine/eggplant

Fish and seafood (peşte)

cegă	sterlet
chiftele de peşte	fish cakes
crap	carp
icre negre	caviar
midii	mussels
nisetru	sturgeon
păstrăv	trout
scrumbie	herring
şalău	pike-perch
ton	tuna

Fruit (fructe)

caise	apricots
căpşune	strawberries
cireşe	cherries
fragă	wild strawberries
mere	apples
pepene galben	melon
pepene verde	watermelon
pere	pears
piersici	peaches

prune (uscate)	plums (prunes)
struguri	grapes
zmeură	raspberries

Desserts and sweets (dulciuri)

bomboane	sweets (candy)
clătită (cu rom)	pancake (with rum)
cozonac	brioche
dulceață	jam (served in a glass)
ecler	éclair
gogoși, langoș	doughnut
halva	halva
ânghețată	ice cream
măr in foietaj	baked apple in pastry
mascotă	chocolate fudge cake
miere	honey
papanași	sweet cheese doughnut
pască	Easter cake
plăcinta cu brânză	cheese pie (like cheesecake)
plăcintă cu mere	apple pie
plăcintă cu vișine	cherry pie
prăjitură	cake
rahat	Turkish delight
ruladă	sponge and jam roll
strudel cu mere	apple strudel

Drinks (băuturi)

apă minerală	mineral water
suc de fructe	fruit juice
cafea filtru	filter coffee
cafea mare cu lapte	large white coffee
cafea neagră	sweet black coffee

cafea naturală	plain black coffee
cafea turcească	Turkish coffee
o ceașcă de ceai	a cup of tea
bere	beer
vin roșu/alb	red/white wine
șampanie	sparkling wine
sticlă	bottle (of beer)
țuică	plum brandy
vodca	vodka
rom	rum

Common terms

aveți...	do you have a...
aș/am vrea	I/we would like
cină	dinner
cu maioneză	with a mayonnaise sauce
cu mujdei de usturoi	in a garlic sauce
dejun	lunch
fiert	boiled
friptură	roast
la grătar	grilled
meniu/listă	menu
micul dejun	breakfast
murăti	pickled
pahar	a glass
piure de	mashed
prăjit	fried
prânz	lunch
pulpă de... la tavă	roast leg of ...
rasol	poached
tare/moale	hard/soft boiled
umplut	stuffed

L

LANGUAGE | Food and drink glossary

Glossary

Alimentară food store.

Ardeal "forested land", the Romanian name for Transylvania.

Baie bath, spa (plural Băile; not to be confused with Baia or mine).

Biserică church.

Biserici de lemn wooden churches.

Bivol buffalo, introduced from India by the Gypsies.

Boyar or **Boier** feudal lord.

Bucium alpine horn used by shepherds, also known as a Tulnic.

Bulevardul (B-dul/Blvd) boulevard.

Calea avenue.

Căluş traditional Whitsun fertility rite performed by Căluşari in rural Wallachia and southwestern Transylvania.

Câmpulung or **Cîmpulung** meadow or long field, for which settlements like Câmpulung Moldovenesc are named.

Capră masked "goat dance" to celebrate the New Year.

Casă house.

Cetate fortress or citadel.

CFR Romanian railways.

Chei gorge.

Csángó Hungarian "Wanderers" in Moldavia.

Dacians earliest established inhabitants of Romania.

Deal hill.

Drum road.

Erdély the Magyar name for Transylvania.

FSN Frontul Salvării Naţional, the National Salvation Front that took power during the revolution.

Gadjé Roma (Gypsy) term for non-Gypsies.

Gradiniţa garden.

Grind raised silt bank in the Danube Delta.

Gură mouth.

Horă traditional village round dance.

Iconostasis literally "icon-bearer", decorated screen in an Orthodox (or Uniate) church containing tiers of icons, that separates sanctuary from nave and priest from congregation during the Eucharist.

Judeţ county.

Lac lake.

Legion or Iron Guard, Romanian fascist movement, 1927–41.

Lipovani ethnic group living by fishing and gardening in the Danube Delta, descended from Russian "Old Believers".

Litoral the coast.

Magyars Hungarians, many of whom live in Romania, mainly in Transylvania.

Mănăstirea monastery or convent.

Maxitaxi minibus.

Moară mill.

Muntenia the eastern half of Wallachia, paradoxically not at all mountainous.

Nai panpipes.

Naos nave or central part of an Orthodox church, lying below the central cupola and in front of the iconostasis.

Narthex entrance hall of an Orthodox church, often decorated with frescoes.

Nations or **Nationes** historically, the privileged groups in Transylvania.

Nedeia village fair or festival characteristic of the mountain regions.

Oltenia the western half of Wallachia, flanking the River Olt.

Pădure woods.

Pas a mountain pass.

PCR Partidul Communist Roman – until 1989, the Romanian Communist Party; now the Socialist Party of Labour (PSM).

Peştera cave.

Piaţa square; also a market.

Piatra stone or crag.

Plaur floating reed islands, common in the Delta.

Popă or **Preot** Orthodox priest.

Pronaos see Narthex.

Răscoala peasant rebellion; usually refers to the great uprising of 1907.

Râu river.

Regat the "Old Kingdom", as Moldavia and Wallachia were known after they united in 1859.

Rom or Roma Gypsies.

Sanctuar sanctuary or altar area of a church, behind the iconostasis.

Sat village.

Saxons name given to Germans who settled in Transylvania from the twelfth century.

Schwaben (Swabians) name given to Germans who settled in Banat in the eighteenth century; others who moved to Transylvania at this time are known as Landler.

Securitate Communist security police, reborn as the Romanian Information Service (SRI).

Siebenburgen Saxon name for Transylvania (literally "seven towns").

Şoseaua (Şos.) long tree-lined avenue.

Strada (Str.) street.

Székely Hungarian-speaking ethnic group inhabiting parts of eastern Transylvania known as the Székelyföld.

Ţara land, country (Romanian); Gypsy encampment.

Târg or Tîrg market, fair or festival.

Vad ford.

Vale valley.

Vătaf leader of Căluşari dancers (Romanian); tribal chieftain (Gypsy).

Vlachs or Wallachs foreign name for the Romanians of Wallachia, Moldavia and Transylvania before the nineteenth century.

Voevod or Voivode Ruling prince of Transylvania or Wallachia.

Useful hiking terms

Aven	doline	Potecă/traseu	path/route
Cabana	mountain hut	Refugiu (salvamont)	refuge (with first aid)
Cascada	waterfall		
Colţ	cliff	Şau	col (saddle)
Cota	altitude	Stâna	sheepfold
Hartă	map	Stânca	rock
Izvor	spring	Telecabina	cable car
Nerecomandabil iarna	unsafe during winter	Telescaun	chairlift
		Teleschi	ski-drag
Poiana	glade	Vârf	peak

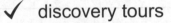

Small print and

Index

A Rough Guide to Rough Guides

Published in 1982, the first Rough Guide – to Greece – was a student scheme that became a publishing phenomenon. Mark Ellingham, a recent graduate in English from Bristol University, had been travelling in Greece the previous summer and couldn't find the right guidebook. With a small group of friends he wrote his own guide, combining a highly contemporary, journalistic style with a thoroughly practical approach to travellers' needs.

The immediate success of the book spawned a series that rapidly covered dozens of destinations. And, in addition to impecunious backpackers, Rough Guides soon acquired a much broader and older readership that relished the guides' wit and inquisitiveness as much as their enthusiastic, critical approach and value-for-money ethos.

These days, Rough Guides include recommendations from shoestring to luxury and cover more than 200 destinations around the globe, including almost every country in the Americas and Europe, more than half of Africa and most of Asia and Australasia. Our ever-growing team of authors and photographers is spread all over the world, particularly in Europe, the US and Australia.

In the early 1990s, Rough Guides branched out of travel, with the publication of Rough Guides to World Music, Classical Music and the Internet. All three have become benchmark titles in their fields, spearheading the publication of a wide range of books under the Rough Guide name.

Including the travel series, Rough Guides now number more than 350 titles, covering: phrasebooks, waterproof maps, music guides from Opera to Heavy Metal, reference works as diverse as Conspiracy Theories and Shakespeare, and popular culture books from iPods to Poker. Rough Guides also produce a series of more than 120 World Music CDs in partnership with World Music Network.

Visit www.roughguides.com to see our latest publications.

SMALL PRINT

Rough Guide credits

Text editors: Lara Kavanagh, Helena Smith
Layout: Ankur Guha
Cartography: Lokamata Sahu
Picture editor: Mark Thomas
Production: Louise Minihane
Proofreader: Jan McCann
Cover design: Jess Carter, Nicole Newman, Daniel May
Photographer: Gregory Wrona
Editorial: **London** Andy Turner, Keith Drew, Edward Aves, Alice Park, Lucy White, Jo Kirby, James Smart, Natasha Foges, James Rice, Emma Beatson, Emma Gibbs, Kathryn Lane, Monica Woods, Mani Ramaswamy, Harry Wilson, Lucy Cowie, Alison Roberts, Eleanor Aldridge, Ian Blenkinsop, Charlotte Melville, Joe Staines, Matthew Milton, Tracy Hopkins; **Delhi** Madhavi Singh, Jalpreen Kaur Chhatwal, Jubbi Francis
Design & Pictures: **London** Scott Stickland,

Dan May, Diana Jarvis, Nicole Newman, Sarah Cummins; **Delhi** Umesh Aggarwal, Ajay Verma, Jessica Subramanian, Pradeep Thapliyal, Sachin Tanwar, Anita Singh, Nikhil Agarwal, Sachin Gupta
Production: Rebecca Short, Liz Cherry, Erika Pepe
Cartography: **London** Ed Wright, Katie Lloyd-Jones; **Delhi** Rajesh Chhibber, Ashutosh Bharti, Rajesh Mishra, Animesh Pathak, Jasbir Sandhu, Swati Handoo, Deshpal Dabas
Marketing, Publicity & roughguides.com: Liz Statham
Digital Travel Publisher: Peter Buckley
Reference Director: Andrew Lockett
Operations Coordinator: Becky Doyle
Operations Assistant: Johanna Wurm
Publishing Director (Travel): Clare Currie
Commercial Manager: Gino Magnotta
Managing Director: John Duhigg

Publishing information

This sixth edition published June 2011 by
Rough Guides Ltd,
80 Strand, London WC2R 0RL
11, Community Centre, Panchsheel Park, New Delhi 110017, India
Distributed by the Penguin Group
Penguin Books Ltd,
80 Strand, London WC2R 0RL
Penguin Group (USA)
375 Hudson Street, NY 10014, USA
Penguin Group (Australia)
250 Camberwell Road, Camberwell, Victoria 3124, Australia
Penguin Group (NZ)
67 Apollo Drive, Mairangi Bay, Auckland 1310, New Zealand
Rough Guides is represented in Canada by Tourmaline Editions Inc. 662 King Street West, Suite 304, Toronto, Ontario M5V 1M7
Cover concept by Peter Dyer.
Typeset in Bembo and Helvetica to an original design by Henry Iles.

Printed in Singapore
© Tim Burford and Norm Longley 2011
Maps © Rough Guides
No part of this book may be reproduced in any form without permission from the publisher except for the quotation of brief passages in reviews.
440pp includes index
A catalogue record for this book is available from the British Library
ISBN: 978-1-84836-887-3

1   3   5   7   9   8   6   4   2

MIX
Paper from responsible sources
FSC® C018179

Help us update

We've gone to a lot of effort to ensure that the sixth edition of **The Rough Guide to Romania** is accurate and up-to-date. However, things change – places get "discovered", opening hours are notoriously fickle, restaurants and rooms raise prices or lower standards. If you feel we've got it wrong or left something out, we'd like to know, and if you can remember the address, the price, the hours, the phone number, so much the better.

Please send your comments with the subject line "**Rough Guide Romania Update**" to ⓔmail @uk.roughguides.com. We'll credit all contributions and send a copy of the next edition (or any other Rough Guide if you prefer) for the very best emails.

Find more travel information, connect with fellow travellers and book your trip on ⓦwww .roughguides.com

Acknowledgements

Tim Burford would like to thank Paul Iacobaş, William Blacker, Colin Shaw, Gavin Bell, Rob & Lia Larcombe, Maria Iordache, George Pop (Maramureş InfoTurism), Pamela & Indrei Ratiu, Claudia Rosca, Corina Crisan & Balogh Beata (Turda), Cristina Parau, Mike & Angy Morton, Dan & Luminiţa, Bogdan Colţea, Tibor Kalnoky, Zoltan Hegedus, Caroline Fernolend, Duncan & Penny Ridgeley, Lucica and family (in Breb), Csilla Hegedus & David Baxter, Robert Roth, Cathy Tin, Cristina & Cornel Nistor, Florin Muntean, Irina Raceu, Oana Milea, Jon & Ioana Matthews, Ruxandra Achitei, Katalin Barabas, Christa Richter & Cristian Sencovici, Giovanna Bassetti, Harry Duda, and Lara Kavanagh, Helena Smith, Katie Lloyd-Jones and all the Rough Guides staff.

Norm Longley would like to thank Lara for her excellent and enthusiastic editing, not to mention her inordinate patience during the course of updating this book. Very special thanks to Maria Iordache at the Romanian tourist office in London for unfailing help and assistance, and Andrei Mahalnischi and the team in Cluj for their continued support. Thanks are also due to Craig Turp in Bucharest for beers and tips, Constantin Rusu and family in Gura Humorului, and John McCarthy and Emilia Croitoru in Bucharest. Thanks, as always, to my colleague and dear friend Tim, to Katy, and most of all, to Christian and Luka.

Readers' letters

Thanks to all the readers who have taken the time to write in with comments and suggestions (and apologies if we've inadvertently omitted or misspelt anyone's name):

Carol Chadwick, Francis Chantree, Giorgio Genter, David Killick, Amanda Loughlin, Andrew Mayo, Margaret Secor, Karen Shaw, Robin, Valerie Towle.

SMALL PRINT

Photo credits

All photography by Gregory Wrona © Rough Guides except the following:

Title page
Sibiu in winter © Superstock/Corbis

Full page
Bran Castle © Gregory Wrona/Rough Guides

Thumbnail
Painted Eggs © Andrei Badau/Fotolia

Introduction
Bucharest street © Sandra Raccanello/Getty Images
Caru' cu Bere restaurant © David Sutherland/ Getty Images
Braşov City Hall © Gavriel Jecan
Skiing in the Transylvanian Alps/Gordon White/ Getty Images

Things not to miss
02 Bucharest © Gavin Hellier/Getty Images
03 River Danube © Richard Packwood/Getty Images
05 Karst formations © Blickwinkel/Alamy
08 Sheep's cheese © Gregory Wrona/Alamy

09 Bear tracking © Nick Turner/Alamy
13 Pageant of the Juni © Florin Andreescu
14 Braşov © Gavriel Jecan
16 Village homestay © Look/Alamy
18 Skiing © PCL
21 Measurement of the Milk Festival © Florin Andreescu
25 Dracula © Kristen Soper/Alamy
28 Folk music © Stephan Siedler/Alamy

Romanian architecture colour section
Secession-era house © Tim Burford
Securitate building, Bucharest © Tim E White/ Getty Images

The great outdoors colour section
Snowboarding, Poiana Braşov © Cozma Iulian/ Alamy
Cabin, Buşteni © David Bleeker/Alamy
Little egret © Julian Hernandez/Alamy
Caving © Salajean/Fotolia

Black and whites
p.122 Braşov © Gavin Hellier/Getty Images

Index

Map entries are in colour.

INDEX

Map symbols

maps are listed in the full index using coloured text

▪▪▪▪▪	International boundary	◉	Accommodation
▪▪▪▪	Chapter division boundary	🏠	Fuel station
▬▬▬	Motorway	P	Parking
═══	Major road	(i)	Information office
───	Minor road	⊠	Post office
▬▬▬	Pedestrianized road	@	Internet access
▥▥▥	Steps	⊞	Hospital
─■─	Railway	�	Gardens
●▪▪▪●	Cable car/Gondola	♟	Museum
▪▪▪▪▪	Footpath	⚠	Campsite
───	River	🕌	Mosque
▥▥▥	Canal	♖	Castle
━━━	Wall	⊙	Statue
‿	Bridge	✡	Synagogue
⊠	Gate	∴	Ruins
🗒	Gorge	♠	Mountain refuge
🗻	Mountain range	■	Tower
▲	Mountain peak	🎿	Skiing
🗻	Waterfall	⬭	Stadium
⌒	Cave	▬	Building
🕯	Lighthouse	╬	Church
✈	Airport	▨	Park
★	Transport stop	⊡	Christian cemetery
Ⓜ	Metro station	▭	Jewish cemetery
♦	Point of interest	▨	Beach
⛪	Monastery	▱	Marshland

So now we've told you about the things not to miss, the best places to stay, the top restaurants, the liveliest bars and the most spectacular sights, it only seems fair to tell you about the best travel insurance around

WorldNomads.com

keep travelling safely

Recommended by Rough Guides